Politics and Policy
in Traditional Korea

Harvard East Asian Monographs, 159

POLITICS AND POLICY
IN TRADITIONAL KOREA

James B. Palais

Published by the Council on East Asian Studies, Harvard University,
and distributed by the Harvard University Press,
Cambridge (Massachusetts) and London, 1991.

Copyright © 1975 by the President and Fellows of Harvard College

Second printing 1991.

Preparation of this volume has been aided by a grant from
the Ford Foundation

Third printing 1997.

Reprinted with the financial support of the Korea Institute,
Harvard University.

The Council on East Asian Studies at Harvard University publishes a
monograph series and, through the Fairbank Center for East Asian
Research and the Reischauer Institute of Japanese Studies, administers
research projects designed to further scholarly understanding of China,
Japan, Korea, Vietnam, Inner Asia, and adjacent areas. Publication of this
book has been assisted by a grant from the Shell Companies Foundation.

Library of Congress Cataloging in Publication Data
Palais, James B   1934–
  Politics and policy in traditional Korea.
  (Harvard East Asian series; 82)
  Bibliography: p.
  Includes index.
  1. Korea – Politics and government.   2. Korea – Economic policy.
I. Title.   II. Series.
JQ1723 1864.P34   320.9′519′02   75-8511
ISBN 0-674-68771-X

For Jane, Julie, Mike, Harry, Henrietta

Acknowledgments

The research for this book was begun in 1962 in preparation of my Ph.D. dissertation under the guidance of Professor Edward W. Wagner of Harvard University. I owe Professor Wagner a great debt because of his full and unstinting support and encouragement of my work for over a decade. In addition to his invaluable advice on scholarly matters, I have also derived great pleasure and satisfaction from my association with this most congenial and self-effacing man.

During the course of research and preparation of the manuscript I received financial aid from the following sources: the Foreign Area Fellowship Program, National Defense Foreign Language grants, the East Asian Research Center of Harvard University, and the Institute for Comparative and Foreign Area Studies, University of Washington. While in Korea I benefited tremendously from the aid and cooperation of Professor Han Woo-keun of Seoul National University. Professor Han helped me locate source materials and instructed me in the meaning of obscure and difficult terms and passages. I will always remember the many hours of valuable and enjoyable discussion we had in his office. Professors Koh Byŏng-ik and Chun Hae-jong also provided me with help during my stay in Korea. I would like to thank the staff of the Kyujanggak collection at Seoul National University Library, Miss Tatebe of the Asian-Africa Section of the National Diet Library in Tokyo, Mr. Kim Song-ha of the Yenching Institute Library at Harvard University, and Mrs. Ch'oe Yun of the Far Eastern Library at the University of Washington. I received useful comments on my manuscript from Professors Gari Ledyard, Lew Young-ick, Gregory Henderson, Kenneth Pyle, Jack Dull, and Donald Hellmann, and I benefited greatly from the criticisms of my colleagues in the China Seminar and History Research Group at the University of Washington. Of course, the views expressed in this book are my own.

The typing of the manuscript was ably done by Mrs. Sharon Giese, and I received excellent logistical support from Frances Greene and Mary Agnes Heath at the Institute for Comparative and Foreign Area Studies, University of Washington. Mrs. Olive Holmes of the East Asian Research Center, Harvard University, provided useful suggestions for the revision of the manuscript.

I would also like to express my gratitude to Chitoshi Yanaga, Professor Emeritus of Yale University, for first giving me the opportunity to enter East Asian studies at the graduate level.

The greatest debt I save for last. This work could not have been completed without the love and sacrifice of my wife, Jane, and my children, Julie and Mike. The burdens of scholarly endeavor often bear most heavily on wives and family who must put up with short-tempered and thoughtless husbands and fathers. It has been my good fortune to have had an understanding wife for all these years. To my parents, Harry and Henrietta, thanks for a lifetime of support and encouragement.

Contents

*Politics and Policy
in Traditional Korea*

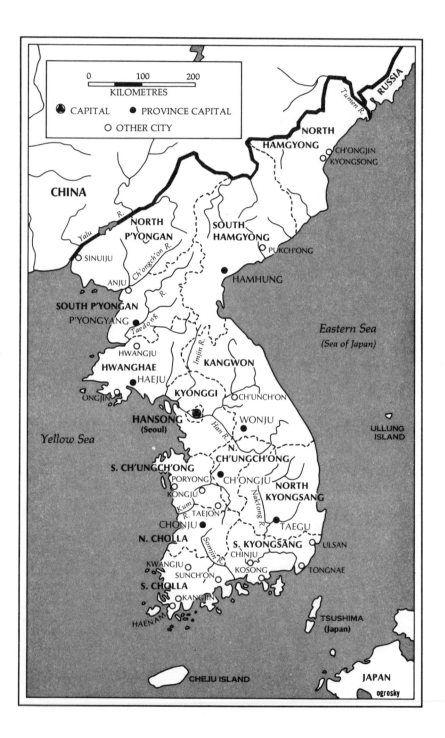

0   100   200
KILOMETRES
▲ CAPITAL   ● PROVINCE CAPITAL
○ OTHER CITY

RUSSIA

Tumen R.

NORTH
HAMGYONG

○ CH'ONGJIN
○ KYONGSONG

CHINA

NORTH
P'YONGAN

SOUTH
HAMGYONG

Yalu R.

Ch'ongch'on R.

○ SINUIJU

ANJU ○

PUKCH'ONG ○

● HAMHUNG

SOUTH P'YONGAN

R.

P'YONGYANG ●

Taedong R.

○ HWANGJU

HWANGHAE

HAEJU ●

○ ONGJIN

Imjin R.

KANGWON

Eastern Sea
(Sea of Japan)

KYONGGI

○ CH'UNCH'ON

HANSONG
(Seoul) ▲

Han R.

● WONJU

ULLUNG
ISLAND

Yellow Sea

S. CH'UNGCH'ONG

N.
CH'UNGCH'ONG

○ PORYONG

● CH'ONGJU

KONGJU ○

Kum R.

TAEJON ○

Naktong R.

NORTH
KYONGSANG

CHONJU ●

N. CHOLLA

S. KYONGSANG

● TAEGU

○ ULSAN

KWANGJU ○

SUNCH'ON ○

Somjin R.

CHINJU ○

○ KOSONG

TONGNAE ○

S. CHOLLA

○ KANGJIN

HAENAM ○

TSUSHIMA
(Japan)

CHEJU ISLAND

JAPAN

ogrosky

1
Introduction

During the last century the Korean people have been subjected to tremendous disruption resulting from the collapse of the traditional order, colonial rule, war, and social change. The first stage of this process began in 1864 when an eleven year old boy known to history by his posthumous title, Kojong, ascended the throne amid growing turmoil and anxiety. The country was plagued by the threat of foreign invasion and peasant rebellion; wealthy landowners and venal officials enriched themselves at the expense of the peasants and the central government; and powerful aristocratic lineages dominated political and economic life. Catholicism and the new Eastern Learning (*Tonghak*) religious movement challenged the ideological unity provided by Confucian thought. In short, the Yi dynasty (1392-1910) faced the most serious crisis in its long history.

For the next decade a major effort at reform was carried out under the leadership of the boy-king's resourceful father, Yi Ha-ŭng, better known as the Taewongun (Grand Prince). The Taewongun gained the opportunity for leadership when his young second son was chosen to fill the vacancy created by King Ch'ŏlchong's decease without male issue. (For details of the succession see Chapter 2.) He proceeded to act in a vigorous and resolute manner to secure the dynasty and the country from the threat of destruction. He met the demands of the foreigner with outright rejection and military force, and thanks to the weakness of the initial foreign thrust and the relative disinterest in Korea he was able to achieve success with a policy that in China or Japan would have led to invasion. No matter how short-sighted, however, the immediate success of his foreign policy afforded him respite to deal with domestic troubles. These, too, he approached directly, repressing rebels, punishing magistrates, changing institutions, and persecuting heretics.

Politics and Policy in Traditional Korea

Nevertheless, after a decade of frenetic activity the Taewongun was forced into retirement, and the process of reform was brought to an end. Although he had some success in eliminating the sources of domestic disruption and weakness and building up the power of the state, in the end the balance of political and social forces remained relatively undisturbed. Furthermore, no sooner had the Taewongun finished his work than the country was forced open by Japan in 1876, and his successors were faced with the formidable task of coming to terms with a new world. Korea failed to preserve her national integrity and in 1910 was incorporated into the Japanese empire as a colony; the old order proved unable to resist the unrelenting pressures of foreign imperialism.

The purpose of this study is threefold: to reexamine previous interpretations of the nature and aims of the reform effort of the 1860s; to identify the major obstacles to reform in terms of some of the salient characteristics of the traditional order; and to emphasize the intimate relationship between socioeconomic interest, ideology, and politics on the eve of the modern era in Korea. A study of the ancien régime in the relative isolation of the twelve years before the Kanghwa Treaty of 1876 will show Koreans responding to demands for reform before foreign intervention limited the range of possible choices. By focusing on such fundamental features of the traditional polity as social and economic organization, the nature and basis of political power, the influence of ideas on policies and action, and the varieties of personal leadership, I may be able to provide a foundation for further studies of the relationship between tradition and modernity in Korea.[1]

Previous Interpretations of the Taewongun

A redefinition of the nature and goals of the Taewongun's reform program is needed to correct misinterpretations and oversimplifications in previous scholarship and to provide an overview of reform in its totality. In the past scholars have regarded the Taewongun in a number of contradictory ways—as an early modernizer,[2] a social revolutionary,[3] a benevolent though tyrannical despot who sought the elimination of popular suffering and bureaucratic factionalism,[4] an idealistic Confucian,[5] a maximizer of power who succeeded in manipulating "mass" society,[6] or as a conservative defender of "feudalism" supported in his reforms by the lower stratum of the ruling class.[7] All these views require modification. The Taewongun should not be regarded as an early modernizer or Westernizer because his domestic reform policies were not inspired by Western ideas and were not aimed at the modern transformation of Korean society; the West at this time only provided a catalyst for reform and not a model.[8] Although some of his reforms injured elite interests, he was not a social revolutionary because he had no intention of destroying the hierarchical status system. He ignored the older factions in his recruitment policies, but factionalism had already become a weak force and played only a minor role in politics in this period. He attempted to alleviate peasant distress, but he was not willing to sacrifice the interests of the state for the peasantry and he did not seek a comprehensive solution to the problem of peasant poverty by any major restructuring of the systems of land tenure and taxation. He was more a pragmatist than an idealist, and in fact was eventually opposed by idealistic Confucian dogmatists. He sought the maximization of royal and central authority, but he did not succeed in this goal and was hardly able to obtain compliance with his directives, let alone manipulate a traditional order that as yet had few of the characteristics of "mass" society. Contrary to Henderson's argument that, because of a high degree of social mobility in the late Yi, Korean society consisted of a mass of atomized individuals subject to central control, in fact the individual was still bound by traditional ties to family, lineage, and village, and social mobility had not led to any significant increase in mass access to positions of political power.[9] The Taewongun sought the preservation of the old order, but the old order should not be regarded as feudal. Nor was he aided by the lower level of the ruling class; on the contrary, he was attacked by several of their members and received most of his support from upper level bureaucrats.

The basic goals of the Taewongun were to preserve the country and the dynasty by removing the superficial causes of peasant discontent (bureaucratic corruption, illicit taxation, official usury), restoring the power and prestige of the throne to earlier levels, increasing the central government's control over financial resources, eliminating subversive and heterodox doctrines, and building up military strength by traditional means. His approach was primarily pragmatic rather than programmatic or idealistic: he preferred direct action that would yield immediate results, and he did not hesitate to step on the toes of the social elite, the older bureaucratic factions, or the Confucian dogmatists. Yet because he possessed no overall Utopian plan for reform, he had no intention of leveling or transforming society, economy, or polity. Therefore, while his reforms were disquieting to many, they never threatened the basis of the traditional order.

It is more important, however, to provide a fuller explanation of the structure and dynamics of the old order than merely to refute previous interpretations or describe the reform program. This task can be achieved by focusing on the causes for the failings and failures of the Taewongun, the reaction against his reform policies, and the cleavages that occurred in Korea after 1873 over policy questions.

The reform effort of the 1860s failed for several interrelated reasons that will be traced throughout the course of this book. The most important cause was the predominance of a landed aristocracy intent upon the preservation of its social, economic, and political privileges. The aggrandizement of monarchical and central government power and the curtailment of elite privilege that was essential for reform could not be accomplished because the position of the elite in society and government was too powerful.

The attempt at domestic reform and adjustment to changing external conditions caused serious differences of opinion over socioeconomic and ideological matters and policy questions with significant political repercussions. There were three major issues that became the foci of dispute: whether the interests of the elite should be sacrificed in seeking an improvement of the central government's control over financial resources and an alleviation of fiscal burdens on the rebellious peasantry; whether violation of fundamental Confucian principles of ethics, social relations, and political economy could be tolerated for the sake of reform; and whether the best means for resisting foreign aggression and avoiding national disaster was unyielding resistance or limited compromise. The conflict over these alternatives split the previous unity of Korean conservatism and created intellectual and political opposition to reform.

Finally, the quality of leadership exercised by the throne was crucial to the problem of reform. In the period under study Korea was led by two men—the Taewongun from 1864 through 1873 and King Kojong from 1874 to 1876. The Taewongun has received the attention of many scholars, but surprisingly the king has been relatively neglected. It has generally been assumed that Queen Min and her relatives seized power in 1874, but in fact their influence did not become significant until later in the 1870s. The king was really the most important political actor in Korea on the eve of the Kanghwa Treaty, and the weakness of Korea's capacity for reform and adaptation was due in part to his shortcomings as a national leader.

Equilibrium and Stability

Although prime responsibility for Korea's eventual subjugation to Japan must be attributed to foreign imperialism, Korea's capacity to adapt to the demands of the modern world in the late nineteenth century was hindered by those factors responsible for the extraordinary stability of the Yi dynasty (1392-1910).[10] This stability was in large measure the result of a state of equilibrium produced by the interrelationship between a monarchical, bureaucratic, and centralized government structure and an aristocratic and hierarchical social system. The yangban elite, which had many of the attributes of an aristocracy, maintained itself by legal and de facto inherited status privileges, landholding, officeholding (in the central bureaucracy), and utilization of Confucian orthodoxy for the legitimization of status and economic interests. King and aristocrat were both mutually antagonistic and mutually supporting; each was dependent on the other for the continuation of his place in the political and social structure.[11] Although the state of equilibrium might shift from one pole to another—from relatively strong monarchy to aristocratic-bureaucratic domination of the throne—the balance of forces was never destroyed. The king remained the best source of legitimacy for aristocrats and bureaucrats, and the bureaucracy and social elite guaranteed the perpetuation of the monarchy. The symbiotic relationship between monarchy and aristocracy checked tendencies toward both the decentralization of power and the aggrandizement of royal or central power. Because the aristocracy identified with the centralized structure as bureaucrats and used it to maintain their social and economic privileges, there was no political decentralization or growth of feudalism. On the other hand, the centralized and autocratic government structure obscured the reality of aristocratic power. In fact, the social elite controlled the bureaucratic structure, kept it relatively weak, and used it to check royal authority.

Thus during the Yi dynasty the Korean people achieved a solution to the problem of political stability, but they could not solve the problem of creating adequate political authority for the achievement of national goals. The balance of power between monarchy and aristocracy was an asset for the maintenance of stability, but it was a liability when Korea was faced with the need to expand central power to mobilize resources for defense and development. The aristocracy had a stake in the preservation of a system that was at the same time centralized and weak, and neither kings nor bureaucrats could provide strong leadership—kings were subject to too many restraints and bureaucrats were always subordinated to royal authority. One of the main problems for the traditional Korean state as it moved toward the twentieth century was, therefore, overcoming the limitations on central authority in order to build national strength in the face of threatening challenges from the outside world.

During the 1860s the Taewongun waged an arduous struggle for a shift in the balance of power from the yangban aristocracy to the throne. It is a testament to his qualities of leadership and political skill that he almost succeeded in his objective, but in the end he failed because of social, political, and ideological restraints against absolute and arbitrary power. During the course of the struggle the Taewongun was called upon to de-

Politics and Policy in Traditional Korea

vise policy to deal with four major problems facing the Korean polity. He had not only to create but to institutionalize centralized monarchical power in the face of the weakness of the throne and checks on monarchical authority. He had to compete with the landed aristocracy for control over national wealth and manpower in an effort to reverse the trend toward the contraction of the tax base that had been in progress since 1600. He had to deal with the Confucian defense of status distinction and Confucian objections to his use of unorthodox means to accomplish his objectives. And he had to formulate a foreign policy that would produce national unity and support in the midst of fear and anxiety.

Restraints on Royal and Central Power

The Taewongun was faced with several major obstacles to the expansion of royal and central authority. The most significant of these was the strength of the yangban aristocracy. In addition, the traditional legitimacy of the crown lacked the powerful symbols and ideological supports that Chinese emperors of the later dynasties had at their disposal. Kings were subjected to powerful restraints inherent in the centralized bureaucratic structure; they could not gain full control over the dispensation of social status and prestige, since those attributes were rooted in the social order; and they were unable to make of Confucian ideology an effective tool in gaining compliance to their authority because the aristocracy also used Confucianism as a means of applying normative checks to royal authority.

The Aristocracy and the Upper Class

Yi dynasty society was divided into three main status groups: the yangban, the commoners, and the lowborn (ch'ŏnmin). At the top of the social pyramid were the yangban, those persons and families who inherited from their forbears their status and prestige, usually land and wealth, and the opportunities for education, academic degrees, and public office. Commoners were free men who had virtually no privileges and all the burdens of taxation. The vast majority were peasants who either owned small plots of land, farmed the land of others as tenants, or worked as landless agricultural laborers. A small percentage were engaged in commerce and artisanry. The ch'ŏnmin consisted mostly of slaves, but also included entertainers, shamans, and outcast groups.[12] In addition to the three main status categories there were smaller groups of intermediate status, such as the hereditary class of specialists (chung'in or middle men) who functioned as interpreters, astronomers, or medical doctors for the state, or the illegitimate sons of yangban who were prevented from taking the civil service examinations.

Introduction

The state in its zeal to freeze society, maintain order, and prevent the disruptive effects of social mobility provided for a personal tally system (*hop'ae*) to identify people in terms of their status.[13] The systems of population and land registration also required the recording of the social status of all individuals.[14] Even the Korean language had been tailored and shaped by the powerful ascriptive values in Korean society to enable the speaker to indicate by his use of honorifics, standard, or blunt forms his position relative to any companion in dialogue. The language had become a perfect vehicle for communication in a status-oriented society.

Although the yangban remained dominant to the end of the dynasty, it has been a difficult problem for historians to determine the specific criteria by which its membership was determined. This difficulty has arisen because Yi dynasty society was not a completely closed caste system in which movement from one status category to another was impossible. As time passed there was growing laxity in the recording of status affiliation in official registers, and there is evidence of both downward and upward mobility, particularly in the last centuries of the dynasty.[15]

Until recently scholars believed that in the Yi dynasty only men of yangban status were eligible to stand for the civil service examinations, so that yangban status could be determined not in terms of degree holding as in the case of the Chinese gentry, but in terms of inherited eligibility for degree holding. The legal regulations for examination eligibility, however, do not contain explicit status restrictions on participation and a few commoners did, indeed, participate in the examinations.[16] But the pattern of success in the examination system, particularly the examination for the highest degree (the *munkwa* examination), indicates that the candidates were drawn from a relatively closed group.[17] Therefore, for all practical purposes, it would still be best to conclude that yangban status was mostly inherited and that it conferred eligibility for participation in the civil service examinations to the exclusion of other status groups.

Recent studies of population and land registers for the eighteenth and nineteenth centuries have shown a large increase in the number and percentage of individuals registered under criteria usually reserved for yangban.[18] Many of these people obtained their titles and status through the purchase of official rank from the government,[19] but it has not been established that any or all of them were eligible to take the civil service examinations, or that they were regarded as bona fide yangban at the time. If they were eligible for the examinations, one would expect to find a large increase of new families among degree holders for the last two centuries of the dynasty, but Wagner's studies have not indicated any such influx of upwardly mobile commoners among the holders of the highest academic degrees.[20] For that reason it seems safe to assume that even though there was an increase in the size of a generalized upper class of well-to-do commoners with increased status, prestige, and privilege, there was not a significant percentage increase of yangban who were either eligible to or actually did participate in the civil service examinations.

Some scholars, notably Shikata Hiroshi and Kim Yong-sŏp, have chosen to define yangban in terms of the distinctions drawn between ascriptive categories in the household and land registers, and not in terms of eligibility for the examinations.[21] Kim has at least distinguished between upper and lower levels of the yangban class, including in the former category the noble relatives of the royal house and holders of high office and high degrees, and in the latter category holders of rank titles which may have been obtained through purchase rather than inheritance. One might therefore define the upper class in terms of two subdivisions: an upper level of hereditary aristocrats or yangban composed of office holders, degree holders, those eligible for participation in the higher civil service examinations, and their close relatives and descendants, who were also large landowners; and a lower level composed of local gentry, large landowners and landlords, and individuals with purchased titles of rank and status. The local gentry may, indeed, have included descendants of royalty, high officials, or degree holders, who still retained a vestige of prestige from inherited social status, but because their family fortunes had declined over the generations, they had become simple landlords, landowners, or even tenants, whose life style hardly differed from that of commoners. Many of these local gentry may still have been treated by the villagers with the deference afforded members of the yangban class even though their families had long since ceased playing a major role in national affairs.

Kim Yong-sŏp, building on the foundation laid down by the work of Shikata Hiroshi, has attempted to provide an economic explanation for the hypothesis that the social status system was breaking down in the last centuries of the dynasty as more and more commoners supposedly obtained yangban status through purchase. In his view the fragmentation of landholdings that occurred in this period increased opportunities for the purchase of land and the accumulation of wealth by members of all social strata after the seventeenth century.[22] Nevertheless, it is possible that the thesis of the breakdown of the social structure and status division has been exaggerated by Kim and others in order to prove the nascent and indigenous growth of capitalism in Korea without foreign stimulus and prior to the impact of the West on Korean society. In my view the evidence for change in the pattern of landholding, the decrease in the average size of private estates, and the increase in the numbers of medium-to-large landowners and people with rank and titles does not prove that a social aristocracy ceased to exist and function in the nineteenth century. Kim's own evidence, for example, can be used to demonstrate that by the end of the dynasty men of yangban status were still the largest landowners relative to other status groups, so that a high correlation between social status and wealth remained intact through the nineteenth century. However one interprets the changes in landholding patterns, there is no doubt that the upper yangban at least were still a hereditary aristocracy. Yet it may be conceded that, from the standpoint of the struggle between the central government and private interests for control over resources of land, wealth, and population, members of the nonaristocratic portion of the upper class of large landowners played a significant role.

Royal Legitimacy and Authority

The legitimacy of the Korean king derived mainly from the fact that there had been kings in Korea since the earliest recorded history and people assumed that the theoretical right to rule was vested in the king. But the legitimacy of the Korean king was weakened by his subordination to the Chinese emperor in the imaginary cosmological hierarchy that formed the basis of the Chinese tributary system. Under the rules of this system the Korean king, queen, and heir apparent had to receive formal investiture from the Chinese emperor, so that ultimate suzerainty lay outside the boundaries of the Korean kingdom.[23] Even though in fact the Chinese emperor never interfered with the Korean succession or the exercise of the king's authority within Korea, his legitimizing role did set limits on the aura of transcendence that surrounded the Korean throne.[24] While Korean kings frequently appealed to the Chinese concept of the mandate of Heaven as justification for their rule, the force of this idea was weakened by the king's inferiority to the Chinese emperor.

Yi dynasty kings functioned at the apex of a system of centralized bureaucracy that was borrowed from Chinese institutions, and on paper it would appear that they could have been as despotic in the exercise of their power as the emperors of the Ming or Ch'ing dynasties in China. As we will see, however, a description of the structure of centralized bureaucratic monarchy can be misleading because in actual practice the kings were much weaker than appeared on the surface. The bureaucratic structure was organized in hierarchical fashion with authority flowing top to bottom. The king theoretically controlled access to the bureaucracy through the civil service examinations and the right to appoint and dismiss officials, and he could supposedly ensure the obedience of his functionaries by remunerative, coercive, and normative inducements.[25] When the inducements provided by opportunities for wealth and prestige failed, the throne could exercise control over offcials by surveillance. All officials were subject to evaluation by their superiors and a biannual review of their performance in office by the ministries of Personnel and War. Individual acts of officials were subject to the scrutiny of the censorate, which could memorialize the throne directly on any acts of malfeasance or impropriety. Secret censors (*amhaeng ŏsa*) were dispatched at irregular intervals by the king to investigate the performance of past and present provincial officials. Furthermore, behind the institutions of surveillance lay the ultimate threat of force. Punishment for officials was handled by the state tribunal (*ŭigŭmbu*), an ad hoc court of justice staffed by judges who were concurrently members of the higher bureaucracy convened for the prosecution of administrative, political, and ideological crimes. The threat to life and limb was impressive: torture under interrogation, exile, enlistment in the army, and a variety of forms of execution. The only right the individual official had against accusation and indictment was the dubious privilege of trial by the state tribunal, but in a system of justice in which the trial was but a means of confirming guilt by forced confession, the state tribunal provided the individual with little protection against the wrath of the state. Finally, the king could use normative standards as a means of inducing obedience to royal authority. Confucian thought stressed loyalty to the ruler, and the body of Confucian thought was made the basis for education, the civil service examination system, and ultimately recruitment into the bureaucracy.

The Yi dynasty kings thus had formidable weapons at their disposal for the exercise of power, and except in the case of weaklings or children who occupied the throne, the king was never transformed into the powerless symbol of legitimacy that the Japanese emperor became after the fourteenth century. The potential for the actual exercise of royal power always existed, and for that reason the relationship between king and yangban bureaucrats must be described in terms of check and balance rather than the complete subjugation of one to the other.

Despite the existence of the apparatus of absolute despotism, the centralized structure of government masked the limitations on royal authority by the yangban aristocracy. The most important reason for these limitations was that the sources of power, wealth, and prestige were not controlled exclusively by the crown; they were also based on inheritance of status and landownership. If not in law then in fact, the hereditary descendents of yangban families also monopolized education, participation in the upper level civil service examination, and membership in the central bureaucracy,[26] and through the process of review and recommendation higher bureaucrats could influence and control the careers of lower bureaucrats.

The yangban bureaucrats even turned the normative standards of Confucian thought against the throne. By insisting that the king conform to moral and ethical standards that transcended his right to the arbitrary exercise of power, by setting themselves up as arbiters of those standards by virtue of their knowledge of Confucian texts, and by insisting on their right to remonstrate and the king's obligation to tolerate remonstrance, yangban bureaucrats and literati sought to reduce kings to puppets of their own desires and interests. These normative restraints on royal despotism were institutionalized in two important ways. The censorate, which was an institution borrowed from the Chinese for the exercise of both surveillance and remonstrance functions, became in the hands of the Koreans a powerful check on royal authority. The daily royal lectures by which young kings were tutored in Confucian learning became agencies for the indoctrination of monarchs in the principles of respect for men of learning and toleration of official remonstrance.[27]

Confucian theory was also used by the ruling class to provide theoretical and moral justification for the existing social structure. Most Korean Confucianists held that a stepladder organization of society was the symbolic embodiment of the distinctions between superior and inferior, father and son, ruler and subject, and elder and younger brother that represented the very essence of Confucian morality. Any attacks on the privileged position of the yangban were therefore stoutly resisted on the grounds that they would destroy the moral as well as the social order. Korean Confucianism thus severely restricted the king's ability to invade yangban rights and manipulate his subjects for the benefit of the throne or the nation.

The weakness of royal prestige and authority was characteristic of Korean states since the formation of the earliest kingdoms. Each of the Three Kingdoms—Koguryŏ, Paekche, and Silla—in the period from the first to the seventh centuries A.D. evolved a kingship that was the outgrowth of a nomadic tribal political organization that had become sedentary. The authority of the throne was generally restricted by the vestiges of a tribal type council, the most prominent example of which was the *hwabaek* council of Silla. Even after Silla's unification of the peninsula in A.D. 668, Silla kings had to deal with the "bone-rank" aristocrats, powerful local magnates, and regional military commanders. In the Koryŏ dynasty (918-1392) despite the development of centralized administration, kings were subjected to the influence of strong aristocratic clans. After 1170 military men seized power, and from 1196 to 1258 Koryŏ kings were hardly more than puppets in the hands of the military-

Politics and Policy in Traditional Korea

aristocratic Ch'oe family, which passed its shogunal type authority down hereditarily through four generations. From the mid-thirteenth to the mid-fourteenth century the royal house reached the nadir of subjugation under the rule of the Mongol invaders. Significantly the effect of Mongol rule on the development of the Korean monarchy was vastly different from what occurred in China. Far from laying the foundation for monarchical despotism, Mongol rule preserved centralized structure but perpetuated weakness by lowering royal prestige. In the Yi dynasty (1392-1910) the trend toward royal impotence was reversed somewhat with the reestablishment of the structure and institutions of centralized rule. There was a trend toward patrilineal succession probably because of the influence of Confucian ideas, and the prestige of the throne was raised by a number of strong kings in the late fourteenth and fifteenth centuries.

In succeeding centuries, however, the power of the throne was effectively checked by the yangban bureaucracy, and in the nineteenth century there was a significant weakening of the king's authority. Because certain kings lacked male heirs and other kings were either infants or youths, and because queens were selected from yangban families, certain yangban lineages were able to dominate the throne. In the absence of a male heir or in the presence of a minor king, the eldest living dowager queen had the right to designate a successor from a collateral line and reign as a regent until the king attained majority. Since the eldest dowager and the other living queens were usually from different yangban lineages, this system prevented the monopolization of power by any single lineage to the exclusion of others as had occurred with the Ch'oe family in the Koryŏ dynasty. As for royal absolutism, however, it suffered as much from its subordination to several aristocratic lineages as to a single one. When Kojong came to the throne in 1864, the Taewongun believed that one of the first orders of business was to reestablish the prestige of the throne—a formidable task in view of the low state to which the crown had fallen.

Weakness of Centralized Bureaucratic Control

Despite the highly centralized appearance of administrative structure, centralized control over the whole country by the top of the bureaucratic hierarchy in the capital had never been complete or thoroughly effective. The Chinese type bureaucratic structure was incompletely centralized, since it did not penetrate deeply enough into the rural villages to ensure efficient or total control over the population. There were only about three hundred and thirty magistrates to govern a population of approximately eight to ten million people by the mid-nineteenth century.[28] The district magistrate was rotated frequently and by the laws of avoidance kept out of his native area. To govern effectively he had to cooperate with local influential families and rely on his clerks and petty officials (*ajŏn, sŏri*) who had virtual permanence of tenure and knew the local scene intimately.

Local clerks and petty officials in the late Yi dynasty were the product of a long institutional development. They were an important group that mediated between the authority of the central government as represented by the district magistrate and the population in the villages. The process of centralization that took place over several dynasties had not included their incorporation into the regular bureaucracy. They were placed outside the realm of emolument and had to fend for themselves by the collection of fees, bribery, and extortion. Many contemporaries and scholars have viewed them as a major cause of dynastic decline, but they were really a part of the system of institutionalized corruption. In earlier dynasties local officials were recruited from among prestigious families in recognition of their social and political position on the local scene and as an inducement to their loyalty to the dynasty. As the process of centralization continued into the Koryŏ and Yi dynasties, the political power of the local magnates was reduced and the position of petty official sank to a lower level of prestige. A clerk's job therefore offered opportunities for illicit wealth for members of the commoner class.

Given the institutionalized position of the clerk and his pursuit of private gain, one could not expect the full and honest implementation of orders from the remote royal court. The magistrate's own remoteness from the villages and the population and the intervening groups of petty officials and local men of influence were in large part responsible for the growth of corruption and the inability of the central government to stem it.

Throughout the Yi dynasty, the government never attempted to extend centralized control and increase its power over all the people. Although in theory the central government expected conformity to its edicts and laws, in practice it was willing to tolerate diversity arising out of adjustment to local and particular conditions. Central control over district magistrates was relatively weak because of distance, poor transportation to all county seats, and the time involved in the transmittal of communications. Instead of trying to improve this situation, however, the central government granted substantial leeway to district magistrates. Since the government's main interest was in the magistrate's ability to fulfill tax quotas and maintain peace, it was more concerned with the results of his administration than with full and complete adherence to the written laws of the land.

Politics and Policy in Traditional Korea

There also seems to have been a bias against forcing the whole population into rigid conformity with fixed and unbending law. It was believed that people varied from place to place in their customs and habits, and that effective administration should not do violence to this variety, but adjust and adapt to it. This willingness to accept diversity would tend to explain the longevity of the dynasty despite relatively inefficient administration. Weak central control may have contributed to diversity, contradictory practices, and administrative confusion when viewed from the top, but by lessening the pressures at the bottom for forced adjustment to unworkable and rigid laws and procedures, the system provided a safety valve for discontent.

Whatever its importance for the longevity of the dynasty as a whole, however, incomplete and inefficient centralization was also responsible for the growing weakness of the central government. When the time came that the king and his officials at the capital decided that something had to be done about both corruption and inefficiency, central control was essential to the success of reform—both institutional change and the weeding out of corrupt individuals—but it was lacking. Both traditional and modern government may benefit from efficient organization to ensure the implementation of plans and programs, but in traditional Korea greater rationalization of government operation and structure was neglected and efficiency was a recessive not a dominant value.

Weaknesses of Bureaucratic Leadership

Because of the check and balance between throne and bureaucracy, the locus of power in the Yi dynasty political system was not clearly established. The lack of clearly defined authority was a serious handicap for an authoritarian order in need of positive leadership from the top. The king was hamstrung by bureaucratic restraints, but the bureaucracy was no more able to exercise positive leadership, not only because of the vertical and horizontal divisions within its ranks, but also because of the weakness of the chief state councilor, the collegial aspects of decision making, and the usual inhibitions against initiative characteristic of any bureaucratic organization.

Because the top of the administrative pyramid was composed of a state council in which the chief state councilor was only slightly more prestigious and powerful than the other councilors, it was impossible for him to exert leadership independently of the king or as a surrogate for the king, even if he had been disposed to do so.

Not only was the state council a collegial body, but major decisions were usually made by a relatively large group of about thirty to fifty officials of *tangsanggwan* rank, usually referred to collectively as *taesin* or chief officials.[29] The *taesin* also included the sinecured elder statesmen of the realm. Therefore, on major questions of state the incumbent officials were subject to criticism by men older and more prestigious than themselves, inhibiting their capacity for independent leadership.

There were other features of bureaucratic structure and behavior that kept the bureaucracy divided and unable to usurp power from the king. One little-noted aspect of the divisive effect of Confucian values on the bureaucracy was the Confucian stress on morality and propriety that created a bureaucratic life full of rancor and enmity. Each official kept on the alert for the slightest violation of Confucian norms by any of his colleagues, partially for the purpose of gaining favor for himself and advancing up the bureaucratic ladder. The meddling of hidebound Confucian moralists in the affairs of others kept the bureaucrats' focus turned inward on each other and diverted their attention from the throne.

Furthermore, conflicts of interest in the administrative structure were not confined to those between the monarch and his officials. Within the bureaucracy there were certain major horizontal cleavages that produced variance of interest and outlook between higher and lower officials. The *taesin* were the people most favored by the throne. They tended to identify with the throne, in particular when criticism of policy or charges of misgovernment were raised by lesser officials or literati. Since policy critics of lower rank had to be careful of attacking the king directly lest they be charged with lèse-majesté, they usually aimed their criticism at the high officials, who had to take responsibility for the crown on sub- stantive policy or administrative matters. For this reason, the entrenched higher officials usually took the lead in suppressing their lower-ranking and less prestigious cohorts, reducing the cohesiveness and power of the bureaucracy as a whole.

The bureaucracy was also riven by vertical cleavage for about two centuries after 1575. Many officials (just what percentage of the total bureaucracy or degree-holding elite has as yet not been established) were members of bureaucratic factions, and sons inherited factional allegiance from their fathers. There were many schisms and recombinations, so that by the beginning of the eighteenth century there were four major factional groupings: the Patriarch's faction (*Noron*), the Disciples' faction (*Soron*), the Southerners (*Namin*), and the Northerners (*Pug'in*). (The latter two were so named because of the location of their founders' residences in Seoul. They were not territorial or regional designations.) By the first quarter of the eighteenth century the Patriarch's faction emerged as the most powerful, with the members of the Disciples' faction in second place. The Northerners and Southerners were not completely excluded from office-holding opportunities but except for brief interludes were in general relegated to minor positions.[30]

Factional division weakened the unity of the upper class and the potential for a direct confrontation between yangban bureaucrats and the throne. Instead of the yangban bureaucrats competing with the throne for the control of the state and developing new types of institutions that would have shifted the locus of power to them, they organized into factional subgroups and competed with one another for the favor of the throne. When they obtained it, they did their best to utilize royal favor to eliminate their opponents. Paradoxical as it may be, bureaucratic factionalism may have been a symptom of the weakness of royal control over the bureaucracy in the Yi dynasty, but by keeping the bureaucracy divided, factionalism also prevented the usurpation of monarchical power by the aristocracy and preserved the structure of centralized administration and the subordination of yangban power to the monarchy. In the Yi dynasty system, the yangban bureaucrat restrained royal authority, but he never fully displaced or replaced the monarch.

Although the influence of the traditional factions had waned by the nineteenth century, the same pattern of factional politics governed the competition between the yangban consort clans for political power, except that intermarriage with the royal house replaced jockeying for the favor of an adult monarch. But the heyday of the factions was the seventeenth and early eighteenth centuries; by 1864 factionalism was no longer the most important basis of bureaucratic politics. It was replaced by cleavage over issues of policy.

Nevertheless it has been necessary to discuss the role of factionalism in Yi dynasty history because it has heretofore been regarded as the indispensable key to an understanding of Korean politics in all periods. Scholars, in writing about the 1860s and 1870s, have usually assigned a primary role to the struggle between a Taewongun and a Min faction, but one of the goals of this study will be to rectify this interpretation. While the Taewongun did have a small clique of supporters personally loyal to him, few of them were important bureaucrats, and his political power did not depend on their support. Furthermore, the Min clan was bound together by familial not factional ties. In other words, court intrigue and palace politics should not be mistaken for bureaucratic factionalism.

Competition for Resources: The Shrinking Revenue Base

The Taewongun was concerned with expanding the central government's control over wealth and manpower, a problem that was by

Introduction

no means confined to the nineteenth-century Korean monarchy. S. N. Eisenstadt has created a model for centralized bureaucratic empires in which the monarchy or central government competes with an aristocracy for free-floating resources and political power.[31] By free-floating resources Eisenstadt means that landed property and its product was not tied up in feudal fiefs or estates but was freely alienable and subject to taxation by the central government. Furthermore, the peasant was not the serf of the feudal manor but the relatively independent landowner, tenant, or laborer, who could be exploited by the state for taxation, corvée, or military service. Thus, in a predominantly agrarian society ruled by a centralized bureaucratic monarchy and a significant aristocracy, the central government and the aristocracy would compete for control of land and population.[32]

Yi dynasty Korea fit this pattern very well and in fact conformed in most respects to Eisenstadt's description of the later Chinese dynasties, with the exception that the upper class during the Yi dynasty was closer in nature to the aristocracy of the T'ang and pre-T'ang eras than to the gentry of the later dynasties in Chinese history.[33] The major forms of land tenure in Korea were ownership and tenancy at least as early as 1424 and probably from the beginning of the dynasty.[34] Therefore, wealth and manpower remained free-floating in the Eisenstadtian sense, but the Korean yangban proved to be a much more formidable opponent of the throne in competition for these resources than the Chinese gentry.

The central government fought a losing battle to maintain a broad tax base and restrict legal and de facto tax exemptions to a small aristocratic elite. In fact, some government policies even exacerbated the narrowing of the tax base. Because the government suffered severe financial shortages as a result of the Japanese invasions of 1592-98 and the Manchu invasions of 1627 and 1636, it began to sell titles and ranks to members of lower social orders as a means of raising funds.[35] This policy only contributed to a permanent contraction of the tax base and redistribution of the tax burden on a smaller number of taxpayers. Central government impoverishment and peasant distress proceeded hand in hand, while a new middle class of well-to-do and intermediate landholders and rentiers grew in size. Even though this new class had a weak claim on membership in the older, narrower elite, it could at least obtain some benefits in the form of raised status and tax exemptions. Thus the economic benefits of the sale of rank to the rich and middle peasants were probably greater than the social or political effects. In addition to legally sanctioned tax exemption, the concentration of private wealth in the hands of a few landlords contributed to the subornation of local officials and permitted the non- and under-recording of land and population for tax purposes with the concomitant depletion of central government revenues.

One other factor that contributed to the decline in the central government's control over resources was the growth in the power of certain private and semiofficial autonomous institutions. These included the estates of princes and princesses, private academies, and lands controlled directly by government agencies, district magistrates, and commanders of military garrisons. The central government felt obliged to provide for the support of princes and princesses, but instead of granting them government stipends from central treasuries, the government allowed them the semiautonomous control of their own lands and estates relatively free from government surveillance. Private academies, which originated in 1543 and underwent a steady growth in the next few centuries, were also allowed to accumulate lands as part of their estates. Last, the government also chose to provide for the system of officially managed rural relief, seed, and credit funds as a major means of increasing state revenues. These funds were loaned out at interest, and the government became increasingly dependent on them because of the inelastic tax structure. Eventually these loans became a source of corruption and were forced on the poorest of peasants, in effect constituting a new and most regressive tax.

By the nineteenth century the central government's control over resources and population had reached a point of crisis that was most difficult to solve because the interests of the central government, aristocracy (or landed upper class), and peasantry were mutually exclusive. Whatever measure taken to benefit one of the three was bound to have adverse consequences for the other two. In any case, the Taewongun sought to reestablish the control over men and resources that had slipped out of the central government's hands in the past few centuries, and by 1873 he succeeded in checking the tendency toward the growth of autonomous control over resources by the social and economic elite. By no means, however, did he succeed in attacking the problem at its roots in the system of land tenure and taxation, and when Korea emerged from seclusion in 1876, the balance between monarchical and aristocratic control over resources had been restored by a reaction against his reforms.

Ideological Opposition: Status Distinction
and Orthodox Methods

The yangban elite of the Yi dynasty was, among other things, an intellectual elite that jealously guarded its social prerogatives and philosophical principles. Late in the 1860s some yangban scholars and officials raised objections to the Taewongun's policies over two fundamental

Introduction

issues: whether in the attempt to save Korea from domestic disruption and foreign invasion the morally superior hierarchical social order should be weakened for the benefit of the state and the alleviation of peasant suffering, and whether fundamental principles of Confucian government should be sacrificed for the benefits of expediency and practical action.

The first of these issues was a product of a certain ambivalence within the Korean Confucian tradition. The Korean aristocracy utilized Confucianism to provide moral justification for a hierarchical society, but this conflicted with the egalitarian strain in Confucian thought and the Mencian dictum that peasant welfare was the basis of the well-ordered state. All good Confucians knew that the suffering peasants had to be relieved of excessive tax burdens if a state were to thrive and if a ruler were to lay claim to moral distinction. Some were even aware that if Confucian thought stressed any hierarchy, it was a moral hierarchy of virtuous men, and not a hereditary hierarchy of social status and landed wealth; a few independent and altruistic thinkers even regarded the existence of a privileged yangban class as an anomalous and untoward development. Therefore, when the Taewongun decided to take limited action against the prerogatives of the upper class—in particular, their tax exempt status and their monopoly over educational institutions and shrines—many officials concerned more with national than class interests concurred wholeheartedly with these measures because they seemed to have as their objective the greater welfare of the peasantry. On the other hand, an influential and vocal minority of literati and lesser officials regarded any tampering with the system of social distinction and special privilege as subversive of the Confucian moral order, especially when it appeared that the main objective of the government was the aggrandizement of income for the state and not necessarily the greater welfare of the peasantry.

The same men also objected to the Taewongun's subordination of Confucian dogma to the attainment of practical objectives. The Taewongun was willing to ignore traditional dogma on tax and monetary policy in order to raise revenue, and he also trampled on Confucian sensibilities in his zeal to raise the prestige of the royal house. The dogmatists, however, were unwilling to sacrifice means to ends; they insisted that taxes be kept low, that the state refrain from monetary manipulation, and that the throne avoid extravagant expenditure no matter how urgent the practical demands of the time.

Foreign Policy and Domestic Politics

The challenge to Korean security posed by the threat of invasion by Western countries and Japan and the gradual spread of Christianity within Korea created the conditions by which the Taewongun built up a powerful national consensus on foreign policy and constructed a solid base of political support for his own authority. In the face of superior force he remained determined to preserve Korean seclusion and isolation despite the threat of violence from the outside world. The French demanded toleration for the activities of their missionaries within Korea and freedom of religious practice for Korean converts. The Americans insisted on protection for shipwrecked American sailors and conclusion of a treaty of trade. And the Japanese asked for a restructuring of foreign relations and changes of protocol along more modern lines. The Taewongun, however, refused to negotiate with the French on the missionary question, refused to admit Korean culpability in the treatment of American sailors, rejected all requests for trade relations, and refused to receive any communications from Japan that deviated in the slightest respect from established forms.

Korean resistance to foreign demands was reinforced by resentment over what appeared to be barbarous Western behavior and by the fear that the Catholic missionary movement was little more than fifth-column political subversion designed to weaken Korean defenses from within in preparation for the attacks of foreign gunboats. The virulence of the Taewongun's anti-Catholic persecution in the 1860s was thus based on the belief that the missionary movement was the vanguard of foreign imperialism.[36] Koreans believed that they were a nation besieged, threatened from within and without, so that perennial vigilance and ruthless extermination of traitors were the only means to their salvation. It was this psychological atmosphere of constant fear that produced the solid consensus of support for the Taewongun's policies during the early 1860s, for few dared criticize objectionable domestic policies of a leader who seemed to be able to keep the nation safe at a time when the Chinese were crumbling under foreign attacks and the Japanese were succumbing to the enticements of Western culture.

Between 1866 and 1871 Korea was attacked twice by relatively small expeditions of regular forces of foreign governments: one launched by the French in 1866 in reprisal for the execution of French missionaries in February and March of that year, and another by a U.S. naval squadron and a small contingent of marines in 1871 against the brave but hapless defenders of Kanghwa Island as an expression of American determination to solve the problems of shipwrecked sailors, trade, and amity![37]

In the same period Korea was raided twice by independent traders and adventurers. In 1866 *General Sherman*, a ship with U.S. registration, an English captain and missionary interpreter, and a mixed crew of Malays

Introduction

and Chinese, arrived off Pyongyang and so terrorized the local populace that they were provoked into setting the ship afire and murdering the whole crew. This incident led to the U.S. expedition of chastisement in 1871.[38]

In 1868 an even more bizarre episode occurred when Ernst Oppert, a German trader adventurer, rebuffed in his first attempt at trade in 1866, returned to Korean shores with what seemed to him a surefire device for ensuring the success of his mission. He raided the tomb of the Taewongun's father in Ch'ungch'ŏng province in order to dig up the remains and then offer to exchange them in return for permission to trade. This grotesque but unique plot to capitalize on filial piety for gain and profit was aborted when Korean troops arrived on the scene and Oppert's group had to beat a hasty retreat to their ships offshore.[39]

Even though the Koreans suffered defeats in pitched battles with the French and Americans, because they had forced the foreigners to leave Korean shores, they felt they had won victories over the Western barbarian, vindicating the Taewongun in his policy of resistance. Moreover, each event only exacerbated the sense of indignation and outrage; in the context of the Koreans' traditions and experience the behavior of the foreigners was both baffling and barbarous.

In the midst of this mood of fear and anger the Japanese began to request a radical readjustment of the form and structure of Korean-Japanese relations. Prior to this time relations between the two countries were strictly regulated and limited in accordance with a treaty concluded in 1609. Japanese were permitted to reside only behind the palisade walls of a trading center at Tongnae near Pusan; trade was restricted by quotas and passports; the exchange of high-level envoys had ceased in 1811; and all negotiations were handled by lowly Korean interpreters.[40]

When a Japanese envoy arrived at Tongnae in November 1868 to report the Meiji restoration and the changes in the government structure of Japan, the Korean interpreter refused even to accept the Japanese communications on the grounds that the Japanese envoy had discarded the use of the Korean seal of authorization and was using a new and unacceptable title, and that the words, emperor, imperial decree, and imperial house, used in the official communication in reference to the Japanese emperor were not permissible because those terms were reserved for the Chinese emperor alone.[41] From 1868 to 1873 the Japanese attempted to obtain Korean recognition of the new Japanese government and the establishment of relations on the basis of equality, but the Koreans rejected all Japanese messages outright, kept the envoys waiting under various ruses and pretexts, refused to allow a direct interview even with the local magistrate, cut off provisions to the Japanese residence, and boycotted trade.[42] These actions provoked the Japanese to the decision to invade Korea during the *Seikan* (conquer Korea) debates of 1873, but with the return of the Iwakura mission from Europe to Japan in the fall of 1873 the Japanese government reversed the decision.[43]

Korea was spared the horror of war with Japan by a hair's breadth thanks to Japanese preoccupation with her own development. For that matter, the Taewongun had escaped unscathed from a whole decade of adamant resistance to the foreigner. When he was forced out of power because of domestic politics, he bequeathed to his successors the difficult task of dealing with foreign powers on realistic terms. He never had to suffer the humiliation of capitulation and remained a symbol of national pride and independence even during the period of his political eclipse in the 1870s. It was not until 1882 when he was unceremoniously abducted to China by the Chinese that the myth of his invincibility was shattered. In the meantime the onus of capitulation was born by his son. When the Taewongun retired at the end of 1873 and King Kojong adopted a conciliatory policy toward Japan, foreign policy became a serious political liability for the young monarch attempting to wield his new-found authority.

The failure of the Taewongun's reform program was a function of three salient aspects of the old order: the power of the elite (which was the major cause of the weakness of centralized government), Confucian dogma, and the weakness of political leadership. Political competition was determined primarily by disputes over concrete policy questions; court intrigue played a minor role in politics, and factionalism none at all, if by factionalism we mean political struggle between discrete bureaucratic factions organized on the basis of personal loyalty. The reaction against reform and the political opposition to the Taewongun stemmed from disaffection with the Taewongun's reform policies even though their main purpose was inherently conservative. Subsequently, the shift of right-wing Confucian conservatives away from Kojong after 1873 was the result of disaffection with his inadequate handling of domestic issues and his compromise with Japan in foreign policy. A study of the interaction between policy and politics against the background of relatively stable political structure, socioeconomic forces, and ideology should provide us with new perspectives on traditional Korea.

2

Problems in the Establishment of Monarchic and Dynastic Power

The Taewongun's attempt to reestablish the power and prestige of the throne and the royal house was hampered by three important factors: the weakness of his own institutional position in the structure of government, his failure to train his son in the exercise of power and convince him of the superiority of his policy goals, and the reaction against his palace reconstruction project and his attempts to upgrade the royal clan.

The Taewongun held power only because the previous king died without heir and his second son was chosen by the eldest dowager to succeed to the throne. Never more than the king's father, he was an institutional anomaly whose lack of legitimacy proved an Achilles' heel to the preservation of his authority. But he was a resolute man who set a certain style of governance and a line of policy. His strength was ingrained in his character, tempered by experience in the politics of the early nineteenth century. Having spent his adulthood as an inconsequential nobleman, neglected or despised by haughty aristocrats, he suddenly found himself in the seat of power with the opportunity and determination to create a strong monarchy. Undoubtedly he must have wished for his son to consolidate his achievements and carry on his work.

What he failed to discern was that the decade of his own authority was also the time of his son's apprenticeship, all the more crucial because of Kojong's inborn timidity, indecisiveness, and diffidence. The king's training was crucial to the forging of central and national power in the long term, but the task was left in the hands of insidious Confucian bureaucratic tutors and scheming courtiers.

Browbeaten by day by long-robed pedants and gulled at night by a quick-witted wife, Kojong emerged from his decade of tutelage an easy mark for the powerseekers around the throne. Armed with his Confucian maxims, he sallied forth to do battle with the real world and was left battered and confused. What his father built in ten years he undid in three, but that is a story for later on. In the meanwhile his father was planning for the restoration of royal and dynastic glory. For this task the elimination of administrative malfunction, popular suffering, and foreign invasion was not sufficient. He wanted a new and expensive palace as a prominent symbol of exalted monarchy and sage rule, but this could not be obtained without risk. He had to gamble with the financial stability of the state and the support of the yangban-official class.

The Throne

Succession

In the first half of the nineteenth century the yangban consort clans or relatives of queens were able to gain control of the bureaucracy and dominate the throne because all four monarchs came to the throne as minors. In some cases this was the result of chance—the lack of male heirs—but it was also produced by the manipulations of the consort clans. When an heir was lacking, the eldest living dowager queen had the right to designate the successor to a deceased king, albeit after consultation with the leading officials. The dowager would also become regent in the case of a minor king. Thus, the strength and position of the consort clans depended on whether they were able to marry their daughters to the young kings or heirs apparent. The power of these women as queens was negligible, but their roles as mothers of future kings or eldest dowagers during brief interregna or regencies were crucial to the continued well-being of their male relatives. The male relatives of queens were given noble titles and special consideration for appointment and promotion in the bureaucracy. Because of clan solidarity the benefits of nepotism extended beyond the immediate relations of the queens to their uncles, cousins, and nephews. Before long the male members of the consort clans monopolized the higher official posts.

No single clan, however, was able to retain hegemony continuously for the whole half-century, because it had to contend with the relatives of other dowagers, members of the royal house, and important officials. At any given time the queen and dowagers might all belong to different clans; the consort clans seldom resorted to naked force to preserve their position,[1] and none ever carried out a full-scale purge of its rivals. If a clan failed to marry one of its girls to a young king or heir apparent, it was willing to abide by the decision and accept the consequences. Because the politics of consort clan rivalry remained civilized and humane, a relative balance among the consort clans was maintained throughout the first half of the century; and in the absence of a male heir to the throne, the position of the dowager-regent could become crucial for determining a sudden shift of political power.

Regencies were established for all four kings of the century. Sunjŏ (r. 1800-34) was but ten years old when he became king under the regency of Dowager Kim of the Kyŏngju Kim clan. Dowager Kim, the second queen of Yŏngjo (r. 1724-26), however, represented the declining forces of the eighteenth century rather than the emerging powers of the nineteenth. She relinquished her regency in 1804 and died the next year.[2] The foundation was laid for the dominance of the Andong Kim clan when the daughter of Kim Cho-sun became Sunjo's queen in 1802.[3] Kim had been tutor to Sunjo when crown prince and he enjoyed the favor of Dowager Kim.[4] He became a powerful figure during Sunjo's reign, but there was no assurance that his influence or that of his clan could be perpetuated, since the crown prince had married a member of the P'ungyang Cho clan.[5] Cho Man-yong, the crown prince's father-in-law, was then promoted to a series of high offices in the 1820s.

Had Sunjo's crown prince (posthumous title, Ikchong) lived to succeed his father, there would have been little opportunity for the Andong Kim to perpetuate their power. But he died in 1830 and his young son became the heir apparent.[6] When Sunjo died in 1834, a regency was established under the eldest dowager, Sunjo's queen of the Andong Kim clan, for the succeeding eight year old king, Hŏnjong (r. 1834-49). Throughout the first few years of Hŏnjong's reign, members of the Andong Kim and P'ungyang Cho clans shared power in the bureaucracy. Cho Man-yong (P'ungyang) was Hŏnjong's maternal grandfather, Dowager Kim (Andong) remained regent until 1840, and an Andong Kim was chosen for Hŏnjong's queen.[7]

Despite Dowager Kim's regency, the balance of power began to shift toward the P'ungyang Cho. In 1838 two of the three top state councilors resigned in protest over one of the dowager-regent's decisions, and the remaining councilor was sympathetic to the P'ungyang Cho.[8] In 1839 the Cho took the lead in the anti-Catholic persecutions of that year, and many of them were appointed to high posts. In 1840 Kim Chŏng-gŭn, the leader of the Andong Kim clan, died, and the dowager-regent found herself isolated and without male support. She relinquished the regency the same year.[9]

The early 1840s were the heyday of the P'ungyang Cho clan who shared power with Kwŏn Ton-in, chief state councilor from 1842 to 1851.[10] They were unable to sustain their position after the deaths of Cho Man-yong in 1846 and King Hŏnjong in 1849. Since Hŏnjong left no heirs and Sunjo's queen, Dowager Kim (Andong), was still the eldest living

Politics and Policy in Traditional Korea

dowager, she was able to use her influence in the selection of the new king, Ch'ŏlchong (r. 1849-64).[11] Ch'ŏlchong was but nineteen years old when he ascended the throne. Certainly in terms of age he was old enough to rule on his own,[12] but Dowager Kim was declared regent from 1849 to 1852. A second and third generation of Andong Kim men came into power, and the daughter of an Andong Kim was chosen for Ch'ŏlchong's queen. Kwŏn Ton-in was replaced by Kim Hŭng-gŭn as chief state councilor and about a dozen members of the lineage were soon placed in important positions in the government.[13]

During Ch'ŏlchong's reign the main challenge to the authority of the Andong Kim came from the royal family, but it was quickly repressed. In 1862 a plot to depose the king and back Yi Ha-jon for the throne was uncovered. Yi had been favored by Kwŏn Ton-in for king after Hŏnjong's death in 1849, and he was now given poison.[15] These were dangerous times for politically ambitious members of the royal house. Yi Ha-ŭng, the later Taewongun, opted for discretion, obscurity, and safety. He acquired a reputation as a ne'er-do-well, which was useful in distracting attention from him.[16]

The Andong Kim lacked the two essentials for the preservation of their power—a male heir and the eldest dowager. Although Ch'ŏlchong's queen was an Andong Kim, all her sons had died prematurely; when Ch'ŏlchong passed away in the beginning of 1864 without a male heir, the eldest dowager was Ikchong's consort, a P'ungyang Cho. According to several historians, Dowager Cho and the Taewongun entered into a conspiracy for the selection of the Taewongun's second son as the new king.[17] Although the conspiracy theory cannot be confirmed, there is some justification for it because the major male relatives of the P'ungyang Cho clan had either died or been forced into obscurity and Dowager Cho lacked political support. It is reasonable to assume that she would have struck some bargain with a member of the royal house to ensure that members of her clan would benefit from the designation of a new king. The Taewongun also benefited from the relative weakness of the P'ungyang Cho clan. Once his son ascended the throne, the P'ungyang Cho would not have the strength to impose their will on him.

In view of these considerations, it is most amazing that the selection of Kojong did not generate more opposition within the ranks of the Andong Kim. Immediately after the death of Ch'ŏlchong, Dowager Cho summoned a conference of chief ministers and declared that the second son of Yi Ha-ŭng (the Taewongun) would be declared king.[18] She specified that the new king would be adopted as the son of her deceased husband, Ikchong, and not Ch'ŏlchong, probably to ensure that she

Problems in the Establishment of Power

would remain as regent instead of Ch'ŏlchong's queen.[19] She also stated that the king's father, now dubbed Taewongun[20] (the title given to fathers of kings who had not themselves been kings) would "assist the king" in the conduct of government. Dowager Cho became regent de jure for the eleven year old monarch, and she did not relinquish that position until March 29, 1866.[21]

One can only speculate on the reasons for the passive acquiescence of the Andong Kim in these decisions.[22] Their inaction was no doubt produced by their own sense of security, their willingness to abide by accepted procedures, and their underestimation of the resourcefulness of the Taewongun.

Regent, Taewongun, and King

Regency

During the first ten years of Kojong's reign, the formal regency lasted for only a little over two years. In fact, three people shared power—the dowager, the king, and the Taewongun. From 1866 to 1873 the country was governed more like a dyarchy than a monarchy. The Taewongun acted as a de facto regent even though he had no institutionalized position, either by custom or statute, in the constitution of the state.

The regulations that defined the positions of king and dowager-regent were drawn up on January 16, 1864. These specified that since the dowager was to take an active role in decision making, the Sung dynasty (the Chinese Sung dynasty, *A.D.* 960-1279) precedent whereby the regent remained in the inner palace and communicated her intentions to the court through eunuch palace officials was not to be followed. Instead, the dowager would attend court in person and sit behind a curtain in the royal audience hall conducting official business conjointly with the king. Officials would present both official documents and private written memorials to the king who would either deal directly with the matter himself or turn to the dowager for her advice. If he decided to follow the dowager's recommendations, officials might then direct their remarks to her. The dowager-regent would also accompany the king to the frequent royal lectures, with the option of sitting behind her curtain or moving out front to take part in the discussion.

Since strict distinctions were to be made by the scribes in recording the remarks and decrees of king and dowager-regent, it is easy to see just which of the pair was involved in various decisions.[23] Because the Taewongun was not regarded as a legitimate participant in the formal machinery of government, he was left out of the regulations and the court records. This is extremely unfortunate for historians for the Tae-wongun played a more significant role in determining important policy questions than either the dowager or the king.

The Taewongun's Role in Decision Making

The position of the Taewongun in the governmental structure can only be estimated by examining the fragmentary references to him in the daily records of the court. Since he is never mentioned in the daily records as in attendance during official court audiences, he must have operated from his own separate palace, the Unhyŏn'gung. Active officials called on him there, and the king's visits to his father's palace were duly noted in the records.[24] He functioned behind the scenes to influence decisions which ultimately were issued in the name of either the dowager-regent or king. On occasion he acted out of complete disregard for prescribed regula-tions. He made arbitrary decisions without prior consultation with the king. He occasionally summoned high officials to his residence to discuss affairs of state. He issued orders directly to government agencies without use of regular bureaucratic channels for discussion and debate. He dispensed funds from his own treasury for official purposes and at times ignored the regular machinery of diplomacy by drafting messages on his own.

The Taewongun was like a "shadow" king who was able to avoid the boring and debilitating ritual that a king had to perform and concentrate his attention on important issues. Under the post-1866 dyarchy, the king was left to handle the daily routine of government. The weakness of this arrangement, however, was to be found in the Taewongun's lack of institutional legitimacy. The single prop of his power was the moral principle of filial piety, for few took issue with the king's obligation to show his father respect and listen to his opinions. On the contrary, to call this obligation into question or to suggest that there was something improper with "two kings" sitting on the throne might lay one open to charges of causing a rift between father and son. An attack on the Taewongun could be interpreted as an attack on the high moral principle of filial piety.[25]

Despite the problem of divided loyalty there was little criticism of the Taewongun during the decade because many officials owed their positions to the Taewongun's favor and many could find no fault with his policies. Had the young king objected to his father's decisions this might have led to the formation of factions among the officials. The personal acquiescence of the young king, therefore, played an important role in muting potential opposition to his father.

The Taewongun's position was still vulnerable, however. Whenever

Kojong might decide to declare personal rule (*ch'injŏng*), the Taewongun would be rendered superfluous. It was not clear when this would occur because the Koreans possessed no firm and legal definition of royal majority. Nor was there any rule which determined at what age (of the king) the dowager-regent was obliged to relinquish her regency.[26] Kojong was a mere fourteen years of age when Dowager Cho formally abdicated her authority; theoretically, he had assumed personal rule in 1866 but was completely lacking in any awareness of his right of absolute authority.[27] When the time arrived for him to assume personal rule, in fact, the obligations of filial piety would take second place to the greater demands of royal authority.

Although the Taewongun was not involved in all the routine decisions of government, there are about a dozen documented cases of his independent exercise of authority. He was responsible for ordering the collection of gifts (so-called voluntary contributions) from private individuals for palace construction; he authorized expenditures for building construction; and he made direct grants from his own treasury for military expenses and relief to peasants. He took particular responsibility for certain matters, such as the minting of the new 100-cash in 1868, land surveys for illegally exempted land and fishing weirs, regulation of the ginseng trade among official interpreters dispatched to China, the new household cloth tax, and the abolition of the private academies.[28]

Toward the end of the decade, the Taewongun's arbitrary actions and bypassing of regular channels caused the king some discomfiture. When the Taewongun issued relief to Kyŏnggi province and Kanghwa Island in 1870, the king was only informed about it several days later by the chief state councilor.[29] The chief state councilor told Kojong he was not sure himself just how the relief rice had been disbursed to the people. In discussing the matter with the governor of Kyŏnggi province, Kojong remarked that henceforth questions of relief should be discussed and determined by the state council. The governor concurred and pointed out the problem involved with such arbitrary disbursements of relief. Better planning would ensure that in the future there could be a wider and fairer distribution of relief funds.[30] Nevertheless, when a similar incident took place in 1871, the governor of Kyŏnggi reported to Kojong ex post facto that the Taewongun had ordered him directly to send out petty officials to make a thorough investigation of all land in the province and to ferret out the source of economic hardship among the people.[31]

The Taewongun was also not above implementing his desires on the spot. On one trip through the countryside, he issued direct orders establishing boundaries for gravesite land. This was subsequently reported to the king by the chief state councilor and others who praised the Taewongun's action. Two weeks later the king issued an edict of his own instructing the mayor of Seoul and governor of Kyŏnggi province to make sure that no individuals were violating gravesite boundaries and monopolizing hillside land.[32]

There are also several examples of the Taewongun's independent actions in the realm of foreign policy. In 1868, when a local official was about to board the American ship *Shenandoah*, anchored off the coast of Hwanghae province on a mission of inquiry, a ferryboat arrived from the shore and delivered a sealed message from the Taewongun to the American captain.[33] The same year when a local official delivered a reply to a note from Ernst Oppert, the German adventurer, it contained a reference to the Taewongun.[34] In 1871, during the American raid on Kanghwa Island, a local magistrate sent a report of his discussion with the Americans directly to the Taewongun's palace and then copied out a separate report for the king. A week later the Taewongun sent a military official back with his own reply.[35]

The Taewongun did not have and was not meant to have responsibility for all decisions. He exercised his authority when he saw fit, and the young king frequently followed the line of policy laid down by his father. Kojong might indicate openly that he had received guidance from the Taewongun on a certain matter, or he might direct responsible officials to memorialize their proposals directly to the Taewongun. In 1870, when Kojong ordered the abolition of corrupt private academies, he declared that he had received instructions for this from his father.[36] In 1869, when he decreed that close relatives of kings would now be eligible to take the civil service exams and hold office, he indicated that he had been instructed to do this by the dowager and ordered that the state council draw up the regulations for this and present them to Taewongun.[37] He referred several matters proposed by officials to his father for decision, such as the repair of shops burned in a fire, the construction of dormitories at the National Academy, the movement of ancestral tablets in royal shrines, the editing of law codes currently being compiled, and changes in rank and title for members of the royal clan.[38]

The Increase of Kojong's Participation and Authority

It would be a mistake, however, to regard Kojong as nothing more than a puppet during his youth; he shared responsibility with his father in ruling the country after 1866, and there was a steady increase in the number and importance of issues that he decided on his own. Even in 1865, when the king was still only twelve years old, he overrode the objections of several high officials to order compensation for some squatters who were being removed from the vicinity of the palace walls.[39] On April 12, 1866, he held his first court audience alone subsequent to the dowager's resignation from her regency.[40]

It was not until 1869, however, that he began to exercise more authority, and it was in the realm of criminal and judicial matters that he appears to have had the most autonomy. Prior to this he was still not completely free of the dowager's influence despite her abdication. In 1866, for example, when Kojong ordered a reduction in sentence for tribute merchants who had hoarded iron to artificially raise prices, he stated that the dowager had instructed him to be lenient in administering punishment.[41] In 1870, however, he acted independently even in the face of opposition from high officials. He insisted on exile instead of execution in the treason trial of Chŏng Man-sik in 1870; and on two occasions in 1872, he ignored the protests of officialdom and reduced the sentences against relatives of criminals.[42] After 1869 he expressed concern over the implementation of orders on land resurveys and the investigation of military service rosters, and he began to discuss problems of logistics and supply in the military establishment.[43] By the middle of 1870 there is no question but that the king was ruling as well as reigning. He asked for a list of outstanding magistrates in Kyŏnggi province and promoted four of them directly, showed some initiative in attempting to control the usurpation of gravesite land by yangban, and consciously took over responsibility for the implementation of orders initiated by the Taewongun.[44] He expressed concern over the compilation of the law codes and proposed to write the preface of one publication himself.[45]

During the American expedition of 1871 he took a backseat to his father; but soon after he attended court with the leading officials and issued direct orders on all business brought before him.[46] He took independent action on all proposals for relief, and in 1873 prohibited the collection of Seoul gate taxes from scholars attending the examinations at the capital.[47] In the same year he independently ordered the creation of grain loan funds for official expenses—an activity previously handled by his father.[48] Thus, the exercise of supreme authority during the decade from 1864 to 1873 cannot be described in static terms because the king's participation in government gradually increased. After 1866 the Taewongun handled major problems either on his own or by referral from his son. The king, in the meantime, continued to operate as the formal head of state—attending court, listening to pleas, receiving instruction from his royal tutors, and generally learning how to exercise regal authority. By 1873 he had obviously become used to the feel of power.

The distribution of power, however, did contain its ambiguities.

Imagine the consternation of the expectant magistrate, who, while his appointment was pending before the court, presented the Taewongun with a gift of a silver utensil, only to find himself dismissed by the young king for improper behavior.[49] What was surprising is that these incidents did not occur more frequently. In general, the officials adjusted quite well to the circumstances.

Father and Son—A Study in Contrasts

The Taewongun spent most of his adult life as a member of an obscure and neglected branch of the royal line during a time when the royal clan in general had fallen on bad days. The late Yi dynasty memoirist, Hwang Hyŏn, has recounted how the Taewongun was humbled by members of the Andong Kim clan, and how he appeared to have had little or no political ambition, spending his time in frivolity and idleness with members of lower social orders.[50] The Taewongun was an educated man who received thorough training in Confucian learning, but he had not been subjected to the rigorous indoctrination that was the standard fare for every heir apparent. When he attained the pinnacle of power, he had been schooled for decades in the realities of politics rather than the abstractions of ethics and metaphysics. He was beholden to few and was soon to display his less than total respect for entrenched interests. The degree of his self-assertiveness cannot be unrelated to his early history.

The youthful experiences of his son were vastly different. Although Kojong had never been heir apparent, he came to the throne at the age of eleven. Thereafter his education in Confucian learning and Confucian precepts for kingship was unremitting and thorough. On the very first day of his reign, the elderly sinecure, Chŏng Wŏn-yong, delivered a speech that was a portent of things to come. He noted that although the young king was bright and intelligent, he had not been diligent in learning and had not read many of the classics and histories; he beseeched the dowager-regent to guide the young king in his studies.[51] The Office of Special Counselors (hongmun'gwan) shortly thereafter drew up a list of regulations for the royal tutoring sessions. The regular lectures (kwŏn'gang) would be held daily with some of the leading scholar-officials of the realm serving in rotation. Only those who had held the honored literary posts of taejehak and chehak in the Office of Special Counselors would be eligible for this service. At least once in every five-day "week" the king would be examined on the texts studied. As if this were not enough, a second lecture session (sodae) might be scheduled for the king to summon members of the Royal Lectures for learned discussions.[52] The progress of the young king was noted with rejoicing; the completion of each classical text was commemorated with a state banquet with the leading civil and educational officials in attendance.[53]

It would have taken the dogged determination of a strong-willed and independent adult to resist the kind of indoctrination that could be accomplished by this rigorous schedule. Kojong, on the contrary, was not only docile and pliant, but even more eager than his tutors. In early 1865 he complained to one of them that he was not receiving enough instruction. "From now on," he told lecturer Pak Kyu-su, "whether in the regular lectures (*kwŏn'gang*) or special lectures (*sodae*), every time I read from a text, if I read it well, then tell me so, and if not, then tell me it is not right." When Pak explained that lecturers were only naturally inhibited and fearful before the august presence, the twelve year old monarch replied in admirable Confucian style that a king could not govern if his officials were afraid to remonstrate with him. "How would I not listen even to those words which grated against my ear?" he remarked on one occasion.[54]

Even in the first decade of his reign, the young king began to display the fruits of his arduous training. In a period of immaturity and limited authority the opportunities for applying his newly learned lessons were meager. Yet even as a youth he demonstrated a heartening compassion for "the people," leniency in the use of punishments, frugality in expenditure, and tolerance of remonstrance. Like all proper monarchs, he was dutifully awed by omens and took care not to offend Heaven by a display of hubris.

Kojong's Confucian training no doubt reinforced latent tendencies in his own personality. At the age of eighteen he issued a classic statement on judicial procedure and standards of evidence that put his elders to shame. In defending his decision to exile Chong Man-sik instead of execute him, as almost all the officials of the central government were demanding, he decreed:

One must be strict in administering the law, and one must be careful in meting out punishment. If a man has been judged guilty, then pardon him. By so doing the laws are strictly carried out, and punishment is given with care.

There have been several trial sessions recently. Some say they were put up to it by someone else, and some say they were guilty of prophesying [the downfall of the dynasty]. To hastily adjudge them guilty of things which one cannot bear to hear, or to say that they are unjustly punished and executed without mercy—how would this be the way to ensure a thorough investigation of the circumstances of the crime? How would this be the way to regard human life as something of the utmost gravity? And not to distinguish between what is bent and what upright, but to first carelessly mete out punishment—when I think of the effects on the polity, without realizing it I am overcome with sadness.

With regard to court trials in the future, no matter who is involved, if there is any matter of unspeakable and unexpected calamity, there must be a thorough investigation and reinvestigation of the matter. If there is an actual violation, the person will be punished according to law. If there is no actual violation, or if the person was put up to it by somebody else, then by decision of the state council, the man will be granted reduction of sentence on the grounds of some doubt as to his guilt . . . I feel that this should be the procedure for the next 10,000 years, and my expectation and desire is that there will be no suits for redress of grievance and no mistakes [in justice].[55]

Kojong then ordered that the motto "Take the utmost care in meting out punishment" be inscribed on a signboard and hung at the state tribunal.[56]

Kojong's sense of justice and his compassion for the accused were put to the test time and again. He often found himself isolated against the protests of high officials, who, though trained like he was in Confucianism, thought that the laws of the state had to be maintained strictly by severe punishment of the slightest offense. In 1872, when Kojong reduced the penalties on the fathers and sons of certain convicted criminals, the censorate, state tribunal, the highest three state councilors, and many of the other officials repeatedly demanded restoration of sentence. On the third day of protest, the three state councilors demanded an audience with Kojong; and when he refused to reverse his decision, they stubbornly remained on their knees in the audience hall and refused to respect his command to depart. After long delay they finally consented to withdraw, only then to submit three special joint memorials of protest (*pinch'ŏng yŏnmyŏng-gye*). Kojong ultimately prevailed, and finally took the extreme measure of dismissing the entire censorate. Less than two weeks later, however, the process was repeated when Kojong sent two men accused of plotting rebellion to exile instead of death.[57]

Leniency in the use of punishment was not the only way in which Kojong expressed his compassion for people. In 1865, despite the resistance of several prestigious officials, he insisted on compensating squatters who were being removed from their illegal encampment outside the palace gates.[58] In 1870 he expressed his concern for the sufferings of the people who were being exploited by the corrupt petty officials. He reminded his officials that "the people are the basis of the state" and was delighted to hear from one of his ministers that King Yŏngjo in the eighteenth century had ordered the hanging of this maxim in all official yamen throughout the country.[59] Three years later he expressed concern about unauthorized arrests of people by officials and instructed that anyone guilty of such acts would be punished. He recounted how his own experiences as a youth in the countryside had made him aware of such problems.[60]

Kojong was particularly concerned about the administration of relief. After the floods of 1873 he instructed councilor Kang No to issue orders to the provinces to ensure the faithful reporting of relief disbursements and equal distribution of grain. Kang replied that the dispensation of relief was limited by the resources of the state. Relief applications had to be examined and grants could not be made to all. Kojong responded by paraphrasing "the ancients." "If the people are wealthy, then the state is wealthy. If the people do not have enough, then how can the state have enough?" How would it be right for the state to have grain stored in state treasuries when the people had none stored in their homes? When given a choice between the needs of state and people, the people had to be considered first.[61] Frugality was another of the cardinal virtues that the young king repeatedly emphasized. He often stated at court that the people were the source of all state revenues and that it was the responsibility of the officials to make frugal use of them.[62]

By the time Kojong was twenty-one, he had learned his lessons well. He was now instructing his tutors on the principles of government. His remarks in some of the lecture sessions of 1873 provide a synopsis of Confucian doctrine on kingship. He had learned that the key to perfect government was the cultivation of virtue by the ruler. A king could not rely on force to maintain order. The people were the "root" or basis of the state, and their loyalty could best be won by the ruler's attainment of virtue. The king could attain virtue and win the loyalty of the people by being "serious and sincere." If the people were united in loyalty, the state would be strong no matter how small the population. The people should be allowed to cultivate the fields in the proper season, and their labor should not be used by kings for more than three days per year, the example set by the ancient sages. They should be taught to be frugal and not waste their meager resources. And the king could further ensure the security of the state by appointing princely men (*kunja*) to office and shunning the small men (*soin*).[63]

While his father was wrestling with the concrete problems of state and setting new precedents in the exercise of royal authority, Kojong was learning lessons in humility and virtuous kingship from his Confucian mentors. It should be no surprise that the style of rule was changed when Kojong took over control of government affairs in 1874. In the meantime, his father set out to reorder the state in accordance with somewhat different principles.

Politics and Policy in Traditional Korea

Bolstering the Prestige
of the Royal Clan

After Kojong came to the throne, the Taewongun made a concerted effort to restore prestige to the royal house. Members of the royal clan who had formerly been prosecuted and punished were rehabilitated. Yi Se-bo, Prince Kyŏngp'yŏng, who had been stripped of his rank and title and exiled in 1860 for his criticism of Kim Mun-gŭn, Ch'ŏlchong's father-in-law, was released from exile and subsequently appointed to office.[64] On March 28, 1864, the wife of Yi Ha-jon was released from exile. Yi had been ordered to commit suicide in September 1862 for plotting the usurpation of the throne.[65] On August 12, after an investigation of all royal clansmen unjustly punished in the past, ranks and titles were posthumously restored to eighteen princes.[66] The court set to work investigating the official genealogies of the royal clan. Posthumous "adoptions" were arranged for all lines that had come to an end for the lack of a male heir.[67] In 1868 orders were issued to rectify irregularities in the genealogies and make uniform the generation names of all the descendants of King Sŏnjo's father, the Tŏkhŭng taewŏn'gun.[68]

The three official agencies that dealt with royal clan affairs—the Office of the Royal Genealogy (chongch'inbu), the Office of the Royal Clan (tollyŏngbu), and the Office of the Princesses' Consorts (ibinbu)—were raised in status and function. In 1865 high officials of the Office of the Royal Genealogy were allowed to attend grand conferences of former and incumbent *taesin,* and officials of that agency and the Office of the Princesses' Consorts were permitted to attend court on a regular basis with civil and military officials.[69]

On March 7, 1869, a completely revised set of regulations was drawn up for the ranks, official titles, and posts of members of the royal clan and the Office of the Royal Genealogy. The number of those eligible for noble titles was expanded by the creation of new lower-level posts. New titles were provided for members of illegitimate lines of nobility and husbands of minor princesses;[70] and honorary titles were given to members of the royal family who were civil, military, or protected (*ŭm*) officials. Many of the new posts were to be filled by sons and grandsons of princes still within four generations of descent from a king, a group previously barred from special consideration. The recommendation of people for minor posts in the Office of the Royal Genealogy was made the responsibility of that office rather than the Ministry of Personnel. Members of illegitimate ancestry were also provided for; those in the fifth generation of descent from a king and after were allowed to stand for the civil and military examinations, but care was taken to maintain distinctions between them and those of legitimate descent, especially in regard to marriage regulations.[71]

Problems in the Establishment of Power

The most important adaptations made for the benefit of the royal clan members were the creation of special examinations for them and permission for close relatives of kings to participate in the regular civil service examinations and be appointed to office. There is, however, a discrepancy between the official court decrees that indicate a significant widening of opportunity for royal relatives and the actual *munkwa* examination rosters themselves, which do not demonstrate any unusual increase in the number of royal Chŏnju Yi clan members who actually obtained the highest academic degrees in the period from 1865 to 1872. It would seem, therefore, that the throne may have provided mainly honorary privileges and possibly greater opportunities for participation at preliminary levels of the examinations only.

On April 10, 1865, the king decreed that all members of branches of the royal house and the P'ungyang Cho clan (that is, those who were students preparing for the examinations) would be listed at the end of the roster of successful candidates in the upcoming regular triennial examination. The Office of the Royal Genealogy and the Office of the Royal Clan were to take responsibility for drawing up the lists of names, which would then be sent to the Four Schools (sahak) in the capital. The students so listed and enrolled in those schools would then go directly to take the examinations.[72]

The dowager-regent added about one hundred members of the royal clan to the examination roster (*pangmok*); but since only three members of the Chŏnju Yi clan passed the *munkwa* examination in 1865, the list of names probably refers to candidates for the examination, and not passers.[73] The dowager-regent provided a banquet at the Office of the Royal Clan for these men, and Kojong ordered that all holders of the literary licentiate degree (*chinsa*) who were members of the royal family and over seventy years of age be put on a special list (of high degree holders) by the Ministry of Rites.[74] In 1867 Kojong also allowed the names of royal relatives who had contributed to the costs of repelling the French invasion of 1866 to be placed at the end of the examination roster.[75]

Later in 1867, after the completion of the supplement to the royal genealogy (*Sŏnwŏn kyebo*), Kojong ordered a special examination to be held for royal relatives (called the *chongch'inkwa*). The candidates for this test were to bypass the initial examination and go directly to the palace examination.[76] Other special examinations of this nature were ordered in 1869 and 1872, but the examination rosters themselves only indicate that five members of the Chŏnju Yi clan passed a special *chongch'inkwa* in 1869.[77]

On March 3, 1867, the king issued an edict that allowed for the first time all members of the royal clan except the first two generations of

Politics and Policy in Traditional Korea

relatives in direct descent from a king to take the civil service examinations. Prior to this time all those royal relatives within four generations
of a king were ineligible.[78] In his edict Kojong asked rhetorically why
there should be any discrimination against able members of the royal
clan, especially since they had committed no crimes deserving of such
treatment; his desire was to protect the descendants of his line for 10,000
generations.[79] Nevertheless, the examination rosters themselves indicate
that from 1865 to 1872 out of a total of slightly over three hundred
passers of the *munkwa* examinations, only forty-two or forty-three were
members of the Chŏnju Yi clan.[80] While this was by no means an in-
significant figure, it does not indicate an abnormally large or sudden increase of degree-holding royal relatives.

Despite the lack of overt opposition to these measures, many officials
must have harbored resentment. In 1866 a censor objected not to the new
laws but to the appointment to office of several ennobled members of the
royal clan some years before.[81] In general, however, officials were cowed
by a resurgent throne. The prevailing mood among officials was reflected
by the remarks of Chief State Councilor Kim Pyŏng-hak, who praised
the measure to allow the high nobility to take the examinations and be
appointed to office as a plan of great foresight.[82]

The restoration of royal prestige was not confined to the royal Chŏnju
Yi clan, alone. The attempt to rehabilitate the Wang clan of the Koryŏ
dynasty and the repair of the tombs of the kings of the Silla dynasty were
also part of the plan to restore the dignity of the royal house.[83]

Palace Construction

The revived kingship also needed a new symbol of authority. This was
provided by a massive construction program which required the largest
expenditures of the dynasty for such purposes. The construction included
not only the rebuilding of royal palaces, but the repair of government
buildings as well. It was inspired by the desire to produce tangible
evidence of a successful restoration of dynastic fortune.[84] The
Taewongun was also moved by his love of the past grandeur of the
dynasty to restore many earlier institutions. As part of his administrative
reorganization, he reestablished the state council (*ŭijŏngbu*), restored the
older Three Armies Command (*samgunbu*), and upgraded the position of
the Office of the Royal Genealogy.[85] Orders were also issued for the reconstruction and repair of the buildings housing these agencies as well.[86]

The most ambitious project of all, however, was the rebuilding of the
Kyŏngbok palace, ordered on April 26, 1865. The Kyŏngbok palace had
originally been occupied by King T'aejo, the founder of the dynasty. It
was burned during Hideyoshi's invasions in the 1590s and had never been
rebuilt. Its reconstruction was planned by Ikchong, the dowager's

Problems in the Establishment of Power

husband, while he was acting king (*taeri*) in the late 1820s. King Hŏnjong (r. 1834-49) also accumulated large sums of cash in his royal treasury for reconstruction, but both men died before their plans could be brought to fruition.[87]

The dowager-regent, the Taewongun, and most of the high officials saw the reconstruction of the Kyŏngbok palace as an obvious act of dynastic "restoration" (*chunghŭng*). The dowager stated this in her April 26 decree, and many officials spoke of the task not only as a restoration but also as the renewal of the mandate of Heaven (*kyŏngmyŏng yusin*).[88] Although none of the officials directly opposed the project, many were concerned with the financial and fiscal problems that would be involved. They observed that state treasuries were depleted and the people would have to bear heavy burdens of taxation and labor. They urged that the pressures on the people be kept to a minimum and urged the throne to be frugal. They reported that the people were all rejoicing at the idea and would come to work "as a child comes [to help his father]."[89]

While the assessments of the officials about the rejoicing of the people taxes our credulity, it appears that the morale of the workers was fairly high at the beginning of the project. Commoners were organized into work brigades of a hundred, each marching to work with banners and decorations. Troops of dancers entertained the workers on the job, and housing was provided for them near the construction site.[90] Laborers were paid fees, and in the first days of construction as many as 30,000 people were mobilized for construction.[91]

The eventual completion of the Kyŏngbok palace was testimony to the Taewongun's tenacity and his ability to tap the existing financial system for hidden resources. As the high officials had pointed out, the regular fiscal structure could not have borne the burden of the costs of palace construction.[92] The state council took this into account a few days after the initial order for construction was issued. It suggested that limits be imposed on labor service requirements and that everyone in the country, regardless of class or status, be required to contribute to the project. It deplored the use of force and advocated granting rank and title to those who made voluntary contributions (*wŏnnap*).[93] The official records are relatively silent on the details of the voluntary contribution system, but Yi Nŭng-hwa, writing in the early twentieth century, reported that the requisition of funds went far beyond the state council's proposals. Agents were supposedly sent out to investigate people's property, and police coerced reluctant contributors. Heads of households were summoned and threatened into volunteering percentages of their wealth and property. Some supposedly committed suicide as a result of the pressures applied to them.[94]

Few were spared the Taewongun's zeal. He himself established a pre-

Politics and Policy in Traditional Korea

cedent by contributing 100,000 yang of cash from the royal treasury.[95] Members of the nobility were solicited for funds by the Office of the Royal Genealogy. The dowager reported that in the first two days after the order for construction was issued, 100,000 yang in contributions had been collected from the capital and another 20,000-30,000 yang was received from the members of the royal clan.[96] In 1872 the Construction Bureau (yŏnggŏn-dogam) reported the grand total of all voluntary contributions. The palace treasury had accounted for 110,000 yang of cash, 5,000 kŭn of wood, and 3,000 kŭn of white alum. Members of the royal clan had given 340,913 yang of cash, and other individuals contributed a total of 7,277,780 yang of cash and 124 sŏk of white rice.[97] This was a considerable figure considering that the yearly average of taxes paid in cash was in the range of 100,000-500,000 yang per year.[98]

Financial difficulties were compounded by two major fires which destroyed part of the palace and wood accumulated for construction purposes.[99] Construction was also interrupted by the French expedition in 1866.[100] The Taewongun, however, refused to be deterred by these obstacles. It took over four years to complete the construction, and during this time he resorted to several extraordinary measures to provide for finances and labor service.[101] In 1866 the government minted new large cash[102] (see Chapter 8). In 1868 a land surtax of 100 pieces of 100-cash/kyŏl was levied which yielded an additional two million yang of cash revenue.[103] Voluntary contributions and the sale of rank and office were continued.[104] Extraordinary measures were also taken for the procurement of wood. Limits were put on the amount of inviolate gravesite land which could be retained by yangban and commoners, and more trees were cut from the hillside land liberated by this means. The Taewongun ignored objections against the taking of large holy trees supposedly inhabited by spirits.[105]

Throughout the period of palace construction, there were repeated complaints of financial difficulty, especially by Chief State Councilor Kim Pyŏng-hak. In early 1868 he asked that the workers be given some relief and that the state cut down on its expenditures for construction.[106] The king also urged frugality in the use of resources. He ordered the chief officials in charge of construction to make a report on expenditures every five days.[107] Even on the day the palace was completed, Kim Pyŏng-hak was apologetic in reporting the news. While praising the completion of the palace, a project planned but delayed for three hundred years, he expounded at length on the desirability of frugality and economy. Construction had gone on for years and expenses had expanded beyond expectations. Since state finances had been depleted and the burdens on the people were great, the most urgent business of the day was frugality and relief for the people. To be sure, the palace had to be rebuilt, but in the future construction had to be limited.[108]

These admonitions were not heeded. Later in 1868 the state council announced plans for the repair of the buildings housing the Office of Ministers-without-Portfolio (chungch'ubu), Office of Inspector-General (sahŏnbu), and the Six Ministries (yukcho). It also reported with dismay the rundown conditions of the Four Schools in the capital, the prison of the state tribunal, and the walls and gates of the capital. The Construction Bureau was ordered to carry out repairs. Kojong approved these measures but warned against excessive expenditures and labor service requirements.[109] The ambivalence between the desire for construction and the need for economy continued.

Economy in expenditure proved difficult to achieve. In 1869 the Construction Bureau reported a depletion in its cash reserves and its inability to meet outstanding bills. The Tribute Bureau (sŏnhyech'ŏng) was ordered by the state council to transfer 100,000 yang of its funds to the Construction Bureau.[110] Later that year, Kim Pyŏng-hak again complained about the failure of the government to heed his recommendations for frugality even though the king had on every occasion agreed with his position. This time, too, Kojong agreed with Kim.[111] Within a week, however, the king ordered the Construction Bureau to begin repairs on other buildings, including the shrine to ancestors of the royal house.[112] He justified this as essential to the "defense of orthodoxy and the rejection of heterodoxy (*wijŏng ch'ŏksa*). Throughout 1869 and 1870, funds were continually allocated from the Tribute Bureau to the Construction Bureau.[113]

The Taewongun and Royal Restoration

The Taewongun came to power by a turn of good fortune created by King Ch'olchong's lack of a male heir and an eldest dowager sympathetic to his interests. As the living father of a reigning king, he found himself in an institutionally anomalous situation. He capitalized on the respect due him as the king's father, a respect that was reinforced by the universally accepted Confucian value of filial piety, in order to exercise de facto regal authority. With his enormous personal strength and tenacity he dominated the age, but he made no move to depose his son and become king himself. Eventually, however, he would have to relinquish power as the young king came of age. As Kojong grew older he became more independent, but he still failed to realize that his father's presence detracted from his own authority. After 1866 father and son shared power in a dyarchy, the lines of which were never clearly drawn. In the meanwhile, the king was receiving a strict education in Confucian values. A conscientious student, his acceptance of these values gave him an outlook on government different from that of his father, who was preeminently a man of action and purpose.

One of the Taewongun's aims was the restoration of the royal house and the dynasty. The greatness of the fifteenth century was to be re-created in form and substance by the duplication of old institutions and the erection of palaces and official structures. So great was this desire that the Taewongun refused to be stayed from its accomplishment by even the most frustrating of obstacles. He achieved the greatest fund-raising effort in the history of the dynasty, but he was compelled thereby to take important compensatory actions in the realm of finance and taxation. His readjustments in tax policy and his flouting of Confucian norms were to act as goads to the emergence of political opposition.

The Taewongun's attempt at royal restoration was unlike the restoration of imperial prerogative in Meiji Japan. It was not the outgrowth of a period of intellectual ferment as had occurred in Japan with the redis-covery of national history. The Andong Kim were never regarded as usurpers of royal authority as was the bakufu. There were no *shishi* or men of will from yangban or official ranks who led the movement. Instead, it was imposed from the top and the restoration of royal prestige cut into the privileges of all strata of the yangban-official class. Nor can the royal restoration be regarded as an alliance between the throne and the people—one which might have led to a greater focus of national loyalty on a refurbished kingship.

There was also no ideological or religious underpinning for the creation of a truly transcendental absolute authority. The Kyŏngbok palace never became a symbol of a new exalted monarchy around which the people could rally although there were signs that this might have been achieved in the early days of the reign. The palace became instead an extravagant construction project which consumed resources that might have been put to better use elsewhere. Instead of a symbol to rally support, it became a focus for attack.

3

Merit and Privilege in the Recruitment of Men

Recruitment of officials on the basis of merit is a feature of modern organization that may also be characteristic of a traditional bureaucracy caught in the midst of a vigorous reform movement. But the ascriptive values of a traditional hierarchical society will serve to check or reverse the trend toward rationalization unless the demand for performance is great enough to break the barrier of social restraint. The Taewongun felt an acute need for widening the opportunity for office holding and basing recruitment on administrative and military skills in order to eliminate corruption and the causes of peasant rebellion, promote the efficient collection of taxes, and forge a strong military establishment. The creation of a more powerful and efficient national government was dependent on his ability to destroy the bastions of special privilege and overcome the restraints imposed by hereditary social status, hereditary factionalism, and nepotism.

The main route to higher office was the civil service examinations, but the vast majority of higher degree holders came from a relatively small number of aristocratic lineage groups despite the absence of legal restrictions against participation by commoners. Even within the group of degree holders, access to office was further restricted by preferential treatment for relatives of the powerful consort clans of the early nineteenth century and discrimination against descendants of members of the Northerner and Southerner factions.

The Consort Clans

Historians have commonly assumed that the Andong Kim were the enemies of the Taewongun largely because of the testimony of the late Yi dynasty gossip, Hwang Hyŏn, about the personal animosity between them. After 1864, however, there is little evidence of conflict with the

Politics and Policy in Traditional Korea

Andong Kim. They made no effort to block Kojong's enthronement or the Taewongun's acquisition of power. Although the lineage as a whole gradually lost power, the older members were appointed to sinecures and attended court as prestigious elder statesmen while several of the younger men continued their careers in the bureaucracy.[1] The most successful by far was Kim Pyŏng-hak, who was appointed minister of personnel in 1864, second state councilor in 1865, and chief state councilor in 1867. He left that post briefly in 1868 but was reappointed to it the same year and remained chief state councilor until November 13, 1872.[2]

Most historians have also tended to lay the blame for corruption, administrative inefficiency, and peasant rebellion at the door of the consort clans, but the Taewongun never gave any indication that he held them responsible for these developments. In fact, contrary to the popular wisdom, at the end of Ch'ŏlchong's reign the Andong Kim were leading architects of policies later adopted by the Taewongun. They advocated restrictions on private academies, abolition of official grain loans, reductions in taxes and labor service, punishment of corrupt clerks, and the adoption of a "hard line" toward Japan.[3] They continued to support the Taewongun's policies after 1864, and Kim Pyŏng-hak in particular sponsored much of the legislation of the 1860s.[4]

The Taewongun did not consider the presence of the Andong Kim as necessarily inimical to his own rule and his vision of a strong monarchy even though their privileged position in the bureaucracy was antithetical to the Confucian ideal of impersonal standards of recruitment and the Taewongun's desire to obtain men with administrative and military skills. Nepotism was not considered particularly abhorrent because status, lineage solidarity, and family loyalty were recognized by all as legitimate. Moreover, the Taewongun only made inroads into aristocratic power when necessary and in a limited way, for he was as dependent on them as they on him. He was fully aware of the importance of mutual dependence.

The Taewongun's tolerance of the consort clans also stemmed from his pragmatic approach to government. Instead of purposely altering the political system to eliminate imperfection, he often preferred to manipulate it. Once the Andong Kim were under control he could have adopted an institutional solution to the problem of consort clans by forbidding any relative of a queen from holding public office. He could have entitled and ennobled all consort relatives and left them to spend their lives in affluence and political obscurity. On the contrary, the Taewongun sought to prevent the emergence of another powerful consort clan by choosing a queen for his son from a lineage that would be loyal and obedient. He found a girl in his own wife's lineage, the Yŏhŭng

Min; and on May 4, 1866, this fifteen year old girl was invested as queen.[5] The choice was an unfortunate one for the Taewongun, for Queen Min proved to be the ablest female politician in the history of the dynasty. Her ability was only part of the reason for her influence, for in the absence of institutional checks on her male relatives they soon began a rapid advance up the rungs of the bureaucratic ladder right under the nose of the Taewongun. It was therefore the Yŏhŭng Min clan, and not the queen alone, which eventually challenged the Taewongun's authority.

By 1873 at least six major members of the clan had risen to high rank and office. Min Sŭng-ho, the queen's brother by adoption and the nominal leader of the clan until his assassination in 1874, moved from rank 3A in 1866 to 2A in 1873 and held a number of posts in the six ministries. His brother, Min Kyŏm-ho, was second ranking minister in the Ministry of Punishments by 1873; and his father, Min Ch'i-gu, the adoptive father of the queen, held several high posts in the late 1860s. Other figures like Min Kyu-ho, Min T'ae-ho, and Min Ch'i-sang advanced to rank 2A or 2B posts.[6] By 1873 the Min clan had still not achieved the highest posts in the state council, but many of them were now *taesin* and they began to sit in on important deliberative conferences. The queen was still young and her relatives had not yet achieved overt control of government, but the foundations of their future political hegemony were laid in the decade of the 1860s.

Queen Min might have found the presence of the Taewongun at court too restrictive in any case, but certain events at court in the late 1860s soured their relations. Two years after she became queen, one of the palace concubines gave birth to a son, Prince Wanhwa (Wanhwagun), who constituted a potential threat to the position of the Min clan if the queen failed to produce an heir. The Yŏhŭng Min must have been acutely aware of the problem because it seems that both Kojong and the Taewongun regarded the young prince as a potential heir to the throne. Then, in 1871, Queen Min bore a son of her own who passed away only three days after birth. It is rumored that the boy died after the Taewongun administered some kind of ginseng palliative. Even if the story is false, it appears that animosity between the queen and the Taewongun originated at this time and that after 1871 the queen waited for an opportunity to help oust the Taewongun from power.[7]

During the 1860s the queen and her relatives were not important participants in the determination of domestic and foreign policy. Whatever role they may have played in helping to force the Taewongun's retirement in late 1873 remains shrouded in mystery. But after 1876 they became the architects of policies that were anathema to the Taewongun, and he had nobody to blame but himself. His failure to deal with the institutional problem of the consort clans in the 1860s was one of the sources of his own fall from power. He attempted to manipulate the system instead of change it, and failed.

The Factions

In theory the Yi dynasty was a centralized state in which an absolute monarch ruled through a loyal and obedient bureaucracy. Officials were supposed to submerge their private interests on behalf of a higher loyalty to their king. In fact, however, factionalism and group loyalty was a predominant feature of political life, especially from the sixteenth to late eighteenth centuries. In China, except for brief periods during the Sung and Ming, the formation of cliques or factions within the bureaucracy was stigmatized as subversive because it placed the private political interest of the official ahead of the greater interest of the throne and state. In the Yi dynasty, however, the formation of distinct bureaucratic factions began in the late sixteenth century. Factional solidarity was quite strong and factional affiliation was in many cases passed on hereditarily. The game of bureaucratic politics was waged for the most part among groups of officials who moved in and out of office on the basis of the political fortunes of their party rather than impartial standards of evaluation. By the nineteenth century the intensity of factional disputes had diminished and other political forces like the consort clans tended to displace the older factions.

Factional solidarity was aided by strong familial and clan ties. The Confucian emphasis on loyalty probably inhibited rash and impulsive transfers of personal allegiance, but the self-righteous moralism that was so characteristic of the Confucianists also tended to reinforce and perpetuate animosity engendered by contests for political power and disputes over substantive issues. One's opponent's wrongdoings were frequently castigated as morally heinous acts which had to be punished even after death. The Koreans were also highly conscious of the immortality conferred by history and fearful of the judgments of posterity on their own deeds and on those of their forebears and companions. It was essential that one redress past grievances and set the historical record straight. Bygones could not be bygones. The rehabilitation of those wrongly maligned in the past was regarded with the utmost importance, and this frequently took the form of posthumous appointments to high office and canonization in Confucian shrines.

While personal ties and group loyalty were powerful forces in the formation of bureaucratic factions, some writers have overemphasized these factors and played down the commitment to issues in traditional

The Recruitment of Men

politics.[8] There were independent-minded men who took their own stands on issues, but it was more common for differences of opinion on substantive issues to lead to transfer of allegiance and intrafactional schism.

Although the political history of the period 1575-1800 is consumed for the most part with the ebb and flow of political fortune among competing bureaucratic factions, this did not mean that the locus of power had necessarily shifted away from king to administration. On the contrary, many kings manipulated the factions, and the success of a faction depended ultimately either on royal favor or on connections with rival heirs to the throne. By the latter part of the seventeenth century there were four major factional groupings, usually referred to as the four colors (sasaek). These were the Patriarch's Faction (Noron), Disciple's Faction (Soron), Southerners (Namin), and Northerners (Pugin). (The territorial designations had nothing to do with regionalism, although regionalism was often a factor in politics.) The Northerners had achieved their greatest influence in the period 1600-23, but after the deposition of Kwanghaegun and the Injo Restoration of 1623, the Northerners suffered a disastrous decline in their fortunes.[9] The Southerners, who were active in the seventeenth century, sustained a serious reverse at the hands of King Sukchong in 1694; and they were subsequently relegated to a secondary place in the competition for office and prestige.[10]

In the eighteenth century a slight change took place in the locus of political struggle. The involvement of the palace or inner court in bureaucratic politics became more pronounced. Among the officials, members of the Patriarch's Faction were generally pitted against the Disciple's Faction, which also had some Southerner support. Toward the end of Sukchong's reign in the second decade of the century, the Patriarch's Faction emerged as supporters of the current crown prince, the future Kyŏngjong (r. 1720-24), while the Disciples-Southerner coalition backed Prince Yŏn'in (Yŏn'in'gun), later Yŏngjo (r. 1724-76). After Kyŏngjong came to the throne a major purge of Patriarch officials was carried out in 1722, and the Disciples gained the favor of the throne. The Disciples' position was soon undermined with the death of Kyŏngjong and the accession of Yŏngjo in 1724. Thereafter, the Patriarch's Faction remained dominant.

Yŏngjo is renowned for his attempt to mitigate the evils of factional politics through his so-called equalization policy (t'angp'yŏngch'aek). While this equalization policy has been highly praised by historians for allowing access to office on the basis of merit, it meant little more than a refusal by the king to wreak vengeance on either the Patriarch's or Disciple's Factions for crimes committed in the past.[11] There is little

Politics and Policy in Traditional Korea

evidence to show that the Southerners or Northerners fared very well during Yŏngjo's reign. In fact, it appears that the major reason why Yŏngjo had his own son, Crown Prince Changhŏn (or the sado seja) starved to death in 1762 was because the latter was a supporter of the pro-Kyŏngjong Disciples-Southerners clique.[12] The murder of Prince Changhŏn then spawned a dispute which was to dominate the politics of the rest of the century. Those nobles and officials who resented Changhŏn's murder and coalesced around his son, the future King Chŏngo (r. 1776-80), came to be called the sip'a. Those who supported Yŏngjo's act were called the pyokp'a and were led by the relatives of Yŏngjo's second queen.[13] The sip'a-pyŏkp'a dispute split the ranks of the dominant Patriarch's Faction and the others of the four colors as well.[14] When Chŏngjo came to the throne in 1776, some of the pyŏkp'a were purged; and by the end of the century, sip'a, Disciples, and Southerners had returned to office. The Patriarch's Faction and pyŏkp'a, however, were by no means eliminated from the scene.[15]

In addition to the splintering of the four colors by the sip'a-pyŏkp'a dispute, the rise of Catholicism further complicated the political picture. In the 1790s, even though many members of the Southerners had converted to Catholicism, some were anti-Catholic or neutral.[16] When Sunjo came to the throne in 1800, he was still a minor and Dowager Kim, Yŏngjo's second queen and leader of the pyokp'a faction, became regent. In 1801 she carried out the first major persecution of Catholics and used it also as a means of eliminating her Southerner and Patriarch-sip'a political enemies.[17]

By 1800 the solidarity of the four colors had obviously been weakened by court politics, the sip'a-pyŏkp'a dispute, and Catholicism. While the four factions had not disappeared, nominal affiliation in any one of them had less significance than a century before. After 1800 the establishment of consort clan political hegemony tended to reduce the importance of membership in the four colors. Kim Cho-sun, the founder of the Andong Kim fortunes in the early nineteenth century, was probably a Patriarch-sip'a, but he also had no difficulty in working with Dowager Kim, a pyŏkp'a. Furthermore, his power did not derive from his Patriarch affiliation but from his blood ties to the throne.[18] Policy toward Catholicism in the nineteenth century may also have been influenced by factional politics. One scholar has written that the sip'a affiliation of the Andong Kim was the reason for the relaxation of anti-Catholic persecution while they were in power at court.[19]

Factional politics was by no means a dead issue by 1864. The memory of centuries of political conflict did not fade so readily from the minds of men. The years had taken their toll of scores of officials—purged, executed, exiled, and cast into disgrace. Their sins were visited on their descendants, who were prohibited from holding office; and kings were frequently petitioned by such unfortunates seeking release from inherited discrimination. In the first year of Kojong's reign the dowager-regent indicated that the regime was making a new departure. She ordered the state tribunal to draw up a list of past criminals to be granted pardons in honor of her forthcoming birthday. She declared the amnesty would be a sign of restoration, a cleaning of the slate, and an act of benevolence, which would ensure a successful and harmonious reign for the young king.[20] When in mid-August a list of about one hundred and fifty men was presented by the state tribunal, it caused a tremendous furor among the highest officials, the censoring bodies, and the Royal Secretariat, who protested that the standards of morality and the integrity of the laws had been undermined. The dowager-regent replied that enough time had passed since the criminals had been punished, and their descendants should not be penalized:

There ought not be any laws which implicate people [in the crimes of their ancestors] and prevent the sons and grandsons [of criminals] from holding office in perpetuity as if they were things cast off withou. any place to stay between heaven and earth. People who have been placed in this position can be numbered in the hundreds and thousands. Why are they to blame for the crimes of their ancestors?[21]

The dowager-regent refuted the charges that the severity of the laws was being weakened. She did not deny the seriousness of the original crimes but merely "opened the path for self-renewal" and "transformed hidden feelings of resentment" by means of amnesty.

The protest did not cease despite repeated rejections and warnings by the dowager-regent.[22] The opposition movement culminated in one joint memorial signed by several Confucian scholars (*yusaeng*), who directed the brunt of their wrath against four of the pardoned men. One of the four was a Great Northerner (Taebuk), a Northerner splinter group, which in 1618 had been responsible for the downgrading of the dowager or queen mother.[23] The others were Southerners involved in the deposition of Sukchong's Queen Min in 1689.[24] At the time, members of the Patriarch's Faction who supported Queen Min had been purged by the Southerners.[25] The scholars charged the four men with treason for their actions against the two queen mothers. They also pointed out that several petitions presented in the past for their pardon had been denied. And they insisted that all the extant writings of the criminals be searched out and burned.[26] The dowager-regent was not cowed by the pressure. She ordered the exile of five of the cosigners of the above memorial and the transfer of all members of the censoring bodies. The five men were pardoned a few days later, however, suggesting that the throne was not completely free to deal with them in an arbitrary way.[27] The dowager-regent's actions seem to indicate that the previous discrimination against Southerners and Northerners would no longer be practiced and that the Patriarch's Faction could not count on privileged treatment. Indeed, this interpretation of the Taewongun's policies was put forward most forcefully by Hwang Hyŏn in his memoirs, the *Maech'ŏn yarok*.[28] According to Hwang, the Taewongun reversed the discrimination against the Southerners and Northerners by appointing members of both factions to high official posts.[29] The Patriarchs were supposedly so dissatisfied with the appointment of Southerners and Northerners to the prestigious Royal Library (kyujanggak) that they dubbed the library "the Taewongun's Library" (un'gak).[30]

There are other indications that the Taewongun went out of his way to humiliate the Patriarch's Faction. As part of his reform of the private academies he abolished the Mandogmyo, the shrine established at the recommendation of Song Si-yŏl, the founder of the Patriarch's Faction. In 1873 the Taewongun adopted as an extra title for himself "Great Elder" (Taero), which happened to be part of the title of Song Si-yŏl's shrine in Yŏju. Since Taero was now a royal taboo name, the title of Song's shrine had to be changed.[31]

The effects of the Taewongun's treatment of the factions should not be exaggerated. The number of Southerners and Northerners who attained high office was still only a fraction of the total posts in the bureaucracy.[32] Lacking more detailed studies, we would have to surmise that the Patriarch's Faction remained dominant. In any case, those who benefited from the patronage of the Taewongun in the 1860s suffered retribution from his enemies after 1874.[33]

Henchmen and Lackeys

The Taewongun was as much interested in men he could manipulate as he was in efficient administrators. Yi Kyŏng-ha, for example, who held several important posts during the decade in the military, police, and capital guards, was described by Hwang Hyŏn as the Taewongun's tool and as a ruthless inquisitor.

> The Taewongun once said that Yi Kyŏng-ha was not better than any one else. It was just that he was good at killing people, and therefore could be used in office. He also said of Yi that he did not execute people to excess, and that all those [he did execute] were heretics [Catholics] and counterfeiters, and hence ought to have been killed.[34]

Hwang also remarked that the Taewongun preferred disreputable types to men of refinement and substance. Drunkards, gamblers, slanderers, and the like were appointed to office, and fortune tellers and shamans were shown favor while men of learning, age, refinement, and accomplishment were cast off.[35] Hwang's testimony must be partially discounted because of his own obvious pro-literati bias. Hwang probably had to rely on hearsay evidence from older men for his information about this decade. Yet it is still likely that the Taewongun utilized lower-class henchmen and fringe elements for political purposes.

The Taewongun is also supposed to have maintained surveillance over the inner court through four men who were related to palace ladies.[36] Five officials in particular were also reputed to be the most trusted of the Taewongun's personal men. He supposedly instructed all of them to go into hiding after 1874, and two were later executed for their part in the An Ki-yŏng plot against the throne in 1881.[37] The Taewongun undoubtedly required a corps of henchmen to stave off his personal enemies. Some he disliked, but others like the relatives of the Dowager Cho and the Taewongun's own brother, son, and son-in-law resented him because they had not been shown enough favor.[38]

The granting of amnesty to the Southerners and Northerners and the selection of some of them for high office were certainly bold steps. While they were intended to remove discrimination against large numbers of yangban excluded from office on factional grounds, it does not prove that the Taewongun believed in total impartiality in the use of men. The vigorous protest raised against the pardoning of Southerner and Northerner criminals—even those punished in the seventeenth century—reflects the strong influence wielded by the Patriarch's Faction and the nonofficial literati. Most of the high officials at the capital also joined in the opposition. The throne rejected these protests, but the authors of the protest could not be eliminated. They constituted an ever-present counterforce against any attempt at a major shift in the political balance.

Privilege versus Merit and the Widening of Opportunity

The ideal of recruitment based on rational criteria of talent and merit was never abandoned in the Yi dynasty, but it had always been subordinated in practice to discrimination on the basis of social status. Within the limits of legitimate status discrimination, however, the search for the talented could be pursued. Several edicts were issued in the 1860s for the purpose of removing de facto regional restrictions of office holding. Residents of Songdo (modern Kaesŏng), the northern provinces, and Cheju Island were given special consideration. Songdo was singled out for notice because the throne was determined to rehabilitate the royal Wang clan of the Koryŏ dynasty as part of its program for restoring royal prestige in general. The northern part of Korea had traditionally produced a proportionally smaller number of degree holders than the south, and the discontent caused by this had flared up in the Hong Kyŏng-nae rebellion of 1811.[39] To counter the neglect of Cheju Island, special examinations were also held there; and orders were issued for local officials to recommend men for appointment to office.[40]

The one area where the Taewongun tended to place greater weight on performance than on ascriptive criteria was military training and recruitment. The throne declared that the military establishment had fallen into a state of decrepitude because military posts had been treated in the past simply as sources of income with little regard for military accomplishment. One edict in 1869 mentioned that commanders of border garrisons along the frontier and the coast were supposed to be staffed by men skilled in bowmanship and horsemanship, but instead they were filled with untrained men and "idle officials who scatter in the morning and come back again at dusk." To rectify this situation the king authorized special examinations to test men in military skills and ordered military officers to proceed through a regular system of advancement gaining experience and training at lower levels before qualifying for higher positions. He ordered that border garrison commanders be appointed from the ranks of military officers and not civil officials and instructed the ministries of war and personnel to adhere to regular processes of recommendation when irregular appointments had to be made. He abolished certain traditional sinecures in the military and authorized investigations to prevent interference by civil officials in military appointments.[41] Although these measures were issued in the name of the king, we might safely assume that they were inspired by the Taewongun out of his great concern for national defense.

The true test of the regime's determination to pursue the goal of efficiency came when rational criteria of recruitment came into conflict with traditionally accepted social barriers. I have found only one such case in the period, indicating by its very isolation the resistance to unlimited opportunity across class lines. This occurred in 1866 when an official slave had finished first in a firearms marksmanship contest. The Ministry of War requested the state council's approval before awarding the man his passing degree, since such a step would have shattered existing precedent. The state council replied that the law specified that private or official slaves were ineligible to participate in such examinations and ordered the test to be held again and another man selected. In this case, however, the throne overrode the state council's decision. The king decreed that the examination had been held for the purpose of encouraging and stimulating the improvement of military defenses. No discrimination should therefore be made because the man had been a slave. Instead of ordering the man to be given his military degree directly, however, the throne made its accommodation with the existing system by granting him commoner status prior to awarding the degree.[42] Two conclusions derive from this single case. The throne raised the criterion of performance in military affairs higher than it had been placed before, but traditional norms were still powerful enough to ensure that upward mobility would be severely limited by social status.[43]

There are other examples which show that the throne's concern for performance was not meant to break down status divisions. In 1869 Chief State Councilor Kim Pyŏng-hak reported that clerks were participating in the governor's special selection and recommendation convocations in the northwest and that this was not the intention of the king when he ordered the recruitment of talented men from the area. Kim recommended that the governor be more careful in the future.[44] In 1872 Kim complained about the problem of clerks taking examinations when this was strictly prohibited by law. From now on," he recommended, "those clerks who are currently in a post should not take the examinations!" The king approved.[45]

A fine distinction has to be made with regard to the throne's attitude toward the lower orders of society. In 1870, for example, the king rescinded the old law that the offspring of a slave mother and commoner father—the so-called matrilineal succession law (*chongmobŏp*)—had to be a slave.[46] This was not an unprecedented measure, since that particular law had been changed several times in the past; but it had always been an important means for enabling upward mobility from the slave to commoner class.[47] It did not necessarily indicate, however, that the throne was interested in the elevation of slaves to the status of officials.

The search for talent did not affect certain types of special privilege. The descendants of former merit subjects prohibited from holding office for some crime committed by their forebears were made eligible for office. The throne also continued to give special recognition to descendants of royalty, merit subjects, and former high officials.[48]

Recommendation, Review, and Qualification

The conflict between standards of performance and ascription was also a major theme in decisions made about the civil bureaucracy. The use of recommendation, stricter adherence to review procedures prior to appointment, and insistence on proper qualification for certain posts were aimed at countering the nonrational aspects of personnel recruitment and procedure.

The use of personal recommendation for the selection of officials was a time-honored device in Chinese and Korean history for supplementing the shortcomings of the examination system as a method of recruitment. There was no guarantee that a literary examination would elicit the most competent or most moral men—whatever the standards for judgment. Personal recommendation, although ostensibly less objective, might well produce better results. Recommendation was also deemed more attractive when the integrity of the examination system was undermined by corruption.[49] In early 1870 orders were issued for the recommendation of men to be given first appointments as local magistrates. Judging from the list of the recommendees, however, it would appear that the throne intended that all of them were to come from the privileged class— descendants of former magistrates and degree holders. The king also allowed all *taesin* to recommend several persons who were lesser degree-holders, and even family relations.[50] Although the use of recommendation was supposed to provide opportunity for the discovery of merit and talent, it still was to be confined to the elite stratum of degree-holding yangban. No impersonal standards were established for the recommendation process, and the throne was not disturbed by the dangers of favoritism.

Another illustration of the ambivalence between merit and privilege is to be found in the normal operating procedure of the bureaucracy, particularly the special requirement that people recommended for appointment to certain posts had to have held certain other lower posts as prerequisites. This regulation was especially applied to positions connected with literary matters, the royal lectures, the compilation of edicts and documents, and the state educational establishments.[51] Requirements for prior service in certain posts were justified on the grounds of proper professional preparation and administrative experience.[52] On the other hand, such restrictions ensured conformity and uniformity in ideological matters and placed priority on routine performance and seniority as criteria for advancement.

The normal device for ensuring efficiency and proper performance in the bureaucracy was the regular review procedures conducted in the lunar sixth and twelfth months, but the system was not functioning effectively. In 1865, for example, the dowager-regent complained that the reviews of official performance had been carried on in a most perfunctory way. Officials were uniformly graded as lower-middle in terms of performance—even the best ones. The failure to conduct proper evaluations had resulted in a lowering of morale among officials. She ordered the ministries of personnel and war to cease promoting and demoting officials at the review sessions in the future, thereby challenging the independence and autonomy of the bureaucracy.[53]

One of the chief devices for surveillance over provincial officials was the institution of traveling secret censors, who were dispatched on an ad hoc basis by the throne. Sporadic use was made of the secret censors in the early part of the decade, but in 1868 they were dispatched throughout the country. As a result of their investigations, over a hundred incumbent and former officials were punished or rewarded on the basis of past performance.[54] Censors, however, were also susceptible to bribery and corruption. Several indictments brought against them for their failure to report wrongdoing uncovered through other channels does show, however, that the regime made an extra effort to rid local government of corruption and evaluate officials on the basis of their performance as administrators.[55]

Sale of Office

At the same time that care was exercised to reward merit and eliminate incompetents from office, people were allowed to obtain magistrate's and other posts by cash contributions. There are scattered examples of the sale of office in the records of the court; the largest single list of several dozen appointees by purchase was submitted on November 7, 1866.[56] It need hardly be mentioned that the sale of office is in principle contrary to the idea of recruitment on the basis of talent, but the state needed revenue almost as much as it needed to eliminate corruption and inefficiency. Since the tax base was restricted by statute and was relatively inflexible, the state had to rely on extraordinary means to raise revenue. The sale of office is therefore a good example of the practical limitations in the use of rational criteria for recruitment.

Rotation of Posts and Continuity of Personnel

The Yi dynasty system of bureaucratic organization did provide for the weeding out of incompetents at lower levels and the selection of the most experienced men for higher office, but once these men had attained high rank and office, the system rendered them partly dysfunctional. The officials of the higher bureaucracy were rotated in their posts with such unbelievable frequency that it is hard to understand how any of them could have accumulated the experience on the job necessary for efficient administration. This phenomenon was particularly noticeable in the six ministries which were the chief administrative arm of the central government. From 1864 to 1873 forty-eight people were appointed to the post of minister of personnel, an average of one appointment every seventy-six days; in 1873 alone eight persons were appointed to the post.[57] For the Ministry of Works for the same period there were eighty-two appointments to the post of minister of works, or one appointment every fifty-two days; the usual tenure was about two months, and the longest term by any individual was six months. In one month in 1866 four different men held the post.[58] Only in the Ministry of Taxation was there any longevity in office. From 1865 through 1874 only two men occupied the post of minister of taxation—Kim Pyŏng-guk, a member of the Andong Kim clan, from 1866 to 1872, and Kim Se-gyun, from 1872 to 1874.[59] One possible explanation for this game of musical chairs is that the bureaucracy was being used as a vehicle for providing prestige and status to the upper class at the expense of administrative efficiency. Since the eligible office-holders probably far outran the number of available posts, frequent appointments and rapid rotation ensured the granting of titles to the largest possible number of persons.

Despite the frequency of appointments and transfers, there was a remarkable degree of continuity among the high officials. When Kojong was formally enthroned as king on February 16, 1864, Kim Chwa-gŭn was chief state councilor, Cho Tu-sun was second state councilor, and Chŏng Wŏn-yŏng was first minister-without-portfolio.[60] At the time the order was handed down for the reconstruction of the Kyŏngbok palace on May 7, Kim was now first minister of the Office of the Royal Clan. Cho was chief state councilor, and Chŏng was first minister-without-portfolio. Of the chief ministers who signed the joint memorial calling for the prohibition of Christianity on February 25, 1866, Kim, Cho, and Chong held the same posts as in 1864. At the court conference convened on September 3, 1866, to discuss the *General Sherman* incident, Kim held the same post and Cho was now first minister-without-portfolio.[61]

Even though certain officials either resigned or were transferred from top administrative posts, it did not mean the end of their role in government. Many were subsequently appointed to the Office of the Royal Clan or to the ministers-without-portfolio (*chungch'ubu*), where they were entitled to royal audience and were almost always summoned to court to discuss major policy questions. This system ensured the retention of older men at high levels almost indefinitely. While retirement was always an option, sinecures enabled older officials to exercise generally conservative influence at policy conferences. The Taewongun did nothing during this regime to counter the frequency of appointment or the retention of elderly officials. On the contrary, by continuing both practices he seems to have sacrificed opportunities for administrative efficiency and the recruitment of fresh talent.

The conflict between merit and privilege can be seen in the several issues dealt with in this chapter, and in certain respects advances were made in the direction of greater rationalization of recruitment and procedure. Restrictions against office holding were lifted and greater opportunities were provided for members of the royal clan, yangban affiliated with minority factions, descendants of people punished for political and other crimes, residents of particular regions like the northwest and Cheju Island, and Wang clan of Koryŏ royalty. Special examinations in traditional military skills were held, and the court insisted that coastal and border garrisons be staffed by men with military experience instead of the usual time-servers. Personal recommendation was used to recruit men ignored by the regular channels of evaluation. Regular procedures of the bureaucracy like review and surveillance were used to ensure that the able be promoted and the corrupt punished.

The emphasis on performance, merit, and efficiency was, however, still limited by considerations of status, privilege, politics, and state finance. Special advantages were accorded to members of the royal clan and descendants of merit subjects. The Andong Kim were retained in high posts and the Yŏhŭng Min were able to build a solid position in the bureaucracy, since the Taewongun failed to initiate institutional restrictions against consort relatives. Members of lower social orders were prevented from moving upward in the military hierarchy and clerks were prohibited from access to civil examinations. Entrenched high officials were the only ones allowed to recommend men for office, and the recommendees were limited to officials and degree holders. The shortage of revenues forced the government to sell offices. The Taewongun relied partly on favorites and henchmen in his manipulation of the existing order. The Patriarch's Faction remained powerful despite the relaxation of restrictions against minority factions, and the entrenched bureaucrats and country scholars still constituted a powerful vested interest. Posts were rotated frequently, preventing the acquisition of administrative expertise. The bureaucracy was topheavy with older officials who stayed on in sinecures closing off opportunities for younger talented officials. In short, there was some widening of opportunity and some attempt to substitute merit for privilege in the recruitment of men but hardly enough to undermine the existing system.

To fault the Taewongun for failure to adhere to rational standards of recruitment would be an anachronistic imposition of modern values on a premodern situation. The essence of the traditional Yi dynasty bureaucratic and social system was balance—a balance reflected in dichotomy between merit and privilege. Given the system, the Taewongun should be given some credit for his vigorous efforts to restore the balance that had been lost in the previous period when consort clan and factional power had gone relatively unchallenged and administrative inefficiency and military weakness had increased to severe proportions. On the other hand, his policies did little to remove the most serious restrictions against recruitment on the basis of merit or curtail the aristocratic monopoly of access to the centralized bureaucracy.

4

Land Distribution and Taxation

In the late Yi dynasty the problems of revenue shortage and peasant unrest were both caused primarily by the aristocratic landowning class's monopoly over the land and free-floating resources of the country.[1] One of the main reasons for the weakness of the central government was its inability to tax land effectively to meet its needs in a time of domestic crisis and foreign challenge. The basic cause of this deficiency was the fusion of aristocratic status with private landownership, an amalgam that was almost as resistant to the fiscal encroachments of the central government as a bona fide feudal nobility, despite the fact that privately owned land was legally subject to direct taxation. The existence of a centralized bureaucratic structure—as opposed to a decentralized or feudal political order—was no guarantee of greater centralized control over land and the tax revenues accruing therefrom.

Peasant poverty and, by extension, the threat of peasant rebellion also derived indirectly from aristocratic landowner control over economic resources in the countryside. Privately owned land was concentrated in the hands of a few large landowners and landlords, most, but not all, of whom were of yangban status. The peasant cultivators, who were predominantly commoners or slaves in social status, were either small-holders, tenants, or agricultural laborers. The concentration of wealth produced by the pattern of land tenure and distribution provided the rural upper class with the resources and influence to control and subvert the land tax system for their own benefit to the detriment of both the central government and the peasantry. Through bribery of local magistrates and clerks they were able to keep their lands off the tax registers, and through their connections with officials in the central bureaucracy they were able to preserve a regressive land tax structure.

Land Distribution and Taxation

Thus, underregistration of taxable land narrowed the tax base of the central government, and regressive taxation increased the burdens of the peasantry.

The alternatives open to the central government on the revenue question were all invidious: it could only increase its revenues from the land tax at the expense of either the social elite—the aristocratic land-owners—or the poor peasant smallholders and tenants. If it chose to raise the tax burden on the upper class, it would encounter strong opposition not only from the large yangban landowners, but also from the bureaucrats who defended landlord interests. On the other hand, if it chose to raise the land tax burden on the poor peasant, it risked provoking open rebellion. The only other alternative was to cut expenditures, an option that was ruled out in the 1860s because of the threat of foreign invasion. When the Taewongun came to power in 1864, he was thus faced with conflicting demands: the central government needed more revenue and the peasants required alleviation of their poverty and tax burden, but the yangban landowners resisted alteration of the fiscal status quo.

Previous studies of the Taewongun's land and land tax policies have usually emphasized his willingness to challenge entrenched private interests and his accomplishments in expanding land tax revenues by improved survey and registration of cultivated land and by restricting and confiscating the estate lands of princes, princesses, and private academies. What lends credence to this view is other evidence of the Taewongun's audacity in challenging the yangban aristocracy over the military support tax and the private academies. Notwithstanding these other matters, however, the Taewongun's land and land tax policies cannot be regarded as either a significant expansion of central power or a solution to the basic causes of peasant poverty. In fact, the Taewongun only made weak, partial, and temporary inroads into the economic foundations of yangban power. He failed to do more because he did not view monarchic interests in direct opposition to yangban interests, and did not dare to launch a direct attack against the yangban landowners; true to the nature of the symbiotic relationship between aristocracy and central power, the Taewongun demonstrated in deed his awareness of the need for mutual support and reliance between throne and aristocracy by avoiding a direct struggle with the major social and economic class over the problems of land and land tax reform.

With regard to the taxation of land the late Yi dynasty land tenure system can be divided into two broad categories: the private sector comprising the majority of arable land subject to the direct taxation of the central government as administered by its local magistrates, and the

Politics and Policy in Traditional Korea

so-called tax-exempt sector of lands or estates controlled by a variety of institutions and semi-corporate bodies. My argument that the Taewongun failed to achieve a significant expansion over land revenues and a solution to peasant poverty because he avoided a direct confrontation with yangban landowners is based on an analysis of the Taewongun's policies toward each of the two sectors, the private and the tax-exempt.

In the Taewongun's approach toward the private sector he emphasized the elimination of administrative corruption because it was the immediate cause of peasant rebellion and he made some progress in resurvey and registration of land, but he did little to eliminate the fundamental causes of revenue shortage, peasant poverty, and aristocratic privilege—concentrated landholding patterns, tenancy, and regressive taxation. Even though the private sector was subject to direct taxation by the state, it was most resistant to the fiscal pressures of the central government; any attempt to redistribute land or raise tax rates was certain to elicit the opposition of the yangban landowners and their representatives in the central bureaucracy.

Conversely, what was ostensibly the most protected sector of the land tax structure—the tax-exempt lands of various institutions—was in fact most vulnerable to an attack by the central government. Many of these institutional and semi-corporate lands, such as palace estates, post-station lands, official colony lands, and private academy estates, were either under the jurisdiction of the central government or subject to its restraints in other ways. These bodies were least able to resist the conversion of their lands to the system of private ownership and direct taxation. Furthermore, the tax-exempt lands were but a minor fraction of the total arable land in the country, yet under the Taewongun's guidance the central government launched a relatively feeble attack on the private sector while directing the brunt of its effort against the tax-exempt sector—the one that was least independent and least able to resist. The Taewongun's avoidance of a frontal attack on the large landowners, landlords, and rich peasants—whether aristocratic or nonaristocratic—reveals the strength of private economic interests and the inherent weakness of the central government, in particular its inability to solve the major problems related to land tenure and taxation.

A corollary to the above interpretation will be taken up in subsequent chapters, namely that the Taewongun was able to avoid a direct confrontation with the yangban landowner class by utilizing other devices for raising revenue, such as forced contributions, transit taxes, currency

Land Distribution and Taxation

manipulation, and grain loan interest. The net effect of these methods was to leave the existing system of elite tax privilege intact.

The Private Sector

Revenue Shortage and Peasant Poverty

The main problems the government faced with regard to land tenure and taxation in the 1860s were revenue shortage and peasant poverty. The two immediate causes of low revenues were underregistration of land and a low and regressive tax rate. As a result of Hideyoshi's invasions of Korea (1592-98) the amount of registered land was reduced drastically from 1,500,000 kyŏl to about 500,000 kyŏl.[2] Thereafter, land surveys were carried out infrequently even though the law stipulated that the land was to be surveyed once every twenty years.[3] Two incomplete land surveys were carried out in 1600-04 and 1627-34, the latter in the southern three provinces only. For the rest of the dynasty, major surveys were conducted in 1663-69, 1718-20, 1820, and 1898-1904; the 1820 survey was the first one in a hundred years.[4] By 1769 there was 1,310,000 kyŏl of registered land, but only 800,000 kyŏl was taxable (silgyŏl).[5] Over a century and a half after the Japanese invasions the central government's land tax base had still not attained the prewar level. Land surveys were conducted infrequently because of high costs, laxity in administration, and obstruction by the large landowning interests. Even when they were carried out, land was falsely registered to the benefit of the wealthy landowners.[6] The government's inability to keep up with land registration meant that changes in landholding patterns and reclaimed land was not recorded and taxed.

The crop damage inspection and assessment system also contributed to underreporting and reduced revenue. During flood or drought the government provided for temporary "crop damage" tax exemptions as a relief measure, but because of corruption the rich landowners obtained exemptions on undamaged land while the poor peasant owner was often forced to continue paying taxes on land that should have been exempted. Because of overreporting of "damaged land" and failure to return reclaimed land to the tax registers, the central government suffered serious long-term reductions in revenue.[7] During the first half of the nineteenth century about 70,000 kyŏl per year on the average were exempted from taxation on the grounds of natural disaster and damage.[8]

A regressive tax structure also resulted in restricted revenues for the central government because of undertaxation of fertile and productive land. In the late fourteenth century the tax rate was supposedly set at 10 percent of the crop or 30 tu/kyŏl. In the early fifteenth century a graded tax scheme was put into effect and tax rates varied from 4-20 tu/kyŏl in accordance with the quality of the land, but by 1635 the graded system had been abandoned and most land was taxed at the uniform rate of 4 tu/kyŏl.[9] By the end of the seventeenth century the land tax had three components: the original land tax assessed at the relatively low rate of 4 tu/kyŏl, the converted tribute tax that averaged 12 tu/kyŏl, and a variety of surtaxes to provide for labor services and the expenses of a host of unsalaried clerks and petty officials. One source estimates that by the end of the eighteenth century regular land taxes (the original land tax plus the converted tribute tax) amounted to 21 tu/kyŏl, but that the total of all regular taxes and surtaxes was as high as 100 tu/kyŏl. Since the yield from one kyŏl of land varied from 150 tu/kyŏl for the poorest land to 900 tu/kyŏl for the best, the actual land tax rate varied from 11 percent of the yield on good land to 76 percent on the poorest land.[10] These figures probably represent the extremes, for another source estimates the total land tax at about 60 tu/kyŏl, which is equivalent to 6.65 percent of the crop on the most fertile land or 40 percent on the least fertile.[11] Obviously a regressive tax rate caused hardship for the poor peasant cultivating marginal lands, but it also caused reduced revenues for the central government because the most fertile and productive lands were in effect undertaxed.

The proportion of total land taxes that was collected by the central government in the capital was relatively low. Whether total taxes per kyŏl were 60 or 100 tu, only 21 tu was earmarked for the central government. Most of the surtaxes went for local needs or to defray the administrative costs of tax collection. In other words, only 20-30 percent of the total taxes collected found its way to the capital; and this percentage might be reduced still further if there were any way to calculate illicit surcharges, gratuities, and extortion. Therefore, not only did the rural landowning elite control most of the land and wealth, but the local officials and their hangers-on controlled most of the land tax revenues.

Regressive taxation and undertaxation of the best land were exacerbated because the government failed to maintain records of land quality for the purpose of adjusting taxation to actual production.[12] For that matter, the basic unit of areal measurement, the kyŏl, contributed to manipulation and falsification because of the complex calculations that were required. After 1653 one kyŏl was defined in terms of six different sizes of land area from 2.2 acres for the most fertile land to 8.8 acres for the least fertile. Grade six kyŏl was thus four times the area of grade one kyŏl.[13] The system was designed to ensure equitable taxation by an automatic adjustment for fertility and productivity, mitigating the effects of a

Land Distribution and Taxation

uniform and regressive single tax rate. In fact, however, false measurement corrupted the system and several scholars and officials proposed the adoption of Chinese-type constant units of area with no adjustments or grades for productivity, but to no avail.[14] For that matter, even if the Chinese units had been adopted, some type of graded taxation scheme would have been necessary to eliminate inequalities of tax burden and ensure full taxation of the most productive land, which generally was owned by aristocrats and rich peasants.

Laxity and corruption in the registration of land and assessment of crop damage also contributed to the regressive tax structure. The wealthier households obtained the greatest benefits from corruption resulting in de facto lower rates of taxation on their holdings, certain portions of which were unregistered and untaxed altogether. The central government suffered losses in revenue while the poorer households generally paid higher tax rates in fact than the wealthy landowners.

Peasant poverty also became a serious problem for the government in its search for revenues in the mid-nineteenth century because of the outbreak of rural rebellion. The revenue problem was inseparable from the question of peasant poverty because the economic livelihood of the peasant had to be stabilized before the central government would be able to ensure a constant flow of tax revenues from the agricultural sector. Since the "equal service" reform of 1750 the central government had evidenced little fear of the excessive tax burdens on the peasantry, but the large-scale rebellion in south Korea in 1862 made it clear that the limit had been reached in the exploitation of the poor peasant.

There were seven probable or possible causes of peasant poverty and rebellion in the nineteenth century: a skewed or concentrated pattern of landholding; small average per capita holdings; high rates of tenancy; a regressive tax structure; false registration of taxable land; extortion and illegal charges and gratuities at tax collection time; and usury, especially official usury in the management of the grain loan system. Of the above only extortion and usury were direct and immediate causes of peasant rebellion; the major peasant rebellions of 1862 and 1894 were directed specifically against the officials responsible for extortion and grain loan usury and mismanagement, and not against landlords and landowners. On the basis of available evidence, it would appear that class consciousness and class struggle (in the economic sense) were still very weak. Even from a Marxist point of view it would be difficult to regard the nineteenth century rebellions as antifeudal, except for the fact that social leveling and egalitarianism were explicit features of Tonghak ideology. One might regard these rebellions, however, as the beginnings of social transformation, a process that extended into the twentieth century.[15]

The regressive tax structure and false registration of land for taxation were obviously direct causes of peasant poverty. The other factors—skewed landholding patterns, small average per capita holdings, and tenancy—were possible but not necessary causes of peasant poverty and rebellion.

Private landownership prevailed from the beginning of the dynasty, official statements about royal or national ownership to the contrary notwithstanding. The right of purchase and sale was recognized explicitly in an edict of 1424, an act which undoubtedly merely affirmed what was already current practice.[16] The so-called land allotment schemes of the first century of the dynasty—the rank-land system (*kwajŏn*) of 1391 and office-land system (*chikchŏn*) of 1466—were really only grants of tax collection rights to people with official rank, and not systems of national ownership and distribution.[17] Furthermore, only a small fraction of all land was controlled in this way. As these allotment systems broke down by the late fifteenth and early sixteenth centuries, tax collection rights over office-land were undoubtedly converted to private ownership; but this process did not signify a major change in the system of land tenure, which was already based in large part on private ownership.

Although landholding patterns varied with time and place, generally a small percentage of landholders owned the majority of land in a given area. In one study of several districts in the seventeenth and eighteenth centuries about 10 percent of the landholders owned 40 to 50 percent of the registered land, while middle or poor peasants comprising about 60 percent of the registered landholders controlled only about 10 to 20 percent of the land.[18] In another case study, in one district 5.4 percent of the landholders owned 62.3 percent of the land.[19] There was a high degree of correlation between social status and landholding; most but not all of the larger landowners were probably of yangban status. The skewed or concentrated pattern of landholding provided an economic base for the yangban aristocracy; it also meant that the majority of smallholders possessed only marginally economic holdings and were probably kept at subsistence levels of income.

There is also convincing evidence of the decrease over time in the size of the average per household or per capita landholding at all levels probably because of population increase and inheritance practice. Since dynasty population figures are extremely unreliable, one can only guess at a mid-nineteenth century population figure of ten million with probably as much as a 10 percent margin of error.[20] The rate of population growth cannot be safely measured since the figure of approximately one million people for the early fifteenth century is also dubious. Yet we may assume that population growth coupled with the custom of dividing the inherited patrimony relatively equally among legitimate sons was

Land Distribution and Taxation

mainly responsible for the decrease in the size of the average land-holding. In the early Yi dynasty those holding less than five kyŏl of land were regarded as poor peasants while large landowners had over fifty kyŏl. By the end of the dynasty anyone with over one kyŏl of land could be classified as wealthy, and the poor peasant held below one quarter kyŏl.[21] Since the kyŏl at this time varied in size from 2.2 to 8.8 acres depending on the quality of the land, many peasant families had to subsist on a holding of a half acre.[22] As noted above, in one area of several districts about 50 to 60 percent of the registered landholders were poor peasants who owned an average of one quarter kyŏl of land or less per household, and their total holdings comprised only 10 to 20 percent of the total land owned.[23]

Kim Yong-sŏp has also estimated that in the districts he studied the after-tax income of 30 to 58 percent of farm households was less than what they required for subsistence. The lower the social status of the landholder, the lower the income and the greater the number of poor peasant families; but close to half the number of households of putative yangban status hovered about the poverty line as well.[24]

Kim's calculations, however, are not based on concrete evidence of productivity in the districts he studied but on general estimates derived from scattered references to production from other sources.[25] In the light of studies of other countries it may not be possible to conclude as Kim does for Korea that fragmentation of landholdings in association with population growth necessarily meant reduced per capita income. As Geertz points out, given a constant level of agricultural technology, productivity in rice cultivation will rise with increased labor input resulting in relatively constant per capita production even in times of rising population.[26]

High rates of tenancy also prevailed in nineteenth century Korea. On one palace estate in 1830 about 65 percent of the cultivated land or 41 percent of the total land area was tilled by tenants. Yet in the same district the rate of tenant-cultivated land on individual parcels varied from 10 to 90 percent.[27] In six select districts studied on the basis of the land survey of 1898-1904, 50.9 percent of all households were owner tenants and another 24.0 percent were pure tenants; in other words, in this area 74.9 percent of the registered households rented either some or all of the land they tilled.[28]

Tenancy per se did not necessarily indicate low levels of income, for some tenants were also landowners and landlords, and some tenants held large parcels that could yield adequate income even after rent and taxes. Nevertheless, most tenants rented less than 0.50 kyŏl, and in the south they were required to pay taxes in addition to the usual 50 percent sharecropping rent.[29] Usually the tenants who cultivated large parcels were those who rented them from palace estates or official colony lands (the tax-exempt sector) and then sublet it to others.[30]

Not all tenant contracts were disadvantageous to the tenant. In ordinary tenancy the tenant's tenure and rights were relatively weak; his contracts were short-term and renewable only at the pleasure of the landlord. There were two forms of tenant fees, fixed rent or share-cropping; but the usual arrangement on short-term rented land was a sharecropping agreement calling for a rent of 50 percent or more of the crop. A more powerful type of tenant right called the *tojikwŏn*, however, was tantamount to partial ownership. In this case the tenant had permanent tenure, which he could pass on through inheritance, gift, or sale to others. The landlord's sale of the land did not affect the tenant's rights. His rent was pegged at a sharecropping rate lower than the usual 50 percent short-term standard. Records of the sale of *toji* rights show that they averaged in value about one third the value of the land itself.[31] Since relatively secure *toji* tenancy arrangements prevailed throughout the country to a rather high degree in the latter part of the dynasty, tenancy alone was not necessarily responsible for peasant poverty. Furthermore, increased labor inputs on rented land may also have increased output.

There is one additional piece of indirect evidence that suggests that a skewed pattern of ownership, small per capita holdings, and tenancy were not necessarily the prime factors in peasant poverty: peasant re-bellions in the nineteenth century were not directed against landowners or landlords. It would appear at least that the peasants did not consciously think of their small holdings or share-cropping arrangements as the cause of their poverty, even though certain scholars and officials recognized them as such.

There were, however, two causes of poverty and distress that were recognized by the peasantry and goaded them to rebellion: corruption in the taxation system and usury. Both were the responsibility of the local magistrates and their clerks. As regressive and burdensome as the land tax was, it is still unlikely that it alone was sufficient to spark rebellion, even after the conversion of the tribute tax to a land levy in the seven-teenth century.[32] Peasant risings were usually directed against corrupt officials who practiced extortion and bribery and registered and graded land falsely and inaccurately.

Another area of corruption and source of peasant discontent was usury and corruption in the administration of rural grain loans. This matter will be taken up separately in Chapter 7. Suffice it to say here that the main source of oppressive and usurious loans was the official grain

Land Distribution and Taxation

loan system. Private usury must have been common in the capital-short rural areas, but the private grain lenders were rural aristocrats, gentry, and landowners and not the absentee landlord moneylenders of late Ch'ing China. One might assume that the more familiar face-to-face relationship between peasant borrower and gentry lender mitigated some of the harsher aspects of indebtedness. At any rate, the peasant uprisings of 1862 were directed against the granary clerks and not the private lenders.

In summary, the main causes of peasant poverty in the nineteenth century might be described as follows: a skewed pattern of landownership, small per capita holdings, and high rates of tenancy kept households at subsistence levels but not necessarily below it. Peasants were pushed below the poverty line by a regressive land tax, administrative corruption, and usury. Prima facie evidence of this interpretation is provided by the fact that peasant violence in the nineteenth century was directed against officials and clerks rather than landlords, landowners, rich peasants, or private lenders.

Approaches to Reform in the Private Sector

Land reform proposals should not be lumped together indiscriminately as if they all had the same goal and effect. There were several alternatives that reflected different motives and objectives. Solution of the revenue shortage problem required resurvey and registration of land to increase the amount of taxable land and more efficient assessment of crop damage and temporary exemptions to reduce loss by falsification. Upward revision of the tax rate on fertile land was necessary to achieve more efficient and equitable taxation of large aristocratic landowners and rich peasants. Solution of the problem of peasant poverty and rebellion required a two-pronged attack on both immediate and fundamental causes. Extortion and graft had to be eliminated by better surveillance, punishment of administrative malfeasance, and better recruitment of officials and clerks. False registration of land and "crop damage" exemptions had to be rectified not just to increase government revenue, but also to provide a basis for a downward revision of tax rates and quotas on the middle and poor peasant. In other words, a highly regressive tax rate had to be modified or converted to a progressive schedule. The oppressive effects of official grain loan usury also had to be eliminated.

With regard to the indirect or fundamental causes of poverty, a more equitable system of landholding and distribution might have alleviated the inequalities produced by the existing skewed pattern of landholding, but this would not have solved the problem of small average per capita holdings. The only solution for that would have been increased output by land reclamation, better technology, more inputs from fertilizer or better seed, or more efficient utilization of land and labor. The problem of tenancy could have been solved by total elimination through a program of nationalization and redistribution of land or by reduction of tenant rents.

When officials and scholars turned their attention to the problems of revenue shortage and peasant poverty in the late seventeenth century, some of them believed that the only permanent and effective solution to both problems was radical reform of the land tenure system, either limitations on private holdings or confiscation of all land by the state and egalitarian redistribution to all cultivators. The inspiration for this radical approach came from the Confucian tradition and past precedent in Chinese history, particularly that aspect of Confucian economic thought which stressed the equal distribution of land as the proper means to the end of a contented and secure peasantry.

Yi Ik (1682-1764) hoped to create an egalitarian order based on the individual peasant proprietorship by limiting the size of holdings, guaranteeing a plot for all peasants, and protecting them against forced sale and foreclosure. He believed that the landowners and social elite were too powerful to allow for the elimination of private property and status privilege and that the only hope for meaningful reform was a gradualist approach by establishing legal limitations on ownership—a device borrowed from Han dynasty China.[33]

Yu Hyŏng-wŏn (1622-74) proposed that the state nationalize all land and grant equal allotments to all commoners. Slightly greater shares of land would be given to aristocrats, bureaucrats, and nobles in ascending order of status and function. His plan would have put an end to private property, ensured a solid base of income and production for the common peasant, and provided an economic base for the social and political elite. In effect, Yu modified the T'ang "equal field" system to meet the needs of the Korean hierarchical social order by providing land allotments to aristocrats with no specific government functions.[34]

The most radical solution to the land distribution and taxation problem was proposed by Chŏng Yag-yong (1762-1836). Chŏng wanted to put an end to both private property and social privilege by replacing private ownership with communal ownership with the community integrated into a hierarchical political structure. Since land would be communally owned, there would be no egalitarian distribution of land but an egalitarian distribution of wealth.[35]

As fascinating as Chŏng's proposals are to the historian of ideas, so much the less significant were they in terms of their influence on government policy. He wrote many of them while in exile, and his physical separation from the capital was symbolic of the remoteness of his ideas from the realm of the practical and the possible. What was possible is revealed by the open debate on the land question held under King Chŏngjo in the late 1790s. Chŏngjo made a formal request for advice on agricultural and land questions from people in and out of office all over the country. The most radical suggestion, however, did not go beyond the land limitation scheme of Yi Ik. Not only did Chŏngjo and his high officials reject land limitation as impractical, they also rejected milder requests for equal tenancy holdings by forced redistribution of rented land to landless peasants; it was argued that this would have been an improper assertion of governmental authority over the rights of private owners.[36]

After Chŏng Yag-yong there were few who seriously advocated any major program of nationalization and redistribution. Advocates of land and tax reform in the nineteenth century turned their attention to administrative measures, such as the reform of the land survey and registration system, the reduction of excessive amounts of untaxed land, the simplification and reduction of tax rates, and the elimination of administrative corruption. They felt that these measures were the best means for increasing state revenues and alleviating excessive tax burdens on the peasantry in a period when private property rights were unassailable.[37]

The scholar, Yi Kyu-gyŏng, writing in the first half of the nineteenth century, and the officials, Hŏ Pu and Kim Yun-sik, who memorialized the throne on the land problem during the 1862 peasant rebellion, all rejected the Chinese well-field, limited-field, and equal-field systems. They pointed to the failure of these systems even in China because of the fact that equal distribution could not succeed in the face of the aggrandizement of landholdings by the wealthy and powerful.[38] In comparing contemporary Korean society with China of the Han and T'ang they acknowledged the even greater power of private property and the yangban social elite in Korean society. They concluded that the yangban were too solidly entrenched to be eliminated and that egalitarian redistribution was out of the question. Instead they shifted their attention to the fair distribution of tax burdens through better land registration.[39]

The Chinese "fish-scale register" system, in particular, appealed to many Koreans as the best solution to the problem of accurate survey and registration. In 1709 it was adopted in the survey of four districts in Hwanghae province but was never extended to any other area. It was advocated by Yi Ik and Chŏng Yag-yong, discussed by officials at court in the 1790s, and mentioned by Hŏ Pu and Kim Yun-sik in 1862.[40] Its proponents complained that one of the reasons for inaccurate and false land survey and registration was that under existing regulations only written records of landowners and their parcels were made. The "fish-scale" system, however, required maps or drawings of the topography and the boundaries of individually owned parcels.

Discussions at court during the peasant uprising of 1862 reveal clearly that the wind had long since been taken out of the sails of those who advocated whole-scale land confiscation and redistribution. The most radical proposal made at this time was the adoption of the Chinese fish-scale registers, but it too was not adopted. To many it would have been sufficient if the central government were able to simply to maintain land resurveys every twenty years as called for in the statutes. The main thrust of reformist thought, therefore, was directed toward the reduction of tax exemptions on land, the reporting and taxation of unregistered cultivated lands, the elimination of falsified records, and the abolition of irregular surcharges. The concentrated pattern of landholding was to be left alone. It was generally agreed that rectification of the existing system would be sufficient to create a lightly taxed, stable, and contented peasantry, and a fiscally balanced budget, since there were no expectations of expanded expenditures. As Kim Yong-sŏp has pointed out in his study of this period, even proposals for a nationwide survey were rejected; the government decided only to conduct partial surveys and to investigate more thoroughly cultivated and fallow land.[41]

Reform in the Private Sector: 1864-73

In view of the wide range of alternatives available for reform in the private sector, the Taewongun's policies were exceedingly conservative. The most effective action taken during his regime was probably the punishment and replacement of corrupt officials and the reform of the grain loan system, the latter to be discussed in Chapter 7.[42] But these problems were precisely the immediate and direct causes of peasant rebellion; the more fundamental causes were hardly touched. After 1864 there was virtually no discussion at court of the radical plans of land confiscation, redistribution, and limitation that had so consumed the thoughts of eighteenth century intellectuals. In August 1864 a minor official did recommend to young King Kojong that he peruse the writings of Yu Hyŏng-wŏn for ideas on the reform of all institutions, in particular the land system. Kojong agreed he would, but after this there was no further mention of any major scheme for land redistribution.[43] Nor were any proposals made to provide security for tenants or rent reduction. For that matter even the Chinese fish-scale registers were ignored; the idea was not revived until 1895. The only two areas of concern were land surveys and land taxes, but the results were not particularly outstanding.

Land Distribution and Taxation

Despite the throne's frequent rhetorical denunciations of yangban land-owner privilege, land resurveys were only limited in scope; and despite the urgent need for alleviation of the regressive tax structure, the only action taken was to add still another surtax and to attempt to prohibit cash commutations of tax payments in kind.

It would appear from the number of edicts and directives issued from the court during this decade that the government was doggedly deter-mined to investigate the actual conditions of cultivation and bring more taxable land onto the tax ledgers. In fact, however, the new regime was reluctant to initiate a massive and total land resurvey project.[44] This caution had been characteristic of Yi dynasty policy on land resurveys, for officials had frequently warned the throne against the consternation, confusion, and protest that might result from too sudden and sweeping a reform. The government feared protest by the landed and property interests against confiscatory taxation and discontent among the common peasant landowners over fear of extortion and falsification by officials during a resurvey.[45]

The tone of this determined though cautious approach was set soon after Kojong took his seat on the throne. The first man to articulate the basic principles of this policy was Chief State Councilor Kim Chwa-gŭn—an Andong Kim and a holdover from Ch'ŏlchong's reign. Kim pointed out that a major survey had not been carried out since 1720. State revenues had been curtailed, the corruption of the clerks and officials had grown more rampant, and the peasants were suffering. Land surveys had to be carried out, but they should not be carried out in all provinces at the same time. Only a few districts in each province should be surveyed. While he admitted that this might prolong the process, it could be expected that in two to three years' time, the resurvey of the whole country could be completed. He recommended that the work should begin in the winter by the regular provincial administration, and Kojong granted his approval.[46]

Unfortunately for the historian the delegation of responsibility to the regular provincial administration for land registration meant that regular reports of all newly registered land were not recorded in the daily records of the central government. Occasional reports do appear from time to time, but they are too fragmentary to provide an overall picture of the success of the effort. While reliable quantitative evidence is lacking, there is much qualitative evidence in the reports to the throne and discussions at court that clearly reveals an appalling gap between orders and implementation.

A year and a half passed by with little to show for the king's approval of Kim Chwa-gŭn's recommendations in 1864.[47] On June 28, 1866, the king issued an edict deploring the breakdown of the land registration system and the necessity for land surveys, particularly in Kyŏnggi and the southern three provinces of Ch'ungch'ŏng, Chŏlla, and Kyŏngsang; he ordered the magistrates to redouble their efforts in this regard.[48] The tone of his edict, however, indicates that little had been done since 1864, and that land surveys were only now getting under way. On July 13 Kojong approved a recommendation by the state council for land registration with a report of the results to be made to the throne and punishment for false reporting.[49] Only three months later, however, the king declared that despite his previous orders for the elimination of illicit exemptions and false reporting, he had heard that these practices were still continuing. He ordered the state council to conduct another investigation and mete out punishments for malfeasance.[50]

Reports from provincial governors and secret censors dispatched to the provinces during 1867 and 1868 were hardly encouraging. In Kyŏnggi province the land registers were reported to be in a state of total confusion.[51] Officials were still talking about beginning land surveys in Ch'ungch'ŏng and Chŏlla province in one or two districts and then extending it to the remaining areas.[52] In 1869 the governor of Chŏlla province finally reported the addition of 3,060 kyŏl to the tax rolls, but he also complained of large amounts of land granted tax exemptions because of permanent registration as ruined or damaged waste land. The state council urged that the investigations be resumed again the next year.[53]

Late in 1869 the court seemed to be awakening to the fact that land registration results were less than what had been hoped for. The king complained on November 23 that his recent order for the registration of cultivated land along dikes and streams had been ignored and that the provincial governors and magistrates could not be trusted to carry out his commands. He directed the state council to investigate and punish the guilty officials.[54] Several days later he asked Chief State Councilor Kim Pyŏng-hak whether his order of the twenty-third was being carried out. He deplored the failure of people to pay taxes on land and instructed Kim to send out further orders to the provinces to report all tax evaders.[55] On March 31, 1870, Kojong again expressed anxiety over tax avoidance; and during the rest of the year, reports trickled in on the results of new surveys.[56]

Seven years had gone by since orders for land resurveys were issued. Undoubtedly some progress was made in registering taxable land, but repeated complaints from the throne indicate that the decision to proceed slowly and the inertia of the administrative system had reduced the effectiveness of the program considerably. In 1869 Chief State Councilor

Land Distribution and Taxation

Kim Pyŏng-hak remarked that the Taewongun thoroughly understood the failure of the magistrates to record all cultivated land because of their desire to avoid trouble.[57]

One of the chief sources of the problem of underregistration of land was the desire of the large landowning families to protect their interests. The king and his state councilors were well aware of this and ostensibly they showed no reluctance to attack these interests directly. In 1864 Chief State Councilor Kim Chwa-gŭn protested the loss of post-station and state grazing lands to powerful private households, and later the king expressed the hope that he would be able to "shut the mouths of the powerful households who have been accumulating private landhold-ings."[58] In 1866 he declared that the wealthy and powerful families in the villages held the vast majority of high-grade land. He held them responsible for using illicit methods to obtain exemptions from taxation and acting in collusion with the clerks to keep their holdings off the tax registers. He also accused the yangban in the capital of having their estates registered as tax-exempt and allowing their agents and stewards to cheat the government of taxes even when the land was registered.[59] When the state council made similar accusations against the "powerful households" on July 13, 1866, the king's rescript ordered magistrates to begin their investigations of unregistered land with the estates of the capital yangban and the local powerful houses. They were to make sure that taxes were collected from all of them.[60] In September, Kojong prohibited the private taxation of fishing weirs and salt flats and unau-thorized tax collections by local yangban and great houses.[61]

In 1870 Kojong directed his attention to the problem of gravesite land of yangban households that had been granted tax exemption privileges. He pointed out that such land became taxable if it were under cultivation, ordered investigations made of gravesites, and complained that the yangban had no right to escape taxes.[62] The next month he repeated the order just in case his previous command had not been carried out.[63]

Yet Kojong's open expression of pique at the yangban landowner monopoly of landed wealth and evasion of taxation should not be mistaken for substantive policy. Despite an occasional vituperative outburst, there was no serious attack on yangban landowner wealth by a restructuring of either the tenure or taxation systems. The only substantial change in the land tax system during this decade was the introduction of small cash and grain surcharges on land. One of these was called the "artillery provision rice" tax (p'oryangmi) introduced in 1871 after the American expedition to provide for the expenses of new artillery units on Kanghwa Island. There is some evidence that levies for artillery provisions were previously adopted in coastal towns in Kyŏngsang province. These were abolished in 1868 because of complaints that they were too great a burden on the peasant, but when no alternative sources of revenue could be found, they were reestablished at the request of the provincial governor.[64] On July 12, 1871, Chief State Councilor Kim Pyŏng-hak suggested that the "artillery provision rice" surtax be imposed on the 700,000 kyŏl of registered land in all provinces except P'yong'an and Hamgyŏng in the north. The new tax rate would be one peck per kyŏl (1 tu/kyŏl) and would provide about 50,000 sŏk of additional revenue. He cited the precedent of the surtax introduced in 1593 to provide funds for the Military Training Agency (called the *samsuryang*). Kojong approved of the idea and made only one modification; he insisted that the tax be levied on the landowners rather than the cultivators.[65] One other surtax, a cash surtax on land was introduced about the same time to help finance the construction of the Kyŏngbok Palace.[66] The new surtaxes do not appear to have provided a solution to the central government's long-term revenue shortage. Furthermore, the proliferation of taxes, surtaxes, and miscellaneous charges was one of the main causes of peasant poverty; the new taxes merely reinforced an already regressive tax structure.

The Tax-Exempt Sector

Type and Quantity

The most vigorous action taken by the Taewongun to expand central control over land and the land tax was directed against the tax-exempt sector of land, in particular land controlled by the palace estates (*kungbang*) of princes and princesses and the private academies (*sŏwŏn*) of the local Confucian literati. While the conversion of these lands to privately owned taxpaying land did increase central government revenues, the land area involved was only a small percentage of total taxpaying land, and the categories of land affected were already subject to some controls and restraints by the central government. The gains made in this sector should therefore not be overestimated.

In addition to palace estates and private academy lands the tax-exempt sector also included post-station land (*yŏkchŏn*), colony lands (*tunjŏn*) under both civil and military jurisdiction, and lands controlled by individual agencies of the central bureaucracy, provincial governors, magistrates, and local garrison commanders. In many instances the above institutions might receive revenues from the treasuries of the central government as well as from the tax-exempt lands under their jurisdiction.

The tax-exempt sector of the Yi dynasty represented a survival of

Land Distribution and Taxation

earlier prebendal land allotments. Under the rank-land (*kwajŏn*) and office-land (*chikchŏn*) systems of the fifteenth century, the state made putative land grants—actually tax collection rights or stipends—to people with rank and office and to most agencies of the central and local government. The system of prebendal grants to individuals began to break down in the late fifteenth century. It was no longer functional even before the Japanese invasions, but the delegation of tax collection rights or control of land to state agencies persisted. After the invasions the peasantry was driven off the land and large areas were left uncultivated. Because of the lack of adequate tax revenues to pay administrative costs, salaries, and stipends, and because of the difficulty of resettling the peasants on the land, the central government chose to issue grants of land to various state agencies and institutions in order to provide for their needs. By shifting responsibility for expanded cultivation and resettlement to these agencies, it voluntarily surrendered a measure of control over land and people, creating a host of autonomous and semiautonomous vested interests that undercut central control even after the country had achieved rehabilitation of the agricultural order. Since tax collection rights were delegated to agencies of the central government itself, this did not necessarily lead to a decrease in overall taxation; it did, however, cause a permanent and institutionalized reduction of revenues under the control of the central government's treasuries. The central government also found it difficult to reallocate resources for changing goals and to monitor taxation procedures and rates.

There were two modes of tenure in the tax-exempt sector. If an agency or institution owned lands outright (*yut'o*), it exercised autonomy over cultivation, peasant cultivators, and tax collection. It was granted certain types of tax exemptions and used distinctive tax rates. In the case of colony land, sharecropping, fixed rent, or total collection of the crop could be used.

The second type of control was the grant of taxation rights only over specified lands owned by private individuals (*mut'o*). The tax rates were generally the same as on regularly taxed lands in the private sector. Theoretically, the land was owned by a private individual who paid taxes to an institution or its agents in lieu of the magistrate. Over time, however, there was a blurring of the distinction between these two types of land and ownership rights. Institutions might expand de facto control and ownership rights over private land, and conversely tenant rights on land owned by an institution might evolve into a limited ownership right that could be sold. Since rents continued to go to the institution, there was little interference with frequent transfers of tenant rights.[67]

The tax-exempt lands (*myŏnseji, myŏnsejŏn*) were thus not really exempted from taxation per se; they were merely exempted from the tax collection processes of the central government. On land owned outright by various institutions (*yut'o myŏnseji*) only the land tax was diverted from the central government to the institution; cultivators were supposed to continue paying the tribute tax to the local magistrate. In the case of nonowned tax-exempt lands (*mut'o myŏnseji*) both the land and the tribute tax were diverted to the institutional surrogate. The local magistrate would usually remit land and tribute tax receipts to the Ministry of Taxation at the capital, and the ministry would issue grain or cash to the institution.

Although the cultivators of lands owned by institutions were not really exempted from land and tribute taxes, they did benefit from exemptions from miscellaneous labor service. Futhermore, on certain types of tax-exempt land the tax rates were lower than rates on land in the private sector. Many cultivators who preferred to escape the onerous labor service, surtaxes, and illegal exactions of the magistrates eagerly commended (*tut'ak*) their lands to the tax-exempt institutions, both overtly and covertly. This resulted in a reduction of the land under the direct control of the central government greater than the limits prescribed by law. Government attempts to return illegally commended lands to the regular tax rolls were ignored and obstructed by the joint efforts of both institutional landowners and cultivators; commendation provided extra income for the institutions and a tax haven for the oppressed small peasant landholder.

Institutions constantly expanded their estates. In addition to direct royal grants and commendation, they could purchase land directly with their own funds, obtain land confiscated from criminals, or use their influence for the false registration of privately owned land as their own. As their power grew greater they were also able to extort greater taxes than the legally stipulated rates. The slaves, agents, and stewards of palaces, the Palace Treasury, and other institutions, and the local garrison commanders lined their pockets at the expense of the peasant cultivators and the central government.

By the nineteenth century this so-called tax-exempt sector consisted of about 200,000 kyŏl of land. Table 1 shows the breakdown by category for 1807, and Table 2 calculates the size of the tax-exempt sector by subtracting the figures for "uncultivated" land from the total untaxed land in the period from 1801 to 1861.

The limits of the central government's control over land and land taxes is clearly shown by these tables. By 1801 the amount of taxable land was only 56.0 percent of the total amount of registered land, and this percentage decreased to 53.5 by 1861. Over one third of the untaxed land

Land Distribution and Taxation

Table 1. Tax-exempt lands, ca. 1807

Category	Amount	(in kyŏl)
Temple, tomb, park land	2,018	
Palace estates (kungbang)	37,927	
yut'o		11,380
mut'o		26,547
Government yamen lands	46,104	
Miscellaneous	118,584	
Total	204,635	
Total registered land	1,456,592	
Currently cultivated	840,714	
Damage-exempted	29,895	
Taxable land (silgyŏl)	811,819	
Tax-exempt land/taxable land — 204,635/811,819		25.3%
Tax-exempt land/cultivated taxable land		19.9%
Tax-exempt land/total registered land		14.9%

Source: Man'giyoram chaeyongp'yŏn, 247-73; Yi Sang-baek, Han'guk-sa kŭnse hugip'yŏn, table facing p. 162.

or about 15 percent of all land belonged to the tax-exempt sector. Tax-exempt lands also comprised about one fifth of all taxable land in the country (that is, the sum of cultivated taxable land and tax-exempt land). Although this represented a significant delegation of control and exploitation to institutions, that portion of the tax-exempt sector that the

Table 2. Taxable, untaxed, and uncultivated land (in kyŏl)

Year	Taxable	Untaxed	Untaxed land	
			Uncultivated	Tax-exempt[a]
1801	802,857	625,719	413,583	212,136
1816	789,721	618,754	414,500	204,254
1831	781,872	640,403	428,815	211,588
1846	787,228	640,403	436,921	203,482
1861	766,299	655,234	451,633	203,601

Source: Kim Chin-bong, "Imsul millan ŭi sahoe," 94-96, based on Asō, Chōsen tenseikō, appendix.

[a]Figures in this column were obtained by subtracting the uncultivated area from the untaxed.

Politics and Policy in Traditional Korea

Taewongun sought to reform was only a fraction of the tax-exempt sector. In 1807 the palace estate lands amounted to about 38,000 kyŏl, and the largest estimate of private academy lands is about 50 percent of the miscellaneous category, or a total of approximately 60,000 kyŏl.[68] Palace estate and private academy lands taken together constituted about 10 percent of all taxpaying land or 7 percent of all registered land. Even a total transfer of these lands to the private sector would only have meant a fractional increase in the central government's tax base. As we shall see, only the private academy lands were converted to the taxpaying private sector.

Reform of the Tax-Exempt Sector

Although the tax-exempt sector included post-station lands, military and civil colony lands, and yamen lands, these were relatively neglected by the Taewongun, who was most concerned with land controlled by the palace estates, Royal Treasury, and private academies. In terms of the solution of the fundamental problems of land distribution and taxation, the Taewongun's reforms in the tax-exempt sector had little effect, for they hardly touched upon matters like concentrated ownership, high rates of tenancy and rent, and regressive taxation. Their main purpose was to reverse the trend toward autonomous control over land and land taxes by certain institutions. To this end institutionally controlled land was either returned to the private sector, or its tax or rent collection rights were transferred from private stewards to public magistrates. As a result some tax revenues were funneled back to the central government, but from the standpoint of the cultivator there was very little reform at all; the major change was a slight shift in the recipient of tax or rent from the semiautonomous institution to the central government.

In the case of the palace estate and Royal Treasury lands, the Taewongun's reforms were aimed at the solution of two problems: illicit expansion of palace estate lands and illicit conversion of their tax collection privileges to ownership rights; and the growing power of the estate stewards (tojang) and their interference with local control. In the early Yi dynasty there were no palace estates at all because royal relatives were given "land grants" (probably prebendal tax collection rights) under the provisions of the office-land system. With the breakdown of this system, it may be assumed that the central government provided for the upkeep of royal relatives, but after Hideyoshi's invasions it no longer had sufficient revenue to continue this.[69] The throne then began granting lands throughout the country directly to princes and princesses. A royal grant (sayŏ, sap'ae) of land and slaves confirmed by a royal warrant with the king's seal could be held either hereditarily or for one generation only.

Land Distribution and Taxation

Palace estate lands could also be obtained upon petition (*chŏlsu*). If the king approved, the Ministry of Taxation would issue a permit (*ib'an*) to the petitioner. Palace estate lands were either owned directly or were limited to tax collection rights only. They were expanded by transfer of state lands, land confiscated from criminals, commendation, and direct purchase of privately owned land.[70]

Since palace estate lands consisted of small parcels scattered about the country, a type of stewardship developed for management and revenue collection. Originally slave agents of the palaces were sent out to collect taxes, but by the 1660s contractual arrangements were entered into with local people called *tojang* for the performance of this service. The *tojang* received a warrant from the palace estate, was required to remit a specific tax quota and could either sell or bequeath his *tojang* rights and obligations. *Tojang* rights were often granted in return for commendation of the *tojang's* privately owned lands to the estate. The *tojang* benefited from the protection of the estate and from opportunities for surcharges and extortion from the cultivators, who might either be slaves or commoner tenants.[71] The *tojang* and the palace estates frequently interfered with the local magistrate's jurisdiction; the estates issued directives (*kamgyŏl*, *p'aech'ik*) to local magistrates informing them of their *tojang* contracts, and they intervened in lawsuits over their estate lands and the property of their *tojang*.[72]

The Royal Treasury (*naesusa*) also controlled land in the manner of the palace estates. In the early Yi dynasty the Royal Treasury had been given tax grants over specified lands (*konghaejŏn*), but these had been converted into ownership rights. The Royal Treasury expanded its holdings, issued warrants to its *tojang* and directives to local officials. Its powers were based on its close ties to the throne and its ability to memorialize the king directly. The regular officials resented its growing strength all the more because some of its higher posts were staffed by eunuchs of the royal palace.[73]

Many officials at court objected to the expansion of the palace estates and the Royal Treasury lands, which they regarded as an incursion by private interests into the realm of state control over revenues. They deplored the exemptions of palace estate cultivators from labor service, the palace estates' confiscation and forced purchase of private property, the transfer of military colony lands (*tunjŏn*) to palace estates, and the depredations and high-handed behavior of the *tojang*.[74] Although kings were generally concerned about these problems too, they were reluctant to reduce their relatives to penury by taking their land grants away. Nevertheless, after the mid-seventeenth century several kings began to approve a policy of limited curtailment on the palace estates. Between

1663 and 1695 limits were set on the amount of tax-exempt land, restrictions were imposed on expansion by purchase, chŏlsu grants by petition were discontinued, and tax collection on Royal Treasury lands was transferred to local magistrates.[75] These measures, however, did not succeed in checking the expansion of the palace estates. In the eighteenth century limits on palace estate lands were reimposed and incorporated in the 1746 code (Soktaejŏn). The limit on tax-emempt palace estate land was set at a maximum of 1,000 kyŏl; tax rates were set on mut'o at 23 tu/kyŏl of polished rice and on yut'o at 200 tu/kyŏl of unhulled rice (100 tu/kyŏl of polished rice); further chŏlsu grants were prohibited; and except for the highest nobility inheritance of palace estate land was limited to four generations.[76] In 1750 salt flats and fishing weirs were taken away from the palace estates, and in 1776 the collection of taxes on mut'o or nonowned land was shifted from the tojang to the local magistrate.[77]

The government was content to hold the expansion of palace estate lands in check by fixing statutory limits and maximum tax rates and by expanding the magistrate's authority at the expense of the tojang. The result was a mediocre record of accomplishment: restrictions on land area were exceeded by commendation, purchase, and outright expropriation; fixed tax rates were ignored; and the tojang system continued albeit on a reduced scale.

During the Taewongun's regime the central government made a significant advance in its protracted struggle with the palace estates by eliminating the fiscal independence of the palaces and the tyranny of the tojang. It converted the type of tenure by the palace estates over their lands from outright ownership to taxation only; it completed the transfer of tax collection rights from the tojang to the local magistrate; and it converted the royal relatives to a stipended nobility paid out of the central government treasury.

The attack on the palace estates began on February 13, 1864, when the Dowager-Recent decreed the abolition of all excess tojang in Hwanghae province and the collection of palace land taxes by the local magistrates.[78] The second step was the conversion of palace estate lands from yut'o to mut'o status. On March 17 Second State Councilor Cho Tu-sun complained that the palace estates in the three southern provinces had been collecting taxes directly on nonowned mut'o lands in direct violation of the laws of 1776, which had transferred tax collection rights on palace estate mut'o lands to the local magistrates. Kojong approved Cho's request that further orders be issued against this.[79]

It was not until 1866, however, that the government began to adopt more radical measures for the control of the palace estates. In the meanwhile, grants of cash, grain, and tax-exempt land were provided to prin-

Land Distribution and Taxation

cesses in accordance with statutory regulations.[80] In 1866 new proposals were made to convert all palace estate land to the nonowned category. The regulations of 1776 had only taken away tax collection rights on *mut'o* land from the *tojang*, leaving them and other estate agents to handle the taxes on land directly owned by the palaces. The keynote of this policy was sounded when Minister of Personnel Yi Chae-wǒn, the king's first cousin, returned an estate granted to his ancestor by King Yǒngjo in the eighteenth century. The estate was the island of Ch'ongsan off Ch'ungch'ǒng province, which was owned outright by Yi's family.[81] What was more important, however, was the king's approval of Yi Chae-wǒn's suggestion that in the future whenever a collateral prince established a separate palace, the Ministry of Taxation should give him a grant of nonowned tax-exempt land only. This, of course, did not eliminate all land in the *yut'o* category, just future grants.[82]

On January 9, 1868, the king issued another edict that revealed clearly the throne's awareness of the reduction of central government revenues caused by the grants by petition (*chǒlsu*) of tax-exempt lands to the palace estates. The edict stated that the withdrawal of these lands from taxation also caused the imposition of excessive burdens on the common taxpayers, and that whatever had been the policy before Kojong's accession, the new policy allowed only tax allotments (nonowned lands) and not direct ownership. It was to be expected that even these grants would be discontinued when the requirements for ancestral sacrifice ran out in the fifth generation (*ch'injin*). At that time the tax revenues from the designated land parcels would revert to the central government. Furthermore, all palace lands obtained by transfer or purchase were to be returned to the taxpaying category.[83]

Evidently some time was required for the Ministry of Taxation to obtain a full record of the amount of palace estate land to be returned to the tax rolls by this order, for it was not until June 3, 1868, that the ministry sent out orders to the provinces for the return of these lands to the magistrates' jurisdiction. The ministry further instructed the provincial officials to remit the land tax to the Ministry of Taxation and the tribute portion of the land tax to the Tribute Bureau in accordance with regular tax collection procedures. The ministry would now take responsibility for paying out to the palaces and the Royal Treasury sums equivalent to the taxes they formerly used to collect from their lands. The local magistrates were also instructed to keep separate tax records for these old palace lands, both *yut'o* and *mut'o*, even though they were to be forwarded to the Ministry of Taxation along with regular land tax revenues.[84]

One report a few months later in 1868 revealed that in one town the amount of palace estate land was so great that the local magistrate was short of funds for expenses.[85] In 1869 high officials at court reported that both the Royal Treasury and the various palaces had illegally taken over unregistered land for their own profit along the coast. *Tojang* from these estates acquired domain over cultivated land that was even registered as taxable in the land registers by claiming that such lands had been granted to them by royal decree, even though this had been forbidden. Furthermore, estate managers collected excessive taxes from fishing weirs and salt flats along the coast which were legally under their jurisdiction. In other instances where the land was registered officially as "empty" or without a landowner, the palace and Palace Treasury agents either took them over directly or induced officials in both the capital and provinces to make up false deeds of ownership (*ib'an*). Chief State Councilor Kim Pyŏng-hak praised the Taewongun for turning his attention to this problem and reported that all these false exemptions had been eliminated. Kim recommended that if this were to occur in the future, stiff penalties should be meted out to the palace agents and the magistrates.[86]

The illegal appropriation of unregistered land along waterways was, of course, not confined to the palace estates alone. On November 6, 1869, the king decreed that surveys of this type of land were to be carried out to take it away from the families of high officials in the capital and local magnates who were also engaging in this practice.[87] The new policy evidently put great pressure on members of the nobility, and shortly thereafter one of them voluntarily returned 500 kyŏl to the state that had been in his family for generations.[88]

There is no reason to believe that the implementation of reform edicts directed against the palace estates was accomplished with any greater degree of efficiency than with the land surveys. The court itself was not so naive as to believe that this was the case, and in a remarkable display of perseverance, it issued a stream of edicts and prohibitions for the next few years. In 1870 Kojong declared on two occasions that he had received reports that the palaces, Royal Treasury, and ex-provincial governors were still appropriating land from dikes and river banks, drafting peasants for labor projects, and obtaining illegal tax exemptions. He criticized false registration and commendation in Hamgyŏng province and prohibited both palace estates and private yangban from clearing gravesite land for cultivation.[89] Yet in spite of the government's inability to obtain full compliance with its orders, the palace estates were no longer a formidable force.

The private academies were also an important component of the tax-exempt sector. In an age of Confucianism the private academies of the Yi dynasty played an economic role similar to the Buddhist monastic estates

Land Distribution and Taxation

of the Koryŏ dynasty. The growth in the number of academies, the area of their estates and tax-exempt lands, and the number of their corvée-exempt cultivators, slaves, tenants, and students constituted a drain on the central government's revenues, just as the Buddhist monastic estates had been to the Koryŏ state. The first of the private academies was established in 1543 but by the eighteenth century there were over six hundred of them.[90]

The attitude of the government toward the academies was ambivalent. On the one hand, the king and high officials as believers in Confucianism sought to aid and support the private academies, which were educational institutions devoted to the propagation of true learning. Kings issued charters to some academies along with grants of land, books, slaves, and other material. Where the private granting of lands to monasteries had been an act of piety in the Koryŏ dynasty, so was the gift of lands to the private academies an act of virtue in the Yi dynasty. On the other hand, the central government was aware of the economic loss to the state represented by the economic privileges of the academies, and it tried to restrict this economic power by setting statutory limits on academy lands and tax-exempt personnel, but these limits were generally ignored. In the eighteenth century the limit on registered students was twenty for a chartered and fifteen for a nonchartered academy, but some academies had several hundred students.[91] In 1657 the limits on academy slaves were set at seven for a chartered and five for an unchartered academy, but these limits were exceeded.[92] The 1746 law code also imposed a limit of three kyŏl of tax-exempt land for chartered private academies, but academy land expanded beyond this limit through gifts, direct purchase, the assignment of confiscated criminal land, the transfer of official or institutional land, and commendation. As mentioned above, the private academies may have controlled as much as 60,000 kyŏl by 1807.[93]

The Taewongun's curtailment of the private academies will be discussed separately in Chapter 6. Suffice it to say here that his abolition of all but forty-seven chartered academies must have returned almost all the academy lands to the private, taxpaying sector. Just how much land was involved is not revealed in the court records, but the figure may be as high as the maximum estimate for academy lands noted above. Yet as radical as this action was, still only about one quarter of the total amount of tax-exempt lands was transferred to direct central government control. It should be remembered that the reform of the palace estate lands did not end their tax-exempt status; it merely transferred about 27,000 kyŏl from the yut'o to the mut'o category. The income from these lands still went to defray the expenses of the various palaces.

During the 1860s the government also did little to reduce the other categories of tax-exempt land: yamen, post-station, military and official colony lands. In 1864 the government issued orders to abolish the use of special tax collection agents (*kyŏngch'ain*) by the Ministry of Taxation, Tribute Bureau, and other capital agencies on lands assigned directly to them, but the order was virtually ignored.[94] In the same year provincial governors were ordered to investigate the post-station and horse-grazing lands to prevent their illegal takeover by yangban, but this measure was designed to preserve their tax-exempt status, not curtail it. In 1868 the state council complained that the collection of gratuities by tax collection agents of the government's military bureaus and units in Right Kongch'ung (Ch'ungch'ŏng) province on land controlled by them had become a serious problem. The council recommended that these taxes henceforth be paid directly to the Tribute Bureau which would then make allocations to the various military yamen.[95] As in the case of the palace estates, the government transferred administrative responsibility over military yamen land to the regular central government apparatus, but it was done only in response to bad conditions in one province and not as part of a comprehensive policy for reform.

As a matter of fact, the government had no intention of eliminating this decentralized system of assigning tax responsibilities to individual yamen. The governor of Kyŏnggi province pointed out in 1870 that the expenses of his yamen had been provided for out of interest on grain loans. After a time, however, the peasants had defaulted on their debts and there was no way to collect the principal. In 1860, 9,300 kyŏl of land was granted special tax-exempt status so that the tax proceeds would go directly to the governor's yamen for its expenses. The governor requested now that another ten-year extension be permitted for this arrangement, and the king approved.[96]

The Taewongun's Land and Land-Tax Policy

In terms of the overall structure of land distribution and taxation the decade after 1864 cannot be regarded as a major period of institutional reform. On the land question the Taewongun was not a Utopian visionary or even a reformer who thought in terms of institutional transformation. He lacked the prescience of intellectuals like Yi Ik and Chŏng Yag-yong and he sought to do the best he could within given conditions. Although he did attack established interests on occasions, he did not do so as a means to the reordering of society. The strength of private property and status privilege in the nineteenth century was too great to allow for any major program of state confiscation and redistribution. The principle of egalitarian distribution had emerged from and been nurtured by

Land Distribution and Taxation

the Confucian tradition. It could be discussed openly without being condemned as heretical, but it was ignored by the government and by the mid-nineteenth century even intellectuals agreed that the times were no longer suitable for it. The vestiges of the egalitarian ideal remained only in the proposals for rectification of the land survey system as a means of ensuring fair and equitable tax distribution, not equal distribution of land.

In the private sector the Taewongun attempted no solution of the fundamental causes of peasant poverty, such as concentrated landholding, small per capita holdings, and tenancy. He did not try to increase land taxes on the wealthy large landowners and made no reduction of taxes on poor smallholders, and his efforts at a cadastral survey were extremely limited in scope. He directed most of his activity against corrupt officials, the immediate but superficial cause of revenue shortage and peasant poverty. In the tax-exempt sector he curtailed the autonomy of the palace estates and the private academies, but the increase in central government revenues and the effect on peasant income was negligible. The Taewongun's land policy thus failed to provide the economic basis for a strong national monarchy and centralized power and preserved the economic interests of the dominant yangban landowning class at the expense of the peasantry.

5

The Household Cloth Tax

Reform of the system of military service and taxation was of crucial importance for the achievement of the Taewongun's goal of building up the strength of the monarchy, the central government, and the nation. But it was also a prime focus of contention between the central government and the aristocracy in the struggle for resources and manpower because of the traditional exemption of the yangban class from service obligations and the reduction in the size of the population available for actual service and payment of military support taxes.[1]

The Taewongun's policies toward military taxation serve to illustrate the main aspects of his style of rule and the nature of the social and systemic restraints on his power. The Taewongun was essentially a man of action, pragmatic and flexible in many respects despite his famed intransigence on foreign policy. When he imposed the military cloth tax on yangban as well as commoner households for the first time in the dynasty in 1870, he did not do so to satisfy any Utopian vision of the perfect egalitarian society but merely to help alleviate the problem of revenue shortage. Yet in spite of his relatively conservative and practical intentions, the household cloth tax produced a reaction on the part of the yangban that contributed to the growth of a vocal political opposition; the entrenched interests of the yangban were too great to expect tacit acceptance of any curtailment of their privileges. Thus, we might conclude that for a revolutionary transformation of the tax structure to have taken place, it would have required two things: more determined and purposive revolutionary leadership than the Taewongun was capable of providing, mainly because he was too much a part of the ancien régime himself; and some weakening of the yangban-landowner-bureaucrat complex of interests and power. In the 1860s the times were not ripe for either possibility.

The Household Cloth Tax

The Taewongun's household cloth tax reform can best be understood by placing it in historical perspective. The main reason why the radical nature of the Taewongun's policy has been exaggerated and the pragmatic aspect of it has been ignored is because of a tacit assumption that the circumstances in the mid-nineteenth century were similar to those of the mid-eighteenth.[2] By 1750 the military service system had been replaced in large part by the payment of a cloth tax by commoners for the support of duty soldiers, and the percentage of registered commoners in the population relative to both yangban and ch'ŏnmin had declined considerably making the commoner cloth tax probably the most regressive tax in the whole fiscal structure. The mid-eighteenth century was also the high point of Confucian social radicalism when several scholars and officials were putting forward comprehensive plans for the egalitarian redistribution of tax burdens. Yet despite radicalism in the intellectual sphere, the solution achieved in 1750 was relatively conservative: yangban tax exemption privileges were still too powerful to be challenged, so the government chose instead to alleviate the burden on the commoner peasant by cutting the cloth tax rate in half and to offset the ensuing revenue shortage by cutting back on expenditures.

After this solution was achieved—the so-called equal service law of 1750—two major changes in the social and taxation systems took place. There was a growth in the number of putative yangban especially because of the sale of rank and title by the government; yangban status was cheapened and government leaders became less reluctant to challenge the privileges of a diluted "aristocracy" and to impose taxes on a class that now included many upstarts and social climbers. In the second place, there was an evolution of the so-called village cloth tax system (tongp'o) according to which cloth tax quotas were levied on villages as a whole and distributed relatively equally among member households, irrespective of status. In other words, by the middle of the nineteenth century yangban households were already sharing in the payment of military cloth taxes in many villages. Because of these developments the imposition of a cloth tax on yangban households in 1870 was by no means as radical a measure as it could have been in 1750. In fact, as Han Woo-keun has remarked, because the Taewongun allowed yangban households to pay the household cloth tax in the name of their slaves, he was in fact taking a step backwards by helping to preserve yangban dignity.[3]

Furthermore, if the Taewongun's household cloth tax is compared to the egalitarian reform plans of the eighteenth century and the policies followed in 1750 under the "equal service" reform, it also appears that his objectives were neither as radical nor idealistic as formerly assumed. The eighteenth century Utopians wanted a return to the ideal of a farmer-soldier militia system with universal military service imposed on all; they attacked status distinction and explicitly sought social leveling. The Taewongun, on the other hand, was not interested in the destruction of the yangban class or the elimination of status distinction; he was hard pressed for revenue and viewed the household cloth tax primarily as a fiscal measure. In fact, the household cloth tax had been advocated by several reformers in the eighteenth century but rejected on the grounds that it was by nature too regressive because it called for a uniform tax on all households without adjustment for variance in the number of household members or able-bodied males in each household. The Taewongun, by contrast, paid no attention to these considerations at all.

The Taewongun's willingness to impose taxes on the yangban contrasts with the equal service reform of 1750, but it obviously was made possible by a cheapening of yangban status, precedents established by the village cloth tax, and a demand for revenue that could not be ignored. Whereas alleviation of commoner peasant tax burdens had been a prime motive in 1750 and resulted in a 50 percent reduction of the cloth tax rate at that time, the Taewongun only showed limited concern for peasant welfare in 1870—he did not reduce the tax rate; he only broadened the tax base.

The Commoner Cloth Tax:
Status Exemption and the
Shrinking Tax Base

Status exemption had always been a feature of the military service system, but it did not become a serious problem until the end of the sixteenth century. In the early part of the dynasty exemption from service was granted to a relatively small number of nobles, merit subjects, and government functionaries as well as to slaves and other members of the ch'onmin class. Members of the exempt elite could, however, serve voluntarily in special capital guards units as officers and many took the military examinations. By the end of the sixteenth century military service had declined in prestige and the yangban sought to dissociate themselves completely from the stigma attached to ordinary service. About the same time the system of rotating tours of duty by which peasants off duty paid cloth taxes in support of those on duty changed to one in which the commoner peasant remained on his fields and paid a military cloth tax (*kunp'o*) or commoner cloth tax (*yangyŏk*) for the expenses of semiprofessional duty soldiers. Support taxes were converted to a fixed charge on an essentially sedentary and civilian peasant population of commoner status.

The Household Cloth Tax

The fiscal pressure on the commoner peasant was then exacerbated as the proportion of commoners in the population relative to tax-exempt yangban and *ch'onmin* began to shrink and the number of soldiers available for military service declined. This situation proved intolerable when the Japanese invasions in the 1590s and the Manchu invasions of 1627 and 1636 placed an additional strain on the system and forced the government to expand its control over revenues and manpower for service by leaving yangban exemption intact but eliminating it for the *ch'onmin*. Even this was difficult to accomplish because any attempt to abolish *ch'onmin* status and slavery was opposed by slaveowners and ideologues who harped about the sanctity of status distinction.

The government allowed slaves or *ch'onmin* into the Military Training Agency (Hullyŏn-dogam) or recruited them as regimental troops (*sog'ogun*) and granted them commoner status for merit earned on the battlefield, membership in certain military units, or the payment of grain to state treasuries (*napsok, songnyang*).[4] The government also sold ranks, titles, posts, and exemption from military service requirements to commoners and yangban as well. In the early seventeenth century there was an active market in blank warrants of title or rank; but since many of these warrants granted exemption from military taxes, the government was mortgaging future revenue in order to meet immediate needs. Eventually it had to reverse this policy by selling titles without exemption from military service and by recruiting more *ch'onmin* into the military to make up for the continuing shortage of commoners.[5]

Granting commoner status to slaves for military merit and as compensation for grain contributions was not sufficient to offset the reductions in the registered commoner population. Evidently more people bought their way out of military service than bought their way in. Part of the reason for this was the continuing resistance of slaveowners, who protested against the liberation of their private slaves, and conservative officials, who feared that manumission would disrupt the social order.[6] By the middle of the seventeenth century the demand for troops and taxpayers increased with the creation of new troop units, and some officials felt that the existing system of hereditary slavery would have to be modified in order to increase the supply of taxpaying commoners.

By the late seventeenth century the government also made changes in the laws governing mixed marriages of commoners and *ch'onmin* in order to grant their offspring commoner status. According to a law promulgated in 1039 in the Koryŏ dynasty, the status of the mother in marriages involving *ch'onmin* determined the status of all offspring. There is little evidence, however, that this law was ever used as a means of liberating children of commoner mothers and slave fathers. On the contrary, it was used by slaveowners who married their female slaves to commoner males in order to increase the number of their private slaves. Even this was done illegally, since there was another law in effect which prohibited commoner-slave intermarriage altogether in order to prevent any egress from *ch'onmin* status.[7] Between 1414 and 1432 there was a relaxation of the law of matrilineal succession to accommodate members of the upper class who wanted something better than slave status for their children by *ch'ŏnmin* concubines. In such cases the children were allowed to assume their father's status.[8] In 1432, however, King Sejong reestablished the matrilineal succession law, but in practice if either parent were of *ch'ŏnmin* status, then the children became *ch'ŏnmin*.[9]

By the middle of the seventeenth century, some officials began to recommend providing commoner status to the children of slave fathers and commoner mothers in order to increase the commoner population and satisfy the demands of the state for military service and taxation. The law for the matrilineal inheritance of status (*chongmobŏp* or *chongmoyokpŏp*) was finally promulgated in 1669, but because of the resistance of slaveowners and the involvement of the issue in factional politics, the law was reversed in 1675, restored in 1681, abolished again in 1689, and not restored again until 1731, after which it remained unchanged.[10] Slavery as an institution did not die out until much later: in 1801 all 61,000 official slaves were manumitted, and in 1894 slavery was abolished.[11]

Institutional historians have usually emphasized the role of the government in weakening the status barrier between *ch'ŏnmin* and commoners as a means to expanding the tax base of the commoner cloth tax. Those interested in social change in general, on the other hand, have stressed the role played by private ownership and small-plot farming in enabling slaves to accumulate wealth by more efficient cultivation of their plots, thereby providing them with the wherewithal to purchase commoner status or act in collusion with local officials to obtain military tax exemptions. A third factor explaining the breakdown of status distinction between commoners and slaves may have been a rising demand for labor caused by the slow growth of commerce and the market system after the seventeenth century, but as yet there have been no significant studies on the problems of labor shortages, labor demand, and differential wage rates between town and country in this period.

Whatever the cause for the blurring of class lines at the lower level, it did not result in an expanded taxable commoner population. With the weakening of the rigid distinctions of status division more people moved out of the commoner class and military taxes than moved in. The sale of rank continued; the number of people with high status titles and exemption from military tax payments increased; and the number of commoners decreased.[12] Commoners were also able to escape taxation by commendation to certain institutions like colony lands, yamen lands, and palace estates and by registration as students in official schools and private academies.[13] Tax evasion was abetted by the machinations of local clerks who enriched themselves by the falsification of the military tax registers. And then to make up for the losses in taxes due, the clerks began to shift tax burdens arbitrarily. If people fled from the village or died, the clerks would demand tax payment from relatives and neighbors and would record infants and legally tax exempt elderly persons over sixty years of age.[14] The names on the military registers ceased to represent adult males who could be recruited in time of war and became instead units of taxation which determined tax quotas from villages, districts, and provinces. The figures bore no relation even to the total number of taxpayers. By the seventeenth and eighteenth centuries many villages were required to provide cloth tax revenues three or four times greater than their actual population warranted.[15]

Available figures of military taxpayers reflect the growing burden of the military cloth tax on the commoner population. In the middle of the seventeenth century, taxes averaging two p'il of cloth or four yang of cash per able-bodied male were levied on 300,000 able-bodied commoner males.[16] By 1750 this figure had increased to 500,000, representing the tax base for revenues of one million p'il or two million yang for the six southern provinces (P'yŏng'an and Hamgyŏng provinces in the north were excluded from the system).[17]

According to one report submitted in 1750, there were 1,340,000 households in the country at the time. Of this figure, about 720,000 households were composed of "the poor, and households with a single male for the support of the family" (*chandok*), categories obviously exempted from cloth tax payments. Tax exempt *ch'ŏnmin* were probably included in this group, since they are not mentioned elsewhere in the report. The report stated that this left about 620,000 "true households" (*silho*) of which four fifths also belonged to tax-exempt categories: *sabu* (officials and their families?), people with official rank living in the countryside (*hyangp'um*), yamen functionaries and clerks, post-station personnel, and monks. Only about 100,000 households or 8 percent of the total were left to meet the cloth tax quotas of 500,000 able-bodied males—a total of one million p'il of cloth or two million yang of cash.[18]

According to another estimate in the early part of the eighteenth century, between 150,000 and 250,000 men were burdened with the military tax requirements of 400,000 able-bodied males.[19] But other estimates run considerably higher: one official in 1750 put the total at 750,000, and

Chŏng Yag-yong estimated that at the turn of the nineteenth century several million commoners were paying the military tax.[20]

A better gauge of the proportion of commoner taxpayers might be obtained from recent studies of population and land registrations. In the districts around Taegu that Shikata Hiroshi studied, he found that 58 percent of the population in the 1780s were commoners, and that this figure was reduced to 28 percent by 1858.[21] In calculating the household military cloth tax burden for one district at the turn of the nineteenth century, Kim Chin-bong estimated that only 60 percent of the registered households were liable for the military cloth tax.[22] According to Kim Yong-sŏp's studies of the percentages of registered landholders in two districts in the period 1720-38, 56 and 43 percent of landholders were commoners.[23] Of course, if landless tenants and laborers were included in the calculation, the commoner population would be higher. It would thus appear safe to say that in the middle of the eighteenth century about 30 to 60 percent of the population of any village was subject to military service or the commoner cloth tax. By this time there was a general consensus that the system was in need of reform.

Egalitarian Idealism in the Seventeenth and Eighteenth Centuries

In the seventeenth century Confucian scholars and officials directed their attention to the reform of the commoner cloth tax and began to study military organization and taxation in Chinese and Korean history in a search for models and precedents for reform. The result of these studies was a strong trend toward idealism and Utopian egalitarianism, in particular the elimination of standing armies and a return to the militia ideal and an egalitarian restructuring of service and tax obligations. The egalitarian ideal colored the thinking of most reformers in this period, but it was not powerful enough to be incorporated into legislation. The equal service reform of 1750, which marked the culmination of the protracted debate over the reform of military service and taxation, represented the victory of the privileged yangban over both egalitarian idealism and the fiscal interests of the central government. For that matter, the Taewongun's household cloth tax of 1870 was a far cry from the Utopian egalitarianism of eighteenth century intellectuals even though it did extend military cloth taxes to yangban households.

The search for historical precedents in the seventeenth and eighteenth centuries produced a surprising unanimity of view concerning certain fundamental precepts. Almost everyone agreed that the ideal system of military organization and service was to be found in the Three Dynasties of ancient China when the well-field system of land distribution and the

The Household Cloth Tax

farmer-soldier system of military service supposedly operated in perfect harmony. The beauty of this system was to be found in several important features. During wartime farmers served in the army as soldiers, and when the war was over they returned to their fields. There was total mobilization during war and total demobilization during peace and thus no need for standing peacetime armies and high taxes to maintain idle troops. All soldiers were peasants who were granted land by the state and were thus provided for economically. The system was, in other words, completely self-supporting.

The armies of this period were believed to have had a high degree of morale and cohesiveness because the local community functioned as the fundamental civil-military unit. People who lived together fought together. Their sense of comradeship was high, as opposed to national armies where the rank-and-file troops were recruited from all over the country. Furthermore, each community was organized into interconnecting civil and military hierarchies of mutual surveillance units. In peacetime they functioned as structures for control and government, and in wartime as a tightly knit military organization.[24]

This ideal system of ancient China (which according to modern historians never existed at all) had not lasted past the Chou dynasty in the opinion of the Korean scholar-officials. The Han dynasty witnessed the emergence of capital guard units which were professional standing forces supported by national tax revenues. While the T'ang dynasty nobly attempted a restoration of the farmer-soldier principle by the institution of the *fu-ping* system, in the later T'ang period there was a reemergence of permanent long-term professional soldiers. By the late T'ang the fall from grace was fairly complete. The farmer-soldier had been replaced by the hired soldier; self-sufficiency was replaced by taxation; and local community cohesiveness was replaced by nationally recruited forces with isolated individual troops unbound by community ties and loyalties.

Most scholars also agreed that the early Yi dynasty military system was a closer approximation to the farmer-soldier principle and the T'ang *fu-ping* than the system of the seventeenth and eighteenth centuries. Even though there had been no land grant system to compare with the well field, the system was based on the principle of militia service with duty troops supported by off-duty farmers. The degeneration of this system to one of hired soldiers supported by the commoner cloth tax was no different in kind from the degeneration of the military system from the Chou to the late T'ang in China. Professional standing armies, especially during peacetime, were a drain on revenues, a cause of oppressive taxation of the people, and a potential political threat to the state.[25]

Politics and Policy in Traditional Korea

There was virtually unanimous agreement on these fundamentals; disagreement arose over the means of rectifying the situation. The first point debated was whether or not the farmer-soldier system of the Chou or the *fu-ping* of the T'ang dynasty could be restored in Korea. This was essentially a sterile argument, for only the most nostalgic hoped for a fundamentalist restoration. Most agreed that the change of circumstances over time obviated the possibility of restoration. As one scholar, Yu Su-won, pointed out, the true farmer-soldier system was inseparable from the well-field system, and the well field was part of feudal structure characterized by the granting of fiefs (*ponggŏn, feng-chien* in Chinese). Since the Yi dynasty was not feudal, feudal institutions could not be applied to it.[26] Yu, however, advanced this argument in order to support his view that the existing system of standing armies and taxation had to be acknowledged as unavoidable and reformed on its own terms. There were many others who insisted on at least applying the principles of the farmer-soldier system to the reform of existing military taxation system, which was criticized for having split the healthy symbiotic union of farmer and soldier asunder. This explains why there was an attempt during the seventeenth century to structure the financing of military units aroung the support personnel (*poin*) concept—even though in fact the support personnel were only taxpayers and not rotating militiamen.

To some extent, therefore, the advocates of reform were frustrated men making the best of an undesirable but unavoidable situation. The ideal was the Chou or T'ang farmer-soldier system, but the passage of time and change of circumstance meant that it could never be acccomplished. Yet some men devoted to reform distilled from their conception of the farmer-soldier and well-field systems what they felt was the essence of those systems and then tried to use it as a foundation for the rational reform of the military taxation system of the Yi. Some saw this essence as farmer-soldier interdependence. Others saw it as equal distribution. The real debate in the period from the late seventeenth century to 1750 took place between those who advocated equal distribution and those who maintained that ideal Chinese systems had to be adapted to Korean circumstances, the most important of which was the strong tradition of social status distinction and privilege.

Some aspects of the debate lay outside the egalitarian-status distinction conflict. Many officials, for example, were concerned specifically with alleviating tax burdens on the people and proposed as the best means for doing so the reduction of troop levels, economizing on expenditures, reductions in the tax rate, and elimination of illegal tax exemptions through better surveillance and administrative techniques. While it is true that these proposals were made by advocates of *both* egalitarian tax distribu-

The Household Cloth Tax

tion and preservation of elite tax exemption, in the case of the latter these methods were proposed as the means to prevent the extension of taxes to the yangban class. Those who most ardently argued for the inclusion of the yangban in military taxes did so on the grounds that it was essential to a total program of equal taxation. But the proposals for yangban taxation were opposed by the advocates of narrow class interest and stymied by the inability to achieve consensus on what constituted the fairest and most equal of tax systems.

There is no great difficulty in understanding why some officials opposed yangban taxation on class grounds: they wanted to preserve their advantageous positions of wealth and prestige. Some extracted the notion of status distinction (*myŏngbun*) from the Confucian tradition and converted it into a cardinal principle of faith. For them, any lessening of the rigidity of status distinction threatened the collapse of the social and moral order, for hierarchy was the basic principle of the hallowed Confucian five relationships. To them, egalitarianism was anathema, for how would people be able to distinguish between what was noble and what was base, or, in other words, what was fine and worthy of emulation and what was beneath contempt and deserving of derision?[27]

The proponents of yangban taxation, on the other hand, suggested that status discrimination in taxation was an undesirable feature of the mid-Yi dynasty justified neither by moral principle nor historical precedent. They pointed out that in ancient China there had been no discrimination on the basis of status, that in the early Yi dynasty all social classes had been required to perform military service, and that there were no discriminatory status exemptions in the contemporary land or tribute taxes.[28]

Because the notion of equal distribution was also contained within the Confucian tradition, the defenders of status distinction could not attack it as illegitimate or immoral. As a matter of fact they were able to show some enthusiasm for its application in a limited way—for example, that equal treatment was desirable but it should be reserved for the lower classes. The yangban should remain exempt while the state ensured that all commoners (and possibly all *ch'ŏnmin*) paid taxes equally.[29]

The most popular proposals for the reform of the military cloth tax— that is, in addition to simple rate reduction, troop reduction, and administrative reform—were plans to establish new systems based on some subject of taxation other than the commoner able-bodied male. Some advocated that the commoner cloth tax be replaced either totally or in part by a land surtax as in the manner of the *taedong* tribute tax reform, because the regular land tax rate was still light and could bear raising

Politics and Policy in Traditional Korea

without imposing excessive burdens on cultivators.[30] Some questioned, however, whether surtaxes on taxable land, estimated in the mid-eighteenth century as anywhere between 500,000 and 800,000 kyŏl, would be sufficient to replace the one million p'il of taxes that would be lost by the elimination of the commoner cloth tax.[31] Of course, Koreans traditionally attached value to a low land tax rate, since it constituted a symbol of a lightly taxed populace and sage rule, but rationalists like Yu Su-wŏn criticized the state's failure to exploit the one source of wealth regarded as truly legitimate in the Confucian value system—agricultural production. It was difficult to persuade kings and high officials of this, however. And others also pointed out that while the central government's tax rates on the land were comparatively low, the burden on the landowners and tenants was high because of the surtaxes, extra charges, and squeeze at the local level.[32] The government was therefore reluctant to transfer the commoner cloth tax from commoner males to land.

Another popular proposal was a capitation tax (kujŏn) or a levy either on every member of the population or every able-bodied male irrespective of status. In 1711 Yu Pong-hwi argued that all connotations of "military" service could be eliminated from a neutral capitation tax and that this would remove the objection of the upper class to paying it.[33] Yu's faith in the gullibility of the yangban was unwarranted, however, and his plan was attacked specifically on the grounds that it would have violated Korean respect for status distinction.[34]

Undoubtedly the most fiercely debated of all plans for enlarging the tax base was the household-cloth (hop'o) plan. Its advocates held that a cash or cloth levy on all households in the country without discrimination as to status would yield sufficient revenues to enable the abolition of the commoner military cloth tax. Since detractors of the plan usually pointed out that a single tax rate on all households would lead to unequal taxation because of variations in the number of persons per household, several plans were put forward for grading households in accordance with the number of family members.[35]

The household cloth tax plan was resisted stoutly by those who objected to any taxation of the yangban class.[36] It also failed to satisfy the demands of egalitarians who argued that gradation by the number of persons per household did not really account for variations in wealth.[37] Yu Su-wŏn, an ardent opponent of status privilege, for example, found the household tax proposal too regressive. He devised a comprehensive system based on a combination of proper household and population registration and a dual land and household tax, with grading based not only on household population but wealth.[38] A third argument raised against the plan was that it would simply not yield the requisite one million p'il to offset the loss of the existing commoner cloth tax revenues.[39] Kings Sukchong and Yŏngjo of the seventeenth and eighteenth centuries were initially in favor of the household cloth plan but were dissuaded from adopting it, no doubt for all the above reasons.[40]

In 1750 reform of the commoner cloth tax was finally achieved under the leadership of King Yŏngjo, but the changes made were far from radical. Yŏngjo reduced the military cloth tax rate by half to benefit the commoner taxpayer, sacrificed a considerable proportion of state revenues, and preserved the tax exemption privilege of the yangban. In spite of the fact that Yŏngjo held no brief for aristocractic interest and even wanted to extend the cloth tax to yangban households, his final decision represented a surrender to their interests.

Under the terms of the so-called equal service reform of 1750, 15 percent of the old revenues from the military cloth tax was made up by a new surtax on land.[41] This undoubtedly had the effect of reducing the benefit of the new law to the commoner cultivator, since the new land surtax was probably shifted to owners and tenants, the majority of whom were commoners and *ch'ŏnmin*. On the other hand, the new laws also provided for a levy on the select military officers of relatively higher status than ordinary commoners and for curtailment of the privileges of the palace estates over fishing, salt, and boat taxes. These measures did represent a partial shift of tax burdens to privileged groups.

In sum, the commoner peasant was granted direct tax relief through rate reduction but had to bear new land tax burdens; the yangban was saved from a direct levy of the military cloth tax, but had to absorb some new costs; and the central government suffered some loss of revenue. Yŏngjo's policy may have failed to satisfy the demands of the minority of Confucian egalitarians because it did nothing to create a more equal distribution of military taxes, but at least it conformed to the Korean Confucian stress on frugality in state spending, sacrifice by the throne for the benefit of the peasantry, and maintenance of aristocratic privilege. The Taewongun's objectives stand out in bold relief by contrast with Yŏngjo: his main purpose was to increase the state's control over resources rather than to sacrifice state interests for peasant welfare. In fact, he sacrificed yangban interests for the welfare of the state, even though he had no intention of destroying the hierarchical social order.

Yangban Status and the Village
Cloth Tax: 1750-1862

The difference between the policies of the Taewongun and Yŏngjo was as much a reflection of different conditions as of different personalities.

Politics and Policy in Traditional Korea

By the mid-nineteenth century the yangban aristocracy was diluted by an increase in its membership through the sale of title and rank, and the cheapening of elite status made yangban exemption from taxation less sacrosanct than it had been before. De facto redistribution of military cloth taxes on all households in some villages under the so-called village cloth tax made the adoption of a household cloth tax in 1870 a far less radical innovation than it would have been in 1750. Furthermore, the state of crisis caused by foreign and domestic troubles in the 1860s prevented budget cutting as a feasible solution to the military service and tax problem. On the contrary, more revenue was needed than ever before.

The equal service reform of 1750 left the old tax structure with all its weaknesses virtually intact. The military establishment was still supported by the same variety of sources as before: commoner taxpayers (still called support personnel as in the early Yi dynasty system), colony lands, interest on grain loans, and central government tax funds.[42] Moreover, the reduction in the tax rate was offset by a proliferation of the numbers of duty soldiers, requiring more military cloth taxpayers to support them. Chŏng Yag-yong estimated that by the turn of the nineteenth century, there had been a fourfold increase in the number of persons paying the military cloth tax.[43]

The unequal distribut n of the military cloth tax was aggravated by the considerable growth of tax-exempt individuals. Yi Kyu-gyŏng, writing in the 1830s, deplored the exemption of the yangban from military taxes, especially when their numbers were growing so large. He agreed that a hierarchical social order and the maintenance of elite privileges in society were desirable in principle, but the yangban had multiplied so greatly that they could no longer be treated in the same manner as a small privileged elite.

In the past, the number of sa [yangban] were no more than one quarter of the population, but at present they take up almost half the population. Do they engage in agriculture or commerce? Can they be recruited into the royal guards or the army? Can you at present implement the well-field system and have them contribute their labor to the cultivation of the lord's fields (kongjŏn)? Can you make them pay silk, cloth, or ramie for the land, labor or tribute taxes? Can you limit their landholdings with the ming-t'ien [name fields] system of the Wei dynasty? Can you put into practice the fang-t'ien [square field] system of the Sung? [Koreans used the term fang-t'ien to refer to land registration and survey systems like the fish-scale registers, which used maps with grid patterns in squares to measure accurately individual landholdings for taxation purposes.]

Because the orders of the court are not applied to the yangban, the household, miscellaneous labor service, and the personal service taxes

The Household Cloth Tax

(*sinyŏk*) are not applied to the yangban. In a system of land taxation, nothing is more important than equalizing distribution of taxes among people, but the evil of unequal distribution exists because of them [the yangban].[44]

Unequal distribution was exacerbated by false registration and administrative corruption, as always. People forged yangban genealogies and sold off the extra office warrants of their ancestors to others.[45] The taxable population decreased as the district tax quotas remained constant or increased, so that the burdens were shifted to the poorest and least powerful of the commoner peasants. Magistrates in desperate search for taxable individuals were registering babies, old men, and even dogs on the military tax rolls.[46] Some villages were saddled with as much as ten times the legitimate tax quotas.[47] While other villages with private academies, post-stations, and tombs of powerful families were able to obtain reduced tax quotas.[48] By the 1860s tax exemption on the basis of putative yangban status was so extensive that it would no longer be feasible to maintain such a narrow tax base, especially after the French attack in 1866.

Another important development after 1750 was the redistribution of military tax burdens within villages by the formation of voluntary associations. The voluntary associations were varieties of the *kye*—groups of individuals who pooled financial resources for loans and investment purposes. Two types of *kye* were formed for the purpose of paying official grain loans and military taxes. The village *kye* were composed of households within a village, and the household *kye* were made up of as many as one hundred families bound together by lineage or blood ties. The *kye*-type association may have benefited its members by distributing cloth tax requirements equally among them, but it often contributed to the inequalities of taxation. In certain villages, well-to-do commoner families organized in groups called *kyebang* were so powerful that they were able to avoid military taxes altogether, and the burden was shifted to other commoners within the village.[49]

Chŏng Yag-yong observed that in addition to the *kyebang*, which distributed military cloth tax burdens among a restricted membership, some villages in Hwanghae and P'yŏng'an provinces in the northwest had formed military cloth *kye* (*kunp'ogye*) on a village-wide basis, and these *kye* distributed taxes among all households of the villages equally and with no discrimination based on social status. Some villages had also set aside certain land within the village for the purpose of defraying military taxes (*yŏkkŭnjŏn*). When someone moved from the village, he was required to donate some of his land to the village to pay off his military tax obligations, since it was unlikely that they would be removed by the magistrate after he left. In other cases the land and property of those who died without heirs were taken over by the village. Over time such lands were all converted to village property which could not be bought or sold.[50]

Chŏng pointed out that the institutions of the military-cloth-*kye* and military-service-land were tantamount to levying a cloth tax on either households or land because they ensured equal distribution.[51] In fact, he regarded them as better than the household cloth system. He recognized that the quotas of commoner able-bodied males no longer really represented living persons. Since they had become tax quotas, the important problem was now the equal distribution of such quotas within the village. The existing system, which required the registration of individuals for military taxes only, provided opportunities to the clerks for bribery and false registration. Furthermore, the problem with the household cloth tax, although admirable in principle, was that it would have required truthful and accurate registration for it to succeed. He pointed out that back in 1750 it had been opposed by commoners as well as yangban because they feared the evil effects of a re-registration process. The village *kye* and land systems, however, represented a successful effort at local initiative. It was up to the state to support the extension of this system wherever possible.[52] Chŏng also recommended that military taxes be graded in accordance with the type of service and tax rate and an attempt made to adjust village tax quotas in accordance with the wealth of the village and its residents.[53]

Other proponents of reform harked back to the old solutions. Yi Tŏng-mu (1741-93) proposed levying a capitation tax (the mouth-cash tax) on all persons. He reasoned that, since it would not be labeled a military tax, no pejorative connotations would be attached to it—an argument used prior to the 1750 reform as well. He also proposed doubling the land tax and using the revenues for hired soldiers, implying that the system of hired or professional soldiers had become a fact of life.[54] As we will see, however, the capitation tax was not adopted, but the *kye* association provided the foundation for the village cloth tax system that antedated the household cloth tax reform of 1870.

The 1862 Rebellion and Reform of the Military Tax System

When rebellion broke out in the south of Korea in 1862, the military service and taxation system was condemned as one of the major causes of the rebellion. It was reported that the commoner cloth tax base had narrowed because of false registration by petty officials and excessive exemptions of people from taxes.[55] Many commoners continued to gain exemptions by registering as students in official schools and private academies. Others organized into *kyebang* or made false claims to family relationship with the royal house.[56] The practice of levying military taxes on babies and elderly persons and holding neighbors and relatives responsible for the taxes due from people who had fled their villages continued without abatement.[57] Troops were still ill trained and the number of soldiers who could be called up for actual service was only a fraction of those listed on the military registers.[58] Magistrates who were authorized by the equal service law of 1750 to levy local taxes on their own authority (*punjŏng*) in order to make up for revenue lost from the 50 percent tax reduction had created a patchwork of taxes over which the state had little control.[59] Palace estates (*kungbang*), families of officials (*sabuga*), and various official yamen had ignored the provision of the equal service reform, which turned over revenues from salt production, fishing, and boat taxes to the Office of Equal Service (Kyunyŏkch'ŏng), and continued to arrogate these revenues to themselves.[60] Officials were ignoring fixed cash commutation rates for the cloth tax and requiring payment in cash at the current market rates of one p'il of cloth.[61] Magistrates were abolishing required military service and substituting cash taxes arbitrarily.[62] The oppressive grain loan system was used by officials to raise funds for military expenses.[63]

The reform of the military service and taxation system begun in 1862 in response to the peasant rebellion reflected several historical developments referred to above. The idealistic plan for restoration of the militia system was ignored, and proposals for capitation taxes, land levies, and a household cloth tax were eschewed on the grounds of impracticality. As in 1750 a frontal attack on yangban tax exemption privilege was avoided in favor of an oblique approach to the problem. It was decided to attempt to eliminate illicit exemption by more honest and efficient administration and to encourage the trend toward the adoption of the village cloth tax system at the discretion of individual magistrates.

When King Ch'ŏlchong issued an order for officials and scholars to submit their written opinions,[64] Fourth Deputy Commander (*puhogun*) Hŏ Pu argued for the reorganization of the military on the basis of the ideal farmer-soldier militia system of antiquity. He praised the Five Guards system of the early Yi, since it was an approximation of the T'ang *fu-ping*, but lamented the creation of the Five Military Commands in the seventeenth century, comparing it to the creation of permanent soldiers in the later T'ang.[65] He proposed cutting the capital guards down to only a small unit of 10,000 men to be recruited from the residents of Kyŏnggi province surrounding the capital. The men would serve on rotating shifts and each would be granted land from Kyŏnggi province for maintenance. Hŏ's plan, in other words, was not only a return to the Five Guards system of the early Yi, but an improvement on it. The provision of land grants to duty soldiers would have added one of the essential elements of the farmer-soldier well-field system of the Chou dynasty that had not been incorporated into the Five Guards system.[66] He also advocated the use of ancient models of systems of mutual surveillance as a guarantee for truthful registration.[67]

Not all recommendations were as fundamentalist in tone as those of Hŏ Pu. One anonymous official raised the question of the use of household and land tax substitutes for the commoner cloth tax, but he pointed out that the problem of military finance had become more complicated than in 1750. Finances for the military were being provided not only from the commoner cloth tax but also from interest on government grain loans. Thus, if the household cloth tax were to be used as a substitute levy, its revenues would have to be sufficient to replace income from both loan interest and military taxes. He stated that the current total of grain loan funds in the country stood at 9.9 million sŏk, of which 50 percent was loaned out (at 10 percent interest), yielding 500,000 sŏk of yearly revenue. He estimated the number of military cloth taxpayers in the military system at 1.6 million (paying a total of 1.6 million p'il?) and the number of households in the country also at 1.6 million (for some reason quoting the 1768 population figure). He concluded that a household tax would not generate enough revenue to replace both these sources of income. If the grain-loan revenues for military expenditures alone were abolished and replaced by a household tax, this would also be undesirable, since the support personnel would be paying a double tax—the commoner cloth and a household tax.[68] Furthermore, if a household tax were imposed on all the population, the 20 to 30 percent of the population that comprised the upper class would object to it; and if it were confined only to the commoner class, commoners would certainly be displeased. But any attempt to grade households according to size would only play into the hands of the corrupt clerks.[69] This official also discussed the use of a land tax substitute and pointed out that there were 1.4 million kyŏl (The 1.4 million kyŏl was an overestimation which did not take into account tax-exempt lands.) of land in the country to provide for the support of 1.6 million support troops and substitute for interest on grain loans. He opposed the use of a land surtax on the grounds that the land tax was already too high and a large extra levy would be needed to provide for military finances as well.[70]

Another essay on the military system is preserved in the collected writings of Kim Yun-sik, later to become an important figure in the late nineteenth century. Kim also expressed disapproval of household and

The Household Cloth Tax

capitation taxes because they were inapplicable to the current situation. He preferred instead elimination of the military cloth tax altogether to be replaced by an increased land tax.[71]

The majority of recommendations presented by various officials in 1862 were concerned with specific problems rather than comprehensive plans. The proposal for re-registration of the population was the one most frequently made.[72] The purpose of it was naturally to cut down on the excessive number of students registered at schools in order to avoid military taxes. Other recommendations included abolition of the *kyebang* and reduction of troops units and military expenditures.[73]

One matter which received considerable attention at this time was the village cloth system.[74] Several officials referred to a phenomenon that Chŏng Yag-yong had reported in his writings a half-century before, that the administration of the military tax system in individual villages conformed to one of two major patterns. Either all individuals eligible for the commoner cloth tax were recorded on the military registers and taxes levied on them, or quotas of military tax revenues for villages were set in a lump sum and distributed equally on all households in the village.[75] The former system—the taxation of individual able-bodied commoner males—was the legally sanctioned system and was referred to by a number of terms, most frequently *myongp'a* or *kup'a* literally, name-scars or mouth-scars, alluding to the branding (read: registration) of individuals for military service.[76] The village levies were called *tongp'o* or village cloth. Court officials in 1862 ackowledged that the village cloth system was illegal but most recommended, as Chŏng Yag-yong had, that it be preserved where convenient. As one official pointed out, the village cloth system was close to the principle that "every one with a body is required to perform labor service."[77] In other words, the system recommended itself because it was tantamount to a capitation tax of uniform rate on all people.

At the end of the debate over the reform of the military system, a list of regulations was drawn up by the Reform Bureau on October 12, 1862. It was recommended among other things that registration of babies, children, and those who had passed the age limit for military service be prohibited. *Kyebang* and support personnel attached to official schools and private academies were to be abolished, and all people affected by this would be returned to regular military service. A thorough investigation was to be made of all individuals who claimed under false pretenses that they were students (*yusaeng*) or descendants of merit subjects. Households of so-called tomb villages (*myoch'on*) previously exempted from military service would now be required to pay taxes. Officials would be allowed to utilize either the mouth-scar or village cloth system at their

Politics and Policy in Traditional Korea

own discretion. Provincial governors were to try and achieve a balance between the military tax quotas due from each village and the number of households in those villages, and provision was made for the punishment of magistrates and clerks for false registration and excessive exemption.[78]

The regulations of 1862 ignored completely the recommendations of people like Hŏ Pu for a restoration of the farmer-soldier system. This had become as irrelevant to the solution of the military tax as the well-field system had to land distribution. Even the enthusiasm for the household-cloth system, which was so noticeable prior to 1750, seems to have dissipated by 1862. As Chŏng Yag-yong and others had pointed out, the village cloth system made the household-cloth plan less attractive than it had been in the eighteenth century. The household-cloth system had always been criticized because it relied heavily on registration procedures and the probity of the army of petty clerks for efficient implementation. Scholar-officials of the nineteenth century tended to place more weight on the dangers of administrative corruption. Despite the fact that the village cloth system was illegal, it was appealing because it had achieved fair or equal redistribution and operated without the intervention of the petty officials. The central government had now taken note of the village cloth system, but in typical Yi dynasty fashion chose only to tolerate it and made no attempt to impose it on all villages.

As for the other elements of the 1862 reform program, schools and academies were again subjected to government pressure in order to return support personnel and students to the tax rolls. The usual list of punishments for corrupt clerks was promulgated one more time, but there was no attempt at any rationalization of procedure as suggested by several scholars at the turn of the century. Troop training and palace estate usurpation of fishing and salt revenues were left untouched. And while much thought was given to the grain-loan problem (see Chapter 7), there was no effort to dissociate it from the military finance structure.

Military Finance, 1864-73: The Artillery Provision and Household Cloth Taxes

After 1864 armed conflict with foreign expeditionary forces and the constant threat of foreign invasion brought a sharp increase in the demand for funds to pay for more troops, weapons, forts, and provisions.[79] The crisis situation of the 1860s, however, did not evoke any comprehensive financial planning. Instead, the government responded to problems of military finance as they arose. At the beginning of Kojong's reign, the dowager-regent ordered the disbursement of funds directly from the royal treasury to meet military expenses; interest from grain loans was used frequently for raising funds; a land-cash surtax was approved for

P'yŏng'an province; rewards were given for voluntary contributions from private individuals; and new recruits were financed by land resurveys.[80]

Fishing, salt, and boat tax revenues, which had been turned over to the central government in 1750, evidently still remained in the hands of the palace estates and other agencies according to the Reform Bureau reports of 1862. Nothing had been done about this situation in 1862, but in a series of edicts issued during the 1860s, the government ordered these revenues turned over to local government mainly for financing military costs.[81] The various measures used to raise revenue were still not sufficient to meet military needs. In 1871, after the U.S. expedition had departed, the government decided to levy a new land surtax of one tu/kyŏl on the estimated 700,000 kyŏl of taxable land in the southern six provinces to yield additional revenues of 50,000 sŏk of grain. The provisions would be used to support the stepped-up defense of Kanghwa and other islands, and the new tax was dubbed the artillery provision rice tax (*p'oryangmi*). Authorities cited the precedent of the three soldiers provision tax (*samsuryang*) used to support the new Military Training Agency during Hideyoshi's invasions. The new law was supported by a number of other revenue-raising measures; such as transfer of the Songdo (Kaesong) ginseng tax revenues, and allocation of funds from the Tribute Bureau and Ministries of Taxation and War, designed to support an additional 3-4,000 troops.[82]

The land surtaxes and the other fiscal measures show that the government could no longer afford the luxury of budget cutting as a means to the alleviation of the regressive commoner cloth tax. On the contrary, the government's need for additional funds acted as a stimulus for the enactment of the household cloth tax in 1870. Even though this tax has been regarded as an attack on yangban privilege, its main purpose was to increase government revenue by more efficient taxation and not to destroy social status privileges or barriers.

Because of serious lacunae in the historical records after 1864, there is some difficulty in tracing the development leading to the promulgation of this law. It appears probable that the recommendations of the Reform Bureau of 1862 were approved by King Ch'ŏlchong, and sometime between 1864 and 1866 an edict was issued in the name of the dowager-regent which in particular reconfirmed the abolition of the *kyebang*, the prohibition of military tax exemptions for support personnel attached to private and official schools and residents of yangban tomb-villages, and the authorization for the use of the village cloth system in those villages where it was found to be appropriate.[83] In 1866 Kojong also ordered the government to have records drawn up for individual villages

Politics and Policy in Traditional Korea

showing the distribution of military taxes according to the tax system in use in any village—that is, either by registration of all eligible individuals or by the village quota system.[84]

Han Woo-keun in a recent study has emphasized the fact that the village cloth system was indeed one which distributed taxes on an equal basis among all the households of a village—yangban as well as commoner.[85] If this view is accurate, and it would seem to be borne out by material presented earlier in this chapter, then it would hold that the taxation of yangban households in some villages had become a fact of life at least since the turn of the nineteenth century. It had not been recognized as permissible, however, until the Reform Bureau regulations of 1862, and it had evidently been reconfirmed after Kojong ascended the throne. Thus, a household cloth tax system existed in fact in some fraction of the villages of the country already, even though the government had made no attempt to establish the taxation of yangban households as a universal principle in law.

There is much evidence to indicate that the village cloth system had not proved to be an unmitigated blessing. In 1867 the secret censor for Chŏlla province reported that one district had converted from the name-scar system to a village cloth system, but that this had resulted in heavier taxes.[86] In 1868 the secret censor for Hwanghae province reported that in those villages where individuals were registered for military taxes the clerks were registering too many names, but that the village cloth system did not provide an adequate alternative. While it might redistribute tax burdens more equitably within a village, it usually resulted in a decrease in tax revenues. Then, in order to make up for the shortages other unauthorized levies like the land-cloth tax would be added on as a sur-tax.[87] A report from Kongch'ung province in 1867 also mentioned the use of both village cloth and land-cloth taxes in certain villages and pointed out that neither system was lawful; they had only been tolerated by the government as temporary expedients.[88] Obviously, there was some confusion over the question of legality. The village cloth system had been recognized by the government and its use permitted in those villages where it was more convenient, but, since it had not been promulgated as universal law for the whole country, it was obviously still regarded as illegal by many officials.

The problems with the administration of the village cloth tax and other measures derived from the weakness of central government control over districts in the provinces. In 1867 the secret censor for Kyŏnggi province pointed out that there had not been thorough investigations of excessive exemptions for yangban and tomb villages and that the village cloth system was not being administered equally.[89] in 1868 the secret censor for

The Household Cloth Tax

Kongch'ung Right province reported that a cloth tax on land was being used in some districts. Since it had proved to be an excessive burden on taxpayers, he recommended that the provincial governor be given discretion whether to impose an individual registration or village cloth system in the villages in those districts. The state council replied that it did not understand how a cloth tax on land had come into use in the provinces. Since it was illegal, it could not be used. The councilors, therefore, endorsed the censor's recommendations.[90]

Sometime in 1870 the Taewongun issued a private directive (*punbu*) to the nation ordering yangban households to pay the military cloth tax and allowing them to pay it in the name of their household slaves. Unfortunately, the order is not to be found in the court records; it is only referred to indirectly in a royal edict in 1871.[91] Other evidence indicates that this directive must also have set a uniform tax rate of the two yang per household.[92] Until the study by Han Woo-Keun, scholars had interpreted this notice as signifying a revolutionary imposition of the military cloth tax on yangban.[93] There is little doubt that this was the first instance of a government decree providing for the universal taxation of yangban households. As Han has pointed out, however, it was not the first instance of yangban taxation, since this had been a feature of those villages which used the village cloth system.[94]

In any case, the Taewongun's initiation of the household cloth tax did not represent an intentional attempt to level Korean society by lowering a fiscal bludgeon on the heads of the yangban elite. Indeed, in the view of Han Woo-keun, the opposite is true. Whereas the village cloth tax provided for the direct payment of taxes by the heads of yangban households, the new household cloth tax allowed yangban to pay the household cloth tax in the name of their slaves. In other words, the Taewongun was trying to soothe the ruffled feelings of the discontented yangban who were upset with the social implications of a tax they were already paying under the village cloth system.[95]

The household cloth tax and other revenue-raising measures had obviously alleviated the financial stress on the government. The minister of war reported on April 1, 1873, that his ministry, at least, had been able to accumulate a surplus because of the policies of the Taewongun over the previous eight to nine years.[96] More effective taxation was obviously a result of the new household cloth tax.

The intentions of the Taewongun can only be surmised because of the lack of any clear statement of purpose by him. His secretary, Kim Kyu-rak, wrote that the Taewongun's purpose in instituting a tax on both aristocrats and commoners was to alleviate the distress of the impoverished peasantry caused by the military cloth tax.[97] Unlike the equal service reform of 1750, however, the new law was not accompanied by rate reduction, indicating that the Taewongun gave priority to state finance over peasant welfare. The king and the chief state councilor were clearly opposed to the idea of social leveling, and it is not unlikely that their views coincided with those of the Taewongun. On January 2, 1873, Chief State Councilor Hong Sun-mok reported to Kojong that the military registers were full of vacancies and that as a result double taxes were being levied on legal taxpayers to make up for shortages. The court had no choice but to distribute taxes by household and provide for the uniform taxation of all—even including the "silk-clad" gentry. The only exceptions to the law were exemptions for impoverished *sajok* (aristocrats), students, and people who were the sole support of their families. The commoners and *ch'ŏnmin*, however, had taken note of the fact that the upper class was now required to pay the same tax as they and now were refusing to accept an inferior status position. They could no longer tolerate being despised by their social superiors.[98]

Hong said that he was shocked by this situation. On a recent tour of inspection in the provinces he had been swarmed by petitioners suing their grievances over this issue. Things were in a confused state and the improverished yangban were hard pressed. The foundation of order in the state was under attack because order depended on the maintenance of proper social distinctions. He claimed that it had never been the purpose of the household cloth tax to undermine this basic principle. He quoted the Book of Changes to the effect that: "Distinguishing between superior and inferior settles the minds of the people. I have never heard of a case where the minds of the people were settled when distinctions between superior and inferior were not made."[99] Hong recommended that the Three Armies Command issue orders for the punishment of the ignorant and recalcitrant in matters of the registration of people for military service and taxes in order "to maintain distinctions of social status and the basis for establishing order."[100]

Kojung in his rescript expressed agreement with Hong's views. Kojong pointed out that the levying of a household tax on both commoners and yangban was justified by ancient precedent. It did not, however, give commoners the right to look down on yangban. "The great people [yangban] are not to be placed in a position where they are held in contempt."[101]

The worst fears of the opponents of the household-cloth tax over the previous two hundred years seemed to have been materializing. It appeared to them that the taxation of the yangban was indeed destroying the foundations of Korean society. But the Taewongun was a pragmatist who was little concerned with the theoretical implications of the household cloth tax. He needed revenue for military defense, so he authorized a tax on all households—an act which was far easier in 1870 than 1750 because the tax-exempt yangban had increased in size out of all proportion to what was tolerable in a fiscal sense.

While he was willing to sacrifice yangban economic interests for the benefit of the state, he did not do so on the basis of any logical or theoretical analysis of the weaknesses of Korean society. The egalitarian intellectuals of the eighteenth century wanted to level society in order to spread tax and service obligations throughout all the population, thereby reducing the burden of the commoner peasant. The Taewongun, on the contrary, wanted to raise funds, so he taxed the yangban, but with no attempt to destroy the social system, and with relatively less concern for reducing taxes or tax burdens on the population.

Because of the long precedent of relatively equal tax distribution at the village level under the village cloth system, the household cloth tax of 1870 was hardly as revolutionary as it would have been in 1750. It was simply a handy revenue-raising measure instituted by a practical statesman who had no intention of overturning the social order. One must conclude that while the Taewongun proved to be a skillful fund raiser, he retreated from the direct confrontation with the aristocracy that would have been necessary for a successful establishment of monarchical, central, or national political and economic power.

6

The Abolition of the Private Academies

One of the most famous acts of the Taewongun was his radical reduction of the number of authorized private academies and shrines. This policy served notice on the aristocracy that the throne would assert its authority in the educational and spiritual realms as well as in the fiscal, and it constituted no less an affront to aristocratic sensibilities than the imposition of the household cloth tax. Despite the radical aspects of the Taewongun's abolition of private academies and shrines, however, the overall effects of this action must not be exaggerated. The elimination of the private academies as an important institution in Yi dynasty society did not result in any significant weakening of the power and influence of the social elite.

In the first place, the power of the elite was not based on autonomous institutions or organizations, but on more diffuse considerations, such as inherited status, degree holding, office holding, and landholding. Control over private academies was never an essential element of aristocratic power. In fact, the institutional basis of the aristocracy was to be found in those structures that ostensibly were designed to function as agencies of central authority—the bureaucracy and the examination system. Even in the area of education the private academies were not crucial to yangban control because institutionalized education was always supplementary to the predominant system of private tutorial. It was because the central government itself showed little interest in providing and maintaining a school system that the literati were able to capitalize on this official neglect to build up a system of private academies in the sixteenth and seventeenth centuries. Yet even at the height of their influence, it still could not be said that elite control over education was a function of the private academies.

The central government, of course, was always jealous of its authority. Its benign neglect of educational institutions reached a limit when its political and economic interests were threatened, and this is just what happened when the local private academies became politicized, interfered with the local magistrates, and built up tax-exempt estates. In the late seventeenth century the throne began to impose restrictions and quotas on the academies, and by the late eighteenth century a balance was achieved between central and local literati interests that lasted to the 1860s. When the Taewongun eliminated the private academies as an institutional threat to centralized authority, he was dealing with an institution that had already been substantially weakened. But since the basis of aristocratic power was diffuse, the abolition of the academies did not eliminate the countervailing power of the aristocracy as a whole.

Furthermore, even though the Taewongun's academy policy produced limited results in the concentration of power at the center, it also had the adverse effect of stimulating literati resistance to his regime. This was inevitable as long as the yangban remained the foundation of Yi dynasty society; partial attacks on their power were counterproductive because they would only serve to stimulate political opposition. In terms of education and criteria for office holding there were only two policies sufficient for breaking the back of aristocratic or yangban power—abolition of the examination system and total elimination of class distinction in the selection of officials—but these were policies the Taewongun was unwilling and unable to sponsor in the 1860s. It took another generation of extreme pressure before the abolition of the examination system in 1894.

Government Neglect of the Educational Establishment

Even though the Yi dynasty government utilized education as a means of ensuring loyalty to the dynasty, inducing conformity to ideological orthodoxy, and recruiting officials for the bureaucracy, except for the first few decades of the dynasty it neglected its own network of official schools. It achieved its objectives without undue organizational effort mainly because the educated elite voluntarily shared the premises of neo-Confucian orthodoxy, assumed private responsibility within the family for education by the hiring of tutors, and complied with the examination system. The yangban elite served its own interests as well because it was able to maintain its monopoly over access to education and office holding by these means.

In the first decades of the dynasty the monarchy did show interest in establishing a system of official schools in the capital and provinces as part of an effort to build up the authority of civil government in the wake

Politics and Policy in Traditional Korea

of the powerful military elite of the mid-Koryŏ dynasty. Both the government and the new civil elite were also promoting Confucianism against a still popular Buddhism as well as consolidating the political power of the new dynasty. According to the 1474 law code, the Kyŏngguk taejŏn, the system of official schools consisted of the district schools (*hyanggyo*) in the provinces and the Four Schools (*sahak*) in the capital, which handled secondary education, and the National Academy (*Sŏnggyun'gwan*) in the capital, which had charge of tertiary education. Primary education was left completely to private initiative; it was taken care of either by the hiring of private tutors in the home or by the establishment of private schools (*sŏdang*) for elementary education.[1]

At age fourteen or fifteen, the student could, if he wished, enter a district school or one of the Four Schools in the capital. At around age eighteen or nineteen, he would then probably stand for the classics or literary licentiate examinations (*saengwŏn, chinsa*, respectively, referred to collectively as the *sama* examinations.). If he passed, he was then eligible for admittance to the National Academy in Seoul. The age of students at the National Academy was usually between twenty and twenty-three, and these students took the *munkwa*, the highest civil service examination, somewhere between the ages of twenty-two and twenty-six on the average.[2] There were no regulations requiring school attendance as a prerequisite for participating in the examinations, even though attendance at school did confer certain advantages.[3]

The National Academy had a quota of two hundred students. The Four Schools had quotas of one hundred each (a total of four hundred), and the quotas of district schools varied from thirty to ninety depending on the size of the district and its rank in the hierarchy of administrative subdivisions.[4] The maximum quota of students allowed to attend the district schools in three hundred and twenty-nine local districts, the Four Schools and the National Academy, combined, came to 15,750 persons.[5]

As Ch'oe Yŏng-ho's studies have revealed, it is most likely that in the early Yi dynasty, contrary to established belief, there were no legal restrictions against men of commoner status either taking the civil service examinations or attending official schools.[6] Ch'oe argues that registration or attendance at an official school as a student (*kyosaeng*) may have been one of the primary determinants of yangban or elite status in the early Yi.[7] It certainly conferred exemption from military service and may have provided the means for a few men of commoner birth to climb the social ladder in the early Yi dynasty. In any case, in the first decades of the dynasty the government schools appeared to have performed a significant educational and social function.

In the late fifteenth century, however, the official schools began a steady and consistent decline. The quality of their teachers fell, their reputations suffered, student attendance was poor, and student behavior substandard. Officials frequently complained that the students in the official schools were ignorant and that they were attending merely to gain *kyosaeng* status and exemption from military service.[8] The state was now content to intervene in educational matters in only a partial and limited way by providing state schools as an alternative to private education, by appointing supervisory officials in the provinces to oversee the actual conduct of education at private or semiprivate institutions, by acting as a final court of review on all matters of education, and by reserving its right to punish and abolish ex post facto whatever activity it disapproved. Such a desultory system of control contributed to the power of the local educated elite and created a vacuum that was soon to be filled when a wave of neo-Confucian zeal overcame the literati in the sixteenth century.

Emergence of Private Academies

Several trends were associated with the emergence of private academies in the sixteenth century. In addition to a decline in the quality of official schools, private education at the primary and secondary levels was becoming more institutionalized.[9] Political conflict in the late fifteenth century created groups of disenfranchised scholar-officials who returned to the countryside to found study centers and schools.[10] The influence of neo-Confucian thought produced a greater concern for moral cultivation as opposed to careerism as the main purpose of education,[11] and there was a rise in quasi-religious piety expressed in the establishment of shrines to scholars and exemplars of virtuous behavior both living and dead.[12] It was the fusion of the private school with the local shrine that produced the new type of private academy of the mid-sixteenth century.[13]

The neo-Confucianist movement of the sixteenth century was in many respects an exercise in conscious cultural borrowing. Not only was Chu Hsi revered as the source of utimate wisdom, but everything he did was taken as a model of correct policy. His resurrection and promotion of private academies in the early Southern Sung dynasty was well known to the Koreans, and the first of the new type of academies—Paeg'undong sŏwŏn of 1542-43—was modeled after Chu Hsi's *Pai-lu-t'ung shu-yüan* even to the adoption of his set of regulations for the governance of the school.[14] The famous Ming gazetteer *Ta-Ming i-t'ung-chih*, which listed the academies in China, was also used as a reference book by Koreans.[15]

The rise of the private academies also represented the recrudescence of the system of discipleship in education which had been quite strong in the

Koryŏ dynasty. This had been institutionalized in the late Koryŏ by the performance of a ritual act between examiner and examinee which made personal loyalty and favoritism one of the chief obstacles to the state's search for talent on the basis of an objective evaluation of scholarly merit. In fact, it would appear that one of the motives for the construction of a strong system of state schools in the early Yi dynasty was a desire to get away from the strong personal bonds of the Koryŏ examination system.[16] By the late fifteenth century, however, the establishment of private schools by eminent scholars driven out of public life—men who were at the same time imbued with a strong sense of Confucian loyalty and piety—strengthened the master-disciple bond of vertical loyalty that had been obscured for a time. This, too, became an important feature, not only of the private school system, but also of scholarship in general after the sixteenth century.

After the seventeenth century the private academies and the government's attitude toward them underwent important changes. In the first place, the number of private academies grew prodigiously. Eighty-eight were founded between 1542 and 1600, and by the beginning of the eighteenth century there were over six hundred in existence. By the nineteenth century, the cumulative total of academies founded since 1542 came to about 680, although it is doubtful that all of them were still functioning at that time. The greatest period of growth occurred in the years from 1650 to 1725 when 400 were founded. After 1725 only thirty-six new ones were established.[17] The ratio of private academies to population was much larger in the Yi dynasty than in any Chinese dynasty, a fact which undoubtedly reflects the lesser degree of central control and greater degree of local literati strength.[18]

This growth was accompanied by a change in the nature and function of the private academy. In the sixteenth century the private academies were centers of learning and contemplation and havens for scholars seeking solace from the vicissitudes of politics. They reflected the growth of neo-Confucian piety and were an institutional manifestation of the search for moral self-cultivation. By the nineteenth century, however, the purity of the earlier vision had been sullied by the growing political and economic functions of the academies. Academies were founded by scholars and officials with ties of loyalty to bureaucratic factions. During the seventeenth and early eighteenth centuries, both political and intellectual life were marked by partisanship, which produced schismatic splintering into smaller groups.[19]

From the outset the state had granted the academies autonomous control over their internal affairs, which included administrative, legal, and economic functions in the handling of students, land, slaves, and income,

The Abolition of Private Academies

and their authority came into conflict with the powers of the local magistrate. Their economic functions also became more important. Like the Buddhist monasteries of the Koryŏ dynasty, their registered students, functionaries, and slaves were exempted from military service, most of their lands were exempted from taxation, and they were the recipients of patronage from the throne and local officials and gifts and grants from the wealthy.[20] At the beginning, all these things had looked to the government like proper acts of Confucian piety, guaranteeing the perpetuation of the word through education and educated men. Before long, however, the private academy came to be viewed as a private institution threatening to state interests.

One scholar has estimated that by 1807 private academies and shrines held a total of 60,000 kyŏl of tax-exempt land, anywhere from 7 to 10 percent of the total taxable land in the country.[21] The private academies also became havens for tax dodgers. Students, academy functionaries, and slaves all obtained exemption from military service, and this kind of protection attracted even more people to them. Some people purchased student status and peasants commended themselves to academy estates.[22]

These factors undoubtedly contributed to a decline in the original pedagogical purpose of the private academy. To a large extent they had become gathering places for local literati and centers of political and intellectual cliques paying homage through the performance of ritual sacrifice to scholars and bureaucrats of the past.[23]

Government Ambivalence

The government never could escape a fundamental ambivalence in its treatment of the academies. It was the government that in 1550 had granted legitimacy to the academies by the issuing of charters (*saaek*), usually in the form of signboards in the calligraphy of the king, and royal grants of land, slaves, and books.[24] State authorization of the corporate nature of the academy was based, however, on the premise of its apolitical, educative, and noneconomic character. When this premise was destroyed, the government began to impose more stringent restrictions by limiting landholdings, tax exemptions, and the number of students and slaves. The 1746 law code (*Soktaejŏn*) stipulated that chartered private academies would be limited to three kyŏl of tax-exempt land, and that unchartered academies would have none.[25] The throne also issued decrees against excessive gifts of land to the academies, but these measures were not effective in limiting the size of academy holdings. By the early eighteenth century, there were an estimated 620 academies, of which about 250 were chartered.[26] Theoretically, only 750 kyŏl of land should have been tax exempt, but it is more than likely that

Politics and Policy in Traditional Korea

almost all the estimated 60,000 kyŏl of shrine and academy land in 1807 was tax exempt.

The government had limited success in restricting the number of academy students and slaves. At first the academies set their own limits on students. The Paeg'undong sŏwŏn set stringent entrance requirements and limited its students at first to ten, and then later to thirty.[27] Other academies had easier entrance requirements and probably larger student bodies. In 1646 some officials proposed a fifty-student limit; King Injo preferred six or seven, and the Ministry of Rites suggested twenty, but no decision was reached.[28] In 1710 limits were set of twenty students for a chartered academy, fifteen for an unchartered one, and thirty for (an academy with?) a Confucian shrine (munmyo) where sacrifices were performed.[29] In 1786 King Chŏngjo had to reissue orders for the twenty-student restriction, indicating that the law had been ignored.[30]

In 1657 King Hyojong set a limit of seven slaves for chartered academies, five for unchartered, and one for local shrines. All slaves above these quotas were ordered released from their attachments to the academy.[31] Yet the Paeg'undong sŏwŏn had as many as eighteen slaves as early as 1545.[32] Later in 1675 King Sukchong endorsed Hyojong's limits on academy slaves,[33] but as in the case of student quotas the reiteration of decrees indicated laxity in the enforcement of the laws.[34]

The period of greatest ambivalence in the throne's policy toward private academies occurred in the century after 1650, and in particular, during Sukchong's reign from 1674 to 1720. It was under Sukchong that the greatest number of private academies were founded in any single reign, a total of four hundred. But it was also a period when severe restrictions were imposed. Several times during his reign Sukchong prohibited construction of academies without government authorization. He placed limits on the number of academy students, forbade the construction of more than one shrine in memory of any single individual, established a scale of punishments for those participating in unauthorized rituals, and in 1720 set the three kyŏl limit on tax-exempt academy land.[35] The trend of repression continued into Yŏngjo's (r. 1724-76) and Chŏngjo's (r. 1776-1800) reigns with noticeable results. Only eighteen academies were founded in the period 1725-50 and only thirteen new ones in the last half of the eighteenth century.[36] Furthermore, many of those already founded were abolished. In 1738 Yŏngjo ordered an investigation of all shrines built privately since 1725; in 1741 he upgraded the schedule of punishments for unauthorized shrine and academy construction and decreed the abolition of over three hundred shrines and academies built without permission since 1714.[37] King Chŏngjo continued Yŏngjo's policy of restriction. In 1786 he reimposed the twenty-man

The Abolition of Private Academies

limit on academy students, ordered punishment for officials who permitted illegal rituals at academies, and prohibited all shrines to living people.[38] In 1800 he ordered all chartered academies to cease performing unauthorized sacrificial rites.[39]

On the other hand, neither Yŏngjo nor Chŏngjo were committed to the total destruction of the private academies. Yŏngjo took a dim view of overzealous magistrates and scholars who destroyed the shrines and academies of their enemies.[40] Chŏngjo sent officials to perform rites to Song Si-yŏl at the Hwayang academy, and he unwittingly contributed to the proliferation of local shrines by refusing in 1783 to allow the incorporation of tablets to lesser worthies in established shrines, insisting that separate shrines be established for them instead.[41]

For the half century after 1800 there were few examples of overt struggle between the central government and the private academies until in 1858 King Ch'ŏlchong (r. 1849-64) abolished the so-called Happiness Wine Villages or Happiness Wine Households that had been established by academies for the purpose of escaping regular taxes.[42] In 1859 Ch'ŏlchong also prohibited the unauthorized construction of private academies.[43] When rebellion broke out in 1862, firmer measures were taken against the academies, which were deemed sources of peasant oppression. The king abolished all rites at unchartered academies built since 1850 and eliminated all shrines to living persons.[44]

Although Ch'ŏlchong did not live long enough to carry out extensive reforms, during his reign it became evident that the throne had been unable to check the power of the private shrines and academies. An official in Kyŏngsang province reported that military taxation on the poor had doubled because of the total exemption of the population in places where shrines and academies were located.[45] One of the chief critics of contemporary conditions, Fourth Deputy Commander Hŏ Pu, accused scholars of pursuing private advantage and officeholding instead of true moral cultivation, and of studying Buddhism, Taoism, or Western Learning instead of Confucian orthodoxy.[46] He held these false scholars responsible for the decline of the school system. He found that the National Academy was empty and overrun with weeds, the district schools converted into bases for political struggle, and the private academies exercising despotic and tyrannical power on the local scene.[47] "It has been a long time since anybody bothered to ask whether there were any teachers or students there."[48]

By 1862 the stage had been set for more radical action by the Taewongun. The crisis caused by the 1862 rebellion lay bare the residual influence of the private academies, created a sense of urgency, and led to a departure from the ambivalent policy of the eighteenth century. In the final contest the private academies were too weak an institution to withstand a frontal and concerted attack by the throne supported by the high officials of the central government.

Abolition of the Academies
and the Mandongmyo

On May 27, 1864, Dowager-Regent Cho ordered the Border Defense Command (myodang) to obtain reports from the provinces on the private academies, shrines to local worthies and living persons, their lands, and the people under their protection.[49] In the summer, however, she complained that people had continued to construct academies and shrines despite the prohibition against it, and that the academies were using their power to harass the people. She instructed the Border Defense Command to consult with the provincial governors to decide which shrines and academies should be abolished.[50] On September 17 she declared that the prime cause for the shortage of men for military service was the extension of private control over population at the expense of the central government and invidiously compared the academies with the powerful aristocratic households, which had extended their protection over dependent households (yangho) and obtained exemption from military and labor service for them. The most egregious example of this was the three hundred dependent households located at the site dedicated to the Taewongun's own father. She reported that the Taewongun had been disturbed about this and ordered all persons outside the regular tomb guards to be assigned either to duty in the army, the grain-loan administration, or household labor service.[51]

This order was immediately followed by a second edict on September 17 which specifically set limits on academy and shrine land and personnel and ordered the return of able-bodied men to military service registration. The dowager indicted the academies and shrines for the corruption of their original purpose. She stated that scholars of the past had built schools and shrines in the memory of worthy men for the purpose of promoting learning and extolling the true way and for this reason the court had frequently granted royal charters, land, and tax exemption for their personnel. They had been corrupted, however. They fought for food and wine; they protected people attempting to avoid military taxes and service; they oppressed the common people and extorted funds from them; and they were established without authorization in great numbers. She announced that the time had come for a radical reform of the situation. In order to eliminate extortion and the intimidation of the common people by the academies, provincial governors and magistrates were ordered to ensure a thorough investigation of every suit against the

The Abolition of Private Academies

people initiated by those relying on the power and authority of a shrine or academy. The officials were enjoined against covering up the facts and ordered to report the results of their investigation to the throne. Any scholars found guilty of extortion or intimidation would be threatened with the loss of their scholarly status and privileges.

The restriction on tax-exempt land provided for in the Soktaejŏn code of 1746 was reconfirmed at three kyŏl per chartered academy, and an investigation was to be conducted to make sure that academies had not taken over privately owned land even for the purpose of obtaining a full three kyŏl. The state council was also instructed to fix quotas for academy personnel exempted from service obligations—the taxpaying support personnel of the students (wŏnsaeng posol), slaves and servants (wŏnbok), and warehouse clerks (kojik)—and return the rest to military service. Local shrines were not to be authorized any tax-exempt support personnel (posol) whatever. The edict referred to the abolition in 1858 of the Happiness Wine Villages and pointed out that the proscription against them had proved ineffective. Officials in all villages where this kind of tax-exempt household was located were ordered to draw up a report and reissue the prohibitions against them. Finally, the edict prohibited all private and unauthorized construction of shrines and academies and any establishment of more than one shrine or academy in honor of a single individual. In case of violation of this order, the shrine would be destroyed immediately and the persons responsible punished.[52]

The September 17 edict was a bold though not unprecedented measure. It marked a return to the restrictive policy of the eighteenth century, and had the Taewongun been content to go no further, it is possible that the local literati would have tightened their belts and adapted to the situation. But in 1865 he abolished one of the most important shrines in the country—the Mandongmyo—and between 1868 and 1871 he took steps to eliminate once and for all the private academies as an important institution. His audacity was rewarded with success, but it was a Pyrrhic victory that cost him his power.

The Mandongmyo

The Mandongmyo, the shrine to the Ming dynasty located at the Hwayang Academy in North Kongch'ung (modern Ch'ungch'ong) province, was the citadel of the Patriarch's faction.[53] It was established in 1704 in memory of the Wan-li emperor (r. 1573-1620) of the Ming dynasty, who had sent troops to aid Korea against Hideyoshi's invasions. During the reign of the last Ming emperor, the Ch'ung-chen emperor (r. 1628-44), a Korean envoy to Peking brought back a four-character motto personally inscribed by Ch'ung-chen—"Make no move that is not in accordance with propriety (*li*)." It was given to Song Si-yŏl, the founder of the Patriarch's faction, who had it incised in the walls of a temple in Hwayangdong. On his deathbed he pledged his disciple, Kwŏn Sang-ha, to establish a shrine to both the Wan-li and Ch'ung-chen emperors. Kwŏn built the Mandongmyo and later King Yŏngjo had it repaired and granted it a twenty kyŏl tax exemption. In 1809 it was built again, and in 1844 the provincial governor was ordered to conduct regular sacrifices in the spring and autumn of every year.[54]

By the mid-nineteenth century, the Hwayang Academy had become one of the most predatory private academies. Royal edicts in 1858 and 1864 had prohibited the Happiness Wine Households that were attached to it, but because of the existence of the Mandongmyo on its grounds, its association with Song Si-yŏl, and its long history of royal patronage, the Taewongun had to be cautious in his attempts to reduce its power. The tactic he adopted in 1865 was to dissociate the shrine from the academy and check the objections of the pious Confucians and Ming loyalists by transferring its rituals to a new shrine within the palace grounds, the Altar of Great Retribution (Taebodan). The edict abolishing the Mandongmyo issued by the dowager-regent on April 24, 1865, was couched in almost apologetic terms. It praised Song Si-yŏl as an official whose virtue was no less than that of the great King Hyojong (r. 1649-59) under whom Song had served. Song's adherence to principle (that is, his resistance to the Manchus and his loyalty to the Ming) had prevented all Koreans from descending to the status of amoral beasts, and just when his lofty purpose was about to die out, it was preserved by the greatest of his disciples by the construction of the Mandongmyo. King Sukchong (r. 1674-1720), however, had decided that in emulation of the way in which the feudal lords used to pay court to the king (*wang*, of the Chinese Chou dynasty), the proper way to express gratitude to Heaven for its benevolence was by the establishment of an altar (*tan*) at court, and not by the erection of a separate shrine (*myo*).[55] "It was because of this that the memory of the great Ming dynasty had been preserved in this small corner of our Green Hills [*ch'onggu*, another name for Korea] and had never been forgotten." It was by this means that the great purposes of Song Si-yŏl would be preserved; it would not be necessary to have duplicate construction of private shrines in the countryside. Furthermore, the edict justified the abolition of the Mandongmyo on the grounds that conditions at the shrine had deteriorated since the time it was founded. It was ordered that all ritual at the Mandongmyo would cease once ceremonies had been conducted at the new royal altar. The Mandongmyo signboard was to be brought to the royal palace grounds and hung over another structure (the Kyŏngbonggak). May 16 was chosen as the day that rites would be conducted at the Altar of Great Retribution.[56]

The Abolition of Private Academies

The personal memoir of the Taewongun's private secretary, Kim Kyu-rak, penned in 1871, sheds a little more light on the Taewongun's purpose in eliminating the Mandongmyo. Although Kim's account is a totally uncritical paean of praise written by a loyal servant about the merits of his master's policies, it does provide some valuable insights into motivation. Kim Kyu-rak repeated the same type of fulsome praise for Song Si-yŏl that was included in the dowager's edict, but he also pointed out that after Song's death scholars began to split into groups which no longer paid respect to Song's teachings and no longer bothered to visit his shrine at the Hwayang Academy. People were still afraid to criticize the problems that had developed at the academy because of its great prestige. The Taewongun, however, had once visited the shrine and had gained personal knowledge of the bad situation there.[57] Kim also stressed the fact that the removal of the altar to the Taebodan signified the continuation of the dynasty's respect not only for three Ming emperors but also for seventy-two Chinese and Koreans who were loyal to the Ming dynasty.[58]

Kim also presented the arguments of the scholars who opposed the abolition of the Mandongmyo. They had protested that the Mandongmyo housed tablets to the Ming emperor, that it was a great symbol of moral standards, and a holy shrine. The maintenance of shrines to the Ming in Korea was especially important because there could be no commemorative shrines to the Ming in China itself now that it had been overrun by the Manchus. As Kim quoted the scholars:

At the present time the land of the gods [China, *shen-chou*] is submerged. The rank smell of fresh meat and fish [is there] as far as the eye can see. The spirits of the Ming emperors in Heaven have no place to descend to. But in our eastern land, in one barren place in the corner of the world, there are an altar and a shrine at which [the spirits of the Ming emperors] can just barely take refuge.[59]

They also insisted that there was no reason to abolish shrines in the countryside just because there was one in the palace.[60]

Kim's reply to these arguments reveals that the Mandongmyo problem was, indeed, closely related to the question of royal prestige in Korea. Kim reminded his readers that in the Chou dynasty, it was not proper for the small state of Lu to perform imperial sacrifice, something which Confucius himself, a native of Lu, had deplored. The feudal lords were also not allowed to make sacrifice for the Son of Heaven. Similarly, the Taewongun transferred the Ming shrine to the royal palace because only the Yi ruling house could rightfully perform rites to the fallen Ming dynasty. Kim also pointed out that the Mandongmyo was not as special as the scholars said it was. It had not housed any imperial tablets; "No

Politics and Policy in Traditional Korea

vessels of sacrificial wine and no incense was burned there. It had the appearance of a shrine, but there was no shrine there."[61] Kim's remarks thus reveal that the Taewongun objected to the control over an imperial shrine by local literati because it detracted from the Korean monarchy's monopoly over the symbols of dynastic legitimacy.

Another question which is somewhat more difficult to resolve is whether the abolition of the Mandongmyo was an attack on all scholars and all factions, or only a partial thrust against the Patriarch's faction. Circumstantial evidence supports the view that the Taewongun was motivated at least in part by personal animosity for the Patriarch's faction and favor for the Southerners. Throughout the interminable political battles of the late seventeenth century, there was a fairly consistent pattern of division among political factions, scholarly groups, and geographical regions. Song Si-yŏl, a member of the broad category of Westerners and later founder of the Patriarch's faction, was usually associated with the literati of Ch'ungch'ong province and the tradition of scholarship which originated with Yulgok (Yi I).[62] On the opposite side of the fence were to be found the members of the Easterner splinter groups, in particular, the Southerners, the local literati from Kyŏngsang province, and the line of scholarship stemming from T'oegye (Yi Hwang).[63]

Of all the factional issues of the seventeenth century it was the dispute over the deposing of Sukchong's Queen Min which may be most germane to the problem of the Taewongun's bias. Sukchong's favorite palace concubine, a lady surnamed Chang (granted the title of Hŭibin in 1689), gave birth to his first son (later King Kyŏngjong, r. 1720-22) in 1688. In 1689, when Sukchong deposed Queen Min, Song Si-yŏl opposed Sukchong's investiture of lady Chang's son as heir to the throne, providing the Southerner faction an opportunity to outflank him by supporting Sukchong. In 1689 Song and the Patriarch's faction were purged from office, the Southerners took their place, and Song was given poison while he was being brought to the capital under arrest.[64]

The Southerners who were closely associated with Queen Min's deposition and the purge of the Patriarch's faction in 1689, Mok Nae-sŏn and Yi Hyŏn-il,[65] were two of the people who were posthumously absolved of criminality in the early part of Kojong's reign. Members of the Southerner faction were also appointed to high office during the 1860s.[66] And in addition to the abolition of the Mandongmyo, on August 12, 1873, the king approved a request from students at the National Academy that the Taewongun henceforth be honored with the title Great Patriarch (taero). Because of a taboo against the use by a subject of any title associated with royalty, the signboard over the shrine to Song Si-yŏl at Yŏju inscribed with the words Great Patriarch (*taero*) had to be changed.[67] Although Kim Kyu-rak implied in his memoirs that the Taewongun was disturbed about factionalism in general, and not just the Patriarch's faction, one would still have to agree with the observation of Hwang Hyŏn that the Taewongun intended to cut the Patriarch's faction down to size.[68]

On June 25, 1865, shortly after the dowager-regent's decree of April 24 abolishing the Mandongmyo, the first salvo of literati protest was fired by a fourth deputy commander (*puhogun*), Im Hŏn-hoe. Im's argument conformed rather closely to the summary of literati protest made by Kim Kyu-rak. Im portrayed the Mandongmyo as an expression of the utmost sincerity of local scholars acting on their own initiative to express their gratitude to the Ming dynasty. King Chŏngjo had patronized it, and past officials had praised it. Even Kings Sukchong and Yŏngjo, who had established an altar in the palace to the Ming, had never shown any discrimination against shrines in the countryside. Palace altars and local shrines each had their own proper place—the existence of one did not justify the abolition of the other. Im agreed with the dowager that the Mandongmyo was run-down and decrepit, but he asked if this was not due to the court's neglect of it. Since the shrine had been in existence for one hundred and sixty-two years, to abolish it overnight simply left the scholars and people without any way to express their own private feelings of sincerity. While it was true that the depredations of the Hwayang Academy scholars and students on the local population were deplorable and should be rectified by the court, this was the fault of the scholars and not the shrine. Im's request for rescission of the order, however, was disallowed.[69]

The protest was intermittent but persistent, the court documents revealing only the tip of the iceberg of repressed literati resentment, which was to emerge more clearly in late 1873. A scholar from Ch'ungch'ŏng province submitted a memorial on September 15,[70] and on January 12, 1866, 1,468 scholars from Kyŏngsang province signed a petition for the restoration of the Mandongmyo.[71] This memorial was particularly significant, since it came from a region that had opposed the Patriarch's faction and Ch'ungch'ŏng scholars in the seventeenth century. The abolition of the Mandongmyo was such a clear-cut case of monarchical attack on scholarly interests that factional differences were dropped as all literati coalesced in opposition to the throne.

On November 27, 1867, a minor official suggested that the abolition of the Mandongmyo would weaken Korea's reputation in the world as a civilized country. Even though Korea was small and isolated, she was known to the world as a small China. It was all right to punish the unruly scholars of Ch'ungch'ŏng, but this did not justify the abolition of the shrine.[72] As this memorial reveals, the literati were for the most part heavily committed to Chinese culture, for it gave them and their country status in the world, and it made them part of a universal civilization. Since they had suffered grievously at the hands of the Manchus, whom they regarded as cultural barbarians anyway, contemporary China meant much less to them than the remote and idealized Ming. The appeals to Chinese culture and loyalty to the Ming were abstractions that stood higher in the scheme of values than the Korean king's right to issue orders and demand obedience. In fact, however, abstract ideals, cultural values, and political and economic interests were intertwined. The literati believed in what they were saying, but they also used cultural and moral appeals as a weapon against the throne and as a means for the preservation of more concrete interests.

Eventually the throne had to do something to dampen the protests of the literati; not, however, by acquiescing to literati demands for the restoration of the Mandongmyo, but by making the performance of rites at the shrine to the Ming emperor part of the king's permanent responsibility. On April 9, 1867, the king decreed that it was the duty of the throne to allow the descendants of those righteous and loyal individuals who died in battle against the Manchus to participate in the rituals to the Ming emperors at the royal altar. Because of the loyalty and merit of Crown Prince Sohyŏn and Grand Lord Inp'yŏng (the partrilineal ancestor of the Taewongun)[73]—sons of King Injo (r. 1623-49)—at the time of the Manchu invasions in 1636, their descendants were allowed to participate in the rituals.[74] This was undoubtedly a sop to those literati who had petitioned in 1864 for the establishment of a separate shrine to Grand Lord Inp'yŏng and a means of exalting the Taewongun's ancestry.[75] Finally, on April 29, 1871, during the height of the campaign against the private academies, Kojong personally performed rites at the Altar for Great Retribution for the first time in his reign.[76]

The Private Academies

1866 and 1867 were busy years for the dynasty because of the General Sherman incident, the French expedition to Kanghwa Island, and the persecution of Catholics. Undoubtedly the Taewongun had to set aside his concern about the private academies during these years until quieter times allowed him the opportunity for more action.

On October 18, 1868, without any prior discussion at court, the king ordered that all students in excess of fixed quotas for the academies be returned to military service; that all land granted to the academies for the maintenance of sacrificial ceremonies be registered as taxpaying land by the Tribute Bureau; that no new construction of academies be permitted; that ritual sacrifice only be allowed at chartered academies; and that the post of academy director (*wŏnjang*) be taken over by the district magistrate.[77] The first three provisions were little more than a repetition of the dowager-regent's edict of September 17, 1864, indicating that there had been little compliance with these provisions. The last two, however, represented a further tightening of the screws of government regulation.

Even these measures, however, did not achieve the curtailment of academy power that the Taewongun was seeking. On October 4, 1870, the king issued another edict which stated that the chartered academies were being controlled hereditarily by the descendants (of the founders?). They had formed cliques which were doing great harm to the common people. If the state were to leave them alone, it would lead to the dissolution of the polity itself. Kojong ordered that any chartered academies which were guilty of acts of oppression—notwithstanding the fact that they possessed charters from former kings—would be destroyed and their sacrificial tablets would be buried. He noted that this order was in accordance with a directive issued by the Taewongun.[78]

The pressure from the throne was unrelenting. On April 28, 1871, the day before Kojong first performed rites to the Ming emperors at the palace altar, he expressed further dissatisfaction with the conduct of rites by individual academies. He stated that this was not in accordance with the practice of ancient China, that there were anywhere from four to six places conducting rites to an individual, and that too many academies had been founded in honor of local worthies and too many royal charters had been granted to them. He ordered that there should be only one shrine to a person, whether they had charters or not, and that the Ministry of Rites present a list of duplicate academies to the Taewongun for approval. Only those people worthy of posthumous rites would be so respected, and all other shrines would be abolished. In the future, any persons noted for learning in the Way would be honored in academies devoted to learning, and any noted for their loyalty and virtue would be honored in academies devoted to loyal persons. These were to be permanent regulations incorporated into the newly revised *Convenient Reference to the Five Categories of Rites* (*Orye p'yŏn'go*).[79] The investigation of the Ministry of Rites subsequently revealed that there were 1,700 shrines, two thirds of which were duplicate shrines to the same individual.[80]

On May 1, when Kojong was performing a ceremony at the National Academy, he summoned a group of scholars and students and repeated the order of the twenty-eighth, adding that people should not be enshrined anywhere until a hundred generations had passed without change in public opinion as to their merit. He again served notice that in the future there would no longer be indiscriminate permission granted for the founding of academies.[81]

A conversation between Kojong and Chief State Councilor Kim Pyŏng-hak on May 5, indicates not only that the initiative for policy on academies had come from the Taewongun, but also that the high officials had been bypassed in the process. Kim told Kojong that he had not had a chance to hear of the admonitions that Kojong had given to the students at the National Academy. Kojong repeated the gist of the remarks to him, adding that the erection of shrines to living people had been most inappropriate. He also told Kim that the Taewongun had his mind set on this policy right from the beginning of the reign in 1864, when he rejected the request of certain scholars for the construction of an academy in honor of Grand Lord Inp'yŏng. Kim dutifully agreed with the king that the Taewongun's policy was, indeed, a wise one.[82]

The failure to consult the high officials in this matter was certainly indicative of the more arbitrary exercise of monarchical power during this period. It also illustrates the flexibility of the governmental structure. It was not necessary for strong kings to change the structure of government to alter the relationship between throne and bureaucracy. The locus of real power—whether in the throne or the high officials—depended on actual circumstances and not on any legalistic prescriptions regarding the process by which decisions were made. High officials simply adapted themselves to the style of the ruler.

In the next week, the decisions of April 28 were followed by a number of edicts. Kojong decreed that only men honored at the shrine to Confucius could have rites performed for them in the academies, and that permission for the honoring of truly loyal and virtuous men would only be granted after it was clear that there were no rites performed for them elsewhere. The minister of rites was instructed to report such matters to the Taewongun.[83] The minister reported back with instructions from the Taewongun. Rites were to be conducted only at the shrine to Confucius and at shrines in forty-seven academies that had been in existence for a hundred years. In all other cases, rites were to be discontinued and royal signboards taken back.[84] On May 14, Kojong told his officials during an audience that tax exemptions had been granted to academies in excess and ordered the minister of taxation to petition the Taewongun as to the means of rectifying this. High officials like Kim Pyŏng-hak and Hong Sun-mok expressed their agreement.[85]

As we have seen elsewhere, however, royal edicts did not ensure full implementation, and on September 30, the king complained that local officials had been lax in reporting the destruction of all academies in

The Abolition of Private Academies

excess of the authorized forty-seven. He accused them of trying to avoid trouble and ordered the investigation of all governors and magistrates who had failed to carry out orders. Kojong also said that he had heard that the academies had avoided the order by changing their names to lecture halls (kangdang). He ordered that such places should also be investigated and eliminated.[86]

The testimony of the Taewongun's private secretary, Kim Kyu-rak, tends to corroborate the evidence provided by the official record as to the motives of the Taewongun in taking the action he did against shrines and academies. Kim explicitly mentioned the Taewongun's concern about the fiscal and political problems involved with these institutions. He also estimated that the number of tax-exempt households attached to private academies and shrines ranged anywhere from fifty to three hundred households per institution.[87] Furthermore, Kim wrote that the academy students wasted their time in frivolity and the academies oppressed the people with their notorious black warrants (hŭkp'ae)—the orders that they issued to the local populace. "The officials could not check or restrain them, and the people could not support themselves (against them)."[88] According to Kim, the Taewongun gave due warning to the academies that he was serious. He bagan by reducing the number of student support personnel (yubo) and issuing admonitions to students about their behavior.[89] Only when the situation failed to improve did he order shrines to local worthies abolished completely.

Kim praised the Taewongun's actions against the scholars. When they showed up en masse at the National Academy to protest government policy, he sent them away with instructions to "go home, read their books, expend all their efforts in self-cultivation, and not strive for reputation in the outside world and interfere in the orders of the court."[90] Those who obtusely and stubbornly persisted in their protest he drove outside the boundaries of the capital. As Kim put it, "If orders had not been given in a courageous and resolute way . . . , then how could anything ever have been determined and brought to completion?"[91]

There could have been no better illustration of monarchical distemper and discontent with scholars in a state which was supposed to rest on the firm foundations provided by an intellectual elite. But in a Confucian state, the intellectual underpinnings of society and polity could not be neglected. As Kim Kyu-rak pointed out in his memoir, the private academies were an anomaly; the system of official schools, the model for which was provided in the Chou-li, was supposed to be the prime vehicle for education. Accordingly, after the Taewongun abolished the private academies, he took steps to upgrade the district schools and the National Academy. He repaired the buildings of the academy and added four dormitories to it, and he also directed local authorities to "select scholars of diligence and application in self-cultivation to be local educational officials."[92] Kim was referring to the set of regulations for the rectification of the official school system promulgated on November 2, 1869. These were submitted by the state council, but judging from Kim Kyu-rak's account, at the behest of the Taewongun. These regulations were designed to ensure student attendance at the National Academy and make it a more prestigious institution. The models for academy regulations were to be taken from those of Chu Hsi's *Pai-lu-t'ung shu-yŭan* and the *Regulations for Schools (Hakkyo samok)* and *Models for Schools (Hakkyo mobŏm)* drawn up by Yulgok in the sixteenth century.[93] Daily and weekly examinations of students both in and outside the academy were to be held, and the best students would be reported to the throne. Dormitory students who failed to appear for examinations without a legitimate excuse were to be suspended. Three students were to be selected at the spring and autumn examination and allowed to proceed directly to the second-level reexamination in the *munkwa* test.[94]

Furthermore, in recognition of the fact that the National Academy and official schools could not ferret out completely the best scholars in the realm, a regulation in the *Soktaejŏn* of 1746 that provided for a stepladder system of recommendation was reinstituted. Each village in a province would recommend one man to the provincial governor who would then select the best two men for examination. The governor would personally conduct a written examination and send the results to the state council. The best scholars were then to be given rewards and their names sent to the Ministry of Personnel for appointment to office.[95]

It is difficult to estimate how successful this policy was in recruiting men of talent. It was certainly of limited effectiveness in soothing the ruffled feelings of the local literati who continued to be alienated from the Taewongun's regime. But, as the events of late 1873 demonstrate, it did succeed in creating a group of loyal supporters for him among the students of the National Academy who leaped to his defense when his policies came under attack.

The Taewongun's Pyrrhic Victory

The history of the rise and fall of the private academies and shrines in the Yi dynasty reflected the major trends in the struggle between monarchy and aristocracy for authority. In the early fifteenth century, the central government was in command and the strength of the state school system was at its zenith. By the late fifteenth and early sixteenth centuries, the decline of central authority stimulated the rise of private

The Abolition of Private Academies

initiative in education at the local level. The sixteenth century was the period in which private initiative in education and thought was institutionalized in the academies and shrines, which continued to grow in number until the middle of the eighteenth century. From the mid- to late eighteenth century, a reaction against this set in as the throne tried to limit the academies. From 1800-1864, when the throne was dominated by the consort clans, there was a swing back toward local control, but in the same period, the power of the bureaucratic factions was weakened. From 1864-73, under the strong leadership of the Taewongun, who was under pressure from the threat of foreign invasion and rebellion, the exercise of monarchical power reached its greatest extent, and the shrines and academies were eliminated as a meaningful institution in Yi dynasty life.

There were two aspects to the rise and fall of the shrines and academies: the material and the spiritual. As the academies grew in number they became corporate institutions with political and economic power. They competed with the central government for control over land and population. In this respect they became a direct threat to monarchical authority, and the restrictions imposed on their power in the eighteenth century and in the 1860s by the throne were designed to eliminate this source of fiscal and political competition.

The spiritual aspect of the private academies and shrines is a much more subtle problem because it is intimately bound up with the role played by Confucian thought and the Confucian-educated scholar in Korean society. Confucian ideas and Confucian education in a Chinese-style monarchical system were naturally used by the monarchy to gain the loyalty of intellectuals and divert them to the politically harmless activity of study and self-cultivation. One sees this quite clearly in the Ch'ing dynasty in China where an alien ruling class used Confucianism in a much more explicitly utilitarian way to reduce Chinese opposition to Manchu rule. A similar phenomenon occurred in the Tokugawa period in Japan where Confucian thought was used to domesticate the warrior class and convert it to an obedient bureaucracy. In the Yi dynasty, however, Confucianism was an important weapon of the yangban bureaucrat and local scholar, used to reinforce their own standing in society and check monarchical authority. The scholar in particular used the appeal to Confucian piety to justify the independent and semi-autonomous existence of his private educational institutions. The degree of success that was possible in this regard, however, was limited and defined by the very nature of Confucian thought and the relationship of yangban-scholar-bureaucrats to monarchical and state authority and structures. The this-worldly nature of Confucian philosophical humanism and the semireligious aspect of Confucian symbolism meant that there was no clear-cut division between the spiritual and temporal. Confucianism contained concepts of the world of the spirit and the existence of superordinate Heaven, but it lacked a notion of omnipotent deity. Confucian scholars could appeal to Heaven, spirits of deceased sages, and overriding moral principles in their contest with monarchical power, but these were much vaguer and weaker than appeals to God, Christ, or the pope. And since the monarch shared these symbols and made his own appeals to them for legitimacy, scholars could not gain a monopoly over these spiritual symbols.

The scholar could never become the exclusive representative of divinity on earth; he could never become an unquestioned interpreter of divine purpose on earth—in short, he could never become a priest, and lacking the status and role of priest the scholar could never create an institutional complex like "the church" separated clearly from temporal authority. In the contest with the throne for authority and the religious symbols of authority, the scholar stood at a disadvantage when compared with the prelates of Western European countries after the tenth century. Despite this inherent weakness, however, the Korean scholar-aristocrat milked his religio-educational institutions for all they were worth. And because the throne shared the same symbols and sought to use them for its own purposes, it was enticed into a position from which it was most difficult to retreat.

The upsurge in shrine and academy building which took place in the sixteenth and seventeenth centuries seemed to most monarchs to fit in with their hopes for the dissemination of an ethic which stressed loyalty to king and superior. But their hopes were frustrated because they focused on the peasant, or more accurately, the vague and undifferentiated mass of "the people," as the object of indoctrination. The monarchy lost sight of the aristocracy in between. Not only did the throne lose a degree of economic and political control to the academies, it also surrendered a degree of its monopoly over religious symbols of legitimacy. It surrendered to private persons not only the right to organize educational institutions but also the right to perpetuate ritual ceremonies to the sanctified spirits of past culture heroes and idealized Ming emperors. The Taewongun's abolition of the Mandongmyo was as much an attempt by the throne to reestablish its monopoly over theocratic symbols and religious legitimacy as it was an attack on the private political and economic power of the yangban-scholar. While the Taewongun's abolition of the shrines and academies was a victory of the monarchy over a major bastion of literati privilege, it was, however, a Pyrrhic victory. The strength of the aristocracy was based on diffuse considerations, rather than on discrete corporate institutions like academies and shrines. Private academies and shrines were in any case preserves of local literati and not of the aristocracy as a whole. Abolishing them was

The Abolition of Private Academies

tantamount to treating the symptoms and not the cause of elite power. While the Taewongun imposed the household tax on the yangban, re-arranged the distribution of political power among their factions, and robbed them of their academies, he never did identify the aristocracy as the main enemy of the centralized state. Their privileged position in the control of land and office holding was preserved.

Thus, the very totality of his victory over the academies and shrines constituted an affront to the group whose support would be needed to govern if it were not to be eliminated. The rural scholars were alienated en masse and many bureaucrats shared their views. The unity that the Taewongun had achieved by his antiforeignism was split asunder as some of the most vocal of the Yi dynasty intelligentsia turned against him, helped ease him out of power in 1874, and raised a clamor for the reversal of his policies. It is all the more to the Taewongun's credit that even after he retired, the private academy did not reemerge as a powerful institution, but the conservative reaction that was triggered by his success in this regard helped put a stop to the trends he had set in motion.

Finally, it must be recognized that the struggle over academies and shrines did not revolve around the same problems plaguing officials in China in the same period. There was no debate over incorporating Western language and science into the curriculum or creating Western types of schools. These questions were not raised in Korea until the 1880s. The Taewongun and the scholars were agreed on the content of education: theirs was a struggle for authority and control that arose out of conflicts inherent in traditional society.

7

Reform of the Grain Loan System

The preservation of aristocratic power and privilege in the Yi dynasty was purchased at the price of a regressive tax structure and a contracted revenue base. Forced to the wall in an almost desperate search for revenue, the government risked the violation of Confucian values and sensibilities when it began to utilize interest on state-sponsored grain loans as a means of supplementing its income, converting an institution devoted to the relief and welfare of the peasantry into one geared to the exploitation of the peasantry. Because some means had to be found to disguise the moral contradiction involved in this policy, the government maintained the fiction that it was operating a relief and loan system when in fact it had created a new kind of tax. Officials in the central government also deluded themselves with the idea that the evils of the grain loan system were due mainly to corruption—forced loans and unauthorized usury. They blamed corrupt magistrates and clerks for peasant oppression and held themselves innocent of any complicity; in fact, however, the central government had become a willing partner in a scheme to fleece the peasant. The government's self-deception only delayed the day of reckoning by postponing remedial action. When it was revealed that the grain loan system was a major cause of the peasant rebellion of 1862, the government then had to acknowledge that it had a serious institutional problem on its hands, and not merely a matter of bureaucratic corruption.

One of the objectives of the grain loan reform of the 1860s was to alleviate peasant distress caused by forced loans, corrupt administration, and usurious interest rates, and thereby to eliminate one of the major causes of peasant rebellion. The Taewongun succeeded in ameliorating these problems by debt cancellation and by transferring administrative responsibility for grain loans from the local magistrates to local notables, but he was also unable or unwilling to discontinue the use of interest on

Reform of the Grain Loan System

peasant loans for revenue purposes. His policy therefore relates to the problem of elite power and privilege in two ways: the Taewongun was forced to continue his reliance on loan interest because of an inflexible, restrictive tax base that was the product of the hierarchical social system; and by continuing to rely on loan interest revenues the government relieved the pressure for imposing greater taxes on the yangban, either by capitation or land levies. Thus, when the Taewongun had to choose between three partially conflicting alternatives—state revenue, peasant relief, and yangban privilege—he at first sought to balance the needs of the first two without damaging the economic position of the latter, thereby preserving the status quo in social and economic relations. Eventually, however, he chose to subordinate peasant needs to state and yangban requirements, and he also failed to achieve a permanent solution to the problems of credit, relief, and usury.

The Taewongun's solution for the grain loan problem was also consistent with one wing of reformist thought that had developed since the seventeenth century, what I call the pragmatic-statist orientation, which placed priority on the maintenance of state revenue through the utilization of interest on loans, reliance on administrative or institutional reform to eliminate corruption, and tolerance or protection of yangban economic interests.

The other wing of reformist thought—the moralistic-popular welfare approach—emphasized the subordination of state interests to the welfare of the people either by the removal of interest on grain loans or by the elimination of official grain loans altogether. In some instances the reformists advocated refunding relief loans by an expansion of tax revenues that would have even sacrificed yangban interests to popular needs. Although the Taewongun did make popular welfare one of his objectives for reform, he did not do so for moralistic or idealistic reasons but for the practical objective of preventing peasant rebellion, and he was unwilling to abandon the use of interest on grain loans as a means of subsidizing the financial requirements of the state.

Loans and Grain Reserves

Unfortunately the utilization of state grain stocks for revenue purposes interfered with the important reserve and relief functions of those stocks. The Yi dynasty economy was overwhelmingly dependent on agricultural production, which was susceptible to fluctuations in natural conditions. The government had to assume responsibility for storing grain for relief purposes during the famine periods, ensuring adequate provisions for the military in case of war, providing funds for commodity price stabilization operations, and furnishing seed and working capital in the form of food loans to peasants to tide them over the planting season. There were thus four main functions of the grain storage system in the Yi dynasty: relief, military provisions, price stabilization, and working capital loans. The government made some attempt at the rationalization of the grain storage system by establishing separate institutions to handle each of the four functions. At the provincial and district levels there were three types of granary: the Ever-Normal Granaries (sangp'yŏngch'ang) for price stabilization, the Military Provision Granaries (kunjach'ang), and the Righteous Granaries (ŭich'ang) for relief and ordinary loans.[1] Central coordination was provided in the capital by the Military Provisions Agency (kunjagam), the Ever-Normal Agency (sangp'yŏngch'ŏng), and the Relief Agency (chinhyŏlch'ŏng).[2]

Because of immediate needs and special conditions, however, it was very difficult to maintain functionally separate grain reserve and loaning systems. In normal years when there was little demand for relief but serious demand for seed and working capital, relief grain and ever-normal reserves were loaned to peasants. Since there was little demand for military provisions during the long period of peace that prevailed in the late Yi dynasty, military reserves were also converted for use in relief and lending.[3] The reserves of the price stabilization system were also diverted to ordinary lending operations. This ever-normal system, which was copied from Chinese institutions, was designed to maintain fairly constant commodity and grain prices. When there was a bumper crop and the price of grain fell, the state was supposed to use its cloth reserves to purchase rice on the market at a price higher than the current market price. Conversely, when there was a poor crop and the price of grain was high, the state would sell its grain reserves for cloth at a price lower than the current market price. But this system presupposed at least some commercialization of agriculture and a relatively well-developed market system, both of which were lacking in the early to mid-Yi dynasty. Therefore, despite the existence of a discrete ever-normal granary system, it was usually underfunded and its price stablization operations were often taken over by the Righteous Granaries in the district towns. At best price stabilization activities of the Ever-Normal Granaries were confined to a few market towns, and its reserves were frequently used for relief and loan purposes, since there was frequent demand for the former and constant demand for the latter.[4]

There was one other factor that led to the practice of lending reserves from all the state's granaries. In order to prevent rotting and spoilage old grain had to be exchanged for new. Rather than carry out this exchange at harvest time it seemed quite logical to loan the old grain out during the winter or spring planting season and replenish the stocks in the fall when the harvest was in.[5]

Since the contracted fiscal base of the late Yi dynasty did not produce

Reform of the Grain Loan System

adequate surplus revenues to enable the independent financing of relief and reserve operations, the government chose to rely on loans as the chief method of refunding the relief and reserve systems. Not only did this appear to be eminently practical, it also conformed to the time-honored tradition in both China and Korea of treating relief as loans rather than as nonrepayable grants. While the state did dispense direct grants of relief in times of famine, the fact remains that despite all the rhetoric about the compassion of sage rulers in dispensing relief to starving peasants, when given a choice the state preferred to loan grain rather than give it away. Unfortunately the use of loans for refunding purposes was based on a fallacy—that the impoverished peasants in need of relief could produce the surplus for state reserves that the restricted fiscal system was incapable of providing. At best the peasants could repay only a fraction of their obligations; in the worst of times they could repay nothing at all.[6] The government, however, refused to acknowledge these truths.

This contradiction produced several very serious effects. The continued use of loans for reserves and relief delayed the search for a fundamental solution to the problem of the independent financing of relief and reserve requirements through tax reform. The fiscal system became more regressive than before because the poorest peasant was obliged to maintain relief, loan, and military reserves, but reserves were continually being depleted because of the inability of the peasants to repay their debts. Furthermore, local officials became more corrupt because unrealistic obligations were imposed on the district magistrate for the collection of principal and interest.

The Use of Loan Interest for
Refunding and Revenue

In the early part of the dynasty, grain loans from the Righteous Granaries and Military Provision Granaries were given out to the peasants interest-free.[7] Of course, the government tried to keep the interest rate low. In 1423, when the Righteous Granary system was refunded, the new regulations required only a 2 percent interest charge on loans to make up for incidental losses in handling and storage.[8] When it became evident in the mid-fifteenth century that relief and other reserves could not be replenished by this means, the government concluded that the problem could be solved by raising interest rates, even though it had already been demonstrated that the peasants were incapable of repaying the principal, let alone the interest.

The utilization of interest by the state passed through three stages of development. In the first stage interest was used as a means of ensuring adequate repayment of the loan or reserve funds. By the middle of the Yi dynasty, however, portions of the interest payments were then taken for the expenses of the district magistrate, as revenue for the Ministry of Taxation, and as capital for the Ever-Normal Granaries. The final stage came when the government expanded grain loan operations beyond the Righteous and Military Provision Granaries and freely granted the right to loan reserves and collect interest to almost any government agency. Provincial governors' yamen, post-stations, military garrisons, and even bureaus of the central government in the capital were given permission to make loans to peasants.

The first step in this process ironically began as part of the experimental application of Chu Hsi's village granary (*sach'ang*) system in ten select districts between 1451 and 1470—a system which was originally devised to benefit the people, and not the state.[9] To be sure, Chu Hsi's original intention and the aim of the Korean officials in levying a 20 percent interest charge in 1451 was not to accumulate revenue for the state, but to create a surplus for refunding the grain loan reserve itself. Viewed in perspective, however, the unprecedented 20 percent rate of 1451 represented an acknowledgment by the government of the failure of non-interest or low-interest bearing loans to maintain a permanent reserve and of the need for adequate interest charges for reserve maintenance purposes.[10] Raising the interest rate, however, was no guarantee that the peasants would be any better able to make repayment. As a matter of fact, the village granary system was opposed at this time on the grounds that the Righteous Granaries already granted interest-free loans and that the collection of interest would mean that only the rich would be able to afford borrowing grain while the poor would get nothing.[11]

The 20 percent interest charge of the village granary system was followed in 1458 by a 40 percent charge on grain loaned from the Military Provision Granaries. The rate was reduced in 1460 to 20 percent to bring it into line with the village granary rate.[12] These direct and relatively high interest charges passed out of use by 1471.[13] By the end of the century, however, the 2 percent wastage surcharge (*mogok*) of 1423-24 had been raised to 10 percent and that remained the legal rate on grain loans for the rest of the dynasty.[14] One scholar suggests that the rate was legalized at 10 percent because officials were actually collecting that much anyway, despite the 2 percent limitation, and that legalization was designed to prevent extortion in excess of 10 percent.[15] The 10 percent surcharge had been tacitly approved by the government even prior to its legalization on the grounds that the magistrate's salary was insufficient for his needs. After the legalization of the 10 percent rate, the income from it did not immediately become part of the central government's revenues. It was left to the local magistrate to dispose of as he saw fit.

By the mid-sixteenth century officials began to consider taking a share of the wastage surcharge for other purposes, and by the early seventeenth century the government had begun to assign 10 percent of the surcharge, or 1 percent on principal, to the Ministry of Taxation. This 1 percent portion was called a recording fee (*hoerok*) and its inauguration marked the second stage in the transformation of grain loans from instruments of relief to sources of revenue for the state.[16]

After the Manchu invasions of 1636 the government decided to take an additional 3 percent on principal as a separate recording fee to be used to defray the expenses of Ch'ing and Yi dynasty envoys.[17] In 1650 the special 3 percent portion was transferred to the Ever-Normal Agency at the capital that had been given jurisdiction over envoys' expenses as well as price stabilization operations.[18] The 3 percent Ever-Normal Agency recording fee together with the 1 percent Ministry of Taxation fee left only 6 percent interest on loans for the use of the district magistrate. The new 3 percent charge also triggered an expansion in the use of loans by other government agencies for meeting their expenses.[19]

The government then increased the proportion of interest taken out as recording fees, and in the 1746 law code a schedule of varying rates of recording fees was established in accordance with the size of the loan funds of any district yamen. In all cases the Ministry of Taxation recording fee amounted to 1 percent of the principal of any loan, but the Ever-Normal Agency fee varied from zero to 5.7 percent. The amount available to magistrates of large districts was less than it had been before, the central government had a greater stake in the grain loan system as a source of revenue, and more pressure was brought to bear on magistrates for supplementing their income by irregular means.[20]

The third stage in the development of state utilization of grain loan interest came when the system was expanded beyond the level of the district magistrate. Because of revenue shortages produced by Hideyoshi's invasions in the 1590s and the Manchu invasions of 1637, both civil and military yamen and garrisons began to loan out their grain stocks at interest in order to raise funds. In 1672 measures were also approved for using loan interest to fund mountain fortresses, the so-called *sansŏng hwan'gok* (mountain fortress grain loans).[22] By the eighteenth century almost every government office whether in the provinces or the capital was loaning out its grain reserves at interest. In 1716 the Office of the Censor-General complained that even the state council and the Office of Ministers-without-Portfolio were engaged in this practice. Governors, magistrates, and border military commanders personally permitted loans. Provincial authorities borrowed cash from administrative agencies in the capital under the pretext that they needed the money for relief, but in fact they loaned it out at interest.[23]

The profitability of loans as a source of revenue had become too great

Politics and Policy in Traditional Korea

Breakdown of grain loan interest allocation.
by percentage

District	Ministry of Taxation recording fee	Ever-Normal Agency recording fee	Interest for district mag.
10,000 sŏk loan fund, or more	1	5.7	3.3
6-10,000 sŏk loan fund	1	4.0	5.0
3-6,000 sŏk loan fund	1	3.5	10.0
0-3,000 sŏk loan fund	1	0	9.0
Kyŏnggi and Hwanghae provinces	All was allocated as a border defense recording fee		
P'yŏng'an province	All was allocated as a recording fee[21]		

for the government to discontinue the system. It was not until the late eighteenth century, however, that restraint was cast aside in favor of the full and complete exploitation of loans at interest for state purposes. In 1725 the national total of grain loan reserves was 416,900 sŏk, but by 1776 this had tripled to 1,377,000 sŏk. By 1807 the national total reached the astronomical figure of 9,995,599 sŏk.[24]

By this time there were different types of loan funds depending on the reserve requirements (see tabulation). Grain loan granaries were spread throughout the country at the district and the subdistrict or *myŏn* levels. According to one report there were as many as two hundred in Kyŏnggi province alone.[25]

Interest on 6,699,499 sŏk of grain came to 727,028 sŏk; 612,164 sŏk was spent leaving a surplus of 114,863 sŏk.[28] The grain loan funds as well as the interest from them were assigned to agencies of the central government in the capital, capital guards, provincial governors' and army and navy commanders' yamens, local garrisons and post stations, and certain high-ranking district magistrates' yamen. Of the 3.7 million sŏk of no-reserve grain alone, the following agencies in the capital had jurisdiction over about one million sŏk.

Reform of the Grain Loan System

Types of grain loan in 1797

Reserve requirement[26]	Amount
no reserve	3,751,660 sŏk
1/2 reserve	4,937,800
2/3 reserve	372,940
1/3 reserve	500
varying reserve requirements	41,720
	9,104,620
no reserve[27]	3,746,154
1/2 reserve	2,686,039
fixed amounts loaned out	40,105
2/3 reserve	125,314
1/3 reserve	335
1/4 reserve	102,550
Total	6,699,499 [6,700,497]
Grand total, all grain loan funds	9,369,777

Despite the reserve requirements, figures for 1807 show that of the total of 9,995,599 sŏk of grain in the loan funds 7,308,319 sŏk was loaned out.[30]

Comparison with the rice revenues of the Ministry of Taxation and Tribute Bureau will give a rough idea of the enormity of the grain loan revenues in the period 1797-1807. While large amounts of cash and cloth were also taken in by these agencies, they will not be considered here because of the difficulty in converting them to rice equivalents. In 1807 the Ministry of Taxation's rice revenue came to 117,000 sŏk,[31] and the maxi-

Grain loan funds of central government agencies (in sŏk)[29]

Agency	No-reserve grain loan fund	All grain loan funds
Tribute Bureau	4,160	110,000
Ever-Normal-Relief Agency	169,622	2,491,392
Equal Service Agency	232,901	511,443
Border Defense Command	582,661	2,438,713
Ministry of Taxation	35,179	793,194
Ministry of Punishments and Seoul Magistracy	892	892

mum possible rice tribute of the Tribute Bureau was probably under 200,000 sŏk.[32] These were maximum, not average figures, yet the income from grain loan interest in the same period was three to four times this total.

One cannot help but wonder how the state was able to accumulate such a vast reserve of grain for loan purposes when the evidence from previous centuries shows a high rate of defaulting on loans and difficulty in refunding reserves. Only one explanation seems feasible: the figure of ten million sŏk of grain loan and reserve funds was a fiction. The government pawned what reserves it had for a yearly 10 percent return on its investment. A fictional reserve was maintained on paper and theoretically principal was recalled yearly along with interest. In fact, however, the bulk of the principal was probably left outstanding, masking the large percentage of nonrepaid and nonrepayable debts. The reserve system was bankrupted, but the government closed its eyes to this as long as it continued to collect the annual 10 percent interest payments. Because interest was not ploughed back into the system but was diverted for funding general administrative expenses, there was even less chance that the relief reserve could be maintained. Put another way, the interest on grain loans was converted into a permanent tax (the original loans having long since been forgotten), but it was a tax which was obtained at the sacrifice of reserves. When the country suffered from recurrent famine conditions after 1800, the government was hard put to meet the demand for relief. Grain stocks had to be shifted from one province to another or allocated from central government revenue agencies, and much use was made of the sale of blank office warrants and private contributions to provide relief to the starving.[33]

Violations of Confucian Sensibilities

The use of interest on loans for revenue and profit created problems for many scholars and bureaucrats because it constituted a violation of Confucian moral prescriptions. The virtuous man was not supposed to dirty his hands in the marketplace. How much less was a sage ruler to engage in profit-seeking manipulations particularly when it was done at the expense of the common peasant? The use of loans at interest by the state also smacked of the type of centralized authoritarian rule that was anathema to moralistic Confucians. Wang An-shih, a kind of anti-Christ to some neo-Confucian Korean thinkers because of his legalistic manipulations of state institutions, had used crop loans at interest back in the Sung dynasty.[34] State loans were justified on the grounds that state interest rates were lower than the usurious rates of private lenders, but because this argument had also been used by Wang An-shih, it did not produce much of a defense against the criticisms of the moralists who regarded Wang's motives as suspect.

Reform of the Grain Loan System

On the other hand, Chu Hsi, the virtual founder of what had become philosophic orthodoxy by the Yi dynasty, had authorized the use of interest on loans in his village granary system, albeit as a means of refunding the grain reserve and not as a means of providing for regular state expenses. The respect for Chu Hsi by Korean Confucians helps explain the contradiction in the reform recommendations of some scholar-officials that loans had to be abolished because of the evils of interest and the oppressiveness of the loaning system, while relief and credit at the village level could be operated by Chu Hsi's village granary system, which indeed did depend on interest for refunding.[35]

Thus the debate over grain loans had an ideological dimension that made the search for solutions on rational grounds alone more difficult. The fact that state loans with interest were regarded as evil by some led to frequent requests for the total abolition of the grain loan system. Since total abolition would have transferred a large burden to the regular fiscal structure for funding reserves and relief, it would have required the raising of tax rates and the imposition of heavier tax quotas on the lightly taxed sectors of the population—precisely those people who were politically most powerful. The government, however, was incapable of doing this. Instead it chose to write off bad debts while continuing to authorize the use of loans and interest. Writing off bad debts provided immediate relief to the indebted peasantry at the expense of the central government, but once the debts had been written off, the credit of the peasants was good again, and future expenses could be obtained by new loans at interest. Thus, the rigid and regressive tax structure based on aristocratic privilege forced the government into the utilization of a method of finance that was roundly condemned in Confucian literature.

Corruption as an Institutional
Not a Moral Problem

The grain loan system proved highly susceptible to administrative corruption, but not as a result of any particular decline in the moral standards of bureaucrats. On the contrary, the magistrate was *forced* to be corrupt by the irreconcilable contradictions in the government's policy. As explained above, it was unrealistic to expect the peasant to be able to repay loans even in the best of times, but rather than abandon loans and interest and expand the tax base the government found it easier to blame the district magistrate for the failure of the system. While the peasant borrower was indirectly responsible to the district magistrate for repayment of his principal and interest, the local officials were legally responsible for debt collection and grain reserve maintenance. Given the high rate of default on peasant debts, the only way the magistrate could meet revenue and reserve requirements was by manipulation of grain stocks, falsification of granary ledgers, and extortion. Corruption was necessary for the maintenance of the system, and it was not surprising that officials and clerks raked off what they could for themselves as well.

The magistrate forced loans on peasants who did not need them in order to obtain interest payments. He took advantage of territorial price variations to profit by shifting grain reserves from areas of glut to areas of shortage, selling off the grain at high prices and restocking at low prices. He used short measures in loaning out grain and filled the measures to overflowing in receiving repayment. And he manipulated cash-grain conversion rates to profit from loan transactions.[36] The point is not, however, that these deceptions were simply methods for private profit, but that they were forced on the magistrate as the only means of maintaining reserves which otherwise would have decreased over time because of basic peasant penury. Since the central government refused to take official cognizance of this simple fact, the magistrate had to keep records which upon inspection would reveal a full complement of grain in the granaries. Falsification of grain reserve records provides the only adequate explanation for the fantastic figure of ten million sŏk of grain reserves supposedly on hand in 1807. The government's willingness to treat falsified reserve figures as valid was the consummate piece of deception in the system founded on self-delusion. Because of the Confucian stigma attached to peasant exploitation, the government could not acknowledge its own responsibility, and instead made a scapegoat of the magistrate. It chose to treat the grain loan problem as one of maladministration and corruption rectifiable by stricter laws, greater surveillance, and harsher punishments.

The Pragmatic-Statist and the
Moralist-Popular Welfare Viewpoints

Since the seventeenth century there had been a spectrum of opinion on grain loan reform limited at either end by two sets of fairly distinct and opposed orientations which we might label the pragmatic-statist and the moralist-popular welfare viewpoints.[37] Scholar-officials of pragmatic orientation regarded loans as a legitimate means of administering welfare, attached no moral stigma to the use of interest, and sought to finance relief, reserves, and regular administrative expenditures out of income from interest on loans.[38] Although concerned with the welfare of the people, they felt that greater surveillance, stricter punishment for malfeasance, and greater rationalization of administrative procedures to eliminate corruption and falsification of records would serve to alleviate the oppression of the common people without sacrificing the opportunity for obtaining revenue through loan interest. Some of this group advocated the use of Chu Hsi's village granaries in order to put grain loan administration into the hands of villagers instead of the magistrates and their clerks as a means of eliminating bureaucratic corruption. But they also regarded the village granary system primarily as the means for preserving loan interest as a source of revenue for the state.

Reformers of the moralist-popular welfare orientation, on the contrary, regarded interest as intrinsically bad and state usury as an unmitigated evil. They saw the prime objective of grain reserves as providing relief rather than loans to the starving peasant. Some who were willing to tolerate a system of state-sponsored loans wanted them to be funded by a fiscally sounder and more responsible method based on the use of regular land or household taxes. The moralists were ambivalent on the question of bureaucratic corruption: some felt that it could be reformed through surveillance and punishment, while others felt that the bureaucracy had to be bypassed altogether, and in this regard they proposed the use of either the ever-normal or village granary systems. Some thought that the Ever-Normal Granaries could provide the ultimate solution to the grain loan problem and bureaucratic corruption by managing relief exclusively through price stabilization operations and abolishing the system of loans and interest altogether.

The ever-normal system, however, was designed to maintain a low price of rice and was based on the presupposition that the peasants had some cloth or cash reserves with which to buy rice. But the majority of impoverished or subsistence cultivators probably had little but grain and not enough of that. With few cash resources to buy rice during bad times even at artificially lowered prices, the peasant's need for relief could not possibly be solved by the ever-normal system alone. Some of its advocates who were aware of this problem also proposed that the ever-normal stocks could be used directly for relief purposes when the situation required it, but had such a system been tried, the ever-normal reserves would have been depleted by relief grants and its market operations paralyzed. One is therefore led to the conclusion that the advocates of the ever-normal system must have been more concerned about the welfare of salaried officials, petty functionaries, and soldiers at the capital and in major towns than they were about the peasants in the countryside.

The village granary system was also advocated by men of the moralist-popular welfare persuasion. What differentiated them from the pragmatic-statists in their support for village granaries was their plan for the use of interest on loans. Even though they usually disdained the use of interest in principle, they justified the use of it in village granaries on the grounds that the village granary system had been introduced by the exalted Chu Hsi, and that the major feature of Chu Hsi's system was the use of interest as a means of building up the relief reserve, and *not* as a source of revenue for the central government.

Given the fact, however, that the most conspicuous anomaly of the tax structure was the undertaxation of the privileged aristocracy, it would appear that the logical solution not only to the problem of financing relief loans, but also of financing central government expenditures in general would have been to expand taxation of the lightly taxed landowning aristocrats. In fact, however, the pragmatic-statists were not willing to increase state revenues at the expense of the aristocracy, and the moralist-popular welfarists were usually not willing to lighten the burdens on the peasantry by the same means. The essence of the pragmatist-statist position was that government in its search for revenue had to compromise with the existing reality of aristocratic privilege rather than pose a direct challenge to it. Interest on loans had been proved a worthy and necessary alternate source of revenue in a system founded on the preservation of tax privileges for the landowning aristocracy. The pragmatists by seeking to preserve the use of interest as a source of revenue were in effect perpetuating a system which exploited the poor peasant for the benefit of the state in order to maintain the privileges of the upper class intact.

A few of the moralists came closest to an attack on aristocratic privilege in advocating the total elimination of loans and interest and the funding of reserves and relief through expansion of the tax base. Most, however, envisioned the competition for resources as a conflict between the state and the peasantry, and on this issue they sought the alleviation of peasant distress at the expense of the state rather than the aristocracy.

The Reform of 1862: Refunding
The Grain Loan System

The peasant rebellions of 1862 sparked the reform of the grain loan system just as it had the reform of the land and military tax systems. One of the special pacification commissioners, Pak Kyu-su (second state councilor in 1874), believed that the corruption of the grain loan administration was the main cause of the rebellion.[39] At his suggestion King Ch'ŏlchong created a Reform Bureau (ijŏngch'ŏng) and issued a request for all officials to present their recommendations for reform.[40]

In his plea for advice, Ch'ŏlchong stated that, since the relief and grain loan system had existed in ancient times in the Silla and Paekche kingdoms, there was nothing wrong with the institution itself. With the passage of time, however, it had become necessary to collect interest on relief loans and to use that interest for official expenditures. Clerks and petty officials had corrupted the system with their illicit manipulations. The time had come for reform.

Ch'ŏlchong remarked that excellent precedents for the reform of the grain loan system were provided by the Ever-Normal Granaries of the Han and the Righteous Granaries of the Sui dynasties in China, but the wastage surcharge that had been used for supplementing expenditures could not so easily be abandoned. He could not cut down on palace expenses, nor could he abolish grain loans and interest charges because of the need for funds. Hard-pressed by the conflicting needs of the state and the people, Ch'ŏlchong beseeched his officials to help him search for a way out of the dilemma.[41]

The proposals made in the seventeenth and eighteenth centuries undoubtedly influenced the men who presented recommendations on grain loan reform to King Ch'ŏlchong in 1862. Hŏ Pu,[42] who submitted a lengthy memorial on the subject, was opposed to both loans and interest as a matter of principle.[43] Echoing the moralist-popular welfare orientation of Yu Hyŏng-wŏn, albeit without specific reference to his writings, he proposed the replacement of grain loans by ever-normal and village granaries. Like Yu, he advocated use of the ever-normal system in order to eliminate the need for loans at interest, but he also approved the use of the village granary system with interest charges on loans. His approval of village granaries, however, was predicated on the tacit assumption that loans and interest would be used for refunding relief reserves at the village level, and not for supporting general administrative costs of the central government. He also proposed the independent funding of relief and reserves by the land tax to be achieved by a more efficient survey and registration of taxable land, citing Li K'uei's system of independent financing of the ever-normal system in the Chinese T'ang dynasty.[44]

Another set of proposals on grain loan and relief reform in 1862 came from the pen of Yun Chŏng-ŭi, a high official of the time.[45] Yun's views were much more of a compromise between extremes than those of Hŏ Pu, and for that reason were probably more representative of majority opinion.[46] Yun was opposed to change for the sake of change and was concerned about the problems that would be created by the proposed solutions. He approved of the idea of abolishing grain loans at interest but also felt that serious consideration had to be given to the problems involved in using alternate sources of revenue. Although he favored the use of a household cloth tax in place of the military cloth tax, he opposed removal of yangban exemptions. He also objected to the use of an extra land levy on the grounds that this device had been used too many times in the past. He approved the ever-normal system in principle, but pointed out that if interest were abolished, a grain loan reserve for relief purposes could not be maintained. He was also ambivalent about the advantages of a village granary system. He felt that it was a good idea to take administration out of the hands of officials and clerks, but he was not convinced that moral standards were any higher in the villages. A village granary system was also likely to produce mismanagement, shortages in reserves, haggling over repayments, and strife among villagers. On balance, he felt the village granary system would cause more trouble than it was worth.

Yun advocated the stricter enforcement of the reserve requirements of the existing system by the secret censors and district magistrates and proposed immediate relief for the peasants by declaring a moratorium on the repayment of loans for a three-year period. As an alternative, interest alone could be collected and repayment on principle deferred. He saw no reason why the state had to rely on loan interest for expenses, which could be met by tapping other types of tax sources. Relief grants could be made on an ad hoc basis from the Ever-Normal Granaries, in which case there would be no need for a separate system of relief granaries. The practice of loaning grain for the purpose of renewing reserve stocks could be reduced by constructing better granaries with stone floors to cut down on rotting due to moisture.

In late July and August of 1862 the Reform Bureau submitted individual proposals for reform of the grain loan system.[47] Then at the request of second State Councilor Cho Tu-sun on September 23, the bureau submitted a complete set of regulations for reform.[48] The reform program called for abolition of the use of grain loan interest for revenue purposes, write-off of most of the bad debts, refunding of the grain reserves at a lower and more realistic level, and replacement of lost revenue with new taxes.[49] Had this plan been approved it would have converted the grain reserve and loan system to a fund for peasant relief; it would have taken pressure off both peasant debtors and magistrates responsible for reserve shortage; it would have put the relief system on a solid fiscal basis by providing for reserves out of regular tax revenue; and it probably would have contributed to better distribution of the tax burden by raising tax revenue from previously exempt and protected groups.

The bureau's proposals set forward very liberal terms for refunding the reserve. It divided grain loan funds into two categories: grain actually on reserve and grain on loan, the repayment of which could be expected (*silhwan*); and grain which was recorded as on reserve but which was missing from the granaries, the repayment of which had become impossible (*hŏryuhwan*). In the first category, there was a total of 2,361,698 sŏk[50] still remaining in the country, and all of this was to be called in and repaid in its cash equivalent over a three year period. The cash would be used to establish by purchase a permanent grain reserve of 1,500,000 sŏk, which would not be loaned out but rotated for fresh grain stocks in two year intervals.

The second category of falsely recorded grain totaled 1,877,944 sŏk. Two thirds of this would be written off (*t'anggam*) as a loss and the remaining third, a total of 938,972 sŏk, would be paid back. An investigation of the account ledgers would be made, and the clerks responsible for debt collection would be required to make restitution to the Equal Service Administration without interest over a period of ten years. The responsibility was thus placed in the hands of the regular and petty officials, but liberal repayment terms eased the pressure on them and the peasant debtors. A grant of 50,000 yang of cash from the palace treasury was proposed to help finance the permanent reserve fund of the system.

The bureau also recommended that a cash surtax on land of two yang/kyŏl be imposed to make up for revenue lost by the abolition of loan interest for state revenue. This proposal was made as the result of lengthy debate on the subject. Back on July 31, the Reform Bureau had proposed that all fishing, boat, and salt taxes which had been expropriated by palace estates and official households and yamen be turned over to the Equal Service Administration.[51] On August 2 the bureau had also requested that all tax-exempt land assigned to the palace estates (*kung-bang*) in excess of amounts prescribed by law in the *Taejŏn t'ongp'yŏn* be made subject to taxation.[52] These provisions were not included in the September 23 regulations, however. Evidently they had been discarded in favor of a general land surtax.

In its report the Reform Bureau noted that there were really only two alternatives to the use of interest for revenue purposes—household or land taxes. The land tax was the best choice, since a household tax would be difficult to supervise and "no distinction would be made between the rich and the poor." This last point was an argument that had been used frequently in the past against the household cloth tax proposal by the defenders of yangban exemption who argued cynically that a household levy was undesirable because it was too regressive a tax. The Reform Bureau explained that land, after all, was the chief source of wealth and that a land surtax had previously been used at the time the equal service reform of 1750 had been adopted. The Reform Bureau called its policy liquidating the grain loans and reverting to the land tax (*t'anghwan-gwigyŏl*).

The Reform Bureau also rgistered its disapproval of the use of the village granary system. Although no harm would be done if the administration of loans were entrusted to the people as provided for under this system, in Korea it had long been the practice to use interest from loans for official expenses and *this was not in the tradition of the ancient village granaries.* Furthermore, the regulations for Chu Hsi's village granary system called for the registering of village households in a mutual guarantee network. It was not now possible for the Korean government to abruptly order the restoration of the village contract (*hyangyak*)[53] or local mutual-guarantee organizations. Yet without these, it would not be possible to coerce idlers and vagrants to repay their debts and maintain the village granary grain reserves.

The Reform Bureau program of September 23, 1862, was as close as the moralist-popular welfare plan ever came to fruition. It would have replaced loan interest for state revenue with increased land taxes, although this did not signify a frontal attack on aristocratic privileges. The land tax was chosen instead of a household tax for the purpose of avoiding just such a confrontation. The village granary system was rejected on the grounds that in Korea it would have become a device for collecting loan interest revenue for the central government rather than an agency for rural peasant relief. In sum, the program represented an uncompromising position against the exploitation of interest and emphasized peasant relief as the prime objective of reform. This formula was acceptable at this time because the main concern of the government was the elimination of the causes of peasant rebellion and because there was also little pressure on the government for raising revenue for military or defensive purposes. However, the chance for the adoption of the moralist-popular welfare plan was missed; by 1866 when the threat of foreign invasion had become a matter of real concern and demands for revenue were rising, state loans were too valuable a source of income to discard.

In the debate that followed the presentation of the Reform Bureau proposals, Chŏng Wŏn-yŏng, first minister of the Ministers-without-Portfolio, opposed the abolition of the grain loan system and the imposition of new land taxes. He believed that it would be better to provide stricter regulation of the existing system by adjusting grain loan quotas in proportion with the size or population of the given district, requiring that peasants repay only the original interest charges, prohibiting illegal transfer of granary stocks, and ensuring that adulterated grain would not be loaned out to the peasants.[54] Ch'ŏlchong finally decided not to adopt the Reform Bureau's proposals but instead to take some remedial measures in the southern three provinces of Kyŏngsang, Chŏlla, and Ch'ungch'ŏng, where corruption in the grain loan system was particularly flagrant. Grain loans at interest were continued, but two thirds of the falsely recorded grain was written off as a loss. The remaining one third was to be repaid if outstanding and used as principal for the grain loan reserves. Furthermore, quotas of grain for loaning purposes were fixed by the government and orders were issued that these were not to be exceeded.[55] By writing off two thirds of its bad debts, the government undoubtedly eased some of the pressure that had led to the peasant uprisings of 1862, but Ch'ŏlchong and his ministers were not bold enough to implement the rest of the Reform Bureau program, in particular, the elimination of interest as a source of revenue and its replacement by land or household taxes, which would have cut into the wealth of the aristocracy.

Reform of the Grain Loan System

Grain Loan Policy under the Taewongun

The reform of the grain loan system under the Taewongun's regime has been publicized by some scholars as possibly the greatest and most successful of his reform programs. Such an evaluation, however, derives from too great a concern with his adoption of the village granary system. If one views the grain loan policy of the Taewongun in the larger context, it would appear that it was hardly as radical as the initial plan of the 1862 Reform Bureau, and that it much more closely resembles the pragmatic-statist program as described above. At the beginning of Kojong's reign in 1864, however, government grain loan policy was ambivalent: sympathy for peasant distress was coupled with concern over shrinking revenues and reserves. The government tried to steer a middle course between the two extremes of debt cancellation and reduction of grain loan funds (moralist-popular welfare) and maintenance of grain loan reserves and interest (pragmatic-statist).

Investigations of the grain loan situation after 1864 also revealed a level of corruption and peasant suffering that roused intense feelings of indignation against corrupt officials and overt sympathy for the oppressed peasantry. The feeling of disillusionment over official corruption was reflected in a lengthy edict issued by the dowager-regent on October 9, 1864 in which she bewailed the corruption of clerks and petty officials throughout the country. She issued orders to the state council that after grain loans were paid back and sealed up in the granaries, any clerks who in the future were in arrears in their collections of loans due would be reported and punished.[56]

In the recompilation of the dynastic law code completed in 1865, the *Taejŏn hoet'ong*, severe punishments were provided for officials guilty of corruption in administering grain loans. Magistrates who were behind 10 percent in their grain loan accounts were to be given sixty strokes of the bamboo with additional strokes for every additional 10 percent shortage in loan funds, up to a limit of one hundred strokes. Those who were in arrears on their loan funds after their three year term of service were to be exiled for three years and prohibited from holding office for five years. Clerks in the governor's yamen guilty of falsification of the account books, irrespective of the amount involved, would be decapitated and their heads displayed as a warning. Clerks in charge of the ledgers in such cases would be exiled and the governor would be stripped of his office warrant. Magistrates who were in arrears but not aware of it, or who had not discovered it, would be required to pay one third the amount due out of their own pockets. Magistrates who had failed to uncover shortages from the previous administration would be required to pay one fourth. In either case the magistrate would be exiled and prohibited from holding further office. Clerks responsible for shortages of 1,000 sŏk or more would be decapitated.[57]

Indignation against the corrupt officials was matched by sympathy for suffering peasants and wherever possible the central government approved of debt cancellation. There was a limit, however, to the government's freedom to cancel debts. Reserves had to be maintained for emergencies and future lending operations, and local officials were still dependent on loan interest for expenses. The government, therefore, chose to respond on an ad hoc basis to requests for remission of debts by local authorities. At the same time it authorized the creation of new loan funds at interest wherever reserves had been wiped out and interest revenue had been lost.[58]

The government was really hard pressed to find substitute funds for the loss of revenue resulting from the debt cancellations of 1862 and after. Only in the case of two provinces, however, did the government adopt the one policy that was most likely to solve the grain loan question once and for all—the substitution of land and household levies for grain loan interest as a source of revenue.

On August 27, 1864, the governor of P'yŏng'an province, Hong U-gil, made three recommendations to the court for the reform of the grain loan system and asked the throne to choose which of the three it preferred. The first recommendation called for a recall of outstanding grain loans and a reduction of the total authorized grain loan fund. Hong also mentioned that if this alternative were chosen, interest collections would naturally have to be suspended while the principal was being called in and substitute revenues found. The second proposal called for establishing grain loan capital funds at reduced prices. The phrasing is vague and may have meant authorization for the capitalization of new loans at cash-grain conversion rates that would be fixed below market prices in order to benefit peasant borrowers. The last suggestion was for suspension or abolition of the grain loans and the replacement of interest income by substitute levies (*kŭptae*). Hong stated that the only sources of substitute levies were land and household taxes which could be used to make up for the 84,000 sŏk of yearly interest that would be lost by cancellation or elimination of grain loans. He suggested levying a tax of 5 tu/kyŏl on the 84,000 kyŏl of taxable land in the province, which would generate 28,000 sŏk of revenue. A household levy of 4 tu per household on the 210,000 registered households in the province would yield an additional 56,000 sŏk.[59]

The state council approved heartily of Hong's proposals for substitute land and household levies, but its memorial to the throne revealed the ambivalence of government policy.

Reform of the Grain Loan System

All the states of the world obtain their revenues either from the land or the people. The collection of interest on grain loans for meeting [official] expenditures has been practiced for a long time, and it has been a long time since evils and corruption appeared in the system causing the people to suffer.

If we stick stubbornly to a corrupt system, in the end it will produce [nothing but] empty account books. We have carried out an exploitive system but said that it could not be abolished because it was law. There has been no correlation between name and fact.

Now, instead of making these excessive exactions and avoiding calling them "land tax" or "household levy," it would be better to collect taxes as levies on land or people. Then names would be rectified and words put in order and nothing would be hidden or embellished . . . The governor's suggestion for a household tax is in effect a levy on the people. His suggestion for a tax on kyŏl is a tax on land. The amounts collected from these taxes . . . would indeed be sufficient to give some relief to the people.[60]

Despite the state council's preference for direct taxes instead of loan interest, it could not bring itself to abolish the system of state-sponsored grain loans, since it provided the foundation for the nation's emergency reserves. Because the government was in the process of calling in loans and refunding the grain loan reserves, the councilors were also concerned that additional land and household levies would cause even greater hardship among the people. The council, therefore, recommended that the government wait until the grain loan administration was reformed before making any decision on land or household taxes. As for the grain reserves of the mountain fortresses, the state council claimed that these funds had to be maintained and authorized that they be loaned out in accordance with law. Surplus grain loan funds in the control of the district towns would be converted to cash and stored in treasuries.[61]

This policy decision was confirmed two months later by the state council's treatment of grain loans in Ch'ungch'ŏng province. On October 13, 1864, the council approved the cancellation of 190,000 sŏk of outstanding debts and authorized the use of the surplus from the existing cash tax on land (kyŏlchŏn) and other taxes to make up for revenue shortages. The council also abolished land and household taxes previously imposed by magistrates on their own authority on the grounds that loan interest had been insufficient to meet revenue needs.[62] True to its word, the state council on February 6, 1865, approved the recommendation of Hong U-gil for the use of land and household surtaxes in P'yŏng'an province.[63]

The government showed that it was willing to approve the use of land

Politics and Policy in Traditional Korea

and household taxes in order to alleviate the burdens placed on the grain loan system for raising tax revenues for the state, but it was not willing to abolish the grain loan system altogether or to refund it by a total reliance on regular taxes. It also showed no desire to expand land and household levies to all provinces. One explanation for this is that government preferred to approve ad hoc requests by local governors rather than establish uniform regulations for the whole country. The court was still committed to the use of the grain loan system for reserve and revenue purposes, but as the bankruptcy of that system was revealed and the problem of revenue shortages became more serious, it found that it could no longer aprove requests for debt cancellation. It came to a decision to refund the loan system once and for all, so that normal operations could be resumed.

This change of attitude is revealed in the government response to conditions in P'yŏng'an and Kyŏnggi provinces in 1865. On May 3 the governor of P'yŏng'an province, Hong U-gil, submitted a report on the difficulty he was having putting the grain loan administration back in order. He reported that all the granaries were empty and it was virtually impossible to find out who the people were who owed grain to the officials and how much they owed. Some of the records were burned in fires, and others had mysteriously disappeared about four or five years before. Hong wrote that he had expected that the dowager-regent's decree for providing alternate sources of revenue while the grain loan system was being put in order would have provided a breathing space for reform, but his optimism had proved unwarranted because he had no idea of the enormity of peasant indebtedness. He concluded that it would be impossible to investigate all unpaid debts and punish all the responsible officials. The only alternative was for the throne to cancel all back debts in order to signal a new beginning.[64] In an edict issued in response to this memorial the king did not agree to the liquidation of all indebtedness, but he did reveal his growing anger and impatience with the situation. Kojong ordered that an investigation be made of all clerks in the taxation section of the P'yŏng'an governor's yamen since 1847 and that all officials on duty there be questioned by the state tribunal.[65]

On October 20 the state council, in response to a request from Kangwŏn province for authorization of substitute revenues made necessary by the loss of loan interest, commented that it would be difficult to continue granting exemptions from repayment of loans because of the difficulty in finding substitute revenues. It recommended that henceforth debt cancellation would be accompanied by punishment for the responsible parties. The council also decided to wash its hands of the matter and transfer the burden to the magistrates. It proposed that in future cases of cancellation throughout the country magistrates would have the responsibility of finding the best way to make up for the loss. Kojong approved these proposals.[66]

By 1866 the court came to the realization that it was impossible to refund the grain loan system by calling in overdue loans and that the central government would have to take responsibility for refinancing the system. A report from the governor of Kyŏnggi province on June 22, 1866, triggered this decision. The governor reported that a total of 154,300 sŏk of falsely recorded grain had been written off the books. Third State Councilor Kim Pyŏng-hak stated that he doubted that the remaining one third of the total grain loan fund for that province would ever be collected and he recommended that it too be exempted from repayment. Since there were at present only 20-30,000 bags of rice actually on reserve in the province, there was no way to provide for interest revenue due from the falsely recorded grain. Appropriate amounts would have to be taken from actual reserves, which were sure to be used up in a few years' time. He recommended that new funds be established as capitalization for loans at interest to provide for yamen expenses.[67]

Later the same day Kojong issued an edict which stated that the dowager-regent had been concerned over the yearly depletion of grain loan reserves. The royal house had been able to accumulate a reserve of 300,000 yang of cash through frugal spending practices and the state council would now distribute it to all the provinces for refunding grain loans. If in the future there should be any reduction in the interest obtained from loans as a result of collusion or corruption, "this would be because the governors and magistrates will have turned their backs on the sage virtue of our Dowager."[68] Two days later a memorial from the state council spelled out the terms of the grant. The money was to be divided among all provinces except P'yŏng'an and Hamgyŏng in the north. The new cash fund would be called the 1866 Special Reserve Grain (*pyŏng'in pyŏlbigok*], and all of it would be loaned out *at interest* with repayment in grain. The two northern provinces could be eliminated from the plan, since in P'yŏng'an province the grain reserve of fortress rice provisions had been maintained in full and in Hamgyŏng province actual grain was on hand in the granaries.[69] On July 9 another edict granted special remission of interest payments on the new loans for the current year, since there were only a few months remaining to harvest time.[70]

Between July 1866 and July 1867 the government tried to operate with the interest available from the severely reduced grain loan funds left over after the reorganization of the last few years had eliminated the nonrepayable portions. This became very difficult to do because of increasing demand for revenues caused by the French expedition of 1866.[71] The grain loan system had been bankrupted by half a century of corruption, and the court decided in July 1866 to refund the system, but the initial

Politics and Policy in Traditional Korea

allotment of 300,000 yang proved insufficient for the task. Then in July 1867 the government adopted the dubious expedient of utilizing the over-valued new 100-cash (*tangbaekchŏn*). The new cash had been used prior to this in April to provide for some military expenses and grain loans.[72] On July 4, 1867, a royal decree stated that the funds that had been issued last year for refunding the grain loan system had not been sufficient to restore the requisite capital fund. Accordingly, 1,500,000 yang of recent-ly minted 100-cash would be distributed to the provinces to be converted into grain for distribution. The new fund would be called the Ministry of Taxation Special Reserve Account (*hojo pyŏlbi hyŏllok*). Following the precedent of the year before a one year moratorium on interest payments on the new loans was allowed.[73]

The use of newly minted currency for funding the grain loan system was not a measure that had been advocated by scholars and officials in the past. On the contrary, they had recommended that loans be funded by the expansion of the regular tax base. The use of multiple-denomina-tion currency—in which the face value of the coin was many times the intrinsic value of the metal—was an alternative chosen because of the government's desire to avoid a direct fiscal challenge to the landowners and aristocrats. Furthermore, the reestablishment of the grain loan system by the use of the 100-cash was purchased at the price of inflation and monetary instability, as we will see in the next chapter.

On July 7, 1867, three days after the refunding order was handed down, Minister of Taxation Kim Pyŏng-hak requested the restoration of the village granary system as the means of administering grain loans in the five provinces of the south. The adoption of the village granary system was not the cornerstone of the Taewongun's grain loan reform but an adjunct to the refunding of the entire grain loan system. The pur-pose of the village granaries was not simply to help eliminate corruption, alleviate the oppression of the peasantry, and guarantee a stable reserve, but to ensure a more efficient collection of interest revenues. Of course, the justification for the establishment of village granaries was couched in the Confucian rhetoric of royal benevolence and concern for the people. As Kim Pyŏng-hak put it in his recommendation, the previous policy had led to fiscal crisis without solving the old problems.

The T'ang minister, Lu Chih, reported to his ruler saying, "you investi-gate the feelings of the people. What they desire most should be done first, and what they dislike the most should be done away with first." Alas! When I consider what the people today dislike the worst, [I find that] nothing is as bad as grain loans. Yet we cannot rashly decide to do away with them.

For the last five or six years the court has been discussing ways to reform the system, and in general all the reform measures were designed to benefit the people at the expense of the state. In the end debt cancellations have amounted to ten million [yang] with the result that the funds on reserve have been depleted and there is nothing left for expenditures. Nor have the people received the benefits they were supposed to receive.[74]

Kim also pointed out that despite the grant of funds from the royal treasury the previous year, the peasants were still unable to repay their loans and interest payments had to be cancelled. In his view only Chu Hsi's village granary system would ensure a corruption-free system and a stable source of interest revenue.

Kim's plan called for a capitalization of 600 sŏk for each village granary to be provided by converting the 100-cash grant from the national treasury to grain. Loans would be made at 10 percent interest with a 2 percent wastage surcharge. After fourteen years when a reserve of 2,100 sŏk had been accumulated the original 600 sŏk would be returned to the magistrate.

The final regulations as presented on July 12 by the state council differed in several important respects from Kim Pyŏng-hak's proposals. Village granaries were to be established in the five provinces of Hwanghae, Kyŏnggi, Ch'ungch'ŏng, Chŏlla, and Kyŏngsang— the rice-producing areas of central and southern Korea. Half the fund in every granary was to be kept in reserve and the other half would be loaned out at 10 percent interest. Surcharges amounting to about 2 percent on principal would cover fees for the granary supervisor (*sasu*), granary clerk (*chikko*), clerical costs, and wastage. There was no explicit mention of the use of the 100-cash for financing, or Kim's recommendations for initial funding and repayment. Since provision was made, however, for the special exemption of the interest portion of *this year's* interest on loans—a corollary to the grant of one and one half million yang of 100-cash on July 4—it is safe to assume that the new system was indeed funded by the new currency.[75]

The regulations do, however, explicitly state that the 10 percent interest charge would be paid to the district magistrate, collected (from the magistrate) by the provincial governor, and remitted to the Ministry of Taxation. This represents a significant modification of Kim Pyŏng-hak's original recommendations which, in accordance with the system of Chu Hsi, would have ploughed the interest back into the reserve funds of the village granaries. The reason for the modification is obvious—the village granaries were to function primarily as a source of revenue.

Other regulations help corroborate this view. Since the whole 10 percent interest charge was now to be remitted to the central government, this represented a more intense utilization of interest by the central government than before when a fraction of the interest was left to the magistrate for his expenses. Furthermore, in case of any debtors who absconded without repaying their loans, the amounts owed would be reapportioned equally among their fellow villagers for repayment—a practice that had been condemned in the past as a major source of unjust exploitation.[76] Finally, another recommendation of Kim Pyŏng-hak was conspicuously left out of the final regulations. Kim had proposed that when the harvest was poor half the loan would be cancelled, and in times of famine all of it would be exempted from repayment.[77] The final version, however, indicates that the government was more interested in revenue than relief.

The fourteenth of the regulations also stipulated that any grain loan funds established by agencies or bureaus of the capital would be kept separate from village granary operations. Thus, the initiation of the village granary system by no means signaled an end to the policy of raising revenue by loan interest through any civil or military agency of the government on an ad hoc basis. The village granaries only supplanted the Righteous Granaries in the district towns.

The government was, of course, not disinterested in the alleviation of peasant distress. It was stipulated, for example, that no consideration was to be made whether borrowers were yangban or commoners in granting loans in order to ensure that the needy were provided for. An extensive system of duplicate record keeping was also established to eliminate the possibility of falsification. Peasant relief, however, was a secondary consideration. The village granaries were designed to increase the efficiency of revenue collection by reforming the administrative apparatus.[78]

The village granary system was also the government's answer to the problem of corruption, but it was an answer that constituted an admission by the government of its inability to eliminate corruption among magistrates and petty officials at the local level through the normal processes of surveillance and punishment. For the village granary system removed direct responsibility for the administration of grain loans and interest collection from the hands of the district magistrate and put it in the hands of local notables.

According to the regulations promulgated on July 12 by the state council, the administration of the new village granaries was to be carried out at the subdistrict level. Village granaries (*sach'ang*) were to be established in those *tong* in the district with the largest concentrations of population. The *tong* (or *i*) was the smallest administrative territorial unit comprised of several natural villages. Several *tong* were combined to form a *myŏn*, a slightly larger territorial subdivision. Neither the *tong* nor the *myŏn* was administered by magistrates from the central government. Granary supervisors were to be chosen under the new law from among the "diligent and somewhat intelligent" inhabitants of each *myŏn* by the *myŏn* council (*myŏnhoe*), which would then report the selection to the district magistrate. The magistrate would confirm the appointment, but he was not enjoined against imposing his choice on the *myŏn* council. The granary supervisors would have jurisdiction over the *tong* chiefs (*tongjang*) who would be selected by *tong* residents in a manner not spelled out, and the *tong* chiefs would supervise the work of the granary clerks. The granary supervisor at the *myŏn* level would have the right to appoint the granary guards and measuring clerks. He would also take account of the varying size and wealth of the villages and rank them in grades for the purpose of distributing grain to them for loans.[79]

The village granary system by its very nature revealed two unhappy aspects about government in the 1860s. Exploitation of peasant relief loans for revenue remained indispensable to a government whose control over resources was still severely limited, and the provincial bureaucracy could not be trusted for the faithful implementation of national policy.

Aftermath of the Village Granary Reform

It is very difficult to assess the effect of the grain loan reform after 1867 because archival records are incapable of providing a balanced picture. Like modern newspapers, they faithfully reported instances of institutional malfunction but remained silent whenever things were running smoothly. The village granary reform was obviously no panacea for all the ills of the grain loan system. Peasants continued to default on their loans because of poverty and famine conditions, which were particularly severe in 1869-70.[80] Corruption and falsification of records was not entirely eliminated.[81] The government still lost revenues it expected to obtain through loan interest[82] and continued to cancel unrepaid debts[83] and refund bankrupted loan funds in order to maintain a steady flow of interest income.[84] Cash reserves in official treasuries were frequently converted to grain by loaning them out in the spring and collecting repayment in grain in the fall at fixed cash-grain conversion rates beneficial to the government.[85] Emergency demands for funds required by the construction of new military garrisons were also financed by the establishment of new loans with or without interest provisions.[86] Grain stocks were moved from one place to another to cover areas of shortage and currency was minted to fund new loans.[87]

Conditions were not the same everywhere, however. In Ch'ungch'ŏng province the chief difficulty came from an oversupply of grain loan stocks rather than a shortage. In 1867 it was reported that the recapitalization of the grain loan system by using surpluses from the land-cash levies had created a large reserve, which was being loaned out at interest. Officials had evidently felt obliged to loan as much of the increased fund as possible in order to obtain more revenues from interest, and this had proved a great burden to the peasantry. In 1867 the government had declared an upper limit on loan funds, and in 1869 a portion of them were converted to cash and paid in to the Ministry of Taxation. This was repeated in 1871.[88] The accumulation of a well-funded reserve in Ch'ungch'ŏng province had paradoxically failed to lighten the burdens on the peasantry. Certainly, the reform program of debt cancellation, refinancing, and village granaries in no way signified any loss of faith in loans at interest as an important method of raising revenues. Whenever funds were needed loan funds were established on an ad hoc basis under the jurisdiction of either capital or local yamen to provide for expenses.[89]

On January 2, 1873, a most interesting discussion was held at a court conference over the grain loan and revenue problems six years after the village granary reform and at least two years after the imposition of the household cloth tax when one would have expected state finances to have been put back in order. On this day, however, the new chief state councilor, Hong Sun-mok, reported to the king that finances had never been in worse condition. Minister of Taxation Kim Se-gyun revealed that while his ministry's rice revenues were a little higher than average, he still did not have enough to meet expenditures. The governor of Ch'ungch'ŏng province asked for a new grain loan fund of 15,000 yang of cash to meet the expenses of his yamen, and loans were authorized for expenses of the provincial military commanders in Hamgyŏng province. For the first time since 1862 grain loans were authorized for P'yŏng'an province to cover revenue requirements there. The Taewongun also personally authorized the allocation of a capital fund of 100,000 sŏk to be lent out in 1873 as a means of producing an annual 10,000 sŏk of interest income.[90]

In the case of the fund for P'yŏng'an province, Hong Sun-mok reported that after the debt cancellations of 1862, the province had been short of revenues. He proposed capitalization of a loan fund with 600,000 yang of cash, to be converted to rice through loans at the rate of 3 yang/sŏk to produce a reserve of 200,000 sŏk of grain. He proposed that the whole fund be loaned out at interest and that no cancellations of debts be permitted in the future. "There has never been a worse time than the present for shortages in revenues for expenses," he stated.[91] He expressed his regret at having to do this, since the initial solution of 1866-67 had provided for the substitution of land levies for grain loan interest. The new fund was to be called the 1973 Special Reserve Loan Fund (*kyeyu pyŏlbimi*) and the first year's interest would be cancelled as an act of benevolence.[92]

These acts do not prove that the village granary system was a failure. It had undoubtedly eliminated much of the corruption that was characteristic of the system prior to 1867. The basic problem was that the grain loan system simply could not carry out the contradictory functions that were assigned to it: maintaining an emergency reserve for loans and military provisions, providing direct relief in times of famine, and obtaining revenues for the government from loan interest. Peasants still had trouble repaying the capital, let alone the interest that was supposed to help fund government expenses.

The Taewongun's regime is to be given credit not only for its willingness to take action in difficult circumstances but for policies which succeeded in eliminating burdens of past indebtedness and removing a large measure of bureaucratic corruption. To this extent the government heeded the advice of the moralist proponents of popular welfare in the past who had complained bitterly about the oppression of the peasantry caused by the grain loan system. The Taewongun, however, was unwilling, and possibly unable, to adopt the total moralist-popular welfare program, which called for the eradication of loans and interest and the expansion of regular land or household taxes. He and his government opted for a more pragmatic solution to the grain loan problem by acknowledging that loan interest had become indispensable to the state as a source of funds, particularly in a period when the costs of military defense had risen sharply. Debt cancellation was therefore followed in the main by a refunding of the grain loan system. Borrowers of grain who were for the most part poor peasants retained the burden of having to help finance the costs of government. Furthermore, because of the shortage of resources, the government was unable to refinance grain loans except by the use of overvalued currency—a policy which contributed to inflation and reduced public confidence in the new currency itself.

In fine, the long-term interests of the peasantry were sacrificed in favor of the short-term demands of the state. Little was done to alter the balance of forces in which a wealthy and privileged aristocracy was maintained at the expense of an exploited peasantry while the central government teetered on the edge of bankruptcy.

8
Monetary Policy

It was under the Taewongun's aegis that for the first time in the history of the dynasty the government authorized the use of the so-called large cash (*taejŏn*) explicitly for the purpose of providing greater revenue for the state. The term large cash simply referred to a coin the face value of which was some multiple of the smallest coin in circulation. The 100-cash that was put into circulation under the Taewongun was supposed to be equivalent to one hundred of the ever-normal circulating treasure (*sangp'yong t'ongbo*), the standard Korean copper currency of the time. Since its metallic content was only five or six times greater than the ever-normal cash, its face value was approximately fifteen to twenty times higher than its intrinsic or metallic value. The government minted the new coins, paid its bills with them, and hoped that the public would accept the cash at face value.

No new monetary principles were introduced by the minting of the 100-cash. Back in the seventeenth and eighteenth centuries when copper currency was first minted by the government in volume, profits on the minting of the ever-normal cash were sometimes as high as 50 percent. In other words, the face value was double the production cost of the coin. When the government in 1866 tried to increase its revenue by minting large cash, it was only doing on a larger scale what had been tried before. But the introduction of the 100-cash was carried out despite justifiable fears of the inflationary effects of such currency, and in defiance of traditional Confucian biases against currency per se.

The Taewongun's inflationary monetary policy roused the ire of conservatives who carried over many of the moralistic attitudes toward the market and currency characteristic of an earlier, simple economy despite the fact that the volume of metallic currency in circulation had expanded greatly since the seventeenth century. When the Taewongun sacrificed

Monetary Policy

price stability for financial gain as a means of solving the revenue crisis, the monetary conservatives turned against him.

Growth in the Circulation and Volume
of Metallic Currency

By the early seventeenth century metallic and paper currency played a limited role in the Korean economy. The Korean government had frequently tried to introduce currency into the economy as a means of stimulating commerce. Currency could not, however, be forced on a society without a developed market system, and all the early efforts to do so ended in failure. Cloth and grain had long performed the function of currency in Korea, but the first attempt to circulate metallic currency on any scale came in 996 when the government put iron cash into circulation and prohibited the use of coarse hemp cloth as a medium of exchange. When this proved unworkable because of the unfamiliarity of the public with metallic cash, the policy was modified to allow the people to continue the use of cloth and grain as media of exchange in market transactions.[1]

Metallic currency was revived again in 1097 when an Officer of the Mint was established. At this time a silver coin called the silver jar money (unbyŏng) had been minted; its value ranged anywhere from ten to fifty sŏk of rice, and it was suitable for large transactions only.[2] Copper cash was not used until 1102 when 15,000 strings of copper cash were minted and put into circulation through the shops of the state liquor monopoly.[3] Not long after, however, there was a reversion to cloth and grain as the main media of exchange.

During the period of the Mongol conquest in the thirteenth century, Yüan dynasty paper money circulated in Korea.[4] At the end of the Koryŏ dynasty in 1390 paper money was printed by the government, but it went out of circulation with the fall of the dynasty in 1392. In 1401 the printing of paper money was resumed, and in the early fifteenth century, paper money, cash, and cloth were used in conjunction as media of exchange. When the value of paper money and cloth fell, the people lost faith in them.[5] Paper money, however, was still in use in the late fifteenth century, and the 1469 law code, the Kyŏngguk taejŏn, included fixed conversion rates for paper money in terms of cloth and rice.[6] Paper money probably went out of circulation sometime around 1537. This was the date of the promulgation of the military cloth receipt law (kunjok sup'obŏp), which provided for cloth payments of military taxes. Sometime earlier this cloth had been substituted for paper money in the requirements of the slave tribute law. By Yŏngjo's reign in the mid-seventeenth century paper money had become a curiosity.[7]

For most of the Yi dynasty the currency system was bimetallic. Both silver and copper cash were used, but silver currency played a small role in Korea. In 1408 restrictions were placed on the use of silver in Korea because of limited domestic production of the metal, but it continued to be used in foreign trade and was still in circulation in the early sixteenth century in the northern provinces. A considerable amount of silver was brought into Korea by Chinese armies during Hideyoshi's invasions in the 1590s, but firm opposition by the government to silver currency at this time inhibited any increase in its supply. In the 1620s the amount of silver cash in circulation increased in quantity, and the value of copper cash was fixed by the government in terms of silver. While this situation lasted to the end of the dynasty, in the eighteenth century copper cash became the dominant medium of exchange, and silver was held mainly as a reserve currency.[8]

The early seventeeth century marked a major turning point in the history of copper cash in Korea. There were closer contacts with China, and a few officials sought to bring Korea up to the level of commercial development in China by introducing and promoting metallic currency. Furthermore, the minting of cash appeared to be a feasible method for solving the state's financial problems.

Copper cash was first minted under government auspices in 1625. Minting was suspended and then revived again in 1626, only to be interrupted by the Manchu invasions of 1627.[9] In 1626 the government established wine shops as a means of promoting the circulation of the new cash and decreed that fines for misdemeanors would be payable in cash.[10] In 1633 a copper coin struck with the inscription ever-normal circulating treasure was minted for the first time and the government also provided that a portion of the land tax and slave tribute tax and 10 percent of the *taedong* rice tax would be payable in cash. As before fines were also collected in coin. Minting operations were decentralized and conducted at major market centers like Andong (later shifted to Taegu), Chŏnju, and Kongju. The face value of copper cash minted in the provinces was also set higher than in the capital in order to attract currency out of Seoul and into the provinces. Official stores were also established along major thoroughfares and in market towns to promote circulation.[11]

/Although the use of metallic currency was once again suspended because of the second Manchu invasions in 1636, it appears that cash began to circulate permanently in the market area in Hwanghae province around the town of Kaesong. Circulation in that area was sustained by an active brassware industry, an extended network of distribution, and private minting. In 1650 Kim Yuk, the architect of the *taedong* tribute tax system, brought back 150,000 mun of Chinese cash and put it into circulation in Pyongyang and Anju on the Yalu River.[12]

There had always been opposition to the use of metallic currency, and the seventeenth century was no exception. Some officials expressed doubt as to whether there was sufficient commercial activity in Korea to sustain the use of metallic currency; the yangban landowning class regarded cash and commerce in general as a threat to the primacy of agricultural production which provided the economic base for their superior position in society, and there was concern over the shortage of copper.[13] Opposition to copper cash was voiced in 1652, and in 1656 King Hyojong issued an order prohibiting its use.[14] In the 1660s, however, minting was resumed by the government and private parties.[15]

Government demand for revenue in the context of a narrowing tax base provided one of the prime motives for the minting of additional cash under official auspices. There was a decline in agricultural production and recurrent famine in the 1660s. Land and military cloth taxes and slave tribute payments had to be reduced at the same time that demand for relief rose.[16] Government officials also began thinking of establishing monopoly control over minting operations as they became aware of the profits to be obtained thereby.[17]

In 1678 King Sukchong ordered the additional minting of the ever-normal circulating treasure.[18] Cash was distributed to shops by government agencies as loans to be repaid in three years without interest. Minting was decentralized in order to eliminate transportation costs. Special commissioners were sent out to encourage circulation, a task which was later transferred to provincial officials. Fines and grain loan repayments were permitted to be paid in cash, and certain proportions of the *taedong*, military cloth, and slave tribute taxes were commuted to cash payments.[19]

The new policy was, however, attended by the usual types of economic dislocation. Because copper cash was overvalued with respect to silver (at 400 mun/yang, then 200 mun/yang), it did not circulate at face value in the market. This produced a rise in prices, and the value of cash on the open market dropped to 800 mun/yang, half the original fixed exchange rate, and one quarter of the amended rate. The government was forced to undertake price stabilization operations through the distribution of cloth from government warehouses in order to bid down prices and maintain the value of copper currency. Finally, in 1680, the government abandoned attempts to fix cash exchange rates.[20] These difficulties, however, did not lead to any government ban on the use of metallic currency as in former times. After 1678 there was no longer any need for the artificial promotion of copper cash. On the contrary, demand outran supply, and the problems faced by the govrnment were now of a different order.

The introduction of the *taedong* tribute tax reform in the seventeenth century was a major stimulus to the development of an exchange market

Politics and Policy in Traditional Korea

and the use of metallic currency. The new law substituted a grain tax on land for payment of tribute products in kind and required the government to purchase tribute articles on the open market. Several times in the seventeenth century the government encouraged the circulation of currency by requiring partial payment of the *taedong* tribute tax in cash. By the end of the century, just about the time that the ever-normal circulating treasure was minted on a more or less permanent basis in 1678, the *taedong* system was extended to most of the country.[21]

In the early eighteenth century there was increased demand for cash because of the conversion of land rents from grain to cash payment during this period. The equal service reform (*kyunyŏkpŏp*) of 1750 also substituted a cash tax on land for a large portion of the military cloth tax.[22] The government in the early eighteenth century found itself pressed by the public to provide a greater supply of currency. This was something new and the government was not used to it. Now the throne and some high officials resisted the spread of metallic currency, which they held responsible for some of the disruptions of the changing economic order.

Opposition to the Spread of Metallic Currency

For the period from 1697 to 1731, no king approved any recommendation for the minting of additional copper cash despite the expanding demand for it. While private minting or counterfeiting continued, the refusal of the government to mint additional currency for the market contributed to deflation. In 1731, when a famine put great pressure on the government for relief funds, King Yŏngjo finally relented, relaxed his opposition to copper cash, and agreed to the resumption of minting.[23] By the middle of the eighteenth century minting was changed from an ad hoc to a regular and periodic activity.[24]

The government's capitulation to the rising demand for copper cash did not signify a basic conversion of general attitudes toward currency but retreat and compromise in the face of necessity. While Korean officials did finally decide to mint more copper cash, they did not regard the growth of commerce and currency as an inexorable and irreversible trend but as an aberration that eventually could be reversed or at least brought under control. In their frustration government officials viewed metallic currency as a prime cause of economic disruption and as a corrupting influence that distracted the diligent and frugal peasant from the arduous cultivation of his fields by enticing him into a desire for the acquisition of material goods. It was believed that cash stimulated conspicuous consumption, undermined the traditional values of saving and hard work, and caused a decline in agricultural production.[25] Cash was also held responsible for usurious lending practices, an increasing gap in the distribution of wealth, risk taking, and counterfeiting. Cash was associated with the growth of commercial activity which made it easier for people of lower social status to accumulate wealth in competition with their social betters. As Wŏn Yu-han has put it, the yangban elite sought the restoration of the primacy of agriculture in order to restore the economic advantages of their own class.[26] The prejudice against cash, in other words, was part of the general antipathy toward commercial development and its disruptive effects on the social order. Some concluded that undesirable economic and social change could be reversed if only the throne would declare metallic currency illegal and abolish its use forever.

A typical example of the resistance to cash in the seventeenth century was a memorial of Yi Kyŏng-yo presented in 1654, two years prior to Hyojong's abolition of metal currency. Yi pointed out that metal cash had not been unknown to the sage rulers of the past, and yet they had chosen not to adopt it. He expressed concern about Korea's inadequate resources of copper and iron and the eventual necessity of having to import raw materials from foreign countries.[27] His major objection to cash, however, was his inability to comprehend the utility of cash in an agrarian subsistence economy. In his view, commerce could only be justified if there were surplus agricultural production, but from what he could see the people of Korea were poor and had no surplus wealth. Even if the peasants had been able to obtain a surplus, it would be of no use to them, since they would only exchange it for cash which they would save in the hopes of a small profit from moneylending. What people needed in order to live were food and clothing. If peasants sold their crops on the market for cash, how would cash help them feed their hungry wives and children? Furthermore, cash would cultivate an unhealthy spirit of profit making in the minds of the people and deter them from the production of tangible and consumable goods.[28]

The attitudes represented by Yi Kyŏng-yo were reflected in King Yŏngjo's resistance to the spread of metallic currency in the 1720s. In 1727 he prohibited the commutation into cash of all or part of the *taedong* tribute, military cloth, and slave tribute levies in order to alleviate the demand for more currency by restricting its use for tax payments. More cash would thus be freed for circulation in the market, and there would be no need to mint more of it. To Yŏngjo and some others, however, this measure was a compromise, for what they really wanted was the abolition of metallic currency. Second State Councilor Hong Ch'i-jung believed that after the abolition of cash the minds of men would become pure and all artifice and deceit would come to an end.[29]

This attempt to reverse the growth of the cash nexus proved abortive, and in 1727 Yŏngjo was forced to rescind his previous order and allow a

50 percent cash commutation of the various taxes involved. It is possible that because of increased specialization of production for the market, requiring payments in kind forced taxpayers to purchase grain and cloth at high prices. Subsequently officials at court debated the idea of substituting paper money and common cotton cloth for metallic currency, but each of these proposals was rejected in turn. But when the drought of 1731 brought demands for relief on depleted government treasuries, Yŏngjo was forced to authorize the minting of more cash to meet this demand.[30] This signified his final capitulation to copper currency, but the anticash bias, which he shared with others, was carried over into the eighteenth and nineteenth centuries—long past the time that copper cash had become an acknowledged necessity. After 1751 cash was minted on a yearly basis, and by 1800 about one billion yang of cash was put into circulation by government mints. If one includes privately minted cash, the volume of copper cash must have reached several billion yang in that period.[31]

Another indication of the increasing importance of metallic currency in the economy and tax structure is the increasing proportion of cash in government revenue collections. The increase is clearly demonstrated in the revenue figures for the land tax which was collected by two agencies—the Ministry of Taxation for the original land tax, and the Tribute Bureau for the converted tribute tax (*taedongmi*). Throughout the eighteenth century the Ministry of Taxation collected on the average about 100,000 sŏk of rice. The year-to-year volume of grain revenue fluctuated with the harvest, but no long-term increase is noticable. There was, however, a definite increase in cash revenues from the land tax. In the period 1700-13, the Ministry of Taxation received 66,000-84,000 yang of cash. By the middle of the century the mean of yearly cash collections rose above 150,000 yang. By the end of the century, 200,000 yang appears to have been a common figure in yearly tax receipts, with a peak of 410,000 yang collected in 1790. The receipts for 1807 were 300,000 yang.[32]

The figures for the Tribute Bureau show the same trend. Grain collections of this bureau fluctuated between 75,000 and 200,000 sŏk per year with the median about 130,000 sŏk. In the period 1759-63 between 247,000 and 288,000 yang of cash was collected per year. In the period 1785-96 the range of receipts had risen from 350,000 to 419,000 yang, and the figure for 1807 was 378,000 yang.[33] In sum, between 1700 and 1800 the cash receipts of the Ministry of Taxation increased by 400 percent, and between 1750 and 1800 the cash receipts of the Tribute Bureau increased by about 60 percent. Lacking data on prices and cash commutation rates for the land tax in this period, it is difficult to judge the increase in real value or constant prices of the government's cash receipts. It is probably safe to assume some increase in government revenues in real terms from greater agricultural production.

Profits from Seigniorage

The enormous expansion in the volume of copper currency in circulation in the marketplace in the late eighteenth century must have required a significant increase in the demand for copper and other metals from mining and import, but the supply of metals for currency evidently failed to keep pace with the demand with the result that the price of metal raw materials was bid up. Consequently, the government's profit margin from seigniorage charges on the minting of ever-normal cash declined, and an important source of revenue was lost.[34] Chronic cash shortage and the rising price of metals were caused by the conservatism of government policy on the minting of additional cash, the insufficiency of domestic mining production, and restrictions on the import of metals from foreign countries. Even though the government had committed itself to regular minting operations, it still imposed quotas on the amount of cash minted.[35] Domestic mining of metals suffered from a low level of technology, lack of rational management, and government restraints on private mining. The government sometimes closed down private mines so that it could maintain a monopoly on production. Government lease and tax arrangements on private mining were designed to milk profits rather than promote expansion, so that private profits from mining were held to a low level.[36]

The government restricted the import of metals mainly because of its fear of silver outflow to pay for the imports. The government placed restrictions on the import of zinc from China because Korean merchants along the northern frontier were smuggling silver out of Korea on the pretext of purchasing zinc, when in fact they were buying Chinese commodities for resale on the domestic market. The government was also concerned about the outflow of silver to Japan to pay for imports of Japanese copper. Up to 1747 Japanese copper had been paid for, at least in part, by Chinese products imported into Korea, but after this date Korean traders were forbidden from going to Peking and the Sino-Japanese trade shifted to Nagasaki.[37]

Thus, while the absolute amount of the metal supply undoubtedly increased, demand constantly outran supply. Shortage of supply led to rising prices of metals and decreased profits from seigniorage. Wŏn Yu-han has argued that the profits from minting the ever-normal cash declined from 50 percent in 1679 to 10 percent in 1814.[38] Additional data from the *Munhŏnbigo* indicates, however, that Wŏn may have underestimated profits. The return to the government from two large mintings in 1829 and 1830 were as high as 37.6 percent and 31.4 percent calculated as profit on investment.[39] This would appear to be a high rate of profit from seigniorage, but the method of calculation may be misleading. Herbert Heaton, in describing currency minting costs in seventeenth century Europe, has pointed out the cost of gold and silver coins was approximately 5 and 25 percent of the face value, and that the cost of copper coins was relatively so high that it was hardly worth the time to make them.[40] The cost/value ratios for three mintings of copper cash in Korea in 1825, 1829, and 1830 were .92, .73, and .73, respectively.[41] By comparison with European standards the cost was prohibitive, but in Europe specie played a major role in currency, while in Korea specie was a negligible factor. If the Korean government were to make money by minting cash, it had no choice but to make copper coins. In this situation, it may have regarded the profit margin as sufficient to justify the effort.

One indication that the government did find minting profits too low as the practice of debasement by reducing the weight of individual coins. From the early eighteenth to the early nineteenth century, the weight of a copper coin was reduced by about 50 percent.[42] Evidently this was still not sufficient to keep pace with the rising price of metal, and it was obvious by the middle of the nineteenth century that, if the profits from seigniorage were to remain as a useful source of revenue, some way of increasing the margin of face value over production cost had to be found.

Large Cash and Chinese Cash

Three proposals were put forward throughout the eighteenth century as means for increasing revenue and the money supply: the minting of large-cash, the importation of Chinese cash, and the use of a bimetallic silver-copper currency system.

Large cash was deemed advantageous since a single coin would have the purchasing power of several of the ever-normal cash. This would reduce the requirements of raw materials and increase the profitability to the government from minting operations. There is one report of some large cash in use in 1727, but it is unlikely that it circulated widely. In 1742 proposals for a 10-cash and a 100-cash were rejected, and in 1750 Yŏngjo evinced his distaste for large cash on the grounds that it would disturb the people.[43] In 1798 in response to proposals for a 5-cash and 10-cash, it was argued that large cash should not be used because the prime function of copper cash was currency and not a means of profit for the government.[44]

Large cash was consistently opposed in the eighteenth century because of the fear of inflation. Copper cash had already been debased by reducing its weight, and this had not only spurred inflation, but also decreased public trust in the currency. It was feared that the public would equate large cash with blatant debasement and that this would wreck the currency system and domestic commerce altogether.[45] In an economy in which paper money, bills of exchange, and banking operations had hardly developed, the public was not prepared to accept large cash at face value, and many officials believed that if such cash were forced on the public, its market value would soon decline to its intrinsic value causing inflation.[46]

As an alternative to large cash, it was proposed in 1675, 1742, and 1792 that Chinese cash be imported into Korea. In 1675 the Chinese refused to allow the export of cash because it was forbidden by law.[47] In 1742 the proposal was shelved on the grounds that it would make Korea dependent on China for her currency supply, and in 1792 it was rejected because of the fear that China would be inclined to refuse all requests for the export of her copper cash anyway and that this would prove a serious embarrassment for Korea.[48] This proposal was also contrary to the accepted policy of insulating Korea from foreign currencies. In 1737, for example, a noncash buffer zone had been established along the Yalu River by government order to prevent the import of Chinese cash.[49] In 1779 the throne also announced that anyone guilty of importing Chinese cash would be punished according to law.[50] As much stigma was attached to the use of currency from Ch'ing China as to large cash.

The third proposal was for the combined use of silver and copper cash. It was argued that if merchants and the government could be induced to maintain their currency holdings in silver currency, more copper would be released for circulation in the market for small transactions.[51] It was commonly believed that one of the causes of cash shortage in the countryside was the hoarding of currency by wealthy merchants and moneylenders. The main objections to bimetallism, however, were that there was not enough silver in the country to warrant its use as currency, that silver was not currently used in the southern provinces, and that, if it were, then it would draw silver out of the north and reduce the monetary capital in that region for the financing of foreign trade.[52] The idea of large-scale bimetallism was dropped and not revived again through the period to 1876.[53]

Monetary Policy under the Taewongun

Unfortunately no monographic work on currency problems in the first half of the nineteenth century has been done, but it is probably safe to assume that there had been no generic change since the late eighteenth century in the nature of problems associated with currency. In the 1860s the demand for revenue became more acute; additional minting of the ever-normal cash was no longer a feasible alternative for raising revenue because of the low profit margin, and traditional biases against currency and the inflationary effects of excessive minting and the use of large cash persisted. The scattered references to currency problems in the court records in the period 1864-66 reveal that metallic currency per se was still viewed with mistrust and trepidation. In 1864 the dowager-regent ordered the cessation of minting operations, and later in the year, Second State Councilor Yi Yu-wŏn complained that the minting of cash was an incurable disease in that province. Despite the order suspending minting, in the Kapsan area of Hamgyŏng province there was an active market in forged and counterfeit copper notes, probably negotiable paper which appeared after further minting was prohibited.[54] In any case, the prejudice of government officials against currency was still strong.

When Second State Councilor Kim Pyŏng-hak proposed the minting of 100-cash (*tangbaek taejŏn*) on December 6, 1866, his justification for it curiously reveals the same suspicion and fear of currency that characterized previous attitudes toward currency—attitudes which in the past had been responsible for the opposition to large cash. Kim justified the policy on the basis of necessity. He made his proposal shortly after Oppert's visit to Korea, the French expedition to Kanghwa Island, and the General Sherman incident at Pyongyang. He complained about the "poor financial condition of the people and the lack of state funds for the repair of garrisons and for the maintenance and support of official and private business." He recommended the minting of 100-cash as the best way to produce surplus revenues for the state, but only as a temporary expedient. He pointed out that whenever large cash had been authorized in past Chinese dynasties, it was always regarded as a temporary measure. In Kim's view, large cash was definitely a dangerous measure but one justified by the circumstances.[55]

In a second memorial presented the same day Kim revealed just how little his thinking had departed from the conservative position on economic and currency matters. He ascribed the current poverty of both the people and the government to profligate and wasteful expenditure of limited resources. He expressed faith in the traditional theory of the fixed volume of production, which would be sufficient for the people's needs only if they exercised frugality in the consumption of goods. Similarly, the problem of revenue shortage could only be remedied by greater frugality on the part of the government. The basic problem as Kim saw it was that consumption outran production in the private sector and expenditures exceeded revenues in the official sector.[56]

Because copper cash had been traditionally regarded as responsible for commercial activity (rather than vice versa), conspicuous consumption, and the decline in frugality and because large cash had been opposed because it was sure to produce inflation, Kim was forced to justify its use on the grounds of temporary expediency. The minting of 100-cash would rectify the immediate problem of revenue shortage, after which stability

Monetary Policy

would be ensured by a return to frugal spending practices and a balance between production and consumption. The contradiction between the policy and its justification was too great, however, to be glossed over by such feeble rationalization. As it later turned out, few were fooled into thinking that the 100-cash policy was anything but a sacrifice of sound monetary practice for the immediate advantage accruing from increased revenues. When anger over unorthodox monetary policy was coupled with discontent over the wasteful expenditure of state funds on palace construction, the alienation of the more conservative intellectuals was complete.

The decision to go ahead with the minting of the 100-cash was a collective one and not the act of the Taewongun or any one man. All former and incumbent officials of *taesin* rank were asked to give their views on the matter on December 12, 1866, and they generally agreed with Kim Pyŏng-hak that the use of large cash was certainly justified. Such currency would meet the needs of both the state and the populace—in the first place by providing large profits from minting operations, and in the second by relieving the currency shortage and stimulating the flow of goods in the market. No one expressed outright opposition to the minting of 100-cash, although some foresaw the potential inflationary consequences. Brevet Minister-without-Portfolio Cho Tu-sun commented that the people might have no confidence in the new 100-cash. If that occurred, the government should respond by substituting 10-cash for 100-cash. Better still, the 10-cash could be tried first, on the grounds that the smaller the differential between the face value and the intrinsic value of the coin, the more likely the people were to accept it at face value.[57]

Brevet First Deputy Commander Kim Hak-sŏng also proposed the initial use of a small denomination coin, like a 5-cash or 10-cash. If that succeeded, then larger denominations could be put into circulation. Brevet Second Deputy Commander Sŏ Sŏng-sun warned that public confidence in the 100-cash would first have to be established before the coin could be used successfully. Hong Sun-mok, a Second Deputy Commander at this time, also held that the success of the 100-cash depended on whether the "small people" obeyed the law in good faith and had no doubts about it.[58]

Since there was little opposition from the high officials, the throne issued orders for the minting of 100-cash the same day, and circulation began on January 15, 1867.[59] On January 7 the state council declared that both the existing ever-normal circulating treasure and the new 100-cash would be regarded as legal tender for official and private transactions. For taxes and other payments to official agencies, cash payments would be made in a ratio of two thirds 100-cash to one third old cash.[60] The nominal value of the 100-cash was, of course, one hundred times that of an ever-normal coin, but only five to six times greater in its intrinsic metallic value.[61]

The minting of 100-cash was continued until June 16, 1867.[62] The government used the new currency to pay for weapons repair, the maintenance of provincial garrisons, support for local civil yamen, funding of new grain loans, and boat and bridge construction. It has been estimated that sixteen million yang of 100-cash was minted during this period by the government.[63] Counterfeiting also contributed appreciably to the increase in the volume of cash in circulation.

As anticipated, inflation was an immediate consequence of the flood of new currency into the market. The price of rice rose by five or six times.[64] On July 4 the state council reported that the new cash had driven ordinary cash out of the marketplace (à la Gresham's law). The state council expressed its amazement at this phenomenon especially since an edict had been issued in 1866 expressly permitting the circulation of both types of currency! The council noted that it would certainly be helpful if all this currency were put back into circulation "to provide some relief and aid for the transaction of official and private business," and it urged that the situation be made known to all officials to that they could remedy the situation.[65]

On November 7 the state council reported a rapid rise in commodity prices but blamed it on counterfeiting. An edict was issued ordering the decapitation of counterfeiters, and one unfortunate individual was executed two weeks later—a sacrificial lamb to the gods of economics.[66] On January 27, 1868, Kojong expressed the view that counterfeiting and laxity of official enforcement were responsible for inflation.[67] Both were useful scapegoats for the failure of government policy.

Finally, on February 23, 1868, the Taewongun decided to intervene directly. By this date it had become obvious to him that the lack of public trust in the new currency was a major stumbling block to the government's monetary policy and that more efficient and zealous enforcement of the regulations of 1866 would serve to ensure the healthy circulation of the new cash. The Taewongun's response to the crisis produced by the 100-cash illustrates as well as anything could his abiding faith in the power of a monarch to effect his will on any issue, if only he had the courage to take resolute action. The complexities of economics, an ignorant and recalcitrant populace, and an untrustworthy and conniving bureaucracy—all these were as nothing to a man of will with the reins of royal authority grasped firmly in his hands.

Were shopkeepers hoarding regular (ever-normal) cash? He summoned them to the palace and ordered them to put it back into circulation. Were criminals counterfeiting currency? He forbade it. Were local officials remiss in their enforcement of currency regulations? He dispatched twelve secret censors to the provinces to proceed directly to the marketplaces to oversee cash transactions, prevent counterfeiting, and ensure the collection of taxes in 100-cash, with the right to make arrests on the spot. And did the people show a lack of faith in the new currency? He issued a set of regulations designed to instill the confidence that was lacking.[68]

In order to underline the central government's confidence in the new 100-cash the Taewongun ordered that henceforth all taxes and other payments to agencies of the government throughout the country be made exclusively in 100-cash. Any clerks found accepting tax payments in regular copper cash and remitting tax payments to the central government in 100-cash would be punished as criminals. In the future all private commercial transactions involving amounts of one yang or more would be made in 100-cash. As he instructed his secret censors prior to dispatching them to the provinces, these regulations would ensure that all cash would be liberated for the market. They were told to put an end to the machinations of the petty clerks and to summon all the people of an area, great and small, and tell them that "the 100-cash will be put into use forever. . . . If there should be any stubborn and perverse types who do not follow instructions, punish them first and report them afterwards."[69] His faith in the efficacy of royal command was unbounded.

And yet, in the end, it was all to no avail, for inflation could not be checked. By 1868 the government could no longer avoid responsibility for the failure of its monetary policy. In November of that year, the court ordered a one-time voluntary contribution on people of all social strata in the form of land and capitation levies payable in 100-cash for the financing of palace construction. This prompted the opposition of Ch'oe Ik-hyŏn—a man eventually to play a key role in the forced retirement of the Taewongun—against excessive taxation and the use of the 100-cash.[70] Sometime soon after, the 100-cash was withdrawn from circulation.[71]

No sooner had the 100-cash proven a failure, however, than the government turned to an alternate solution of the same genre—the importation of Chinese cash. Chinese cash was already in use in 1867, and in 1868 it was imported in increasing quantity.[72] By 1874 there was an estimated three to four million yang of Chinese cash in Korea.[73] The intrinsic metallic value of Chinese cash was only one half that of the ever-normal cash, but they both circulated at the same face value. The means by which Chinese cash was imported into Korea at this time—whether by direct government purchase on tribute missions or by private merchants—is not clear, but it appears probable that the Korean government purchased Chinese copper coins because they were cheaper in China than in Korea by one third, and then paid for goods and services

Politics and Policy in Traditional Korea

with them. The difference in the value of the copper coins of the two countries was probably made possible by trade and exchange barriers between the two countries which prevented equalization of value by normal trade and currency movements. The influx of the Chinese currency into Korea increased the volume of currency and produced inflation just as the 100-cash had.[74] The same tactic was tried twice in one decade with unfavorable results.

A narrow and restricted tax base was put to the test by a sudden increase in the demand for revenue in the 1860s. The government turned to profits from seigniorage on the minting of copper currency as an alternate solution to the problem of revenue shortage and as a means of avoiding the wrath of the privileged elite, but by doing so antagonized the conservative monetists who possessed a moralistic distaste for currency and a fear of inflation. The notion of currency as a source of evil was grounded in the Confucian disdain for commercial activity and a fear of the weakening of the moral values of diligence and frugality that were so essential to the maintenance of agricultural production. The growth in the volume of copper cash had been fought in the early eighteenth century by those who preferred a return to the stability and security of a natural economy where barter and the use of grain and cloth in a smaller range of transactions prevailed. Even though the battle against cash was lost by 1731, the conservative bias against the evils of cash was carried over into the nineteenth century.

Furthermore, by the nineteenth century copper cash had come to play such an important role in market transactions and government revenue that the economy was affected more seriously by price fluctuations than it had ever been before. There was general consensus that an imbalance between the money supply and the volume of commodities led to either deflation or inflation, neither of which was desirable. Deflation and a shortage of cash could be remedied by additional minting, but caution had to be exercised lest excessive minting overturn the balance producing commodity price inflation.

By the late eighteenth century the minting of cash at a profit had become an accepted alternative for raising revenue, but as the cost of metal rose and the profitability of minting ever-normal cash declined, the inducement for relying on large cash became greater. Large cash was no different in essence from minting cash at a profit or debasement of copper coins—both of which were practiced in the eighteenth century, but large cash involved higher profits from seigniorage than either of the above methods. By the middle 1860s the government's finances were strained to the breaking point and minting cash at a profit seemed to be a feasible way to raise funds in an emergency, but the margin of profit on ordinary

Monetary Policy

ever-normal cash was by now too low. Only the minting of large cash promised to yield adequate income. Caution was therefore abandoned in the face of the immediate crisis but not without some trepidation, for officials were still aware of the potential inflationary effects of large cash. Yet the fear of inflation—great as it was—was less formidable an obstacle than a total revamping of an inequitable tax structure. When the predicted and predictable inflation and withdrawal of ever-normal cash from the marketplace did take place, the Taewongun personally stepped into the breach. He tried to force the new currency onto the market and create public confidence in it by exhortation and coercion. When this failed, he imported Chinese currency but with the same untoward results.

The social elite, landowning class, and conservative intellectuals would not accept a tax policy that seriously threatened their interests. Neither would they tolerate an inflationary monetary policy that violated the tenets of economic and moral dogma. Had they been in power they would have solved the revenue problem by curtailing expenditures, especially on palace construction because they had no stake in restoring the grandeur and prestige of the throne. For the Taewongun palace construction, military defense, and relief for the peasantry could not be abandoned, and the consequences of currency manipulation were less serious than the failure to achieve these objectives. He failed to see, however, that the conservative opposition to his monetary policies would lead to the shattering of the consensus he had achieved on his domestic and foreign policies.

9

Consensus Destroyed: The Retirement of the Taewongun

At the end of 1873 the Taewongun was forced into retirement, an event that was accompanied by a change of administrative personnel and a revision of domestic policy. It has been frequently held that the Taewongun's forced withdrawal from politics was the opening round in a protracted factional struggle between his cohorts and those of Queen Min, a struggle which consumed the energies of the Korean people and distracted them from the more important task of defending national integrity.[1] The factional explanation, however, fails to take into account the role of the king and the fundamental philosophical conflict between the Taewongun and his critics over domestic policy.

The king's role in the Taewongun's retirement was crucial and decisive. The only source of legitimacy for the Taewongun's exercise of authority derived from his position as the father of the king. As long as Kojong was young and pliable he did not challenge his father's leadership, but the potential for a challenge was present from the time that the Dowager Cho relinquished the regency in 1866. This potential was realized when the king came of age in a real rather than in a legal sense in 1873. His attainment of adulthood, signified only by his own consciousness of independence, was the touchstone to the shift in political authority that took place at that time. For the Taewongun to have retained power in the face of an unwilling adult king would have required some act of usurpation in the manner of the attempted deposition of Kojong in 1881 or the military uprising of 1882. Failing this, the king's sovereignty remained supreme.

During Kojong's minority the source of the Taewongun's political support was not to be found in any discrete "faction" of bureaucrats loyal to him on an exclusively personal basis, even though there were some who obviously fit that category. The acceptance of his leadership

Consensus Destroyed

rested more on general support for his policies throughout the bureaucracy. This consensus was lost just about the time that the king became an adult. It was broken by a small but vocal group of officials and scholars who took issue with some of the Taewongun's domestic policies on the grounds that they violated their conception of orthodox Confucian principles of government. This opposition was politically significant despite the fact that it represented minority opinion because political power was not determined by obtaining majority support within the bureaucracy, but by influencing or gaining the favor of a king who had come to maturity.

The queen and her relatives probably could not have turned the king against his father for purely political reasons. The Confucian opposition contributed to the politics of the situation by convincing the king of the dubious nature of some of his father's policies. Kojong's conviction that his father was in error gave the otherwise timid young fellow the courage to challenge his parent directly. Once challenged, the Taewongun decided to retreat from the scene of action, rather than force the issue and oppose his legitimately enthroned son.

The Consensus on Foreign and Domestic Policy

The consensus of the 1860s was built around the Taewongun's foreign policy and domestic program. His foreign policy was by far the more significant of the two in terms of its effect in solidifying domestic political support for his regime because it appealed to the sense of pride and self-esteem of the Korean people. Although there were some who harbored reservations about the risks involved in his policies, they were cowed into silence by the immense popularity of his resolute resistance to foreign demands.

His foreign policy was simple and straightforward: no treaties and no trade with the Westerners, no toleration of Catholic proselytization within Korea, and no reordering of relations with Japan. Initially this stance appeared dangerous and risky for the Koreans when all about them had succumbed to foreign power. The "victories" over the French in 1866 and the Americans in 1871 vindicated the Taewongun in his boldness and gave reassurance to his people. Confucian intellectuals in particular were heartened by his courageousness, for they felt that the Manchus had failed to defend Chinese civilization, that the Japanese had put up virtually no resistance at all and had sold out to the West, and that Korea remained the last and best hope for the preservation of Eastern culture. On these grounds, the intellectual leaders of the nation, in particular the local scholars and literati who provided the country with moral fiber and backbone, provided solid support for the Taewongun's foreign policy.

Politics and Policy in Traditional Korea

The Confucian intelligentsia was also heartened by the Taewongun's uncompromising suppression of heterodox and subversive thought within Korea. Although the Tonghak movement of the early 1860s had been partially based on opposition to Western thought, to Confucians it appeared heterodox because of its Western accretions and its egalitarian appeal to the lower classes, and they were encouraged by the suppression of the movement in 1862. Catholicism was, of course, regarded as much more dangerous because it appeared to be a vehicle of fifth-column subversion as well as a threat to Confucian orthodoxy. Ever since the capture of Hwang Sa-yong and his "silk letter" in 1801 (requesting French military aid for the support of Catholicism in Korea) the link between native Catholics and foreign military force was established firmly in the minds of many Koreans. Because of several cases of actual complicity of French missionaries and Korean Catholics in Western expeditions to Korea in the 1860s, the subversive potential of Catholicism was feared more than ever before. Even when evidence of collusion was lacking, it was assumed.[2] Therefore, Confucian intellectuals and officials responded with zeal to the Taewongun's call for the persecution of Catholicism, which for all practical purposes was wiped out by 1871.

The Taewongun also had strong support for his domestic policies at the outset of his regime because there was general awareness of the need for reform in the wake of the 1862 rebellions. Yet any program of reform or national salvation contained within it the seeds of discontent and division. The basic question was simply this: at what price was national salvation or reform to be achieved? Were the preservation of the dynasty or the reform of inequities in government and taxation to be purchased at the expense of elite interests or Confucian orthodoxy?

The weakness of national consciousness contributed to the difficulty of achieving solidarity and support for national needs. While Korea possessed several aspects of nationhood—a single language, racial and ethnic homogeneity, a long historical tradition, an undivided polity, a distinctive life-style, a consensus on culture and values, and even a sense of the uniqueness of the Korean people—in the absence of a focus of loyalty to the nation-state the divergent interests of dynasty, social class, family, lineage, and Confucian culture could be held in higher esteem than national interest.

Although the Taewongun was no social revolutionary, he gave priority to the interests of the dynasty and monarchy over those of the social elite. As a man of action he was also willing to ignore certain aspects of Confucian dogma in order to achieve his objectives. His critics, however, opposed him on both counts: they were unwilling to tolerate any subversion of the status quo in economic and social relations and they were intolerant of any compromise with Confucian norms and values, for they believed that there was no nation worth saving without a yangban elite and a Confucian tradition.

The First Signs of Rift: Conflicting Approaches to Government

The first sign of opposition to the Taewongun's policies was voiced in 1866 at the time of the French expedition to Kanghwa Island when the elderly scholar-official, Yi Hang-no, submitted a memorial to the throne which combined an affirmation of the Taewongun's foreign policy with an attack on his domestic program. Yi's memorial was doubly significant because it represented the protest of a man whose influence far outweighed his bureaucratic position. Yi Hang-no had the kind of reputation for learning and integrity and undeviating commitment to principle that ultimately would have the most effect on a young king who was then being indoctrinated in the fundamentals of Confucian government. The Taewongun as a man of practical action was less inclined to give heed to the doctrinaire rantings of a semi-recluse than his son, but even he had acknowledged the prestige of Yi Hang-no by purposely bringing him into his government to borrow the aura of his prestige for his own regime. On October 16, 1866, just after the occupation of Kanghwa Island by the French, the seventy-four-year-old Yi had been appointed Sixth Royal Secretary.[3]

Yi Hang-no was the kind of man who represented one extreme of the polarity in the Confucian tradition, so well described by Benjamin Schwartz, between the contemplative and the active, between the inner world and the outer, and between the ideals of self-cultivation and the ordering of the world.[4] Throughout his life Yi had spurned opportunities for office in preference for a life of study and moral self-cultivation, but not with the idea that he was to remain forever detached from public affairs. On the contrary, a life of detachment in study and contemplation was designed to provide a better and more fundamental knowledge of government than participation in the bureaucracy. Men who devoted their lives to contemplation and self-cultivation waited for the time when the circumstances were right, when their services would be in demand, and when the results of their study could be put to best use. It was not until 1866 that the true opportunity for which he had been preparing himself for a lifetime presented itself. The country was in a state of crisis for the barbarians were at the gates of the capital. The time had come for Yi Hang-no to proffer his advice for "ordering of the world."

On October 20, 1866, just four days after his appointment to office and four days before the French were defeated in battle on Kanghwa Island, Yi submitted his recommendations to the throne. He indicated total support for current foreign policy. There was to be no compromise with the barbarians, and those who talked of peace were betraying their

Politics and Policy in Traditional Korea

country. There had been some talk of adjusting to the circumstances by retreating in the face of the French forces and evacuating the capital, but this was not to be tolerated. Yi declared that there were only two ways of conducting affairs—adhering to principle or adjusting to the circumstances—and only a sage had the requisite knowledge and wisdom for adjusting to the circumstances. Ordinary men had to hold fast to principle and defend the capital.

Yi expressed himself in defense of the fatherland with a kind of militant patriotism that formed the basis for the reactive or negative antiforeign nationalism of ensuing decades. He delved back into history for a precedent with which to rally king and country to defend against barbarian attack. The Chinese Sui dynasty (581-618), he pointed out, though outnumbering the Koreans of Koguryŏ times by huge margin, were rendered helpless by the brave deeds of the general Ulchi-mundŏk. Emperor T'ai-tsung of the T'ang failed in his seige of Korean cities and "became the laughing-stock of the world." The hordes of Red Turban bandits who invaded Korea during the Koryŏ dynasty were repelled and crushed.

For Yi the correct domestic policy was also essential for success in resisting the invaders, but the essence of his domestic program was an appeal to fundamental moral virtues and not the suggestion of concrete plans for action.

> If from now on the King starts by rising early and going to bed late, and if the ministers take oaths among themselves to cut out the evils of parties and merriment, be diligent in cultivating frugality and virtue, do not allow private considerations from taking root in their minds, and do not use artifice as a method of operation in government affairs, then the officials and common people will all cleanse and purify their minds and be in great accord with his will . . .
>
> What I wish the King would do is to consult with men of sagacity and with his ministers . . . Their face-to-face remonstrance with the King will be sufficient to rectify the King's errors and encourage the King in his habits. Their purification and cleansing of government affairs will be sufficient for reviving the subjects of the King. Their talent in and knowledge of military affairs will be sufficient to stand up against the hated enemies of the King.[5]

Since Yi Hang-no had spent most of his life in Confucian self-cultivation, it is not surprising that in his formula for the rectification of the outer world he fell back on the norms by which he had attempted to rectify his own self. Yi did not concern himself with laws and institutions, for he believed that all problems could be solved by the recruitment of moral men and adherence to moral standards.

Furthermore, as Schwartz has pointed out, men who believed that the cultivation of morality was more efficacious in ordering the state than institutional reform also had their special view of economic policy. They believed that the common people had to be guaranteed a minimal level of subsistence and security before they could be led to ethical behavior—an idea at least as old as Mencius. Government had to "refrain from heavy taxes, excessive corvee, ambitious military ventures, and displays of pomp and luxury."[6] Yi Hang-no also subscribed to such views. He reminded the king that his mandate to rule rested on the support of the people, which was to be obtained by guaranteeing their livelihood. But he found that since 1864 the interests of the people had been sacrificed to the needs of the monarchy and the state, and he demanded a return to fundamental Mencian values.

Put a stop to construction projects; put an end to government which exacts taxes from the people; abandon the habits of luxury and extravagance; make the palace humble and partake simply and sparingly of food and drink; shun fancy clothes and devote all efforts to the people's affairs . . . Then the strength of the people will be greatly extended and public opinion will be in harmony, and the people will look up to you as a father and mother . . . Only after things are done like this can the Western barbarians be driven off and the state preserved.[7]

Yi Hang-no's remarks could have been construed as an attack on the Taewongun, but on October 22 he was promoted to the post of second minister of works. He declined and was subsequently appointed to two other posts, which he also refused to assume.[8] In the absence of solid evidence, one can only surmise the reasons for this generous treatment of Yi. The Taewongun may still have desired to keep him in office in order to display his sincerity in the search for talented men, or he may have been more pleased by Yi's support of foreign policy than disgruntled by his critique of domestic policy. It is also possible that the king or queen intervened to protect Yi.

Whatever the source of his good fortune, Yi Hang-no was not fearful of the loss of an official position which he had shunned for so long. On October 27 he repeated his initial criticism, and on November 28 he requested the restoration of the Mandongmyo, the shrine to the Ming that had been abolished by the Taewongun in 1865, (see Chapter 6). Yi Hang-no was concerned about the Mandongmyo because it was a spiritual symbol of righteousness that signified Korea's commitment to moral values and superior culture. He reminded the throne that the shrine had been constructed in commemoration of the great benevolence of the Ming in dispatching troops to Korea to oppose the Japanese and that it was especially incumbent on Korea to preserve this ritual expression of respect and loyalty because the Manchus had snuffed out the Ming dynasty and because King Hyojong and Song Si-yŏl had been frustrated in their ambition to wreak vengeance on the Manchus.

Politics and Policy in Traditional Korea

Furthermore, several kings had paid homage to the shrine and granted it support. When it was abolished the literati and yangban of Ch'ungch'ŏng and Chŏlla provinces raised a hue and cry, but public opinion was flouted and the decision was not reversed. Now that the barbarians were at the gates of Korea, it was no time to discontinue rites that had long been practiced, for the "rites observed by rulers and subjects are what distinguish the cultured and civilized from the barbarians." If the king were to order the restoration of the Mandongmyo, Yi urged, "then the people of the state will know their righteous duty of expelling the barbarians and the foreign pirates will tremble with fear. Our spirit and strength will, on the contrary, be greater than the force of three armies."[9] Although the government failed to heed Yi's request, his protest was the first crack in the Taewongun's solid phalanx of support. It sounded the death knell for the Taewongun's regime.

Ch'oe Ik-Hyŏn

The standard raised by Yi was taken up by his leading disciple, Ch'oe Ik-hyŏn. Born in 1833, Ch'oe was taken by his father to study with Yi Hang-no in 1846. In 1854 he entered the National Academy and passed the *munkwa* examination the next year. Unlike his mentor, Ch'oe chose to serve in office. He was appointed to a district magistracy in 1862 and subsequently held some minor posts in the capital. His mother died in 1866, and mourning requirements took him out of circulation until the middle of 1868.[10]

Soon after his appointment to the post of third inspector in the Office of the Inspector General on November 13, 1868, Ch'oe submitted a memorial calling for an end to useless construction projects and excessive taxation, and the abolition of the 100-cash and the transit taxes collected at the gates of Seoul. Ch'oe's criticism was based on unadulterated Mencian dogma: ostentatious expenditure by a ruler caused the ruination of his people, while frugality on his part spared them the oppression of excessive taxation. Ch'oe held that all Chinese history was a testament to this simple proposition, and he pointed out that sage Chinese emperors of remote antiquity lived in humble quarters eating coarse food and devoting themselves to the welfare of the people. On the contrary, the last ruler of the Hsia and Shang dynasties and the infamous Shih Huang-ti of the Ch'in dynasty ruined their states by building magnificent palaces and terraces and constructing long walls. "Since the Han dynasty, was there ever a sovereign who maintained his state and enjoyed great peace who did not devote himself to putting a stop to corvée and winning the minds of the people? Was there ever a sovereign who did not lose his state and was not overthrown because he had undertaken too many construction projects and had exhausted the strength of the people?"[11] Kojong praised

Consensus Destroyed

Ch'oe's love of country and concern for the people. Although Kojong failed to heed his advice and discontinue either palace construction or gate taxes, this was the first concrete example of Kojong's sympathy for the moralistic critique of his father's policies.[12]

Several days later a censorate official, Kwŏn Chŏng-nok, impeached Ch'oe and demanded his exile. Kwŏn asked why it was that Ch'oe had decided to issue his wild accusations just when palace construction was about completed and the currency problem solved? Kwŏn claimed that gate taxes were no more than part of the standard regulations governing roads and transportation, and that both Ch'oe and Yi Hang-no were only interested in establishing their reputations. He demanded Ch'oe's exile because of his use of disrespectful language.[13]

Kojong excused Ch'oe on the grounds that he was an ignoramus from the country, but he dismissed him from office.[14] Four days later on November 21, however, Ch'oe was appointed First Secretary in the Royal Clan Administration, a promotion from senior fourth to senior third rank.[15] This appointment was probably a mild act of defiance by the king against his father, especially since it was likely that the Taewongun had directed Kwŏn Chŏng-nok to impeach Ch'oe.[16] The king's action was a harbinger of things to come.

Ch'oe Ik-hyŏn's First Memorial

On December 14, 1873, two weeks after his appointment to the Royal Secretariat, Ch'oe Ik-hyŏn submitted a memorial to the throne. At the time Ch'oe was still at his home in the countryside and had not yet proceeded to the capital to take up his official duties. He handed his memorial over to the local magistrate for transmission, but when it arrived at the office of the governor of Kyŏnggi province, the governor was so shocked by its contents that he personally delivered it to the Taewongun. Enraged, the Taewongun ordered it sent back to Ch'oe's district. Talk about the memorial began to spread through Seoul. The king, who had been wondering why Ch'oe had not come to Seoul to assume his post, heard about the memorial and summoned him to court.

The Taewongun reputedly dispatched a commander of one of the royal guard regiments with a note for Ch'oe telling him that his memorial could not be presented in its original form, and that it would be best for him to feign illness and decline his recent appointment. If he did not do so, then "the court would not be pleased." Ch'oe, however, refused to retract his memorial, which was finally presented at court.[17]

The memorial contained a slashing attack on the current state of affairs.

> Recently, old governmental regulations have been changed. Men have been chosen for their pliability. Decisions have been made without the

recommendations of the high officials of the six ministries. The censors try to avoid charges of meddling [and thus make no remonstrance.] Those at court talk stupidly and act willfully. What ought to be done and what is upright has been extinguished. Sycophancy runs rampant. Upright men are hidden, and there is no rest from taxation. The people [have become] fish and meat, and morality has been destroyed. Serving the public interest is regarded as most deviate, and serving private interest is thought of as the best policy. We are inundated with men who know no shame and who have gained favor. Men of integrity are rare and are dying off. Thus has it come about that we have had natural disasters in heaven and on earth. Rain, sun, cold, and heat are all out of conjunction with their proper seasons.[18]

Ch'oe's strident diatribe was directed against practically every high official in government service, and his contention that government, morality, and nature were out of kilter called into question the state of the king's virtue.

Kojong, however, took no offense. He praised the memorial as "coming straight from the heart," and ordered that Ch'oe be promoted to the post of second minister in the Ministry of Taxation. The next day, at the royal lectures on the classics, the king said he was delighted to see such an example of upright, forthright remonstrance, so rare in recent times. He admitted that it might be grating to the ear, but that this recommended it all the more as good counsel. "What I respect and desire is the opening of the pathways of speech," said Kojong, and he urged that officials at court pay respect to the errors pointed out in the memorial.[19]

Within the next week, eight of the highest government officials tendered their resignations, the majority of officials in the Royal Secretariat and the three censoring offices were dismissed from their posts, and two officials were exiled for protesting Ch'oe's memorial. While it has been common to regard these dismissals as a political purge engineered by the Min faction against the Taewongun faction, as the evidence will show, the officials who were dimissed for defending the policies of the Taewongun's regime were not necessarily members of a discrete faction; the pattern of dismissals does not clearly indicate a purge of pro-Taewongun men alone; the high state councilors resigned from office rather than being dismissed, and Kojong even tried to prevent their resignations.

On December 15 and 16, Second State Councilor Kang No, Third State Councilor Han Kye-won, and First Minister of the Royal Clan Administration Hong Sun-mok submitted their resignations on the grounds that Ch'oe had charged them with laxity and malfeasance in office.[20] These three men owed their positions to the Taewongun's patronage. Kang No, a member of the minority Northerner faction, had

Consensus Destroyed

been appointed to important office first in 1866 and was made second state councilor in 1872. Han, of the minority Southerner faction, had been appointed third state councilor in 1872. Hong Sun-mok had held a series of important posts including the governorship of Hwanghae province, minister of personnel, chief magistrate of Seoul, and in 1869 third state councilor. He had been appointed chief state councilor on November 13, 1872, and had resigned on May 25, 1873. The post of chief state councilor was left vacant until the appointment of Yi Yu-wŏn on January 1, 1874, but during this half-year period Hong performed the advisory if not the administrative functions of chief state councilor from his sinecure in the Royal Clan Administration.[21]

Kojong reaffirmed his approval of Ch'oe's memorial but refused to accept the councilors' resignations, indicating that the Ch'oe incident was more complicated than a simple political purge. If the Min faction were in control with Kojong acting as their puppet, there is no reason why they should have failed to seize this opportunity to remove pro-Taewongun officials. Kojong did, however, accept the resignations of other officials. On December 16, members of the Royal Secretariat and the three offices of the censorate—the Office of the Inspector General, the Office of the Censor-General and the Office of Special Counselors—resigned en masse. They charged that Ch'oe's statement that "old governmental regulations have been changed and morality destroyed" failed to distinguish clearly what was meant and who was responsible for such a state of affairs, and his accusation that the censorate had failed to make remonstrance impugned their integrity.[22]

One must be cautious about assigning important political significance to a dismissal of a censorate roster because frequent and indiscriminate changes in the make-up of the three censorate offices had become common practice. For example, between 1864 and 1873, there were about fifteen to twenty changes *per year* in the posts of censor-general and inspector-general. In 1864 alone, ninety-four men held these two posts. Obviously higher censorate posts were hardly functional, and the rapid turnover in censorate appointments may have been a traditional device in Korea to solve the problem of imbalance between the large number of qualified yangban and the small number of available posts.[23]

Furthermore, many of the men dismissed on December 16, were reappointed to office on December 21, and many of those who were appointed on December 16 were dismissed on December 21.[24] One of the new censors appointed on December 21 was none other than Kwŏn Chŏng-nok, the man who impeached Ch'oe Ik-hyŏn in 1868 supposedly at the direction of the Taewongun. But on December 23 he and the other appointees of December 22 were also dismissed from their posts.[25] These dismissals were carried out because the censorate and other offices continued to protest Kojong's actions, but there was no clear picture of a political purge of Taewongun men.

Kojong finally exiled two men for their attacks on Ch'oe. On December 17, An Ki-yong,[26] who was then third minister in the Ministry of Punishments, claimed that Ch'oe's criticisms were not honest remonstrance at all, but merely an attempt to build his own personal reputation. An pointed out that Ch'oe's charge that morality had been destroyed cast aspersions on every decision taken since Kojong came to the throne. For someone to suggest that the king had failed to preserve moral standards without being punished would lead future generations to assume that the charges were true. An asked that Ch'oe be tried by the state tribunal.[27]

Hŏ Wŏn-sik, a former censor, also protested that Ch'oe's charges were tantamount to an imputation that the proper moral obligations between ruler and subject, and father and son were not being fulfilled. He insisted that there had been nothing lacking in the royal family's respect for its ancestors and in the people's filial piety and respect for their elders. The people had been successful in rejecting heterodoxy (Catholicism) and had avoided "falling to [the status of] animals and beasts."[28] Hŏ claimed that Ch'oe's criticism that "old regulations of government have been changed" was also contrary to fact. In governing a state, nothing was more important than rites and music, and during the last few years mistakes in legal statutes had been rectified by the compilation of the law code, the *Taejon hoet'ong*, and by the collation of ritual texts of previous reigns in the *Orye*.[29] Furthermore, the oppression of the peasants by powerful local families had been ended. The people were no longer starving and were all satisfied and content. Hŏ demanded to know specifically who was indicated by the charges of willful behavior and sycophancy and how Ch'oe could accuse all officials of trying to avoid criticism. He too demanded Ch'oe's exile. The newly staffed Royal Secretariat then claimed that An and Hŏ had no right to remonstrate because they were not censors. If they were not to be dismissed from office, at least they should be admonished and investigated. Kojong approved and ordered them exiled.[30]

At the royal lectures that day lecturers Yi Sŭng-bo and Kwŏn Chŏng-ho[31] demanded Ch'oe's impeachment because of his flagrant and unspecified charges and defended An and Hŏ for their loyal remonstrance. Kojong replied that it was Ch'oe, not An and Hŏ, who was following in the tradition of loyal remonstrance and he refused to bring Ch'oe to trial.[32]

The protest expanded to take in a broader spectrum of the high officials than the state councilors or censors. On December 17 memorials of resignation were submitted by ministers of taxation, rites, works and war, and by a former minister of punishment. Kojong refused the resignations but ordered reductions in salary for the men involved.[33]

Student Strike

The protest against Ch'oe Ik-hyŏn was by no means limited to a few officials who might be construed as members of a Taewongun clique. On December 17 the students of the National Academy in Seoul initiated what might be anachronistically called a protest strike. When asked the reason for their act, they presented the academy director with a manifesto defending the king (and by implication the Taewongun) on moral-ethical grounds.

In the memorial Ch'oe said that "morality was destroyed." We do not understand what he meant by this and our hearts are cold and we tremble with fear.

Now, that whereby men are men and a state is a state is only that the laws of Heaven and human morality are carried out by the King. Therefore, if human relationships have crumbled and morality is in decay, then this means there are no such things as ruler and subject, father and son [and the moral obligations that these relationships imply]. Being without ruler or father is the same as being barbarians and animals. How could men act like men and how could a state be a state?

Alas! The culture cultivated by former kings and the teachings nurtured by them have now been extinguished. Our sage King with his illustrious intelligence and great virtue and learning has daily devoted himself to the task of leading and guiding [the people] in the laws and government of former kings. He has clarified the teachings of the sages, defended true learning and rejected heterodoxy, advanced filial piety and friendship and paid respect to the ancestors of the royal house . . .

How can it be that one memorial appears, and in the end it causes a generation in which [proper] teachings have prevailed and enlightenment achieved to be barbarians and animals . . . ? As far as morality is concerned we cannot remain silent when it had been said that "morality has been destroyed." Therefore, we do now presume to open our hearts and petition.[34]

The students had few political motivations and were no doubt as idealistic as students are today. Their rebuttal was couched in the same philosophical and ethical terms used by Ch'oe; it was not an expression of political factionalism. When the students ignored the orders of the director of the National Academy to return to school, Kojong exiled the leaders of the protest and the student who drafted the petition.[35]

On December 19 during the royal lectures Kojong expressed his amazement that the students had dared to go on strike about a matter that did not concern them at all. He also remarked that if he received any more memorials like those of An Ki-yǒng and Hǒ Wǒn-sik, he would mete out proper punishment. Pak Kyu-su, soon to be a leading official in the new regime and an individual who would have benefited from a purge, came to the defense of the students. He told Kojong that the student protest was based on their defense of principle, and that there were instances in the past when students had gone on strike for this purpose.[36]

On December 19 the headmaster of the National Academy submitted his resignation because of his inability to persuade the students to return to their studies.[37] The next day Minister of Punishments Cho Pyǒng-ch'ang suggested that a heavy hand be used with the recalcitrant students, but Kojong was not pleased with this recommendation. Possibly he was upset at the suggestion that coercion was needed to reveal his own virtuous role, and he dismissed Ch'oe from office.[38] But it was not long before he was driven to take the kind of action that Ch'oe recommended. When it was reported that the students had refused to go to supper in the dining hall at the academy and were protesting the exile of their leaders, Kojong again ordered them back to school. The students refused to comply until Ch'oe Ik-hyǒn was punished, and Kojong responded by exiling the new leaders and expelling those who refused to return to their studies.[39]

Hong Si-Hyǒng's Attack

Ch'oe Ik-hyǒn's first memorial had been couched in vague and general terms, and it was not until December 18 that concrete policy issues were raised in a memorial by censor Hong Si-hyǒng. Hong requested the restoration of the Mandongmyo and the private academies, the abolition of the household cloth tax because it confused social status distinctions, and the elimination of voluntary contributions, extra land levies, and other forms of official extortion in order to remove the fiscal burdens on the peasantry. He suggested that financial problems be solved by greater frugality and by returning responsibility for tax collection to individual palaces and yamen, and he requested the withdrawal of Chinese currency, which had caused inflation and disrupted the currency system because it had failed to circulate in Kyǒngsang province and the northwest region. He ended with an attack on An Ki-yǒng and Hǒ Wǒn-sik and a plea to Kojong to summon worthy men and retired scholars to court to lecture on the classics and assume public office. This would be the way for the king to achieve a true restoration (*chunghǔng*) that would enable the dynasty to continue forever. Hong's message to the Taewongun was a direct and simple one: the dynasty was not to be preserved by damaging the status quo in social relations or moral standards.

Consensus Destroyed

Yet Kojong praised Hong's memorial and appointed him to the Office of Special Counselors so that he would be responsible for offering remonstrance in the future.[40]

Kojong declined to restore the Mandongmyo because he felt he had no right to countermand Dowager Cho's decree abolishing it during her regency, but he acknowledged no restriction against his taking action on any law enacted after 1866, when he had formally assumed personal rule. Therfore, he abolished all new levies imposed after that date, such as the voluntary contributions, land levies, and river port taxes.[41] This decision represented the second major policy reversal after the abolition of the Seoul gate taxes.

Ch'oe's Second Memorial

Hong Si-hyŏng's memorial was followed shortly thereafter by a second memorial from Ch'oe Ik-hyŏn on December 22. Ch'oe attempted to provide a detailed explanation of his thinking, a critique of the past decade, and a direct indictment of the Taewongun for interfering in government affairs. In Ch'oe's view, Korean history was the record of a moral order continuing down through time to the present reign. Korea had been converted from her barbarian customs during the Chinese Shang dynasty (in the middle of the second millennium B.C.), and ever since that time a succession of sage rulers and worthy ministers had preserved the moral order. It was only in the last few years, referring indirectly to the Taewongun, that this order had been subverted by imposing voluntary contributions, abolishing the Mandongmyo and the private academies, tampering with the royal clan genealogy to fill in extinct lines of the royal house, absolving certain long-deceased officials of crimes of treason and posthumously restoring them to office, and importing Chinese cash.[42]

Ch'oe repeated the arguments of Yi Hang-no and Hong Si-hyŏng that the abolition of the Mandongmyo and the private academies was a disruption of the moral order. The private academy was a place where young men studied the classics and learned about the true way. To do away with them could only do damage to the cultivation of morality and virtue. Futhermore, local worthies served as models of virtue for the populace by conducting rites at the academy shrines. He promised that if they were restored, "the sacrificial garments and the resonant tones of the musical instruments and incantations would be in no way inferior to the golden age of the past. Would that not be fortunate, indeed?"

It was a vision of the utopia of remote antiquity that Ch'oe kept ever in his mind's eye. He read into the sordid realities of his own day the image of a simple society of moral perfection. He admitted that some of the private academies might be ineffective and corrupt, but as Confucius said

Politics and Policy in Traditional Korea

to one of his disciples, as long as you have a sheep, you always have hope that rites may sometime be restored. Once the academies were abolished, then learning and ritual might be lost forever.

Ch'oe also claimed that royal lines which had become extinct had been improperly extended by tampering with the royal genealogies. Men from branch lines were adopted as heirs from main lines—a dangerous practice because it upset the proper order for ancestral sacrifice. The king had had the best intentions in ordering work done on the genealogy but mistakes were made by certain officials who "have been cut off from the [teachings of] Confucius." Gaps in the genealogy were filled in with "spirits" as if they were true ancestors. Thus, in "embellishing" the line of succession, these men had "sullied ten thousand years of human history."

Ch'oe also regarded as reprehensible the fact that three officials who lived in the sixteenth and seventeenth centuries were absolved of their crimes posthumously.[43] Such a reversal of decisions once rendered was only another way in which the great moral relationships between father and son, and ruler and subject had been subverted in the present reign. To Ch'oe, Heaven's mandate and Heaven's judgment were not things that could be altered by the private desires of men.

The last charge on Ch'oe's list was against the import of cash from China and its circulation throughout Korea. Ch'oe was particularly upset about the moral questions involved. This currency, after all, was "Ch'ing cash" or "Manchu cash." Had not the Manchus invaded Korea twice in 1627 and 1636? Had not the Manchus overthrown the benevolent Ming to establish the Ch'ing dynasty in 1644?

In my humble opinion, the abolition of Ch'ing cash is a matter of making a strict distinction between *hua* [cultured, Chinese] and *i* [barbarian], and of bearing up under suffering [that is, enduring whatever suffering there might be from abolishing Ch'ing cash]. This was the feeling . . . passed on by King Hyojong and Song Si-yŏl, whose merit was the same as that of Confucius and Chu Hsi. I refer to that matter in the past of the just prohibition of goods being brought back [from China] by prisoners [after the Manchu invasions]. The use of Manchu cash at present means that we have forgotten the shame of defeat in war [at the hands of the Manchus]. It confuses the distinctions between *yin* and *yang* and loyalty and treason. The harm done to good government has already been most severe.

Thus it would seem that the opposition movement was led by a small group of pro-Ming cultists among the orthodox Confucianists in Korea. They criticized the abolition of the Mandongmyo and the use of Ch'ing cash on the grounds of disloyalty to the Ming. They still continued to date their writings in the name of the last Ming ruler instead of either the contemporary Chinese reign period or the reign year of the current

Korean king.[44] Their protestation of loyalty to the memory of the Ming was thus no sham to disguise factional political objectives.

Ch'oe then assessed responsibility for the evils he had described. Naturally, the blame was not the king's, for these mistakes had been perpetrated while he was still young and not in control of the throne. "They were particularly due to ministers in charge of affairs, who covered and blocked off the king's intelligence and understanding, and who manipulated power and wealth so that law and order became lax, bringing on the ills and events that beset us today."

Ch'oe suggested that the way to restore good government was for the king to be diligent, attend the lectures on the classics regularly, summon Confucian worthies to court, and practice virtuous conduct and self-cultivation.

If [the king's] mind is as clear as pure water, his desires will be purified and disappear, and Heaven's principles will flow [everywhere]. When it comes to government orders and carrying them out, what should be done will be done with the ferocious force of lightning and wind, and what should be discarded will be discarded with as much vigor as . . . cutting through iron. And when he gives a clear order and admonishes and instructs the court, the Way will be established without doubt.

Self-cultivation was to Ch'oe a mystique for the ordering of the world. By meditation one eliminated desire and clarified the physical endowment which obscured one's true mind. One then would comprehend Heaven's principles or the Way, with which the true minds of all were one. Orders issued by a monarch who had thus become one with the ultimate would be a reflection of the true Way. Ch'oe's meditative, introspective neo-Confucianism formed the philosophic basis for his view of good government.

However, good government was not simply confined to the king's cultivation of virtue, for Ch'oe's feet were still in the world affairs. Government also consisted of a bureaucratic apparatus, of which he himself was a part. The bureaucracy was also an extremely rational creation in which its parts were designed to perform specified governmental functions. To each his proper place and to each his proper function.

Instruction as to the nature of virtue should be made the responsibility of worthy teachers. The promotion or demotion of officials and the administration of government should be entrusted to the chief ministers. Remonstrance and the correction of errors and mistakes should be the charge of the censorate. Speaking one's thoughts and assisting in the cultivation [of the king] and memorializing openly and freely from the depths of one's conscience should be the responsibility of Confucian officials. The training of troops and the improvement of weapons, the defense against enemies and the prevention of insult should be left to the

Politics and Policy in Traditional Korea

administrative officials. The selection of filial and moral men and the selection of men of talent should be entrusted to the provincial governors.

Ch'oe complained, however, that the regular bureaucratic structure of government had been superseded by the Taewongun in the years since 1864. Since the Taewongun was neither king nor bureaucrat, he had no proper role to play and should therefore be removed from involvement in government affairs.

As for he who is not in such a position [that is, one of the regular bureaucratic functions described above], but only occupies a place whereby he receives *the respect due a father from a son*, then we should simply honor his position, and increase his emoluments, and accommodate his likes and dislikes, but *prevent him from interfering in government.* [Italics mine.]

Thus, the tension between monarch and bureaucrat that was part of the Chinese state system was also a factor in the anti-Taewongun opposition. There was, of course, a strong basis for this conflict in Confucian thought. It was the king's duty to seek out virtuous men to assist him in government. Such men were to be found among scholars and officials, who by their mastery over the principles of ethical conduct contained in the classics were qualified to render advice to their prince. In Ch'oe's opinion, however, the Taewongun had ignored these fundamental precepts and had interfered with the proper conduct of government from his extralegal position of authority.

Exile and Protest

In his rescript to Ch'oe's memorial, Kojong again refused to restore the Mandongmyo on the grounds that its abolition had been decreed by the dowager, but he did meet one of Ch'oe's requests by taking away the office warrants of the three deceased officials who had been posthumously restored to office. He also ordered Ch'oe's exile because many of the phrases he had used in his memorial went too far.[45] The next day officials in attendance at the royal lectures complained that exile was insufficient punishment. Hong Sun-mok, Kang No, and Han Kye-wŏn memorialized jointly that Ch'oe had no right to request the restoration of the Mandongmyo after the king had explained previously that he could not reverse an act of the dowager-regent. They charged that Ch'oe was immoral for suggesting that the abolition of the private academies implied the destruction of morality and for accusing the Taewongun of interfering with government affairs.[46] Two joint memorials were submitted by the censorate demanding a trial by the state tribunal, but Kojong refused to change his exile orders and dismissed the total membership of the Offices of the Censor and the Inspector-General just one day after their appointment.[47] Kojong was also called to task during the Royal Lectures for his punishment of the leaders of the student protest movement. The new minister of punishments, Yi U, protested that it was improper to beat students with the bamboo and requested leniency for the students. Kojong refused to modify his orders, insisted that the punishment and exile of the students be carried out, and ordered Yi transferred to the post of magistrate of Kwangju.[48]

Finally, on the evening of December 23, an extraordinary audience was granted to Hong Sun-Mok, Kang No, and Han Kye-won, at their request. They vigorously protested Kojong's disposition of the Ch'oe Ik-hyŏn case, forcing Kojong into the awkward position of defending an official's right to criticize the throne while fellow bureaucrats were attacking that official for lèse-majesté and the king for excessive tolerance. Furthermore, the three officials displayed an almost total lack of the awe and respect for regal authority that one might expect of an Oriental court. Nothing would illustrate this better than a sample from the evening's discussion.[49]

> *King:* What words and phrases in this memorial were [so] extremely outrageous?
>
> *Hong:* The King has already seen the memorial and decreed that its wording went too far, and is aware of everything. Why do you wait for us to speak out on its wording and phraseology? . . .
>
> *King:* The Mandongmyo was abolished when the Dowager was Regent, but it is said that the scholars seemed to have been sorely grieved . . .
>
> *Kang:* If Ch'oe was talking about the distress of the literati, then why did he not say anything about it? Why did he submit these perverse words?
>
> *King:* As for the phrase "morality has been destroyed," the ancients also used it.
>
> *Hong:* When was this ever used in ancient texts? In this sage age, with what perverse and treasonous thoughts did he write this phrase?
>
> *King:* Because of his phrases in the last paragraph I ordered him exiled.
>
> *Hong:* For a criminal like this, how could you stop at the ordinary punishment of exile . . . ? That whereby the state is maintained is rewards and punishments. The King once said that his words were straightforward and rewarded him. Now that his treason has been exposed, how is it that suitable punishment is not applied to him?

The three ministers demanded that Ch'oe be remanded to the state tribunal for trial, and under the pressure of attack, the king shifted his defense.

Politics and Policy in Traditional Korea

King: It was all right that I adjudged him not worthy of serious punishment, because he was an ignoramus from the country . . .

Hong: If an evil and perverse crime such as this is attributed to the fact that he is an ignoramus from the country and severe application of the law is not made, then rebels and traitors will certainly begin to arise one right after the other . . .

Kang: If it is said that he is an ignoramus from the country, then even his first memorial should not have been tolerated . . .

Hong: I saw his memorial. Indeed, it cannot be attributed to an ignoramus from the country. The whole memorial was nothing if it was not an expression of the horrendous feelings he harbored.

The ministers pressed their attack further. They accused the king of stifling remonstrance by refusing to accept the memorials of protest against Ch'oe. Hong instructed Kojong:

Feelings and ideas flow between those above [king] and those below [subjects] . . . As for the decree that the memorials of the censorate not be accepted, if things are like this, then can it be said that there is interchange between the feelings and ideas of those above and those below?

Again they demanded to know why the punishment had not been more severe, and Kojong replied that because of Ch'oe's position as a high official he had ordered exile. The three officials finally retired with the promise that they would submit a *pin'gye,* a formal written memorial usually submitted at court conferences held between the king and the state council and other high officials—an extraordinary procedure connoting their opposition to the king.[50]

One cannot help being struck by the way poor Kojong was intimidated by his official tormentors. It certainly would have been a rather odd performance for a monarch in the midst of a purge of his political opponents. His reticent behavior makes much more sense if it is understood as the first belabored and halting attempt of a young monarch to assert his authority against the solid opposition of the bureaucracy.

There was no respite from the constant bombardment of memorials. A joint memorial from the Office of the Royal Genealogy (*Chŏngjongwŏn*) on December 23 refuted Ch'oe's charges about falsification of the genealogy. Several prestigious names were included among the cosigners, including Yi Sŭng-bo, the royal lecturer of the previous few days, and Yi Kyŏng-ha, the commander of the Special Pacification Command, which had been set up for the defense of Kanghwa Island and the coast of Kyŏnggi province at the time of the French expedition of 1866.[51] The chief official of the Office of the Royal Genealogy was Yi Ch'oe-ŭng, later chief state councilor in 1875, elder brother of the Taewongun, and a man usually regarded as a Min puppet. Kojong's rescript stated that Ch'oe could not have known any of the details concerning the compila-

Consensus Destroyed

tion, hence there was no need for them to be so sharp in criticizing him.[52]

Even the state tribunal refused to carry out Kojong's order to exile Ch'oe on the grounds that it was standard to delay exile whenever an official was under fire by the censorate.[53] Of the members of the tribunal, Pak Kyu-su was soon to become second state councilor and Sin Hŏn was later the chief negotiator of the Kanghwa Treaty. Both reached high office, in other words, after the Taewongun's overthrow, but here they joined in an attack on his chief critic. It was therefore unlikely that they were partners in a conspiracy to overthrow him.

Kojong ordered the state tribunal to carry out Ch'oe's exile forthwith and dismissed all four officials of the tribunal who refused to carry out his orders. As in the case of the censorate, these dismissals were less significant politically than might be imagined because state tribunal posts were ad hoc concurrencies. Furthermore, Pak Kyu-su was reappointed to the post from which he was just dismissed, and Sin Hŏn reappeared sometime later in responsible positions.[54]

Kojong Declares Personal Rule

On December 24 a most interesting discourse took place at a court conference of chief officials. Kojong noted that in last evening's audience he had mentioned two items that he intended to have promulgated in the *Official Gazette*. Since he had assumed personal control over all affairs of government in 1866, however, there was no need to bring up the matter anymore, and for that reason he had rescinded the order to promulgate the edicts in the gazette.[55] The previous day's court records reveal no such orders, but Kojong had evidently issued a decree the night before declaring his independence of the regency and his assumption of personal rule. He was then informed that he already had all the legal justification he needed for the independent exercise of authority since the dowager's resignation in 1866. As Han Kye-wŏn stated in the audience of December 24, "After the retirement of the [dowager] regent, your assumption of power over all affairs was known to everyone in the country. It is not necessary to promulgate this again." Kojong replied that if all ministers were agreed, then he would not promulgate the announcement of the previous day.[56] Kojong was now fully conscious of his authority and determined to use it.

Ch'oe's Trial

On December 24 a *pin'gye* signed by fifty-seven officials—most of the upper bureaucracy—was presented to Kojong. Since several of the co-signers were men who could be construed as supporters of a Min faction, the attack on Ch'oe was obviously not the work of any narrow Taewongun faction.[57] The memorial defended the decree abolishing the

Mandongmyo under the dowager's regency and recommended Ch'oe's investigation and execution.[58] In the face of such massive opposition Kojong conceded and ordered Ch'oe's investigation to be carried out, but he also ordered the dismissal or investigation of four minor officials who had attacked Ch'oe and Hong Si-hyŏng.[59]

On December 27 the membership of the state tribunal was constituted to conduct Ch'oe's trial. All its posts were held as concurrencies by high officials who were the leading critics of Ch'oe Ik-hyŏn and the chief defenders of the regime.[60] For that matter, it may have been impossible for the king to find any defenders of Ch'oe among the higher level bureaucrats. In trying to defend Ch'oe, Kojong found himself pitted against the bureaucracy as a whole in a test of strength.

Ch'oe, meanwhile, was preparing to return to his home at P'och'on, about twenty miles north of Seoul when he was arrested by an official of the state tribunal on December 25. According to one account the king replaced the commissioners of the Right and Left Police Departments with men who were to ensure Ch'oe's safety in the face of the Taewongun's wrath.[61] Ch'oe was imprisoned at the state tribunal jail on December 27, and that evening a man standing outside Ch'oe's cell thrust in a sealed note through the crack in the window. The note supposedly was written in *han'gul* (the Korean alphabet) rather than Chinese, an indication that it might have been sent by the queen. Ch'oe refused to open it on the grounds that it was prohibited by law for outsiders to communicate with prisoners. The stranger then opened it himself, thrust it back in the hole, and asked Ch'oe to look at it. The note stated that during his interrogation Ch'oe was to avoid bringing up the issue of the restoration of the Mandongmyo because the dowager-regent had decreed its abolition. However, as for the other issues—the matter of the posthumous exoneration of the traitorous officials and the criticism of defects in government—he was not to avoid a vigorous attack. Ch'oe returned the note without acknowledgment.[62]

Scholarly opinion has been divided over whether this note came from Queen Min and whether Ch'oe was a tool of the Min faction or engaged in conspiracy with them.[63] The question of conspiracy cannot be proved conclusively one way or the other, but the conspiracy argument implies that men like Yi Hang-no, Ch'oe Ik-hyŏn, and Hong Si-hyŏng were merely insincere political opportunists. Even had these men been engaged in conspiracy with the Min clan, however, their reasons for entering such a conspiracy would have originated from their basic philosophical disagreement with the Taewongun's policies.

Ch'oe's trial began on December 27. He was indicted for secretly harboring evil intentions, submitting a petition to the throne while under

Consensus Destroyed

impeachment by the censorate, and using perverse and detestable phrases. Ch'oe insisted that his memorials were loyal remonstrance, that they were composed privately by himself without assistance from others, and that his remarks about nonbureaucrats interfering in government were merely general remarks (and not directed against the Taewongun). The state tribunal found Ch'oe guilty of lèse-majesté and requested further interrogation under torture, but Kojong ordered Ch'oe exiled immediately to Cheju Island claiming that he was merely a country bumpkin and that the dowager had also requested a light sentence for him.[64] The Royal Secretariat immediately protested the decision in a number of memorials, but Kojong refused to budge.[65]

Dismissal of Chief Ministers

Around 7:00 P.M. on the evening of December 28, the king granted a special audience to the chief officials of the state tribunal—Hong Sun-mok, Kang No, Han Kye-wŏn, Kim Se-gyun, and Pak Kyu-su, among others. Hong protested as spokesman for the group that it was unprecedented to have the king hand down a decision on a criminal case after only one or two "easy" interrogation sessions and requested the trial be continued. The group insisted that Ch'oe was not an ignoramus, that failure to punish him would only lead to similar acts in the future, and that he should be forced to confess his guilt. Hong added that they would even be willing to countenance a delay in the proceedings until the following spring (after the queen gave birth,) but it was important to maintain the law and uphold principle. Kojong was goaded by this: "You ministers are aware of principles, but is it that I am not? Even though it were an obstruction of principle, how is it you do not accept and carry out an edict from the merciful throne?"[66] Hong rejoined, "If the edicts of the King cannot be discussed as to their worth . . . what is to become of state affairs?"

The arguments had come full circle producing a strange reversal of traditional roles. Kojong insisted that Ch'oe's right of remonstrance should be defended, but his officials demanded Ch'oe be executed for lèse-majesté. Kojong rejected this and demanded obedience to his decision, but the officials refused to obey on the grounds that it was their right and duty to remonstrate.

Kojong again fell back on the rather transparent device he had tried earlier. He had received, he said, instructions from Dowager Cho for lenient punishment, and in deference to the dictates of filial piety, he was obliged to carry it out. If his ministers were so interested in principle, how was it that they could not understand this? This defense was a rather feeble one for a monarch who had just reaffirmed his assumption of rule.

Politics and Policy in Traditional Korea

Obviously, he felt that his authority as king was not sufficient to win obedience to his decrees.

Finally, Kojong cut off the conversation by announcing that it was time for him to eat. Hong replied that if the king was going to act like that, they would all withdraw. Kojong protested:

King: If you leave, where will you go? I would like to know where you would go.

Kang: We will await punishment outside the city walls.

King: How is this in accordance with principles to abandon me and leave? How can high officials like you talk like this? How improper!"

The ministers thereupon withdrew and the second and third state councilors, Kang and Han, handed over their palace-entry tallies at the gate. The king, hearing of this, ordered them to return.[67]

On December 29 Kojong sent letters of encouragement to his officials now ensconced in their homes in angry pique. As the text of one of these notes indicates, Kojong had no intention of purging his chief officials.

> Your actions were truly most inappropriate. I have already expounded my intentions fully in the audience. You should have understood, but you recklessly handed in your gate-tallies and left the palace in a huff. What kind of strange action and behavior was this?
>
> I had already set up an investigation of Ch'oe at your request. Several times you received my edicts and also an edict decreeing light punishment [for Ch'oe]. I then say, that when those above [the king] acquiesce and those below [subjects, people] comply then both achieve their due. But, contrary to expectation, you left without a thought to the situation.
>
> If you are so reckless in regarding your importance as ministers of state affairs that you leave the chairs of the top three state councilors empty, this will mean that state affairs will be neglected and government will be disrupted and most confused. There will be errors in everything. All will look up and clearly let loose cries of anger. I do not know what to say.
>
> If you have given a thought to this, how is it you do not forthwith change your plans and return. I herewith give back your summons [tallies] and promulgate this heartfelt decree [as encouragement].

The three officials still refused to heed Kojong's command. Hong Sun-mok replied, "If by next spring the investigation is completed and a final decision is made, we may be somewhat satisfied as to the care and seriousness with which the administration of punishments [has been carried out]."[68] Such arrogance would not be tolerated by any monarch who wished to salvage some of the dignity of his position, and on December 31 Kojong finally dismissed the three men from office.[69] If Kojong were the means by which the Min faction engineered a political

Consensus Destroyed

coup, then either the Min were monumental bunglers or Kojong was singularly inept at carrying out orders. Both these interpretations are preposterous. There is no doubt that had these three officials decided not to present the young king with an ultimatum he would not have dismissed them. Finally, sometime during the above proceedings (the date is not clear), the Taewongun retired from the capital to a country retreat beyond the north gate.[70] This marked his withdrawal from direct participation in government affairs until the military uprising of 1882, except for his attempt to block the conclusion of the Kanghwa Treaty in 1876.

The Taewongun's retirement was brought about by a subtle interplay of political, institutional, and ideological factors. While there may have been a faction of Min relatives and supporters, their role in the affair was not decisive. Nor was the Taewongun supported by anything which could be labeled as a faction. His support came from the upper bureaucracy as a whole and the students. Factionalism, therefore, provides a weak explanation for the Taewongun's fall from power. The king's coming of age and his decision to exercise his authority independently of his father were the most important direct causes of the Taewongun's retirement. In the end the traditional legitimacy of an adult king was more important than the derivative legitimacy or personal charisma of his father.

The Taewongun's power was based on two factors: his position as the king's father, and the creation of a solid consensus of support for his foreign and domestic policies. The former proved too weak a basis for the continuation of the Taewongun's power once his son became conscious of his own authority, and the consensus of support was split by a small group of scholar-officials who objected to the Taewongun's domestic policy. In political terms the loss of consensus by itself would not have been decisive, because the critics of domestic policy were vastly outnumbered by the defenders of that policy in the upper levels of the capital bureaucracy. The criticism was politically significant because it appealed to the king and stimulated him to oppose his father's authority and policies, forcing him into a confrontation with the bureaucracy and students.

The debate over the punishment of Ch'oe Ik-hyŏn turned into a confrontation between the king and bureaucracy in which the weaknesses of both sides were revealed. The high officials and students utilized every institutional restraint on royal authority that was available to them. The state tribunal blocked Ch'oe's exile; the Royal Secretariat refused to transmit the king's commands; the students continued their protest strike against the king's objections; the Royal Lecturers harped at the king during his daily educational sessions; and the chief ministers

Politics and Policy in Traditional Korea

paralyzed government operations by refusing to come to court. They succeeded in obtaining Ch'oe's exile, but they failed to obtain his execution or ensure the continuation intact of previous policy. In the final test of strength, the three top officials gambled their own positions on an ultimatum to the king; their dismissal and the retirement of the Taewongun signified the king's ultimate victory and cleared the decks for a change of both administration and policy.

Although Kojong won the final battle in this struggle, in the process he revealed his own weaknesses. He was forced to defend Ch'oe by the use of transparent and weak arguments. He lacked confidence in his own authority and appealed to the prestige of the dowager-regent for support. He acquiesced to the demand for Ch'oe's exile, and, most important of all, he showed that he could be bullied.

The key to an understanding of Kojong's strengths and weaknesses in this hour of crisis is to be found not only in his own personal timidity, but also in his commitment to Confucian ideas. The criticisms of Ch'oe and the others were based on Confucian dogma and struck a responsive chord in the mind of Kojong. His conviction in the correctness of their views gave him the courage to oppose his father and the bureaucracy as a whole. On the other hand, a decade of indoctrination at the hands of Confucian officials who taught him repeatedly that the ideal monarch placed moral standards above the arbitrary exercise of despotic authority and gave heed to honest remonstrance by sincere officials weakened his determination to resist the flouting of his commands.

Ch'oe Ik-hyŏn and Hong Si-hyŏng opposed the domestic policies of the Taewongun's regime because they placed priority on the maintenance of the status and privileges of the social elite, rigid adherence to moral criteria in the conduct of government affairs, and dogmatic application of Confucian dicta on political economy. No matter how serious the fiscal difficulties of the state, revenue shortage was not to be solved by destroying the proper distinction between social classes by imposing an equal or progressive tax scheme. Excessive taxation of the common people was also forbidden because it was sure to lead to suffering, rebellion, and the fall of the dynasty, and currency manipulation was disdained because it led to inflation which interfered with the economic well-being of the peasantry.

Although the Taewongun and most of the men who held high office under his regime were not determined to change the status quo and destroy status distinction, they were willing to levy taxes on the upper class when dynastic or national interest demanded it. Though they adhered to Confucian standards in a general sense, they were also willing to ignore certain aspects of dogma when practical action was needed. They subordinated the maintenance of the status quo and ideological purity to the interests of dynasty, monarchy, and state.

Consensus Destroyed

As 1874 began, men of the ilk of Yi Hang-no and Ch'oe Ik-hyŏn were undoubtedly optimistic that a king sympathetic to their views had now assumed power. Kojong had given every indication of his support for them by defending their remonstrance against tremendous odds and by adopting their recommendations to lower taxes. They had every expectation that he would adopt the rest of their program on domestic affairs while standing fast against the barbarians on foreign policy.

10

The Abolition of Ch'ing Cash

When Kojong assumed power in 1874 he was virtually the intellectual captive of the Confucian fundamentalists, convinced that the most important criterion of good government was a willingness to subordinate the material interests of throne and state to the welfare of the common people. But the king's faith in the efficacy of dogma to solve real problems was dealt a serious blow by the first major act of the new regime—the abolition of Chinese currency. Kojong's decision to withdraw Chinese currency from circulation and prohibit its use as legal tender at a time when it constituted a large percentage of government treasury reserves was probably one of the most ill-considered measures in the history of the dynasty. Central and local government were forced into virtual bankruptcy and two years were spent in a struggle to make ends meet. Kojong's faith in his fundamental principles and his confidence in his power to govern were shaken irreparably at a time when Korea was about to face a new set of challenges from abroad.

The immediate stimulus for Kojong's decision to withdraw Chinese currency from circulation came from complaints about inflation. On January 2, 1874, an ex-censor, Yi Kyu-hyŏng, memorialized that although the minting of 100-cash had been stopped because of counterfeiting and inflation, the use of Chinese currency had resulted in even worse conditions. Commodity prices had risen a hundredfold and the value of Ch'ing cash had fallen so greatly that "in the capital and countryside if someone obtains but a single piece of Ch'ing cash, he is only afraid of holding on to it . . . and feels he must exchange it for goods." Yi complained that people were hoarding goods and that normal trade activities had been obstructed, and he asked that Ch'ing cash be withdrawn from circulation.[1] On January 3 another official complained of inflation, but there was no indication in the higher councils of government that people were overly concerned about the situation.[2]

The Abolition of Ch'ing Cash

Kojong then took the initiative to order the abolition of Chinese cash on January 22 without consulting his top officials. His edict stated:

> The circulation of Ch'ing cash at the beginning was an unavoidable affair, but by the present time goods have become dear and the currency cheap. It gets worse every day, so that one day it will not be possible to endure it . . . There must be a change. From now on the circulation of Ch'ing cash will be completely abolished.[3]

He also declared that all cash payments to government agencies in Ch'ing cash would only be allowed for the first lunar month, and that ever-normal cash would be required after the second month.[4]

Kojong's decision on the withdrawal of Chinese currency did not represent a new consensus among the upper bureaucracy, for his new ministers were practical bureaucrats who were keenly aware of administrative costs and revenue problems. The contrast between Kojong's idealism and the practicality of his chief officials was revealed in a memorial submitted by the state council after the decision to withdraw Chinese currency was rendered.

> The circulation of this currency at first and now its abolition were both measures which show the King's sage intentions on behalf of the people. Who would not respect greatly a government which does harm to those above to benefit those below [the people]. Yet some thought must be given to the difficult situation regarding "official" expenditures and to the provision of expenses and payment of salaries. Other plans [must be made].[5]

Kojong, on the other hand, was clearly not concerned about state revenues. As he remarked on February 10, "In this abolition of Ch'ing cash, I did not worry about national finances. I did it only for the people because of the evils existing."[6] In the next breath, however, he urged the governor of Kyŏngsang province to expedite the remission of taxes to the central government in view of the insolvency produced by his decision.

Serious discussion of monetary policy did not take place until a court conference held on February 10 when the new high officials pointed out some of the problems involved in Kojong's rather rash action. Chief State Councilor Yi Yu-wŏn and Third State Councilor Pak Kyu-su told Kojong that after Chinese currency had been introduced into circulation and depreciated in value, certain officials had forced the people to pay their taxes in ever-normal cash, while they remitted tax quotas to the central government in Chinese currency at face value. By this method local officials had retained the more valuable currency for themselves while government coffers were filled with Chinese cash that was decreasing in value and purchasing power. Now that Chinese currency was withdrawn from circulation by court edict, the government treasuries were left without liquid assets. Kojong was surprised at Yi Yu-wŏn's report and he told Yi that he had believed that the situation in Seoul, where depreciated Chinese currency had driven the ever-normal cash out of circulation, prevailed throughout the whole country.[7] One might note, however, that even if all ever-normal cash had been driven out of circulation, the government would have ended up holding nothing but Chinese cash in any case.

When Kojong issued his abolition order, he did not even have the slightest idea of how much Chinese currency was in government treasuries or in circulation throughout the country. He did not bother to ask his ministers about these problems until March 1, over five weeks after he had withdrawn Ch'ing cash from circulation. His advisers, however, were unable to provide accurate answers. Yi Yu-wŏn estimated that there was anywhere from three to ten million yang of Chinese currency in circulation, and Minister of Taxation Kim Se-gyun said that although it may have been possible to estimate the total amount of Ch'ing cash in circulation when it was first introduced into the economy, it was impossible to estimate its volume at the present time.[8]

Kim also remarked that no distinction had been made previously between Ch'ing cash and ever-normal cash in the treasury of the Ministry of Taxation—a rather serious lapse in view of the growing worthlessness of the former. He noted that the project to cover the roof of the Kyŏngbok palace with tile had been suspended because of the current fiscal shortage. To pay for ancestral sacrifices at the royal tombs and for repair and construction work related to ritual matters, 11,500 yang was also needed, but only 800 yang of ever-normal cash was on hand for this purpose.[9] Yi Yu-wŏn also expressed his concern over the inability of the Ministry of Taxation to meet the demands of government bureaus for expenses.[10]

Kojong finally began to express some concern over the revenue problem. He decreed that economies should be made in expenditures and that local magistrates be urged to expedite the remission of their tax quotas to the capital. When Yi Yu-wŏn observed that the magistrates had been too interested in showing their love (for the people) and had not been pressing for tax payments, Kojong replied that it had been a long time since the provincial governors had submitted an audit of their account books. Yi Yu-wŏn informed him that an audit on a province-wide basis was part of the normal procedure accompanying the appointment of a new governor, but that their reports would be delayed until the magistrates had time to submit their figures. Kojong ended the conference on March 1 with instructions to the state council to order P'yŏng'an province to remit its taxes to the capital immediately and to require all government bureaus to report the amount of Ch'ing cash on hand.[11]

The Abolition of Ch'ing Cash

Government Cash Reserves Decimated

The most obvious result of the abolition of Chinese currency was that the cash reserves of various government treasuries, both in Seoul and in the provinces, were wiped out by a stroke of the pen. To be more accurate, the value of cash reserves in government treasuries was reduced from either the nominal value of the cash—or probably its depreciated market value—to nothing more than its intrinsic metallic value.

On March 8 Yi Yu-wŏn reported to Kojong that the state council only had a reserve fund of 100,000 yang of (ever-normal) cash. Yi recommended that in view of the poor fiscal situation it would be best to wait and see what the most urgent requirements would be before authorizing the expenditure of these funds. He suggested that the Ch'ing cash in the treasury could be used for immediate expenses (as metal?), and until further supplementary funds arrived, the government could tighten its belt. Kojong stated that he had received the reports from the various government bureaus on their cash reserves and found that there was a total of one million yang of ever-normal cash and two million yang of Ch'ing cash on hand. In other words, two thirds of the cash in monetary value on hand in the government treasuries had now been declared nonnegotiable.[12]

Additional information on the problem of the cash sector in government treasury reserves can be obtained from the quarterly reports submitted to the throne of balances of reserves in the treasuries of various ministries and agencies. These reserve reports included the ministries of Taxation and War, the Tribute Bureau, and the major military commands.

An examination of the figures (see Table 3) from the fourth lunar month of 1873 to the end of the ninth lunar month, 1875, shows that most of the serious reduction in reserves occurred in the cash sector. Fairly constant levels were maintained in gold, silver, rice, and beans, and in the various types of cloth. Although the figures pertaining to cash balances do not coincide exactly with other evidence, there was a steady reduction of cash reserves until a low of 138,863 yang was reached in the final quarter of 1874. Most, if not all, of this must have been ever-normal cash.[13] By the third quarter of 1875, a balance of only 13,927 yang of Ch'ing cash was maintained in the treasuries, and the ever-normal reserves, after a brief rise in the two previous quarters, dropped to a low of 100,000 yang. These figures provided graphic evidence of the tremendous drop in the cash reserves of the central government after the abolition of Ch'ing cash at the beginning of 1874. This paucity of cash reserves prevailed to the end of 1875.

The statistical figures on the shortage of cash are only embellished by the evidence available in the daily court records. On May 5 Kojong was

Table 3. Quarterly treasury balances[a]

Year (lunar)[b]	Gold (yang)	Silver (yang)	Cash (yang)	Ch'ing cash	Silk (tong)	Cotton (tong)	Rice (sŏk)	Beans (sŏk)
1873. 1.15	62	108,793	656,912	-	84	3,780	162,950	24,228
1873. 4.15	151	137,768	785,549	-	90	4,183	174,584	15,964
1873. 7.15	144	139,637	884,214	-	90	6,509	227,187	44,838
1873.10.15	144	151,068	836,543	-	68	6,212	130,779	41,343
1874. 1.15	151	154,933	1,635,498	-	87	5,330	205,794	38,320
1874. 4.15	144	150,908	263,307	2,064,912	39	5,047	179,302	27,147
1874. 7.15	144	151,202	1,819,257	-	39	4,628	199,292	28,284
1874.10.15	128	144,987	522,684	-	37	5,498	199,292	34,597
1875. 1.15	105	116,797	138,863	-	75	2,576	123,647	27,606
1875. 4.15	144	148,935	222,610	-	45	3,310	188,968	17,419
1875. 7.15	167	157,545	342,620	-	37	5,631	196,989	18,618
1875.10.15	144	126,848	108,424	13,927	-	1,974	221,201	26,439

Source: CSS.6.4., KJSL.

aCertain items, like ramie cloth, cotton cloth, and miscellaneous grain have been omitted.

bOn March 25, 1873 (2.27 lunar), it was decreed that henceforth the expenditures and accounts of the Tribute Bureau (Sŏnhyech'ŏng), Ministry of War, the Three Yŏng (military commands), Ch'ongyung-ch'ŏng, and Yanghyang-ch'ŏng tax receipts, expenditures and accounts (balances) would be reported the first day of each quarter. This was amended to the fifteenth day by the Minister of Taxation, Kim Se-gyun. See CSS.6.4.290.

notified that after the abolition of Ch'ing cash there were no funds left in the special reserve fund (*pyolch'i*), except for cotton cloth. Yi Kyŏng-ha, a high military official, reported that the Military Training Agency had nothing but Ch'ing cash on hand in its treasuries, none of which could be used. Kim Se-gyun, the minister of taxation, reported that there was only 6,000 yang of Ch'ing cash left in the special reserve fund of the state council. And Yi Yu-wŏn said that all the special reserve funds of the cash and grain yamen had been rendered useless by the abolition of Ch'ing cash. Finally, Kim Se-gyun reported that the Office of Military Provisions' (Yanghyang-ch'ong) reserve of 8,000 yang was all useless Ch'ing cash.[14]

The provincial governments also suffered from shortages. Between March and June memorials were submitted by the magistrate of Kwangju and the governors of Kyŏnggi, Hwanghae, Ch'ungch'ŏng, P'yŏng'an, and Chŏlla provinces, reporting that all or most of their cash reserves were in Ch'ing cash and could not be spent. They requested permission either for supplementary funds from central government treasuries or for the extraordinary refunding measures.[15] The remarks of Sin Ŭng-jo, governor of P'yŏng'an province, were typical: "At present the situation in this province is so urgent that I do not know what to do. For half a year the local magistrates have been blaming me, and I have been petitioning the court only to request funds to make up for the Ch'ing cash."[16]

General Financial Malaise

Kojong's monetary policy was only one of the factors contributing to a serious and chronic shortage of revenue. The government also suffered a depletion in income from crop failures, the sinking of grain transport ships, nonremittance of taxes by local agencies,[17] embezzlement by officials,[18] expenditures for tribute missions and Chinese envoys,[19] and a narrow land tax base.[20] In February Kojong had to suspend the project to tile the roof of the Kyŏngbok palace and defer the repair of his own quarters, a project that would have consumed 200,000 yang of cash.[21] By March he decided to liquidate and convert to cash large amounts of grain loan funds and on April 14 he suspended all current construction projects.[22]

On April 20 Minister of Taxation Kim Se-gyun reported that in the past his ministry had averaged about 540,000 yang of revenue per year and this had been expected to rise to 600,000 yang in the current year. At present, however, it was anticipated that only 500,000 yang would be collected in 1874. Since regular expenditures came to about 400,000 yang, Kim did not expect that there would be enough left over for extraordinary expenses.[23]

April and May were difficult months for the government. It was forced to wait for the first remittances of liquidated grain loan funds that were not due to arrive in the capital until the period from the end of May through the middle of July. Kojong told Yi Yu-wŏn on April 20 that if the government were frugal and confined its expenditures to income, it could get by.[24] By May 27, however, the financial pressure had still not been relieved. Yi reported to Kojong that although not all taxes due had been received from the provinces, what had been sent in had been all paid out by the middle of May and there were no further resources available until the receipt of taxes in the fall! Kojong noted that the period of greatest difficulty would be in mid-June to mid-August, and Yi replied: "We only have to be frugal to get by."[25]

On June 12 Yi Sŭng-bo, an official in the Tribute Bureau and one of Kojong's favorite lecturers, informed the king that there would not be enough cash for purchasing articles from the tribute merchants until at least June 14. Yi also reported that after the abolition of Chinese currency, provincial officials had been sending tax funds that they usually remitted to the Tribute Bureau to the Ministry of Taxation instead. The ministry had therefore cannibalized the tribute revenues without any plans for replenishing them.[26]

Yi Yu-wŏn expressed fears to Kojong on June 18 that there were insufficient funds to meet emergency expenditures, and on July 8 Minister of Taxation Kim Se-gyun told the king that his ministry usually took in about 530,000 yang of cash in a year and paid out 450,000 yang, leaving a mere 70-80,000 yang, which was not sufficient to meet emergency expenditures. Furthermore, tax revenues had been decreasing every year by close to 100,000 yang, and grain balances were precarious, since rice revenues for the ministry for 1873 were 115,000 sŏk and expenditures were 106,000 sŏk. Fortunately, the government had been able to meet its obligations in 1873, but the prospects for 1874 were poor because of widespread crop failures. Kim also reported that several grain transport ships were filled with rotten grain, and another twelve ships were sunk with a loss of 12,000 sŏk—almost 10 percent of the previous year's total grain revenue.[27]

There was hardly any improvement in the financial situation despite the revenues from the fall harvest. In December Yi Sŭng-bo reported that there would be delays in the remittance of tax grains to the capital because ice formation had obstructed traffic, but he still anticipated shortages even after its arrival at the capital.[28] On February 15, 1875 the Ministry of Taxation memorialized that its resources were so depleted that it had no way to provide for the expenses for the current envoy from China, and it requested that extraordinary allocations be made from other sources for this purpose. Kojong assigned a special allotment of 100,000 yang from the Ministry of Taxation to be spent sparingly and ordered a general paring of all expenditures.[29]

The Abolition of Ch'ing Cash

At a court conference on June 13 Second State Councilor Yi Ch'oe-ŭng deplored the current revenue shortage and blamed it on the lack of frugality.[30] Minister of Taxation Min Ch'i-sang reported on November 22 that his ministry was low in finances and requested that immediate relief be provided by commuting to cash 8,000 sŏk of tax beans from eleven towns, a sum equivalent to 40,000 yang.[31] He stated that revenue for the year was no more than 520,000 yang, but that since the first month of 1875 the amount of cash expended was over 800,000 yang and 500,000 yang more had to be paid to the tribute middlemen for articles received. Min estimated total expenditures at 1,450,000 yang, and remarked, "In one year we have spent three years' revenue."[32] The financial problem in 1875 had turned out to be worse than in 1874 and the government appeared to be faced with a chronic revenue shortage. Kojong and his ministers alike were convinced that the only solution was frugality and economy.[33]

Currency and the Tribute Tax System

The cash shortage also disrupted the normal operation of the tribute tax mechanism, which had become dependent to a large extent on cash. Originally, tribute taxes of local products were paid to the government in kind. After the *taedong* reform of the seventeenth century the tribute tax was converted to a grain payment levied on land. The central government actually received more grain revenues from this tax than from the land tax. Then as currency came into use the practice of commuting tax payments from grain to cash was permitted with more frequency.

The throne and the various capital agencies still required their quota of tribute articles, which were purchased with grain or cash at rates set by the government from licensed tribute merchants (*kong'in*). The rates were determined to allow a profit for the *kong'in*, but there were also times when they were not realistic, that is, when they were almost the same as the market price, allowing almost no profit for the *kong'in*. By 1874 it seems that most of the payments to the *kong'in* for the purchase of tribute articles was made in cash, and for this reason the abolition of Ch'ing cash had curtailed the government's tribute purchases and caused hardship for the tribute merchants.[34] As early as March 5, 1874, Yi Yuwŏn told the king that there was nothing on hand in the treasuries with which to purchase tribute articles from the *kong'in*. Because of the lack of cash there was no way for goods to circulate in the capital, and the tribute merchants or their suppliers were left holding large inventories.[35]

On December 9, 1874, Minister of Taxation Kim Se-gyun told Kojong that between the ninth and eleventh lunar months (October 10-January 7, 1875), a total of 96,000 yang of cash was needed for the purchase of tribute articles, but at the time the Ministry of Taxation had only 70,000 yang of immovable reserve cash, and only several thousand yang of regular funds in the treasury. Kim reported that his ministry at first had 100,000 yang of immovable reserves but "before he knew it" it had been used up. The ministry's resources had also been depleted by the loan or temporary transfer of close to 100,000 yang to the military garrisons for their expenses.

Kim told Kojong that currency was not circulating in the market and the value of cash was appreciating. In other words, prices were falling because of the sudden decrease in demand for goods by the government, and tribute merchants were undoubtedly hard pressed. Kim recommended that 70,000 yang of immovable cash reserves be disbursed to "give the people who furnish tribute cloth respite during which time they could somewhat recoup their strength." Kojong agreed to use reserve funds for this purpose as long as it would be a temporary measure.

Kojong did ask Kim if the immovable fund could be refilled in the current year. Kim replied that it could if all funds loaned out from the ministry were repaid, and if the sums due as royal tribute (*sangnap*) from the provincial administrative towns were all remitted. Kojong asked why there had been a delay in the remittance of royal tribute payments, and Kim said that the delay was caused by the abolition of Ch'ing cash and the machinations of the cash-tax remittance middlemen (*kyohwan juin*).[36]

Disposing of the Chinese Currency

Kojong had given no thought at all to the problem of the disposition of the Chinese currency once it had been withdrawn from circulation. Pak Kyu-su first raised this issue on February 10 when he recommended that the people be allowed to melt the Chinese cash down for making utensils and that the government use what it had to defray the traveling expenses of tribute missions to China by exchanging it for silver in China and using the silver for making payments and purchases there. In this way it would revert to the place whence it came, the amount of it on hand in the treasuries would be reduced, and it would be replaced by good currency. Pak admitted his ignorance about the copper-silver exchange rate and other conditions in China but suggested that some able technician could be selected by the interpreters to handle the details.[37]

Yi Yu-wŏn, however, revealed the naivety and impracticability of this proposal. He pointed out that there was a great variation in the value of a string of cash as expressed in the units of account between Korea, Manchuria, and China proper.[38] Furthermore, the Chinese were in the habit of purchasing their petty commodities with cash and valuable goods with silver. In China it was easy to exchange silver for cash, but not so easy to exchange cash for silver. The Ch'ing cash in use in Korea was also not the same cash that was used in China. When it was transported from China to Korea, it had to be accompanied by customs tickets. It could not now be returned without authorization, for this would be regarded as smuggling. Yi also pointed out that the expenses for a tribute mission to China were about 10,000 liang of silver in China while the total amount of Ch'ing cash on hand in Korea was about three million yang. It would take forever to use this up. Pak asked, "How would the Chinese ever be willing to accept this useless stuff and give us silver in exchange for it?"[39]

Yi was still reluctant, however, to question the sagacity of Kojong's order abolishing the use of Ch'ing cash.

The present abolition of Ch'ing cash was due to the magnanimous and bright intentions of the sage King. All the people are dancing for joy, so how can we now delay matters for several years by [quibbling over] the inconsequential question of profit or loss . . . and allow the people to look for opportunities [to contravene] state laws? If this [the circulation of Ching cash] were not stopped, then in a day or a year or two, I am afraid that it might naturally start circulating again.[40]

Yi concurred with Kojong that the benefit to the people was more important than the inconvenience to state finance.

Pak Kyu-su then suggested that the Chinese cash be melted down into ingots and used for its intrinsic value to defray state expenses. Yi agreed, and Kojong even suggested that the Chinese might accept the copper ingots, if not the cash itself. Pak, however, pointed out that this would be impracticable. Although silver circulated throughout China, cash minted in each province was stamped with the mark of that province and could not pass its boundaries into other provinces. The Chinese also had laws against taking cash out of circulation by melting it down to make utensils, in order to maintain an adequate volume of cash (so that its value relative to goods would remain stable.).[41] They certainly could not allow copper ingots or utensils to come in from Korea.[42] The discussion on February 10 thus ended without any solution to the problem of disposing of the Chinese cash.

Although Yi Yu-wŏn initially opposed the suggestion to ship the currency back to China, by March 8 he had changed his mind. He told Kojong that there was no way to solve the immediate problem of the cash shortage in government treasuries. Kojong replied that nothing could be done until the Ministry of Taxation began collecting ever-normal cash, although he admitted that cash was urgently needed to pay tribute merchants for the purchase of tribute articles, to provide for the expenses of military garrisons, and to pay daily expenses for the Ministry of Taxation. Yi now suggested that Ch'ing cash be used to pay the expenses of the tribute missions to China. Kojong wondered whether the Chinese would accept the cash more than once, and Yi replied, "If we get away with it once, then there is no reason why we cannot do it every year."

Kojong then expressed the fear that if the cash were used this way, Koreans living along the Western route—the route taken by the tribute missions on their way to China—would not believe the edict abolishing the use of Ch'ing cash. Yi, however, discounted the possibility.[43]

There is evidence, however, that the pressure for funds induced Kojong to authorize the use of Chinese currency within Korea at least for its metallic value. Kojong approved a request by the magistrate of Kwangju for spending Chinese cash without specifying how this was to be done. He asked Yi Yu-wǒn about this on March 8, and Yi suggested that the cash be melted down into ingots. On March 12 Kojong approved a similar request from the governor of Kyǒnggi province,[44] and on March 13 Kojong and Yi agreed to allot the reserves of Ch'ing cash in the government treasuries to meet current expenses of 200,000 yang for military needs and tribute purchases.[45] On March 17, however, Yi mentioned that it was inappropriate to disburse one million yang of the more than two million yang of Ch'ing cash on hand,[46] and on March 22 he raised similar objections. He remarked that he had not been able to take part in the discussion of the matter in the state council but had discussed it with the chief officials of the Ministry of Taxation and Tribute Bureau, and it was his feeling now that it would be better to wait until these officials could come to court to deliberate on the question before rendering a final decision. Kojong said that the situation was too urgent to wait until these officials could deliberate on it, but he approved Yi's recommendation that the Ch'ing cash be gathered in one place and used as metal as had been done with the 100-cash.[47]

Yi Yu-wǒn was undoubtedly afraid of the inflationary effects of the release of massive amounts of Chinese currency back into the market, but Kojong was beginning to feel the effects of the financial squeeze. Since he was still unwilling to raise taxes on the people to solve the revenue problem, he was probably anxious to use the Ch'ing cash for whatever it was worth without much concern for its effects on the market.

Price Stability and Government Noninterference

Yi Yu-wǒn and Pak Kyu-su were more concerned than Kojong with combatting inflation and restoring price stability to the market. Pak Kyu-su had a much more realistic view of the motives behind the demand for the abolition of Chinese currency than Kojong. On February 10 he informed the king that the Confucian literati were not the only ones who desired the abolition of Chinese currency. The private coinage and minting interests also desired it, so that they could profit from resumed minting operations. Pak told Kojong that prior to 1864 wealthy individuals had been allowed by the throne to set up private facilities for minting cash, for which privilege they paid a tax to the government. It was thought at the time that this method would be of advantage both to public and private interests, but the result was that excessive amounts of debased currency found its way into circulation and commodity prices rose sharply. Pak charged that all those who minted cash engaged in profiteering, and that they were the ones who had led in the clamor for the abolition of Ch'ing cash. They had claimed that Ch'ing cash was injuring the people and preventing goods from circulating, and they demanded that after the abolition of Chinese currency the private minting of cash be resumed. Pak recommended that careful deliberation of the problem be made before any orders were issued for the resumption of coinage and that those who continued to agitate for private minting be punished.[48]

Pak Kyu-su's primary concern, however, was not simply with preventing illicit profiteering by private coinage. His objective was to restore stability to market operations in accordance with traditional views about money and prices that prevailed prior to the Taewongun's use of the 100-cash. Since Kojong was virtually ignorant of these matters, it was left for Pak Kyu-su to articulate them clearly to the young king.

Pak's solution to the problem of market stability was based on two traditional considerations that had been violated by the Taewongun: maintaining a balance between the volume of cash and commodities in circulation in order to stabilize prices and laissez-faire instead of price fixing and government interference in the market. Since the eighteenth century Korean officials had been aware of the effect on prices wrought by fluctuations in the volume of metallic cash in circulation. The traditionally accepted opinion on monetary policy since that time was that price stability was to be maintained by limited coinage, since the excessive minting of cash resulted in a rise of prices. The government tried to control minting so that the volume of metal currency introduced into the market would not exceed the volume of commodities available for sale at stable market prices. The Taewongun, of course, had violated these maxims by subordinating price stability to revenue demands in order to profit from seigniorage charges on the 100-cash. When this produced inflation, he tried to check it by fixing prices.[49] When price fixing failed, the Taewongun then resorted to importing Chinese cash in order to profit from the cheaper price of copper in China.

Pak Kyu-su argued for a return to a policy of maintaining a balance between the volume of currency and commodities and government noninterference in the market. By recommending restraints on private minting, he intended not only to check private profiteering but also to limit the amount of cash that would be funneled into the market. He placed even greater stress on government noninterference and laissez-faire. Pak urged upon Kojong the necessity for restoring normal market activities because the abolition of Chinese currency had left the government with no cash reserves with which to make purchases, and merchants were left holding inventories. "Only after there is no stagnation in the circulation of currency among the people will the way be opened for the flow of necessary commodities to official yamen." The only way to ensure this, he assured Kojong, was to let nature take its course. There should be no interference with the market, for any restraints would check the flow of goods and enable speculators to profit from the manipulation of prices.[50]

Pak asked that government authorities be constrained from conducting investigations and manipulating commodity prices during trading periods and that officials from the Ministry of Punishments and capital police be prevented from interfering in the Seoul markets. He promised that if the market were left alone, prices would reach their own level and price fixing would not be needed. Yi Yu-wŏn also agreed that price control was "a poor way to conduct government," and Pak admonished Kojong to follow the maxim "Be careful not to disturb the market."[51]

Kojong agreed with both aspects of Pak's and Yi's recommendations. He remarked that he had read in the *Shih-chi* that every time cash was minted it brought on inflation, and for no other reason than that there was a limit to the quantity of goods produced but no limit to the amount of currency that could be issued. He therefore agreed to prohibit the indiscriminate private minting of cash.[52] Kojong also noted that the government had not been able to fix commodity prices at a low level. He agreed with Pak that if things were left to the people to work out for themselves, goods and money would be exchanged as a matter of course.[53]

Pak and Yi were agreed that the ideal of equilibrium between goods and money was in the natural order of things. Manipulation—be it by the government or by private individuals—was to be abhorred. As things left to themselves seemed to acquire a natural balance, so would the economy right itself from the recent imbalance brought about by the Taewongun's inflationary money policies and the abolition of Chinese currency. This naturalistic view of the market—a kind of laissez-faire economics sans profit motive, stressing harmony rather than competition—inhibited any thought of positive action to remedy economic problems. Furthermore, Pak and Yi obviously placed priority on stable market prices and general economic well-being rather than on the state's utilization of money and coinage for revenue purposes. This was contrary to the course pursued by the Taewongun of manipulating coinage for revenue and interfering in the market by price fixing in order to maintain stable prices.

In February Kojong agreed with Pak Kyu-su and Yi Yu-wŏn on these

The Abolition of Ch'ing Cash

matters, but by March he had begun to shift his priorities toward the accumulation of revenue, particularly by using the Ch'ing cash at its intrinsic value to pay government bills. He was still anxious, however, to prevent undue burdens on the common people.

Protecting the Peasants

Kojong had abolished Ch'ing cash in response to complaints that inflation was working a hardship on the people, and he was determined to adhere to this policy no matter how great the financial shortage. By March there was mounting pressure for some kind of modification of his policy in order to permit greater revenue, and on March 13 Yi Yu-wŏn tried to impress the king with the urgency of the situation.[54]

One of the problems the government had to face after the abolition of Ch'ing cash was the disposition of tax payments already collected in that currency. Should it be returned to the taxpayers and ever-normal cash required in its stead? On February 10 Yi Yu-wŏn took the position that such a step would not be taken because it would constitute a double tax on the peasantry. He urged that in such cases the officials be held responsible, and not the people.[55] On March 17 Kojong declared that the land-tax surcharges were indeed a great evil, for not only was the peasant burdened with interest payments on loans, but he had to suffer this extra levy, too. He refused to go along with those who advocated that the land-tax surcharge for P'yŏng'an, Hamgyŏng, and Kyŏngsang provinces, which had already been paid in Ch'ing cash, be returned and collected again in ever-normal cash. Instead he ordered that:

1. If the people had presented [Ch'ing cash] for payment, and this had been rejected, it was to be accepted.
2. If the outer provinces had already accepted [Ch'ing cash in tax payments], and had not yet remitted it to the capital, they were to keep it on hand.
3. What had not yet been collected from the people in the administrative towns would be exempted [from payment].[56]

Yi Yu-ẅon was effusive in his praise for Kojong's benevolence, for allowing the people to pay in Ch'ing cash was as good as exempting them from the tax. But he also expressed concern over low revenues. Kojong replied: "If it is of benefit to the people, even though there might be damage to state finances, what obstacle is there to it? It is only because it is of advantage to the people that I did it."[57]

Kojong also issued orders to protect the peasants of Ch'ungch'ŏng and Chŏlla provinces from double taxation. People living in mountainous and hilly areas in these provinces were responsible for paying their land tax in cash to the grain-transport warehouses, which then purchased the grain that was shipped to the capital. Collections had already been made in Ch'ing cash the previous fall, and the grain shipments were due shortly. Kojong ordered that these people not be required to make payments again in ever-normal cash in place of Ch'ing cash, since it would be too onerous a burden.[58]

Yi Yu-wŏn was alarmed that Kojong might go too far with his magnanimous exemption policy. He pointed out that these same hill people in Ch'ungch'ŏng and Chŏlla provinces also were required to pay the *taedong* tribute tax half in cloth and half in cash. If this too were exempted, there would not be enough in the treasury to meet expenses. Kojong replied that the 150,000 sŏk of rice stored in the capital treasuries should be enough for the year's expenditures. As for Kyŏngsang province, there would be no problem there, since ever-normal cash had always been the medium of exchange.[59] Yi replied that if there were enough rice in the capital treasuries, it would be all right to handle things this way, but he feared that this fall's *taedong* revenues might be less than usual because of a poor crop year. He requested that he be allowed to discuss the matter with the chief officials of the Ministry of Taxation and the Tribute Bureau and petition again.[60]

On March 22 Yi finally gained Kojong's consent to a modification of his previous exemption order. Kojong agreed to Yi's suggestion that the authorities be instructed to collect such taxes as the people were able to pay without any time limit for payment, and he ordered that the officials make no severe exactions in levying the taxes. Yi opined that if the taxes were collected from time to time (rather that at one fell swoop), this would be sufficient to alleviate the burden, and no special order for tax remission would be needed.[61] Given the state of corruption at the time, this modification of Kojong's original purpose might have rendered his concern for the mountain dwellers well-nigh useless. The pressure exerted by financial need had finally taken its toll on Kojong's resolve. It was not an easy matter for him to maintain his moral standards, but he continued to try.

On March 25 a new prince was born to Queen Min, and in an audience of chief ministers on March 27, the king said that something ought to be done in honor of the felicitous occasion. He asked Yi Yu-wŏn if there had been any Ch'ing cash remitted to the capital that was then returned to be replaced by ever-normal cash. Yi replied that 30,000 yang had been sent back from the Ministry of Taxation. Kojong thereupon ordered cancellation of the taxes due in honor of the occasion.[62] The king took the same action with regard to 35,000 yang of Ch'ing cash that had been remitted to the Ministry of Taxation from the Office of Interpreters (sayŏgwŏn.). The ministry had sent this back after the abolition of Ch'ing cash to be replaced by ever-normal cash. Yi Yu-wŏn explained to Kojong that the people were opposed to this because the Office of Interpreters had col-

The Abolition of Ch'ing Cash

lected this revenue from merchants who had brought in goods from China and the burden of another collection would fall on them. Yi recommended that the original Ch'ing cash be accepted by the Ministry of Taxation, but he also pointed out that by doing so there would be a deficit in the 1873 taxes due from the Office of Interpreters. Kojong replied, "If it profit the people, though there be deficiencies, what harm will there be?"[63] This was certainly Kojong's idea of fulfilling Mencian directives to provide for the people's subsistence despite the mounting pressure for finances.

The king also decided to abolish taxes which had recently been imposed on land in Seoul. He asked Pak Kyu-su if taxes had formerly not been imposed in order to attract settlers to the capital. Pak replied that such had been the case. Kojong then decreed that taxes paid in Ch'ing cash and rejected by the authorities would now be accepted and that the new land taxes in Seoul would be abolished.[64]

Further tax relief measures were ordered on March 31. Various taxes were suspended including a surcharge on grain transport sailors for rotten grain, miscellaneous corvee (for two months), and taxes on butcher shops (for thirty days). Tribute middlemen were also granted ten sŏk of rice apiece from the Ministry of Taxation.[65] When Yi Yu-wŏn objected that too many exemptions were permitted, Kojong replied that at such a felicitous time there should be special dispensations and postponements and taxes could be collected later.[66] Throughout 1874 Kojong remained committed to the idea that the people's welfare took precedence over state revenues and he repeatedly approved of tax exemptions.

Inflation

Kojong had withdrawn Ch'ing cash from circulation in order to stem inflation, but inflation persisted. On June 9, 1874, Kojong complained that he had abolished Ch'ing cash to benefit the people but commodity prices were still double or triple the normal level. The answer, however, was not to be found in coercive legislation.

Guiding the people depends on making the people's feelings change of themselves. The feelings of the people are like water. All it may do is flow; you cannot make it flow. Recently cash [Ch'ing cash?] has been circulating in the alleys and lanes, for the people of the marketplace are tricky and deceitful. This is indeed most deplorable.[67]

On October 29 Kojong again deplored the fact that inflation was even worse than before the abolition of Ch'ing cash. Yi Yu-wŏn agreed, but rejoined that Ch'ing cash still had to be abolished. If it were still in use, prices would be even higher. Kojong agreed that its prohibition was essential.[68]

Politics and Policy in Traditional Korea

On November 16 the king made note again of the persisting inflation to Yi Yu-wǒn. Yi confirmed this with a report of conditions in Kyǒnggi province obtained from a recent personal trip through the area. Although he had heard that inflation had spread throughout the whole country, he did not think that prices should be controlled by the government. All that could be done was to wait for nature to take its course and level things off. Kojong agreed and said that he had noticed that whenever he handed down an order, a few days later prices would go up. The solution to this, said Yi, was for the king to induce the people to follow his orders by acting as a model for the people. This had been done by the ancients and was the key to getting his orders obeyed and eliminating confusion in government. Kojong wholeheartedly agreed with this.[69] Despite the fact that the main purpose of his aboliton of Ch'ing cash had not been achieved, Kojong and his chief minister, Yi Yu-wǒn, clung to the idea that the Taewongun's currency manipulation and price fixing were mistaken and that governmental inaction to ensure a free market combined with moral suasion to eliminate excessive profit seeking were the only answers to the problems of money and prices.

The Significance of Currency Policy

The history of currency in Korea shows that there was a long tradition of prejudice against the use of cash itself. Part of this prejudice was based on orthodox Confucian economics, which was concerned with the people's subsistence but not their affluence and which emphasized social stability and frowned on social mobility—especially via business activity. Confucian economics also emphasized the fundamental significance of agriculture as almost the only legitimate occupation for the nonscholar or nonbureaucratic class. Cash smacked too much oñ profit seeking. This basic undercurrent of prejudice persisted despite the growing use of cash in the economy and the payment of taxes. Currency was tolerated by government policy as a necessary evil.

The Taewongun arrived on the scene an active, vigorous leader with several costly ideas for restoring the grandeur of the dynasty and standing up courageously to foreign enemies. In some ways, he was oriented more toward the wealth and power philosophy of political-economic thinking than to the orthodox Confucian emphasis on morality and people's welfare. He needed funds for his projects, and he was not one to let moral nitpicking stand in his way. His minting of large cash and his importation of Ch'ing cash were designed to supply the need for such funds, but these were inflationary measures which evoked cries of anguish from the orthodox, who were the heirs of anti-cash prejudice. Moreover, to offset inflation he attempted to impose controls on the market.

The Abolition of Ch'ing Cash

When Kojong came to the throne he found himself saddled with an inflation induced by his father's currency policies. What surpluses there were in the government treasuries were held in depreciated Ch'ing cash, masking what was really a precarious fiscal position. Kojong felt that it was the duty of the king to give priority to the welfare of the people, a principle he had learned from his training in the proper way of the Confucian monarch, and he was swayed by the arguments of the orthodox literati that depreciated currency and inflation were working great hardships on the people.

Pak Kyu-su and Yi Yu-wŏn, who concerned themselves with such mundane things as market prices and profits—matters which literati like Ch'oe Ik-Hyŏn had not deigned to consider—preferred a minimum of government interference in the market. They believed that the market should be left to its own natural mechanism, and they felt that the Taewongun had tampered with this mechanism by coining large cash and by introducing price controls. Kojong agreed with this view and stuck to it, even though the abolition of Ch'ing cash failed to curb inflation.

What had been a precarious financial situation upon Kojong's accession to the throne became a disastrous one after the abolition of Ch'ing cash. The continuing shortage of funds for state operations was not entirely due to Kojong's economic policies. Crop failures, official corruption, the built-in restrictions of the tax collection and distribution system, and the extraordinary expenditures on tribute missions and Chinese envoys also added to the fiscal crisis, but revenue shortage was exacerbated by Kojong's doctrinaire implementation of orthodox Confucian economic precepts. In almost every situation where he was given a choice between reducing tax burdens on the peasantry and increasing state revenues, he opted for the former.

Whether from inexperience, natural dullness, or just simply a superb job of indoctrination by his tutors, Kojong failed to realize that good government in premodern Korea meant maintaining that precarious balance between the needs of the state and the subsistence of the people. This balance was upset when, adhering rigidly to his ideal view of the Confucian monarch guaranteeing the welfare of the populace against all pressures to the contrary, he virtually liquidated most of the state's cash reserves and obstructed attempts to replenish them.

11

Maintaining the Status Quo

The failure of Kojong's monetary policy resulted in a subtle but significant shift in domestic policy from positive reform to maintenance of the status quo. The new policy was a direct product of the disillusionment with the extremes offered by institutional reform and ethical dogmatism. On the one hand, it became obvious to many officials that the institutional reforms of the Taewongun's decade had not really been that effective in eliminating corruption and providing a stable revenue base for the government, and on the other hand, the disaster of the young king's monetary policy showed that moralist doctrinaire extremism could strip the government of its resources and humble the throne. The king began to realize the necessity of maintaining adequate revenue and to develop a healthier awareness of his own prerogatives as monarch.

By 1875 the state council in particular was content to remedy whatever was malfunctioning but refused to countenance any major changes in government structures or institutions. Adhering to the status quo, however, produced discontent among several groups. Young officials, particularly the secret censors who were active in investigating local conditions, continued to propose institutional solutions for domestic problems, but most of their recommendations were ignored by the state council. Those scholars and officials who demanded the full implementation of the conservative Ch'oe Ik-hyŏn program were frustrated by the reluctance of the king to restore the Mandongmyo and the private academies and to abolish the household cloth tax.

The shift in domestic policy brought with it serious consequences for the welfare of the Korean people. Just when the country was about to be opened to trade and diplomacy and exposed to new dangers by the challenge of foreign powers—a time when the king and all his officials should have been giving thought to the changes and adaptations that would be

Maintaining the Status Quo

necessary for national self-preservation—a consensus had been reached in high government circles that the best policy for domestic affairs was to stand pat with the existing system.

In this chapter several aspects of the shift to a status quo policy in domestic affairs will be explored: the adjustment of grain loan policy in response to extreme fiscal shortage, the struggle to preserve the village granary system without undertaking any extension of it or any institutional innovations; and the king's reluctance to entertain literati demands for the restoration of the private academies and abolition of the household cloth tax.

Pressure on the Grain Loan System:
Liquidation of Special Reserve Loan Funds

The desperate search for revenue by the government after January 1874 almost resulted in the total dismantling of the grain loan system that had been reconstructed by the Taewongun in the previous decade. The central government and its agencies, provincial governments, and military garrisons continued to depend heavily on the interest payments from outstanding loans, for the Taewongun had done very little to undermine this sytem and shift the responsibility for raising revenue to the regular tax structure. In fact, he had strengthened the government's reliance on loan interest by refunding a system that had been bankrupted—cancelling unpayable debts and establishing new loan funds. The recent refunding of the grain loan system, however, meant that a huge amount of capital was tied up in official grain loans and in the village granary system throughout the country, and during the revenue crisis of 1874 the king and his officials began to consider calling in these funds.

Liquidation of the grain loan funds was a difficult decision to make because the government relied on the grain loan system for military and famine reserves and for a steady flow of revenue from interest. Furthermore, the health of the village granary system and ultimately the welfare of the peasantry in the rural villages depended to a large extent on maintaining the capital of the village granaries intact lest the peasantry fall prey to the usurious interest rates of the private moneylender or the old corrupt practices of the local magistrates and clerks. The government was therefore faced with a dilemma: whether to sacrifice the state's reserves, interest revenue, and the welfare of the peasant in order to tide the government over an immediate and difficult financial crisis.

In addition to financial pressures several reports of corruption in the administration of grain loans in the provinces during the first half of 1874 helped convince Kojong of the need to liquidate the loans authorized in the previous decade as a means of raising revenues.[1] At the begin-

Politics and Policy in Traditional Korea

ning of March Kojong decided to call in grain loan funds from P'yŏng'an, Hamgyŏng, and Kyŏngsang provinces over the objections of the ministers, but this proved to be a frustrating and difficult decision. Kojong first proposed calling in the special loan fund in P'yŏng'an province capitalized after 1865 by special land and household levies and voluntary contributions, but Yi Yu-wŏn informed him that in fact the recorded reserves of that fund were almost totally falsified and that there was not even one bag of rice left in the account. Pak suggested that Kojong recall the 660,000 yang 1873 Special Reserve Rice Loan Fund (*kyeyu pyŏlbihwan*) in that province, but Minister of Taxation Kim Se-gyun objected on two counts: the government could not afford to lose the 60,000 yang per year interest revenues, and the governor would have great difficulty in finding 660,000 yang (principal plus first year's interest) of ever-normal cash, since it had been driven out of circulation in P'yŏng'an even before the abolition of Chinese currency. Kojong overrode his objections and observed that P'yŏng'an could get ever-normal cash from neighboring Hamgyŏng province, where it had continued to circulate.[2]

Kojong next proposed to call in the Special Reserve Loan Fund (*pyŏlbihwan*) in Kyŏngsang province, but Yi Yu-wŏn objected on the grounds that the king could not arbitrarily reverse a decision made by the dowager-regent. Kojong then suggested liquidating some of the village granary funds in that province, but Yi objected again on the same grounds. Kojong remarked that he would seek the dowager's advice and proposed calling in a grain loan fund from Hamgyŏng province. When Yi pointed out that his loan fund had been established to benefit the people, Kojong responded that in fact the fund had only led to corruption and distress. He agreed that the village granary system should be left alone but felt it was essential to call in all the special reserve loan funds. Yi replied that he knew of the corruption in the grain loan system from his own experience as provincial governor but nothing could be done about it, and he promised to confer with other high officials to seek alternatives.[3]

Kojong's frustration and depression strengthened his determination to liquidate as much of the grain loan reserves as possible. On March 6 he overrode Yi Yu-wŏn's objections against calling in loan funds. On that day the state council submitted a special report on the total amount of grain in Kyŏngsang province, and Kojong decreed that he had received authorization from the dowager for the recall not only of 50,000 sŏk of grain from the 1866 and 1867 special reserve loan funds, but also of the village granary funds in that province.[4] Two days later Kojong asked Yi Yu-wŏn for an estimate of the amount of grain loan funds in Hamgyŏng province. Yi reported that there were 110,000 yang of loan funds in Hamgyŏng, and if all loan funds were called in from Kyŏngsang, P'yŏng'an (and Hamgyŏng?) provinces, the central government would obtain a total of 1,300,000 yang. Kojong stated that in view of the current financial crisis caused by the abolition of Chinese currency he had no choice but to call in the special reserve loan funds and the loan capital accumulated from the cash surtax on land.[5]

Kojong and Yi Yu-wŏn, however, had not reckoned with the financial problems of the provinces. Revenue shortages forced the provincial governments into competition with the central government for resources and made it difficult for them to recall and remit grain loan funds to the capital. The recall of grain loan funds from P'yŏng'an province had placed an unduly heavy financial burden on the authorities there, and in late May, Governor Sin Ŭng-jo requested that 200,000 yang of the 600,000 yang due to be paid to the capital of the 1873 Special Reserve Loan Fund be exempted from repayment. In the debate that took place at court on May 20 Yi Yu-wŏn pressed for the remittance of the whole amount to the capital in order to alleviate the pressure on central government treasuries for funds, but Pak Kyu-su was more sympathetic to the governor's request, having himself served as governor of that province. He pointed out that after the reform of the grain loan system in P'yŏng'an in 1865, when grain loans were replaced by surtaxes, the province's original grain reserve of 800,000 sŏk was practically wiped out and at the present time there was only 100,000 sŏk of fortress provision rice (*sŏnghyangmi*) on reserve, a fund insufficient for emergencies.[6] On May 22 the governor repeated his request, blaming the financial difficulty in the province on the abolition of Chinese currency. The state council advised the king to disallow the request because of the desperate financial situation in the capital, although it acknowledged that some way to provide a reserve for the province had to be devised.[7] On June 20 the governor resubmitted his request together with his resignation in which he compared the financial effects of the abolition of Ch'ing cash in his province to the losses incurred from a massive crop failure.[8] The state council recommended that P'yŏng'an be allowed only a 50,000 yang deduction and remarked, "Thus, by throwing a glass of wine into the river, we can save it from being dried up. But in the future that province should be ordered to put its finances in order."[9]

On May 6, 1874, the governor of Hwanghae province, Min T'ae-ho, complained that the people would have difficulty paying their taxes and repaying their loans in the current year because of the prohibition of Chinese currency. He reported that at the present time in his province the governor's yamen treasuries, the administrative towns, military garrisons, and post stations had a total of 456,046 yang, but that all of it was in Ch'ing cash. This fund was all the province had for payments of salaries and military expenses and for remittances due to the central government. Furthermore, the repayments of principal and interest on grain loans to the peasants had already been collected. Now that Chinese currency had been withdrawn from circulation, some other way had to be found for meeting the province's obligations.

Min mentioned that there was a grain loan fund of 60,000 sŏk in the province the interest payments from which were usually remitted to the capital. If it were sold for cash, the province could obtain 210,000 yang for it. If the Ch'ing cash reserves in provincial treasuries were also sold for their metallic value, about 60,000 yang (about one ninth the face value) could be obtained by that means. That would give the province a total of 270,000 yang, leaving a deficit of about 200,000 yang. The state council noted that the interest due on this 60,000 sŏk loan fund (equivalent to 210,000 yang of cash) was 21,000 yang, and it suggested that interest on the village granary loans in the province could be allocated for this purpose. Kojong approved, but when Yi Yu-wŏn raised objections to the utilization of village granary interest on May 20, Kojong agreed to rescind the order.[10]

Yi had intervened to preserve the village granary system intact in Hwanghae province, but he could not do the same for Ch'ungch'ŏng province. On June 18 Sŏng I-ho, the governor of that province, reported that he had been unable to make emergency remittances of funds to the capital as well as payments for local expenses. He asked for permission to allocate 5,000 sŏk of village granary funds to meet current demand, and then to make up for it later by transferring surpluses from the collection of the cash surtax on land (*kyŏltujŏn*). Yi Yu-wŏn approved of the request, since Sŏng promised to replenish the amount he would borrow from the village granaries, but Yi also insisted that a deadline of three years be set for replenishing the village granary system with punishment for any failure to meet the deadline. Minister of Taxation Kim Se-gyun protested that the village granary system was the only one of all the grain loan funds that had a full complement of grain, and he urged the king to try and maintain the principal intact. Kojong agreed that, since the village granary system was administered by the people themselves, the grain stocks had to be in proper order, but when Yi Yu-wŏn urged upon him the necessity to alleviate the financial burdens of the province, he agreed to permit Governor Sŏng's request for a three year period.[11]

The recall of grain loan principal did not prove to be the panacea that Kojong had thought it would be. On June 25 Kim Se-gyun mentioned that of the 1,120,000 yang from all loan funds that had been called in from Kyŏngsang, P'yŏng'an, and Hamgyŏng provinces, 985,000 yang had to be paid out to government bureaus and 20,000 yang to the Tribute Bureau, leaving only a little over 100,000 yang to meet other expenses. Kojong asked Kim if most of the cash interest payments from village granary loans had been received from the provinces, and he expressed

Maintaining the Status Quo

concern that the work on the Kyŏngbok palace might not be finished without these funds.[12]

In late July the governor of Chŏlla province, Cho Sŏng-gye, requested permission to take over 50,000 sŏk of grain from the village granaries in his province for the purpose of maintaining provincial revenues. He proposed to call in the whole fund in cash and reinvest it in loans in the conversion rate of three yang/sŏk. The loans would be limited to five years' duration during which time only the interest on the loans would be paid. The principal would be repaid whenever there was a bumper crop. Yi Yu-wŏn told the king that Cho's request was just as illegal as every other request made by provincial governors since the abolition of Chinese currency, but because the request of the governor of Hwanghae had been approved, there was no reason for refusing Cho's proposal. Yi did object, however, to Cho's plan for manipulating cash-grain conversion ratios and delaying the repayment of principal, since this was contrary to standard grain loan practice.[13]

By the fall of 1874 the king had called in most of the special reserve loan funds established under the Taewongun and he showed no inclination to reverse this decision. In September a minor official requested the reestablishment of the 600,000 sŏk grain loan fund in P'yŏng'an province. He complained that the interest from this loan fund had been replaced by land and household surtaxes imposed at the suggestion of ex-governor Hong U-gil in 1865 and that these taxes placed an unfair burden on people who owned no land. He argued that the loan fund could be built up again with surplus tax revenues in six years' time, implying that interest income could replace the land and household taxes.[14] The state council, however, successfully opposed the recommendation because the grain loan system had been the "bane of the people."[15]

Saving the Village Granary System

The village granary system was in grave danger of liquidation because of government demands for revenues and fears of rampant corruption, but the king and his court were inclined to preserve it, since it was supposed to have been designed for the purpose of eliminating corruption. The salvation of the village granaries therefore depended to a large extent on an evaluation of their performance.

In December 1874 secret censors who had been dispatched to the provinces to investigate administrative malfeasance returned to the capital to make their reports directly to the king. The secret censor for Kyŏnggi province, Kang Mun-hyang, in his written report complained about the corruption in the administration of village granaries. The principal of grain loans was often left outstanding for a number of years while the interest alone was collected; there were irregularities in the measuring of

Politics and Policy in Traditional Korea

grain and adulteration of the grain that was loaned out. Kang recommended that in view of the corruption he had uncovered, the administration of the village granaries be changed to conform with the regulations
for the old district granaries (*ŭpch'ang*).[16] During his court audience with
Kojong, Kang reported that the grain loan system in Kyŏnggi province
was the most corrupt institution of all. Kojong commented that the village
granary system had been all right at first, but as time went on it became
corrupted. Kang agreed that this was usually what happened to any new
institution.[17] The state council, however, was unwilling to adopt Kang's
recommendations for reverting to the district granary system.

The district granaries have their own old regulations, and the village
granaries (*sach'ang*) have their own new regulations. What Kang is advocating is the idea that if something is new, do not establish it, and if old,
do not change it. But the village granary administration cannot be
changed rashly. Opinion has to be consulted before making a decision.[18]

The day before the state council submitted its decision on Kang's proposals, the secret censor for Ch'ungch'ŏng Left province,[19] Kim Myŏng-
jin, reported that the village granaries were operating extremely well.
Kim explained, "The reason why at present there is no corruption in the
grain loan granaries is because the clerks are not allowed in, and the
people themselves make the loans and collect the debts." He warned,
however, that if, because of the need for revenue, loan payments were
commuted to cash and called in or loans were made in cash, the officials
could manipulate the cash-grain computation rates for their own profit.[20]
In his audience with Kojong on December 7 Kim said that the village
granary system was operating as provided for by Chu Hsi's *she-ts'ang*
system and that "there was no corruption among officials and no evils."
Kojong asked Kim's opinion about the previous decision to call in 5,000
sŏk worth of funds from the village granaries in that province. Kim
replied that it had been unavoidable at that time, and the five year time
limit on repayment did not seem reasonable, but he repeated his plea that
cash commutations not be allowed in the future.[21] On December 12 the
state council endorsed Kim's remarks about the sanctity of the village
granary system and insisted that funds borrowed from it by the government be repaid within the time limit, especially since the purpose behind
the establishment of village granaries was "to benefit the people."[22]

Therefore, despite the evidence of corruption in some areas in the
administration of village granaries, it appears that by the end of 1874
Kojong and his government were determined to preserve the system
come what may. On January 20, 1875, for example, the secret censor for
Kyŏngsang Left province, Pak Chŏng-yang,[23] reported that grain loan
stocks were being moved about from one place to another in order to

Maintaining the Status Quo

profit from varying market conditions and that grain from the village granaries had recently been converted to cash for the purpose of supplementing official revenues, depleting the government's emergency reserves.[24] Kojong asked Pak if he thought the village granaries had proved effective. Pak said that they actually had rice stored in them and that there had been no trouble with loans from granaries in remote villages. "But, if the clerks and petty officials were allowed to interfere, there would be trouble and corruption."[25] On April 3 the state council again corroborated the basic policy of maintaining the village granaries while attempting to limit corruption.

The basic purpose of the establishment of the village granaries was to benefit the people. How is it that the petty officials work their deceit? We must deliberately stop them from tampering with the regulations that have been established so that there will be no violations of [grain-loan] allotments.[26]

Despite the financial pressure the village granary system was saved because it still represented the best chance for relieving the peasantry of the burdens of corrupt credit and loan practices. The salvation of the village granaries was a more difficult task than their establishment, for when they were created they were funded relatively easily by newly minted cash but they could be kept alive only by a most determined resolve to prevent the cannibalization of their resources in a period of severe financial shortage.

Weariness with Institutional Reform

Despite the preservation of the village granary system, there was a growing mood of disillusionment and weariness with institutional reform among government officials who were no longer convinced that institutional changes would be that efficacious in eliminating corruption and creating new sources of revenue. The mood of the times had changed, and officials were now willing to settle for the maintenance of the status quo. After December 1874 some of the young secret censors still retained some ardor for reform, but their recommendations were directed to specific problems uncovered in individual provinces. The state council was content to accept some of their suggestions but in general refrained from planning on a national basis. It had called in most of the special reserve loan funds but was reluctant to authorize additional loans, and it had preserved the village granary system in five provinces but showed no inclination to extend its benefits to the rest of the country.

Despite reports from secret censors about rampant corruption in the administration of grain loans in Kangwŏn, Ch'ungch'ŏng, Chŏlla,

Politics and Policy in Traditional Korea

P'yŏng'an, and Hamgyŏng provinces, the state council took very little remedial action other than to prohibit illicit transfer of grain stocks and insist on the maintenance of reserve quotas.[27] Probably the best illustration of the new mood occurred when Secret Censor Hong Man-sik reported that in South P'yŏng'an province grain loan interest had previously been replaced by new land and household surtaxes, but that the registration procedures had resulted in overtaxation from collusion and falsification. Household registration had not kept pace with changes in residence patterns and population, and cadastral surveys had not succeeded in recording the increasing amount of uncultivated land. Hong remarked, "The resentment and suffering of the people is no less than it was before the abolition of the grain loan system."[28] He recommended that half the household levy be set in a fixed cash rate to eliminate manipulation by officials.[29] The state council was willing to accept Hong's minor recommendation about household surtaxes, but it was unwilling to undertake any major or radical reform of the system in South P'yŏng'an province. It reported to the throne that the present system had been in existence for ten years, and to keep changing it again and again would only "confuse the people."[30]

Demoralization also led to indecision. The secret censor for Hamgyŏng pointed out in January 1875 that local officials were loaning out their reserves at interest in order to supplement their income, and he asked for the authorization of additional loans to meet the financial shortage. When the state council finally responded to this problem in April 1875 it refused to authorize new loans and remarked that the depletion of reserves by unauthorized loans was sometimes unavoidable. Although at least half the stored grain was supposed to be kept in reserve, because of the financial crisis the council chose to leave the decision on whether to keep a 50 percent reserve or use it all in loans for the local officials to determine "in accordance with the circumstances."[31]

Demands for the Restoration of the
Mandongmyo and Private Academies

Kojong's policy on the grain loan question illustrates the growing reluctance for tampering with the status quo, but government inaction on grain loans did not alienate any important groups in Korean society or create any large-scale discontent. The government's failure to take positive action did have more serious political repercussions, however, with respect to other issues. After Kojong assumed full power he implemented almost all the demands of Ch'oe Ik-hyŏn with the exception of the restoration of the Mandongmyo and private academies and the abolition of the household cloth tax. Kojong was becoming a less pliant tool of the literati and yangban because he was growing more cognizant of the financial

Maintaining the Status Quo

crisis and he was developing a greater awareness of his own power and prerogatives as monarch. As Kojong began to assert his independence he alienated many of those who had supported him in the first place. The same man who had split with the Taewongun over domestic policy now began to lose confidence in the king's ability to adopt their solutions for national salvation. Their discontent with Kojong began with domestic issues and was later fueled by the change of direction in foreign policy.

Even when Kojong took power he proved recalcitrant on literati demands for the restoration of the Mandongmyo and the private academies.[32] Almost immediately after the dismissal of the high state councilors and the exile of Ch'oe Ik-hyŏn in the last days of December 1873, a host of individual memorials and joint petitions were submitted to the throne for the restoration of the Mandongmyo and the academies.[33] Since most of the petitioners were non-officeholding students, scholars, and degree holders were particularly concerned about the moral and ritual significance of the Mandongmyo, by refusing to entertain their demands Kojong was risking the alienation of the literati. For example, Kojong had sought to appoint one eminent literatus, Im Hŏn-hoe, to a post in the government. Sixty-two years old at the time, Im had preferred as a youth to abandon the competition for a degree and devote himself to study, no doubt in emulation of his renowned teacher, Hong Chik-p'il, who had also shunned office.[34] In 1858 at the age of forty-seven Im had accepted his first appointment to office under King Ch'ŏlchong, and was one of those who had protested the abolition of the Mandongmyo in 1865.[35] On January 5 Kojong appointed Im to the post of Royal Lecturer, so that the eminent scholar could help him become a sage ruler, as Kojong expressed it, but Im declined the appointment and petitioned for the restoration of the Mandongmyo.[36] Kojong refused to entertain Im's suggestion to alter the dowager-regent's decree on the abolition of the Mandongmyo, but he sent a second notice of appointment to Im.[37] Im sent another refusal from his home in the country in which he remarked that there was no reason why the king could not reverse an edict of the dowager-regent's. On the contrary, such an act would increase the virtue of the king beyond that of the dowager. Im complimented the king on all the recent governmental decisions that he had made, except for his failure to act on the Mandongmyo question.[38]

The protest was continued by other scholar-officials mainly because of the moral debt due the Ming dynasty for its aid to Korea during Hideyoshi's invasions. As one student, Yi Pyŏng-gyu, put it in his memorial of February 6,

Our Emperor, Shen-tsung [of the Ming dynasty], mobilized the troops of his empire and exhausted the material of his empire in completely driving out the wicked invaders [Hideyoshi] and restoring the rivers and mountains of our ruined country of 3,000 *li*. Not one blade of grass, not one hair did the Emperor spare . . . People of olden times have never been able to forget [the need] to repay this debt even after death to the end of time.[39]

Yi instructed the king that the debt to the Ming dynasty was a never-ending and never-fulfilled one that past Korean kings and scholars had always acknowledged. "Alas," wrote Yi, "I still cannot bear to speak of the overthrow of the Ming. . . . Even stupid and ignorant men and women at that time all said, 'Our flesh and blood are their flesh and blood!' How much more so in the case of the chaste and loyal King Sŏnjo (r. 1567-1608), who did suffer over this?" Yi pointed out that after the Manchu invasion of Korea in 1637, King Injo (r. 1623-49) still privately practiced the rites to the Ming in his garden, "facing north [toward China] and shedding tears like rain over the tragedy." King Hyojong (r. 1649-59) also "could not bear to live on the same earth with his great enemy [the Manchus]," but his and Song Si-yŏl's plan to wreak vengeance on the Manchus was never achieved, and "the great obligation was never fulfilled. As long as it takes mulberry fields to be changed into the sea, this obligation will never be forgotten."[40]

Yi Pyŏng-gyu did, however, acknowledge that the local literati of the shrines and academies had been exercising unrestrained power and "acting like bandits, killing people and destroying families," but instead of punishing these people the government had abolished the private academies and the most important shrines. Yi lamented the decline in moral standards that had ensued upon the abolition of these shrines as illustrated in the current year when some "worthless common clout" had turned over the stele to the illustrious Six Loyal Ministers of Tanjong's reign (1452-55) and wrecked the alter at their shrine in P'och'ŏn.[41] Yi recommended that Kojong petition the ex-dowager-regent for a restoration of the Mandongmyo, the academy to Kija, and the shrine to Confucius. In fine, he expressed some discontent at the exile of Ch'oe Ik-hyŏn and the king's failure to adopt Ch'oe's total program.

Even though the path of remonstrance has been opened at court, words of criticism pointing out faults have not been completely adopted. On the contrary, such men [who have offered criticism] have been exiled. This has served to impede the king's knowledge of things and to cause grievance to the literati.[42]

In his rescript Kojong refused to alter his position on the private academies and shrines but did agree to give consideration to the altar of the Mandongmyo. He also instructed Yi to return to his studies and self-cultivation.[43]

The petitions continued to come in through the end of March, but

Maintaining the Status Quo

Kojong rejected all of them.[44] On April 1, however, Kojong decreed that he had received instructions from the dowager to resume ritual sacrifice at the Mandongmyo.[45] Kojong had finally acquiesced to literati demands, but his capitulation was far from complete for the restoration of the Mandongmyo marked the end of the king's commitment to the program of Ch'oe Ik-hyŏn. Furthermore, even though Kojong had authorized the rebuilding of the Mandongmyo, he took pains to ensure that it would remain under the jurisdiction of local officials. As the edict stated,

Even though the Mandongmyo was first established by an illustrious scholar, the situation [concerning its status] naturally changed when King Chŏngjo granted it a royal charter. Thus, in restoring it now, *it should be under the control of the court.* (Italics mine.)[46]

Kojong ordered that the governor and local magistrate would supervise reconstruction, ritual sacrifice, and the guarding of the shrine.[47] He had no intention of allowing it to become an independent symbol or center of literati power.

Although Kojong was willing to restore the Mandongmyo, on April 14 he rejected the request of a minor inspector for the restoration of the Hwayangdong academy established in honor of Song Si-yŏl next to the Mandongmyo. Kojong stated that the obligation to Song had already been met, and he chastised the official for venturing to lecture the throne on moral principles.[48] The king held fast to this decision despite several other requests—a petition signed by twenty-four students and degree holders on April 22,[49] a joint memorial submitted by 165 from Ch'ungch'ŏng province on April 24,[50] and another submitted by 914 students from Kyŏnggi province on April 28.[51] After the last one he instructed the Royal Secretariat to accept no further petitions on this issue.[52] The matter was now laid to rest and reconstruction work on the Mandongmyo was reported completed on September 10.[53]

Kojong had almost adopted all the demands of the literati for the reversal of the Taewongun's policies and the restoration of Confucian standards of government, but because he had not granted full satisfaction to them, he was unable to dissipate their discontent and win them over wholly to his side. At the same time, he was becoming annoyed with their imprecations now that they were challenging his leadership directly.

Demands for the Abolition of the
Household Cloth Tax

Some scholars and officials were also concerned about the household cloth tax because they feared it would undermine the social order and weaken the respect shown for the upper class by the common people.

Politics and Policy in Traditional Korea

The first of several protests against the household cloth tax was made by Yi Kyu-hyŏng, third censor in the Office of the Censor-General, on January 2, 1874:

> The clans of high officials have been mixed together with commoners [in the application of the tax.]. I sincerely believe that this arose from the exalted intention [of the throne] to extend [tax burdens] equally. Nevertheless the common people are ignorant and dense, and it is difficult for them to understand. If no distinctions are made between classes, people will overstep their places and law will be destroyed. This doctrine of "you and I being the same class" is a confused teaching and [is not proper to] a sage and enlightened reign.[54]

Yi was not unaware of the need to rectify the corruption in the military tax and service system, but he felt that the household cloth tax did not provide the adequate solution. While it was true that youths and elderly persons were illegally carried on the military service rosters, there were still many idlers loafing around the villages who could supply the raw manpower needed to fill the rolls. He laid the blame at the feet of the petty officials in the districts and local towns who were taking bribes to falsify the registers, and recommended tighter administration to eliminate corruption.[55]

Yi's views were corroborated by Sin Ch'ŏl-gu, a former censor, who deplored the failure to distinguish between upper and lower classes in levying the new tax and recommended a more thorough investigation of eligible able-bodied males and more equitable distribution of tax payments. If this did not prove effective, he advised, the government could always revert to the older system in which each eligible adult male was required to perform service instead of paying a cloth tax.[56]

On March 2 another official, Kim No-su, expressed his displeasure at the king's lack of action on the household cloth tax and complained about maladministration in the operation of the village cloth tax system, which had not succeeded in lowering tax burdens on individual households. Clerks had ignored the tax quotas established for each village and were collecting many times the amounts due. He advised Kojong that if he reconfirmed the original tax quotas and ensured the fair administration of the cloth tax, tax burdens on households could be reduced by two thirds.[57]

Not all officials, however, were irrevocably opposed to the household cloth tax despite their yangban status. In a memorial submitted on March 12 a Fourth Deputy Commander, Kim Kyu-sŏp, was able to see both sides of the problem. On the one hand, he reported that because "the household cloth tax was levied without discrimination on both noble and base," it had caused discontent among the elite.

> All the yangban are suing for grievance and saying that those who are

now required to pay tax are the silk-clad scholar-gentry. All of a sudden, one morning, they were required to pay the "equal cloth" [tax] and were mixed up with the commoners, destroying and eradicating all trace of law and order and social status.

On the other hand, Kim was also aware of the sufferings of the people from the military tax system, and he sympathized with their cause.

The commoners all said that generation after generation the cloth tax was levied only on poor households, and because of this they scattered and fled and shed tears. They turned to each other and said they only wanted to give birth to daughters, not sons. How fortunate it would be [they said] if the labor service tax were reduced. Then our desire to repay [such benevolence] would extend to the end of Heaven, and we would only want to give our lives for our country.

As Kim summarized the issue:

Alas! The yangban are the subjects of the king, but the common people are also the subjects of the king. Both are equally subjects, but the commoners were burdened with the cloth tax while the yangban were not. Therefore, social status was made correct and distinctions between those above and those below [were preserved]. State finances prospered, but the people scattered and fled under the cloth tax burdens.

How truly distressing this was for the state and the people! It was unavoidable that for the time being the system of the "equal cloth tax" be devised. The yangban did not understand the basic intent of the court, and it is not unusual that they only raised a big fuss.

I would request that the king give wide [ear] to opinion at court and talk in the village streets and handle matters in accordance with the best [policy].[58]

Kim's exposition made clear a contradiction inherent in the proposals of literati like Ch'oe Ik-hyŏn. They had advocated that the throne pay heed both to the welfare of the peasantry and the interests of the aristocracy on the assumption that the two were not in conflict. By refusing to abolish the household cloth tax Kojong risked the alienation of the yangban class and their literati spokesmen.

Late in 1874 the cloth tax issue was raised again, but this time by secret censors returning to court to report on conditions in the villages. The essence of their reports was not that the tax on yangban was upsetting the social order, but that maladministration had resulted in unequal and burdensome distribution of taxes on households. The government's response to the new situation, however, resembled its policy on grain loans. It was tired of large-scale institutional reform and was now content to maintain the status quo.

On November 28, 1874, the secret censor for Kyŏnggi province, Kang Mun-hyŏng, reported that the village cloth tax was not being fairly administered and in some villages a neighborhood of ten households would have to pay the taxes for twenty. Kang proposed that a survey be made of the original quotas of tax assessments for each village, and that the proper tax levies be advertised and made known to the public to prevent officials from withdrawing certain households from the tax registers and to ensure uniform tax assessments.[59] The state council, however, did not endorse Kang's recommendations.

Even though the evils of the village cloth tax were rectified, there still would be inequalities in trying to fix equal [quotas for payment] in accordance with the actual number of families. Regulations pertaining to the village cloth and households differ from district to district, and they all cannot be unified in one general [law]. The situation has to be rectified in accordance with the circumstances.[60]

The state council was not only declaring its general distaste for positive reform, it was also declaring its lack of concern for more equitable tax distribution. Although the council did not explicitly say so, it would appear that by the end of 1874 yangban and wealthy landowning households had succeeded in lightening their own tax burdens and shifting them to the lower classes by collusion with local officials. The state council showed little enthusiasm for upsetting the status quo in the villages, and its defense of the existing village or household cloth tax systems no longer signified a courageous stand on behalf of the people against the upper class.

Although not all secret censor reports were critical of the military tax system,[61] Secret Censor Ŏm Se-yŏng from Chŏlla Right province submitted proposals for reform similar to those of Kang Mun-hyŏng. On January 13, 1875, he reported that corruption in tax administration had caused many men to flee their villages bequeathing greater burdens for those who remained. Even after the institution of the household cloth tax there had not been any abatement of tax collections from neighbors and relatives of delinquent taxpayers. Assessments on each household exceeded the legal limit; in certain places taxes were levied on land as well as households; no longer was there much uniformity or equality of taxation. Ŏm pointed out that the conscription rosters were falsified and did not represent the actual number of men available for military duty, so that in an emergency there would not be enough men available for troop assignments. He proposed that military agricultural colonies be established so that the troops would be responsible for their own support, that all able-bodied males liable for military support taxes be organized in units, and that a calculation be made of the total amount of land and households in any given area and the tax burdens allotted equally. In his audience with Kojong, Ŏm told the king that there was insufficient revenue from the household cloth tax and argued that equal distribution of

Maintaining the Status Quo

military taxes on the basis of land area would be an efficient method of administering the military tax system.[62]

Ŏm's proposals were designed to restore equity and equality by replacing the household cloth tax with a system that offered fewer loopholes for evasion and maldistribution, but his suggestions were not in tune with the times. The state council did not reply to his recommendations until April 3, 1875 and then they ejected Ŏm's program because:

It has been several years since the household cloth tax was put into practice, and there have been no evils in it, so it would be difficult to change it all of a sudden. Let us put [Ŏm's recommendations] aside for the time being.[63]

Kojong approved the council's suggestion and the military tax issue was laid to rest. Whatever zeal the court once had for equal tax distribution had been dissipated.

Demoralization and the Loss of Idealistic Zeal

In two short years since the retirement of the Taewongun significant changes took place in the mood and style of domestic policy under Kojong. The most significant development may have been the subtle weaning of the king away from his naive faith in the efficacy of orthodox Confucian ideas on political economy. This would not have been so bad had he been able to return to the institutional approach of his father, but he was disillusioned by the apparent failure of such major reforms as the grain loans and household cloth tax to eliminate corruption from government operations.

The consequences of the loss of idealistic zeal were serious, since the government retreated to a status quo policy on problems of administration. The government virtually abdicated its responsibility in the face of overwhelming financial problems and repeated reports of corruption. By liquidating a major part of the grain loan system it withdrew to a lower level of funding. Even more serious was the government's willingness to tolerate an acceptable level of corruption as an inevitable part of the system of government. Vigorous leadership from the throne was necessary for the accomplishment of any major reform or institutional change, but Kojong's disillusionment contributed to a growing vacuum of power. The locus of decision-making authority had shifted subtly to the state council by 1875, for the king had obviously lost confidence in his ability to govern alone.

Despite Kojong's initial adherence to the program of Ch'oe Ik-hyŏn and other literati, he made his last commitment to that program by April 1, 1874, when he authorized the reconstruction of the Mandongmyo.

Politics and Policy in Traditional Korea

After that date he took no further action on the private academies or the household cloth tax, because he was convinced that maintenance of the status quo was the only way to balance the needs of the state and people. He thus failed to create a solid base of support among the literati or the yangban class as a whole. In effect, Kojong was losing his grip over events and men; as we will see, he lost his control over politics, which became increasingly virulent, and he watched helplessly as his country was forced willy-nilly into new treaty arrangements with Japan.

12

The Clamor for the Recall of the Taewongun: The Politics of Dissent

Hitherto, the shift in domestic and foreign policy after 1873 and the internecine political strife that accompanied it has usually been attributed by scholars to the factional political rivalry between Queen Min and the Taewongun, but the feud between these two was as yet still a minor aspect of a complex political situation. A more important cause of political strife in the period 1874-76 was the rise of dissent among certain literati against domestic and foreign policy and their increasingly vocal displeasure with the quality of Kojong's leadership.

Kojong's performance after 1874 was not of a kind to inspire confidence. Although his father had bequeathed a difficult financial situation to him, his disastrous monetary policy nearly plunged the country into bankruptcy. While his attempted return to normalcy and shunning of active policy planning may have given solace to those yearning for a rest from the frenetic activity of the Taewongun, others more aware of impending danger must have been alarmed. Even those few who had supported Kojong in December 1873 in the hopes that he would embody their plan for the establishment of Confucian sage rule were also disappointed by his failure to adopt their total program.

In the space of one year Kojong had shown that he was unsure of himself, his principles, and his ability to lead. As a result a few courageous individuals openly expressed their lack of confidence in him and at first hinted, later directly requested, that the king would do well to recall his father to the capital to provide counsel. Faced with a challenge to his leadership Kojong lost the tolerance for remonstrance that he had professed when his father had been the object of attack and responded ever more angrily and curtly to his detractors, but his determination to stifle their criticism and establish his authority beyond question only led him into a direct confrontation with the upper bureaucracy. Although the

Politics and Policy in Traditional Korea

weakness of Kojong's leadership eventually created a vacuum that the queen and her relatives attempted to fill, they did not establish their dominant position at court until after 1876. Prior to that time palace intrigue was overshadowed by a more fundamental conflict between monarch and scholar-bureaucrats.

The Pak U-Hyŏn Case

The first challenge to Kojong's leadership came in January 1874 in the aftermath of the exile of Ch'oe Ik-hyŏn when a minor official, Pak U-hyŏn, submitted a memorial which attacked Ch'oe, criticized the king for dismissing the country's leading officials, impugned the ability and integrity of the new officials, and suggested that the king had failed to show the proper respect for his father.[1] Pak was not a political tool of any Taewongun faction but an individual scholar-official exercising his traditionally revered right of remonstrance, and he probably represented the views of many literati around the country who were mildly chagrined with some of the Taewongun's actions but still preferred his overall policies and leadership to the present administration. For example, despite Pak's disdain for Ch'oe Ik-hyŏn, he agreed with the latter that the Taewongun had gone too far in abolishing the private academies. He accepted this act as a fait accompli but expressed regret over the abolition of an institution that should have been preserved. He was especially concerned about the regime's neglect of scholars. He complained that only sons of wealthy families were successful in the examinations and selected for office and that "educated men, even though they have the talent and ability, are [not employed] on the pretext that they are rotten scholars. [They are discarded] as if they were worn-out shoes."[2] Pak, in other words, held no brief for narrow political interests; he was speaking on behalf of the educated elite as a whole.

Pak claimed that prior to Ch'oe Ik-hyŏn's submission of his second memorial all had been well. The principle of filial piety and respect for elders, which he called "the root of all action and the basis of all change" and the secret to the proper governance of the state as taught in *The Great Learning*, had been given due respect by the king. The king in those days had met his filial obligations to his father and in spite of danger the accomplishments of the reign had been bright and glorious, the spirit of harmony prevailed throughout the realm, and Heaven showed its pleasure with favorable omens. It was only after Ch'oe's second memorial that harmony was disrupted, bad omens appeared, political life was disrupted by dispute, and decisions on matters of state were "contrary to what was right." The only solution for the situation, Pak averred, was a return to the previous era when the cardinal virtue of filial piety was given due respect.[3]

Recall of the Taewongun

Pak U-hyǒn's innocuous appeal to virtue shook the capital and unleashed a response only slightly less disruptive than the Ch'oe Ik-hyǒn case. At the outset the king himself hardly took note of the memorial, appending a perfunctory acknowledgment at the end of it, but the Royal Secretariat accused Pak of disrespect for the throne by sending a household servant to present his memorial and by his careless choice of words. In his rescript to the Royal Secretariat's memorial, Kojong acknowledged that Pak deserved severe punishment, but at the instruction of the dowager he had decided to show mercy and merely banish him to "a remote and noxious island."[4]

Kojong was still treating dissent with the same tolerance he had shown Ch'oe Ik-hyǒn by ordering Pak's exile before vengeful bureaucrats could vent their wrath. One alert ex-censor did, indeed, call the king to task for rushing the exile order in order to forestall demands for Pak's execution.[5] On January 29 four members of the Royal Secretariat resigned in protest over the failure to punish Pak properly, and on January 30 the censor-general and inspector-general demanded the trial (and execution) of both Ch'oe and Pak.[6] These officials were obviously more concerned with punishing contumely than with politics because Ch'oe and Pak were, after all, adversaries. Kojong refused to recall Ch'oe, but capitulated to the demands for Pak's trial.[7]

Hong Si-hyǒng, the censor who had first defended Ch'oe Ik-hyǒn and later attacked him, now saw an opportunity to gain special favor with the king. He attacked his fellow censors for excessive delay in protesting Pak's memorial, especially when they had been so quick to criticize Ch'oe.[8] The implication of this charge was obvious: that the censorate was more concerned about the dignity of the Taewongun than the king. The censor-general and inspector-general immediately submitted their resignations and explained that they were new appointees and did not have an opportunity to speak out on the Ch'oe case. They asserted that they did, after all, demand Pak's trial. When Kojong refused to accept their resignations, Hong was now placed in a precarious position, and he asked the king that he be relieved of his post, but Kojong rejected his petition.[9]

The interrogations of Pak U-hyǒn at the state tribunal began on February 1.[10] Under torture Pak revealed that his memorial was submitted in protest against the reprimand and dismissal of the state councilors, the reduction of the salaries of the chief ministers of the six ministries, and the dismissal of officials from the three censorate bodies. He had been angered because Ch'oe Ik-hyǒn's criticism had had the effect of alienating Kojong from his father, and he insisted that his criticism of Ch'oe was no worse than that of Hǒ Wǒn-sik, An Ki-yǒng, and Hong Man-sǒp in December. His interrogators, however, refuted this claim and pointed

Politics and Policy in Traditional Korea

out that, on the contrary, these three men had spoken directly and clearly, but Pak's remarks had been vague and suspicious. Indeed, a review of the original memorial and trial transcript does leave the impression that the cause of Pak's downfall was his use of obscure allusions and indirect innuendo, which rendered him more vulnerable to the charge that he "harbored treasonous thoughts."[11]

Kojong now intervened to save Pak from death by the ordeal of interrogation, and on February 4 he decreed that he had received special instructions from the dowager to exile Pak to a remote island.[12] For the next two days a number of memorials were submitted in protest by Yi Yu-wŏn, Pak Kyu-su, the censorate bodies, and individual officials, who called for more severe punishment for both Pak and Ch'oe.[13] But Kojong remained firm and Pak was finally exiled.[14]

The Pak U-hyŏn case illustrates, as the Ch'oe Ik-hyŏn case did before it, that the expression of dissent could be quite risky and dangerous because the borderline between loyal remonstrance and lèse-majesté was not well defined in Korean law. Differences of opinion over policy matters, if expressed in a circumspect manner, were unlikely to result in punishment, but blanket condemnations of the state of affairs couched in terse and obscure phraseology could be construed as impugning the king's virtue. The persecution of men like Ch'oe Ik-hyŏn and Pak U-hyŏn occurred not because the king was so despotic, but because officialdom as a whole loosed their venom on any who impugned their integrity, no matter how indirectly.

The trials of Ch'oe and Pak were thus a product of the failure of the traditional Korean state to define the limits of acceptable dissent, and the result of conflict between individual scholar-officials and the capital bureaucracy, which coalesced into a solid interest group in preservation of their positions and power. The king's task in this situation was to moderate the conflict, to establish limits on dissent, and mediate between bureaucrats in conflict. Kojong was just beginning the independent exercise of regal authority and his officials were putting him to a severe test, demanding that they, and not the king, be the final arbiters of acceptable dissent.

No sooner was the Pak U-hyŏn case laid to rest than a new commotion was raised over another memorial by a minor member of the Office of Special Counselors, Yi Sun-i. On February 13 Yi submitted a comparatively innocuous memorial in which he expounded at length on the virtue of seriousness (kyŏng, ching in Chinese). Yi merely stressed that seriousness was the key to "the rectification of the mind" which was in turn the key to "the study of learning," which was in turn the basis of the good government of past emperors. Kojong took no umbrage at the suggestion that he might need more work on the cultivation of his virtue, but the

Recall of the Taewongun

censorate took a different view and accused Yi of lèse-majesté and demanded his exile. Kojong capitulated to their request.[15]

Recall of Dismissed Ministers

One important indication that factional politics was not a major factor in the disputes of January and February 1874 was the king's conciliatory approach to Hong Sun-mok, Kang No, and Han Kye-wŏn, the three high officials he had dismissed in December 1873. On February 11, just after the final disposition of the Pak U-hyŏn case, the king stated that he had been given no choice but to dismiss these officials a month before and was now reappointing Hong and Kang to office.[16] Kojong apologized for having dismissed them and beseeched them to return to court to be at his side. Being without them, Kojong said, was like "having lost my right and left hands . . . Do not let the events of the previous month be the cause of enmity between us."[17] Hong and Kang refused their new appointments on February 16, but Kojong repeated his request that they assume office.[18] In addition, Han Kye-wŏn, who had been ordered exiled on January 29, was released from exile on February 17.[19]

The king's attempt to conciliate these three officials only confirms the conclusion that he had not attempted to purge them from office for political reasons in December 1873. On the contrary, they had chosen to resign because their honor had been impugned, and because the king had failed to indicate the proper confidence in them by not executing their accuser, Ch'oe Ik-hyŏn.

The Yi Hwi-Rim Case

Politics remained relatively calm until November 28 when a minor military official, Yi Hwi-rim, submitted a memorial urging the king to summon his father back to the capital from the countryside, implying that Kojong was incapable of governing without his father's guidance.[20] Yi stated that the whole country had been dismayed to hear that the Taewongun had moved to quarters outside the capital.

Perhaps he has gone on a trip to rid himself of cares and has not yet returned. Or perhaps the king, out of consideration and obedience, has not yet summoned him back. The Taewongun's utmost feelings of tenderheartedness ought not long be separated [from the king]. The king ought not go for too long without being able to express his most sincere filial piety. How much more so when at present there is trouble along our borders without cease, and the foreign pirates are looking for an opportunity.[21]

Kojong had little trouble grasping the purport of this plea. He stated that

Politics and Policy in Traditional Korea

the Taewongun had only gone to the suburbs to rest and would be returning before long, and he exiled Yi for disrespectful language.[22]

As might be expected, Yi's memorial and Kojong's quick decision on punishment set off a chain reaction of protest by the censorate. One official objected in particular to the implication that the whole country was "doubtful and ill at ease" over the Taewongun's failure to return to the capital, and that the country was in danger from border troubles and "foreign pirates" without the Taewongun's leadership.[23] Kojong acquiesced to the pressure on December 1 by increasing the degree of exile to imprisonment behind a palisade on a remote island.[24]

The Assassination of Min Sŭng-ho

Politics and protest took a more violent turn as the result of two events in January 1875: the assassination of Min Sŭng-ho and the impeachment of Yi Yu-wŏn. The role of Queen Min and her relatives in the politics of this period is most difficult to establish because of the lack of documentation. Most of the evidence pertaining to the Min clan comes from the memoir of Hwang Hyŏn, the late nineteenth century scholar, but Hwang's account of the events of 1873-76 must have been based on hearsay because he was only an adolescent at the time and was probably not living in Seoul. According to Hwang's account the queen and her brother, Min Sŭng-ho, were in firm control of king and court after 1873.

In 1874 the king finally assumed personal rule, but on the inside [the palace] the queen was in control of things, and on the outside, Min Sŭng-ho respectfully carried them out . . . At the beginning, it was as if she were giving orders to the king, thereby purveying her likes and dislikes. Finally, her exclusive [control] and willfullness became worse day after day, and the king, on the contrary, was [even more] under her domination.

Min Sŭng-ho warned [the king] against the exclusive and arbitrary [power] of the Taewongun, and the Taewongun was removed. He urged the king to select men of reputation at court. He took his turn in attendance on the king, and participated in the conduct of affairs.[25]

Hwang Hyŏn also reported that Min Sŭng-ho was evidently unable to exert positive leadership because he was not too bright, weak, easily deceived by others, and incapable of handling government affairs. When his mother died, he withdrew to his home and maintained communication with the palace only through couriers. As Min's authority declined, Hwang explained, his henchmen began to act on their own.[26] However, Hwang Hyŏn's account of the Taewongun's retirement and of Min Sŭng-ho's role in court affairs in 1873-74 is not borne out by the daily chronicles. Nor was Min one of the high officials who attended important court conferences during this period, although it is possible that he may have exerted considerable influence behind the scenes.

On January 5, 1875, Min Sŭng-ho was killed by a bomb contained in a package delivered to his home. In Hwang Hyŏn's version of the assassination, after the explosion Min pointed to the Taewongun's palace two or three times before he expired, convincing the queen that the Taewongun was plotting against her family. Subsequently, when a fire broke out in the home of the Taewongun's brother, Yi Ch'oe-ŭng, a supporter of the new regime, the queen's spies supposedly identified the culprit as a retainer in the home of one of the Taewongun's favorite military officials.[27] Hwang Hyŏn also mentions, however, that Min Sŭng-ho was really killed by his own brother, Min Kyu-ho, who tried to divert suspicion to the Taewongun. Min Kyu-ho's plot was supposedly part of his attempt to seize power for himself by eliminating his brother and making his nephew, Min Yŏng-ik, the son of Min T'ae-ho, the heir to the main line of the Min clan. After he persuaded Min T'ae-ho to allow his son to be adopted into the line of Min Sŭng-ho, Min Kyu-ho then won favor with the queen and became the real leader of the clan and the real power behind the throne.[28]

According to court chronicles, however, on January 18, 1875, Min T'ae-ho protested the adoption of his son, Min Yŏng-ik, by the family of the deceased Min Sŭng-ho on the grounds that it was contrary to law to take the eldest son of a branch line as the heir of the main line of a lineage. Min complained that the decision was made by the Ministry of Rites without obtaining a signed and sealed affidavit from family heads of both sides; he asked that the king rescind the order but Kojong refused.[29] Hwang's account is obviously inaccurate.

Other evidence also indicates that the Min clan was not as powerful at this time as Hwang suggests. During most of 1874 Min T'ae-ho was governor of Hwanghae province. On October 8 he was appointed governor of Kyŏnggi province and he remained in that post through 1875. While governor of Hwanghae, however, he was investigated for corruption in the administration of examinations in his province with the king's approval.[30] Even though nothing came of the investigation, the power of the clan was still not so great as to exclude them from indictment for malfeasance.

As for Min Kyu-ho, at the beginning of 1874 he was a second counselor in the Office of Special Counselors, and on June 27 he was appointed second minister of personnel. Just prior to the death of Min Sŭng-ho, he was appointed to two important posts in rapid succession—minister of rites on November 27 and sixth state councilor on December 16.[31] Sometime prior to March 11, 1875, he was appointed

Politics and Policy in Traditional Korea

commander of one of the capital guard units, a post that he held concurrently with his state council position.[32] Despite his high position,
however, Min Kyu-ho was not immune to attacks from his fellow
bureaucrats. On March 2 the Royal Secretariat complained that Min had
failed to come to court despite two summonses, and Kojong ordered an
investigation.[33] Min refused the third summons and then submitted his
resignation on March 13.[34] Two weeks later, on March 29, the Three
Armies Command[35] asked that Min be dismissed from his post as capital
guard commander because he had failed to make his nightly rounds on
the pretext of illness. Kojong remarked that Min had been admonished
about this several times, yet continued to neglect his duties, "a most
amazing thing to do." Kojong said that dismissal would not be sufficient
punishment, and ordered that Min be stripped of his office warrants. The
Royal Secretariat requested an investigation; Kojong refused but he did
instruct the minister of war to assume Min's post as a concurrency.[36] The
next day, however, Kojong declared that Min had been investigated and
exonerated and reappointed him to his former post.[37] Although Min
Kyu-ho's rapid reinstatement was undoubtedly due to the influence of
the queen or her relatives, Min's near dismissal does not indicate that he
was in any way the power behind the throne at this time. Later in the
year, however, he did rise rapidly through a succession of posts to
minister of personnel and commander of the new palace guard unit, the
Muwiso.[38] The influence of the Min clan on the king at this time was
undoubtedly great, but he was by no means their complete tool. They
were, however, consolidating their power in a mood of increasing bitter-
ness after the assassination of Min Sŭng-ho.

The Impeachment of Yi Yu-Wŏn

Less publicized, but as significant politically as Min Sŭng-ho's assassination, was the impeachment of Yi Yu-wŏn. On January 6, 1875, the day
after the death of Min, a former third inspector in the Office of the
Inspector-General, Son Yŏng-no, requested the recall of the Taewongun
to the capital and impeached Yi Yu-wŏn for misbehavior in office.[39]
Son's memorial was the most unequivocal declaration to date of lack of
confidence in the king's leadership.

Son criticized the king's previous statement that the Taewongun's
absence from court was due to a recuperative vacation in the countryside, and he urged the king to recall his father immediately. Son was
obviously motivated by his displeasure over the conduct of state affairs
since the Taewongun's retirement.

Our king has assumed personal charge of all affairs [of state] and has
striven to rule with all sincerity. [Things] should have attained the

Recall of the Taewongun

heights of T'ang and Yü, but they have sunk to the depths of the Han and T'ang dynasties. Why? Orders are not performed and law and order has become lax. The benevolence of the king does not extend down [to the people], and the people's livelihoods are in difficulty. For what reason?[40]

Son, of course, could not go so far as to hold the king responsible, since this would have been courting certain death. Instead he fixed the blame on the king's most important minister, Yi Yu-wŏn, in an indictment that was as vicious a piece of character defamation as had been made in the past decade.

Really, what kind of man was appointed to the responsibilities of prime minister today? His character is that of a fierce and evil person. His actions have been wily and deceitful. With his viperous venom he bites people upon encountering them. Like a flea on a dog, scurrying about busily in search of the slightest advantage, he only runs after power. Having held posts in the inner and outer [court] he illicitly took advantage of [his position], to [gain] glory and luckily roll into one of the three highest posts . . . Because of his memorials at court, the beautiful statutes [enacted] during the decade [when the Taewongun was in power] were all abolished. The handling of government affairs has all been done in secret and by bribery . . . Look at him cross-eyed, and there is no limit to the fear of his vengeance. Touch a sore spot of his and you are destroyed . . . He conspires to let young boys pass the examinations. He does not care if evil persons serve in attendance on the king. He forgets the hatred [we have] for our enemies—the Western bandits—and on the contrary urges that markets [be set up with them for the exchange of] cloth. His crimes are so many I cannot point them all out, and I cannot write them all down. Ministers at court are afraid and keep their mouths tightly closed. If I did not speak out on behalf of the king, how would the king [ever] hear of it?[41]

Despite Son's vicious ad hominem attack on Yi Yu-wŏn, the real significance of Son's memorial is to be found in his chagrin over what he regarded as the reversal of the Taewongun's domestic reform program and weakness in foreign policy.

Kojong was not so obtuse as to miss Son's message, and he ordered the state tribunal to try him on the charge of lèse-majesté.[42] Kojong's patience was by now wearing thin: he made no attempt to spare Son the rigors of interrogation by shuffling him quickly off into exile as he had done so many times before. On the contrary, after the first interrogation session, Kojong quickly gave his assent to the use of torture. Son, however, insisted that his only purpose was to criticize the behavior of Yi Yu-wŏn and not to impugn the integrity of the king. When the state council requested that Son be exiled lest he die from the beating Kojong gave his approval.[43]

Politics and Policy in Traditional Korea

The state council's request was evidently not an expression of unanimous opinion at court, for Hong Sun-mok, Pak Kyu-su, and the censorate joined in demanding that the king retract the exile order and continue Son's trial. But Kojong refused to change his mind.[44] Hong's position on the Son case is significant if only because he was one of the chief architects of policy during the latter part of the Taewongun's regime. It is unlikely that his contempt for Sŏn Yong-no meant that he disagreed with Son's defense of the Taewongun's policy. For that matter, Pak Kyu-su, who enjoyed high office after 1874, had also been a high official under the Taewongun and remained on friendly terms with him through 1876 at least. Both Hong and Pak were probably offended by the vituperation of Son's attack on a high official and his implied denigration of the king's dignity.

Yi Yu-wŏn, of course, has suffered badly at the hands of historians who have accused him of being a stooge of the Min faction, a self-interested seeker after reputation, and a sponsor of "subservient" diplomacy toward the Ch'ing dynasty.[45] Hwang Hyŏn accused him of perverted sexual practices, cowardice, and avarice.[46] Much of the criticism about Yi is undoubtedly exaggerated. He passed the *munkwa* examination in 1841, held a number of posts and was appointed third state councilor in 1864 and second state councilor in 1865. Later he was elevated to the sinecure of second minister-without-portfolio.[47] He came from an illustrious family: his father and grandfather had both been ministers of rites, and he was descended from Yi Hang-bok, who won fame under King Sŏnjo during Hideyoshi's invasions.[48] Yi was supposedly held in high repute by King Hŏnjong as an able administrator and scholar. He was a prolific writer and in 1871 produced thirty-three volumes of scholarly essays entitled *Jottings in Retirement (Imhap'il)*.[49] He was not really subservient to Chinese interest, he accepted the post of chief state councilor under Kojong only with the greatest reluctance, and there was nothing in his conduct of state affairs that seems suspect.[50] He also displayed none of the ambition of which he was accused after he chose to resign and refused repeated pleas from Kojong to return to his post.[51] On balance, therefore, it would appear that Son Yŏng-no used Yi as a scapegoat in order to express his dissatisfaction with Kojong's leadership. Yi was then attacked by two other minor officials for illegally appropriating a royal stone monument, but he provided an explanation for the act and Kojong punished his two accusers.[52] Meanwhile, the leadership of the administration was taken over by Yi Ch'oe-ŭng and Kim Pyŏng-guk, who were appointed to the posts of second and third state councilors, respectively, on January 24.[53] Yi Yu-wŏn and Pak Kyu-su were given sinecures and as elder statesmen had the right to participate in major court conferences.[54]

Recall of the Taewongun

Yi's impeachment was significant because it symbolized a loss of confidence in the new regime by a segment of the literati. Kojong sensed that his own leadership was being attacked and he responded by punishing Yi Yu-wǒn's critics. He was beginning to lose his tolerance for remonstrance.

Petitions for the Recall of the Taewongun: A Contest Between King and Bureaucracy

Because of the challenge to his dignity, Kojong sought to assert his authority until he overstepped the bounds of propriety and ran headlong into the opposition of his own bureaucracy. Kojong gave evidence of his growing impatience with dissent on August 11, 1874, when he complained to Yi Yu-wǒn about the tumult caused by the literati.

Recently ignorant scholars have been gathering together, and assorted groups have been causing trouble. I have issued many orders [against this], so how dare they continue to do so? Order the Seoul magistrate, the minister of punishments, the two censorate bodies and the Left and Right Police Departments to arrest them.[55]

In adumbration of the conflict that was to occur between the king and his bureaucrats in 1875, Yi objected to the arrest of scholars, but Kojong replied:

How do you deal with students and scholars? They have been appearing here and there throughout the country causing trouble. Nothing is worse than this. What would be wrong with it if we had the police arrest them?[56]

The commotion died down until the spring of 1875. On April 26 Kojong ordered four scholars exiled for submitting scandalous memorials.[57] When a number of local scholars from Kyǒngsang province requested in June that the Taewongun be recalled to the capital, Kojong criticized the petitioners for violating his ban on requests of this kind. He exiled four of the scholars and ordered the rest of them dispersed from the capital.[58]

Late in June Kojong expressed his chagrin over the obstinacy of the scholars in continuing to submit petitions for the Taewongun's recall. He remarked that the Taewongun had gone to the countryside only for a rest, but the public seemed to think that something had happened to cause the Taewongun's departure. He told his top officials that he was particularly upset by their failure to treat these petitions with the proper gravity. He instructed them to withdraw from court and inform the scholars that they had better cease their petitioning and leave the palace area and he promised to prosecute any future offenders as traitors. He

Politics and Policy in Traditional Korea

reported that even the Taewongun had been upset by the petitions for his recall. As a final act of leniency, Kojong ordered a special reduction of sentence for two scholars who had been incarcerated. The officials present commented that the scholars would surely desist now that the king had made his intentions clear.[59]

The failure of Kojong's highest officials to give him full and enthusiastic support against the literati in the spring of 1875 is all the more striking because these men were supposed to be sympathetic to the queen. At this time the six most important officials were the sinecured elder statesmen, Yi Yu-wŏn, Kim Pyŏng-hak, Hong Sun-mok, and Pak Kyu-su, and the second and third state councilors, Yi Ch'oe-ŭng and Kim Pyŏng-guk.[60] Yi Yu-wŏn, Yi Ch'oe-ŭng, and Kim Pyŏng-guk, in particular, were reputed to be loyal members of a Min faction.[61] Yet back on March 16, 1875, all six of these officials had joined the Office of Special Counselors and the censorate in opposing Ch'oe Ik-hyŏn's pardon even though Ch'oe had been the chief catalyst in the removal of the Taewongun.[62] The high officials obviously did not share the king's resentment of the scholars or the queen's antagonism toward her father-in-law. This basic difference of interest and attitude was again revealed when another group of scholars ignored Kojong's recent warning and submitted still another petition on July 18. Kojong declared that the petition was an offense against the crown punishable by death and ordered the execution of the four leaders without even the formality of a trial at the state tribunal.[63]

By this act, however, Kojong overstepped the traditionally accepted limits on royal authority. Even though the state tribunal may have appeared to be the instrument of the throne for the suppression of dissent, it also gave the bureaucrats a say in the punishment of their own kind. For the king to bypass it meant that the rights of the bureaucracy were threatened.

Prior to July 1875 Kojong had intervened in state tribunal trials to exile defendants prematurely in order to save them from the execution demanded by their peers. Now their roles were reversed. The constant criticism of the literati had taken the blush off Kojong's original innocence, and he was now determined to make a display of his monarchical power. When this occurred, his officials, almost to a man, leapt to the defense of the accused, not because of factional politics, but because they were obliged to defend their bureaucratic and aristocratic prerogatives.

On July 21 the state tribunal, headed by Yi Sŭng-bo, hitherto a frequent royal lecturer and one of Kojong's most trusted officials, protested that it was unprecedented for the king to render judgment without trial. "Not only was this a violation of statutes," wrote Yi, "but the case of these four men requires the utmost care and caution. The [state tribunal] could not rashly accept and carry out [the king's order]. We beg the king to understand."[64] Kojong rejected Yi's protest, declared that the matter had already been decided, and ordered the tribunal to carry out the command immediately.[65] Kim Pyŏng-hak, Hong Sun-mok, Pak Kyu-su, Yi Ch'oe-ŭng, and Kim Pyŏng-guk agreed that the literati involved had committed a serious crime but pointed out that because these men had reputations as scholars the king was obliged to take pity on them and rescind the execution order. Kojong replied that he had already discussed the matter with them and really did not expect them to protest his decision.[66]

On July 22 the king summoned the members of the state tribunal and the Royal Secretariat to court. He chastised the former for failing to accept his orders and the latter for not putting pressure on the state tribunal officials to do so. The royal secretaries promised to carry out the king's commands, but the state tribunal officials submitted a joint memorial which stated that despite the king's orders they could not violate the king's laws. "You cannot render a decision on an important criminal case without a trial. This is unprecedented," the tribunal members insisted. Kojong chided them in his rescript for their disobedience but went no further.[67] Then Kim Pyŏng-hak, Hong Sun-mok, and other former and incumbent state councilors stated that they realized that the king wanted to punish the scholars because they disobeyed his orders, and if he failed to do so, it would lead to the collapse of law and order. Nevertheless, the dynasty was nurtured for five hundred years on the primary vital force of literati acting "on behalf of the state." Though these scholars had committed a crime, the king should be benevolent in punishing them. Kojong replied:

> You people are saying that even though a man be guilty of an offense against the crown, if he is a scholar, he cannot be executed. But this means the state has no prince—only scholars. Is what you say right? It seems you are mistaken.[68]

Undaunted, the state tribunal on July 25 again refused to accept the execution order citing many past precedents of officials refusing royal orders of capital punishment. Even if they were to accept it, they stated, "they would not dare carry it out."[69] Kojong then ordered the dismissal of all those officials of the Office of Special Counselors who had signed a protest memorial the day before.[70] Soon after, the king was informed that Kim Pyŏng-hak, Hong Sun-mok, Pak Kyu-su, Yi Ch'oe-ŭng, and Kim Pyŏng-guk were all "awaiting punishment" outside the gate of the state tribunal in protest against the execution order. Kojong ordered them to calm down and go home, but they repeated this action on July 24.[71] The highest state officials were behaving just as the state councilors had in December 1873.

Politics and Policy in Traditional Korea

Kojong summoned all of them to an audience on July 25. Once again they petitioned for leniency toward the scholars, and Kojong finally gave in and reduced the sentences to exile.[72] Kojong had allowed his annoyance with literati dissent to snowball into a major confrontation between himself and his bureaucrats. He had not anticipated this development and was not prepared for it, so that his attempt to assert royal authority resulted in a major setback for the throne. The king's loss of face was too great to be accepted without some sort of quid pro quo. On July 25 he dismissed two royal secretaries and one member of the state tribunal and handed down a new list of ten appointments for the Office of Special Counselors.[73] In September he also exiled Yi Sŭng-bo.[74]

The Setback to the Prestige of the Crown

The period from early 1874 to mid-1875 was marked by an unfortunate trend toward polarization and violence in Korean politics. With the exception of the assassination of Min Sŭng-ho, which was either engineered by the Taewongun or the product of a power struggle within the Min clan, political conflict was chiefly the result of growing dissatisfaction with Kojong's shifts in domestic and foreign policy. The impeachment of Yi Yu-wŏn and the petitions for the Taewongun's recall were not the work of a political faction of bureaucrats loyal to the Taewongun; they were expressions of discontent with the leadership of the king that represented a much wider spectrum of views than a discrete faction. For that matter, despite the shuffle of bureaucratic posts that took place after the Taewongun's retirement, the upper capital bureaucracy was by no means staffed with factional puppets of the Min clan.

As the criticism of his leadership continued, Kojong began to lose his capacity for the tolerance of remonstrance. He became determined to assert his authority as king and put an end to the embarrassing implication that his policies were bankrupt and his father was needed to give him guidance. Since his decrees against dissent had been ignored and the exile of dissenters had not cowed them into obedience, he decided to set a proper example of his authority by executing four scholars. It was this act that brought him into conflict with his own officials, who felt that an excessive assertion of monarchical power had to be checked. The conflict between the Taewongun and the queen was really a secondary issue.

The king lacked a proper understanding of the political process and the extent of monarchical power in his own country. Nor did he possess a clear-cut view of the proper response to remonstrance. He fluctuated from one extreme to the other—from dogmatic tolerance of remonstrance that bordered on lèse-majesté to insistence on an arbitrary and ruthless punishment of dissent. By unwittingly forcing a showdown with his officials for which he was unprepared, he had no choice but to capitulate. A brief half year before the major confrontation with Japan, the king was forced into an open display of ineptitude and weakness that would make it most difficult for him to assert leadership in a time of crisis.

13

The Debate over Accommodation With Japan

Those scholar-officials who had split with the Taewongun because of his domestic policy and looked to Kojong to establish a reign of virtue had been disillusioned with his failure to adopt their total domestic program. They were completely alienated from him and driven back into the arms of the Taewongun when in foreign policy Kojong presided over a shift toward friendlier relations with Japan. In retrospect the political consequences of domestic and foreign policy measures adopted by both the Taewongun and Kojong were ironic: fundamentally conservative policies alienated the leading scholar-official spokesmen of conservatism because of differences over means and methods. The Taewongun's domestic policy was designed to preserve the dynasty and the country from foreign invasion and domestic rebellion without doing serious damage to yangban privilege and traditional culture, but it still engendered a political opposition because of minor violations of elite interest and Confucian dogma. Similarly, Kojong's policy of conciliation toward Japan was designed to protect the Korean people from the potential disruption of foreign contact, yet it earned the resentment of the conservatives who could not tolerate the slightest compromise with foreigners and their insidious Western culture.

The Taewongun and the conservative xenophobes had a very real appreciation of the threat posed to the traditional way of life by even the slightest increase in foreign contact, and they were acutely afraid of it. But they underestimated foreign strength and overestimated Korean military capabilities, and as a result were convinced that Korea could hold out indefinitely against foreign powers. Had the Taewongun continued in power, however, his policy was sure to have led to war and disaster for the Korean people.

Kojong's government, by contrast, possessed a more realistic apprecia-

The Debate over Japan

tion of foreign strength, Korean weakness, and the possibility of invasion and destruction. But Kojong and his officials naively believed that the threat of invasion from Japan could be blunted by a mere change of attitude from hostility to friendship, without any need to compromise on fundamental issues. Thus the new policy of conciliation had unexpected results: instead of appeasing the Japanese it convinced them that the Korean will to resist had weakened and that the Koreans would be vulnerable to pressure. The Japanese sought a pretext for a casus belli and used it to intimidate the Korean government to conclude the Kanghwa Treaty of February 1876 opening Korea to trade and diplomatic intercourse.

When conciliation proved worthless for checking Japanese demands, Kojong was left floundering with no policy save his determination to maintain the peace. As in the case of domestic policy, when Kojong's principles or policies were rendered inoperable, he was left without goals or guidelines and was forced to adjust to changing circumstances beyond his control. The antiforeign conservatives, disgusted with his lack of leadership and incensed by what they regarded as capitulation to Japan, turned against the regime.

The New Policy of Conciliation

The prime catalyst for Kojong's shift in foreign policy was fear of foreign military strength exacerbated by reports from China in the spring and summer of 1874.[1] During a discussion on May 15 with an official recently returned from a mission to China, Kojong expressed awareness of the plight of Vietnam at the hands of the French and fear of a potential Russian threat to Korea. The official also informed him that the Chinese were unable to drive the Westerners out of China.[2]

Korean fears were heightened by a communication from the Chinese Board of Rites on August 4 informing the king of the recent Japanese expedition to Taiwan and the Japanese takeover of the Ryukyu Islands. The Chinese explained that the Taiwan expedition was a device by the Japanese government to siphon off samurai discontent over the decision not to invade Korea in 1873. The board also passed on the rumor that the United States and France might join in an alliance with Japan against Korea, and that Japan might use her 5,000 troops in Taiwan for a Korean expedition. The Tsungli yamen, the Ch'ing dynasty's new foreign office, also passed on its recommendations that the best way for Korea to prevent formation of this kind of triple alliance was to sign treaties with the United States and France in order to check Japanese ambitions.[3]

These reports destroyed whatever mood of confidence had been left over from the Taewongun's regime. Most officials recommended the improvement of military defenses. Pak Kyu-su expressed fears that the people were unused to and unprepared for war, and he urged Kojong to exert greater leadership over the country in order to unify the will of the people. He also criticized Kojong's efforts in military defense, pointing out that the recent creation of a new 500-man palace guard was of negligible value.[4]

The Korean government was unable to accept the Tsungli yamen's advice to conclude treaties with France and the United States because it still regarded Western countries and the Catholic-Western conspiracy as the main threat to Korean security and the traditional order. On August 7 Kojong had mentioned at court that it was necessary to keep a rein on Catholicism because of fifth-column activities and domestic collaborators,[5] and in the August 9 reply to the Chinese communication, he reiterated his father's policy of refusing to open trade with the West. He also asked China to mediate with Japan, France, and the United States in order to prevent them from making demands on Korea.[6] Kojong's government was not content to rely on Chinese mediation to stave off the new threat. It also decided to reduce the possibility of Japanese aggression by seeking a rapprochement with Japan.

The Taewongun, of course, had not only rejected Western demands at every turn, he had also ranked the Japanese alongside the Westerners and treated them in like manner. Their adoption of Western dress and their use of Western steamships and weapons was sufficient proof to him that they had joined the Western camp and constituted a threat to the traditional East Asian order. The result of his attitude, however, was that he had added to Korean burdens by making an enemy of one of her closest neighbors in the Far East.[7]

One of the leading proponents of rapprochement, Pak Kyu-su, acknowledged in a letter to the Taewongun that it was essential for Korean security to eliminate Japanese hostility and convert this powerful neighbor to a friend by compromising on questions of protocol. During the Taewongun's regime the Korean government had refused to accept any communication from Japan that was improperly worded, or to acknowledge any change in the form of foreign relations, even on minor questions of protocol. The Taewongun rejected all references to the Japanese emperor, since that term was reserved only for the Chinese emperor, and he also rejected all changes in the titles of Japanese officials even though they were the result of Japan's restructuring of her own administrative apparatus. Pak Kyu-su argued that these issues could be settled if Korea simply took the position that the wording of communications, the references to the Japanese emperor, the titles of Japanese officials, and minor matters of protocol were internal Japanese matters that had no effect or bearing on Korea or Japan's relations with Korea.

The Debate over Japan

To accede to the Japanese position on these questions would, in his view, have no adverse effects on Korean security. On the contrary, by disposing of minor issues that were the cause of strife, Japanese friendship would be obtained and the situation would revert to the status quo ante.[8] In a letter to the Taewongun in the spring of 1874 Pak also suggested that a good way to demonstrate Korea's sincere desire for friendship would be to place the onus of blame for the fouling of relations with Japan on the shoulders of the responsible officials in Kyŏngsang province.[9]

Some of Pak's recommendations were adopted on August 11 when Yi Yu-wŏn argued at court for the acceptance of Japanese communications. He also accused the Korean interpreter at Tongnae, An Tong-jun, of responsibility for the breakdown in relations with Japan over the past decade, and he recommended the arrest of An, the exile of the ex-magistrate of Tongnae, Chŏng Hyŏn-dŏk, and the dismissal of the former governor of Kyŏngsang province, Kim Se-ho.[10] These moves had probably been contemplated since the beginning of the year, and the communication from China on August 4 provided the stimulus to decisive action. Both the governor and the magistrate had been from their posts in late February. Although the interpreter, An Tong-jun, was kept in office, the secret censor for Kyŏngsang province, Pak Chŏng-yang, had been instructed to review all communications with Japan since 1868 as well as possible evidence of corruption in office.[11] Pak was told that if An or any of his subordinates were guilty of malfeasance in office, Yi was to decapitate them first and report it afterwards.[12]

In May, Yi Yu-wŏn remarked to Kojong that although there had as yet been no word of any crimes committed by An, he had been in office for several years and was due to be replaced. If at some later date he were found guilty of criminal action, it would not be too late to punish him.[13] Later in the month Kojong instructed Yi to keep An in his post until certain business had been cleared up, although he also mentioned that it would be best to change the officials at Tongnae.[14] In June, Moriyama Shigeru, the new envoy from the Japanese Foreign Office in Tongnae, reported to Tokyo that the Tongnae magistrate had been dismissed and that the interpreter, An Tong-jun, was in a precarious position. He advised his government that the time was ripe for the dispatch of an official negotiator to Korea to deal with substantive outstanding issues.[15]

Yi Yu-wŏn then brought indictments against ex-governor Kim Se-ho and ex-magistrate Chŏng Hyŏn-dŏk on August 14.[16] An was arrested and remanded to Seoul for investigation.[17] Further action was taken against all three officials in 1875 when the secret censor, Pak Chŏng-yang, returned to court on January 20 after a year's investigation and detailed a staggering list of misdemeanors, bribes, and embezzlements for all three men.[18] Kim and Chŏng were subsequently exiled and prohibited from ever again holding office,[19] and on April 9, An Tong-jun was ordered executed.[20] Despite scholarly opinion that the purge of these three officials constituted a political stroke against the Taewongun's faction, the prime motive in their dismissal was Kojong's alteration of policy toward Japan.[21] Their punishment, which was not deemed necessary in 1874, was brought about by reports of excessive corruption in office in 1875. Meanwhile, on August 17, 1874, Moriyama Shigeru was told that An had been replaced, and on September 24 he was informed in a private letter from Cho Yŏng-ha, commander of the *Kŭmwiyŏng* and nephew of the dowager, that An's arrest had been ordered for the purpose of demonstrating Korean sincerity in restoring friendly relations with Japan.[22] Moriyama had to be informed about An Tong-jun's dismissal privately rather than by an official communication because of the antagonism to Japan that still prevailed at court.[23]

While the policy of Kojong's government did represent a significant departure from the Taewongun's inflexibility, it did not go as far as Pak Kyu-su's position. Pak advocated that friendship with Japan could be achieved by a willingness to compromise on such substantive issues as the wording of documents and changes in protocol, but the government merely took the position that Japan could be converted from enmity to amity by little more than a sincere expression of good will. It was not prepared for any substantial compromise on substantive issues. During the negotiations with Moriyama in September 1874 Yi Yu-wŏn did approve of one of Moriyama's proposals for the solution of the dispute over the receipt of diplomatic communications by authorizing the draft of a set of new notes in Japan.[24] But when Moriyama returned in late February 1875, the Koreans refused to accept the new messages because of improper wording and the use of mixed Sino-Japanese script. When Moriyama also demanded that he be allowed to confer directly with the Tongnae magistrate instead of through interpreters, and declared that he would be attired in formal Western dress during such an interview, the negotiations broke down completely.[25]

The Korean court had proceeded under the naive belief that diplomatic relations were governed by the same set of moral principles as interpersonal relations. The new administration believed that the Taewongun had erred by failing to show the proper courtesy to guests, no matter what one thought of them, and that adherence to propriety and courtesy in international relations must of necessity lead to the relaxation of tensions. The most succinct expression of this moral approach to diplomacy is contained in a letter sent from Pak Kyu-su to the Taewongun sometime in February or March of 1875, just when the negotiations with Moriyama had reached an impasse. The Taewongun in an earlier letter to Pak had argued that acceptance of improperly worded communications would be tantamount to a display of weakness, but Pak asserted that stubbornness was not equivalent to strength and adherence to proper moral standards of courtesy was not equivalent to weakness. On the contrary, proper adherence to moral standards of behavior was the real criterion of strength.

Generally speaking, strength or weakness depends only on whether or not [we] are "straight" or "crooked" with regard to the principles [of the situation] involved, and that is all there is to it. If in our handling of the situation we treat others with *li* (propriety, courtesy), then we would be "straight" in our principles. Then, even though weak, we would without question be strong. If in our handling of the situation, we treated others without *li*, then our "principles" would be "crooked," and even though strong, we would without question be weak.[26]

In addition, Pak argued that the pursuit of a policy of conciliation would not lead to Korea's destruction as the Taewongun had charged.

It has been said by some that "since ancient times that which has endangered the state is peace [that is, appeasement]." I do not know from what test this was taken. The only case throughout the past when peace brought about the ruin of a state was when Ch'in Kuai brought about the ruin of Sung . . .[27] The Sung's forgetting who their enemies were and making peace with Chin [dynasty] was something which had never occurred throughout all antiquity. How can this be summarily referred to as analogous to the matter of [making] peace with a neighbor?[28]

Pak agreed with the Taewongun's view that the Japanese were indistinguishable from Westerners, but that only meant that the chances of war with Japan were all the greater. The Japanese were obviously looking for an opportunity to commence hostilities, and for this reason it was incumbent upon the Koreans not to provide them with a pretext. By accepting Japanese communications, any pretext for war would be removed, and at no damage to Korean honor; he therefore urged that the government accept Moriyama's request for an interview with the magistrate. But he also told the Taewongun that the mood of hostility to the Japanese at court was so great that he dared not express his views in public.[29]

Pak's assessment of the mood at court was accurate. Kojong's government was almost as unwilling as the Taewongun to tolerate the use of disrespectful language or any serious changes in the form of foreign relations. Even by June 1875 the government still believed that it could reach an accommodation with Japan by merely *accepting* the Japanese communications from Moriyama subject to a later rejection of wording and phraseology. It also failed to take proper cognizance of Moriyama's requests for other changes in the form and substance of foreign relations,

Politics and Policy in Traditional Korea

such as equal relations between officials of the same rank in diplomatic discourse, expansion of trade and commerce, and the use of Western formal dress during official meetings. Because of the inability of the Korean government to appreciate the seriousness of these issues, negotiations at Tongnae reached an impasse.

Ironically, the conciliatory policy of the Kojong government had an effect on the Japanese that the Taewongun had predicted. Moriyama became convinced that Korea was more susceptible to intimidation than ever before and he advised the Tokyo government in April 1875 to seek a casus belli to put pressure on Korea before the Taewongun and the antiforeignists gained control of the government.[30] In September 1875 the Japanese government dispatched three ships to the western coast of Korea to engage in surveying operations. When small boats sent off-shore by one of the ships, the *Unyō*, were fired on by coastal batteries, the Japanese government was provided with a pretext for the use or threat of force against the Korean government.[31] Moreover, in October and December the Japanese in the Tongae area also tried to intimidate the Koreans by firing naval salutes, landing a contingent of sailors and breaking out of their compound to demand an interview with the magistrate.[32]

The *Unyō* incident was then used by the Japanese government as justification for the appointment of a minister plenipotentiary, Kuroda Kiyotaka, to proceed to Kanghwa Island with an armed force of warships and soldiers to demand an apology and negotiate a treaty of amity and commerce with Korea.[33] The Korean court was almost totally unprepared for this development. Its thinking on foreign policy had hardly proceeded beyond the question of the wording of communications, the subject of a major court conference in June 1875.[34] And even on this issue, Kojong had been unable to provide leadership and direction for foreign policy because he had been virtually cast adrift amid the wreckage of his conciliatory policy. Despite the demands of his own ministers at that time that he decide the course of Korean policy on the Japanese negotiations, he refused to do so and left the matter to a consensus decision of the high officials and elder statesmen, who decided not to compromise on the protocol dispute.[35] After the *Unyō* incident, however, on December 12, the court finally decided to have the Tongnae magistrate accept the Japanese communications.[36] But it was now too late, for the Japanese had succeeded in raising the stakes.

When Kuroda appeared on Kanghwa Island in February 1876 the Koreans had no policy aside from a commitment to maintain the peace and continue the policy of conciliation. This attitude was illustrated once again in the contents of the note of "apology" they handed over to Kuroda for the *Unyō* incident. In fact, the note was not an apology at all; it merely restated Korea's good intentions toward Japan and reminded the Japanese that An Tong-jun and Chŏng Hyŏn-dŏk had been dismissed in 1874 in order to show good faith with Japan.[37] The Japanese, of course, were unconcerned that the apology was not really an apology, for the *Unyō* incident was only a device to force the conclusion of a treaty with Korea.

The Korean government was totally unprepared for war, and in the end succumbed to Japanese pressure by concluding the Kanghwa Treaty with but few revisions of the original Japanese demands.[38] All the debates of the previous decade had been rendered obsolete in the space of a few days after the Japanese landed troops at Kanghwa Island in early February.

The Koreans were ignorant of the prolonged Japanese effort to obtain the acquiescence of the Chinese government to the definition of Korea as an independent state so that Japan could deal directly with Korea on her own. They did not receive word of Mori Arinori's negotiations with the Chinese government and Li Hung-chang on this question until March 7, after the Kanghwa Treaty had been signed. They therefore were not concerned about Article I, which contained a statement that Korea was a "self-governing country," since that did not conflict with their understanding about Korean autonomy with the tributary system.[39] They felt that they had blocked the Japanese request for a permanent legation in Seoul. They agreed to the opening of two new ports, but believed that the Japanese could be contained within them much as they had been restricted to the Waegwan (Japan House) in Tongnae under the old system. They did not object to consular jurisdiction, since it merely seemed to give the Japanese juridical rights over their own subjects. They rejected the provision for most-favored-nation rights for Japan because they had no intention of extending treaty or trade rights to any other country,[40] and the Japanese agreed to delete it.[41] And they were satisfied by Japanese acceptance of Korean demands that Westerners be prohibited from entering Korea in the guise of Japanese, and that opium and Christian literature also be prohibited.[42] The Koreans also dropped their previous objections to equality of status between officials of equal rank, and even turned to the defense of this principle as a means of salvaging some dignity for themselves.[43]

By clinging to mistaken views and attitudes the Korean government had achieved a resolution of differences with Japan and succeeded in preserving Korea from invasion and war. The Korean leaders believed, however, that they had reestablished the old system of relations with only the most inconsequential of modifications, whereas in fact they had presided over the transformation of those relations.

Politics and Policy in Traditional Korea

Dissatisfaction with Kojong's Leadership

There was a rising tide of opposition to the king's foreign policy in 1875, because of Kojong's inability to exert decisive leadership and formulate a clear policy line. The most significant event in the rise of domestic dissension was the king's performance at the court conference of June 13, 1875, summoned to debate the acceptance of the new Japanese communications brought by Moriyama and Moriyama's demands for changes in protocol. A survey of the opinions of the officials at court produced a division of opinion. Kim Pyŏng-hak and Third State Councilor Kim Pyŏng-guk argued against accepting any communications with improper wording. Second State Councilor Yi Ch'oe-ŭng agreed with Kim in resisting changes in language and protocol, but he also deplored the worsening of relations and suggested that the use of language might be considered an internal Japanese matter. Pak Kyu-su pressed his position that the communications should be accepted and the Japanese envoys received by Korean officials, and he was given mild but somewhat equivocal support on this by Hong Sun-mok. Yi Yu-wŏn expressed no views at all.[44] While the highest officials seemed to be split on the question, another six to ten minor officials opposed acceptance of the Japanese communications, and no one expressed outright approval of acceptance.[45]

After the opinions were surveyed, Kojong refused to decide the issue. He asked that all the ministers withdraw and hold a separate conference (*pinch'ŏng*) and then submit their decision. Yi Yu-wŏn, however, retorted, "This matter must be decided by the King . . . What need is there for further discussion?" He suggested that if word leaked out that the king could not make up his mind, it would bring shame on the country. Yi Ch'oe-ŭng also urged Kojong to make up his mind, but the king refused.[46]

The fact that the assembled ministers decided in the end not to compromise with the Japanese at this time is of less consequence for our analysis of the domestic effects of Kojong's policy than his almost total failure to exert leadership. Pak Kyu-su was so upset at Kojong's lack of courage that he lost confidence in the king and turned to the Taewongun as the only man left who could ensure the success of his policy.

In a letter to the Taewongun after the June 13 conference Pak pointed out that it was incumbent on the Korean government to resolve the outstanding differences with Japan at this time lest the chance for peace be lost. He claimed that the high ministers at the June 13 conference had intended to advocate acceptance of the communications but were afraid to do so in public because they were intimidated by general opinion. He insisted that bold leadership was needed in the face of a possible Japanese invasion. He ended his letter with an appeal for compromise with Japan and a request for the Taewongun to return to court and exert the kind of leadership of which the king was incapable.

What I have always said has never been in agreement with your Excellency's lofty and brilliant views, and I truly do not have a clear understanding of the ramifications of the situation. At the present time I am bound tight in agony. I here humbly ask what, in general, are the circumstances which make it impossible for us to accept their communications, and I humbly bow down and look up [to you] for your instructions on each matter to guide me out of my stupidity and make me realize what my mistakes are.

Even though your Excellency does not want to [participate] in the matters of the world and [wants just] to stand on the sidelines, still this matter is greatly concerned with life or death, safety or danger. If one slip is made, there is no telling how far the regret will go.

At a time like this [you should] rush to the capital and assume the leadership in policy. It also would not be wrong if you were restored to "facing the mountain" [attending court, guiding the king?] How can you sit around quietly and watch? [Italics mine.][47]

In other words, Pak was asking the Taewongun to assume the leadership of a policy he had never approved and always opposed. Yet so little confidence did Pak have in Kojong's leadership that he decided it was easier to persuade the Taewongun to change his views than to make a leader out of Kojong.

Pak continued to press his case both with the Taewongun and with Yi Ch'oe-ŭng in a series of letters to both of them throughout the summer months of 1875, but to no avail.[48] The Korean government took no new initiatives after the decision of the June 13 conference.

The Opponents of Conciliation

Pak's plea to the Taewongun was, of course, an exercise in futility, but it shows that the leading advocate of conciliation was as disenchanted with the king as the conservative opponents of conciliation, who were numerous and outspoken. On July 5 a former magistrate, Kim Pyŏng-ok, accused the Japanese of deceit, claimed that they had the worst of intentions toward Korea, and charged that they were working hand in glove with the British minister to Japan, Sir Harry Parkes, in a plot against Korea. He held that the only course of action was immediate preparation for war but criticized the Korean government for wasting its time in idle talk about "principle" without making preparations for defense. Like the Taewongun and most other opponents of compromise, he had no doubts about Korea's ability to defend herself, but mainly on the Confucian grounds that the right men could be found to take responsibility for defense. Kim downgraded the importance of military power because he felt that national strength was to be achieved by internal rectification. Even though he acknowledged that Korean society was plagued with corruption and disruption—a local uprising had just occurred in Ulsan, and Kim feared that the rebels might join with the Japanese—he still believed that the rebels could be rounded up, the venal officials decapitated, and the minds of the people united into a "solid wall."

> I would again compare things to a sickness. The incidents and bad conditions in our country today are like an internal malady. The [Japanese] attempts to test us by stirring up trouble on our borders is like an external curse. If you first cure the internal disorder and the original vital force is filled up, then the external ailment will be erased by itself.[49]

Although Kim could not be accused of the naive underestimation of Japanese intent that characterized Kojong's policy, his concern with internal moral rectification rather than with military strength led him to a dangerous underestimation of Japanese power and the probable adverse consequences of war.

On July 16 another former magistrate, Hong Chong-t'ae, argued that, since the Japanese intended to wage war, there was no need to compromise over the acceptance of their communications. The Japanese were the mirror image of the Westerners and had emulated the Western barbarians in committing aggression against China. It behooved Korea to "defend what was right," reject heterodox ideas, and add extra garrisons to the defense of Kanghwa Island. Kojong dismissed Hong's plea, but he showed his concern by warning officials in Kyŏngsang province to prepare their defenses and stay on the alert.[50]

The opposition was muted until Kuroda landed on Kanghwa Island. Then on February 12, the day after Kuroda began his formal talks with Korean officials, the Taewongun made his first public statement since his retirement in December 1873. He sent a letter to the state councilors who had been deliberating daily on the crisis. He remarked that he knew nothing of the content of their deliberations and did not expect that his views would be adopted but that, since the current crisis threatened the destruction of the dynasty, it was his responsibility to speak out. He stated that his position had not changed in the intervening two years. Relations with Japan had continued peacefully for three hundred years until the Japanese had the effrontery to change the wording of their communications. Nor was there any justification for them to change their institutions, their weapons, and even their clothing to conform to the standards of the Western barbarians. Now they were making plans to invade Korea. "How can you just sit by and accept their deceptions and bring on our own destruction?" He concluded by accusing the Korean court of cowardice. The Japanese had had the temerity to violate fixed regulations for the entertainment of envoys, and Kuroda had trespassed into Korean waters with warships with impunity because:

> The whole court is cowardly and fearful, and I have not yet heard one word of firm rejection. The court even secretly intends to accept [the Japanese demands] . . . I would not have expected that court discussion would have been as confused as this. Whether their communications are to be accepted or not is a matter for the state council to decide, but whether our country is to be defended or not depends on me, alone. I have my house servants whom I can lead to die a martyr's death, so how is it that in these 3,000 *li* of green hills there are no descendants who have been nurtured by the sage kings of our dynasty [to fight for the nation]?[51]

Pak Kyu-su's appeals to the Taewongun to change his position had obviously failed.

The extent of the pressure exerted on the court by the opponents of compromise can be gauged by the remarks of the Korean interpreter, O Kyŏng-sŏk, to Moriyama Shigeru on Feburary 13.[52] O informed Moriyama that Chief State Councilor Yi Ch'oe-ŭng and Minister of Personnel Min Kyu-ho favored peace, but that their efforts were opposed by the Taewongun and his supporters. He reported that even the two Korean negotiators, Sin Hŏn and Yun Cha-sŭng, shared the Taewongun's views. Because the Taewongun was strong and the king weak, those who favored peace were afraid to speak out. O also suggested that the negotiations be settled before the Taewongun returned to power.[53]

At the court conference held on February 14 to discuss Korean policy in preparation for the impending negotiations, Yi Yu-wŏn, Kim Pyŏng-hak, and Kim Pyŏng-guk all agreed that Kuroda's arrival with troops and warships was prima facie proof of Japan's aggressive intentions and not her professed desire for friendship. Yet no one, not even the officials most opposed to compromise on the issues, advocated a war policy. Only Kim Pyŏng-guk came close to suggesting the possibility of resistance, but he also believed that the country was incapable of mobilizing sufficient resources for war because taxes had not been collected on time, state treasuries had been exhausted, and the peril of the situation had thrown fear into the people and resulted in an outbreak of thievery, plunder, and lawbreaking.[54] None of the highest officials had any concrete suggestion to make on either overall policy or specific negotiating tactics, leaving the chief negotiator, Sin Hŏn, with full responsibility to hold the line against Kuroda at Kanghwa the best he could. The February 14 conferees could offer no better advice to the king than to suggest that inner rectification was the best means for driving out the foreigner (*naesu oeyang*). This was, of course, the same argument that the most conservative antiforeignists had always used, and it shows the common ground of ideas shared by all officials.

Politics and Policy in Traditional Korea

Yi Ch'oe-ŭng argued that the activities of the Japanese had an adverse effect on the people by stirring them up and confusing them. He feared that uprisings might occur at any time and recommended that the way to counteract this was to maintain social status distinctions (myŏngbun) and preserve law and order. If these two methods were followed, then "trouble coming from the outside will not be sufficient to cause grave concern." Pak Kyu-su insisted that in spite of the possibility of Japanese attack, Korea should preserve her superior moral position and not be the first to commence hostilities. If war should come, then Korea would have to use military force. But Pak had no specific tactical recommendations to make other than internal rectification as the means of expelling the foreigner and of enriching the state and strengthening the military (kukpu pyŏnggang). This slogan was the watchword for the modernizers of Meiji Japan, but to Pak Kyu-su it represented the strength of a nation united by the spiritual force of moral rectitude.[55]

Some of the lower ranking officials at court, however, had stronger views on the situation. On the same day as the court conference a minor military officer memorialized that the Japanese ought to be chased out by force, and a former censor Yi Hang-nyŏn, deplored the failure of the government to press into action the troops trained for defense along the coast.

The bandit troops are no more than pirate plunderers. We should attack them in one fell swoop with the rifles we have accumulated in the last ten years and defeat them. If they are allowed to grow big like a dragon in his lair, then it will be difficult to suddenly attack and destroy them. I humbly beg the king to immediately order troops to be sent to attack the evil and dirty [scum], so they will not dare to squat all over our borders.[56]

Kojong had, however, committed himself to a policy of peace. He instructed Yi that the state council would take care of the situation and that he should not pester the throne about it.[57]

The high tide of militant protest came on February 17 when two sharply worded memorials were submitted to the throne. The first was from a former censor, Chang Ho-gŭn. Chang could hardly contain his anger at the court's inaction.

Up to four hundred of the stinking bandits have invaded our territory and landed on Kanghwa, and they have been there for several days. To open our gates to the bandits and let them tramp around on territory which we have defended against harm for four hundred years, how can this be tolerated? . . . Their determination to conclude a treaty of thirteen articles is even more difficult to understand. In a situation like this, ruler and subjects, those above and those below should firmly as one, swear a righteous oath to [fight] to the death to expel them.

The Debate over Japan

But I have not yet heard that the state council, which is meeting every day, has done anything about it. When court officials have something to memorialize [in protest against court inaction], they are dismissed from office and exiled, obstructing loyalty and the pathways of remonstrance.[58]

The Royal Secretariat immediately charged Chang with slander against the state council and demanded his exile. Kojong ordered that Chang's memorial be handed back to him and that he be investigated.[59]

The second protest came from Ch'oe Ik-hyŏn, who by this time was thoroughly disenchanted with Kojong's handling of foreign policy. Ch'oe had been released from exile the year before and was awaiting reappointment to office in the capital. On February 17 he led a band of about fifty scholars to the gates of the Kyŏngbok palace. Holding axes in their hands symbolizing their willingness to suffer execution for their conviction, they submitted a memorial to the Royal Secretariat.

In the memorial Ch'oe declared that every one was up in arms over rumors that the court intended to seek peace with the Japanese, and if it were true, Korea would be no better than a land of bandits. Ch'oe argued that there would be nothing wrong with a peace policy if it were the product of Korean strength and Japanese weakness, but at present Korea was only displaying her own weakness; to make no preparations for war and seek peace only out of fear and cowardice would only deter the Japanese temporarily.

Ch'oe also opposed opening Korea to trade. The Japanese were only interested in material things and profit and their products were merely exotic playthings, whereas Korea produced only what was necessary to life. If trade were allowed, the Korean people would be enticed into exchanging their staples for useless objects. Ch'oe also feared that if the Japanese were allowed to reside in Korea, build houses, and buy land, they would seize Korean property and women. They had no understanding of human principles: they were animals, not humans, and there was no way that one could conclude friendly relations with animals.

Ch'oe believed that the Japanese had truly become Westerners at heart and he criticized Kojong for having insisted that friendly relations could be restored with the Japanese because they were not the same as Westerners. On the contrary, the Japanese wore Western clothes, rode on Western ships, and used Western weapons. If a treaty were concluded with them, it would open the floodgates to the propagation of heterodox teachings. He urged that Catholicism be stamped out as it had been in the reigns of Kings Sunjo and Hŏnjong in 1801 and 1839. "How can the king face these two ancestors of his? What kind of a king will later generations think him to be?" Furthermore, according to the Chinese note of August 4, 1874, Japan was about to launch an attack on Korea in league with France and the United States. "On the day that our old friendship with

Politics and Policy in Traditional Korea

Japan is restored, we will have concluded peace with Westerners." Ch'oe advised the king to inform the Japanese that the main issue between Korea and Japan was the Western threat and not the dispute over the wording of communications. Kuroda had to be told that Japan was being deluded by the Westerners, and that Japan had first to expel the Western bandits from her own country before the Koreans could agree to restoring amicable relations with her. Otherwise, Kuroda was to return home forthwith. Ch'oe even drafted a note for Kuroda.

He ended the memorial with a threat against the court itself phrased in terms reminiscent of the Taewongun's antiforeign steles of 1871.

And if there are any officials at court who advocate peace and sell out their country . . . have them cast out and executed. If this is not done, I will see with my own eyes the people of the capital turned into animals. I do not want to see moral degradation rampant. I beg I be given the ax and my executed corpse shown to the people, enabling me to return by the side of those two kings [Sunjo and Hŏnjong].[60]

Kojong, however, did not take Ch'oe's criticism too kindly, and he ordered him arrested for having memorialized while still under criminal indictment.[61]

Ch'oe Ik-hyŏn had emerged in 1873 as the most articulate and outspoken advocate of militant, dogmatic conservatism on both domestic and foreign policy issues. He treated his beloved tradition as he would a fragile flower sheltering it from the slightest chill. Compromise with Japan was out of the question because any single contact with a foreign and hostile outer world was liable to sow the seeds of ruin in a hothouse cultural environment. The Japanese had been infected by the Western virus, and any contact—through trade or even normal intercourse— would introduce false values into a closed system that could not tolerate any diversity. Was he really far from wrong? It was, indeed, only the anxious and uncompromising conservatives like Ch'oe, and not the pliant and yielding ones like Kojong or Pak Kyu-su, who had the prescience to foresee the consequences to the old order of the slightest breech in the wall of seclusion.

Considering that Ch'oe Ik-hyŏn was expressing opinions that coincided with the Taewongun's views on foreign policy, one would have expected that his petition would have received a warm reception by some of the high officials at court who had served under the Taewongun. Such was not the case, however, for these men were now servants of the king and administrators of the king's policies. Even after his exile order of February 17, a number of memorials were submitted on Feburary 19 and 20 by the censorate, charging Ch'oe with lèse-majesté and demanding an investigation. Ch'oe was also attacked by Kim Pyŏng-hak, Hong Sun-mok, and Kim Pyŏng-guk, all of whom had given solid support in the

The Debate over Japan

1860s to the very policy Ch'oe was now recommending.[62] Kojong issued a decree in which he defended his policy toward Japan. He declared that the Japanese were different from the Westerners and that if Ch'oe's recommendations were implemented, it would lead to the ruin of a whole generation.[63]

No sooner had Kojong issued his royal certification of Japanese uniqueness than he was refuted by a minor official in the Office of Ritual Affairs (t'ongyewŏn), O Sang-hyŏn. O reminded his sovereign that in 1871 he had set up antiforeign monuments around the country which gave warning to anyone who might "advocate peace and sell out the country." (This was really done at the initiative of the Taewongun.) For five years after this, the "foreign devils" committed no aggression, but now the Japanese had trespassed on Korean territory garbed in Western clothes and using Western ships. "They call themselves Japanese envoys, but how are they any different from Westerners?" O also echoed Ch'oe's fears about the potential subversive effects of foreign trade.

According to the way our former kings dealt with the problem of markets and [foreign] trade, [they felt] that if you allowed trade in Western goods, their heterodox teachings, which do not recognize the position of the father or ruler [as objects of respect under the Confucian moral code], would follow after their goods, stealthily enter the country, and [cause] the degeneration of our people into beasts.[64]

O was particularly frustrated at the court's declared policy of meticulously avoiding any responsibility for the commencement of hostilities. He could not understand the reason for the government's timidity, since the Japanese only had a thousand troops with which they had penetrated "a thousand *li*" into Korean territory. He concluded that they could not have done so without help from Korean Catholic collaborators, and he suggested that "if the king were to expel the heterodox groups and strengthen and rectify the nation's punishments, those who favor peace will not be able to carry out their plot." He also urged the king to summon the tiger hunters to wipe the Japanese out before they were able to convert Kanghwa Island to their own base. Finally, O came to the defense of Ch'oe and others, claiming that the censorate and the throne were stifling proper remonstrance by punishing dissent. "How can the prohibition of public debate among the scholar-literati by the legal and punitive agencies [of the state] be [in conformity with] the basic ideal of selecting men of talent?"[65]

After his earlier setback in his attempt to execute dissenting literati, Kojong was no longer prepared to take rash action against scholars, but there was no need for him to do so, since his officials were quite willing to perform that task for him. O Sang-hyŏn was indicted by the Royal

Secretariat for remonstrating without proper qualifications, and the king ordered his exile.[66]

On February 22 Fourth Deputy Commander Yun Ch'i-hyŏn, a minor official who may have spotted a good opportunity to gain favor with the throne, presented a refutation of Ch'oe's and O's arguments, although he did request that the king take care not to "block off the pathways of remonstrance" by excessive action against these men. Despite his low rank, Yun provided as detailed an explanation of the basis of Kojong's policy as any edict ever issued by the throne. Yun argued that there were but two main problems related to the Japan question: whether the Japanese were Westerners or not, and whether there should be peace or war. According to Yun, if it were known that the Japanese were indeed allied with Western countries and maintained friendly relations with the Westerners, it would behoove Korea to reject Japanese demands and wage war, for Koreans could not bear to live on the same earth as the hated Westerner. But he refused to acknowledge that the Japanese were identical to the Western barbarian. On the contrary, Japan had maintained friendly relations with Korea for three hundred years; Kuroda was a *Japanese* envoy, and the Japanese government only intended to present her communications. The dictates of propriety required that the Korean government should treat "guests from afar" with cordiality and "accept and read" their communications. It was not, however, necessary to accept their substantive demands. If Korea failed to conform to standards of propriety, and if Korea were to commence hostilities without justification, she would be condemned by the whole world.[67]

Yun differed from other advocates of conciliation in that his position was based on moral conviction and not on acknowledgement of Korean military weakness. He wrote that if the conciliatory policy failed, Korea could mobilize 30,000 crack troops, call up 60,000 more from the garrisons in the capital, and use the 30,000 men in the new rifle (musket?) units formed in 1866.

Once the proclamation was issued and troops assembled like clouds from the four quarters we could destroy our small enemies totally, like crushing an egg with the weight of one thousand catties. How much more so when we would be fighting on our home territory? How then could we fly in fear and not fight?[68]

Yun also opposed the argument that contact with Japan would lead to the introduction of Western heterodoxy. He argued that even though new consulates were to be established for the conduct of trade by the terms of Kuroda's draft treaty, the penetration of heterodoxy could be checked by strict regulations preventing the Japanese from trespassing into the interior and proscribing Western goods from trade. Yun, in other

The Debate over Japan

words, was committed to the preservation of seclusion but he did not fear that the new treaty would weaken Korea's isolation.

So they [the Japanese] will be they, and we will be we, and no damage will be done to the friendship between neighbors. In addition to doing away with our fears and doubts, [the treaty will ensure that] even though we may continue our friendship with Japan, we will really be rejecting the heterodoxy of the West.[69]

Yun's antipathy to the West was undoubtedly sincere. He deplored the recent tendency throughout the world for people to adopt the clothes and implements of the West, praising their superiority over others. He insisted that this tendency had to be rooted out of Korean life lest it transform moral and virtuous Koreans into amoral animals. An effort had to be made to refurbish orthodox teachings: the books of Confucius and Mencius had to be recited daily in all households as well as in the schools, and the role of the examinations in selecting men of talent had to be made clear. If these steps were taken, heterodoxy could not spread among the people.[70]

Yun Ch'i-hyŏn's memorial provides a fairly complete exposition of the rationale for Kojong's Japan policy. It demonstrates clearly that the new policy in no way signified a departure from a commitment to seclusion and an antipathy for Western culture and values. The basis of Kojong's policy was that Japan could be treated as distinct and separate from the West, that Korea was under moral obligation to show friendship and courtesy to her neighbor, that maintenance of moral integrity and propriety would succeed in transforming an enemy into a friend no matter what the issues between them, and that a new treaty port system with different regulations for trade would not be used as a device for the penetration of Western goods or ideas. While Yun also believed that Korea had the military capacity for defending herself if negotiations broke down, the Korean government was obviously less sanguine than he about the strength of the Korean military establishment.

Yun's memorial marked the end of discussion prior to the signing of the treaty on February 27.[71] On February 29 the leading officials of the country, Yi Yu-wŏn, Kim Pyŏng-hak, Hong Sun-mok, Pak Kyu-su, Yi Ch'oe-ŭng, and Kim Pyŏng-guk, submitted their resignations. As Yi Ch'oe-ŭng put it in his memorial, government policy had been based on a commitment to the preservation of peace and friendship with Japan. Yet he and others had been accused of advocating a policy of peace with the Westerners. Although this accusation was completely false, he asked to be dismissed because of the slur on his reputation. Kojong refused to accept the resignations and told his officials that they should not have been bothered by what others had said. He declared that the conclusion

Politics and Policy in Traditional Korea

of the treaty with Japan was no more than a restoration of old friendship, and so he truly believed.[72]

The Struggle Between Two Alternatives

Between 1864 and 1876 two different plans were adopted by Korean governments as the best means to preserve the security of the country against the threat of violent invasion, the disturbing effects of economic change, and the insidious corrosion of traditional beliefs and values by the introduction of new ideas. Up to 1874 the answer to these problems was a simple one: Korea could not stand the slightest crack in the dikes of seclusion lest a trickle of subversive influence cascade into a flood that would sweep country, tradition, and culture before it. The concept of the hermetically sealed state was, however, an idea that was rapidly approaching the end of its time; it succeeded for the Koreans as long as it did only because Korea was on the outmost periphery of Western interest.

Japan, however, was a close neighbor, not a distant and unconcerned power, and the Taewongun had chosen to treat her as a cultural inferior, tainted by the poisonous ways of the West. He had wounded Japanese pride—a more serious matter than frustrating the mercantile ambitions of the Americans—and the danger of invasion by a people with a martial tradition and a great sense of honor was quite real. In 1873 invasion was averted only by the narrowest of margins, and in 1874 it still appeared imminent, all the more dangerous because of the rumor of a Japanese alliance with France and the United States.

The Taewongun's blind stubbornness had succeeded because the international situation permitted it to succeed, but by 1874 it had become a liability that threatened the destruction of Korea. Korea could no longer afford to make enemies of all foreigners save the Chinese, particularly when the Chinese umbrella had been rent and torn by repeated humiliations at the hands of the West. Kojong's regime devised a new solution. It would neutralize the most dangerous military threat in order to preserve Korea's defenses against the more distant but more insidious Western menace. Western missionaries, Western merchandise, and Western ideas were regarded as the real danger to Korea, not the Japanese. Japan would be converted from enemy to friend by adherence to civilized standards of courtesy and by treating Japanese demands for changes in protocol as curiosities peculiar to the special domestic problems of the Japanese nation.

Kojong was therefore as blind as the Taewongun, but his blindness was of a different order. He grasped the significance of the adverse military situation, but could not perceive the consequences of the new treaty system. When the Japanese were not mollified by Korean demonstrations of friendly intent, continued to press for specific substantive changes in

The Debate over Japan

the mode of relations, and backed their demands with the threat of force, the Koreans were forced to acquiesce and justify the acquiescence by treating the new treaty system as a minor adaptation of the old. The Taewongun had preserved the traditional order at the risk of the country's destruction by war; Kojong had preserved the country at the risk of weakening the traditional order.

The conclusion of the Kanghwa Treaty also brought to a conclusion a shift in the alignment of political forces under way since early 1874. Many conservative scholar-officials who had begun to lose faith in Kojong's leadership and commitment to Confucian principles of government were now convinced of the correctness of their suspicions. They split from the new regime and became a permanent conservative opposition, gaining a moment of glory with the Taewongun's short-lived return to power in 1882. Kojong, on the other hand, was left holding the center in league with the queen's relatives and the moderates, beleaguered by both conservatives and radicals in the following decades as the pressure for change increased.

14

Conclusion

As stated in the Introduction, the purpose of this study is to reevaluate the nature and aims of the Taewongun's reform program, identify the major obstacles to reform in terms of salient aspects of the traditional order, and clarify the relationship between policy disputes and politics in the period just preceding the opening of Korea in 1876. All three of these goals are related to a fundamental theorem about the nature of the traditional order: that the extraordinary stability of the Yi dyansty polity was the product of a balance of power between centralized monarchy and an aristocratic elite, and that any tendency toward the aggrandizement of power by either the throne or the aristocracy was eventually checked by reaction and counterpressure. For the first half of the nineteenth century the yangban aristocracy had increased its control over the throne and the central bureaucracy, but the peasant rebellions of 1862 and the threat of foreign invasion in that decade created a sense of urgency about the need for reform. The Taewongun responded to this challenge in the 1860s by instituting a reform program that was accompanied by a shift in the balance of power back toward strong central and monarchical leadership because it became necessary to expand central control over resources in order to build up the strength of the state to withstand the onslaught of foreign imperialism. But the traditional system was incapable of allowing a major shift in the balance of power toward strong central and monarchical leadership, and the challenge to yangban privilege posed by some of the Taewongun's policies gave rise to a reaction against reform and a reversion to limited monarchy.

The Nature and Aims of the Taewongun's Reform Program
Even though this book has concentrated on aspects of the Taewongun's reform program, the elimination of corruption and the reform of

Conclusion

institutions were not the primary issues of the time. These were but means to the end of increasing royal prestige and authority and expanding central control over resources to preserve both the dynasty and the nation.

The Taewongun was a conservative because he sought the preservation of the dynasty without any major changes in the political system or the status quo in social and economic relations. For that matter, everyone in this period was conservative; yet the Taewongun has been regarded by some scholars (and also by some of his contemporaries) as a social revolutionary because of his willingness to intrude on the privileges of the yangban class. But his lack of respect for yangban privilege did not stem from any desire for social leveling; it was the product of a style of rule characterized by pragmatic adaptation to changing circumstances and emphasis on the needs of the state over those of the social elite or the peasantry.

In short, the Taewongun was a traditional reformer whose main purpose was the creation of a strong monarchy and strong central government. His goals were conservative, but his pragmatic methods led him to limited intrusions into the area of yangban privilege and factional interest. He shared with the literati a commitment to Confucian ideals, but his pragmatic orientation toward policy led him to violate certain Confucian priciples which earned him the enmity of the Confucian dogmatists. In his approach to reform, he ignored the programs of the idealistic, Utopian Confucianists of the seventeenth and eighteenth centuries in favor of practical action for the benefit of the state. He sought to conserve the old order and yet earned the resentment of a portion of the social elite who misconstrued his purposes and adhered to a narrow view of class interest and ideological orthodoxy.

Obstacles to Reform

Institutional Problems

Despite arduous efforts, the Taewongun was not able to overcome the institutional obstacles to the expansion of monarchical power and the establishment of strong centralized control over the nation. One of the most serious problems in this regard was the weakness of his own position in the structure of government. Since he was never regent, he had no legal basis for his exercise of authority, but as long as he could count on the active support of the dowager-regent and the passive acquiescence of the young king, his directives were not questioned. Furthermore, because of the popularity of his foreign policy, there were few who even desired to challenge his leadership in a time of crisis.

The Taewongun's position was, however, highly vulnerable, because

Politics and Policy in Traditional Korea

once his son came of age, or more accurately, became conscious of his authority and his right to exercise it independently, the Taewongun would become superfluous. It might therefore be said that one of the Taewongun's main problems was to prepare the way for his son by removing restraints on monarchical authority so that Kojong would be able to carry on his example of forceful leadership. But the Taewongun failed to create the basis for a powerful kingship because he neglected the important problem of training his own son to the exercise of power, and he overlooked the problem of a resurgent and dominant consort clan. While he was leading the country through the vicissitudes of reform and foreign troubles, his son was undergoing intensive indoctrination at the hands of his official Confucian mentors in the twice daily Royal Lectures on the principles of Confucian statecraft. When Kojong emerged from this decade of instruction in 1874, he had become the disciple of his Confucian tutors and a believer in the propriety of limited and restricted royal authority, and not the heir of his father's forceful and pragmatic style.

The Taewongun also failed to ensure that the queen and her relatives would be prevented from future interference in government and politics, a problem that had plagued Korean kings during the first half of the century. He sought to control the consort clan by selecting a queen from a yangban lineage with relatively little power, but he underestimated the abilities of Queen Min and did nothing to check the rise of her relatives through the bureaucratic structure even while he was in control of the government. Therefore, after he withdrew from involvement in the government, the queen and her relatives were able to dominate the court because King Kojong was incapable of controlling them. This development did not reach its zenith, however, until after the Kanghwa Treaty.

While he was in power, the Taewongun was not troubled by opposition from the upper levels of the bureaucracy, which, on the contrary, provided loyal support for his leadership. Many of them owed their high position to the Taewongun's policy of expanding opportunities for advancement to many bureaucrats previously discriminated against because of their hereditary affiliation with minority factions. Another reason for their support was their sympathy for his efforts at reform: they had no real objection to the restoration of monarchical and dynastic prestige, the increase of the central government's abilities to tax, and the build-up of national strength. High officials usually identified with the policies of the throne, since in the presence of strong leadership from the top, they were willy-nilly forced to do their best to execute these policies or suffer damage to their careers. The Taewongun was also unsuccessful in his attempt to create a more efficient bureaucracy by recruiting

Conclusion

officials on the basis of merit because he was unwilling to allow any serious weakening of status barriers to office holding.

The Taewongun was unable to overcome the traditional inefficiency and decentralization of the regular bureaucracy. Although he did use the secret censors to advantage, he made no attempt at greater rationalization of bureaucratic organization and did not offer any solutions to the problem of weak central control over district magistrates and rural villages. In fact, in one of the major institutional reforms of his regime—the establishment of the village granary system to handle the administration of grain loans—the Taewongun virtually acknowledged his inability to control administration at the magisterial level by transferring responsibility for the grain loan system to nonofficial leaders at the *myŏn* level. The district magistrate and his clerks could neither be trusted nor controlled.

There was one area of activity where the Taewongun's efforts to expand monarchical authority were rewarded with a large measure of success. By abolishing all but forty-seven of the chartered academies, the Taewongun crushed the institutionalized power of the literati in the provinces. And by transferring the shrine to the Ming emperors, the Mandongmyo, to the royal palace, he took over an important national symbol of semi-religious loyalty. The greater the degree of success in the handling of the academy and shrine question, however, the greater the political liability for the Taewongun. Literati resentment over the treatment of the academies and shrines was a major factor in stimulating their political opposition to his regime, and their political opposition proved crucial in stimulating Kojong's decision to assume full power in December 1873.

Central Control of Resources and Population

The central problem of the Taewongun's regime was really his attempt to increase the control of the central government over the resources and population of the nation. The major obstacle to the accomplishment of this task was the opposition of the yangban elite and rural landowners to any attempt by the central government to increase its income at their expense.

The control and taxation of land was undoubtedly the most important aspect of the government's attempt to control wealth. The Yi dynasty economy was overwhelmingly agrarian and land tax revenue was the most important sector of the state's fiscal structure. From the seventeenth century on, many scholars and officials believed that private control over land was the fundamental cause of both the shortage of government revenues and the oppression of the peasantry through tenancy and overtaxation. They advocated a program of nationalization of all landhold-ings by the state and redistribution to the peasantry on a basis of equality as a means of increasing government revenues and equalizing tax bur-dens among the entire population. Nationalization and redistribution proved impossible goals to achieve, and by the nineteenth century, most reformist-minded intellectuals were concentrating on plans for the more efficient survey of cultivated land for tax purposes. By this time it was obvious that the inequalities of the land tax structure were due to under-registration of the cultivated landholdings of the wealthy landowners and the over-taxation of the impoverished small holders and tenants. Land resurvey became the catch phrase of agrarian reformers, and the Taewongun was heir to this trend of thought when he assumed power. He did his best to return untaxed land to the tax registers, but because he failed to order a complete resurvey of land in all provinces during his regime, his actions were too limited to produce significant results. The Taewongun preferred to avoid any radical solution that would threaten the stability of the existing socioeconomic order, despite his desire for the aggrandizement of state revenue.

On the other hand, it was under his leadership that the state ordered the levying of a household tax on all households, yangban as well as commoner, sometime between 1870 and 1871. It might be argued that this policy proved his fearlessness in the face of aristocratic opposition and his willingness to attempt radical solutions, but because of two im-portant developments that had taken place in the previous century, the household cloth tax was no longer as radical and extreme as was once thought. In the first place, there had been a significant increase in the number of households and individuals who had gained rank titles through purchase and other means, thereby narrowing the tax base for the military cloth tax. By the middle of the nineteenth century, many officials felt that it was unreasonable for such large numbers of people to retain exemptions from the cloth tax. There were thus far fewer officials who resisted the extension of the military cloth tax to yangban house-holds in 1870 than in 1750 (when the household cloth tax failed of adoption) simply because too many people of watered-down yangban status were enjoying tax exemptions at the expense of both the central government and the commoner population. In the second place, from the turn of the nineteenth century, villages were assigned military cloth tax quotas (under the so-called village cloth system), and in many villages these quotas were distributed on a more or less equal basis among house-holds irrespective of the status of the head of the household. Therefore, the household cloth tax plan of 1870-71 was hardly as radical a departure from standard practice as it would have been in 1750.

In two respects, the Taewongun did achieve minor victories of sorts in his campaign to increase government revenue: by his curtailment of the

Conclusion

control over land and population by the palace estates of the princesses and royal in-laws and by the private academies and shrines. The lands of the palace estates, academies, and shrines were easier to control than the holdings of the landowning class in general. The palace estates were, after all, granted to members of the royal house itself, and it was not a serious problem for the Taewongun to change the method by which princesses and their consorts were supported from a system of semi-autonomous control over allocated lands to the granting of stipends from central government treasuries. As for the local literati and their academies, although they were important figures on the local scene, their semi-autonomous control over land and population was resented by both the local magistrates and the rural population. Because the estate lands of the academies were scattered, the political power of the academy estates was not significant. Despite the affiliation of some academies and some of the local literati with traditional bureaucratic factions, they obtained little support from high officials and were not strong enough to prevent the Taewongun's confiscation of their lands. Although the abolition of their academies and estates represented one of the Taewongun's major victories in the fiscal field, it did not seriously damage the economic base of yangban power.

In terms of the overall picture of central control over resources, the land resurveys, the household cloth tax, and the confiscation of palace estate and academy lands were not sufficient to create an adequate revenue base to meet the expanding demands for resources by the central government. The Taewongun therefore chose to increase his revenues by means that in effect left the regressive tax structure of the dynasty and the privileged position of the aristocracy and upper economic class intact. He levied a few land surtaxes for special purposes; he imposed river, boat, commercial transit, and gate taxes; and he forced the upper class to make "voluntary contributions" for special purposes like palace construction. These were all ad hoc measures that proved successful in the short term. But in addition, he also relied on two questionable devices for fund raising: interest income from official grain loans and the minting of cash for profit.

The Korean government had been cannibalizing its rural credit, relief, and military emergency grain reserves for over a century in order to supplement the revenue needs of local magistrates, provincial military commanders, and central government agencies. Furthermore, the rural credit and relief loan system had been corrupted by its local official administrators, who forced unwanted loans on peasants as a means of extorting interest and fees. Because the grain loan system was one of the chief causes of the peasant uprisings of 1862, there was a considerable body of opinion that favored its total elimination.

The Taewongun, to his credit, was responsible for one of the major

Politics and Policy in Traditional Korea

institutional reforms of the dynasty when he presided over the initiation of the village granary system. Although he intended the reform to benefit the peasantry by reducing the potential for corruption, he had no intention of abandoning the valuable source of income that the interest on grain loans represented to the state. The regulations of the village granary system provided that interest on loans would be forwarded to the central government and not used to refund and maintain a stable reserve as provided for in Chu Hsi's model system. Moreover, the village granary system was only applied to five provinces and did not cover all types of grain loans. The government continued to authorize agencies of the central government, provincial officials, and military garrison commanders to lend out their reserves or tax income at interest in order to provide a yearly return for expenditures.

By continuing to rely on a source of revenue that in fact was tantamount to a tax on the peasant populace, and the poorest segment of it at that, the government alleviated the need for any greater taxation of the wealthier portion of the population. The Taewongun may not have consciously set out to achieve this result, but by preserving a system of fund raising that exploited the impoverished peasantry for the benefit of the state and left the privileged class relatively unscathed, he unwittingly helped alleviate those pressures that threatened the stability of the existing social order.

The same conclusion might also be drawn for his monetary policy. Since the Taewongun's efforts to expand income from regular taxation had not produced adequate results, he also resorted to the highly questionable device of minting what amounted to debased copper cash in order to benefit from the profits of seigniorage. Minting cash at a profit was not an idea that originated with the Taewongun's regime, but by his authorization of the so-called large cash he was responsible for putting into circulation the most debased coin in the history of the dynasty. In a way, he was forced to do so, because the cost of copper and the cost of production had risen so high in the past century that some high multiple of the existing ordinary cash had to be used as the face value of the new coin if any profit were to be made at all. Furthermore, the government not only used the new 100-cash for regular purchases, it also used it to refund the defunct grain loan system and capitalize the new village granaries.

The new currency caused inflation, and the disruption of stable market prices imposed added burdens on the peasantry and certain merchants. These effects were certainly not unanticipated, for there had been a long tradition of opposition to currency manipulation because of the fear of inflation, but the government decided to gamble on inflation in order to take its profits from seigniorage. Then when price fixing and market controls failed to stem inflation, the Taewongun withdrew the 100-cash

Conclusion

from circulation. He was still pressed for funds, however, and he soon reverted to another inflationary monetary policy when he imported overvalued Chinese coins to help pay government bills.

Both the grain loan and monetary policies of the Taewongun show his preference for expedient measures that were sure to yield immediate and certain profits for the central government, no matter what the long-term negative consequences for the peasantry. And, as indicated above, the Taewongun's grain loan and monetary policies redounded to the benefit of the upper class because they satisfied the government's immediate demand for revenue and precluded the need for a more thoroughgoing revision of the tax structure. It is therefore not completely accurate to speak only of the resistance of the landed interests and the wealthy upper class to taxation as the cause of the difficult fiscal situation of the central government and the failure of the Taewongun to find a permanent solution to the problem of regressive taxation and peasant economic oppression. For the Taewongun himself preferred to avoid a direct confrontation with the upper class, especially when alternative means to the raising of funds were readily available.

The Taewongun had to balance the needs of the state for power and revenue against the demands of the upper class for the preservation of their privileges and the demands of an impoverished peasantry for relief. He would have preferred to accomplish all three objectives at the same time, but it was impossible to meet the needs of all three groups equally. He favored the fiscal needs of the state over all other considerations, and he worked to relieve the burdens on the common peasant only when the adverse effects on the upper class were minimal.

Policy and Politics: The Emergence of a Political Opposition

Conventional interpretations of the politics of this period usually stress the role of factionalism in the overthrow of the Taewongun. In fact, however, the political opposition to the Taewongun was made up of three forces: those who opposed his policies because they threatened the socioeconomic base of the yangban; those who objected to his pragmatism on ideological grounds because it violated hallowed principles of Confucian dogma; and the queen, her relatives, and a small number of other bureaucrats who sought political power for themselves. In the end, however, none of these groups would have succeeded had the young king not chosen to assert his authority, and in this decision he was moved chiefly by ideological arguments rather than by his desire to defend yangban economic interests or promote the political ambitions of his consort relatives.

The supreme irony of the Taewongun's regime is that he was regarded

Politics and Policy in Traditional Korea

by many aristocrats and literati as the archenemy of their class interests, when in fact he helped preserve the social system and their preeminent place in it. At the time, however, it appeared to many yangban intellectuals that the Taewongun was bent on destroying their privileges and their power. The abolition of the private academies and shrines and the imposition of the household cloth tax on yangban households were particularly irksome to aristocrats. Certain intellectuals insisted that both these measures were destructive of the moral order as well as the social order. They opposed the abolition of the academies because they claimed it would weaken the education of the youth of the country in fundamental Confucian moral principles. They criticized the removal of the shrine to the Ming emperors to the palace because it would prevent private individuals from fulfilling their moral obligation to display loyalty to past benefactors. And they deplored the imposition of a household tax on the yangban because it would destroy the proper distinction between superior and inferior that was fundamental to a system of morality based on respect.

The opposition to the Taewongun's policies was thus not wholly confined to conflicts of economic and class interest. Objections were also raised to the Taewongun's violation of Confucian norms and fundamental principles of government in his practical approach to affairs and in his eager search for workable solutions to problems. Many conservative scholars demanded adherence to three fundamentals of good government: frugality on the part of the monarch and the government, concern for the welfare of the peasantry, and maintenance of status distinction in society. It was felt that if the king reduced his expenditures to a minimum, there would be no need for oppressive taxation of the peasant population, and no need to increase taxes on the yangban.

Some literati felt that the Taewongun had violated these fundamental principles. They could not object to his demands for revenue for the military establishment, but they did object strenuously to expenditures for palace construction, the only purpose of which was to create exalted symbols of royal prestige and authority. They demanded that palace construction be stopped and that the extra levies and imposts that he introduced be rescinded. Thus, many of the yangban literati demanded that the throne sacrifice its own interests for the benefit of both the peasantry and the aristocracy and reduce its income to a bare minimum.

The literati opponents of the Taewongun also objected to his monetary policies, primarily for two reasons. They deplored the inflationary effects of the new debased coins, and they also objected to currency on principle. Since they believed that agriculture was the only real legitimate pursuit for the common people and that crops and food were the only things of real value, they believed that money only served the interests of

Conclusion

parasitic middle men, distracted peasants from their prime task of cultivating the fields, and lured them into a useless pursuit of profits from
commercial transactions in luxury goods. In demanding the abolition of
first the new 100-cash, and then the overvalued Ch'ing cash, they really
desired a reversion to a natural economy that was untainted by the profit
motive and not necessarily the replacement of debased coins by sounder
currency.

The opponents of the Taewongun's policies also raised two other
minor issues. They objected to his tampering with the genealogies of the
royal clan as a means of strengthening the lineage groups within the royal
family, and they also objected to his rehabilitation of the descendants of
certain political criminals of the past because it weakened the standards
of law and order.

By his violation of the economic and status privileges of the yangban
class, and by his violation of certain norms of Confucian government,
the Taewongun had created a vocal opposition to his rule. But this opposition was limited to the rural literati and a few of their courageous
spokesmen. By itself, it would not have been sufficient to topple him
from power. Two other factors contributed to his forced retirement in
December 1873.

The first of these is a relatively unknown quantity because of the lack
of specific evidence; that is, the role of the queen and her relatives of the
Yŏhŭng Min clan. It seems likely that the queen had grown to resent her
father-in-law and may, indeed, have influenced her husband to assert his
independence. Furthermore, several of her male relatives had been
working their way up the bureaucratic ladder under the very nose of the
Taewongun. They were joined by discontented nephews of the dowager-
regent, members of the P'ungyang Cho clan, who felt that they had not
been rewarded sufficiently with high office. They may also have been
supported by the Taewongun's own brother, Yi Ch'oe-ŭng, who was appointed to high office after the Taewongun's retirement. In addition,
many officials, most notably Pak Kyu-su, may also have felt that some
modification of the Taewongun's Japan policy would be necessary if
Korea were to be spared a disastrous war.

But the immediate cause of the Taewongun's retirement was the decision of Kojong to declare his capacity for the independent exercise of
his royal powers. He was brought to this decision mainly by his sympathy
for the arguments of the yangban literati dogmatists. His general philosophical outlook was the product of a decade of training at the hands of
his literati mentors, and he was convinced that his father had violated
Confucian prescriptions against extravagant expenditure and overtaxation of the peasantry. He was determined to reverse these policies and go

Politics and Policy in Traditional Korea

down in history as a model of virtuous kingly behavior—as a monarch who would willingly sacrifice royal interests for the greater welfare of the common people. The opposition of the literati thus provided a catalyst for the king to declare himself the sole, independent ruler of the state. Once he did this, the Taewongun realized that his own position was superfluous, and lacking the will or the political support necessary for a usurpation, retired to the countryside.

Kojong's Regime, 1874-76

As soon as Kojong took over responsibility for government affairs on his own, he immediately adopted that part of the conservative literati platform that called for the alleviation of peasant distress. He therefore rescinded many of the extra taxes and levies introduced by the Taewongun, stopped palace construction, and ordered the withdrawal of Chinese coins from circulation. But Kojong's abolition of Ch'ing cash proved his undoing. He felt that he would be able to stem inflation by eliminating the currency that was its cause, but he did not foresee the adverse consequences for the fiscal and revenue position of the central government. Ch'ing cash had driven the older and more valuable ever-normal cash out of circulation, so that the government treasuries were left holding mostly Ch'ing cash as reserves. By withdrawing the use of Ch'ing cash as legal tender, the king had immediately bankrupted his government and many provincial yamen as well. He was plunged forthwith into a situation of insoluble difficulty and was unable to provide even minimal funds for government operations.

The order to abolish the use of Ch'ing cash had two important effects. It shook the king's confidence in the advice of his Confucian mentors and the validity of the conservative literati program for good government, and it forced him to scramble for funds to meet payments due. He was now reluctant to adopt other aspects of the literati program, and refused to rescind the household cloth tax. In any case, his main desire was to benefit the peasantry and not necessarily the aristocracy, and now that his government was short of funds, he was in no way anxious to give up a lucrative source of income.

Kojong also proved recalcitrant on the question of the private academies and shrines. He rejected requests for the reestablishment of the academies, and he reluctantly authorized the rebuilding of the Mandongmyo but only with strict magisterial supervision over its operations. Now that he was king in fact as well as name, he began to realize the importance of maintaining some sort of edge over the aristocrats and literati in the contest for power.

Because of the financial shortage, Kojong abandoned his earlier re-

Conclusion

straint against the raising of revenue and decided to call in the large amounts of capital that were tied up in the refunding of the grain loans. It was only with the greatest effort, after extensive investigation of the village granary system by the secret censors, that he prevented its cannibalization and destruction. He finally decided to leave it intact, because it had been relatively successful in eliminating bureaucratic corruption and relieving peasant distress.

Once Kojong abandoned the literati program and refused to carry out their every wish, they lost confidence in him and began to attack his policies and his regime. Certain individuals even suggested that the king summon his father back to the capital to provide the proper leadership for government affairs. Kojong, who had insisted in December 1873 that the government must tolerate criticism of the throne (when that criticism was really directed against his father), now began to resent the attacks against his own leadership.

One of the casualties of the new tide of dissent was Yi Yu-wŏn, one of Kojong's leading advisers. Yi was blamed for the failures of the new government and forced to resign from his post. Despite Kojong's entreaties for him to return to office, he refused to do so. Kojong now became determined not to allow further criticism, and he attempted to silence his critics, especially scholars and students of the National Academy, by exile and execution. But his high officials refused to support him in this and obstructed his attempts to impose punishments on the literati in a completely arbitrary manner. In the end, he was forced to back down and reveal to his officials that he did not have his father's fortitude and resolution. Kojong had unfortunately chosen the wrong issue on which to take a stand. Had he continued his policy of toleration for remonstrance, or had he at least chosen to mete out reasonable punishment, he would not have forced a confrontation with his own bureaucracy that resulted in the weakening of his prestige as king.

One of the effects of this setback was that Kojong lost some of his confidence in his ability to rule and began to turn over more decision-making responsibility to his officials. At the same time, he and his officials began to lose faith both in the effectiveness of institutional reform and the efficacy of Confucian dogmatism. For that matter, many of Kojong's official advisers had resisted the conservative Confucian platform from the start because it was sure to lead to the bankruptcy of government finances. Disillusioned both by pragmatism and dogmatism, Kojong's regime began to move toward a do-nothing policy of standing pat with existing institutions whatever their shortcomings. Reports from the secret censors convinced them that the benefits of the Taewongun's reforms were marginal at best. They decided that a certain level of corruption was inevitable and unavoidable, and that the best policy was to work on improving the administration of existing institutions. Maintenance of the status quo became the cornerstone of government policy by about 1875. This solution did not satisfy either the practical reformers or the Confucian dogmatists. The latter, in particular, became totally disillusioned with Kojong's leadership on domestic affairs and were converted into opponents of the king even before the negotiations with Japan reached a crisis.

Kojong's foreign policy put the finishing touch on the alienation of the Confucian conservatives and xenophobes. Kojong and his court were in basic agreement with the Taewongun's objectives of insulating the country from foreign contact, but they believed that the best way to ensure this was to reach some compromise and accommodation with the Japanese. Eventually they capitulated to almost all Japanese demands for a reordering of relations between the two countries, but they deluded themselves into believing that they could maintain Korean isolation even under the new treaty system. Their naivety on this score was balanced by a realistic appraisal of Korean military weakness, in contrast to the views of the Taewongun and the literati, who possessed a naive overconfidence in Korea's military capacity combined with a realistic understanding of the effects of compromise with Japan and the West. They realized that once Korea's doors were opened, things would never be the same again.

Kojong's foreign policy thus helped drive the conservative Confucian proto-nationalist literati back into the arms of the Taewongun. In the decade after 1876, Kojong, the queen, and the government found themselves in the center of the political and policy spectrum, hemmed in from the right by the Taewongun and his conservative supporters, who sought a return to the old days before Kanghwa, and from the left by radical progressives like Kim Ok-kyun. In the space of two brief years (1882-84), however, both the right and the left were eliminated and driven out of the country after abortive coups, thanks mainly to Chinese aid and intervention. Thus, the leadership that emerged in 1876 was preserved to the Sino-Japanese War of 1894.

In the twelve years prior to the Kanghwa Treaty of 1876, the Koreans were involved in a fundamental conflict over the control and distribution of political and economic power. This conflict was brought about by the Taewongun's drive to bolster the authority of the crown, increase central control over the resources and population of the nation, and strengthen the capacity of the country to defend itself against attack. Had the Taewongun pursued these goals to their logical limits, it would have led to a transformation of the basic structure of the Yi dynasty state by the concentration of power in the hands of the monarch, the subjugation of the

Conclusion

bureaucracy to the orders of the king, the centralization of control over wealth and people, and the weakening of the hereditary aristocracy and landed gentry.

These goals were not achieved for three reasons. The Taewongun succeeded neither in rationalizing, centralizing, and strengthening the administrative apparatus, nor in subordinating it in a permanent way to royal authority. He had no intention of destroying the aristocratic basis of the social order, and, in fact, helped to preserve it by meeting government demands for revenue by the manipulation of fiscal and monetary policy. And he could not satisfy the rigid and narrow normative standards of the intellectual leaders of society in his choice of methods. As a result, the Taewongun was forced to retire from government affairs and his active and pragmatic style of leadership was replaced by the inactive and passive approach of his son, King Kojong. When Korea's doors were opened to the outside world, she was led by a king once again subjected to the restraints of the bureaucratic and social structure and the traditional value system, a man who in seeking solace from trouble became the victim of changing circumstances rather than the master of events.

In a very real sense the major struggle for expanded central authority was waged in the decade prior to the opening of the country, and not in the generation that followed it. The struggle was lost, and in the course of it confidence in the validity and efficacy of both conventional Confucian wisdom and active institutional reform was lost, too. The Korean government after 1876 therefore lacked both conviction in the ability of the old order to save the state and commitment to the purposive adoption of new and foreign institutions. It was eventually pressured into the implementation of some modernizing reforms, either to please its Chinese advisers or to mollify the Japanese predators, but its main concern was to preserve the social and political status quo based on the traditional formula of a dominant aristocracy combined with weak monarchical and central authority. It was, therefore, not unusual that the drastic measures of the kabo reform of 1894 were carried out by a government operating under the protective wing of Japanese armed forces, an external source of authority that was in no way restrained by domestic social and political forces. It was furthermore not surprising that in the fifteen years after 1894 many Korean officials aligned themselves with foreign interests and power, either Russian or Japanese, for in the absence of a powerful and pervasive nationalism and in the presence of a weak and discredited monarchy, many yangban bureaucrats tended to gravitate toward actual sources of power even though they were foreign. For the traditional order on its own was never capable of creating strong and effective central authority.

The traditional monarchy and yangban aristocracy were destroyed in

Politics and Policy in Traditional Korea

the period of Japanese colonial rule from 1910 to 1945, and in the period after Liberation in 1945 Koreans were still left with the problem of creating political authority, a task that was not made easier by the long tradition of restrained central power. But the political and social bases of the old equilibrium had disappeared with the result that contemporary Korean governments in both North and South Korea developed more powerful centralized authority than had ever existed in traditional times.

Notes
Bibliography
Index

Abbreviations Used in the Notes

CSJMJS	*Chōsen jimmei jisho*
CSS	*Chōsenshi*
GKMJ	*Dai Nihon gaikō monjo*
ILSN	*Ilsŏngnok*
KJSL	*Kojong sillok*
KSDSJ	*Kuksa-daesajŏn*
MCYR	*Maech'ŏn yarok*
MHBG	*Chŭngbo munhŏnbigo*
RCZS	*Richo jidai no zaisei*
*SJW**	*Sŭngjŏngwŏn ilgi*
TMHG	*Tongmun hwigo*

*Two types of citation are used in the footnotes to refer to the *Sŭngjŏngwŏn ilgi.* *SJW* alone refers to the original documents in the *Kyujanggak* collection of Seoul National University library. If *SJW* is followed by a reference like "Kojong I," it refers to the appropriate volume in the Kuksa p'yŏnch'an wiwŏnhoe edition of the *Sŭngjŏngwŏn ilgi.* This discrepancy arises from the fact that part of the research for this book was done in the United States where only published versions of documentary materials were available.

Notes

1. Introduction

1. See the remarks of S. N. Eisenstadt on relating different aspects of tradition to social structure and organization. "Post-Traditional Societies and the Continuity and Reconstruction of Tradition," *Daedalus* (Winter 1973), 4.

2. Yi Sŏn-gŭn has emphasized the Taewongun's supposed introduction of new military technology, in particular a "flying ship" with crane feathers for sails, an abortive attempt to build an armored steamship modeled after the *General Sherman*, captured in 1866, and underwater mines. *Han'guksa ch'oegŭnsep'yŏn* (Seoul: Uryu munhwasa, 1961), 215-18.

3. Hayashi Taisuke and Ching Young Choe have praised the Taewongun for his revolutionary imposition of the household cloth tax on yangban, Hayashi Taisuke, *Chōsen tsūshi* (Keijö, 1912), 505-524, 536-542; Ching Young Choe, *The Rule of the Taewŏn'gun, 1864-1873: Restoration in Yi Korea* (Carﬧbridge, Mass.: East Asian Research Center, Harvard University, 1972), 40.

4. Hayashi also stressed the tyrannical aspects of the Taewongun's rule, and both Hayashi and Choe praised his attack on factionalism. See note 3 and Choe, *The Rule of the Taewŏn'gun*, 52; Gregory Henderson, *Korea: The Politics of the Vortex* (Cambridge, Mass.: Harvard University Press, 1968), 65-66.

5. Han Woo-keun regards the Taewongun as an idealistic Confucian reformer incapable of realizing the need for modernizing change. *The History of Korea* (Honolulu, Hawaii: East-West Center Press, 1971), 362-377.

6. Gregory Henderson emphasizes the Taewongun's expansion of royal power, but he exaggerates its extent, *Korea: The Politics of the Vortex*, 60-62.

7. One North Korean history views the Taewongun as a conservative reformer who sought to build up his own power, restore the "feudal" structure to a state of health, and pacify the people to inhibit their struggle against the ruling class. It also claims that the Taewongun was supported by the lower yangban and upper commoners, but no evidence is presented to support this kind of class analysis. Chosŏn minju juŭi inmin konghwaguk kwahagwŏn yŏksa yŏn'guso, *Chosŏn t'ongsa*, I, (P'yŏngyang, Kwahagwŏn ch'ulpansa, 1962), 811-816. Another North Korean historian, Ch'oe Ki hwan, emphasizes the Taewongun's lack of concern for either modernization or capitalism. *Chōsen kindai kakumei undōshi* (History of the modern

revolutionary movement in Korea), compiled by the Chosŏn minju juŭi inmin konghwaguk kwahagwŏn yŏksa yŏn'guso and translated into Japanese by the ZaiNihon Chōsenjin kagakusha kyōkai shakai kagaku bumon rekishi bukai (Tokyo: Shin Nihon shuppansha, 1964), 42-44.

8. Paul A. Cohen's observations on nineteenth century China are also appropriate for Korea. "Ch'ing China: Confrontation with the West, 1850-1900," in James B. Crowley, ed., *Modern East Asia: An Interpretation* (New York: Harcourt, Brace and World, Inc., 1970), 31-32.

9. See Bruce Cuming's critique of Gregory Henderson's thesis of mass society in late nineteenth century Korea, "Is Korea a Mass Society?" in *Occasional Papers on Korea*, no. 1 (June 1972), 66-83; Henderson, *Korea: The Politics of the Vortex*, 36-55.

10. Cf. Kwang-Ching Liu's remarks on stability in Late Ch'ing China. "Nineteenth-Century China: The Disintegration of the Old Order and the Impact of the West," in Ping-ti Ho and Tang Tsou, eds., *China in Crisis*, vol. I, bk. 1 (Chicago: University of Chicago Press, 1968), 95.

11. See James B. Palais, "Stability in Yi Dynasty Korea: Equilibrium Systems and Marginal Adjustment," paper presented at the Conference on Tradition and Change in Korea, Seoul, Korea, Sept. 1, 1969; published in Korean in Han'guk yŏn'gusil, ed., *Han'guk ŭi chŏnt'ong kwa pyŏnch'ŏn* (Seoul: Koryŏ Taehakkyo, 1973), 283-312. See also *Occasional Papers on Korea*, no. 3 (forthcoming).

12. Slavery in the Yi dynasty is a subject that deserves extensive treatment. Suffice it to say here that while slaves were treated as chattel, they could also own property of their own, including other slaves. Furthermore, one of the most important modes of slavery in Korea was the "outside resident slave" (*oegŏ sano*, or *oegŏ nobi*), whose relationship to his master was similar to landlord-tenant relations. For landownership by slaves, see all of Kim Yong-sŏp's articles on land tenure in Chapter 4 below, notes 1, 3, 9, and Chapter 5, notes 21 and 23. For other material on slavery, see Shikata Hiroshi, "Richo jinkō ni kansuru ichi kenkyū," in *Chōsen shakai hōseishi kenkyū* (Tokyo, 1937), 81-112; Kim Sŏk-hyŏng, *Chōsen hōken jidai nōmin no kaikyū kōsei*, trans. from the Korean by Suematsu Yasukazu and Yi Tal-hŏn (Tokyo, 1960), 1-79, 112-143. See also Han Woo-keun, *The History of Korea*, 247ff.

13. Yi Sang-baek, *Han'guksa kŭnse chŏn'gip'yŏn* (Seoul, 1962), 429-430.

14. See Kim Yong-sŏp's articles on land tenure, Chapter 4 below, note 1.

15. See Susan Shin, "The Social Structure of Kumhwa County in the Seventeenth Century," in *Occasional Papers on Korea*, 1 (June 1972), 9-35; Kim Yong-sŏp, "Chosŏn hugi e issŏsŏ ŭi sinbunje ŭi tongyo wa nongji chŏmyu: Sangju yang'an yŏn'gu ŭi ildan," in *Sahak yŏn'gu*, 15 (April 1963), 1-46.

16. See Ch'oe Yŏng-ho, "Commoners in Early Yi Dynasty Civil Examinations: An Aspect of Korean Social Structure, 1392-1600," *Journal of Asian Studies*, 33:4 (August 1974), 611-631; Ch'oe Yŏng-ho, "The Civil Examinations and the Social Structure in Early Yi Dynasty Korea: 1392-1600," Ph. D. diss., University of Chicago, 1971, passim.

17. See note 16 and Edward W. Wagner, "The Ladder of Success in Yi Dynasty Korea," in *Occasional Papers on Korea*, 1 (June 1972), 1-8; Edward W. Wagner, "The Korean Chokpo as a Historical Source," in Spencer Palmer, ed., *Studies in Asian Genealogy* (Provo, Utah: Brigham Young University Press, 1972), 141-152; Song June-ho, "The Government Examination Rosters of the Yi Dynasty," in ibid., 153-176; Song June-ho, *Yijo saengwŏn chinsa si ŭi yŏn'gu* (Seoul: Taehan min'guk tosŏgwan, 1970).

18. See Chapter 4, notes 1, 3, 9; Chapter 5, notes 21 and 23

19. See note 30 below and Chapter 5.
20. Edward W. Wagner, "The Ladder of Success."
21. See note 18 above.
22. Chapter 4, note 1.
23. For a discussion of the tributary system see John K. Fairbank, ed., *The Chinese World Order* (Cambridge, Mass.: Harvard University Press, 1968), in particular, Hae-jong Chun, "Sino-Korean Tributary Relations in the Ch'ing Period," in ibid., 90-111, and John K. Fairbank, "A Preliminary Framework," in ibid., 1-19; Fairbank and Teng, "On the Ch'ing Tributary System," in *Ch'ing Administration: Three Studies*, Harvard-Yenching Institute Studies 19 (Cambridge, Mass.: Harvard University Press, 1961), 107-218; M. Frederick Nelson, *Korea and the Old Orders in Eastern Asia* (Baton Rouge, Louisiana: Louisiana State University Press, 1945).
24. See Sohn Pow-key, "Social History of the Early Yi Dynasty, 1392-1592: With Emphasis on the Functional Aspects of Governmental Structure," Ph. D. diss., University of California at Berkeley, 1963, chap. 1, "The Monarchy and Ideology."
25. This is a phenomenon in Chinese history that has been well studied. See, for example, Chang Chung-li, *The Income of the Chinese Gentry* (Seattle, Washington: University of Washington Press, 1962), 7-42; Ch'ü T'ung-tsu, *Local Government in China under the Ch'ing* (Cambridge, Mass.: Harvard University Press, 1962), 22-32. For a discussion of compliance, see Amitai Etzioni, *A Comparative Analysis of Complex Organizations* (New York: The Free Press, 1961).
26. Edward W. Wagner, "The Ladder of Success."
27. Edward W. Wagner, "The Literati Purges," Ph. D. diss., Cambridge, Mass., Harvard University, 1959, 29-31, for a discussion of the royal lectures; et passim, for a discussion of the censorate. For the effects of training and tutorial on princes in eighteenth century China, see Harold L. Kahn, *Monarchy in the Emperor's Eyes: Image and Reality in the Ch'ien-lung Reign* (Cambridge, Mass.: Harvard University Press, 1971), 115-181.
28. Kim Un-t'ae, *Chosŏn wangjo haengjŏngsa: kŭnsep'yŏn* (Seoul: Pagyŏngsa, 1970), 96. The names of administrative subdivisions based on different sources at different times in the dynasty are given in Kwŏn Sang-no, *Han'guk chimyŏng konghyŏk-ko* (Seoul: Tongguk munhwasa, 1961), 338-404. The average figure is about three hundred and fifty. For a discussion of population estimates for the Yi dynasty, see Chapter 4, note 20.
29. It is my belief that the term, *taesin*, was used synonymously for *tangsanggwan*. In a system of eighteen official ranks, from 1A to 9 B, the *tangsanggwan* included all those from 1A down to a select portion of those in the 3A category. The number of officials in this category varied, since some of the posts were sinecures, but judging from a head count of those listed in attendance at special court conferences, it would seem that thirty to fifty officials usually attended these sessions. Regular and periodic convocations of the *taesin* were called *ch'adae* conferences. When the *taesin* were summoned irregularly or for emergency meetings, the meetings were termed convocations of "all incumbent and former taesin" (*siwŏn'im taesin*). For a chart of this rank division, see Ch'oe Yŏng-ho, "The Civil Examinations and the Social Structure in Early Yi Dynasty Korea: 1392-1600," 13.
30. On factionalism, see Han Woo-keun, *The History of Korea*, 298-303; William E. Henthorn, *A History of Korea*, (New York: The Free Press, 1971) 192-195; Key P. Yang and Gregory Henderson, "An Outline History of Korean Confucianism," in *Journal of Asian Studies*, 18:1-2 (November 1958-February 1959). A good but undocumented survey in Korean of the factional problem is Sŏng Nak-hun, "Han'guk

tangjaengsa," in *Han'guk munhwasa taegye*, II, (Seoul, 1965), 221-390. A survey of factionalism in Sukchong's reign has recently been published. See Kang Chu-jin, *Yijo tangjaengsa yŏn'gu* (Seoul: Seoul Taehakkyo ch'ulp'anbu, 1971).

31. Eisenstadt theorizes that in a centralized bureaucratic monarchy with a significant aristocracy, the monarchy may seek to restrain not only the political and economic power of the aristocratic class, but also any tendency toward political autonomy by its own bureaucracy. See S. N. Eisenstadt, *The Political Systems of Empires* (New York: The Free Press of Glencoe, 1963), 18, 20, 72ff., 91, 115-130, 132-137, 144, 149-150, 175-221, 257-260, 318, 331, 337, et passim.

32. Ibid., 33ff., 91, 95, 122ff., 136, 253, et passim.

33. Ibid., 17ff., 204ff. I was fortunate to read the interesting seminar paper by David Johnson, "Remarks on the Medieval Chinese Oligarchy," presented to the Columbia University Seminar on Traditional China, ca. 1972. See also Mark Elvin, *The Pattern of the Chinese Past* (Stanford, Calif.: Stanford University Press, 1973).

34. *Sejong sillok*, Sejong 6.3. kihae, cited in Pak Pyŏng-ho, *Han'guk pŏpchesa t'uksu yŏn'gu: Yijo sidae ŭi pudongsan maemae kŭp tanbobŏp* (Seoul, 1960), 1-2; Pak Pyŏng-ho, "Han'guk kŭnse ŭi t'oji soyukwŏn e kwan han yŏn'gu," in *Seoul taehakkyo pŏphak*, 8:87; *Chōsenshi* (Keijō: Chōsen sōtokufu, 1935), series 4, no. 3, p. 16, hereinafter cited as *CSS*. 4.3.16. This notice, and other evidence cited by Pak that was dated a year or two before this time, indicates that land and property sales occurred even before 1424. The governor of Kyŏnggi province memorialized that people had been forced to sell their lands because of funeral expenses, debts, payment of fines, or poverty, but that the officials had been confiscating the sale price (cash), evidently because the sale of land was in violation of the law. The governor noted that the sale of house sites and vegetable plots in the capital were legal. It was only in the outer areas (of the province) where land sales were prohibited. He asked that the prohibition against sales be lifted, and his request was approved. The *Chōsenshi* mistakenly records that this was not approved by the king. For a fuller discussion of land tenure, see Chapter 4.

35. The sale of titles and ranks is discussed in a number of articles. See Chapter 5 and Susan Shin, "The Social Structure of Kumhwa County."

36. Ibid., 91-96; Palais, "Korea on the Eve of the Kanghwa Treaty, 1873-76," Ph. D. diss., Harvard University, 1968, 439-489, 513ff.; Yu Hong-nyŏl, *Han'guk chŏnjugyohoesa* (Seoul: Kat'orik ch'ulp'ansa, 1958); Urakawa Wasaburo, *Chōsen junkyōshi* (Tokyo: Zenkoku shobō, 1944); Charles Dallet, *Histoire de l'église de Corée*, 2 vols. (Paris: Victor Palme, 1874); Yu Hong-nyŏl, *Kojong ch'iha Sŏhak sunan ŭi yŏn'gu* (Seoul: Uryu ch'ulp'ansa, 1962); Pak Kyu-su, *Hwanjaejip*, 10:21b-25b. Yu Hong-nyŏl estimates that over 10,000 Korean Christians lost their lives during the persecutions of 1866-71, and that if those who starved to death or died from illness were added, more than half the estimated 23,000 Korean Catholics of the time probably lost their lives. Yu, *Kojong ch'iha Sŏhak*, 308-309, 350; Dallet, *Histoire de l'église*, II, 588.

37. For an extensive treatement of these events in English, see Ching Young Choe, *The Rule of the Taewŏn'gun*, 91-133.

38. Ibid., 118-119.

39. Ibid., 112-114.

40. See Ching Young Choe, *The Rule of the Taewŏn'gun*, 134-139; Palais, "Korea on the Eve," 536-539; George M. McCune, "The Exchange of Envoys between Korea and Japan during the Tokugawa Period," *Far Eastern Quarterly*, 5:3 (May 1946), 308-325; Yi Hyŏn-jong, *Chosŏn chŏn'gi tae-Il kyosŏpsa yon'gu* (Seoul, 1964);

Nakamura Eikō, *Nissen kankeishi no kenkyū*, 3 vols. (Tokyo, 1965-69); Oda Shōgo, "Rishi Chōsen jidai ni okeru Wakan no hensen," in *Chōsen Shina bunka no kenkyū* (Tokyo, 1929), 93-140.

41. Ching Young Choe, *The Rule of the Taewŏn'gun*, 139-165.

42. The best chance of a settlement of these questions came in the spring of 1870 during the mission of Urase Saijō from Tsushima. He used the old Korean seal, and presented communications without the term for "emperor." But the talks were aborted when Max von Brandt, the North German minister to Japan, accompanied by a Japanese interpreter, arrived in Pusan harbor on a Western steamship on a sightseeing trip. The Koreans suspected a Japanese-Western conspiracy and broke off the negotiations. Three attempts by the Japanese to continue the negotiations after this ended in failure: the Yoshioka mission of December 1870, the Sagara mission of February 1872, and the dispatch of Hanabusa from the Foreign Office to the Waegwan in October 1872. See Choe, *The Rule of the Taewŏn'gun*, 151-161.

43. The most recent study of the *Seikan* debate is Marlene J. Mayo, "The Korean Crisis of 1873 and Early Meiji Foreign Policy," in *Journal of Asian Studies*, 31:4 (August 1972), 793-819. For other studies in English, see Hilary Conroy, *The Japanese Seizure of Korea, 1868-1910* (Philadelphia, Pa.: University of Pennsylvania Press, 1960), 17-77; Nobutaka Ike, "Triumph of the Peace Party in Japan in 1873," *Far Eastern Quarterly*, 2 (May 1943), 286-295. For events in Korea, see Choe, *The Rule of the Taewŏn'gun*, 139-165.

2. The Throne

1. One exception was the case of Kwŏn Yu, who died under torture because of his opposition to the selection of Kim Cho-sun's daughter for Sunjo's queen. See Yi Sang-baek, *Han'guksa kŭnse hugip'yŏn* (Seoul: Uryu munhwasa, 1965), 327-328.

2. Birth dates of kings and queens can be found in *Han'guksa: yŏnp'yo* (Seoul: Ŭryu munhwasa, 1959), 346-373. These pages include a reproduction of the *Sŏnwŏn kyebo* (Genealogy of the royal family).

3. Ibid., 370. Kim Cho-sun, ca. 1765-1831. For short biographies, see *Chōsen jimmei jisho* (Keijō, 1937), 998, and *Kuksa-daesajŏn* (Seoul, 1962), I, 300. These two dictionaries will hereinafter be referred to as *CSJMJS* and *KSDSJ* respectively.

4. *CSJMJS*, 998; *KSDSJ*, I, 300.

5. *Han'guksa yŏnp'yo*, 283, 370-371. The crown prince married Cho Man-yong's daughter in 1819. Yi Sang-baek, *Han'guksa kŭnse hugip'yŏn*, 334.

6. Ibid., 370-371. Ikchong died on 1830.5.6 lunar. The later King Hŏnjong was designated heir apparent (literally, *wangseson*, or grandson of a king in the line of legitimate succession) the same year.

7. Hŏnjong's queen was designated queen in the third lunar month of 1837. Ibid., 287.

8. Yi Sang-baek, *Han'guksa kŭnse hugip'yŏn*, 346. Another sign of waning Andong Kim power was the recall in 1838 of Kang Si-hwan from exile. Kang had criticized the government and the regency before, in 1836, second lunar month. *Han'guksa yŏnp'yo*, 285.

9. Ibid., 346.

10. In 1848 one of the leading members of the Andong Kim clan, Kim Hŭng-gŭn, was exiled to his registered domicile in the country. See Hwang Hyŏn, *Maech'ŏn yarok* (Seoul: Kuksa p'yŏnch'an wiwŏnhoe ed., 1955), 2. Hereinafter referred to as *MCYR. CSS.* 6.3. 215-216. On August 15, 1848, the censor-general (*Taesagan*) impeached Kim for conspiracy on rather vague grounds.

Notes to page 26

11. Yi Sang-baek, *Han'guksa kŭnse hugip'yŏn*, 350.

12. The ages of kings during regencies in the nineteenth century are arranged in the following tables:

Regency by kings

King	Birth (lunar)	Accession and beginning of regency	Western age	Age in se	End of regency	Western age	Age in se
Sunjo	1790.6.8	1800.6.28	10	11	1804.1	13	15
Hŏnjong	1827.7.18	1834.11.13	7	8	1840.12	13	14
Ch'ŏlchong	1831.6.17	1849.6.6	17	19	1851.12	20	21
Kojong	1852.7.25	1863.12.8	11	12	1866.6	14	15

Regency by dowagers

Dowager	Years of regency	King	King's western age
Kim (Kyŏngju, Yŏngjo's second queen)	1801-04	Sunjo	10-13
Kim (Andong, Sunjo's queen)	1834-41	Hŏnjong	7-13
Kim (same person as above)	1849-52	Ch'ŏlchong	17-20
Cho (P'ungyang, Ikchong's consort)	1864-66	Kojong	11-14

Sources: Hanguksu yŏnp'yo, passim: Yi Sang-baek, *Han'guksa kŭnse hugip'yŏn*, 320-353.

13. For a list of Andong Kim officeholders, see Yi Sang-baek, *Han'guksa kŭnse hugip'yŏn*, 351. Kim Hŭng-gŭn was appointed chief state councilor in 1851, and Kwŏn Ton-in was impeached the same year. For the biography of Kim, see *KSDSJ*, I, 315, and *CSJMJS*, 1092. For Kwŏn, see *KSDSJ*, I, 205, and *CSJMJS*, 1865.

14. In 1860 the Kyŏngp'yŏnggun, or Prince Kyŏngp'yŏng, was impeached for his criticism of members of the consort Andong Kim clan, Kim Chwa-gŭn and Kim Mun-gŭn. He was exiled and stripped of his princely status. See *Ch'ŏlchong sillok*, kwon 12, Ch'ŏlchong 11.11.2 sinmyo, 11.4 kyesa, 11.9 musul; *CSS.* 6.3, same dates; Yi Sŏn-gŭn, *Han'guksa ch'oegŭnsep'yŏn* (Seoul, 1961), 156-157.

15. After Kwŏn's fall from power, an official implicated Yi in a treasonous plot on August 18, 1862 (7.23 lunar), and Yi was executed.

16. Several stories are told about the humiliations suffered by the Taewongun prior to 1864. According to one undocumented source, the Taewongun wanted his son, Yi Chae-myŏn, to pass the civil service examinations. He invited Kim Pyŏng-gi and Nam Pyŏng-ch'ŏl to a banquet, evidently to enlist their aid. They agreed to go but failed to appear. See Hayashi Taisuke, *Chōsen tsushi*, 510.

According to Hwang Hyŏn's memoirs, the Taewongun visited the home of Kim Chwa-gŭn during his impoverished youth to seek a favor. After he left, one of those present, Sim Ŭi-myŏn, remarked to Kim: "That fool ought to stay in the palace and leave it at that. What is he doing always dragging his tail around to the homes of the chief ministers?" The story leaked out and the Taewongun resented it. According to Hwang, the Taewongun later took revenge against Sim's family. Hwang Hyŏn,

MCYR, 20, 30; Yi Sŏn-gŭn, *Han'guksa ch'oegŭn-sep'yŏn*, 158, 163; Tabohashi Kiyoshi, *Kindai Nissen kankei no kenkyu*, (Keijō, 1940) I, 23.

17. Kikuchi Kenjō, *Kankoku kindai gaikōshi: Taiinkun-den* (Tokyo, 1910), 7; Kikuchi Kenjō, *Kindai Chōsen shi* (Keijō, 1937), I, 68; Hayashi Taisuke, *Chōsen tsūshi*, 506ff.; Yi Sŏn-gŭn, *Han'guksa ch'oegŭnsep'yŏn*, 158-160; Tabohashi Kiyoshi, *Kindai Nissen kankei no kenkyū*, I, 24. According to Hwang Hyŏn, King Ch'ŏlchong had favored Kojong for the throne and the Andong Kim wanted to help carry out his wishes, even though they objected to having a king with a living father. Hwang, *MCYR*, 2.

18. *KJSL*.I.1ff., 1863.12.8. Ching Young Choe, "The Decade of the Taewongun," I, 97. All the kings after the seventeenth century traced their lineage back to Injo (r. 1623-49). See the table facing p. 302 in Yi Sang-baek, *Han'juksa kŭnse hugip'yŏn*. In general, if a king died without male heirs, his grandson was chosen to be the next king. This was true of Chŏngjo (r. 1776-1800), who was the grandson of Yŏngjo (r. 1724-76), and Hŏnjong (r. 1834-49), who was the grandson of Sunjo (r. 1800-34). Kings were usually of the first or second generation of descent after their predecessors. There was no hard and fast rule about this, since Ch'ŏlchong (r. 1849-64), who was chosen to succeed the heirless Hŏnjong, was a cousin of Hŏnjong's deceased father. Kojong, who was chosen to succeed the heirless Ch'ŏlchong, was Ch'ŏlchong's cousin.

It would also appear that in choosing a king to succeed a king who had died without heirs, there was no rule requiring that first sons be chosen over second sons. The Taewongun (Hŭngsŏn taewŏn'gun) was the fourth son of Namyŏn'gun (Prince Namyŏn), and his three elder brothers all had sons of their own. Kojong was also the Taewongun's second son. In other words, Kojong was not chosen because of fixed rules of blood line, generational descent, or age. Since there was a range of choice, it might mean that the dowager's influence could have been a major factor in the choice of an heir. Young boys may have been preferable to adults because they lent themselves to control by regents and others. This would explain the selection of Kojong. See table in Yi Sang-baek, *Han'guksa kŭnse hugip'yŏn*, facing p. 302.

19. According to Hwang Hyŏn, on the day that Kojong was chosen to be king, the *wŏnsang*, or acting official in charge of affairs during the interregnum, Cho Tu-sun, wrote out a decree designating Kojong as the heir of Ch'ŏlchong. But Dowager Cho "raised an angry shout and said, 'Write that he is inheriting the great royal line from Ikchong [her deceased husband].' Cho Tu-sun did not dare go against her will." Hwang explained that the same thing had happened when Ch'ŏlchong first came to the throne. He should have succeeded to the line of Ikchong, but Sunjo's queen, an Andong Kim, wanted the regency and ordered that Ch'ŏlchong succeed to Sunjo's line. Hwang pointed out that by Kojong's being adopted into Ikchong's line Dowager Cho's regency was legitimized. Hwang, *MCYR*, 9. Hwang's information is not recorded, however, in the *Kojong sillok*.

20. Ch'ŏlchong's father was also granted the title of Taewŏn'gun; that is, the *Chŏn'gye taewŏn'gun*. Yi Sang-baek, *Han'guksa kŭnse hugip'yŏn*, 350.

21. *KJSL*. I.353-55, 1866.2.13.

22. A discussion was held at court on the protocol to be followed for the Taewongun on January 21, 1864. Chŏng Wŏn-yong, the first minister-without-portfolio, remarked that the court was bound to follow earlier precedent, but this situation (with a living Taewongun) was unprecedented. New regulations had to be established. Kim Chwa-gŭn noted that he had not had much chance to meet with the Taewongun. He remarked that they could discuss matters of etiquette and protocol after conferring with him. *KJSL*.I.11-12, 1863.12.13.

Hwang Hyŏn reported that sometime later in 1864, after the Taewongun gradually began to take part in the conduct of affairs, Kim Hŭng-gŭn objected to his participation in government: "Since ancient times the close relatives of the king have not interfered in government. It would be proper if [the Taewongun] were made to return to his private quarters and for the rest of his life retain his wealth and privileges [instead of interfering in government]." Hwang, MCYR, 2.

Kikuchi Kenjō and Hayashi Taisuke, in their general histories, reported that when the officials were discussing regulations for the king's formal visits to his father once a month, Kim Hŭng-gŭn and the other ministers did not object. Cho Tu-sun, however, supposedly remarked that if the king had to pay calls on his father, it would actually mean that the state would have two lords. See Kikuchi, Kindai Chōsen shi, I, 68; Hayashi, Chōsen tsūshi, 508. These items are not to be found in the daily court records. They would indicate, if true, that objections to the Taewongun were mild at first, and only after he began to exercise his authority did people openly express their dissatisfaction.

23. KJSL.I.4, Ch'ŏlchong 14.12.8. The eldest dowager's function as regent during a royal minority was not practiced in the early part of the dynasty. In the fifteenth century, officials called wŏnsang deliberated and decided matters of state during minorities. The post of wŏnsang was created by King Sejo (r. 1455-68) at about the same time that the Royal Secretariat was upgraded in importance. Sejo, a strong king, weakened the state council, and as a result certain favorite officials held long terms in the Royal Secretariat, the agency that handled the flow of official documents. These officials came to be called wŏnsang. During Yejong's brief reign in 1468, Sin Suk-chu acted as the wŏnsang to give aid and advice to the young king. He continued this function until the seventh year of Sŏngjong's reign (1476).

In the sixteenth century, the wŏnsang functioned in conjunction with dowager-regents, especially during the early parts of Myŏngjong's (r. 1544-67) and Sŏnjo's (r. 1567-1608) reigns. See Yi Sang-baek, Han'guksa kŭnse chŏn'gip'yŏn, 160; KSDSJ, II, 998.

24. See note 22. For a notice of Kojong's visit to the Unhyŏn palace, see KJSL.I.379-380, 1866.3.21. In 1864 a new gate was built between the Unhyŏn palace and the royal palace to give the Taewongun greater access to the court. Yi Sŏn-gŭn, Han'guksa ch'oegŭnsep'yŏn, 162; KJSL.I.135, 1864.6.6.

25. See Harold L. Kahn's discussion of the importance of filiality in the determination of policy during the reign of Ch'ien-lung of the Ch'ing dynasty. "The Politics of Filiality: Justification for Imperial Action in Eighteenth Century China," Journal of Asian Studies, 26:2 (February 1967), 197-203.

26. See note 12.

mr 27. Kojong declared the assumption of "personal rule" on December 23, 1873, but rescinded the decree the next day after he was reminded by officials that he had already assumed "personal rule" when the dowager-regent abdicated her regency in 1866. ILSN 142:26b-27a; Tabohashi Kiyoshi, Nissen kankei no kenkyū, I, 45-46; Choe, "Decade of the Taewongun," 518.

28. KJSL.III.246; KJSL.III.249, and Sŭngjŏngwŏn ilgi (Seoul: Kuksa p'yŏnch'an wiwŏnhoe ed., 1967), Kojong III (third volume, Kojong's reign), 619-620. Hereinafter referred to as SJW, Kojong III. When the original is cited, the notation will simply be SJW. KJSL.I.234; KJSL.II.12-13, 149-150, 224, 252, 299, 307-308, 317; KJSL.III.240-241, 288, 310; SJW, Kojong III, 538-539, 586-587, 632, 765, 773.

29. KJSL.III. 246, 1870.10.15.

30. The governor was royal lecturer that day. KJSL.III.249, SJW, Kojong III, 619-620, 1870.10.24.

31. *KJSL*.II.299, 1871.2.20.

32. *KJSL*.III.233, *SJW*, Kojong III, 573, 1870.8.25; *KJSL*.III.238, 1870.9.6. See also Yi Nŭng-hwa's remarks on the Taewongun's obtaining wood from gravesite land, Yi Nŭng-hwa, *Chosŏn kidokkyo kŭp oegyosa* (Keijō, 1928), II, 5-7.

33. *KJSL*.II.23, 1868.4.3.

34. *KJSL*.II.28, 1868.4.21.

35. *KJSL*.II.324, 1871.4.10; *KJSL*.II.328-329, 1871.4.17.

36. In ordering the abolition of corrupt private academies and the burial of their royal signboards or charters, Kojong declared that he had been so instructed by the Taewongun. The term for the order handed down by the Taewongun in this case was *punbu*, a term that was also utilized for other directives sent by the Taewongun to high officials. *KJSL*.III.240-241, *SJW*, Kojong III, 586-587, 1870.9.10; *KJSL*.III.310, 1871.3.10.

37. *KJSL*.II.121, 1869.1.2. Kojong also ordered that the regulations for the changes in title and rank of members of the royal clan be submitted to the Taewongun. *KJSL*.II.128, 1869.1.24.

38. The repair of shops burned in a fire was to be petitioned to the state council and reported to the Taewongun. *KJSL*.II.166, 1868.9.3. A similar case appears in *KJSL*.II.166, 1869.9.4. Kojong asked the headmaster of the National Academy (*Sŏnggyun'gwan*) to propose to the Taewongun the construction of additional dormitories, *KJSL*.III.167-168, 1869.9.13. Kojong asked the Ministry of Taxation to recommend to the Taewongun moving certain royal ancestral tablets to different shrines, *KJSL*. III.197, 1870.1.1. Kojong told the chief state councilor that revisions in the compilation of the *Orye p'yŏn'go*, a collection of regulations on ritual, should be petitioned to his father, *KJSL*.III.220, *SJW*, Kojong III, 520, 1870.5.20. In addition, Kojong also paid homage to two Taewongun of the past by visiting the shrines of the *Chŏn'gye taewŏn'gun*, Ch'ŏlchong's father, and the *Tŏkhŭng taewŏn'gun*, Sŏnjo's father, *KJSL*.I.601, 1867.8.16.

39. *KJSL*.I.256-257, 1865.4.12. He issued an edict in 1865 to include the P'ungyang Cho clan members on an examination roster. This was later rescinded when the dowager objected. *KJSL*.I.240-241, 1865.3.15; *KJSL*.I.243, 1865.3.17.

40. *KJSL*.I.365-372, 1866.2.27.

41. *KJSL*.I.393-394, 1866.5.6.

42. *KJSL*.III. 240, *SJW* Kojong III, 587, 1870.9.10; *KJSL*.II. 450-452, 1872.5.16-20; *KJSL*.II.454ff., 1872.6.7.

43. *KJSL*.III. 183-184, 1869.11.7; *KJSL*.III.223-224, *SJW*, Kojong III, 538, 1870.6.29.

44. *KJSL*.III.249-250, *SJW*, Kojong III, 620, 1870.10.24; *KJSL*.III.26, 1870.11.21; *KJSL*.II.317, *SJW*, Kojong III, 773, 1871.3.25.

45. *KJSL*.III. 220, *SJW*, Kojong III, 520, 1870.5.20. For a follow-up inquiry by the king, see *KJSL*.III. 223, *SJW*, Kojong III, 538, 1870.6.29.

46. *KJSL*.II. 362-363, 1871.7.20.

47. *KJSL*.II. 540, 1873.7.10; *KJSL*.II.544, 1873.8.26.

48. *KJSL*.II.518-519, 1873.3.5.

49. *KJSL*.III. 273, 1870.12.20.

50. See note 16.

51. *KJSL*.I.8, Ch'ŏlchong 14.12.13.

52. *KJSL*.I.43, 1864.1.15.

53. Kojong started with the *Classic of Filial Piety* (*Hyogyŏng, Hsiao-ching* in Chinese) and then proceeded to the *Small Learning* or classic for the young (*Sohak, Hsiao-hsüeh*), which he completed on November 1, 1867. He finished the *Great*

Learning (Taehak, Ta-hsüeh) in the next month and then started the Analects (Non'o, Lun-yü). KJSL.I.617, 1867.10.6; KJSL.I.620, 1867.11.1.

54. KJSL.I.210, 1864.12.13.

mn55. KJSL.III.240, SJW, Kojong III, 587, 1870.9.10. While it is true that major edicts were drafted by scholars for the king, Kojong's other actions on criminal matters and political crimes indicate that the sentiments expressed in this edict are his, if not the wording.

56. Ibid.

57. KJSL.II.450-452, 1872.5.16-20, 28; KJSL.II.454ff., 1872.6.7, 6.26.

58. KJSL.I.256-257, 1865.4.12.

59. KJSL.III.260-261, 1870.11.14.

60. KJSL.II.520, 1873.3.22.

61. KJSL.II.540, 1873.7.10.

62. KJSL.II.472, 1872.9.20; KJSL.II.543-544, 1873.8.10; KJSL.III.220, SJW, Kojong III, 520, 1870.5.20; KJSL.I.618, 1867.10.12.

63. SJW, 1873.10.27, 10.28, 10.30, 12.24, 12.28.

64. Choe, "Decade of the Taewongun," 121-122.

65. Ibid.; KJSL.I.175, 1864.8.27. On this latter date an order was issued for the restoration of ancestral rites to Yi Ha-jon. An heir was found for Yi in 1872, KJSL.II.465-466, 1872.7.30.

66. Choe, "Decade of the Taewongun," 121-122.

67. Ibid., 123; KJSL.I.151, 1864.7.11; KJSL.I.157, 1867.7.18; KJSL.I.158, 1864.7.20; KJSL.I.163, 1864.7.27; KJSL.I.169-70, 1864.8.11; KJSL.I.170, 1864.8.13; KJSL.II.465, 1872.7.25; KJSL.II.466, 1872.8.1; KJSL.II.492-93, 1872.12.16; KJSL.-II.514, 1873.2.22. Early in 1873, one of the leading officials of the Office of the Royal Genealogy, the Taewongun's elder brother, Yi Ch'oe-ŭng, reported to the throne that his agency had filled in all the missing places in the royal genealogies, changed the titles of nobles as ordered, and "washed out" the false crimes attributed to members of the royal family in the past. See KJSL.II.492-493, 1872.12.16.

According to Hwang Hyŏn, the Taewongun had a Grand Genealogy (Taedongbo) compiled and held a banquet for the royal clan at the Office of the Royal Genealogy, at which 60,000-70,000 men participated. The Taewongun was supposed to have remarked that he had obtained 100,000 crack troops for the state (i.e., the royal clan). Hwang Hyŏn, MCYR, 9.

68. Common generation names (tollimja) were not uniform for members of the same generation as they should have been. KJSL.II.13-14, 1868.3.2.

69. KJSL.I.220, 1865.1.5; KJSL.I.315, 1865.10.5. The Office of the Royal Genealogy (chongch'inbu) was in charge of the keeping of the genealogies of kings and branch lines of the royal house as well as all clothing and portraits or likenesses of royalty. Many of the office titles associated with the office had unlimited quotas, and they were usually assigned as sinecures or concurrencies to royal relations. Several new positions were created by the Taewongun.

The Office of the Royal Clan (tollyŏngbu) was in charge of all affairs pertaining to relatives of kings and female relations of royalty, including the consort families. Posts in this office were often given as sinecures to ex-chief state councilors or other high officials.

The Office of Princesses' Consorts (ibinbu) seems to have had no other functions than those implied by the title. Royal sons-in-law were given titles and posts in the office. See Taejŏn hoet'ong (Keijo, 1939), 68-73; Yi Sang-baek, Han'guksa kŭnse *chŏn'gip'yŏn*, 146-149. For the roster of incumbents in the Office of the Royal Genealogy in 1872, see *KJSL*.II.492-493, 1872.12.16.

70. The term "illegitimate" is used to describe the offspring of nobles and concubines. It would be more accurate to say that such people were of a lesser degree of legitimacy rather than illegitimate. In the case of the king, all the women of his harem—that is, in addition to the queen—had title and rank. Their sons could be designated crown prince in the absence of a son by the queen.

71. *KJSL*.II.122-123, 1869.1.2; *KJSL*.II.128, 1869.1.24; for the list of new regulations (*pyŏltan*), see *KJSL*.II. 128-132, 1869.1.25; *KJSL*.II.136, 1869.2.8; for the order granting posthumous posts to fathers and wives of *taegun* (princes by the queen) and *wangjagun* (princes by other palace ladies), see *KJSL*.III.241, 1870.9.13; for edict on marriage regulations for illegitimate nobility, see *KJSL*.II.122, 1869.1.2; for another edict restoring titles to nobility, see *KJSL*.II.436, 1872.7.16. Other minor posts were also opened up to the royal clan; *KJSL*.III.218, *SJW*, Kojong III, 510, 1870.5.5; *KJSL*.III.221, 1870.5.21.

72. *KJSL*.I.240-241, 1865.3.15. The dowager-regent, however, protested that members of her clan should not be given treatment equal to the royal house, so Kojong rescinded that portion of the previous day's order that pertained to the P'ungyang Cho clan. *KJSL*.I.243, 1865.3.17.

73. I am indebted to Edward W. Wagner for information on *munkwa* passers from 1865 to 1872.

74. *KJSL*.I.247, 1865.4.2; Hwang Hyŏn, *MCYR*, 9. In the early part of 1873 the king rewarded members of the royal clan who had made monetary contributions for military expenses and the construction of buildings by ordering that their names be added at the end of the literary and classics licentiate lists (*saengwŏn-chinsa pangmok*), *KJSL*.II.511, 1873.1.29; *KJSL*.II. 513, 1873.2.11. See also *KJSL*.II.514, 1873.2.20.

75. *KJSL*.I.548, 1867.2.5.

76. *KJSL*.I.631, *SJW*, Kojong III, 737, 1867.11.30. The event was marred, however, when it was discovered that ten men had taken the examination under false pretenses. Their names were not actually listed in the royal genealogy. It was ordered that in the future, the Office of the Royal Clan would have to examine the genealogies of all candidates in such examinations before allowing them to receive their degrees. *KJSL*.II.17, 1868.3.20. On this occasion five men were passed in the civil examinations and an indeterminate number in the military examinations. Another royal clan palace exam (*chŏnkwa* or *chŏngch'inkwa*) was held concurrently with a special *munkwa and mukwa* examination in 1868.4.11, *KJSL*.II.26.

77. *KJSL*.II.125, 1869.1.9; *KJSL*.II.416, 1872.1.7. Information on rosters supplied by Edward W. Wagner.

78. All members of the royal clan except *taegun, wangjagun, chŏk wangson* and *wangson* were eligible; that is, legitimate sons of kings (by queens), sons of kings by palace ladies, legitimate grandsons of kings, and grandsons of kings who traced their descent from a palace lady rather than a queen, respectively. *KJSL*.II.121, 1869.1.2. In 1873, it was ordered that four nobles be appointed to posts when vacancies occurred. *KJSL*.II.526, 1873.5.9.

79. *KJSL*.II.121, 1869.1.2. See article 39 of the new regulations pertaining to the royal clan, *KJSL*.II.131, 1869.1.25. King Kojong's half brother, Yi Chae-myŏn, passed the *munkwa* examination in 1864, before this decree was issued. Possibly he qualified on the grounds of distant relationship to King Yŏngjo. Kojong's cousin, Yi

Chae-gŭng, passed the *munkwa* in 1873. See Edward W. Wagner, ed., "The Harvard Edition of the *Mansŏng taedongbo*" (1967), 64a.
80. Information supplied by Edward W. Wagner.
81. *KJSL*.I.403, 1866.6.11.
82. *KJSL*.II.139, 1869.3.8.
83. *KJSL*.I.535, 1867.1.14; *KJSL*.I.535-536, 1867.1.15; *KJSL*.I.481, 1866.10.3; *KJSL*.I.576, 1867.5.7; *KJSL*.I.621, 1867, 1867.11.3; *KJSL*.II.235, 1870.8.25.
84. For a discussion of restoration in the Chinese context, see Mary Wright, *The Last Stand of Chinese Conservatism* (Palo Alto: Stanford University Press, 1957), chap. 4. In note *c*, p. 45, and in the text on that page, Mrs. Wright defines *chung-hsing* (Korean, *chunghŭng*) as "a new lease on life" or "restoration," and *wei-hsin* (Korean, *yusin*) as a new form of government under Ch'in Shih-huang-ti (221-210 B.C.), and as a modern term denoting general reform and modernization on the Meiji pattern (the *ishin* of *Meiji ishin*). The term had the connotation of spiritual spring cleaning and freshening up but was rarely used in mid-nineteenth century China.
85. For information on these institutions, especially in the early Yi dynasty, see *KSDSJ*, I, 670, II, 1100-1101; Yi Sang-baek, *Han'guksa kŭnse chŏn'gip'yŏn*, 145-166, especially the chart on p. 156, for administrative changes in the late fourteenth and early fifteenth centuries.
86. *KJSL*.II.55, 1868.7.2.
87. *SJW*, Kojong I, 639, 1865.4.1.
88. *KJSL*.I.246-247, *SJW*, Kojong I, 639, 1865.4.1; *KJSL*.I.248-250, *SJW*, Kojong I, 640-643, 1865.4.3.
89. *KJSL*.I.248-250, *SJW*, Kojong I, 640-643, 1865.4.3.
90. Yi Nŭng-hwa, *Chosŏn kidokkyo kŭp oegyosa*, II, 5. This is an uncorroborated secondary source.
91. Yi Sŏn-gŭn, *Han'guksa ch'oegŭnsep'yŏn*, 189; *SJW*, Kojong I, 668, 1865.4.29; *SJW*, Kojong II, 333, 1866.10.1; *SJW*, Kojong I, 678, 1865.5.5.
92. *SJW*, Kojong I, 640-643, 1865.4.3.
93. *KJSL*.I.250, *SJW*, Kojong I, 646, 1865.4.5. For a list of contributors and the awards in rank and office they received, see *KJSL*.I.480, *SJW*, Kojong II, 333-334, 1866.10.1. Referred to in Yi Sŏn-gŭn, *Han'guksa ch'oegŭnsep'yŏn*, 195.
94. Yi Nŭng-hwa, *Chosŏn kidokkyo kŭp oegyosa*, II, 5-6. Hwang Hyŏn also reported the people punning the term, *wŏnnap*. By substituting another Chinese character, its meaning was converted to "resented contributions" instead of "voluntary contributions." Hwang Hyŏn, *MCYR*, 4.
95. *KJSL*.I.252, *SJW*, Kojong I, 648, 1865.4.8.
96. *KJSL*.I.250, *SJW*, Kojong I, 646, 1865.4.5.
97. *KJSL*.II.470, 1872.9.16.
98. *Man'gi yoram*, *Chaeyong-p'yŏn* (Finance), compiled ca. 1808, 488-490, 553-567, hereinafter referred to as *MGYR*; *Chŭngbo munhŏnbigo*, preface dated 1907, 155:17b-20b. Hereinafter referred to as *MHBG*.
99. *SJW*, Kojong II, 92, 1866.3.6; Kikuchi Kenjō, *Kindai Chōsenshi*, 89, which refers to a fire in the *Kyŏnghoeru* on 1867.2.9. *KJSL*.I.549, 1867.2.9.
100. Ibid., 87.
101. For a report of Kojong's move to the completed palace, see *KJSL*.11.58, 1868.7.2.
102. For debate on the minting of the 100-cash (*tangbaekchŏn*), see *KJSL*.I.512-513, 1866.11.6; *SJW*, Kojong II, 375, same date. For the memorial reporting that the

Notes to pages 40-44

100-cash would begin to circulate on January 4, 1867, see *KJSL*.I.521, *SJW*, Kojong II, 399, 1866.12.1.

103. Kikuchi Kenjō, *Kindai Chōsenshi*, 87. This source notes that a land surtax (*kyŏltujŏn*) of 100 mun of cash per kyŏl on Kyŏnggi province alone netted an additional two million yang of cash. The *Kojang sillok* records that in 1868 the Taewongun issued a directive for a land surtax on the whole country. It was to be paid by all classes, including all those persons exempted from personal labor service. The new surtax was labeled a voluntary contribution. See the addendum to the entries for the day, *KJSL*.II.89, 1868.9.6. There is no corresponding entry for this day in the *Sŭngjŏngwŏn ilgi. KSDSJ*, I, 60, gives 1867 as the date. Yi Sŏn-gŭn remarked that the rate on the land tax, hitherto called the *kyŏltujŏn*, was raised, but he made no reference to primary sources. Yi Sŏn-gŭn, *Han'guksa ch'oegŭn-sep'yŏn*, 195, 196, 203.

104. Kikuchi, *Kindai Chōsenshi*, 89.

105. Yi Nŭng-hwa, *Chosŏn kidokkyo kŭp oegyosa*, II, 5.

106. *KJSL*.I.632, *SJW*, Kojong II, 748-749, 1867.12.17.

107. *KJSL*.II.26-27, *SJW*, Kojong II, 854, 1868.4.14.

108. *KJSL*.II.62, 1868.7.4.

109. *KJSL*.II.81, 1868.9.7.

110. *KJSL*.II.133, 1869.1.27.

111. *KJSL*.II.151-152, 1869.5.29.

112. *KJSL*.II.153, 1869.6.3; *KJSL*.II.155, 1869.6.11; *KJSL*.II.155, 1869.6.11. Construction work on the *munmyo*, or Confucian shrine, was completed on *KJSL*.II.167, 1869.9.10.

113. *KJSL*.III.199, 1870.1.12; *KJSL*.III.201, 1870.1.24; *KJSL*.III.206, 1870.2.27. Various estimates have been made by scholars of the total sum used in palace construction. Kikuchi Kenjō estimated that from mid-1865 to mid-1869, six million yang in voluntary contributions were collected and that the total cost of the Kyŏngbok Palace was fifteen million yang, *Kindai Chōsenshi*, 84, 89. Yi Sŏngŭn wrote that total expenses on Kyŏngbok Palace were 7,700,000 yang of "voluntary contributions" and several million man-hours of forced labor. *Han'guksa ch'oegŭnsep'yŏn*, 192, 198.

The figure of 7,700,000 yang is corroborated by the sources, but since this amount represents the total of voluntary contributions alone and does not take into account transfers of regular tax funds, Kikuchi's estimate may be closer to the mark. See *KJSL*.II.470, 1872.9.16. On this date the Construction Bureau reported a total of 7,838,694 yang of cash collected in voluntary contributions.

3. Merit and Privilege in the Recruitment of Men

1. Kim Chwa-gŭn, the brother of King Sunjo's queen, had been appointed chief state councilor for the fourth time in his career on October 20, 1863. He resigned from this post on May 23, 1864, at the age of sixty-seven. For the next two years he held sinecures in the Office of Ministers-without-portfolio (*chungch'ubu*) and the Office of the Royal Clan (*tollyŏngbu*). In June 1864 he was appointed to the commission for the compilation of *The Veritable Record of King Ch'ŏlchong* (*Ch'ŏlchong sillok*), and two months later was made chief of this committee. On May 7, 1866, only three years before his death, he was appointed the chief of the newly restored Three Army Command (*samgunbu*), probably the highest military agency under the Taewongun. Despite the fact that the responsibilities of this post may only have been nominal, his appointment to it indicates a certain degree of favor by the Taewongun. Kim Chwa-gŭn's continued access to the throne as an elder statesman was guaranteed by his

prestigious sinecures. See *KJSL*.III.119-120, 1864.4.24; *CSS*.6.4.20, 1864.4.29; *CSS*.6.4.23, 1864.6.2; *KJSL*.III.340, 1866.1.11; *CSS*.6.4.199, 1869.4.25; *CSS*.6.4.166, 1868.3.23.

Kim Hŭng-gŭn, a third cousin of Kim Chwa-gŭn, resigned from his post as first minister in the Office of the Royal Clan on February 4, 1865, on the grounds of illness. He was sixty-nine at the time. *CSS*.6.4.34, 1865.1.9.

Kim Pyŏng-gi, the son of Kim Chwa-gŭn, was appointed minister of war, and on March 28, fifth state councilor in the state council. On November 4, 1867, he became minister of personnel, and on April 15, 1868, the second ranking official in the newly restored Three Army Command. Finally, on May 13, 1873, he was appointed again to the post of minister of personnel only two years before his death in 1875 at the age of fifty-seven. *CSS*.6.4.37, 42, 64, 155, 166, 293. According to Yi Sŏn-gŭn, Kim Pyŏng-gi was the actual leader of the Andong Kim at this time. In Yi's view, most of the Andong Kim leaders left their posts or were transferred to minor ones as a result of a purge by the Taewongun, but this is not confirmed by the evidence. *Han'guksa ch'oegŭnsep'yŏn*, 165.

2. *CSS*.6.4.9, 10, 42, 43, 52, 129, 146, 147, 175, 252.

3. *CSS*.6.3. 319, 435, 533, 541, 554, 629, 632, 640-641, 660. Andong Kim officials also participated in the Reform Bureau of 1862. See the *Imsul ijŏngch'ŏng tŭngnok* in *Imsullok* (Seoul, 1958 ed.), 297ff.

4. As second state councilor in 1866 he proposed the minting of the 100-cash. *CSS*.6.4.129, 1866.11.6. In 1871 he asked for the surcharge on the land tax to provide funds for the defense of Kanghwa Island, *CSS*.6.4.252, 1871.5.25. He supported the construction of the Kyŏngbok palace. See Chapter 2.

5. The queen was the adopted daughter of Min Ch'i-rok. The Taewongun's wife's brother, Min Sŭng-ho, the reputed leader of the clan, had been adopted as Min Ch'i-rok's son. Yi Sŏn-gŭn, *Han'guksa ch'oegŭnsep'yŏn*, 343-344.

6. The following table lists the most important relations of Queen Min and the posts that they held up to 1873.

Name	Relationship	Post (official rank)	Year of appointment
Min Sŭng-ho	Queen's brother by adoption. Son of Min Ch'i-gu. Real brother of Min Kyŏm-ho and Min T'ae-ho	Headmaster of the National Academy	1866
		Third Minister in the Ministry of Personnel (3A)	1866
		First Counselor in the Office of Special Counselors	1866
		Second Minister in the Ministries of Taxation, Works, Personnel (2B)	1867
		Minister of Rites, Punishment (2A)	1872
		Magistrate of Suwŏn	1872
		Minister of War	1873

continued

Name	Relationship	Post (official rank)	Year of appointment
Min Kyu-ho	Brother of Min T'ae-ho (not the same person as the brother of Min Sŭng-ho). Son of Min Ch'i-o	Third Minister in the Ministry of Personnel (3A)	1867
		Second Minister of Punishments (2B)	1869
		Second Minister of Personnel	1873
		Minister of Rites (2A)	1874
		Sixth State Councilor	1874
		Deputy Director of the Office of Special Counselors	1875
		Seventh State Councilor	1875
		Magistrate of Seoul	1875
		Commander of the *Muwiso* palace guards	1875
Min T'ae-ho	Brother of Min Kyu-ho. Real father of Min Yŏng-ik.	Governor of Hwanghae province (2B)	1873
		Governor of Kyŏnggi province	1874
Min Ch'i-gu	Father of Min Sŭng-ho, Min Kyom-ho, and Min T'ae-ho. Father-in-law of the Taewongun.	Third Minister of Works	1863
		Minister of Works	1864
		Magistrate of Kwangju	1865
		Chief Magistrate of the State Tribunal (1B)	1868
		Deputy Director of the Office of the Royal Clan) (1B)	1868
		Minister of Works (2A)	1869
Min Ch'i-sang	Shares common fourth generation ancestor with Min Ch'i-gu	First Royal Secretary at the time of Kojong's accession (3A)	1864
		Minister of Punishments (2A)	1870
		Minister of Rites	1872
		Minister of Works	1872
		Minister of War	1872

The above information is based on Yi Sŏn-gǔn, *Han'guksa ch'oegǔnsep'yŏn*, 347, note 1, and Kim Haeng-ja, "Minbi chipkwŏn'gi Hanjŏn taeoe kwan'gye ǔi kukche chŏngch'ijŏk koch'al," Master's thesis, Ihwa taehakkyo, 1966, 104-122. Miss Kim's chart includes posts to 1894. Supplemental information was added from the *Mansŏng taedongbo* (Seoul, n.d.), II. For a genealogical chart of the Min clan, see Yi Sang-baek, *Han'guksa kǔnse hugip'yŏn*, facing p. 396.

7. Yi Sŏn-gŭn, *Han'guksa ch'oegŭnsep'yŏn*, 343-344; Yi Sang-baek, *Han'guksa kŭnse hugip'yŏn*, 395, note 1.

8. Gregory Henderson, *Korea: the Politics of the Vortex* (Cambridge, Mass., 1968), 265.

9. Song Nak-hun, "Han'guk tangjaengsa," in *Han'guk munhwasa taegye* (Seoul, 1965), II, 282-288.

10. Ibid., 319-345.

11. Ibid., 383ff; Yi Sang-baek, *Han'guksa kŭnse hugip'yŏn*, 56-62. Pp. 1-56 cover the earlier history of factionalism in the Yi.

12. Sŏng Nak-hun, "Han'guk tangjaengsa," 378-383.

13. Ibid., 378-383; Yi Sang-baek, *Han'guk kŭnse hugip'yŏn*, 62-66; Oda Shōgo, "Richō no hōtō o ryakujo shite Tenshukyo ni oyobu," in *Seikyū gakusō* (1931), I, 9-10; Tabohashi Kiyoshi, *Kindai Nissen kankei no kenkyū* I, 2-7; Yi Nŭng-hwa, *Chosŏn kidokkyo kŭp oegyosa*, I, 113; Urakawa Wasaburō, *Chōsen junkyōshi*, 94-95.

14. Oda Shōgo, "Richō no hōtō," I, 9-10; Urakawa, *Chōsen junkyōshi*, 95. Many officials remained neutral on the question. See Oda, 9-10; Urakawa, 95. In *KSDSJ*, I, 807, it states that most of the *sip'a* were Southerners and most of the *pyŏkp'a* were Patriarchs. This opinion does not seem to be justified in the light of the opinions of the scholars quoted here.

15. During Chŏngjo's reign, Hong Kug-yŏng, a brother of a royal concubine, gained royal favor and first place at court. Hong's factional credentials are not clear, but we know that when both his sister and the prince whom he was backing for investiture as crown prince died, he was forced out of power by the attacks of the *pyŏkp'a*, led by Dowager Kim, Yŏngjo's second queen. Tabohashi, *Kindai Nissen kankei no kenkyū*, I, 6.

16. In the 1790s, Ch'ae Che-gong, who has been identified as a Southerner-*sip'a*, became second state councilor and achieved a brief period of dominance at court. At this time there happened to be many Southerners who were Catholics and most of the important ones reputedly belonged to Ch'ae's *sip'a* faction. There was also a Southerner-*pyŏkp'a* faction opposed to Ch'ae, and in 1791 one of its members, Ch'oe Hŏn-jung, attacked the Catholics. Under Ch'ae's protection Catholic persecution was muted and Southerner Catholics like Yi Ka-hwan were also shown favor by Chŏngjo. Ch'ae Che-gong lost power around 1795, but the Catholics were saved from persecution by Chŏngjo. Ch'ae Che-gong, however, was neither Catholic nor pro-Catholic.

Oda Shogō has suggested that there was a change in the nature of factionalism in the eighteenth century. The *sip'a-pyŏkp'a* dispute served to shift the locus of political struggle from the outer bureaucracy to the inner court, a process that had begun at the time of the contest over Kwanghaegun's succession in the early seventeenth century.

For the above, see Urakawa, 94-96; Yi Nŭng-hwa, I, 54-57; Ching Young Choe, "The Decade of the Taewongun," 256; Oda Shogō, 8, and *Chŏngjo sillok*, Chŏngjo 12.8.3, for Ch'ae Che-gong's attitude on Catholicism.

17. Urakawa, 97; Yi Nŭng-hwa, I, 113; Tabohashi, I, 8; Yi Sang-baek, *Han'guksa kŭnse hugip'yŏn*, 320-325.

18. Yi Pyŏng-do, *Han'guksa taegwan* (Seoul, 1964), 460; Tabohashi, I, 7; Yi Sang-baek, *Han'guksa kŭnse hugip'yŏn*, 328ff.

19. According to the study by Yu Hong-nyŏl, the Andong Kim, who were *sip'a*, were lenient toward the Catholics, many of whom were Southerner-*sip'a*. Thus, Chŏng Yag-yong, the famous *Sirhak* scholar, Catholic, and Southerner, was released from exile in 1818.

When Hŏnjong became king in 1834, Sunjo's queen, daughter of Kim Chosun and a Patriarch-*sip'a*, became regent; and there were no persecutions of Catholics. But Cho Man-yong of the P'ungyang Cho clan and a relative of Ikchong's queen took over hegemony at court from the Andong Kim in 1839 and held it until his death in 1846. It was then, in 1839, that a persecution of Catholics was carried out.

Yu did not mention what Cho's factional affiliation was. Whether his anti-Catholicism made him pro-*pyŏkp'a*, anti-*sip'a*, and anti-Southerner, we cannot know. The P'ungyang Cho clan was not without its own Catholics. In 1868 Cho Ch'ŏl-chung, a member of the clan and a Catholic, was forced to commit suicide to escape arrest for his religious beliefs, for aiding and abetting native Catholics in escaping to China, and for helping Western gunboats come to Korea.

Hŏnjong died in 1849 without an heir, and his successor, King Ch'ŏlchong, was chosen by Dowager Kim, Sunjo's queen and a Patriarch-*sip'a*. Ch'ŏlchong was a grandson of Prince Un'an (Un'an-gun), a younger brother of King Chŏngjo. During Chŏngjo's reign, Prince Un'an and his youngest son were exiled, and his eldest son, Prince Sanggye, was executed for treason in 1786. It is not clear why these princes were punished, but Yu Hong-nyŏl pointed out that the wives of both Prince Un'an and his son, Prince Sanggye, were baptized by the Chinese missionary, Chou Wen-mo, at the turn of the century. They were later executed during the persecution of 1801. Prince Un'an was given poison even though he was not a Catholic.

Yu believes that Ch'ŏlchong carried out no persecutions of Catholics because he had Catholics in his own family, and also because his reign was dominated by the lenient Patriarch-*sip'a* Andong Kim. See Yu Hong-nyŏl, *Kojong ch'iha Sŏhak sunan ŭi yŏn'gu*, passim, and *Han'guk Ch'onjugyohoesa*, passim.

20. *KJSL*.I.128, *SJW*, Kojong I, 272, 1864.5.18, June 21.

21. *KJSL*.I.153, *SJW*, Kojong I, 335, 1864.7.14. For protests, see *KJSL*.I.149, *SJW*, Kojong I, 328, 1864.7.10; *CSS*.6.4.25-26, *KJSL*.I.150-151, *SJW*, Kojong I, 329-331, 1864.7.11. See also Hwang Hyŏn, *MCYR*, 14, 18.

22. *KJSL*.I.153, 1864.7.15; *KJSL*.I.156, 1864.7.18; *KJSL*.I.156, 1864.7.18; *KJSL*.I.157, 1864.7.19; *KJSL*.I.157-158, 1864.7.20; *KJSL*.I.158, 1864.7.21; *KJSL*. I.160, 1864.1.25.

23. This was Han Hyo-sun who brought charges against Sŏnjo's queen, the Inmok-daebi. Han was second and third state councilor during Kwanghaegun's reign. The *Sŏin* (Westerners—parent faction of the Patriarch's and Disciples' factions) were responsible for the deposing of Kwanghaegun and the Injo Restoration of 1623. Han Hyo-sun was posthumously stripped of his office and rank. For details in English, see James B. Palais, "Korea on the Eve of the Kanghwa Treaty," Ph.D. diss., Harvard University, 1968, 831, note 60; *Han'guksa yŏnp'yo*, 243; *CSS*.5.1, 1618.1.4. (Kwanghaegun 10); *CSJMJS*, 1800; *KSDSJ*, II, 1247, 1690; *KSDSJ*, I, 165; Yi Pyŏng-do, *Han'guksa taegwan* (Seoul, 1964), 406ff; Yi Ki-baek, *Kuksa sillon* (Seoul, 1961), 251.

24. These were Mok Nae-sŏn, Yi Pong-jin, and Yi Hyŏn-il. For descriptions of the incidents involved in the 1689 and 1694 incidents see Ching Young Choe, "Decade of the Taewongun," 513, note 51; *KSDSJ*, I, 478, II, 1236; *CSJMJS*, 470-471; Yi Pyŏng-do, *Han'guksa taegwan*, 413ff.; Song Nak-hun, "Han'guk tangjaengsa," 334-345; Yi Sang-baek, *Han'guksa kŭnse hugip'yŏn*, 43ff.; Hwang Hyŏn, *MCYR*, 14, 18.

25. For the text of the memorial, see *KJSL*.I.156-157, *SJW*, Kojong I, 343-344, 1864.7.18.

26. Ibid.

27. *KJSL*.I.157-160, 1864.7.19, 7.20, 7.21, 7.25. They were released on 7.25 in

honor of the dowager-regent's birthday. For the transfer of the censorate members, see *KJSL*.I.153, 1864.7.15.

28. Hwang Hyŏn, *MCYR*, 3.

29. Yu Hu-jo and Han Kye-wŏn of the Southerners and Im Paek-kyŏng and Kang No of the Northerners were appointed state councilors. The Southerner Cho Sŏng-gyo and the Northerner Kim Se-ho were both appointed *taejehak* in the Office of Special Counselors. Ibid., 4. These issues have been covered in Ching Young Choe, *The Rule of the Taewŏn'gun*, 52-63.

30. Hwang Hyŏn, *MCYR*, 5, 21.

31. Ibid., 5, 21.

32. Choe, *The Rule of the Taewŏn'gun*, 58-59.

33. Hwang Hyŏn, *MCYR*, 4, 18. Hwang wrote that Han Kye-wŏn and Kang No were both exiled later because they were "guests" or henchmen of the Taewongun. Ibid., 45.

34. Ibid., 7. Hwang Hyŏn mentioned several other military officials also known as the Taewongun's "tools." Sin Kwan-ho (later known as Sin Hŏn) was favored by the Taewongun for his military skills.

35. Ibid., 9.

36. Yi Nŭng-hwa, *Chosŏn kidokkyo kŭp oegyosa*, II, 6.

37. The five men were Han Ki-dong, Ch'oe Pong-gu, Ch'ae Tong-sul, and Kwŏn Chŏng-ho, and also Chŏng Hyŏn-dŏk. Kwŏn and Ch'ae were the ones involved in the plot. Hwang, *MCYR*, 21.

38. According to Hwang the Taewongun resented the Andong Kim, the Yŏhŭng Min and some of the Sim clan, *MCYR*, 3, 4, 20. For Kim Po-hyŏn, who was later favored by the Min, see *MCYR*, 22-23. Those who resented the treatment they received included relatives of Dowager Cho, the Taewongun's own brother, Yi Ch'oe-ŭng, and his son and son-in-law, Yi Chae-myŏn and Cho Kyŏng-ho. Hwang mentioned the supposed conspiracy between Kojong and his brother Yi Chae-myŏn against their father's usurpation of power. *MCYR*, 9, 17, 22.

39. The traditional view about discrimination against inhabitants of the northern provinces in examinations and appointments to office has been refuted by Edward Wagner, who reported a sharp rise in the number of degree-holders in the northern provinces after 1775. He found no evidence of unusual discrimination against this section of the country. In fact, the northerners may have fared better in proportion to their population than examination candidates from Kyŏngsang province. See Edward W. Wagner, "The Ladder of Success in Yi Dynasty Korea," in *Occasional Papers on Korea*, 1 (June 1972), 7-8. For the more traditional view, see Ching Young Choe, *The Rule of the Taewŏn'gun*, 59-62; Yi Sang-baek, *Han'guksa kŭnse hugip'yŏn*, 335-344; *KSDSJ*, II, 1739-1740.

40. *KJSL*.I,126, 1864.5.12; *KJSL*.I.481, 1866.10.3; *KJSL*.I.514, 1866.11.13; *KJSL*.I.535, 1867.1.14; *KJSL*.I.535-536, 1867.1.15; *KJSL*.II.426, 1872.3.4; *KJSL*.II.428-429, 1872.3.5.

In 1872 special examinations for the Wang clan were held in conjunction with a royal progress to the Kaesong detached palace where Kojong performed rites at the Confucian shrine and at the shrine of T'aejo of Koryŏ. At the time, five men passed the *munkwa* examinations (a *chŏngsi*) and twenty-six passed the military or *mukwa* examination. One of the passers was appointed directly to the Office of Special Counselors (*Hongmun'gwan*). *KJSL*.II.426-429, 1872.3.4,3.5. Kojong was accompanied at the time by the royal secretary, Wang Chŏng-yang, who had passed a special Songdo examination in 1867, and had at that time been promoted directly to the post of third minister of the Ministry of War. *KJSL*.I.535, 1867.1.14.

In one case the new policy providing special opportunity for certain regions came into conflict with regulations for objectivity and impartiality. When one scholar from Cheju Island publicly revealed that he came from Cheju, he was indicted by a censor for breaking the rule forbidding candidates to reveal their place of origin. The king ordered the man conscripted into the army, but he also reconfirmed the decision to show special consideration for Cheju. See *KJSL*.I.126, 1864.5.12.

41. *KJSL*.III.178-179, *SJW*, Kojong III, 341, 1869.10.11.

42. *KJSL*.I.514, 1866.11.11.

43. Recruitment into the leadership ranks of the military was still based on skill in the use of archaic weapons such as the bow and musket. My conclusions about the significance of this incident are diametrically opposed to the view of Ching Young Choe, who regarded this case as a good example of the widening of opportunity. See Choe, *The Rule of the Taewŏn'gun*, 63.

44. *KJSL*.II.140, 1869.3.8.

45. *KJSL*.II.446, 1872.4.30. Some concern was also shown for illegitimate sons of yangban and for providing opportunity for office for them. Without further study, it is hard to say whether they were actually given such opportunity. See *KJSL*.I.282, 1865.6.10.

46. *KJSL*.III, 274, 1870.12.26.

47. Between 1669 and 1731 the law was changed five times. The offspring of slave fathers and commoner mothers were alternately *ch'ŏnmin* and commoner. After 1731 they were commoners. Shikata Hiroshi, "Chōsen jinkō ni kansuru ichi kenkyū," 90-92. See notes 4-8, chap. 6, especially the articles by Hiraki Makoto.

48. *KJSL*.II.116, 1868.12.15; *KJSL*.II.514, 1873.2.12; *KJSL*.I.548, 1867.2.4; *KJSL*.II.306-307, 1871.3.15.

49. Hwang Hyŏn's account of the examination system deplored the degree of corruption in it, especially the sale of degrees. *MCYR*, 34-41.

50. *KJSL*.I.404-405, 1866.6.18; *KJSL*.III.205, 1870.2.16; *KJSL*.III.206, *SJW*, Kojong III, 447, 1870.2.30. For the list of those recommended by Minister-without-portfolio Yi Yu-wŏn, Chief State Councilor Kim Pyŏng-hak, and Third State Councilor Hong Sun-mok, see *KJSL*.III.212, *SJW*, Kojong III, 468, 1870.3.19. For other references to special recommendations, see *KJSL*.III.212, 1870.3.19; *KJSL*.II.348, 1871.5.25, which order was issued after the U.S. expedition to Kanghwa Island and was designed to recruit able military officials; *KJSL*.II.462, 1872.7.10; *KJSL*.II.488, 1872.12.4, which simply exempted specially recommended first appointees to magistrate's posts from the ordinary review procedure (*sŏgyŏng*) of the censorate.

51. *KJSL*.III.216-217, *SJW*, Kojong III, 504, 1870.4.27; *SJW*, Kojong III, 539. These orders required that candidates for posts for the Office of Special Counselors and Office of Literary Affairs (*yemun'gwan*) were to be recommended for posts in the Royal Lectures, and that those who held posts in the Royal Lectures and the other of the above two offices were to be directly recommended for second minister of personnel, or for service in the National Academy (*sŏnggyun'gwan*).

52. Chief State Councilor Kim Pyŏng-hak stated that police officials had to have prior military service in military agencies. Kim deplored the appointment of two men lacking these qualifications. *KJSL*.II.366, 1871.7.29.

53. *KJSL*.I.284, 1865.6.15. For a list of awards to good magistrates after a review session (*chŏnch'oe*), see *KJSL*.I.404-405, 1866.6.18.

54. *CSS*.6.4.14, 1864.3.3; *CSS*.6.4.60, 1865.11.10. On this date censors were sent out to Kyŏnggi and the three southern provinces to check on the disbursement of relief. *CSS*.6.4.145, 1867.4.23; *CSS*.6.4.149, 1867.6.5; *KJSL*.I.609-610, 1867.9.17; *CSS*.6.4.151, 1867.7.23; *CSS*.6.4.154, 1867.9.17; also consult *CSS* from 1868.10.8 to 11.10.

55. The secret censor for Kongch'ung province (modern Ch'ungch'ŏng) was arrested for failing to report crimes and failing to investigate cases of some local bad magnates (*t'oho*). *CSS*.6.4.145, 1867.4.23. The censor for Kyŏngsang province was dismissed for failing to report on a bad local magnate. *CSS*.6.4.151, 1867.7.23.

56. *SJW*, Kojong II, 333-334, 1866.10.1, for the most complete list; *CSS*.6.4.129, 1866.11.8; *KJSL*.I.591-592, 1867.7.10; *KJSL*.II.153, 1869.6.3, which provided that those who contributed to the establishment of artillery batteries in Chŏlla and Ch'ungch'ŏng provinces were to be given first posts as magistrates; *KJSL*.II.417, 1872.1.10, records people who contributed to relief in Hamgyŏng province with the promise of an appointment to office.

57. The information on appointments was gathered from the pertinent volume of the *Chōsenshi*; that is, *CSS*.6.4. This work does not include all appointments to all offices, and there may also be omissions in the appointments to higher offices; but it probably can be relied on to give a general picture, if not a completely accurate one.

The number of appointments to the posts of second and third minister of personnel, as found in the *Chōsenshi*, are much lower than those for first minister. During this period, only six persons are listed as having occupied the post of second minister and thirteen persons for third minister. This may be due to the incompleteness of the *Chōsenshi* or it may be possible that lesser officials were the duty officers and spent longer periods of time on the job.

58. As in the case of the Ministry of Personnel, only two or three men are listed in the *Chōsenshi* as having been appointed second and third ministers.

59. Kim Pyŏng-guk held the post from May 29, 1866 (4.16 lunar) to October 30, 1872 (9.29 lunar). See *CSS*.6.4. under the pertinent dates. Kim Se-gyun held the post from October 30, 1872 (9.29 lunar) to December 15, 1874 (11.7 lunar). *CSS* 6.4., passim.

60. Kikuchi Kenjō, *Kindai Chōsenshi*, I, 70.

61. Ibid., 80, 101, 148. Chŏng was missing from this conference.

4. Land Distribution and Taxation

1. Several excellent studies of the late Yi dynasty land, population, and tax systems have come out in recent years. Kim Yong-sŏp has probably achieved the most prodigious effort in this field, and most of his articles have been collected and published in two volumes, *Chosŏn hugi nong'ŏpsa yŏn'gu: nongch'ong kyŏngje, sahoe pyŏndong* (Seoul: Ilchogak, 1970), and *Chosŏn hugi nong'ŏpsa yŏn'gu: nong'ŏp pyŏndong, nonghak sajo* (Seoul: Ilchogak, 1971). The first of these volumes contains articles of more relevance to this chapter; such as his work on land registers, patterns of land tenure, ownership and tenancy, palace estates, the role of social status in land tenure, and social change in the late Yi dynasty.

One very important article of his that is not included in these two volumes is his "Kwangmu yŏn'gan ŭi yangjŏn saŏpe kwanhan ilyŏn'gu," *Asea yŏn'gu*, 11.3 (September 1968), 81-202, English summary, 203-210.

Other recent works of great value are Han Woo-keun (Han U-gŭn), *Tonghangnan kiin e kwanhan yŏn'gu* (Seoul: Seoul Taehakkyo mullikwa taehak, Hanguk munhwa yŏn'guso, 1971), esp. pp. 88-121, and Kim Chin-bong, "Imsul millan ŭi sahoe kyŏngjejŏk paegyŏng," Sahak yŏn'gu, 19 (April 1967), 89-127. A useful reference is the recent publication by the North Korean scholar Pak Si-hyŏng, Chosŏn t'oji chedosa, II (Pyongyang, 1961).

Other useful more general works of slightly older vintage are Han Woo-keun, Yijo hugi ŭi sahoe wa sasang (Seoul, 1961), 1-131; Ch'ŏn Kwan-u "Han'guk t'oji chedosa," II in Han'guk munhwasa taegye, II (Seoul, 1965), 1381-1430; Yi Sang-baek, Han'guksa kŭnse chŏn'gip'yŏn (Seoul, 1962), 40-51, 344-385; Yi Sang-baek, Han'guksa, kŭnse hugip'yŏn (Seoul, 1965), 155-80 et passim; Yi Sŏn-gŭn, Han'guksa, ch'oegŭnsep'yŏn (Seoul, 1961), 36-90 et passim; Kim Yong-sŏp, "Nongch'on kyŏngje," part of the Conference on Social Change in the Late Yi Dynasty, Sahak yŏn'gu, 16 (December 1963), 96-105.

For important Japanese summaries of the Yi dynasty land system, see Richo jidai no zaisei (Chōsen sōtokufu, 1936); Wada Ichiro, Chōsen no tochi seido oyobi jisei seido chōsa hōkokusho (Keijō, 1920); Chōsen tensei-kō (Keijō: Chōsen sōtokufu, chūsūin, 1940).

2. Yi Sang-baek, Han'guksa kŭnse chŏn'gip'yŏn, 407; Richō jidai no zaisei, hereinafter referred to as RCZS, 38; MHBG 141:15a-b; Han Woo-keun, Yijo hugi, 13-16, points out that by 1769 there was 1,310,000 kyŏl registered, but only 800,000 was silgyŏl or taxable land. Cho Ki-jun, Han'guk kyŏngjesa, 188ff., reported 1,655,234 kyŏl during Sejong's reign (1418-51), and 1,701,000 kyŏl before Hideyoshi's invasions.

3. MGYR, chaeyongp'yŏn, 197; Kim Yong-sŏp, "Yang'an ŭi yŏn'gu: Chosŏn hugi ŭi nonka kyŏngje," pt. 1, in Sahak yŏn'gu (May 1960), 3. The article is reprinted in Kim's Chosŏn hugi nong'ŏpsa yŏn'gu (1970). Taejŏn hoet'ong (Keijō, 1939), 208.

4. For land surveys, see MHBG 141:15a-23a; Yi Sang-baek, Han'guksa kŭnse hugip'yŏn, 170; RCZS, 38-39, 41; Kim Yong-sŏp, "Yang'an ŭi yŏn'gu," pt. 1, 34; MGYR, chaeyongp'yŏn, 201ff.

5. See note 2.

6. Han Woo-keun, Yijo hugi, 14-18; RCZS, 37-61; Yi Sŏn-gŭn, Han'guksa ch'oegŭnsep'yon, 54; Kim Yong-sŏp, "Yang'an ŭi yŏn'gu," I, 32-45; Kim Chin-bong, "Imsul millan ŭi sahoe," 33. Kim also cited reports of resistance to a resurvey in 1819 by large landowners.

7. Kim Chin-bong, "Imsul millan ŭi sahoe," 98-100; Han Woo-keun, Tonghangnan kiin e kwanhan yŏn'gu, 88-109, Han's survey focuses mainly on the period from 1864 to 1894.

8. Kim Chin-bong, "Imsul millan ŭi sahoe," 99, based on Asō Takekame, Chōsen tensei-kŏ.

Year	Amounts of Tax-exempt "Damaged Land" (in kyŏl)
1802	23,296
1814	195,777
1838	89,468
1844	26,907
1853	82,221
1855	24,309

9. *MHBG* 148:12a, 13b. For material on the land tax and surtaxes, see *MHBG*, 148, 149; Yi Sang-baek, *Han'guksa kŭnse hugip'yŏn*, 169-180; Hong I-sŏp, *Chŏng Yag-yong ŭi chŏngch'i kyŏngje sasang yŏn'gu* (Seoul, 1959), 113-114; Wada, *Chōsen no tochi seido*, 641-688; Yi Sŏn-gŭn, *Han'guksa ch'oegŭnsep'yŏn*, 54-60; *RCZS*, 69ff., 86-112, 169-191, 200-203, 206-246; Han Woo-keun, *Yijo hugi*, 33-38; Kim Yong-sŏp, "Yang'an ŭi yŏn'gu," pt. 2 in *Sahak yŏn'gu*, 8 (November 1960), 104-107; Pak Si-hyŏng, *Chosŏn to'oji chedosa*, 313-325; Han Woo-keun, *Yijo hugi*, 34; *RCZS*, 69; Wada, *Chosen no tochi seido*, 648; *Soktaejon* (Keijō, 1935), 158.

On 1874.4.12 (May 15), both Kojong and royal lecturer, Kim Se-gyun, deplored the heavy tax burden on the individual peasant. In addition to the regular tax burden, the peasant suffered the extortion of corrupt clerks and officials. Kim Se-gyun noted that the tax levies on each kyŏl of land were as follows,

Kind of tax	Tax rate
Land tax	4 tu/kyŏl (where 15 tu equal 1 sŏk
Taedong (tribute)	12 tu/kyŏl
Samsuryang (military support surcharge)	1.5-2.5 tu/kyŏl
Kyŏlchŏn (cash surtax on land)	5 chŏn/kyŏl (where 100 chŏn equal 1 yang) (equivalent to approximately 5-1 tu/sok at at a 3-7 yang/sŏk commutation rate)
P'oryang (military tax)	1 tu/kyŏl
Total	Approximately 20 tu/kyŏl maximum

This estimate was only one fifth that of contemporary scholars, *SJW, ILSN* 151: 44b-45b.

10. *RCZS*, 86ff., 94ff.; Hong I-sŏp, *Chŏng Yag-yong*, 114. Kim Yong-sŏp, relying on the material presented in Chŏng Yag-yong's works, estimated the total of regular taxes as 21 tu/kyŏl, but the total of all taxes including surcharges as over 100 tu/kyŏl. *MGYR*, chaeyongp'yŏn, 197, also estimates 100 tu/kyŏl. See Kim Yong-sŏp, "Yang'an ŭi yŏn'gu," pt. 2, 106ff., for estimates of net agricultural income; this article is also reprinted in his *Chosŏn hugi nong'ŏpsa yŏn'gu* (1970). Wada, *Chōsen no tochi seido*, 651.

11. Kim Chin-bong estimated the per kyŏl tax rate in two areas he studied at 57.9 and 63.4 tu/kyŏl. Calculating also the grain equivalents of the military cloth tax and grain loan obligations, however, the total per kyŏl burden on the cultivator came to 134.8 and 172.7 tu/kyŏl. Kim Chin-bong, "Imsul millan ŭi sahoe," 108-114, chart on p. 112.

12. Kim Yong-sŏp, "Chosŏn hugi ŭi nong'ŏp," 81.

13. *MGYR*, chaeyongp'yŏn, 198; *RCZS*, 42; Yi Sang-baek, *Han'guksa kŭnse chŏn'gip'yŏn*, 166.

14. Kim Yong-sŏp, "Kwangmu yŏn'gan ŭi yangjŏn," 113, 119.

15. Franz Schurmann, *Ideology and Organization in Communist China* (Berkeley, Calif.: University of California Press, 1966, 2nd ed.), xxxvii.

16. *Sejong sillok*, Sejong 6.3.kihae, cited in Pak Pyŏng-ho, *Han'guk pŏpchesa t'ŭksu yŏn'gu: Yijo sidae ŭi pudongsan maemae kŭp tanbobŏp* (Seoul, 1960), 1-2; Pak Pyŏng-ho, "Han'guk kŭnse ŭi t'oji soyukwŏn e kwan han yŏn'gu," 1, in *Seoul*

taehakkyo pŏphak, 8:1 (1966), 87. This notice, and other evidence dated a year or two before cited by Pak, indicates that land and property sales occurred even before this date. The governor of Kyŏnggi province memorialized the throne that people had been forced to sell their lands because of funeral expenses, debts, payment of fines or poverty, but that the officials had been confiscating the money paid for the purchase of land (because the sale of land was a violation of the prohibition against land sales). The governor noted that the sale of house sites and vegetable plots in the capital were legal. It was only in the outer areas (of the province) that land sales were prohibited. He asked that the prohibition against sales be lifted, and this was approved by the king.

The same item is carried in *Chōsenshi* (Keijō: Chōsen Sōtokufu, 1935), series 4, no. 3, p. 16. Hereinafter cited as *CSS*.4.3.16, but it mistakenly records that this request was not approved by the king.

In addition to Pak Pyŏng-ho, other advocates of the view that land was privately owned in the early Yi dynasty, and even before, are Ch'ŏn Kwan-u, Kang Chin-ch'ŏl, and Arii Tomonori. See Ch'ŏn Kwan-u, "Han'guk t'oji chedosa," II, in *Han'guk munhwasa taegye*, II (Seoul, 1965), 1381-1430; Kang Chin-ch'ŏl, "Han'guk t'oji chedosa, sang," in *Han'guk munhwasa taegye*, II (Seoul, 1965), 1229-1379; Pak Pyŏng-ho, "Han'guk kŭnse ŭi t'oji soyukwŏn," in *Seoul taehakkyo pŏphak*, 8:1 (1966), 63-93; 8:2 (1966), 78-104; and 9:1 (1967), 157-185; Arii Tomonori, "Richō shoki no shiteki tochi shoyū kankei," in *Chōsen shakai no rekishiteki hatten, Chōsenshi kenkyukai rombunshū*, 3 (October 1967), 63-92. For a good short survey of views on land tenure, see Arii Tomonori, "Tochi shoyū kankei: kōdenron hihan," in Hatada Takashi, ed., *Chōsenshi nyūmon* (Tokyo: 1970), 125-154. For Sudō Yoshiyuki's studies on land deeds and bills of sale, see "Chōsen kōki no dendō bunki ni kansuru kenkyū," 1, *Rekishigaku kenkyū*, 7:7 (July 1937), 2-48; 2, ibid., 7:8 (August 1937), 39-65; 3, ibid., 7:9 (September 1937),23-68.

17. For interpretations on the *kwajŏn* system, Pak Pyŏng-ho, "Han'guk kŭnse ŭi t'oji soyukwŏn," 3 parts; Fukaya Toshigane, "Sensho no tochi sedo, ippan, jō: iwayuru kadenhō o chūshin to shite," pt. 1, *Shigaku zasshi*, 50:5 (1939), 47-82, and pt. 2, ibid., 50:6 (1939), 32-78; "Chōsen ni okeru kinseiteki tochi shoyū no seiritsu katei," pt. 1, *Shigaku zasshi*, 55:2 (1944), 1-37; pt. 2, ibid., 55:3 (1944), 77-98. Fukaya's chief contribution is his theory of multiple rights to land under both the *chŏnsikwa* land allotment system of 976 and the *kwajŏn* system of 1391: the state's right to control and dispose of land, the designated recipient's right to the *cho* tax or land rent, and the peasant holder's right of cultivation. The designated recipient was given a putative "land allotment" by the state. Fukaya's theories are reviewed by Pak Pyŏng-ho, "Han'guk kŭnse ŭi t'oji soyukwŏn," 1, 66-70.

The *kwajŏn* system seems to conform closely to Max Weber's use of the term prebends or "life-long assignment to officials of rent payments deriving from material goods, or of the essentially *economic* usufruct of land or other sources of rent, in compensation for the fulfillment of real or fictitious duties of office." Max Weber, *Economy and Society* (New York: Bedminster Press, 1968), 966-967.

18. Kim Yong-sŏp, "Yang'an ŭi yŏn'gu," I, 84, 74, for classification scheme; Kim Yong-sŏp, "Kwangmu yŏn'gan," 179.

19. Ibid., 173ff. The land survey of 1911 shows a similar pattern of stratification. Based on the figures of land tenure for all provinces, 55 to 64 percent of registered landholders held less than 0.20 kyŏl of land, and 81 to 87 percent of registered landholders held less than 0.50 kyŏl of land, depending on the province. Conversely, 4.7-8.5 percent of landholders in each province were wealthy peasants, holding one

kyŏl or more of land. Kim Yong-sŏp, "Yang'an ŭi yŏn'gu, I, 91, chart 61, based on Yamaguchi Toyomasa, *Chōsen no kenkyū*, 330.
20. The problem of population in the Yi dynasty awaits the efforts of a demographer. My estimates are purely conjectural, and are based on two assumptions: that the population records of the dynasty provide figures that were probably lower than the true population because it was in the interest of the people to avoid registration to escape taxation, and that the estimate of eight to ten million for the middle of the dynasty is probably conservative in view of the population figure of 13,091,000 for the year 1909. For the latter figure, see Andrew J. Grajdanzev, *Modern Korea* (New York: The John Day Co., 1944), 73. Yi Sang-baek's collation of traditional population figures is as follows:

Year	Population
1406	370,365 (excluding the capital)
1419-50	801,847
1648	1,531,365
1657	2,290,083
1669	5,018,644
1717	6,846,568
1753	7,298,731
1807	7,561,403
1852	6,810,206
1904	5,928,802

See Yi Sang-baek, *Han'guksa kŭnse chon'gip'yon*, 428. See also *MHBG* 161. According to Pak Ir-wŏn, *Takchiji* dated 1796 (Seoul National University Classics edition, Seoul, 1967), 77, the population in 1786 was 7,356,783. Yi Sang-baek, citing this source, remarked that the population for the reign of King Chŏngjo (r. 1776-1800) as recorded in the *Takchiji* was ten million, but I was unable to find the exact reference for this figure. Yi Sang-baek, *Han'guksa kŭnse hugip'yŏn*, 168.
In view of the Korean population figures for the early part of the twentieth century, the figures for 1852 and 1904 as presented in Yi Sang-baek's chart are obviously low.
21. Kim Yong-sŏp, "Yang'an ŭi yŏn'gu," I, 74-88.
22. For a summary of problems on the size of the kyŏl, see a forthcoming Ph.D. dissertation by Susan Shin at Harvard University on the Korean land system, untitled manuscript, appendix 1, "Yi Dynasty Measurements," 1.
23. See note 18.
24. Kim Yong-sŏp, "Yang'an ŭi yŏn'gu," II, 109. Kim did not include income from by-employments. Kim Chin-bong reached similar conclusions from his study of two districts in the south, one dating from 1866. Kim Chin-bong, "Imsul millan ŭi sahoe kyŏngjejok," 108-114.
25. Kim Yong-sŏp, "Yang'an ŭi yŏn'gu," II, 49ff.
26. Clifford Geertz, *Agricultural Involution* (Berkeley, Calif.: University of California Press, 1970), 32-37; Dwight Perkins, *Agricultural Development in China, 1368-1968* (Chicago: Aldine Publishing Co., 1969).
27. Kim Yong-sop, "Sok, Yang'an ŭi yon'gu, sang: Chosŏn hugi ŭi chŏnho kyŏngje," *Sahak yŏn'gu*, 16 (December 1963), 28-30.

28. Kim Yong-sŏp, "Kwangmu yŏn'gan ŭi yangjŏn," 180. Studies on tenancy in the first decade of the twentieth century reveal that about 60 to 70 percent of the rural population rented. land. See Kim Yong-sŏp, "Yang'an ŭi yŏn'gu," pt. 2, 61-63.

29. Kim Yong-sŏp, "Sok Yang'an ŭi yŏn'gu," 31ff., esp. p. 44; Kim Yong-sŏp, "Kwangmu yŏn'gan ŭi yangjŏn," 186ff.

30. Ibid., 189; Kim Yong-sŏp, "Sagung changt'o ŭi chŏnho kyŏngje," *Asea yŏn'gu*, 19 (September 1965), 113-146.

31. Sin Yong-ha, "Yijo malgi ŭi tojikwŏn kwa ilcheha ŭi yongsojak ŭi kwan'gye: sojangnong tojikwŏn ŭi soyukwŏn ŭro ŭi sŏngjang kwan mollak e taehayŏ," *Kyŏngje nonjip*, 6:1 (March 1967), 29-75.

32. For an article in English on this reform, see Choe Ching-young, "Kim Yuk (1580-1658) and the Taedongbŏp Reform," *Journal of Asian Studies*, 23:1 (November 1963), 21-36. Arii Tomonori's studies have also revealed conversion of one type of labor service to an additional land levy, in "Richō shoki no yōeki," *Chōsen gakuhō*, 30-31.

33. Yi Ik, pen name, Sŏngho, was a Southerner and a son of a high official. He passed the qualifying examination for the *munkwa* examination, but evidently never took the final. (I am indebted to Edward Wagner for this information.) He gave up his interest in an official career after his elder brother was involved in factional politics. He refused appointments tendered by King Yŏngjo and devoted himself to scholarship. He was interested in Western science and Catholic theologic writings as well as questions of institutional reform. See *KSDSJ*, II, 1199; Han Woo-keun, "Sŏngho, Yi Ik ŭi sahoe wa sasang," in *Yijo hugi ŭi sahoe wa sasang* (Seoul, 1961), 133-325.

34. P'an'gye is the pen name of Yu Hyŏng-wŏn. He obtained the *chinsa* degree in 1653 but took no official posts. King Chŏngjo ordered the publication of his works in 1770. For general information on his life and ideas, see Ching Young Choe, "The Decade of the Taewongun," 33, 35-36, 45-48, 53-54; *KSDSJ*, II, 1045; Ch'ŏn Kwan-u, "P'an'gye, Yu Hyŏng-wŏn yŏn'gu, sang," *Yŏksa hakpo*, 3 (January 1953), 87-139. See also Chŏng Ku-bok, "P'an'gye Yu Hyŏng-wŏn ŭi sahoe kaehyŏk sasang," *Yŏksa hakpo*, 45 (March 1970), 1-53.

35. Chŏng Yag-yong was the son of a scholar and passed the *munkwa* examinations in 1789. He held a succession of high posts in the government before becoming involved with his relatives in the Catholic persecutions of 1801. He was then exiled to the countryside until 1818. He compiled the works of the former Sirhak thinkers, Yu Hyŏng-wŏn and Yi Ik. See *KSDSJ*, II, 1358-1359; Choe, "Decade of the Taewongun," 38-40, 61-62; Hong I-sŏp, *Chŏng Yag-yong*; Pak Chong-gŭn, "Tasan, Tei Jyaku-yō no tochi kaikaku shisō no kosatsu: kōsaku (nōryoku ni ojita) tochi bumpai o chushin to shite," *Chōsen gakuhō*, 28 (July 1965), 75-112; Yi Ŭl-ho, *Tasan kyŏnghak sasang ŭi yŏn'gu* (Seoul, 1966); Kim Kwang-jin, *Chŏng Tasan ŭi kyŏngje sasang* (P'yŏngyang, 1962).

36. The first "request for advice" on agricultural and other problems during Chŏngjo's reign occurred in 1786. See Han Woo-keun, "Chŏngjo pyŏng'o sohoe tŭngnok ŭi punsŏkchŏk yon'gu," *Seoul taehakkyo nonmunjip*, 11 (November 1965), 3-51. A more extensive survey of opinion on agriculture, land, and taxation was held in 1798. See Kim Yong-sŏp, "Chosŏn hugi ŭi nong'ŏp munje: Chŏngjo mallyŏn ŭi ŭngji chinnongsŏ ŭi punsŏk," *Han'guksa yŏn'gu*, 2 (December 1968), 53-103.

37. An excellent illustration of this point is to be found in the reform proposals of Yi Ki (pen name, Haehak), presented in 1895. Yi Ki deplored the unequal distribution of wealth but felt that the system of private property was too strong to be overturned by either well-field type land distribution or land limitation schemes. For that reason,

he turned his attention to equalization of tax and rent burdens. By lowering rents drastically and raising land taxes slightly, he hoped to improve the economic condition of tenants and increase the state's revenues at the expense of the landlord class. While his rent limitation scheme was never adopted, he did inspire the national land survey effort of 1898-1904. See Kim Yong-sŏp, "Kwangmu yŏn'gan ŭi yangjŏn," 104-141.

38. This position was about the same one taken by Yi Ki. See note 27.

39. Yi Kyu-gyŏng, *Oju yŏnmun changjŏn san'go* (Seoul, 1959), II, 308-310; for the long memorial of Hŏ Pu, see *Imsullok* (Seoul, 1958), 364-403; Kim Yun-sik, *Unyangjip* 16 kwŏn, preface dated 1913, 7:10b-19b.

40. *MHBG* 142:3a-b, 16b-17a. Yi Ik's suggestion is listed after an entry for the date, 1767. Hong-I-sŏp, *Chŏng Yag-yong*, 107; Kim Yong-sŏp, "Chosŏn hugi ŭi nong'ŏp," 82; *Imsullok*, 370; *Unyangjip*, 7:12a-13a. It was also a part of Yi Ki's recommendations in 1895 and after, Kim Yong-sŏp, "Kwangmu yŏn'gan ŭi yangjon," 119.

41. Kim Yong-sŏp, "Kwangmu yŏn'gan ŭi yangjŏn," 85-87.

42. Choe Ching-young, *The Rule of the Taewŏn'gun*, 33-35.

43. *KJSL*.I.153-154; *SJW*, Kojong I, 336, 1864.7.15.

44. Kim Yong-sŏp, "Kwangmu yŏn'gan," 87-88. Kim maintains that the policy in this decade was the same as that of 1862.

45. *MHBG* 142:1a, 2a-b, 10a-b.

46. *KJSL*.I.64, *SJW*, Kojong I, 99, 1864.2.10. Kim Yong-sŏp, "Kwangmu yŏn'gan," 87.

47. There is one report from the governor of Hwanghae province in 1865 about the addition of 246 kyŏl of reclaimed land to the tax registers. *KJSL*.I.295, *SJW*, Kojong I, 811, 1865.8.1.

48. *KJSL*.I.397-398, 1866.5.16.

49. *KJSL*.I.402, 1866.6.2.

50. *KJSL*.I.445, 1866.9.7.

51. *KJSL*.I.613, 1867.9.25; *KJSL*.II.99, 1868.10.27.

52. *SJW*, Kojong II, 539, 1867.4.27, for Kongch'ung province; and *KJSL*.II.109, 1868.11.18 for Chŏlla Right province. The secret censor for Kyŏngsang province reported on August 19, 1867, that there had not been a resurvey of the land there for 148 years. *KJSL*.I.593-594, 1867.7.20. For the report from the governor that a total of 321 kyŏl had been added to the registers from one hyŏn, see *KJSL*.II.142, 1869.3.27.

53. *KJSL*.II.177-178, *SJW*, Kojong III, 336, 1869.10.3.

54. *KJSL*.II.179-180, 1869.10.20.

55. *KJSL*.II.183-184, 1869.11.7.

56. For Kojong's complaint, see *KJSL*.II.207, *SJW*, Kojong III, 447, 1870.2.30; a report from the magistrate of Suwŏn recorded 779 kyŏl added to the tax rolls. The state council praised this. *SJW*, Kojong III, 523, *KJSL*.II.221, 1870.5.26. The governor of Kyŏngsang reported an additional 391 kyŏl recorded in Tongnae, *KJSL*.II.264, 1870.11.25; and 204 *kyŏl* from Ŏnyang-hyŏn, *KJSL*.II.388, 1871.10.25.

57. *KJSL*.II.224, *SJW*, Kojong III, 538-539, 1869.6.29.

58. *SJW*, Kojong I, 99, 1864.2.10; *SJW*, Kojong I, 336, 1864.7.15.

59. *KJSL*.I.397-398, 1866.5.16.

60. *KJSL*.I.402, 1866.6.2.

61. *KJSL*.I.433, 1866.8.6.

62. For the original edict, see *KJSL*.II.261, 1870.11.17; for Kojong's discussion with Kim Pyŏng-hak at court, see *KJSL*.II.263, 1870.11.21.

63. *KJSL*.II.272-273, 1870.12.13.

64. *KJSL*.II.4, 1868.1.7; *KJSL*.II.54, 1868.6.18.

65. *KJSL*.II.345, *SJW*, Kojong III, 823, 1871.5.25; Ching Young Choe, "The Decade of the Taewongun," 192; *KSDSJ*, II, 1625; *Ajia rekishi jiten*, 8:279.

66. I was not able to find a notice for this in the court records, but it is cited in Ching Young Choe, "The Decade," 191. Choe refers to Yi Nŭng-hwa, *Chosŏn kidokkyo kŭp oegyosa*, 11:5, and Chŏng Kyo, *Taehan kyenyŏnsa* (Seoul 1957), 1:1. *KSDSJ*, I, 60, provides a date of 1867 and a rate of 100 mun of cash per kyŏl.

67. Yi Sang-baek, *Han'guksa kŭnse chŏn'gip'yŏn*, 156-162; Takchiji, 136ff; Wada, *Chōsen no tochi seido*, 128, 144ff.

68. Min Pyŏng-ha, "Chosŏn sŏwŏn ŭi kyŏngje kujo," *Taedong munhwa yŏn'gu*, 5 (August 1968), 87.

69. The sources consulted on the problem of the palace estates were Yi Sang-baek, *Han'guksa kŭnse chŏn'gip'yŏn*, 156-162; Han Woo-keun, *Yijo hugi*, 18-25; *Takchiji*, 134-144; *MGYR*, chaeyongp'yŏn, 240, 243ff.; Wada, *Chōsen no tochi seido*, 93-101, 119-184; *RCZS*, 80-92, *MHBG* 144:7b-21b, passim; Kim Yong-sŏp, "Sagung changt'o ŭi kwalli: Tojangje rŭl chungsim ŭro," *Sahak yŏn'gu*, 18 (September 1964), 573-626.

70. Wada, *Chōsen no tochi seido*. 126-127; *MGYR*, chaeyongp'yŏn, 24-43; Kim Yong-sŏp, "Sagung changt'o ŭi kwalli," passim.

71. Kim Yong-sŏp expressed reservations about whether a *tojang* who had obtained his position by commendation (*tut'ak tojang*) was really the same as the steward-type who was a contractual manager and tax or rent collector. Because commendation was illegal, there were very few *tojang* contracts that recorded such transactions explicitly. Kim Yong-sŏp, "Sagung changt'o ŭi kwalli," 607. The nature of *tojang* rights are treated fully in Kim Yong-sŏp, "Sagung changt'o ŭi kwalli," passim.

72. *MGYR*, chaeyongp'yŏn, 99ff.

73. Wada, *Chōsen no tochi seido*, 124ff., 149-159.

74. *Takchiji*, 134-135, 142; Han Woo-keun, *Yijo hugi*, 18-24; Yi Sang-baek, *Han'guksa kŭnse chŏn'gip'yon*, 157-159; Wada, *Chōsen no tochi seido*, 96, 98, 132, 152-153; *MHBG* 144:7aff.

75. Yi Sang-baek, *Han'guksa kŭnse chŏn'gip'yŏn*, 156; *Takchiji*, 136, 138, 142; *Soktaejŏn*, 141-143; *MHBG* 144:7a-9b; Han Woo-keun, *Yijo hugi*, 22-25; *MGYR*, chaeyongp'yŏn, 252. The limit on palace estates was 1,000 kyŏl, with one exception of 1,500 kyŏl; Wada, *Chōsen no tochi seido*, 152-153.

76. Han Woo-keun, *Yijo hugi*, 25; Yi Sang-baek, *Han'guksa kŭnse hugip'yŏn*, 159; *Soktaejŏn*, 141-143; Wada, *Chōsen no tochi seido*, 96, 129. All these items except the four-generation provision are included in the *Soktaejŏn*. The prohibition for Kangwŏn province was added in 1754. *Takchiji*, 142; *Taejŏn t'ongp'yŏn* (Seoul: Pŏpchech'ŏ, 1963;, 170.

77. Ibid., 162; *MGYR*, chaeyongp'yŏn, 243; Wada, *Chōsen no tochi seido*, 99, gives the date 1784, but this is the date of the promulgation of the *Taejŏn t'ongp'yŏn*. See *Taejŏn t'ongp'yŏn* (Seoul: Pŏpchech'ŏ ed.), 170. The *MGYR* clearly records the date as 1776. According to this edict, both *mut'o myŏnse* and the dispatch of *tojang* (to collect taxes) on these palace estate lands were abolished. It specified that the taxes of 23 tu/kyŏl of polished rice or 7 yang, 6 chŏn, 7 pun of cash would be paid directly to the Ministry of Taxation, which would then dispense funds to the palaces.

The *MGYR* records that on *yut'o* land, the palace dispatches *tojang* to collect the taxes, while on *mut'o* land the local magistrate collects the taxes and forwards them to the Ministry of Taxation. It also noted, however, that the palaces continued to send their agents to collect taxes directly, and in *mujin* year (1808?) it was ordered that this be punished.

78. *KJSL*.I.31, *SJW*, Kojong I, 5, 1864.1.6. For a survey of the palace estate problem, see Han Woo-keun, *Tonghangnan kiin e kwanhan yŏn'gu*, 109-117.

79. *KJSL*.I.66, *SJW*, Kojong I, 100, 1864.2.10.

80. See *KJSL*.I.355ff., 1866.2.13 and 1866.2.15, where the nine-year old daughter of Ch'ŏlchong and her mother were given titles and stipends. The mother obtained in addition a grant of 200 kyŏl of tax-exempt land.

81. *KJSL*.I.432-433, 1866.8.6. He was the son of Yi Ch'oe-ŭng, the Taewongun's brother.

82. Ibid., 433; *KJSL*.I.434, 1866.8.9. The state council added its approval.

83. *KJSL*.I.632, *SJW*, Kojong II, 746, 1867.12.15.

84. *KJSL*.II.42, 1868.i4.13. See a follow-up memorial from the Tribute Bureau, *KJSL*.II.43-44, 1868.i4.17.

85. *KJSL*.II.53, 1868.6.16.

86. *KJSL*.II.163, 1869.8.20; *KJSL*.II.224, *SJW*, Kojong III, 538-539, 1869.6.29.

87. *KJSL*.II.177, *SJW*, Kojong III, 336, 1869.10.3.

88. *KJSL*.II.176-177, *SJW*, Kojong III, 335, 1869.10.2. In this case the king allowed him to keep 50 kyŏl.

89. *KJSL*.II.207, *SJW*, Kojong III, 447, 1870.2.30; *KJSL*.II.256, 1870.i10.22; *KJSL*.II.395, 1871.11.12; *KJSL*.II.516-517, 1873.2.29.

90. For material on the economic aspects of the private academies, see Min Pyŏng-ha, "Chosŏn sŏwŏn ŭi kyŏngje kujo," 75-96. A doctoral thesis on the academies has just been completed; see Warren Smith, "The Rise of the Sowon: Literary Academies in Sixteenth-Century Korea," Ph.D. diss., Berkeley, Calif.: University of California at Berkeley, 1972.

91. Min Pyŏng-ha, "Chosŏn sŏwŏn," 78.

92. Ibid., 91ff. Min gives two cases of academies with eleven and eighteen slaves recorded.

93. Ibid., 77-78, 87; *Soktaejŏn*, 140.

94. The taxes were to be collected by district magistrates instead. See Han Woo-keun, *Tonghangnan kiin e kwanhan yŏn'gu*, 91, and note 24, p. 91. For original citations, see *Pibyŏnsa tŭngnok* (*PBS*), 2, Kojong 1.1.6; 9, Kojong 1.1.6; 9, Kojong 1.4.22; 10, Kojong 1.5.13, Kojong 1.10.5.

95. *KJSL*.II.105, 1868.11.5.

96. *KJSL*.II.207-208, *SJW*, Kojong III, 447, 1870.2.30.

5. The Household Cloth Tax

1. Detailed description of the Yi dynasty military organization and service system will not be provided here, since it is not of great relevance to the main themes of the chapter, but the following materials were consulted in preparation of the chapter.

Ch'a Mun-sŏp, "Sŏnch'o ŭi kapsa e taehayŏ," pt. 1, *Sach'ong*, 4 (November 1959), 115-136; pt. 2, *Sach'ong*, 5 (November 1960), 38-55; "Imnan ihu ŭi yangyŏk kwa kyunyŏkpŏp ŭi sŏngnip," pt. 1, *Sahak yŏn'gu*, 10 (April 1961), 115-131; pt. 2, *Sahak yŏn'gu*, 11 (July 1961), 83-146; "Sŏnch'o ŭi Ch'ung'ŭi, Ch'ungch'an, Ch'unsunwi e taehayŏ," *Sahak yŏn'gu*, 19 (April 1967), 1-48; "Sŏnjojo ŭi Hullyŏndogam," *Sahakchi*, 4 (November 1970), 11-30; "Chosŏnjo hugi ŭi yŏngjang e taehayŏ," *Sach'ong* 12-13 (September 1968), 495-518.

Ch'ŏn Kwan-u, "Yŏmal sŏnch'o ŭi hallyang," *Yi Pyŏng-do Paksa hwagap kinyŏm nonch'ong* (Seoul, 1956), 333-356; "Chosŏn ch'ogi Owi ŭi hyŏngsŏng," *Yŏksa hakpo*, 17-18 (June 1962), 515-546; "Chosŏn ch'ogi Owi ŭi pyŏngjong," *Sahak yŏn'gu*, 18 (September 1964), 59-95.

Yu Sŭng-u, "Chosŏn hugi kunsu kwanggong'ŏp ŭi palchŏn," *Sahakchi*, 3 (July 1969), 1-35; Arii Tomonori, "Richō hojūgun kō," *Chōsen gakuhō*, 31 (April 1964), 58-101; Miyahara Toichi, "Richo no gun'eki seido, ho, no seiritsu," *Chōsen gakuhō*, 28 (July 1963), 112-131; Yi Sang-baek, *Han'guksa kŭnse chŏn'gip'yŏn*, 213-255.

For additional material on the Five Military Commands (*Oyŏng*) of the seventeenth century, see *MGYR*, kunjŏngp'yŏn, passim; Yi Sang-baek, *Han'guksa kŭnse hugip'yŏn*, 143-150; *RCZS*, 119-152.

What appears to be an extremely valuable survey of the early Yi military system was just published as this manuscript was completed. *Han'guk kunjesa: kŭnse Chosŏn chŏn'gip'yŏn* (Seoul, Yukkun ponbu, 1968).

2. According to Ching Young Choe, "The establishment of the *hop'o* [household cloth tax] was revolutionary, since it equalized the military obligations among the social classes." *The Rule of the Taewŏn'gun*, 40.

3. See notes 85 and 94.

4. Ch'a Mun-sŏp, "Hullyŏn-dogam," 20ff; Hiraki Makoto, "Sipch'il segi e issŏsŏ ŭi nobi chongnyang," *Han'guksa yŏn'gu*, 3 (March 1969), 100ff.

5. Ch'a, "Yangyŏk," pt. 2, 94-97; Ch'a, "Hullyŏn-dogam," 20ff.

6. Hiraki Makoto, "Sipch'il segi," 104, 106, 113, 118-121.

7. Yi Sang-baek, "Chŏnja sumo-go," *Chindan hakpo*, 25-27 (December 1964), 157-162.

8. Ibid., 162-167.

9. Ibid., 168; Hiraki Makoto, "Jūshichi-hachi seiki ni okeru muryōsai shosei no kisoku ni tsuite," *Chōsen gakuhō*, 61 (October 1971), 48.

10. Ibid., 45-75; Yi Sang-baek, "Chŏnja sumo-go," 173ff.

11. Ibid., 182-183.

12. Shikata Hiroshi, "Richō jinkō ni kansuru mibun kaikyūbetsuteki kansatsu," *Chōsen keizai no kenkyū*, 3 (Tokyo, 1938), 363-482; Kim Yong-sŏp, "Chosŏn hugi e issŏsŏ ŭi sinbunje ŭi tongyo wa nongji chŏmyu: Sangju yang'an yŏn'gu ŭi iltan," *Sahak yŏn'gu*, 15 (April 1963), 7.

13. Ch'a, "Yangyŏk," pt. 2, 98-100.

14. Illegally registered persons over sixty years of age and under sixteen were usually referred to as "bleached bones" and "yellow mouths," respectively (*paekkol*, *hwanggu*).

15. Ch'a, "Yangyŏk," 111. *MHBG* 156:4a; Han Woo-keun, *Yijo hugi ŭi sahoe wa sasang*, 59ff.

16. *Kyunyŏk sasil ch'aekcha*, which is recorded in *Yŏngjo sillok*, Yŏngjo 8.1. ŭlhae. (1752). Also, according to the memorial of Yi Chong-sŏng in 1750, when the late Prime Minister Kim Sŏk-chu proposed the household cloth tax in 1677, the expenses of capital and provinces (disbursed from military cloth revenues) came to about 600,000 p'il. *Yŏngjo sillok*, Yŏngjo 3.1.1 (1727). This item was discovered by Han Woo-keun, *Yijo hugi*, 63, note 178.

17. There are many sources for these figures. See "The True Facts about the Equal Service Reform," in *Yŏngjo sillok*, Yŏngjo 8.1. ŭlhae; Chŏng Yag-yong, *Mongmin simsŏ*, 8:13a (Seoul, 1961 ed.), 476; Yi Chong-sŏng stated that when the Commoner Cloth Bureau (*yangyŏkch'ŏng*) was established in 1723, the number of persons paying the two p'il cloth tax was 459,000, yielding revenues of 918,000 p'il. There were also people paying the tax at a one p'il rate. Total revenues from both rates were about one million p'il. *Yŏngjo sillok*, Yŏngjo 26.6. kyesa (1750); Ch'a "Yangyŏk,"

318

Notes to pages 91-92

111; Ching Young Choe, "The Decade of the Taewongun," 23. The ms. of "The True Facts about the Equal Service Reform" is in the *Kyunyŏk samok*, dated 1752, last section, 1a-9b.

There is one conflicting piece of evidence, however. In 1750 one official reported that the expenditures of military support cloth taxes (probably equivalent to revenues) for the capital and provinces had increased recently from 604,000 p'il to 633,708 p'il. These figures were broken down in the following way:

1. Revenues from the two p'il tax rate:	
Support cloth from the Five Military Commands	456,543
Support cloth paid to the capital bureaus	46,116
2. Provincial expenses, including both two and one p'il tax rates:	
Yongnam (Kyŏngsang) provincial army commander's headquarters	43,012
Honam (Chŏlla) provincial army and navy commander's headquarters	46,207
Hosŏ (Ch'ungch'ŏng) provincial army and navy commander's headquarters	15,952
Kyŏnggi (governor's?, army commander's?) hdqs.	3,664
Expenses for Hosŏ (Ch'ungch'ŏng) province	22,214
Total	633,708

Source: Yŏngjo sillok, Yŏngjo 26.5 kyŏng'o; Han Woo-keun, *Yijo hugi,* 63, note 178.

These figures would have to exclude some categories of cloth tax payments. *MGYR* reveals that the number of cloth tax paying support personnel for the Ministry of War in 1807 was approximately 100,000 men, paying a one p'il tax rate. This figure alone would be greater than the second item above, which gives expenditures for capital bureaus. *MGYR, kunjŏngp'yŏn,* 136. I would thus assume that the revenues of the Ministry of War, at least, were not included in the above figures, and that one million p'il should still be regarded as the best figure for total tax revenues from the commoner cloth tax in the several decades before 1750.

18. "The True Facts of the Equal Service Reform," in *Yŏngjo sillok,* Yŏngjo 28.1.ŭlhae (1752); Ch'a, "Yangyŏk," 111. Another official in 1750 estimated the total population at 1,700,000 households, but did not give an estimate of taxpaying households. *Yŏngjo sillok,* Yŏngjo 26.5.kyŏng'o (1750).

19. Ch'a, "Yangyŏk," 111.

20. *Yŏngjo sillok,* Yŏngjo 26.5.kyŏng'o (1750), cited also in Ch'a, "Yangyŏk," 133. In 1743 a survey of commoners liable for military service was conducted and the results published in 1748. According to this survey, there were 525,000 commoners, not including Kyŏnggi province. With Kyŏnggi province included, I would estimate a total of 600-700,000 men. For Chŏng Yag-yong's estimate, see Chŏng Yag-yong, *Mongmin simsŏ,* 8:13 (1961), 476.

21. Shikata Hiroshi, "Chōsen jinkō," 386-389, 410.

22. Kim Chin-bong, "Imsul millan ŭi sahoe," 110. Kim found that the average per household rate for the two districts was 1.2 and 1.4 yang/household. After 1750 the legal tax rate was 2 yang or 1 p'il (of cloth) per able-bodied male. Considering that the

average number of males per household would at least be about two (equivalent to 4 yang/household in taxes), Kim's household average is relatively low. Since it is an average figure, however, it would not indicate the actual distribution of taxes from household to household.

23. Kim Yong-sŏp, "Chosŏn hugi e issŏsŏ ŭi sinbunje ŭi tongyo wa nongji chŏmyu," 7. Kim's figures for the population of the two areas are as follows (in percent).

Status	Area 1		Area 2	
Yangban	28.3		38.8	
upper		10.0		15.5
lower		8.3		23.3
Commoner	56.0		43.0	
upper		46.0		34.0
lower		10.0		9.0
Slave	19.0		17.0	
private		18.4		15.6
official		0.6		1.4

N.B. It should be remembered that these are not percentages of the total population, but just of the registered landholders (kiju), those people whose names are carried on the land registers.

The above figures might be compared with the distribution of landholders (kiju) by social status group in the three areas (myŏn) of Hoein-hyŏn in Ch'ungch'ŏng province, studied by Kim for the year 1669.

Status	Area 1	Area 2	Area 3	Total
Yangban	15.8	42.4	45.3	31.4
Commoner	55.5	24.3	22.6	37.7
Ch'ŏnmin	28.7	33.3	32.1	30.9

These figures did not include landless peasants (tenants, laborers, and so forth), which were estimated as comprising about 30 percent of the rural population in 1458. See Sejong sillok, 7, 249, cited in Kim, Chosŏn sinbunje, 10. By the seventeenth century, the tenancy rate was probably closer to 40 percent, although only about half of these were pure tenants. If tenant or landless population were added, the percentages of commoners and ch'ŏnmin would be increased at the expense of yangban.

See also Susan Shin, "The Social Structure of Kumhwa County in the Late Seventeenth Century," Occasional Papers on Korea, 1 (June 1972), 15. According to a 1663 Seoul census register (northern section of Seoul), yangban households were 16.6 percent of the total registered households in the area, commoners were 30 percent, and slaves 53.3 percent. See Edward W. Wagner, "Social Stratification in Seventeenth Century Korea: Some Observations from a 1663 Seoul Census Register," Occasional Papers on Korea, 1 (June 1972), 36-54. One might surmise that the greater numbers of slaves and slave households in the capital than in the provinces was due to the concentration of well-to-do households in the capital.

24. For a description of the various pyramidal systems of mutual aid and surveillance in ancient China, see Yu Hyŏng-wŏn, "Pyŏngje kosŏl" (Study of Military

Systems), in *P'an'gye surok*, 23:1a-5a (Seoul, Tongguk munhwasa ed., 1958). The system with the most influence on Korean scholars was the military organization described in the *Chou-li*. Ibid., 23:1a-1b; see 23:3a-b for Chu Hsi's praise of this system. See also Yi Ik, *Sŏngho sasŏl, sang*, I (Seoul: Kyŏnghŭi ch'ulp'ansa, 1967, ed.), 250. For an excellent discussion of the Chinese militia system and the interconnected nature of civil and military roles in Chinese dynasties, see Philip A. Kuhn, *Rebellion and Its Enemies in Late Imperial China: Militarization and Social Structure, 1796-1864* (Cambridge, Mass.: Harvard University Press, 1970), 10-36.

25. The fullest exposition by a Korean scholar of trends in the Chinese military system is the lengthy essay by Yu Hyŏng-wŏn in *P'an'gye surok*, "Pyŏngje" (military system), 21:1a-64a, which deals with the Korean military system, and "Pyŏngje kosŏl, 23:1a-35b, which deals with the history of military systems in China.

For other essays by scholars with references to Chinese systems, see Yi Ik, *Sŏngho sasŏl*, I, "Kunjŏng" (Essay on the military system), 250-294, and "Kunbyŏngbo" (Essay on troops and support personnel), ibid., 356-357; Yu Su-wŏn, *Usŏ* (ca. 1729-37), (Seoul National University Press ed., 1971), 109, 114, 170-171; Pak Che-ga, *Chŏngyujip* (Seoul: Kuksa p'yŏnch'an wiwŏnhoe ed., 1961), 435-436; Yi Tŏng-mu, *Ch'ŏngjanggwan chŏnsŏ*, I (Seoul National University: Kojŏn ch'ŏngsŏ series, no. 1, 1966), 364-365; Chŏng Yag-yong, *Mongmin simsŏ*, 8:12a-31a; 33aff.; Yi Kyu-gyŏng, *Oju yŏnmun changjŏn san'go, ha* (Seoul: Kojŏn kanhaenghoe ed., 1959), "Private views on the mouth-cash tax," 307, and "Essay on grain tax collection and the equalization of service taxes," 308-310; Kim Yun-sik, *Unyangjip*, 7:15a, 8:8a, 10b-19b; for collections of documents with comments on Chinese models and systems, see *MHBG* 156:2b, 5a; memorial of Yu Pong-hwi, *Sukchong sillok*, Sukchong 37.8. kapsul (1711); "Kyunyŏk sasil" ms., dated 1752, 1a; memorial of Hŏ Pu, in *Imsullok*, 371-375; *Imsullok*, 408.

26. Yu Su-wŏn, *Usŏ*, 170.

27. *MHBG* 156:2a; Ch'a, "Yangyŏk," 121; *Sukchong sillok*, Sukchong 37.8. kapsul (1711). See H. D. Harootunian's discussion of *meibun* in Tokugawa thought in *Toward Restoration: The Growth of Political Consciousness in Tokugawa Japan* (Berkeley, Calif.: University of California Press, 1970), 66ff.

28. See the remarks of Yu Kye, in *MHBG* 156:1a; the remarks of Yi Sa-myŏng in *Sukchong sillok*, Sukchong 8.1.kyŏng'o, and the remarks of Yu Pong-hwi, in *MHBG* 156:5b. These arguments were repeated frequently by others as well.

29. Even Yi Ik would not have included the elite in the military taxes, *Sŏngho sasŏl, sang*, 294; Han Woo-keun, *Yijo hugi*, 291-292. He also advocated that ch'ŏnmin be required to perform military service obligations and that slaves be converted gradually to commoners by a variety of laws; such as, prohibition of purchase and sale, manumission of slave children, and limitation on the number of slaves per household. Han Woo-keun, *Yijo hugi*, 291-297.

30. In 1721 Third State Councilor Yi Kŏn-myŏng requested a reduction of the cloth tax rate from two p'il to one p'il with the revenue lost thereby to be supplemented by a land surtax called "the miscellaneous labor service land surtax" (*chŏn'gyŏl chabyŏkka*). Miscellaneous labor service, which had been assigned to people on the basis of units of land area, would then be transferred to households. The Border Defense Command recommended a trial run of this proposal in three administrative towns, and Sukchong approved, only to rescind the order a few days later because of a censor's objections. *MHBG* 156:6a-b; Yu Su-wŏn, *Usŏ*, 113.

31. In 1750 Chief State Councilor Cho Hyŏn-myŏng pointed out that the two northern provinces could not be included in any land tax and the 700,000 kyŏl of land

in the three southern provinces would be insufficient for the 970,000 p'il of state revenues that would be lost by any elimination of the military cloth tax. *Yŏngjo sillok,*
Yŏngjo 26.5. kyŏngsin.

Another official in discussing the land-cash proposal said that the amount of
taxable kyŏl in the southern six provinces in a good crop year came to 700-800,000
kyŏl, and in a bad year, to 500-600,000 kyŏl. If the land tax were to be increased to
replace the revenues from the two p'il cloth tax, this would require an additional levy
of 400-500 cash (mun) per kyŏl. Or if the cloth tax were only reduced by half to one
p'il, the land tax would have to be raised by 200-300 mun/kyŏl. *Yŏngjo sillok,* Yŏngjo
26.6.pyŏngja. One mun was 0.1 chŏn or 0.01 yang. See also a similar proposal by Yi
Chong-sŏng, in *Yŏngjo sillok,* Yŏngjo 6.6.kyesa.

32. Chŏng Yag-yong, *Mongmin simsŏ,* 8:12b-13b (1961), 475-476.

33. For Yu Pong-hwi's plans, see *Sukchong sillok,* Sukchong, 37.8.kapsul; Ch'a
Mun-sŏp, "Yangyŏk," 127-128; *MHBG* 156:4a-5a; Han Woo-keun, *Yijo hugi,* 56-57.

34. See the objections of Third State Councilor Cho Sang-u, in *Sukchong sillok,*
Sukchong 37.8.kapsul.

35. The first comprehensive exposition of the household-cloth tax plan was put
forward in 1682 by Second Minister of War Yi Sa-myŏng. He quoted census figures
for 1678, which set the total of households in the country at 1.1-1. 2 million. Of this
figure, a total of about 430,000 households of *ch'ŏnmin,* the sick and indigent would
have been exempted, leaving 730,000 households liable for the tax. He proposed
dividing households into two classes: complete households (*wanho*) with eight or
more individuals and weak households (*yakho*) with fewer than eight. The complete
households would pay two p'il of cloth per year, and the weak households would pay
one p'il per year. He estimated the total revenue from this at about 800-900,000 p'il.
He thought this would be more than enough to substitute for the current revenue from
the military cloth tax, which he estimated at 500,000 p'il of cloth—slightly less than
the 600,000 p'il cited earlier in this chapter for the mid-seventeenth century. See *Sukchong sillok,* Sukchong 8.1. kyŏng'o; Ch'a Mun-sŏp, "Yangyŏk," pt. 2, 122.

Some of the opponents of the household cloth tax in 1711 mentioned that the
form of the plan then under consideration called for three grades of household paying
three, two and one p'il of cloth, respectively. *Sukchong sillok,* Sukchong 37.8.
kapsul; *MHBG* 156:4b. Sin Wan proposed three rates in 1750 of 1.5, 1.2-1.3 and 1
yang per household. *Yŏngjo sillok,* Yŏngjo 26.5 kyŏngsin.

36. See notes 34 and 35. In 1711 Yu Pong-hwi, an opponent of the household cloth
tax but an advocate of taxes on yangban, stated, "If the idle persons from the *sajok*
(elite, yangban) on down have to pay a tax they have never paid before, they will
surely resent it. The reason why the household cloth tax hitherto was never enacted is
only because of the violent opposition of these people." *Sukchong sillok,* Sukchong
37.8.kapsul.

The arguments brought forth against the household cloth plan were, of course,
not limited to the question of yangban taxation. In 1682, for example, the opponents
of the plan argued that "the people" did not want the household cloth tax; that it
would only benefit a few soldiers and commoners who would receive rate reductions
at the expense of the many who would have to pay the tax; that it had been twice
rejected under Kings Hyojong and Hŏnjong; and that in view of the current crop disasters and famine its implementation would not be appropriate. *Sukchong sillok,*
Sukchong 8.1. kyŏng'o; 8.1. pyŏngja; 8.2. kapsin.

37. Yi Chong-sŏng, a sinecured official in the Office of the Royal Clan, in 1750
advanced four reasons why the household cloth tax should not be approved by King

Yŏngjo. It was "unequal" because it graded taxes on the basis of the number of persons per household and not the wealth of the household. It would not yield sufficient revenue. It would lead to an increase of the land tax in order to make up for financial shortages. His last reason, however, was probably the most significant: it would destroy the morale of the *sabu* (elite) and turn them against the dynasty. *Yŏngjo sillok*, Yŏngjo 26.6. kyesa; Yu Su-wŏn, *Usŏ*, 109ff.; *Sukchong sillok*, Sukchong 37.8. kapsul; *MHBG* 156:4b, which includes criticisms of the regressive nature of the proposed system of graded household taxation.

38. Yu Su-wŏn, *Usŏ*, passim, esp. p. 113.
39. In 1750 Sin Wan proposed tax rates on the three grades of households at 1.5, 1.2-1.3, and 1 yang per household, but another official pointed out that the poorest households comprised 80-90 percent of the total population, so that the state could not expect much revenue from the highest two categories. The minister of taxation told Yŏngjo that Sin Wan's tax rate would mean that anywhere from 670,000 to one million households would be required just to make up for revenues lost from a one p'il or 50 percent reduction in the current two p'il cloth tax. To replace revenues from the entire military cloth tax, 1.35 to two million taxpaying households would be needed. If the *ch'ŏnmin* and the aged and destitute were to be excluded, even with the inclusion of all of the upper class, this would have left only about 600-700,000 taxable households in the country. *Yŏngjo sillok*, Yŏngjo 26.5. kyŏngsin; 26.6 pyŏngja.
40. *Sukchong sillok*, Sukchong 8.2. kapsin *Yŏngjo sillok*, Yŏngjo 26.5 kyŏngsin; cited also in Ch'a Mun-sŏp, "Yangyŏk," pt.2, 134.
41. See "Kyunyŏk samok," ms., dated 1752, and the "Kyunyŏk sasil" (True facts about the equal service reform), attached as an addendum to the former. Ch'a Mun-sŏp, "Yangyŏk," pt.2, 133-142; Han Woo-keun, "Yijo hugi," 64-69; *MHBG* 156:6b-14b; *Yŏngjo sillok*, Yŏngjo 26.5. kyŏngsin; 26.6. kyesa; Yŏngjo 28.1. ŭlhae.
42. The Ministry of War received the largest funds of all military agencies, approximately 170,200 p'il from about 117,000 support personnel divided into nine categories. The following chart is taken from *RCZS*, 119-152, the information for which was taken from *MGYR*, kunjŏngp'yŏn, for 1807 figures. Since there is little variance between the figures for 1807 and 1864, only the figures for 1864 are shown here. The p'il was used as a unit of account, equivalent to 2 yang of cash. The Five Military Commands' cloth tax revenues were as follows:

Unit		1864 support revenues
1)	*Hullyŏn-dogam* (Military Training Agency)	43,000 *p'il*
2)	*Kŭmwiyŏng* (in 1795 the system of rotating shifts was abolished, and taxes were collected from those off duty)	89,000
3)	*Oyŏngch'ong*	85,000
4)	*Ch'ongyungch'ŏng* (nine different sources of revenue, only one of which came from taxpayers paying the military support tax)	7,000
5)	*Suŏyŏng*	10,500
6)	Select Military Officers (*Sŏnmu kun'gwan*) (created in 1750; required one p'il cloth tax payment from previously untaxed scions of the well-to-do [commoners?])	25,750
	Total, including Ministry of War revenues	430,450

This figure is lower than the 500,000 p'il reported to be the military cloth tax revenue in 1750. Possibly the figure of 7,000 p'il for the *Ch'ongyungch'ŏng* is too low. The information pertaining to it in the *MGYR* kunjŏngp'yŏn, is much less specific than for the other four Military Commands. Or, it is possible that other sources of military funding—from the Ministry of Taxation—were not reported here. One last possibility is that about 70,000 p'il of military cloth taxes were diverted to civil agencies.

The calculations in p'il are my own. Conversion rates were 2 yang/p'il and 6 tu or 0.4 sŏk/p'il.

Chŏng Yag-yong listed the following types of soldiers and military support taxpayers at the turn of the nineteenth century: troops attached to the governors' and provincial military commanders' yamen, those on duty at the local magistrate's yamen, soldiers conscripted privately for the protection of granaries and offices, support personnel at schools, palaces, and private academies, support personnel composed of petty officials and official slaves, and others. *Mongmin simsŏ*, pyŏngjŏn 1, 8:13a (1961), 476. For a general but short survey of Chŏng's ideas on military affairs, see Hong I-sŏp, *Chŏng Yag-yong ŭi chŏngch'i kyŏngje sasang yŏn'gu*, 161-172.

43. Chŏng Yag-yong, *Mongmin simsŏ*, 8:13a-b (1961), 476.

44. Yi Kyu-gyŏng, *Oju yŏnmun, ha*, 309.

45. Chŏng Yag-yong pointed out that people frequently stole the genealogies (*chokpo*) of aristocrats and filled in names from their own families wherever they could find branch lines that had died out in the past. They did this to prove they were descendants of merit subjects, royal sons-in-law, or court nobles. There was a market in royal genealogies and office warrants, too. Families would, for example, keep all office warrants held by their ancestors over generations, retain the most prestigious and sell off the rest. Chŏng reported that the price was as high as 100 yang for a warrant. Purchasers of the warrant would then register one of their ancestors as an office holder in their genealogies, change their household registration, and petition the magistrate for exemption from military taxes. Ibid., 8:25b-28a (1961), 482-483. See also, Edward W. Wagner, "The Korean *Chokpo* as a Historical Source."

46. Chŏng Yag-yong, *Mongmin simsŏ*, 8:13b-15a (1961), 476-477.

47. Ibid., 6:19b (1961), 425. He also reported that in the past military taxes on one household came to 100 cash (*chŏn*) per year, but now even several thousand cash was not sufficient to meet household tax requirements.

48. Ibid., 8:25b (1961), 482.

49. Ibid., 6:19a-b (1961) 425; 8:25b (1961), 482.

50. Ibid., 8:15b-20b (1961), 477-479; *Taejŏn hoet'ong*, 224.

51. Ibid., 8:18a-b (1961), 478.

52. Ibid., 6:22a-23a (1961), 426-427; 8:15b-17a (1961), 477-478.

53. Ibid., 8:22b-23a (1961), 480-481. Chŏng, by the way, placed the regimental soldiers (*sog'ogun*) in the category of "base service" (*ch'ŏnyŏk*), indicating a probable drop in prestige of these soldiers since the early seventeenth century.

54. Yi Kyu-gyŏng, *Oju yŏnmun, ha*, 307-310.

55. The last part of this chapter was written in the United States. Unfortunately, I did not have access to the SJW or ILSN for Ch'ŏlchong's reign. The *Ch'ŏlchong sillok* is woefully inadequate and contains only minimal information on this period. The best available source is the collection of documents in the *Imsullok* (Documents on the Rebellion of 1862), one section of which contains a chronological account of important memorials presented at court during 1862. For the problem of the falsification of registers, see *Imsullok*, 227, 299, 304, 311, 320, 326, 336, 363.

56. For the problems of students at official schools (*kyosaeng*) and private academies (*wŏnsaeng*) and the *kyebang,* see *Imsullok,* 227, 229, 304, 311, 317, 336, 363, 410; *Ch'ŏlchong sillok,* 1862.7. chŏnghae.
57. *Imsullok,* 311, 322, 326, 335, 372, 410.
58. Ibid., 317, 363.
59. Ibid., 310, 313-314; *Ch'ŏlchong sillok,* Ch'ŏlchong 1862.7. pyŏngsin.
60. *Imsullok,* 304, 310.
61. Ibid., 329. See p. 373 for the memorial of Hŏ Pu, which states that in remote villages eight or nine yang of cash was being collected in lieu of one p'il of cloth.
62. Ibid., 329.
63. Ibid., 322, 410.
64. *Ch'ŏlchong sillok,* Ch'ŏlchong 1862.6. sinyu.
65. *Imsullok,* 371-372.
66. Ibid., 373.
67. Ibid., 374-375. See Hŏ's discussion of the mutual surveillance type of organization for the purposes of military registration. See note 23.
68. Ibid., 408-411.
69. Ibid., 411.
70. Ibid., 411. Second State Councilor Cho Tu-sun also opposed the transfer of taxes to land for the same reasons. Ibid., 322.
71. Kim Yun-sik, *Unyangjip,* 7:14b-15a.
72. See notes 55 and 56 and *Imsullok,* 312, 317, 372, 408-410.
73. See note 57.
74. *Imsullok,* 266, 271, 311-312, 317, 320, 322, 331, 335, 372; *Ch'ŏlchong sillok,* 1862.8. chŏngch'uk.
75. *Imsullok,* 266, 277, 311-312, 317, 320, 322, 331, 373.
76. Han Woo-keun, "Taewŏn'gun ŭi sŏwŏn kwangjangch'aek ŭi iltan," in *Kim Chaewŏn Paksa hoegap kinyŏm nonch'ong* (Seoul, 1969), 297-300. With regard to the term, *p'a* (to scar), "The Regulations for the Household Tally System" (*Hop'ae samok,* dated 1625.7.28, ms.), required that for certain categories of tally, namely the Small Wood Tally to be used to identify students, clerks, and other types, and the Large Wood Tally for soldiers, "distinguishing body marks were to be recorded [on it] (*p'agi*)." In this case, however, *p'a* does not seem to indicate branding of people liable for military service.
77. The phrase is *yusin yungji, Imsullok,* 311.
78. *Imsullok,* 331-336 (1862.i8.19). There seem to be many lacunae in the *Ch'ŏlchong sillok.* There is no entry on 1862.i8.kihae that corresponds to the nineteenth day of the month about the promulgation of the list of regulations. On the eleventh day (*sinmyo*), there is a memorial from an official, which states that "the list of regulations of the Reform Bureau was promulgated yesterday." The previous day, however, is missing, and I was not able to locate the complete text of the regulations in the *Sillok.*
79. *KJSL.*I.164-165, 1864.8.1; *KJSL.*I.167, 1864.8.2; *KJSL.*I.173-174, 1864.8.20.
80. *KJSL.*I.71, 1864.2.20; *kjsl.*I.426-427, 1866.8.1; *KJSL.*I.443, 1866.9.1; *KJSL.*II.107, 1868.11.9. For a two chŏn/kyŏl cash tax for P'yŏng'an province, see *KJSL.*II.179, *SJW,* Kojong III, 342, 1869.10.13; for rewards for voluntary contributions from private individuals, see *KJSL.*I.86, 1868.9.24; and for land surveys for increasing tax revenues, see *KJSL.*II.221, *SJW,* Kojong III, 523, 1870.5.26. For a 100 cash/kyŏl land surtax in 1868, see Ching Young Choe, "The Decade of the

Taewongun," 191. Choe cites Yi Nŭng-hwa, Chosŏn kidokkyo kŭp oegyosa, 11:5, and Chong Kyo, Taehan kyenyŏnsa (Seoul, 1957), 1:1.
Throughout the period, the demand for financing remained a serious problem. See the request from the Ch'ongyungch'ŏng in 1867 for an allotment of 300,000 yang of cash as a fund for providing 3,000 sŏk of rice provisions per year (probably in grain loan interest). KJSL.I.603, 1867.8.23. Even the Three Armies Command was established without proper financing. The chief state councilor pointed out in 1870 that the agency had no funds of its own and asked for 5,000 yang per year to be allotted to it. KJSL.II.201, SJW, Kojong III, 415, 1870.1.22.

81. KJSL.I.423, 1866.7.30; KJSL.II.177, 1869.10.3; KJSL.II.224, 1869.10.3, cited in Ching Young Choe, "The Decade," 193.

82. KJSL.II.345, SJW, Kojong III, 823, 1871.5.25; RCZS, 96; Ching Young Choe, "The Decade," 192; KSDSJ, II, 1625; Ajia rekishi jiten, 8:279. There is also evidence that a p'oryangmi or musketeer rice tax was in use prior to this in 1868 in Kyŏngsang province in coastal villages, and that it had been abolished because it led to corruption. KJSL.II.4, 1868.1.7; KJSL.II.54, 1868.6.18.

83. KJSL.I.401-402, 1866.6.2; Hwang Hyŏn, MCYR, 12, states that the Taewongun ordered a levy of two min per household on yangban as well as commoner households in 1864. As Han Woo-keun pointed out, this seems to be mistaken. There is no such notice from the dowager-regent to be found in the court records, only the indirect reference to it. Han interprets two min as equivalent to two yang. Han Woo-keun, "Taewŏn'gun ŭi sewŏn kwangjang," 299.

84. KJSL.I.402, 1866.6.2; Han Woo-keun, "Taewŏn'gun ŭi sewŏn kwangjang," 299; Ching Young Choe, "The Decade," 200, note 228. In 1867 the governor of Kongch'ung province reported that the Reform Bureau regulations of 1862 had succeeded in eliminating corruption no matter whether the villages used the village-cloth or the name-scar systems (1867.3.25).

85. Han Woo-keun, "Taewŏn'gun ŭi sewŏn kwangjang," passim.

86. Ibid., 300.

87. Ibid., 300-301; KJSL.II.94, 1868.10.17.

88. KJSL.I.572, SJW, Kojong II, 540, 1867.4.27.

89. KJSL.I.610, 1867.9.17; this notice is not in SJW; also KJSL.I.613, 1867.9.25.

90. KJSL.II.104, 1868.11.5.

91. KJSL.II.317, SJW, Kojong III, 773, 1871.3.25. See another reference to it in an edict in KJSL, 1871.8.25, cited in Ching Young Choe, "The Decade," 200, note 228.

92. MHBG 156:17b, which notes that the rate was increased to three yang per household in the kabo reforms of 1894. See also Hwang Hyŏn's reference to a two min levy, in MCYR, 12, which Han Woo-keun has interpreted as two yang. See note 91 above.

93. Yi Sŏn-gŭn, Han'guksa ch'oegŭnsep'yŏn, 204-205; Hayashi Taisuke, Chōsen tsūshi (Keijō, 1912), 522-523; Yi Sang-baek, Han'guksa kŭnse hugip'yŏn, 384; Chosŏn t'ongsa, sang, (Pyongyang, 1962), 814; Ching Young Choe, The Rule of the Taewŏn'gun, 35.

94. Han Woo-keun, "Taewŏn'gun ŭi sewŏn kwangjang," 303.

95. Ibid., 303.

96. The ministry's special and immovable reserves at this time totaled 47,000 yang of silver and cash and 60,000 p'il of cloth, KJSL.II.518-519, 1873.3.5.

97. Kim Kyu-rak, "Unha kyŏnmunnok" (ms., ca. 1871), 73, pagination mine. This information is included in Kim's chapter on "The Establishment of Village Gran-

aries, the Equalization of the People's Cloth Taxes, and the Creation of a Surplus in State Revenues."

98. *KJSL*.II.487, 1872.12.4 cited in Ching Young Choe, "The Decade," 200, note 229.

99. See the tenth hexagram, *lü*, in *The I Ching or Book of Changes*, trans. Richard Wilhelm, rendered into English by Cary F. Baynes (New York: The American Book, Stratford Press, 1950), I, 45-47.

100. *KJSL*.II.487, 1872.12.4.

101. Ibid.

6. The Abolition of the Private Academies

1. *Kyŏngguk taejŏn*, promulgated 1471 (Keijō: Chōsen sōtokufu ed., 1934). For descriptions of the early Yi educational and school systems, see Yi Sang-baek, *Han'guksa kŭnse chŏn'gip'yŏn*, 268-274; *Chōsen kyōikushi* trans. Song Chi-hak from the North Korean original (Tokyo: Kuroshio shuppan, 1960), 51-60; Yi Sŏng-mu, "Sŏnch'o ŭi Sŏnggyun'gwan yŏn'gu," *Yŏksa hakpo*, 35-36 (December 1967), 219-268.

2. Watanabe Manabu, *Kinsei Chōsen kyōikushi kenkyū* (Tokyo, 1969), 124.

3. *Kyŏngguk taejŏn*, 207.

4. Ibid., 240, 243.

5. Ch'oe Yŏng-ho, "Commoners and Yangban in the Civil Service Examination in Early Chosŏn Dynasty Korea, 1392-1600," ms., delivered at the 23rd annual meeting of the Association for Asian Studies, Washington, D. C., March 28-31, 1971, 9; Watanabe Manabu, *Kinsei Chōsen*, 162, gives a figure of 333 local districts for the country in 1413. Neither Ch'oe nor Watanabe discussed whether these legal quotas were always filled.

6. Ch'oe Yŏng-ho, "Commoners and Yangban," passim; Yi Sang-baek, *Han'guksa kŭnse chŏn'gip'yŏn*, 279, states that only yangban could take the *saengwŏn*, *chinsa*, *and munkwa* examinations, but no primary reference is cited. Yi admitted, however, that there were no restrictions against commoner attendance at school. "One cannot say that the route to education was closed off to youths of commoner status and below, but it would be no exaggeration to say that most of it was restricted to the sons of yangban." Ibid., 268.

7. There is some question as to whether a student had to be registered at an *official* school in order to obtain student (*kyosaeng*) status. Students at the National Academy were given tax-exempt status (*pokho*), *MHBG* 203:la. "The Regulations for the Household Tally System" (*Hop'ae samok*), ms., dated 1625, to take effect 1626.1.1, indeed, define the term, *yuhak* (literally, "Confucian student") as one who was registered in a school.

8. Yu Hong-nyŏl, "Chōsen ni okeru shoin no seiritsu," pt. 1 *Seikyū gakusō*, 29 (August 1937), 66; pt. 2, *Seikyū gakusō*, 30 (October 1939), 59ff.; Watanabe Manabu, *Kinsei Chōsen*, 163-168.

9. In the early fifteenth century, in addition to the use of private tutors in the home, individual scholars took on students in their private studies or libraries—what Watanabe Manabu terms the library-study (*sŏje*) type of private school (*sŏdang*). In the early sixteenth century the government encouraged the formation of village primary schools, which were sometimes attached to private academies when the latter were first founded. By the seventeenth century, however, the private elementary schools (*sŏdang*) were split off from the private academies guaranteeing them an independent existence, which they preserved into the early twentieth century. Watan

abe Manabu, *Kinsei Chōsen*, 170ff; "The Regulations for Schools in Capital and Provinces" (*kyooe hakkyo chŏlmok*) of 1545 in *MHBG* 203:8b.

10. The persecution of scholars by Yŏnsan'gun (r. 1494-1506) forced many of them to take refuge in the countryside. During the literati purge of 1504 Yŏnsan'gun turned the National Academy into a pleasure park and abolished one of the Four Schools. King Chungjong (r. 1506-44) found it difficult to restore the official school system and decided to encourage private and local initiative in the reconstruction of education. Yu Hong-nyŏl, "Chōsen ni okeru shoin," pt.1, 66-71; *MHBG* 203:6b; Watanabe Manabu, *Kinsei Chōsen*, 202, note 11, 203.

11. Yi Sŏng-mu, "Sŏnch'o ŭi Sŏnggyun'gwan yŏn'gu," 240ff.; Watanabe Manabu, *Kinsei Chōsen*, 200.

12. Yu Hong-nyŏl, "Chōsen ni okeru shoin," pt.1, 42-43, 75-89; *MHBG* 202, 203 et passim.

13. Ibid., 89. For similar developments in the late T'ang and Southern Sung dynasties, see Terada Gō, *Sōdai kyōikushi gaisetsu* (Tokyo: Hakubunsha, 1965), 23, 369.

14. Yu Hong-nyŏl, "Chōsen ni okeru shoin," pt.2, 82-84.

15. The first extant reference to this text was in 1481. It was also presented to the Korean court by Ming envoys in 1494. Ibid., pt.1, 84, pt.2, 87-88.

16. Ibid., pt.1, 75.

17. See the chart in Watanabe Manabu, *Kinsei Chōsen*, 204.

18. Terada Gō regards as noteworthy the establishment of twenty-three *shu-yüan* between 1246 and 1274. Terada, *Sōdai kyōikushi gaisetsu*, 315-317; Taga Akigorō records that there were 300 official *shu-yüan* in the Ch'ing dynasty, Taga, *Chūgoku kyōikushi* (Tokyo: Kawasaki Shoten, 1955), 99; Yu Hong-nyŏl reported a total of 320 or 412 *shu-yüan* in China founded from the Sung through the Ming, evidently a cumulative total. Yu, "Chōsen ni okeru shoin," pt.1, 57.

19. For an account in English of the splinter groups in Yi dynasty intellectual life, see Key P. Yang and Gregory Henderson, "An Outline History of Korean Confucianism," *Journal of Asian Studies*, 18:1-2 (November 1958 and February 1959).

20. Yu Hong-nyŏl, "Chōsen ni okeru shoin," pt.2, 106-108; Min Pyŏng-ha, "Chosŏn sŏwŏn ŭi kyŏngje kujo," *Taedong munhwa yŏn'gu*, 5 (August 1968), 76. See also Gregory Henderson, *Korea: the Politics of the Vortex*, 27.

21. Ibid., 86-87. The percentages are based on an estimate of 600-800,000 kyŏl of taxable land.

22. Ibid., 75, 78, 88.

23. See Yi I (Yulgok)'s criticism of the academies in 1578 in *MHBG* 210: 2b, also 210:3b, 9a.

24. *MHBG* 210:1a-b.

25. *Soktaejŏn*, 141, cited by Min Pyŏng-ha, "Chosŏn sŏwŏn," 78. Compare these limits with 400 kyŏl for the National Academy, 10 kyŏl for each of the Four Schools, 7 kyŏl for district schools (*hyanggyo*) in *chu* and *pu*, and 5 kyŏl for those in *kun* and *hyŏn*.

26. *Watanabe Manabu*, Kinsei Chōsen," 204; Min Pyŏng-ha, "Chosŏn sŏwŏn," 86, which cites Yi Kŭng-ik, *Yŏllyŏsil-kisul*, *pyŏlchip*. See the first volume of the Chōsen kosho kankokai ed. (Keijō, 1913), 201-278.

27. Min Pyŏng-ha, "Chosŏn sŏwŏn," 78.

28. *MHBG* 210:3b.

29. There was a request for a twenty-man limit in 1700, *MHBG* 210:13b. For the limits of 1710, see *MHBG* 210:15b.

30. *MHBG* 210:22b-23a.

31. *MHBG* 210:4b, Min Pyŏng-ha, "Chosŏn sŏwŏn," 92. It is not clear what was done with surplus slaves.

32. Ibid., 94-95.

33. *MHBG* 210:5b.

34. Min Pyŏng-ha, "Chosŏn sŏwŏn," 94-95.

35. The *MHBG* contains evidence of several instances of government restriction on academies in the quarter century prior to Sukchong's reign in 1646, 1655, and 1675. *MHBG* 210:4a-5a. For Sukchong's restrictions, see *MHBG* 210:14b-17b.

36. Watanabe Manabu, *Kinsei Chōsen*, 204. The nature of repression in Korea differed from that in China during the Ming dynasty. In Korea during the Yi dynasty, the lines of conflict between king and literati were more clearly drawn than during the sixteenth and seventeenth centuries in the Ming, when the repression of academies was led by high officials at court. Academy involvement in factional politics played a major role in both dynasties. See John Meskill, "Academies and Politics in the Ming Dynasty," in Charles O. Hucker, ed., *Chinese Government in Ming Times: Seven Studies* (New York: Columbia University Press, 1969), 149-174; Charles O. Hicker, "The Tung Lin Movement of the Late Ming Period," in John K. Fairbank, ed., *Chinese Thought and Institutions* (Chicago: University of Chicago Press, 1957), 132-163.

37. *MHBG* 210:18a-19a.

38. *MHBG* 210:22b-23a.

39. *MHBG* 210:25a.

40. *MHBG* 210:17b, 18b.

41. *MHBG* 210:23a.

42. *CSS*.6.3.533, 1858.7.10. In the index volume of the *Chōsenshi*, there is only one citation for the period, in 1801, when unauthorized rites performed by scholars at private academies in three administrative towns were prohibited. *CSS*.6.1.48, Sunjo 1.8.9 (1801).

43. *CSS*.6.3.554, 1859.4.5.

44. *CSS*.6.3.642, 1862.5.29.

45. *CSS*.6.3.643, 1862.6.1.

46. This statement suggests that there was possibly more syncretism under the surface of Chu Hsi orthodoxy than is presently thought to have existed in the Yi. Cf. with Sakai's comments about the late Ming. Tadao Sakai, "Confucianism and Popular Educational Works," in Wm. Theodore de Bary, ed., *Self and Society in Ming Thought* (New York: Columbia University Press, 1970), 331-366.

47. The term Hŏ used for this phrase was *mudan*, literally "rule by military (force)."

48. *Imsullok*, 390-392.

49. *KJSL*.I.118, 1864.4.22.

50. *KJSL*.I.136, 1864.6.7 (July 10); *KJSL*.I.163, 1864.7.27 (August 28).

51. *KJSL*.I.171-172, *SJW*, Kojong I, 391, 1864.8.17.

52. *KJSL*.I.172, *SJW*, Kojong I, 391, 1864.8.17.

53. The shrine was located in Kongch'ung province, Ch'ongju-mok, Sŏwŏn-hyŏn, Hwayang-dong, *CSS*.6.4.44, 1865.3.29.

54. *KSDSJ*. I, 459; Ching Young Choe, *The Rule of the Taewŏn'gun*, 70-72.

55. For details on these rites as performed by Sukchong and Yŏngjo, see *KJSL*.II.304-305, 1871.3.9.

56. *KJSL*.I.245-246, *SJW*, Kojong I, 636, 1865.3.29; *SJW*, Kojong I, 638, 1865.4.1. A Royal Secretary was also ordered to proceed to the Hwayang Academy to conduct rites there.

57. Kim Kyu-rak, *Unha kyŏnmunnok*, 61-62, pagination mine. According to the spicier but less reliable account of Hwang Hyŏn, it was because the Taewongun had once been insulted by the students of the Hwayangdong Academy that he took revenge on them when he came to power. Hwang Hyŏn, *MCYR*, 5.

58. Kim Kyu-rak, *Unha kyŏnmunnok*, 61. Emperors with tablets there were T'ai-tsu, the founder of the Ming, and Shen-tsung and I-tsung, or the Wan-li and Ch'ung-chen emperors, respectively.

59. Ibid., 68.

60. Ibid., 68.

61. Ibid., 69.

62. Yi I (Yulgok) himself, however, was reluctant to get involved in political factionalism.

63. There are innumerable examples to be found in support of this. During Injo's reign (1623-49) when the Westerners requested Yulgok's enshrinement in the Confucian shrine (*munmyo*), scholars from Yŏngnam (Kyŏngsang province) objected to it. Sŏng Nak-hun, "Han'guk tangjaengsa," 288. During the long dispute over the length of mourning to be performed by a member of the royal house—a dispute that lasted from 1659 to 1674—the Southerner officials and Yŏngnam literati were united against Song Si-yŏl, many of the Westerners, and the Ch'ungch'ŏng literati. Sŏng Nak-hun, 300-302. See also a memorial signed by 1400 Yŏngnam scholars attacking Song on the mourning question. Ibid., 166; an attack by scholars from Ch'ungch'ŏng against the Yŏngnam scholars, ibid., 302; and an attack on Song by a scholar from Chinju, the northwestern part of South Kyŏngsang province, ibid., 309. In 1683 the Westerner, Kim Su-hang, attacked the Yŏngnam scholars, ibid., 324; in the 1680s a member of the Disciple's faction (*Soron*) accused Song of downgrading T'oegye's scholarship. See the letter of Yun Chŭng to Song, ibid., 328. See Hwang Hyŏn's remarks about the Taewongun's personal animosity, note 57 above.

64. Ibid., 334-344.

65. Yi Hyŏn-il actually defended Queen Min against deposition, but in the course of so doing cast slur on her reputation, for which he was not forgiven by the Westerners. Ibid., 343.

66. See Chapter 3.

67. *CSS*.6.4.296-97, 1873.i6.20.

68. Kim's account merely states that since the beginning of the dynasty, the arguments of the Confucian scholars were not unified, that the four factions of Easterners, Westerners, Southerners, and Northerners existed, that their members would not reside with one another in the National Academy dormitories, and that the Easterners and Westerners held a higher place than the Southerners and Northerners.

The gist of the passage is that the Taewongun had established four new dormitories in the National Academy for student members of the four factions, indicating that he was catering to their traditional exclusiveness at the same time that he probably deplored it. Kim Kyu-rak, *Unha kyŏnmunnok*, 66, pagination mine. Hwang Hyŏn, *MCYR*, 3.

69. *KJSL*.I.269-270, *SJW*, Kojong I, 724-725, 1865.i5.2.

70. *KJSL*.I.292, 1865.7.26.

71. *KJSL*.I.329, *SJW*, Kojong I, 891, 1865.11.26. The arguments of the Kyŏngsang scholars were virtually the same as those of Im Hŏn-hoe.

72. *KJSL*.I.504, *SJW*, Kojong I, 504, 1866.10.21, a memorial from the Fourth Deputy Commander (*Puhogun*), Pak Kyu-sŏ.

73. Choe, *The Rule of the Taewŏn'gun*, xv.

74. *KJSL.*I.557, 1867.3.5. Crown Prince Sohyŏn (*Sohyŏn seja*), 1612-45, was the eldest son of King Injo, and he became crown prince in 1625. He was held hostage by the Manchus together with the *Pongnim-daegun* (later King Hyojong). He was famous for having met Adam Schall and for his role in bringing books on Western science and Catholicism into Korea. *KSDSJ*, I, 763. Grand Lord Inp'yŏng (*Inp'yŏng-daegun*), 1622-58, was the third son of Injo and younger brother of King Hyojong, *KSDSJ*, II, 1253.

75. I have not been able to find the original memorial in 1864 to which this statement refers.

76. *KJSL.*II.305, 1871.3.9; *KJSL.*II.306, 1871.3.10.

77. *KJSL.*II.79-80, 1868.9.3.

78. *KJSL.*II.40-41, *SJW*, Kojong III, 586-587, 1870.9.10.

79. *KJSL.*II.305, 1871.3.9. See *CSS.*6.4.180, 1868.7.2. for the change in the name of the *Ch'un'gwan t'onggo* (Comprehensive record of the Ministry of Rites) to the *Orye p'yŏn'go*.

80. Kim Kyu-rak, *Unha kyŏnmunnok*, 63, pagination mine.

81. *KJSL.*II.306, 1871.3.12.

82. *KJSL.*II.308, *SJW*, Kojong III, 765, 1871.3.16.

83. *KJSL.*II.310, 1871.3.18 (May 7).

84. *KJSL.*II.312-313, *SJW*, Kojong III, 768, 1871.3.20. *KJSL* contains a list of the forty-seven.

85. *KJSL.*II.316, *SJW*, Kojong III, 773, 1871.3.25. See Ching Young Choe, *The Rule of the Taewŏn'gun*, 73-76, for a recent account of the whole episode.

86. *KJSL.*II.374, 1871.8.16.

87. Kim Kyu-rak, *Unha kyŏnmunnok*, 64, pagination mine.

88. Ibid., 64.

89. This probably refers to the dowager-regent's decree of September 17, 1864.

90. Kim Kyu-rak *Unha kyŏnmunnok*, 67. This probably refers to the protest of the scholars from Kyŏngsang province in January 1866.

91. Ibid., 67.

92. Ibid., 60, 67, 129.

93. For references to these regulations, see Watanabe Manabu, *Kinsei Chōsen*, 31, 35, 176. For other regulations, see the *Hakkyo mobŏm*, comp. 1580, the *Hakkyo chŏlmok* comp. Cho Ik, 1630, and the *Kwŏnhak samok* comp. Kwŏn Kŭn, 1407.

Chōsen kyōikushi, 66, states that both Yi I (Yulgok)'s *Hakkyo samok* and *Hakkyo mobŏm* were compiled in 1582. The former provided regulations for the selection of teachers, and the latter set out the purposes of education.

94. *KJSL.*II.172-175, 1869.9.29.

95. *KJSL.*II.174, 1869.9.29. For Ching Young Choe's account of the reestablishment of the National Academy, see his *The Rule of the Taewŏn'gun*, 76-79.

7. Reform of the Grain Loan System

1. For a review of relief and lending institutions in Chinese dynasties, see Hsiao Kung-chuan, *Imperial China: Rural Control in the Nineteenth Century* (Seattle, Wash.: University of Washington Press, 1960), 144-183, 549-552; *Ajia rekishi jiten*, 2:360-361; 4:411-412, 9:183, 2:3; Palais, "Korea on the Eve of the Kanghwa Treaty," notes 4-6, 853-856; Derk Bodde, "Henry A. Wallace and the Ever-Normal Granary," *Far Eastern Quarterly*, 5 (1946), 411-426.

According to Hsiao's account the major difference between the Chinese and Yi dynasty granary systems seems to have been the greater degree of official control and involvement in the Righteous Granaries (*uich'ang, i-ts'ang*) in the Yi dynasty. In the later Chinese dynasties the *i-ts'ang* was funded by contributions from the populace and was also managed by local people with official supervision. In the Yi dynasty, however, they were managed directly by the district magistrates and their clerks. The government took the main responsibility for funding them and voluntary contributions played a minor role in this respect.

In Korea the first recorded instance of grain loans for relief was in A.D. 194 in the Koguryŏ kingdom. The founder of the Koryŏ dynasty, T'aejo (r. 918-945), is supposed to have established the so-called black granaries (*hŭkch'ang*) for relief. The name was changed to Righteous Granaries (*ŭich'ang*) in 986, and one such granary was supposedly placed in each of the prefectural units (*chu* and *pu*) throughout the country. They were still in operation in 1392 when the Yi dynasty was founded. They were administered by the district magistrate and loans were distributed from them interest free. After 1405 central surveillance over them was exercised by a bureau in the Ministry of Taxation.

The first example of the Ever-Normal Granaries (*sangp'yŏngch'ang*) occurred in 993 when one was established in each of the two capitals and twelve provincial-level units in the Koryŏ dynasty. They were only used for emergency situations in this period, however.

For information on the granaries in Korea, see Asō Takekame, *Shakanmai seido* (Keijō: Chōsen sōtokufu, Chūsūin, 1933); *KSDSJ*, II, 1775; *RCZS*, 1, 322-323; *Ajia rekishi jiten*, 2:361; *MHBG* 166:1aff; Song Ch'an-sik, "Yijo sidae ŭi hwanja," *Yŏksa hakpo*, 27 (April 1965), 25; Pak Kwang-sŏng, "Chosŏn ch'ogi ŭi ŭich'ang chedo e taehayŏ" *Sach'ong*, 7 (November 1962), 48-79. For the notice concerning the Righteous Granaries in 1392, see *T'aejo sillok*, T'aejo 1.9.im'in.

2. The Ever-Normal Granaries (*sangp'yŏngch'ang*) were revived in the Yi dynasty in 1458, and in 1608 the name was changed to the "Agency of Royal Benevolence" or the Tribute Bureau (*sŏnhyech'ŏng*), as it is referred to in these pages. This agency was created mainly for handling rice and other revenues from the conversion of local tribute taxes to a land tax. In 1626 the independent Ever-Normal Agency (*sangp'yŏngch'ŏng*, est. 1617) and the Relief Agency (*chinhyŏlch'ŏng*) were both incorporated into the Tribute Bureau. Although these offices were combined into one administration, the old names were still used in association with the particular function performed. *KSDSJ*, I, 181, 696, 734; II, 1775; Song Ch'an-sik, "Yijo sidae ŭi hwanja," 49-52; Asō Takekami, 13-14, 84-91; Pak Kwang-sŏng, "Chosŏn ch'ogi ŭi ŭich'ang," 50.

3. *Kyŏngguk taejŏn*, 192; *Taejŏn hoet'ong*, 230.

4. *Kyŏngguk taejŏn*, 192; Asō, 6, 12, 69-84; Pak Kwang-sŏng, "Chosŏn ch'ogi ŭi ŭich'ang," 49-50. Ever-Normal Granaries were never very effective in the Ch'ing dynasty in China and disappeared from view by the end of the dynasty. See Hsiao Kung-chuan, *Imperial China*, 146-147.

5. Asō, 3.

6. Hsiao Kung-chuan, in commenting on relief loans in China, stated, "Many of the defaulters failed to repay because they had nothing to pay with. Most of the peasants were hard pressed even in normal years. It was no surprise that they could not honor debts incurred during a famine . . . The best solution would have been to give them outright relief instead of giving them grain loans. But a new problem would have arisen: how to replenish the reserves thus expanded." Hsiao, 166, 181.

7. *T'aejo sillok*, T'aejo 1.9.imin; Asō, 29; *Kyŏngguk taejŏn*, 192; Pak Kwang-sŏng, 53, 62.

8. Asō, 31.

9. Palais, "Korea on the Eve of the Kanghwa Treaty," 241-246; *RCZS*, 325-329; Song Ch'an-sik, 30-33. According to Hsiao Kung-chuan, the interest charge in Chu Hsi's system in the twelfth century only amounted to 10 percent, which was then waived after the original capitalization had been returned to the prefectural government and a reserve had been built up in the granary. See Hsiao Kung-chuan, 175-176, 551. While the fifteenth century Korean village granaries did include a 20 percent interest charge, this was supposed to be reduced to a 6.7 percent wastage surcharge after the original capitalization was repaid. *Munjong sillok*, Munjong 1.6.kisa.

10. For reports of depleted reserves, see Pak Kwang-sŏng, 56-58; Asŏ, 38-39.

11. Asō, 60-64; *Munjong sillok*, Munjong 1.6.kisa.

12. Song Ch'an-sik, 32-33; *RCZS*, 329; Pak Kwang-sŏng, 62; *Sejo sillok*, Sejo 5.8.kimi; Asō, 67.

13. Since the 1471 law code, the *Kyŏngguk taejŏn*, does not include any provision for the collection of interest on military provision grain, the 20 percent interest charge was probably dropped prior to this date.

14. The 1746 law code, *Soktaejŏn*, provided for a 10 percent wastage surcharge (*mo, mogok*) on all loans of grain from the Military Provision, Ever-Normal, and district (Righteous) granaries. *Soktaejŏn*, 146. According to Song Ch'an-sik, between 1425, when the wastage surcharge (*momi*) was abolished, and 1554 there is no mention of such a surcharge. In 1554 an official's memorial contained the information that the current surcharge was 0.67 percent on principal (1 sŭng/tu). Song believed that the 10 percent surcharge became law sometime between 1425 and 1554. Song Ch'an-sik, 35-40.

15. Ibid., 35-40.

16. Recommendations were made in 1554 that the wastage surcharge (*mogok*) be regarded formally as state revenue and that account books be kept of it. It was also suggested that 1 percent be assigned to the central government as *hoerok* (recording fee), but this was not approved. Ibid., 42-46.

A memorial of 1642 noted that the 10 percent surcharge had been appropriated as *hoerok* to provide for traveling expenses. Another notice in 1654 stated that the wastage surcharge rate was 10 percent and that one tenth of this was *hoerok* and the other nine tenths was used by the magistrate. Song Ch'an-sik believed that the 1 percent *hoerok* was imposed sometime before 1636 because the later 3 percent *hoerok* was decreed just after the Manchu invasions of 1636.

The term *hoerok* was an accounting term, rendered in full, *karok hoegye* ("recording [said items] in the official accounts"). The items in question were recorded in the *hoean*, which were probably the account files or case files in the Ministry of Taxation. Ibid., note 64, pp. 44, 46-47.

17. Ibid., 49-50; *MHBG* 166, sijogo; *Takchiji*, 12, Hyojong 1; *MGYR*, chaeyongp'yŏn, chojŏk-cho (Section on grain loans); Chŏng Yag-yong, *Mongmin simsŏ*, 5, kokpu-cho; *Imsullok*, samjŏngch'aek-cho.

18. Song Ch'an-sik, 50-56. In 1648 the name of the Relief Agency was changed to Ever-Normal Agency and put in charge of expenses for Ch'ing envoys as well as price stabilization.

19. Ibid., 56-57.

20. Ibid., 60; *Soktaejŏn*, 146.

21. *Soktaejon*, 146; Asō, 96-97.

22. Asō, 93-94.

23. For a review of conditions in the eighteenth century, see Han Woo-keun, *Yijo hugi ŭi sahoe wa sasang*, 113-122.

24. *RCZS*, 332; Asō, 97ff.
25. *RCZS*, 334. According to Kwŏn Sang-no, ed., *Han'guk chimyŏng yŏnhyŏk-ko* (Seoul, 1961), 338, 392, 399, there were only about thirty districts (*kun* and *hyŏn*) in Kyŏnggi province. This would indicate that there were Righteous Granaries at the sub district or village level. These must have been administered by clerks and petty officials appointed by and directly responsible to the district magistrate.
26. *RCZS*, 333.
27. Asō, 98ff.
28. Ibid.
29. Ibid., 99ff.
30. For 1797, *RCZS*, 332, gives a figure of 9,269,600 sŏk. Asō gives a total of 9,380,654, but on p. 58, gives 9,369,777 sŏk. For 1807 see ibid., 475, note 28.
31. *MHBG* 155:17b-20b; *MGYR*, chaeyongp'yŏn, 485-490.
32. *MGYR*, chaeyongp'yŏn, 554-555. The largest expenditure in the period was 195,720 sŏk in 1787. Ibid., 563-568, The Tribute Bureau handled receipts from the tribute tax (*taedongmi*) after it was converted to a land tax in the seventeenth century.
33. For the period after 1807 the *Chōsenshi* has too many examples to record. For some examples in the sample period, 1809-14, see the following dates in *CSS.6.1*, 1809.11.21; 1810.2.2, 5.27; 1812.7.30, 10.30; 1813.5.29, 10.30; 1814.2.6, 6.5, 7.30, 9.16, 10.13.
34. Yu Hyŏng-wŏn, *P'an'gye surok* (Seoul, 1958 ed.,), 76. Yu objected to the potential of official corruption in Wang's *ch'ing-miao* loan system and also to putting cash in the form of loans into the hands of peasants, since this was conducive to unrestrained spending on the part of the peasants.
35. See note 9.
36. For the problems of corruption see Han Woo-keun, *Yijo hugi ŭi sahoe wa sasang*, 116-119, and passim; Han Woo-keun, *Tonghangnan kiwŏn e kwan han yŏn'gu*, 154-82; Asō, passim.
37. For the concept of polarity in Confucian thought and behavior, see Benjamin Schwartz, "Some Polarities in Confucian Thought," in Arthur Wright, ed., *Confucianism in Action* (Stanford, 1959), 50-62.
38. The analysis in this section is based on the following: Yu Hyŏng-wŏn, *P'an'gye surok*, 76-81, 143-147 (see Kim Sang-gi's translation into Korean; Seoul: Nong'ŏp ŭnhaeng chosabu, 1959), 289-309; Han Woo-keun, *Yijo hugi*, 311-314; Yi Sŏn-gŭn, *Han'guksa kŭnse ch'oegŭnsep'yŏn*, 72-77; Palais, 63, 263-267; Hong I-sŏp, *Chŏng Yag-yong ŭi chŏngch'i kyŏngje sasang yŏn'gu*, 134-161; Chŏng Yag-yong, *Yŏyudang chŏnsŏ*, V, *Kyŏngse yup'yo*, 12:1a-41b.
39. *CSS.6.3.630* (May 2, 1862); *CSS.6.3.640* (June 18); Pak Kyu-su, *Hwanjaejip*, 6:8b-12a.
40. *CSS.6.3.632-633*, 640-641, 646. Ch'ŏlchong's request for advice was issued on 6.12 (July 8). The complete text is in *Imsullok*, 363-364. 405-406.
41. Ibid.
42. Hŏ Pu was the son of a censorate official, born in 1797. His registered domicile was Yangch'ŏn in Kyŏnggi province. He passed the *munkwa* examination in 1835, and his highest post was minister of works. He died in 1886 at the age of 81. Sin Sŏk-ho styles him "a giant of the *Sirhak* school" and notes that his studies included rites, military affairs, agriculture, law, calendar making, and so on. See Sin Sŏk-ho's introduction in *Imsullok*, 4-5; Kim Sun-dong, ed., *Han'guk kosa taejŏn* (Seoul, 1965), 250, 290, 360. Hŏ was a rank four official at the time he submitted his memorial.
43. Hŏ Pu, "Samjŏngch'aek" (Recommendations for the reform of the Three Institutions), in *Imsullok*, 375-383.

44. Li K'uei was a minister in the service of *Wen-hou*, ruler of the state of Wei (446-397 B.C.). He is famous for his economic and agricultural policies, referred to as *chin-ti-li* (full utilization of the resources of the land). There were two aspects to this policy. One was designed to further the productive effort of the peasants, and the other was the establishment of a price stabilization policy in order to heighten the desire of the peasant to produce. The latter is described in some detail in "The Treatise on Food and Money" (*Shih-huo chih*) of the *Han-shu* (History of the Han dynasty).

Li K'uei believed that because the peasant family was not able to produce enough food to meet the cost of living and taxes, he became discouraged and lost his will to produce. Declining production caused the price of grain to rise. As a remedy Li proposed the establishment of a grading system. Crop yield was divided into three grades of good crop yield and three grades of poor crop yield. For a good crop year, the government would buy up a portion of the harvest, the amount varying with the grade of the year; for a poor crop year the government would sell grain from its reserves. See the article by Nishida Taichirō in *Ajia rekishi jiten*, 9:183.

See *Food and Money in Ancient China*, trans. and annotated by Nancy Lee Swann (Princeton, 1950), 136ff. For other material on granaries and loans in Chinese dynasties, see Dun J. Li, ed., *The Essence of Chinese Civilization* (Princeton: D. Van Nostrand, 1967), 288-306.

45. Yun's rank is not given. He was the descendant of Yun Im, or "Big Yun," a victim of the purge of 1545. Otherwise, little information is available on Yun. *Imsullok*, 4-5.

46. Yun Chŏng-ŭi's proposals are to be found in Yun Chŏng-ŭi, "Sŏk pukch'on chŏnch'o" (A preserved copy-book [composed at?] Sŏkpuk stream), in *Imsullok*, 408-413.

47. *CSS*.6.3.650-651, 1862.7.5; *CSS*.6.3.651, 1862.7.7.

48. *CSS*.6.3.658, 1864.8.27; *CSS*.6.3.659, 1862.8.20 (September 23). An undated memorial from the Reform Bureau containing proposals for reform is in *MHBG* 167:22a-25a. It is also to be found in the *Ijŏngch'ŏng-dŭngnok* (Record of the Reform Bureau), in *Imsullok*, 336-360. Judging from the content, it must be the one submitted on September 23.

49. The following discussion of the Reform Bureau plan is taken from ibid., 336-360.

50. Cf. this figure with the 2,311,690 sŏk given in *RCZS*, 366.

51. *CSS*.6.3.650-651, 1862.7.5.

52. *CSS*.6.3.651, 1862.7.7.

53. The term, *hyangyak* (*hsiang-yüeh* in Chinese), originated in 1076 when a Confucian scholar of the Sung dynasty devised a plan for village self-government called the *Lü-shih hsiang-yüeh*. It was supposed to be a system of voluntary associations of villagers for the support of morality and education and for mutual aid in production. The idea was picked up by Chu Hsi in the twelfth century and by scholars of the Ming dynasty.

Hsiao Kung-chuan in his study of the *hsiang-yüeh* in the Ch'ing dynasty has emphasized that they were originally devised as a local lecture system for the promotion of Confucian morality, social order, and harmony in the village, but that they were converted into a tool of the imperial government for police activities and local self-defense organizations. Hsiao Kung-chuan, *Imperial China*, 184-205. See also Wang Shou-jen, "A Rural Compact," in Dun J. Li. *The Essence of Chinese Civilization*, 309-312.

Koryŏ dynasty scholars were evidently aware of the system, but it was not formally introduced into Korea until 1398, when King T'aejo set up a village compact (*hyanghŏn*) of forty-one articles for his hometown. It was later spread to the rest of the country. The Korean system seems to have adhered more closely to the principle of local cooperation and association than royal control, although elements of the latter were not lacking. The creation of the *hyangyak* in the Yi dynasty has been ascribed to the demise of the *yuhyangso* of Koryŏ, a local institution of self-government that had been established with the object of curtailing the activities of corrupt clerks and petty officials. During Chungjong's reign in the sixteenth century, the articles of the *Lü-shih hsiang-yüeh* were promulgated throughout the country at the request of Cho Kwang-jo and Kim Sik. This village contract or village compact was composed of four articles: mutual encouragement in virtuous tasks; mutual surveillance to detect wrongdoing; mutual cooperation in the maintenance of rites and mores; and mutual relief in time of disaster. The scholars T'oegye and Yulgok and their disciples also set up model village contracts. See *KSDSJ*, II, 1706-1707. Regulations for the five-family mutual guarantee system in 1675 (*oga chakt'ong*) combined loan and relief operations at the village level with this kind of organization. Asō, *Shakanmai*, 95.

54. *CSS*.6.3.660-61, 1862.i8.11. *Ch'ŏlchong sillok*, 14:18a-b.

55. See Palais, 871, note 74, and items in *CSS* and the *Ch'ŏlchong sillok* under the following dates of the lunar calendar: 1862.i8.11, i8.17, i8.19, 10.29, 11.2, 11.15, 12.11.

56. *KJSL*.I.180, 1864.9.7. On several occasions in 1865 the dowager-regent repeated her charge of laxity against governors and magistrates and chastised them for their failure to investigate malfeasance in grain loan administration among the clerks in Ch'ungch'ŏng and P'yŏng'an provinces. *KJSL*.I.208-209, 1864.12.9 (January 6); *KJSL*.I.210-211, 1864.12.13 (January 10). The state council subsequently repeated the same accusations, *KJSL*.I.304-305, 1865.9.1; *KJSL*.I.396, 1866.5.10.

While this manuscript was being completed, Han Woo-keun published his study of the background to the Tonghak rebellion of 1894 that includes a section covering the grain loan problem in Kojong's reign. See Han Woo-keun, *Tonghangnan kiwŏn e kwanhan yŏn'gu*, 154-182.

57. *Taejŏn hoet'ong*, 229-233; *MHBG* 167:32a-b.

58. The governor of Kyŏnggi province revealed that only 14,317 sŏk of an original grain loan fund of 168,631 sŏk of grain was on hand in the province and that all the rest represented unrepaid loans. The government at first agreed to cancel two thirds of the debt and then was forced to acknowledge that there was little chance of collecting the remaining third. This produced serious shortages for current expenses, which, if met by reserves on hand, would have led to the total depletion of granary reserves. By 1866 the government decided that there was little choice but to cancel the old debts and establish new loan funds. The sense of crisis over revenue and reserve shortages was mounting. See *KJSL*.I.293, 1865.7.28; *KJSL*.I.298, 1865.8.9; *KJSL*.I.315, 1865.10.7; *KJSL*.I.395, 1866.5.10.

Reports about peasant difficulties in repaying loans in Kyŏngsang province did not lead to cancellation of outstanding loans, but permission was granted to commute half the repayment to cash in order to allow the peasants to benefit from favorable cash-grain conversion rates. See *KJSL*.I.251-252, 1865.4.5; *KJSL*.I.285, 1865.6.17; *KJSL*.I.296-297, 1865.8.3.

On April 16, 1864, the governor of Kongch'ung province reported that in 1862 two thirds of the grain loans due had been exempted from repayment, but after that date it was discovered that almost all the grain loan records had been falsified. There was supposed to be a fund of 226,683 sŏk in the province, but in fact almost all of it was owed and the granaries were empty of reserves. He praised the benevolence of the 1862 cancellations but also pointed out that because of the existing shortages there was no hope of repeating that policy. The two thirds portion that was exempted from repayment in 1862 came to 380,000 sŏk. See *KJSL*.I.93, 1864.3.11; *KJSL*.I.95-96, 1864.3.13.

On October 20, 1865, the state council memorialized in response to a request from the governor of Kangwŏn province for substitute funds instead of grain loan interest that it would be difficult to continue the policy of granting exemptions from repayment of loans and replacing them with substitute funds. From then on anybody illegally owing funds would be punished. After a debt was cancelled in the future, the magistrate would have to find the best way to make up for the loss. There would be no need to memorialize the throne every time this occurred. *KJSL*.I.305, 1865.9.1.

In 1864 when the magistrate of Suwŏn in Kyŏnggi province requested permission to loan out 10,000 yang of cash at interest to meet his expenses, the Border Defense Command had approved the request even while admitting that it was a violation of current policy. *KJSL*.I.50, 1864.1.21. It at first authorized the establishment of such a fund in Kyŏngsang province but then reminded itself that the policy of 1862 had prohibited further additions to grain loan funds in the southern provinces and requested that the new fund be established in the name of Hwanghae province instead, in order to maintain conformity with the law. *KJSL*.I.71-72, 1864.2.21.

In 1864 the secret censor for Ŭiju on the Yalu River reported that grain reserves used for the rations of border garrisons had been depleted by grain loans and nonrepayment of debts and that something had to be done to replenish the reserves. The only response of the government on this occasion was to rail against unauthorized loans of public funds, empty granaries that were supposed to be filled with grain, and transfers of funds from one agency to another to make up for shortages. *KJSL*.I.94-95, 1864.3.12; *KJSL*.I.134, 1864.6.1.

For one case of a blanket order for reduction and cancellation of loans in honor of the dowager-regent's birthday, see *KJSL*.I.161, 1864.7.25.

59. *KJSL*.I.161, 1864.7.26.

60. Ibid.

61. Ibid.

62. *KJSL*.I.181, 1864.9.13.

63. *KJSL*.I.221, 1865.1.11.

64. *KJSL*.I.253, 1865.4.9.

65. Ibid. For the list of men punished as a result of these investigations, see *KJSL*.I.259, 1865.4.26.

66. *KJSL*.I.304-305, 1865.9.1.

67. *KJSL*.I.396, 1866.5.10.

68. Ibid.

69. *KJSL*.I.397, 1866.5.12. The distribution of cash from the palace treasury by province was as follows:

Province	Cash (in yang)
Kyŏnggi	40,000
Kyŏngsang	70,000
Chŏlla	60,000
Ch'ungch'ŏng	60,000
Hwanghae	50,000
Kangwŏn	20,000
Total	300,000

See also Ching Young Choe, *The Rule of the Taewŏn'gun*, 36.

70. *KJSL*.I.401, 1866.5.27.

71. For notices pertaining to the use of grain loan interest for administrative and defense purposes, see *KJSL*.I.483, 1866.10.4, *SJW*, Kojong II, 338; *KJSL*.I.524-525, *SJW*, Kojong II, 410, 1866.12.14; *KJSL*.I.536-537, *SJW*, Kojong II, 441, 1867.1.15; *KJSL*.I.552-553, 1867.2.20. In this last case the court authorized that half of the 100,000 sŏk of garrison reserve grain in P'yŏng'an province be loaned out at 6.7 percent interest. The state council noted that even though new regulations provided for loans without interest, the need for military expenses justified authorization of this request for an interest charge. *KJSL*.I.595, 1867.3.28; *KJSL*.I.580, 1867.5.23.

There were also some reports that loans to peasants could not be paid back. See *KJSL*.I.571, 1867.4.25; *KJSL*.I.572, 1867.4.27. One report stated that loans due on Kanghwa Island had to be written off because of the destruction caused by the French attack, *KJSL*.I.507, 1866.10.30, *MHBG* 167:32b-33a.

In Kyŏnggi province half the grain reserve, a total of 32,170 bags of rice, had to be distributed as relief to the poor after the French expedition. *KJSL*.I.574-575, 1867.5.1.

72. *KJSL*.I.555-556, 1867.3.1; *KJSL*.I.556-557, 1867.3.4.

73. *KJSL*.I.582-583, *SJW*, Kojong II, 580, 1867.6.3. The distribution by province of the new cash fund was:

Province	Cash (in yang)
Kyŏngsang	600,000
Chŏlla	480,000
Ch'ungch'ŏng	300,000
Hwanghae	120,000
Total	1,500,000

For the order postponing repayment, see *KJSL*.I.587-588, 1867.6.11.

74. *KJSL*.I.584-585, *SJW*, Kojong II, 582-583, 1867.6.6. Lu Chih lived A.D. 754-805 and served under Emperor Te-tsung of the T'ang. A brief biography is in *Ajia rekishi jiten*, 9:193.

75. *KJSL*.I.584-585, *SJW*, Kojong II, 582-583, 1867.6.6.

76. Ibid., *KJSL*.I.587, 1867.6.11.

77. *KJSL*.I.584-585, *SJW*, Kojong II, 582-583, 1867.6.6.

78. *KJSL*.I.586-587, 1867.6.11.

79. Ibid. (not in *SJW*). For Kim Pyŏng-hak's original proposals, see *KJSL*.I.584-585, *SJW*, Kojong II, 582-583, 1867.6.6.

80. *KJSL*.II.292-293, 1871.2.5; *KJSL*.II.369, *SJW*, Kojong III, 874, 1871.8.11; *KJSL*.II.461-462, 1872.7.6; *KJSL*.I.634, *SJW*, Kojong II, 753, 1867.12.22; *KJSL*.I.631-632, *SJW*, Kojong II, 744, 1867.12.11; *KJSL*.II.9, 1868.1.25; *KJSL*.II.254, *SJW*, Kojong III, 636, 1870.i10.15; *KJSL*.II.185, 1869.11.14; *KJSL*.II.419-420, 1872.1.25; *KJSL*.II.417, 1872.1.10; *KJSL*.II.150, 1869.5.22; *KJSL*.II.170, 1869.9.23.

81. *KJSL*.II.461-462, 1872.7.6; *KJSL*.II.176, *SJW*, Kojong III, 332, 1869.9.30; *KJSL*.II.279, 1871.1.4; *KJSL*.II.252, *SJW*, Kojong III, 632, 1870.i10.10; *KJSL*.II.170, 1869.9.23; *KJSL*.II.29-31, 1871.1.29; *KJSL*.II.467, 1872.8.9; *KJSL*.II.157, 1869.6.30.

82. *KJSL*.I.608, 1867.9.14; *KJSL*.II.101-104, 1868.11.5; *KJSL*.I.634, *SJW*, Kojong II, 753, 1867.12.22; *KJSL*.II.254, *SJW*, Kojong III, 636, 1870.i10.15; *KJSL*.II.49, 1868.5.23; *KJSL*.II.512, 1873.2.9; *KJSL*.II.170, 1869.9.23.

83. *KJSL*.II.170, 1869.9.23; *KJSL*.II.461-62, 1872.7.6; *KJSL*.II.547, 1873.9.6; *KJSL*.II.5, 1868.1.8; *KJSL*.II.9, 1868.1.25; *KJSL*.II.491, 1872.12.13; *KJSL*.II.98, 1868.10.27; *KJSL*.II.274, 1870.12.29; *KJSL*.II.150, 1869.5.22.

84. *KJSL*.I.605, 1867.9.2. In this instance 5,000 yang of "newly minted cash" was used, *KJSL*.II.74, 1868.8.11; *KJSL*.II.36-37, 1868.i4.4 (no interest charges on this fund). *KJSL*.II.98, 1868.10.27; *KJSL*.II.169, 1869.9.23; *KJSL*.II.177, *SJW*, Kojong III, 336, 1869.10.3; *KJSL*.II.214, 1870.4.13; *KJSL*.II.241-242, 1870.9.15; *KJSL*.II.262, *SJW*, Kojong III, 657, 1870.11.17. On this date the Taewongun gave authorization for loaning out half the grain reserves on Kanghwa Island without interest for the purpose of renewing stocks. *KJSL*.II.371-372, 1871.8.14; *KJSL*.II.512, 1873.2.9. The Taewongun allocated 10,000 yang to Hamgyŏng province of which 3,000 yang was to be loaned out at interest in the southern part of the province. The interest was to be used for yamen expenses. *KJSL*.II.491. 1872.12.4; *KJSL*.II.488-489, 1872.12.4. On this date the Taewongun personally allocated 8,600 yang. *KJSL*.II.512, 1873.2.9; *KJSL*.II.489, 1872.12.4; *KJSL*.II.311-312, *SJW*, Kojong III, 766-767, 1871.3.19; *KJSL*.II.512, 1873.2.9.

85. On December 2, 1870, it was reported that cash had been distributed to twelve districts in Kyŏnggi province as loans, which were repaid in the fall in grain at a rate of 1/4 sŏk/yang. The same memorial took note of the contrast with the much more benevolent conversion rate used in 1867 (should be 1866) when the Taewongun authorized the distribution of 300,000 yang for loans. At that time the conversion rate for repayment was 1/100 sŏk/yang. Undoubtedly by 1870 the government was no longer able to authorize giveaway loan funds. *KJSL*.II.252, *SJW*, Kojong III, 632, 1870.i10.10; *KJSL*.I.397, 1866.5.12. In 1873 another fund was established with a stiffer conversion rate of 1/2 sŏk/yang under the Taewongun's authorization. The fund was called the Taewongun's Special Reserve Rice (*unhyŏn'gung pyŏlbigok*), *KJSL*.II.512, 1873.2.9.

86. *KJSL*.II.254, *SJW*, Kojong III, 636, 1870.i10.15; *KJSL*.II.98, 1868.10.27; *KJSL*.II.417, 1872.1.10; *KJSL*.I.605, 1867.9.2; *KJSL*.II.74, 1868.8.11; *KJSL*.II.36-37, 1868.i4.4; *KJSL*.II.169, 1869.9.23; *KJSL*.II.177, *SJW*, Kojong III, 336, 1869.10.3; *KJSL*.II.489, 1872.12.4; *KJSL*.II.489, 1872.12.4; *KJSL*.II.311-312, *SJW*, Kojong III, 766-767, 1871.3.19.

87. *KJSL*.II.45, 1868.i4.29; *KJSL*.II.192, 1869.12.22; *KJSL*.II.417, 1872.1.10; *KJSL*.II.157, 1869.6.30; *KJSL*.I.605, 1867.9.2.

88. For notices pertaining to Ch'ungch'ŏng province, see *KJSL*.I.619, 1867.10.24, *KJSL*.I.631-632, *SJW*, Kojong II, 744, 1867.12.11; *KJSL*.II.176, *SJW*, Kojong III, 332, 1869.9.30; *KJSL*.II.227, 1870.7.19; *KJSL*.II.279, 1871.1.4; *KJSL*.II.360, *SJW*, Kojong III, 860, 1871.7.20; *KJSL*.II.530, 1873.6.1.

89. See note 84.

90. *KJSL*.II.488-491, 1872.12.4.

91. *KJSL*.II.488, 1872.12.4.

92. Ibid.

8. Monetary Policy

1. *MHBG* 159:1b.

2. *KSDSJ*, II, 1773; Chang Kuk-chong, "Sipch'il segi kǔmsok hwap'e (tonghwa) ǔi yut'ong e taehayǒ," *Yǒksa kwahak*, 6 (1961), 52.

3. *MHBG* 159:2a-b.

4. *MHBG* 159:3a.

5. Chang Kuk-chong, "Sipch'il segi," 53. The famous scholar, Yi I (Yulgok, 1536-84), once remarked: "Korea is basically a poor country, and what is used [for currency] among the people is only rice and cloth, and that is all. There is no other material that circulates." Yulgok went on to recommend the minting of copper cash and suggested that strict punishments be meted out in order to enforce circulation. *MHBG* 159:5a-6a.

6. Chang Kuk-chong, "Sipch'il segi," 53; *Kyǒngguk taejǒn*, 199; for tax rates in paper money, see ibid., 169ff., 199.

7. Chang Kuk-chong, "sipch'il segi," 53; for a statement in 1625 by the minister of taxation that paper money had long been out of circulation and that grain and cloth were the only currency, see *MHBG* 159:5a-6a.

8. Chang Kuk-chong, "Sipch'il segi," 52-53. Large exports of silver to China and Japan produced shortages in that metal in the late seventeenth century. Silver currency became too valuable for small transactions, and there was considerable debasement of silver currency. See Wǒn Yu-han, "Yijo Sukchongjo ǔi chujǒn tonggi," *Tongguk sahak*, 9-10 (1966), 44.

9. Chang Kuk-chong, "Sipch'il segi," 44; Wǒn Yu-han, "Yijo Sukchongjo," 37; Wǒn Yu-han, "Yijo hugi ch'ǒngjǒn ǔi suip yut'ong e taehayǒ," *Sahak yǒn'gu*, 21 (September 1969), 145; *MHBG* 159:6a.

10. Only 1,100 strings of cash (11,000 yang) were minted in 1626—the *Tongguk t'ongbo* (Eastern Country Circulating Treasure), and the *sipchǒn t'ongbo* (10-cash circulating treasure). *MHBG* 159:5a-6a; Chang Kuk-chong, "Sipch'il segi," 44-45.

11. Ibid., 45-46; Wǒn Yu-han, "Yijo Sukchongjo," 40-41.

12. Chang Kuk-chong, "Sipch'il segi," 46-49. Kim Yuk noted that he had first gone to Peking in 1636 where he was overwhelmed by the wonders of Chinese civilization. "I wanted to propose copying everything, but it could not be done. Yet of all the things the most beneficial to the people was their use of vehicles and cash."

After another trip to China in 1644, Kim memorialized the throne requesting the minting of cash, but it was not adopted. When he went to assume his post as magistrate of Kaesǒng in 1646, he found to his amazement that the people there "were using cash just like in China." He again requested the throne to circulate cash along the "Western Route" (Hwanghae and P'yong'an provinces), but it was turned down. In 1650 en route to China he made the same request of the throne from Pyongyang, and then proceeded to China. Evidently without any authorization, Kim purchased 150,000 mun of Chinese cash with savings he was able to make from his expense funds. When he returned, he found the court had approved his request for the circulation of cash. *MHBG* 159:9a-b. The term *mun* probably meant either an individual coin or a unit of account similar to the *ch'ien* in China, whereby 1,000 *ch'ien* equaled 1 *liang* or tael.

The regulations for the circulation of cash in 1651 provided that the following proportions of tax and other payments be made in cash: one eighth the *taedong* tribute tax for Kyǒnggi province, one half the fines in lawsuits, one fifth the funds issued by government bureaus to merchants for purchasing tribute, one third the funds issued for hiring workers, and one third of the salaries, usually paid in cloth, of the Ministries of Taxation and War. The king also ordered the prohibition of coarse hemp as currency. MHBG 159:6b-8b.

Later, however, in 1651, Kim Yuk noted that in his travels through the countryside he found that the people were still using coarse cloth and not cash. MHBG 159:9a-b; Wǒn Yu-han, "Yijo hugi chǒngjǒn," 146.

13. Wǒn Yu-han, "Yijo Sukchongjo," 37.

14. MHBG 159:9b.

15. Chang Kuk-chong, "Sipp'al segi ŭi tonghwa chujo wa chǒnhwang munje," Yǒksa kwahak, 1 (1963), 40.

16. Wǒn Yu-han, "Yijo Sukchongjo," 43; Chang Kuk-chong, "Sipch'il segi," 51.

17. Copper was discovered on Kǒje in 1668, and mining was begun. Ibid., 50-51.

18. Pibyǒnsa tǔngnok 34, 1678.1.23, cited in Wǒn Yu-han, "Yijo Sukchongjo," 37,46.

19. Ibid.

20. Wǒn Yu-han, "Yijo Sukchongjo," 43-51.

21. Chang Kuk-chong, "Sipch'il segi," 44; Wǒn Yu-han, "Yijo Sukchongjo," 41-42. The taedong system was instituted in Kyǒnggi in 1609, Kangwǒn in 1624, Ch'ungch'ǒng in 1651, Chǒlla in 1657, and Kyǒngsang in 1677.

22. Chang Kuk-chong, "Sipp'al segi," 42.

23. Wǒn Yu-han, "Sipp'al segi e issǒsǒ ŭi hwap'ye chǒngch'aek: tongjǒn ŭi chujo saǒp chungsim," Sahak yǒn'gu, 19 (April 1967), 55-57.

24. Chang Kuk-chong, "Sipp'al segi," 42.

25. Ibid., 48-49; Wǒn Yu-han, "Sipp'al segi," 49-54.

26. Wǒn Yu-han, "Sipp'al segi," 50-54.

27. MHBG 159:8a; Chang Kuk-chong, "Sipch'il segi," 50.

28. MHBG 159:8a.

29. Wǒn Yu-han, "Sipp'al segi," 55-56, which cites Pibyǒnsa tǔngnok, 81, Yǒngjo 3.5.11.

30. Wǒn Yu-han, "Sipp'al segi," 56-57.

31. Chang Kuk-chong, "Sipp'al segi," 42.

32. MHBG 155:17b-20b; MGYR, chaeyongp'yǒn, 487-490.

33. MGYR, chaeyongp'yon, 553-556, 559-562, 567-568.

34. Wǒn Yu-han, "Sipp'al segi," and Chang Kuk-chong, "Sipp'al segi," passim.

35. Wǒn Yu-han, "Sipp'al segi," 66-67; Chang Kuk-chong, "Sipp'al segi," 43.

36. Wǒn Yu-han, "Sipp'al segi," 79-83. Government officials also looked upon mining as they did commerce—as a threat to agricultural production because it drained the work force away from the fields.

37. Ibid., 78; Wǒn Yu-han, "Yijo hugi chǒngjǒn," 151.

38. Wǒn Yu-han also presents figures for the declining profits from minting: 1679, 50 percent; 1731, 50 percent; 1775, 30 percent; 1798, 20 percent; 1814, 10 percent. "Yijo hugi chǒngjǒn," 73, note 74; Wǒn Yu-han, "Tang'ojon-go," Yǒksa hakpo, 35-36 (December 1967), 313-314.

39. The information from the MHBG is tabulated as follows: (in yang)

Year	Cost	Face value	Profit	Cost/value
1825	337,500	367,500	10.7	.92
1829	533,600	733,600	37.6	.73
1830	574,300	784,300	31.4	.73

See also Ching Young Choe, "The Decade of the Taewongun," 203, note 234.

40. Herbert Heaton, *Economic History of Europe* (New York: Harper and Row, 1948 rev. ed.,) 367.

41. *See note 37.*

42. Wŏn Yu-han, "Sipp'al segi," 73.

43. Chang Kuk-chong, "Sipp'al segi," 51; *MHBG* 159:17a.

44. Wŏn Yu-han, "Tang'ojŏn," 314-315; *Chŏngjo sillok*, Chŏngjo 22.5. ulch'uk; Chang Kuk-chong reports only a proposal for 10-cash in 1798. Chang, "Sipp'al segi," 51; Wŏn Yu-han, "Sipp'al segi," 74.

45. Wŏn Yu-han, "Sipp'al segi," 74; Chang Kuk-chong, "Sipp'al segi," 51-52.

46. Wŏn Yu-han, "Yijo hugi chŏngjŏn," 147.

47. Chang Kuk-chong, "Sipp'al segi," 50-51; Wŏn Yu-han, "Yijo hugi chŏngjŏn," 149-152.

48. *MHBG* 159:16a-b.

49. *MHBG* 159:18a.

50. Chang Kuk-chong, "Sipp'al segi," 52-53.

51. Ibid., 53. These objections were raised in 1742.

52. Chang Kuk-chong regarded this situation as unfortunate. Chang writes that the most logical solution to the currency problem would have been to limit the export of silver to foreign countries, use silver and copper cash, and require the government to make its tax collections in silver currency, but because of the opposition of reactionary officials, these proposals were never adopted. Ibid., 54.

53. *KJSL*.I.159, 1864.7.22.

54. *KJSL*.I.506, *SJW*, Kojong II, 366, 1866.10.30.

55. Ibid.

56. *KJSL*.I.512-513, *SJW*, Kojong II, 375, 1866.11.6.

57. Ibid.

58. Ibid.; *KJSL*.I.521, *SJW*, Kojong II, 399, 1866.12.1.

59. *KJSL*.I.521, 1866.12.2.

60. Wŏn Yu-han, "Tang'o," 315.

61. *KJSL*.I.575, 1867.5.4. On this date it was ordered that minting was to end on 1867.5.15.

62. Ibid.

63. For notices pertaining to military expenditures, see 1867.1.24, 1.25, 2.17, 3.1, 7.27, 9.2, 9.19; for providing for civil expenses, 1867.2.9, 2.15; for grain loan funds, 1867.3.4, 5.23, 9.2, 9.25; for other purposes, 1867.8.15, 11.18, 1868.1.25.

64. Wŏn Yu-han, "Tang'o," 315.

65. *KJSL*.I.583, *SJW*, Kojong II, 580, 1867.6.3.

66. *KJSL*.I.618, 1867.10.12; *KJSL*.I.619-20, 1867.10.28.

67. *KJSL*.II.4, 1868.1.4.

68. *KJSL*.II.12-13, 1868.1.30.

69. Ibid.

70. *KJSL*.II.89, 1868.10.6; *KJSL*.II.91-92, 1868.10.10.

71. Wŏn Yu-han gives the tenth month (lunar) of 1868 as the date for the prohibition of the 100-cash, but I have not been able to locate this notice. See Wŏn Yu-han, "Tang'o," 315. As the debate in 1874 reveals, however, there is no doubt that the 100-cash was withdrawn from circulation.

72. Wŏn Yu-han believes that a reference to "small cash" in 1867 really meant Chinese cash, although I see no reason why it could not have referred to "ever-normal" Korean cash. I am, however, willing to accept the view that large-scale

importation of Chinese cash began around 1868-69. Wŏn Yu-han, "Tang'o," 316; Wŏn Yu-han, "Yijo hugi chŏngjŏn," 154-155; KJSL.I.583, 1867.6.3.

73. It was estimated at this time that there was about ten million yang of ever-normal cash in circulation, but this was obviously a gross underestimate. For that matter, three or four million yang of Chinese cash may also have been a serious underestimate of the total volume in circulation. Ibid., 316; Wŏn Yu-Han, "Yijo hugi chŏngjŏn," 155. In the late eighteenth century the cost of Chinese copper cash was one tenth that of Korean copper cash. Subtracting transportation costs, smugglers were still making 500-600 percent profits. Ibid., 152, note 23.

74. Wŏn Yu-han, "Tang'o," 316.

9. Consensus Destroyed

1. There is a variety of opinion over the role of the Taewongun and the effect of his policies, but there is little disagreement with the view that the Min faction was almost entirely motivated by the selfish desire for political power. Ching Young Choe seems to have suggested that after 1873 there was nobody on the political scene who was able to provide the type of leadership that the Taewongun displayed in the previous decade. See Choe, The Rule of the Taewongun, 176. While most scholars refer to the opposition to the Taewongun's policies, they still put most stress on the Min faction conspiracy as the chief reason for his fall from power. See Hayashi Taisuke, Chōsen tsūshi, 505-524, 536-542; Yi Sang-baek, Han'guksa kunse hugip'yon, 373-396, which seems to follow Hayashi's account almost word for word; Chōsen kindai kakumei undōshi, Chosŏn minjujuŭi inmin konghwaguk kwahagwŏn yŏksa yŏn'guso comp., trans. into Japanese by the ZaiNihon Chōsenjin kagakusha kyōkai shakai kaguku bumon rekishi bukai (Tokyo: Shin Nihon shuppansha, 1964), 42-44; Chosŏn t'ongsa, sang, (Pyongyang, Kwahagwŏn ch'ulp'ansa, 1962), 811-816; Yi Na-yŏng, Chosŏn minjok haebang t'ujaengsa (Pyongyang, 1958; Tokyo: Hag'u sŏbang, 1960, ed.), 15-17, 41-43.

2. Palais, "Korea on the Eve of the Kanghwa Treaty," 476-494, 513-536.

3. KJSL.I.449-450, 1866.9.8.

4. Benjamin Schwartz, "Some Polarities in Confucian Thought," in Confucianism in Action (Palo Alto: Stanford University Press, 1959), 50-62.

5. For biographical data and the text of the memorial, see Yi Hang-no Hwasŏjip, 3, chuso; KJSL.I.460-462, 1866.9.12; Tabohashi, Kindai Nissen kankei no kenkyŭ, I, note 3, pp. 417-419 and p. 34.

6. See Schwartz, "Some Polarities," 56-57; Benjamin Schwartz, In Search of Wealth and Power (Cambridge, Mass.: Harvard University Press, 1964), 10-13, for the contrast between the orthodox Confucian and legalist points of view of politico-economic problems.

7. KJSL.I.460-462, 1866.9.12; Yi Hang-no, Hwasŏjip, 3, chuso.

8. Ibid., purok, 9, yŏnbo, quoted in Tabohashi, Kindai Nissen kankei no kenkyū, I, 35. See note 5, above.

9. Yi Hang-no Hwasŏjip, 3, soch'a, quoted in Tabohashi, I, 35, note 5.

10. For biographical information on Ch'oe, see Myŏn'am sŏnsaeng munjip, purok, yŏnbo, 1:1a-12b; KSDSJ, II, 1559; CSJMJS, 2005-2006.

11. KJSL.II.98ff, 1868.10.10; Ch'oe ik-hyŏn, Myŏn'am sŏnsaeng munjip, purok, yŏnbo, 1:12b-13b; Tabohashi, I, 36, note. 7.

12. See note 11.

13. KJSL.II.93-94, SJW, Kojong III, 38-39, 1868.10.14.

Notes to pages 183-185

14. Ibid.; Ch'oe ik-hyŏn, *Myŏn'am sŏnsaeng munjip, yŏnbo*, 1:14b.

15. Ibid., 15a; *KJSL*.II.95, 1868.10.18. According to the biography in Ch'oe's collected works, when Ch'oe entered the capital, he was surprised to find that he had been appointed to this post. Cho Tu-sun and others had opposed Ch'oe and his new appointment, but they knew that because of "public opinion" they could not block it and so did not resist.

16. Ch'oe Ik-hyŏn, *Myŏn'am sŏnsaeng munjip, yŏnbo*, 1:14a. Tabohashi Kiyoshi believed that the discontent of Kojong chafing under the controls imposed by his father, coupled with the opposition of the Min clan was the force that eventually brought on the retirement of the Taewongun from active politics. The Min clan, led by Min Sŭng-ho, in his view, had tried to influence Yi Hang-no to work with them, but were unable to persuade the stubborn old man to become their tool in their conspiracy to overthrow the Taewongun. They were pleased when the king praised Ch'oe's memorial in 1868, and their efforts were crowned with success in 1873. Yi Sŏn-gŭn generally supports the thesis of a Min conspiracy. See Tabohashi, I, 36-37; Yi Sŏn-gŭn, *Han'guksa ch'oegŭnsep'yŏn*, 343-344. For other surveys, see note 1.

17. Ch'oe Ik-hyŏn, *Myŏn'am sŏnsaeng munjip, purok, yŏnbo*, 1:19b-20b. See also Ching Young Choe, "The Decade of the Taewongun," 505. Choe stated in his dissertation, "The king and his in-laws were soon informed of the incident and managed to obtain an original copy of the memorial by dispatching a clerk of the Royal Secretariat to P'och'ŏn." The text of the *yŏnbo*, however, only mentions that a clerk from the Royal Secretariat was dispatched, and says nothing about the king's in-laws.

18. Ch'oe Ik-hŏn, *Myŏn'am sŏnsaeng munjip, yŏnbo*, 1:19b-20b; *KJSL*.II.551-552, *SJW*, 1873.10.25; *Ilsŏngnok*, 141: 37b-38b, hereinafter referred to as *ILSN*; *CSS*.6.4.302; Tabohashi, I, 38. For an alternate translation of Ch'oe's memorial into English, see Choe, "The Decade of the Taewongun," 504.

19. *ILSN* 141:39a-40a.

20. *ILSN* 141:40b-41a; *SJW*, 1873.10.26, 10.27.

21. For specific appointments of these men, see *CSS*.6.4. passim; for general biographical information, for Kang No, see *KSDSJ*, I, 28; *CSJMJS*, 2003; for Hong Sun-mok, *KSDSJ*, II, 1754, *CSJMJS*, 2003; for Han Kye-wŏn, *KSDSJ*, II, 1643, *CSJMJS*, 2012.

22. *ILSN* 141:n.p., 1873.10.27.

23. The information in this paragraph and the following table were compiled from data in *CSS*.6.4.

Number of Appointments Per Year

Year	Censor-General	Inspector-General
1864	45	47
1865	27	29
1866	25	28
1867	14	15
1868	17	18
1869	10	10
1870	14	15
1871	13	13
1872	14	14
1873	14	13

These posts could hardly have been functional if the average term in office was less than one month. In the first year of Kojong's reign, average tenure was little over a week per appointment. For a comparison with the Ming dynasty for length of tenure, see James B. Parsons, "The Ming Dynasty Bureaucracy: Aspects of Background Forces," in Charles O. Hucker, ed., *Chinese Government in Ming Times* (New York: Columbia University Press, 1969), 175-231, in particular table 1, p. 178. There seems to have been nothing in the Ming dynasty to compare with such brief tenure.

24. Twenty-one of the forty duty officials in the Office of Special Counselors (*hongmun'gwan*), Office of the Censor-General (*saganwŏn*), Office of the Inspector-General (*sahŏnbu*), and Royal Secretariat (*sŭngjŏngwŏn*) were dismissed on December 16. Most of those dismissed seem to have been junior officials. None of the top five officers of the Office of Special Counselors, for example, were dismissed. These were sinecures. Of the eleven eligible positions in ranks 3B to 6B, nine men were dismissed.

Furthermore, the list of names yields no clear evidence that the dismissals constituted a purge of pro-Taewongun men, although the list of those dismissed did include Inspector-General Hong Chong-ŭn, a clansman of Hong Sun-mok, and the third counselor in the Office of Special Counselors, Hong Man-sik, the son of Hong Sun-mok. Since the king later proved reluctant to dismiss Hong Sun-mok, these dismissals cannot be regarded as conclusive evidence of a purge. Furthermore, Min Yong-muk of the Min clan, who had just passed the examinations in 1871 and was murdered in Kim Ok-kyun's coup in 1884, was also among those dismissed at this time. Yun Cha-sŭng, the assistant negotiator of the Kanghwa Treaty, was also dismissed.

The new appointees included Sŏ Tang-bo, chief state councilor in 1881, and O Yun-jung, an important official for the next twenty years. No clear-cut pattern of factional purge emerges from this data. *ILSN* 141:n.p., 1873.10.27.

25. Both Hong Man-sik and Min Yong-muk were reappointed on December 21, and in Min's case, he was demoted from a 4A to a 5B post, a curious demotion for a member of a clan that was supposed to be leading a purge. Min Yong-muk was six generations removed, and Min Sŭng-ho was five generations removed from a common ancestor. For Min Yong-muk, see *Mansŏng-daedongbo*, II, 1466; *ILSN*, *SJW*, 1873.11.2, 11.3, 11.4.

26. *KSDSJ*, I, 874-875; Yi Sŏn-gŭn, *Han'guksa ch'oegŭnsep'yŏn*, 457.

27. *SJW*, *ILSN* 141:*n.p.*, *1873.10.28*.

28. *Ibid.*

29. For a discussion of previous Korean editions of ritual texts, see the dialogue between Kojong and the royal lecturer, Kim Se-gyun, *KJSL*.II.268, 1870.12.7.

30. *SJW*, *ILSN* 141:n.p., 1873.10.28.

31. Kwŏn was also a participant in the attempted deposition of Kojong in 1881. *KSDSJ*, I, 874-875.

32. *SJW*, *ILSN* 141:n.p., 1873.10.28.

33. The men involved were Kim Se-gyun, Taxation; Cho Sŏng-gyo, Rites; Yi In-ŭng, Works,; Sŏ Sang-jŏng, War; and Sŏ Tang bo, the former minister of Punishments. *SJW*, *ILSN* 141:n.p., 1873.11.2.

34. *SJW*, *ILSN* 141:n.p., 1873.10.28.

35. Ibid.

36. *SJW*, *ILSN* 141:n.p., 1873.10.29.

37. Ibid.

38. *SJW*, *ILSN* 142.2a, 1873.11.1.

Notes to pages 188-196

39. *SJW, ILSN* 142:5a-b, 1873.11.2.

40. For Hong's memorial see *SJW, ILSN* 141:n.p., 1873.10.29. Oddly, Hong's appointment was a demotion of five grades in rank from his previous post. It could be possible that an appointment to the Office of Special Counselors carried with it more prestige than a post in the other two censorate agencies.

41. *SJW, ILSN* 141:n.p., 1873.10.29.

42. For the memorial, and for subsequent quotations from it in the text, see *SJW, ILSN* 145:7a-13a, *KJSL*.II.565-73, 1873.11.3; Ch'oe Ik-hyŏn, *Myŏn'am sŏnsaeng munjip,* 3, memorials; Tabohashi, I, 39-43.

43. Ch'oe referred to the posthumous pardoning of Han Hyo-sun, Mok Nae-sŏn, and Yi Hyŏn-il. For a discussion of these men, see Chapter 3.

44. See the *Chonhwarok* (Respect for Chinese Culture), 6 *kwŏn* (1900).

45. See note 42; *ILSN* 142:13b-14a for exact page reference.

46. *SJW, ILSN* 142:15a-18b, 1873.11.4.

47. Ibid; most of the cosigners of the memorial were men appointed after the previous censorate dismissals. One of these was Hong Si-hyŏng, who had been transferred to a censorate post after his defense of Ch'oe on December 18. Another was Min Yŏng-muk, a member of the Yŏhŭng Min clan. Evidently these officials were still fearful of the Taewongun's power.

48. *SJW, ILSN* 142:15b-16a, 1873.11.4. During the lecture session Kojong replied to his critics that the student "strike" did not represent the feelings of all the students and that it had been instigated by certain leaders. He justified his punishment of them on the grounds that he was trying to prevent the formation of a clique. The lecturer, Cho Pyŏng-hǔi, protested that there was no danger of cliques, and that although the students were divided into groups with varying opinions, their refusal to submit to the king's orders was due to the failure of elders and educational officials to train them in the proper spirit.

49. For all references to the conference of this date, see *SJW, ILSN* 142:23a, 1873.11.4; *KJSL*.II.575-579.

50. See *SJW, ILSN* 142:23a, 1873.11.4.

51. Yi Kyŏng-ha was a relative of Dowager Cho's and a leading police official during the Taewongun's persecution of Catholics. During the coup of 1882, however, his son gave refuge to the Dowager and Queen Min. See *KSDSJ*, II, 1108-1109.

52. *SJW, ILSN* 142:28a-b, 1873.11.5.

53. *SJW, ILSN* 142:29b-30a, 1873.11.5. According to the record of Ch'oe Ik-hyŏn's trial, the state tribunal memorial was submitted on December 23. See *Ŭigŭmbu, choein Ch'oe Ik-hyŏn kug'an.*

54. *SJW, ILSN* 142:30a, 1873.11.5.

55. *ILSN* 142:26b-27a; Tabohashi, I, 45-46; Ching-young Choe, "The Decade of the Taewongun," 518.

56. Ibid. Tabohashi attached great significance to this incident, as has Ching Young Choe after him. Tabohashi believed that it proved that the consort clan had set about gaining control of the administration as quickly as possible after Ch'oe Ik-hyŏn's second memorial.

57. The signers of the memorial who might be construed as members of a Min clan faction were: Pak Kyu-su, Kim Se-gyun, the nephews of Dowager Cho, Cho Yŏng-ha and Cho Sŏng-ha, and Min Kyu-ho, one of the leaders of the Min clan.

58. *SJW, ILSN* 142:31a-32a, 1873.11.5; *KJSL*.II.579-581.

59. A Fourth Deputy Commander, Hong Man-sŏp, accused Ch'oe of being a blood relation of a low-class servant family and defended the students of the National

Academy for their attack on him. A former fourth inspector in the Office of the Inspector-General, Ki Kwan-hyŏn, claimed that when Hong was a magistrate he had delayed informing the central government of his father's death for a few days so that he could collect his salary. Later, a minor censorate official went over to Hong's house and accused him to his face of having praised Ch'oe in a memorial one day and then reversing his position by joining in a censorate impeachment of Ch'oe later on. For this last incident, see *ILSN* 142:37a-b. For the text of the other memorials, see *ILSN* 142:34b-38b, 1873.11.7. This material is to be found under the date 1873.11.6 in the *SJW*.

Kojong was incensed at all these accusations. During the royal lectures on December 26, he demanded to know of the officials in attendance how a lowly official in the censorate had the right to make accusations against a high official like Hong? What kind of foolishness was the charge that Ch'oe's family was related to a household servant? What kind of memorial was that by Cho Wŏn-jo a few days before (December 24)? Were all these men country bumpkins, rude and uneducated?

Lecturer Chang Wŏn-sang, an official in the Office of Special Counselors, replied that foolish as these men might be, yet "a sage can choose [what is good] from the words of a crazy man." But Kojong could not abide such petty and trifling charges against Ch'oe. In his rescript, he agreed with Chang's comment that the demented often speak truths, but said that these memorials were just too outrageous and ordered the exile of all four men. See *SJW*, *ILSN* 142:38b-39a, 1873.11.7.

60. For the composition of the tribunal, see *SJW*, *ILSN* 142:42b, 1873.11.8; *Ch'oe Kug'an*, same date.

61. Ch'oe Ik-hŏn, *Myŏn'am sŏnsaeng munjip, purok, yŏnbo,* 1:29b; Choe, "The Decade," 517.

62. Ch'oe Ik-hyŏn, *Myŏn'am,* 1:32b-33a; Choe, "The Decade," 517-518, note 58; Tabohashi, I, 44-45. It is possible that the Dowager Cho sent this note.

63. Tabohashi concluded that the letter must have come from the queen simply because no man would have written in *han'gŭl* (the Korean alphabet), instead of classical Chinese. But Ch'oe refused to act as a tool of the queen, just as he later refused to be used by the king after the Sino-Japanese war. Choe also agreed that the episode proved that Ch'oe had no political ties with the queen. See note 62 for references.

64. *Ch'oe . . . kug'an,* 1873.11.8 (December 27), for all references to the trial. *SJW, ILSN* 142:44a, 1873.11.9. The editor of Ch'oe's collected works stated that Kojong justified the exile on the grounds that the queen was expected to give birth shortly. Ch'oe Ik-hyŏn, *Myŏn'am . . . , yŏnbo,* 1:32a-b.

65. *SJW, ILSN* 142:49b-50b, 1873.11.10.

66. Text of the court conference is in *SJW, ILSN* 142:46a-49b, 1873.11.9; *KJSL.*II.586-589. All subsequent references and quotes in the text are based on this record.

67. Ibid.; the compiler of Ch'oe's collected works wrote that Pak Kyu-su was the only one who stated that it would not be right to reject the king's orders repeatedly. This statement, however, does not appear in the court records of the conference. See Ch'oe Ik-hyŏn, *Myŏn'am . . . , yŏnbo,* 1:33a.

68. *SJW, ILSN* 142:59b, 1873.11.11.

69. *SJW, ILSN* 142:54a-55b, 61b-62a, 1873.11.11 (December 30).

70. I have not been able to discover the exact dates for the Taewongun's movements. Yi Sŏn-gŭn notes that he first went to his "mountain villa at Samgyedong, just outside North Gate in Seoul." Then he went to pay his respects to his father's grave at Tŏksan-gun, Kaya-san, in South Ch'ungch'ŏng province. He then withdrew to his

"mountain villa" at Chikkok, in Yangju-gun, in Kyŏnggi province. See Yi Sŏn-gŭn, *Han'guksa ch'oegŭnsep'yŏn*, 351.

10. The Abolition of Ch'ing Cash

1. *SJW, ILSN* 143:13a-b, 1873.11.14.
2. *SJW, ILSN* 143:18a, 1873.11.15.
3. *SJW, ILSN* 146:22a-b, 1873.12.5.
4. Ibid.
5. *SJW, ILSN* 146:23a-b.
6. *SJW, ILSN* 146:29b, 1874.1.13.
7. *SJW, ILSN* 146:44b-45a, 1874.1.13. Yi Yu-wŏn noted later that day that ever-normal cash circulated in Hamgyŏng and P'yŏng'an provinces, and its circulation in the suburbs of Seoul was greater than in the city itself. *SJW, ILSN* 146:42b, 1874.1.13.
8. *ILSN* 146:43b, 1874.1.13.
9. *ILSN* 146:39b-41a.
10. *ILSN* 146:40b.
11. *ILSN* 146:42b-43b.
12. *SJW, ILSN* 146:69b-70b, 1874.1.20. It would seem that if the term *yang* denoted a unit of account rather than weight, then the figure, two million yang, would mean as many coins of Ch'ing cash as it would take to make up two million of this unit of account. If this were the case, the figure, two million, would refer to its market value just prior to its withdrawal from circulation.
13. Prior to the abolition of Ch'ing cash, the government agencies never recorded the distinction between the two types of cash. Consulting the chart in the text, we find that in the last quarter of 1873 there was a balance of 1,635,498 yang of cash, which one would assume would include Ch'ing cash. The report for the first quarter of 1874, issued on May 30 (4.15 lunar), listed Ch'ing cash as a separate category. This was after the promulgation of the order abolishing Ch'ing cash and after the first day of the second lunar month—March 19—when the government was to refuse payments of tax moneys in Ch'ing cash. At this time there was 263,307 yang of ever-normal cash and 2,064,912 yang of Ch'ing cash. The figure of two million yang of Ch'ing cash that was submitted to Kojong on March 8 or thereabouts jibes with the above figure, but 263,307 yang of ever-normal cash is substantially lower than the figure of one million reported to Kojong at court. Either one million was a grossly inaccurate estimate, or some of the ever-normal cash in the treasuries had been disbursed prior to the accounting report of cash balances on May 30.

The figures for cash reserves from the second quarter of 1874 to the third quarter of 1875 do not note whether the totals are in Ch'ing cash, a composite of Ch'ing and ever-normal cash, or ever-normal cash alone. One would expect the figures to represent reserves of ever-normal cash alone, since this was now the only legal tender, but it is not likely that the reserves of ever-normal cash increased from 263,307 yang in the first quarter of 1874 to 1,819,257 yang in the second quarter. Hence, the latter figure probably is a composite figure of both ever-normal and whatever Ch'ing cash was left in the treasuries.

14. *SJW, ILSN* 149:n.p., 1874.3.20.
15. *SJW, ILSN* 146:67a-b, 1874.1.19; *SJW, ILSN* 146:84a, 1874.1.24; *ILSN* 149:20b-21b, 1874.3.21; *SJW, ILSN* 150:63a-b, 1874.4.28; *SJW*, 1874.5.5; *SJW, ILSN* 150:10b-11a, 1874.4.5.
16. *SJW, ILSN* 151:29b, 1874.5.7.

17. *SJW, ILSN* 171:36a-37a, 39a, 1875.9.23.

18. *SJW, ILSN* 150:64a-b, 1874.4.28; *SJW, ILSN* 151:44b-45b, 1874.5.12.

19. *SJW, ILSN* 172:47a-b, 1875.10.25; *SJW, ILSN* 175:3a, 1875.12.2; *SJW, ILSN* 175:10a-b, 1875.12.5; *SJW, ILSN* 167:35a, 1875.5.10; *SJW, ILSN* 172:47a-b, 1875.10.25.

20. *SJW, ILSN* 151:44b-45a, 1874.5.12.

21. *SJW, ILSN* 146:70b-71a, 1874.1.20; 158:2a, 4a, 1874.11.1.

22. *SJW, ILSN* 146:90a-b, 1874.1.25; 146:10a-b, 1874.1.29.

23. *SJW, ILSN* 148:17b-18a, 1874.3.5.

24. *ILSN* 148:18b.

25. *SJW, ILSN* 150:38b-39a, 1874.4.12.

26. Kojong said that officials who had been sending tax remittances due the Tribute Bureau to the Ministry of Taxation might instead send them directly to the Tribute Bureau, which would then transfer funds to the Ministry. *SJW, ILSN* 150:65b-66a, 1874.4.28.

27. *SJW, ILSN* 151:94a-b, 1874.5.25. Regarding the lost ships, Kim told Kojong that the standard load was 1,000 sŏk, but the sailors' provisions were also aboard, so the loss must have been about 1,200-1,300 sŏk per ship, or a total loss of from 13,200 to 14,300 sŏk.

28. Yi Yu-wŏn also remarked on this day that even though the Ministry of Taxation had several hundred thousand yang of cash on hand, he feared it still would not be enough to meet the demand for 100,000 yang for extraordinary expenses. *SJW, ILSN* 151:11a-b, 1874.5.5.

29. *SJW, ILSN* 162:46a, *KJSL*, 1875.1.10.

30. *KJSL*.III.247, 1875.5.10.

31. According to Min the commutation rate would be 7 yang (per sŏk?). This would have made a total of 56,000 yang. Since Min estimated his ministry would receive 40,000 yang by this means, I must assume that 16,000 yang would have been used for some other purpose.

The 7 yang/sŏk rate seems rather high, since in other instances the government cash-grain exchange rate for grain loans was in the vicinity of 3 yang/sŏk. Either the government was attempting to maximize its revenue, or it was following prevailing market prices in a period of grain shortage.

32. *SJW, ILSN* 172:47a-b, 1875.10.25.

33. Ibid.

34. For a good study in English on the *taedong* reform, see Ching Young Choe, "Kim Yuk and the Taedongbŏp Reform," *Journal of Asian Studies*, 23:1 (November 1963), 21-36.

35. *SJW, ILSN* 146:61a-b, 1874.1.17.

36. Kim reported that 300,000 yang of ministry funds had been spent for the reconstruction of the palace alone, and that 20-30,000 yang more would have to be spent for this purpose. *SJW, ILSN* 158:1a-2a, 4a, 1874.11.1.

37. Pak Kyu-su, *Hwanjaejip*, 6:7b-8a.

38. Yi said that in Korea one string (*tiao*, in Chinese) was worth slightly less than 1 yang, whereas it was worth 1 yang 6 chŏn (*liang, ch'ien*, in Chinese) in *Kuan-wai* ("outside the passes," Manchuria?), and 5 yang (*liang*) in China proper. *ILSN* 146:38b. There is no way to tell if Yi was speaking in terms of Korean or Chinese units of account. I doubt that a Korean yang represented the same value as a Chinese *liang*, even though the Chinese character used is the same.

Yi's remarks do not seem to jibe with the findings of Frank H. H. King that 1 *tiao* was equivalent to 1 *liang*, although the number of coins on a string might vary between 800 and 2,800, or that strings could also be made up of 500 or 1,000 coins. Frank H. H. King, *Money and Monetary Policy in China: 1845-95* (Cambridge, Mass.: Harvard University Press, 1965), 51-68.

39. *ILSN* 146:39a.

40. Ibid.

41. This would happen if, for example, the value of copper rose appreciably above the mint price for copper. See Frank H. H. King, *Money*, passim.

42. *ILSN* 146:39b-40b.

43. *SJW, ILSN* 146:70b-71a, 1874.1.20.

44. *SJW, ILSN* 146:84a, 1874.1.24.

45. On this day Yi Yu-wŏn provided the king with a summary of the current fiscal situation. Word had come from the governor of P'yŏng'an province that the taxes from that province would be remitted to the capital by the first day of the second lunar month (March 19, about one week later). The expenditures required for tribute purchases and military expenses for the second, third, and fourth lunar months came to about 200,000 yang—100,000 for payments for the purchase of tribute articles, and 104,000 to be paid out by the Ministry of War. Yi urged that the most essential requirements be paid for first. Kojong said that the present deficits in government finance meant trouble unless something were done to make them up. Both Yi and the king agreed again to allot the reserves of Ch'ing cash in the treasuries for expenditures (evidently not as money, but as metal or ingots). *SJW, ILSN* 146:90a-b, 1874.1.25.

46. Kojong had evidently decided to use at least half of the Chinese currency, but it is not clear whether Yi was advocating that all of it be used or none of it. At any rate, Yi calculated the requirements of the various government bureaus from the first to the fourth lunar months and found that the Ministry of Taxation needed by far the most funds—close to 600,000 yang in which was included 200,000 yang for palace repairs and 5,400 yang for compilation of *The Records of Daily Reflection (Ilsŏngnok)*, one of the daily court records. *SJW, ILSN* 146:106a-b, 1874.1.29.

47. *SJW, ILSN* 147:12a-b, 1874.2.5.

48. Pak Kyu-su, *Hwanjaejip*, 6:7a-b.

49. Ching Young Choe, "The Decade of the Taewongun," 205.

50. *SJW, ILSN* 146: passim, 1874.1.13.

51. A more complete version of Pak's memorial is to be found in Pak Kyu-su, *Hwanjaejip*, 6:6a-b. See also *SJW, ILSN* 146:36a-37b et passim, 1874.1.13.

52. *SJW, ILSN* 146:37b, 1874.1.13. Kojong asked Yi Yu-wŏn what his experience was when governor of Hamgyŏng province relative to the problem of coinage. Yi's understanding of currency was rather vague, but he did report that the Kapsan copper mines were located in Hamgyŏng near the Chinese border, and that mining operations were accompanied by active competition and trouble among the people who flocked there to make profits. Chinese often crossed the border illegally to engage in mining activities and corrupted Korean officials through bribery. *ILSN* 146:38a.

53. *SJW, ILSN* 146:37b, 1874.1.13.

54. *SJW, ILSN* 146:91a, 1874.1.25.

55. *SJW, ILSN* 146:44b-45a, 1874.1.13.

56. *SJW, ILSN* 146:110b-111a, 105b-106a, 1874.1.29.

57. *SJW, ILSN* 146:105b, 1874.1.29.

58. *ILSN* 146:107b, 1874.1.29.

59. In other words, ever-normal currency had not been driven out of circulation in Kyŏngsang province by Ch'ing cash.

60. *ILSN* 146:107b, 1874.1.29.
61. *ILSN* 146:6b, 1874.1.29.
62. *SJW, ILSN* 147:24a-26a, 1874.2.8.
63. *SJW, ILSN* 147:84b-85b, 1874.3.12.
64. *SJW, ILSN* 147:24a-26a, 1874.2.8.
65. Twenty sŏk of rice was also provided to each *siin,* a term that probably referred to merchants, licensed or unlicensed. *SJW, ILSN* 147:36a, 1874.2.14.
66. *SJW, ILSN* 147:82a-b, 1874.2.28.
67. *SJW, ILSN* 150:58a-59b, 1874.4.25.
68. *SJW, ILSN* 155:46a, 1874.9.20.
69. *SJW, ILSN* 156:21a-b, 1874.10.8.

11. Maintaining the Status Quo

1. *SJW, ILSN* 143:13a, 1873.11.14; *ILSN* 146:86b-87a; *ILSN* 151:98a-b, 1874.5.25.
2. *SJW, ILSN* 146:41a-42b, 1874.1.13.
3. *SJW, ILSN* 146:61a-62b, *KJSL.*III.14, 1874.1.17.
4. *KJSL.*III.15, 1874.1.18.
5. *KJSL.*III.15, 1874.1.20 (March 8); see also *SJW, ILSN* 147:82b, 1874.2.28.
6. *SJW, ILSN* 150:9b-12a, 1874.4.5.
7. *SJW, ILSN* 150:25a-b, 1874.4.7.
8. *SJW, ILSN* 151:29b-30b, 1874.5.7.
9. *SJW, ILSN* 151:31b-32a, 1874.5.8. During the court conference this day Kojong remarked that even if the Ministry of Taxation had several hundred thousand yang of cash, that would still not be enough to meet requirements for extraordinary expenditures. Yi Yu-wŏn replied that not even a million yang would be enough.
10. *ILSN* 149:20b-21a, *KJSL.*III.73, 1874.3.21; *SJW, ILSN* 150:9b, 1874.4.5.
11. *SJW, KJSL.*III.86-87, 1874.5.5.
12. This is an odd statement since village granaries were not established in Hamgyŏng and P'yŏng'an. Kim was probably referring to other types of grain loan interest or capital that had been recalled from these provinces. *SJW, ILSN* 151:46a-b, 1874.5.12.
13. Cho also requested that 30,000 yang of cash be borrowed from the *kyŏlchŏn* or cash surtax on land to meet provincial requirements. He promised that this sum would be paid back to that account in the fall. *SJW, ILSN* 152:39a-b, 1874.6.13.
14. *SJW, ILSN* 154:3a-4a, 1874.8.2.
15. *SJW, ILSN* 154:10a-b, 1874.8.4.
16. See his written report, *SJW, ILSN* 157:37a, 1874.10.24.
17. *SJW, ILSN* 157:20a-b, 1874.10.24.
18. *SJW, ILSN* 157:96b, 1874.10.30.
19. Some provinces were subdivided into two parts for administrative purposes; that is, all but Kangwŏn, Kyŏnggi, and Hwanghae provinces.
20. *SJW, ILSN* 157:88a-b, 1874.10.30.
21. *SJW, ILSN* 157:69b-70a, 1874.10.29.
22. *SJW, ILSN* 158:30a, 1874.11.5; *KJSL.*III.178-179 carries this report on 11.4 (December 12).
23. Pak Chŏng-yang was one of the officials who went to Japan in 1881 on a special investigation mission. In 1887 he was dispatched to the United States as a special minister-plenipotentiary. He later returned to Korea and held a succession of

posts including the prime ministership. At the time, he was thirty-four years old. He had passed the *munkwa* examination in 1866 at the age of 25. *KSDSJ*, I, 537; *CSJMJS*, 1988.

24. *SJW, ILSN* 159:85b-86a, 1874.12.13.

25. *SJW, ILSN* 159:59a-b, 1874.12.13.

26. *SJW, ILSN* 164:86a-b, 1875.2.27.

27. *SJW, ILSN* 157:43a-b, 53b, 1874.10.27; *KJSL*.III.179, 1874.11.3; *SJW, ILSN* 157:69a-70b, 1874.10.29; *SJW, ILSN* 157:88a-89a, 1874.10.30; *KJSL*.III.181, 1874.11.4; *SJW, ILSN* 158:22a-23b, 1874.11.18; *SJW, ILSN* 158:7b, 1874.11.18; *SJW*, 1874.11.25; *ILSN* 158:8a, 24a-b, *KJSL*.III.188, 1874.11.18, 11.25; *SJW, KJSL*.III.188, *ILSN* 158:49b, 1874.11.25; *ILSN* 158:9a, 1874.11.18; *ILSN* 158:26b-27b, 1874.11.18; *SJW*, 1874.11.25; *ILSN* 158:49b, *KJSL*.III.188, 1874.11.25; *SJW, ILSN* 164:87a-b, *KJSL*.III.235, 1875.2.27; *ILSN* 160:106b-107a, 1874.12.29; *ILSN* 158:25a-b, 1874.11.18; *ILSN* 158:8b, 1874.11.18; *ILSN* 160:3b, 13b, 1874.12.16; *SJW, ILSN* 160:13b-14a, 1874.12.16.

28. *SJW, ILSN* 158:7a-b, 1874.11.18.

29. Hong reported that prior to 1864 the total grain loan fund in that province came to 820,000 sŏk, at least on the books. Most of this, however, was either falsely recorded as being in the granaries or defaulted and uncollectable debts. After the grain loan system in P'yŏng'an was virtually abolished by calling in the old loans and writing off the defaulted ones in 1865, the government made up for the 82,000 sŏk that it had been collecting as 10 percent per annum interest on the grain loans by levying a tax of 4 tu of grain on each of the 217,000 registered households in the province, and a land cash surcharge of 1 yang for each of the 98,000 kyŏl of land in the province was levied. These taxes produced 50,000 sŏk of grain and 98,000 yang of cash.

Hong Man-sik's account differed slightly in its figures from the original memorial of Hong U-gil, governor of P'yŏng'an in 1865. Hong U-gil's memorial mentioned 84,000 kyŏl of land and 84,000 sŏk interest on loans. He proposed a 5 tu/kyŏl land tax and a 4 tu/household household tax, to be levied on 210,000 households. See *KJSL*.I.161-162, 1864.7.26.

Hong Man-sik recommended that half the household grain tax be commuted to cash at the rate of 4 chŏn of cash (0.4 yang) per tu of grain (1/15 sŏk). Thus, instead of revenues of 50,000 sŏk of grain and 98,000 yang of cash, the government would receive about 29,000 sŏk of grain and about 274,000 yang of cash. See *SJW, ILSN* 158:7a-b, 1874.11.18.

30. *SJW, ILSN* 158:49a, 1874.11.25.

31. *SJW, ILSN* 146:88b, 1874.2.28.

32. *SJW, ILSN* 143:39a-b, 1873.11.24.

33. Ibid., *SJW, ILSN* 143:16b-17a, 1873.11.5.

34. For a biography of Hong, see *KJSDSJ*, II, 1763. He lived from 1776 to 1852. See also, *CSJMJS*, 1250.

35. For a biography of Im, see *KSDSJ*, II, 1286; *CSJMJS*, 202.

36. *KJSL*.II.597-598, 1873.11.17.

37. *SJW, ILSN* 144:9a-b, 1873.12.2.

38. *SJW, ILSN* 145:n.p., 1873.12.18.

39. *ILSN* 145:19b.

40. *ILSN* 145:19b-20b.

41. Ibid., 21b. This shrine was called the *ch'ungmoktan*. Tanjong was the young king whose throne was usurped by his uncle, later King Sejo.

42. Ibid., 22b.

43. Ibid.
44. *SJW, ILSN* 145:51b-52b, 1873.12.24; *SJW, ILSN* 145:58b-59a, 1873.12.26; *SJW, ILSN* 145:55a, 1873.12.24; *ILSN* 145:70b, 1873.12.28; *SJW, ILSN* 146:52b-53a, 1874.1.14; *SJW, ILSN* 147:21a-22a, 1874.2.9; *SJW, ILSN* 147:27b-28a, 1874.2.11.
45. *SJW, ILSN* 147:30a-b, 1874.2.13.
46. Ibid.
47. Ibid.
48. *SJW, ILSN* 147:79a-b, 1874.2.26.
49. *SJW, ILSN* 148:25b, 1874.3.6.
50. Ibid.
51. *SJW*, 1874.3.10.
52. One more memorial was submitted on May 30 by eight students from Kyŏngsang province. *SJW, ILSN* 150:43a-b, 1874.4.15.
53. *SJW, ILSN* 153:73b, 1874.7.30. There was some financial difficulty along the way, however. See *SJW, ILSN* 149:1874.3.20; *SJW*, 1874.5.5.
54. *SJW, ILSN* 143:12a, 1873.11.14.
55. *SJW, ILSN* 143:12a-b, 1873.11.14.
56. *SJW, ILSN* 143:58b-59a, 1873.11.29.
57. *SJW, ILSN* 146:53b-54a, 1874.1.14.
58. *SJW, ILSN* 146:88a-b, 1874.1.24.
59. *SJW, ILSN* 157:36b-37a, 1874.10.20.
60. *SJW, ILSN* 157:96b, 1874.10.30.
61. Cho Pyŏng-se, the secret censor from Hamgyŏng province, reported that after the village cloth tax was instituted in the village there, "military service tax allotments were really carried out on an equal basis, and there is not even one problem to discuss."
In his audience with Kojong, Cho also remarked that in the province every village was given a special designation when its able-bodied males were on actual duty in the army. When they were off duty, the village paid the village cloth tax (*tongp'o*). *SJW, ILSN* 159:15b, 26a, 1874.12.4.
62. *ILSN* 160:2a, 10b-11a, 1874.12.16.
63. *SJW, ILSN* 164:83b, 1875.2.27. There was one subsequent proposal for administrative reform. A former censor, Cho Kyŏng-sun, on February 3, 1877, recommended an investigation to compare taxes actually paid with the quotas set, and dismissal of magistrates guilty of excessive levies. He also mentioned that eligible males were posing as students to escape military service, and that as a result the military rosters in the village were empty of able-bodied males. Cho's recommendations were later endorsed by the state council on February 5, 1877. *SJW, ILSN* 174:n.p., 1876.12.21.

12. The Clamor for the Recall of the Taewongun

1. *SJW*, 1873.12.12; *KJSL* 10:53a-54a, 1873.12.12; *ILSN* 144:49b-52a, 1873.12.11. *SJW* carries the memorial a day later than *ILSN*. Pak U-hyŏn was a minor official and obscure figure, who enters the pages of history only because of this one memorial. He is so little known even to this day that his biography is carried in none of the major biographical compendia. The only reference to him is in the *pangmok*, or list of Yi dynasty degree holders in the *CSJMJS*. According to this he was a member of a relatively minor lineage, the Koryŏng Pak. (I am indebted to Professor Edward Wagner

for this information.) He was born in 1829 and received his *munkwa* degree in 1870 at the age of forty-one. He was no relation to Pak Kyu-su. *CSJMJS, pangmok,* 54.

2. *ILSN* 144:51a.

3. *ILSN* 144:49b-50a.

4. *ILSN* 144:49b-52a, 1873.12.11. The date for this in *SJW* and *KJSL.* 10:53b-54a is 1873.12.12.

5. *KJSL* 10:54b. See the memorial of the former third inspector of the Office of the Inspector-General, Kang Yŏng-gyu. Kang was a distant relative of Kang No, the minister dismissed by Kojong in December 1873. That is, they belonged to the same lineage but different sublineages within it. Evidently the degree of relationship was not close enough to demonstrate any factional alignment, since in this case Kang Yŏng-gyu was attacking Pak for suggesting the recall of the Taewongun. For biographical data on Kang Yŏng-gyu, see *CSJMJS, pangmok,* 205, *Mansŏng taedongbo,* II, n.p.

6. *SJW, ILSN* 144:58b-59a, 1873.12.12; *SJW, ILSN* 144:62b-63b, *KJSL* 10:54b-55a, 1873.12.13. Two rather prestigious Royal Secretaries who resigned at this time were Kim Po-hyŏn and Pak Chŏng-yang, the latter a secret censor in 1874.

7. *SJW, ILSN* 144:62b-63b, *KJSL* 10:54b-55a, 1873.12.13. Other memorials of protest against Pak followed. *SJW, ILSN* 144:63b-65b, *KJSL.*10:55a, 1873.12.13.

8. *SJW, ILSN* 144:63b-67b, *KJSL* 10:55a, 1873.12.13.

9. *SJW, ILSN* 144:68a-70b, 1873.12.14.

10. Kojong appointed Yi Yu-wŏn, Pak Kyu-su, Kang Mun-hyang, later a secret censor, and two leading censors, Cho Sŏng-gyo and Chŏng T'ae-ho to the state tribunal.

11. For the text of the interrogations, see *Uigŭmbu, choein, Pak U-hyŏn kug'an* and *ILSN* 144:77aff., 1873.12.15. Pak was beaten quite severely, especially on February 2 when a total of twenty-four strokes were administered.

12. *Uigŭmbu choein, Pak,* 1873.12.18; *SJW, ILSN* 145:11a.

13. *SJW, ILSN* 145:11a-14b, 1873.12.18; *SJW, ILSN* 145:17a, 1873.12.19; *ILSN* 145:n.p., 1873.12.20, the date of this memorial in *SJW* is 12.19; *SJW, ILSN* 145:17a-18a, 1873.12.19.

14. *SJW, ILSN* 145:24b, 1873.12.19.

15. *KJSL.* 10:58b, 1873.12.27; *SJW, ILSN* 146:10a-11b, *KJSL* 11:1b, 1874.1.2.

16. *SJW, ILSN* 145:55a, *KJSL* 10:58a, 1873.12.25. Hong was reappointed director of the Royal Clan Administration, *ILSN* 145:57a-b, 1873.12.26.

17. *KJSL* 10:59a-b, 1873.12.29 (February 15).

18. *SJW, ILSN* 145:n.p., 1873.12.30.

19. *KJSL* 10:54b, 1873.12.12. Hong submitted two more refusals on February 17 and 18. He did appear at court on March 25, the day the queen gave birth to a son, but Kang and Han failed to make their appearances. Kojong sent both of them notes deploring their absence. *SJW, ILSN* 146:5b, 1874.1.1; *SJW, ILSN* 146:9b, 1874.1.2; *KJSL* 11:13a, 1874.2.8; *SJW, ILSN* 147:26a, 1874.2.10.

20. *SJW, ILSN* 157:11b, *KJSL.*11:87a-b, 1874.10.20; Ching Young Choe, "The Decade of the Taewongun," 502.

21. *SJW, ILSN* 157:11b, *KJSL* 11:87a-b, 1874.10.20.

22. Ibid.

23. *SJW, ILSN* 157:13b-14a, 1874.10.21; *SJW, ILSN* 157:16a-17a, 1874.10.22.

24. *SJW, ILSN* 157:19a-b, 1874.10.23.

25. Hwang Hyŏn, *MCYR,* 22.

26. Ibid.

27. See Yi Sŏn-gŭn's account of the assassination based on Hwang Hyŏn's *Maech'ŏn yarok*, Yun Hyo-jŏng's *P'ung'un Hanmal pisa*, and Hwang Hyŏn's unpublished *Oha-gimun* (colophon dated 1910) in *Han'guksa ch'oegŭnsep'yŏn*, 359-362. The text of the MCYR account is as follows:

At the time Min Sŭng-ho was in mourning and he had a mountain monk offer prayers for happiness in a quiet place for his son. Then he waited [for word to come]. One day a letter was sent from some place outside. It came from the place where the prayers were being performed. The monk wrote [on the package], "Open this in a private room. Its contents will bring good fortune. Do not let any one else take part [in opening it]."

Min looked around for the man who had brought it, but he had already gone. Half-doubting, half-believing, he followed the instructions and read the letter in a quiet spot. . . . When he tried to [un]lock it [the package], there was a roaring explosion. His son, then ten years old, and his grandfather all died on the spot. Min Sŭng-ho was thrown into the air, and his whole body was [charred] like a piece of coal. Like a dummy he could not speak. He passed the night and died.

When he died he pointed toward the *Unhyŏn'gun* [the Taewongun's palace] two or three times. Outside there was chatter and confusion, and [people] eyed the Taewongun, but in the end it was not known from whom the package came. The "two palaces" [king and queen] grieved over the death. Queen Min also gnashed her teeth at the Taewongun, but there was no way for her to avenge this.

It happened that there was also a fire at Yi Ch'oe-ŭng's house. The queen thought that [it was because] the Taewongun hated them that both these fires were plotted. Subsequently she spied on him and arrested a man named Chang, who was a retainer of Sin Ch'ŏl-gyun. Sin had long ago come from the house of the Taewongun. Consequently, they trumped up a case against him and put him on trial. Hwang Hyŏn, *MCYR*, 26.

28. Hwang, *MCYR*, 27-28. Yi Sŏn-gŭn was able to gain access to an unpublished manuscript of Hwang Hyŏn, the *Oha-gimun* (colophon dated 1910), which confirms the above account. According to this source, Min Kyu-ho sent a man named Kim, who lived for a long while in Manchuria later on, to carry out the assassination. Later Kim made his appearance and confessed and returned to reside in Seoul. (This source was not available to me.) See note 27.

29. *SJW, ILSN* 159:52a-b, 1874.12.11.

30. *SJW, ILSN* 150:32a-b, 1874.4.10.

31. The following list of offices held by Min Kyu-ho in 1874-75 is compiled from various sources:

Date	(lunar)	Post	Source	Rank
March 7	1.19	2nd counselor in office of Special Counselors	KJSL	3A
March 16	1.28	In attendance as *yagwŏn* (medical officer)	KJSL	
June 27	5.14	2nd Minister of Personnel	KJSL	2B
November 27	10.19	Minister of Rites	KJSL	2A

Date	(lunar)	Post	Source	Rank
December 16	11.8	Sixth State Councilor	KJSL	2A
January 5 ('75)	11.28	*Death of Min Sŭng-ho*		
March 5	1.28	Deputy Director, office of Special Counselors	Kim Haeng-ja Minbi, 106	2B
March 23	2.16	Resigns from Commander of Oyŏngch'ŏng	ILSN 164:42a, SJW	
March 30	2.23	Seventh State Councilor	Kim, 106	2A
April 7	3.2	Chief Magistrate of Seoul	KJSL	2A
June 17	5.14	2nd Minister of Personnel	CSS.6.4.330	2B
September 2	8.3	Minister of Personnel	Kim, 106	2A
September 5	8.6	*Muwi tot'ongsa* (Commander of new palace guards)	Kim, 106	

32. *ILSN* 163:74a-b. According to the memorial, he was concurrently sixth state councilor at the time.

33. *SJW, ILSN* 164:42a, 45a, 1875.2.14.

34. *SJW, ILSN* 164:47b, 1875.2.16.

35. See Ching Young Choe, "The Decade of the Taewongun," 164ff., for a description of the restoration of the Three Armies Command (*samgunbu*) in 1868.

36. *SJW, ILSN* 164:71b-72a, 1875.2.22.

37. *SJW, ILSN* 164:74a-b, 1874.2.23. Min submitted a formal declination that was rejected.

38. See note 31. For information on the *Muwiso*, see the article in *KSDSJ*, I. 492. This unit was established in 1874 and placed under the jurisdiction of the commander of the Military Training Agency (*Hullyŏn-dogam*). *ILSN* 153:10a, 1874.7.4.

For notices pertaining to the establishment of the *Muwiso* (also called *P'asugun*), see *SJW, ILSN* 150:58b-59a, 1874.4.25; *SJW, ILSN* 150:68b-70b, 1874.4.29; *SJW*, 1874.5.19; *SJW, ILSN* 152:55a, 1874.6.20; *SJW, ILSN* 153:41a-b, 1874.7.15; *SJW, ILSN* 154:67a-b, 1874.8.28; *SJW, ILSN* 155:62a, 1874.9.26.

Since Min Kyu-ho's appointment as *Muwiso tot'ongsa* came so quickly after his appointment to the post of Minister of Personnel, it is possible that it was intended for him to hold the two posts concurrently. See *KJSL*.12:29b, 1875.8.3, 8.6.

39. Son Yŏng-no was born in 1820, a member of the Kyŏngju Son clan. He passed the *munkwa* examination in 1841 and was fifty-five years old when he submitted his impeachment of Yi Yu-wŏn. *CSJMJS, pangmok*, 227.

40. *SJW, ILSN* 158:59a-b, 1874.11.29.

41. *ILSN*, 158:59b.

42. *ILSN* 158:59b-60a.

43. *Ŭigŭmbu, choein Son Yŏng-no kug'an*, see 1874.11.30, 12.1, 12.2; *SJW, ILSN* 158:79b, 1874.11.30.

44. *Ŭigŭmbu*, 1874.12.3, 12.4, 12.5; *SJW, ILSN* 159:7a-b, 12a. Kim Ok-kyun makes his appearance here as a signatory of one of the protest memorials. He was sixth counselor in the Office of Special Counselors at the time. See *ILSN* 159:9a-b, 1874.12.3.

45. Ching Young Choe wrote of Yi Yu-wŏn that he "actively sided with the Min faction" and that "he was incredibly corrupt and selfish." See "The Decade of the Taewongun," 486, note 2. Yi Sŏn-gŭn has accused Yi of collusion and profiteering

while governor of Hamgyŏng province in the mid-1860s. Yi claims that his refusal to accept the appointment of chief state councilor in 1874 was only a sham and "an attempt to elevate his reputation." Yi Sŏn-gŭn also claimed Yi Yu-wŏn was a trusted subordinate of the Min faction because in 1875 he was sent on a mission to China to ensure the investiture of the crown prince; that Yi Yu-wŏn also negotiated secretly with Hanabusa, the Japanese resident in Pusan, to influence the Chinese authorities in Peking to invest the prince; and that Yi was one of the agents of "subservient" diplomacy toward the Chinese. See Han'guksa ch'oegŭnsep'yŏn, 335-354, 362. Yi Sŏn-gŭn, however, did not document some of these charges. I have not discovered any verification of the supposed secret negotiations with Hanabusa.

Tabohashi Kiyoshi wrote that Yi tried to form connections with the Taewongun in order to strengthen his own position, but the Taewongun regarded him as a base or inferior individual. Because he once insulted Yi, Yi was supposedly driven into the arms of the Min faction and converted into a life-long enemy of the Taewongun. Tabohashi claimed that Yi recommended Min Sŭng-ho for the post of Suwŏn magistrate and Cho Yŏng-ha for the post of commander of the Kŭmwiyŏng in 1872, but failed. He also allegedly plotted for the overthrow of the Taewongun. Tabohashi, however, substantiated none of these charges with any evidence. See Tabohashi, I, 28.

46. Hwang Hyŏn made a series of charges against Yi Yu-wŏn. He reported that Pak Kyu-su once had occasion to reprimand him to his face before the king for cowardice. He also supposedly "picked out young girls and pretended that they were boys, and kept them at his beck and call. His other extravagances and lascivious practices prove this." According to Hwang, his son, Yi Su-yŏng, was "palsied and pockmarked" and "his dirtiness repelled others." After Yi Su-yŏng died at an early age, Yi Yu-wŏn decided to adopt his grandson. Evidently he was not the son of Yi Su-yŏng's legitimate wife, since he was only four or five years younger than her. Hwang Hyŏn reported what followed: "Subsequently mother and son committed incest. Yi Yu-wŏn confessed this to the king and said, 'My grandson has had intercourse with his mother. I venture to end the adoption.' Those present covered their faces." See Hwang Hyŏn, MCYR, 24-25. Hwang's charges are redolent of the gossip columnist and are of dubious value. I have found no instance of a confrontation between Pak Kyu-su and Yi Yu-wŏn in the court records. Also, the clan genealogy of the Kyŏngju Yi clan does not list a wife for Yi Su-yŏng. See "Kyŏngju Yi-ssi sebo," mu-p'yŏn, 3:27a-b.

47. KSDSJ, II, 1193; CSJMJS, 633.

48. Yi had been a "protected official" (umsa), since he had been granted office without a degree on the basis of the merit of his ancestors. See his conversation with Kojong, SJW, ILSN 143:53b, 1873.11.27. He also mentioned to Kojong that his "house" had produced eight state councilors and four chief state councilors. ILSN 143:54a, 1873.11.27. Yi received his educational training from his maternal relative, the scholar Pak Ki-su (1774-1845), a member of the Pŏnnam Pak clan (the same as Pak Kyu-su). See KSDSJ, I, 522. Yi passed the chinsa examination in 1837. His ancestor, Yi Hang-bok, had won renown for escorting King Sŏnjo on his flight from Hideyoshi's invading forces. He suffered impeachment and banishment during the reign of Kwanghaegun (r. 1608-23). See KSDSJ, II, 1232-1233.

49. See the introduction to Yi Yu-wŏn, Imhap'il (Seoul: Sŏnggyun'gwan, 1961), 1-16, by Chŏng Pyŏng-hak.

50. See Kwŏn Sŏk-pong, "Yi Hong-jang ŭi tae Chosŏn yŏlguk imnyak kwŏndoch'ae e taehayŏ," Yŏksa hakpo, 21 (August 1963), 101-130. Since many offi-

cials went through the formality of refusing appointments to high office, it is necessary to show that Yi's refusals were sincere. On December 30, 1874, Yi requested dismissal from his concurrently held posts because of illness, but on January 2, 1874, the king appointed him chief state councilor. Thereafter, Yi submitted resignations almost daily until about the middle of January, and Kojong rejected all of them. On January 12 Yi refused to accept the king's summons because it contained a phrase unacceptable to him. Kojong complied by ordering the objectionable phrase struck out. On January 14 Kojong reminded Yi that he had "spent many days as a child studying hard under you," indicating that Kojong may have selected Yi for high office because Yi had been the king's tutor. On January 15 Yi again claimed that the most recent royal summons also contained unacceptable phrases and demanded a retraction. Kojong asked Yi to come to court to discuss the phrases, but Yi insisted on a retraction first. Then Kojong ordered that seventy words be deleted. Yi did come to court to discuss certain tax matters on January 18, but resigned again on the nineteenth. This marked the end of his protests, for from then on Yi assumed his regular post. Later in the year, however, Yi submitted several more resignations.

For sources for the above discussion, see *SJW, ILSN* 142:61a-b, 1873.11.11; *ILSN* 143:7a, 1873.11.13; *SJW, ILSN* 143:28a, 1873.11.19; *ILSN* 143:41b-42a, 1873.11.24; *SJW, ILSN* 143:45b, 1873.11.26; *SJW, ILSN* 143:49a-b, 1873.11.27; *SJW, ILSN* 143:48a-54b, 1873.11.27; *SJW, ILSN* 143:55a-b, 1873.11.28; *SJW, ILSN* 144:3b-4a, 1873.12.1; *SJW, ILSN* 144:15a-b, 1873.12.4.

For resignations after January 1874: (April 14), *SJW, ILSN* 147:85b, 1874.2.8; (April 20), *SJW, ILSN* 148:18b-19a, 1874.3.5; (April 24), *SJW, ILSN* 148:n.p., 1874.3.9; (May 1), *SJW, ILSN* 148:n.p., 1874.3.16; (May 20), *SJW, ILSN* 150:16a, 1874.4.5; *SJW, ILSN* 156:16a, 1874.10.7.

51. *SJW, ILSN* 158:60a-160:57b, 1874.11.29 to 1874.12.24. On February 3 Kojong dismissed Yi from his post as chief state councilor because he had been so stubborn, but the next day he appointed him to five new sinecures. Yi refused these appointments as well. On March 22 Kojong reappointed Yi chief state councilor and tutor to the crown prince, but Yi refused. *ILSN* 162:56a, 57b, 1875.1.15; *ILSN* 163:5a-7b, 1875.1.17; *ILSN* 163:8b, 1875.1.18; *ILSN* 162:10a-b, 1875.1.19; *ILSN* 161:77a-b, 1874.12.27; *ILSN* 160:80b, 1874.12.28; *ILSN* 164:45b-46a, 1875.2.15; *ILSN* 165:48b-49a, 1875.2.16; *ILSN* 165:50a-52a, 1875.2.17; *SJW*, same dates.

Yi continued to submit resignations through the middle of June, at times almost daily: *ILSN* 165:70a, 1875.2.21 (March 29); *ILSN* 164:94a-b, 1875.2.28 (April 14); *ILSN* 166:17a-18a, 1875.4.11 (May 14); almost daily from May 19 to May 29, *ILSN* 166:44a-67a, 1875.4.15-1875.4.26, and *ILSN* 167:20b-21a, 1875.5.10 (June 13). See also *SJW* same dates.

52. *SJW, ILSN* 160:58b-60b, 1874.12.24; *ILSN* 160:62a-b, 1874.12.24; *ILSN* 160:65b-66a, 70b; *ILSN* 160:77a-b, 1874.12.27; *ILSN* 160:80b, 1874.12.28; *ILSN* 160:108b, 1874.12.29; *ILSN* 161:6a, 1875.1.1; *ILSN* 161:12a-b, 1875.1.3; *ILSN* 161:n.p., 1875.1.4; *ILSN* 162:49a-50a, 1875.1.12. See also *SJW* for the same dates.

53. *ILSN* 160:39b, 34a-b, 35a, 37b-38a, 38b-39a, 40b, 45b-46b, 51a-b, 52b, 53a-b, 53b-54b, 56a-57b, 57a-b, 62b-63b, 64a-b, 66a-67a, 68a, 69a, 71a-b, 72a-b, 72b-73a, 73b-74a, 74b-75a, 79a, 80a, 81b.

54. Yi's appointment was on February 17 (1875.1.12) and Pak's was July 22 (1875.6.20). See *CSS*.6.4. same dates.

55. *KJSL*.11:60a, 1874.6.29. This was the same day that the interpreter, An Tong-jun, was indicted by Yi Yu-wŏn. See Chapter 13.

56. Ibid.

57. *SJW, ILSN* 165:42a, *KJSL* 12:16b, 1875.3.21. The content of the memorial is not reported.

58. There is no mention in *SJW* or *KJSL* 12:15b-16a, 1875.3.5 or 3.6 about the content of the memorial or anything pertaining to the Taewongun. This material is mentioned in *CSS*.6.4.361 and by Yi Sŏn-gŭn, *Han'guksa ch'oegŭnsep'yŏn*, 363. Yi may have used the *CSS*.

59. *KJSL* 12:20b-21a, 1875.5.17.

60. There was no chief state councilor at this time.

61. Hwang Hyŏn related that Yi Ch'oe-ung did not get along with his younger brother, the Taewongun, and that Min Sŭng-ho had him appointed state councilor in order to oppose the Taewongun. See Hwang Hyŏn, *MCYR*, 22, and Yi Sŏn-gŭn, *Han'guksa ch'oegŭnsep'yŏn*, 347. Of course, Min was assassinated on January 5, 1875, and Yi Ch'oe-ŭng was not appointed second state councilor until January 24. This in itself would not disprove that Yi's appointment was in accordance with Min's wishes, but it would make it very unlikely that Min engineered the appointment.

Yi Sŏn-gun also described Kim Pyŏng-guk as one of the Andong Kim enemies of the Taewongun but without any corroborative evidence. Ibid., 346.

62. *KJSL* 12:9b, 10a, 1875.2.9.

63. The other cosigners were released. *SJW, ILSN* 168:n.p., 1875.6.16, *KJSL* 12:23a has 6.17 for the date of this edict. The execution was ordered the next day, July 19, according to *SJW, ILSN*, and on the twentieth according to *KJSL*.

64. *ILSN* 168:n.p., 1875.6.19.

65. Ibid.

66. *SJW, ILSN* 165:n.p., 1875.6.19.

67. *SJW, ILSN* 168:n.p., 1875.6.20.

68. *SJW, ILSN* 168:n.p., 1875.6.20.

69. *SJW, ILSN* 168:n.p., 1875.6.21.

70. The cosigners included both Min Chong-muk and Kim Ok-kyun, ibid.

71. *SJW, ILSN* 168:n.p., 1875.6.22.

72. One died later in exile, Yi Sŏn-gŭn, *Han'guksa ch'oegŭnsep'yŏn*, 363.

73. *SJW, ILSN* 168:n.p., 1875.6.23. Five of the new appointees had been dismissed on July 23. They were merely reappointed, their dismissal evidently indicating nothing more than the usual pro forma expression of royal displeasure.

74. *SJW, ILSN* 169:n.p., *KJSL* 12:26b-27a, 1875.7.9; *SJW, ILSN* 170: 29a-b, *KJSL* 12:27a, 30b, 1875.8.12.

13. The Debate over Accommodation with Japan

1. While foreign relations will be discussed in this chapter, no attempt will be made to give a full account of those relations or negotiations with the Japanese. For surveys on this period, see James B. Palais, "Korea on the Eve of the Kanghwa Treaty," 439-796; Ching Young Choe, *The Rule of the Taewŏngun*, 134-165, Hilary Conroy, *The Japanese Seizure of Korea, 1868-1910.*

2. *ILSN* 149:64b, 1874.3.30.

3. The Tsungli yamen memorial was submitted on 5.30 lunar, July 13. See *Tongmun hwigo, wŏnsok, Waejŏng*, 2b-4b, 1874.6.22. Hereinafter referred to as *TMHG*. See also *KJSL*, same date; Yi Sŏn-gŭn, *Han'guksa ch'oegŭnsep'yŏn*, 369-370.

4. *ILSN* 152:77a-78a, 1874.6.25.

5. *ILSN* 152:75a-b, 1874.6.25.

6. *TMHG, wŏnsok, Waejŏng*, 3b-4b, 1875; Yi Sŏn-gŭn, 370.

7. The Taewongun's views are contained in Pak Kyu-su's private letters to the Taewongun. Unfortunately, the letters from the Taewongun are not included, but some of his attitudes are described directly by Pak, and others can be deduced by Pak's counterarguments. See Pak Kyu-su, *Hwanjaejip*, 11:1a-5b, 10b-11a, 1874. For a fuller discussion in English of this correspondence, see Palais, "Korea on the Eve of the Kanghwa Treaty," 590-595, 618-628.

8. Pak Kyu-su, *Hwanjaejip*, 11:1a-3b.

9. Ibid.

10. *SJW, ILSN* 152:94a-95a, *KJSL* 11:59a-b, 1874.6.29; *KJSL* 11:61a-b, 1874.7.3. Chŏng was exiled the next day, August 15 (7.4 lunar), and Hong Wŏn was appointed the new governor of Kyŏngsang on August 20 (7.9 lunar). *ILSN* 153:n.p., above dates.

11. This information comes from Japanese sources. *Dai Nihon gaikō monjo* (*GKMJ*), VII, 364, doc. 210. See Moriyama's report on June 21, in Tabohashi, I, 340, and 332.

12. *KJSL* 1:2b-3a, 1874.1.10.

13. *SJW, ILSN* 149:n.p., 1874.3.20.

14. *SJW, ILSN* 150:12a-b, 1874.4.5.

15. *Chōsen kōsai shimatsu*, chap. 3, cited in Tabohashi, I, 341; Yi Sŏn-gŭn, 369.

16. *KJSL* 11:61a-b, 1874.7.3. Chŏng was exiled according to the report of Pak Chŏng-yang, in *ILSN* 159:71a, 1874.12.13.

17. For Yi Yu-wŏn's indictment of An, see *SJW, ILSN* 152:94a-95a, *KJSL* 11:59a-60a, 1874.6.29. Moriyama Shigeru reported the recall of Chŏng Hyŏn-dŏk and An Tong-jun to Seoul to his government, in *GKMJ*, VII, 362-365, doc. 210, supp. 1,2.

18. *ILSN* 159:60a-87a, 1874.12.13; Palais, "Korea on the Eve of the Kanghwa Treaty," 419-423.

19. *ILSN* 161:46b-47a, 163:3a, 13a, 23a, 1874.12.13; *SJW, ILSN* 164: 37b-38a, 1875.2.12.

20. *SJW, ILSN* 165:11b-12a, 1875.3.4. An was not tried by the state tribunal because he was an interpreter and member of the *chung'in* class.

21. Tabohashi, I, 332-333; Yi Sŏn-gŭn provides an account of An Tong-jun's obstruction of Queen Min's attempt to assure Chinese investiture for her son as crown prince, and An's punishment as a purge by the Min faction (specifically, Yi Yu-wŏn and Min Kyu-ho) of Taewongun men. Yi Sŏn-gŭn, 363-366. Yi's source was Yun Hyo-jŏng, *P'ung'un Hanmal pisa*, which was not available to me.

22. *GKMJ*, VII, 404-414, doc., 218, supp. *GKMJ*, VII, 409, doc. 218.1; Tabohashi, I, 346-347; Yi Sŏn-gŭn, 371.

23. Tabohashi, I, 347.

24. *SJW, ILSN* 154:17a-b, 1874.8.9; Tabohashi, I, 349.

25. For the account of these negotiations, see ibid., 358ff.; Palais, 609-618.

26. Pak Kyu-su, *Hwanjaejip*, 11:3a-5a.

27. Ch'in Kuai (1090-1155) was prime minister during Kao Tsung's reign in the Southern Sung. Fearing the strength of the Chin, he advocated peace and was killed by Yo Fei and the other advocates of war. See *Hanhandaesajŏn; Ajia rekishi jiten*, 5:29b-30a; Edwin O. Reischauer and John K. Fairbank, *East Asia: The Great Tradition* (Boston: Houghton Mifflin Company, 1960), 209.

28. Pak Kyu-su, *Hwanjaejip*, 11:3a-5a.

29. Ibid.

30. *GKMJ*, VIII, 71-72, doc. 29; Yi Sŏn-gŭn, 374. For Moriyama's report to Terashima, see *GKMJ*, VIII, 70-71, doc. 28.

31. Sin Kuk-chu, "Kankoku no kaikoku, Unyō-go jiken o megutte," in *Nihon gaikōshi kenkyū: Bakumatsu-Ishin jidai* (Tokyo, 1960), 127ff.; Tabohashi, I, 395-400; Yi Sŏn-gŭn, 375-376; Hilary Conroy, *The Japanese Seizure of Korea*, 61; "Nikkan Kōshō jiken roku" in *Nikkan gaikō shiryō shūsei*, VII (Tokyo: Gannandō shoten, 1963), 3-5; Palais, 668ff.

32. *SJW, ILSN* 173:16a-17a, 1875.11.9; Tabohashi, I, 405.

33. Conroy argues that the *Unyō* incident represents a continuation of the policy of Ōkubo, Iwakura, and the other antiwar leaders who emerged victorious during the *seikan* or "conquer Korea" debates of 1873. It was a policy "which, while further undermining the stand of samurai war-hawks in Japan, would avoid costly military involvement, and would be justifiable in terms of Western international practice." Hilary Conroy, *The Japanese Seizure of Korea, 1868-1910*, p. 62. For detailed accounts of the negotiations, see Palais, 705-796; Martina Deuchler, "The Opening of Korea, 1875-84," Phd. diss., Harvard University, 1967; Tabohashi, passim; Sin Kuk-chu, *Kindai Chōsen gaikōshi* (Tokyo, 1966), 31-65 (Korean edition: *Kŭndae Chosŏn oegyosa* [Seoul, 1965], 38-76).

34. *SJW, ILSN* 167:21b-30a, 1875.5.10; Palais, "Korea on the Eve," 632-640.

35. *SJW, ILSN* 167:29a-30a, 36a-37a, 1875.5.10.

36. *SJW, ILSN* 173:29a, 1875.11.5.

37. *Waesa ilgi*, I, 1876.1.25; *CSS*.6.4.397; *GKMJ*, IX, 103-105, doc. 21, supp.; Tabohashi, I, 498-500.

38. For an English summary of the negotiations from February 19 to 22, see Palais, "Korea on the Eve," 760ff.

39. For a complete text of the treaty in Chinese and Japanese, see *KuHanmal choyak hwich'an* (Seoul: Kukhoe tosŏgwan, 1965), I, 3-16; *GKMJ*, IX, 114-120, "Nikkan kōshō jiken roku," in *Nikkan gaikō shiryō shūsei*, VII, 3-5; Palais, "Korea on the Eve," 761ff.

40. Ibid., 761-769; Tabohashi, passim, esp. 465ff.

41. Tabohashi, I, 484.

42. Ibid., 490-493; *ILSN* 177:8b-14a, 1876.2.5; *Waesa ilgi*, II, same date.

43. *GKMJ*, IX, 105-6, doc. 22; Tabohashi, I, 484-485.

44. Kim Pyŏng-hak, Pak Kyu-su, and Yi-wŏn were all sinecured elder statesmen.

45. *ILSN* 167:21b-30a; Tabohashi, 390-393; Palais, 637.

46. *ILSN* 167:29a-30a.

47. Pak Kyu-su, *Hwanjaejip*, 11:5a-6a, 1875.5.

48. Ibid., 11:6b-7b; Palais, "Korea on the Eve," 657-666.

49. *SJW, ILSN* 168:n.p., 1875.6.3.

50. *SJW, ILSN* 168:n.p., 1875.6.14; *SJW, ILSN* 168:n.p., 1875.6.19, 6.20.

51. *Yŏngho hallok*, 22. I consulted the original manuscript in the *Kyujanggak* collection at Seoul National University. See also Tabohashi, I, 509-510. The Taewongun's letter is not contained in the regular daily court records.

52. Moriyama had accompanied Kuroda and Inoue Kaoru on their mission to Korea.

53. *GKMJ*, IX, 95-97, doc. 19, and supp. Tabohashi has a slightly different account based on the *Shisen nikki* (Daily Record of the Minister to Korea), which was not available to me. According to this, on February 12 the Korean negotiator, Sin Hŏn, sent the interpreter, Hyŏn, to convey a message to the Japanese interpreter, Urase, that two of the Taewongun's followers wanted to obstruct friendly relations with Japan and were planning to lead a force out of the capital. A report about this had been received from those officials who were in favor of maintaining the peace. If these

men were to commit any aggression against the Japanese, the Korean government would have no objection to the Japanese forces executing them on the spot. Once they were "pacified," the Japanese should then submit a report of what had happened.

The Japanese stationed a marine guard around their quarters and ordered Miyamoto to pay a call on Hyŏn the same day to declare that the Korean king was responsible for the pacification of lawbreakers in his country. Although the Japanese plenipotentiary could defend himself against attackers, even if there were several thousand of them, he would have no choice but to regard such an attack as grounds for breaking off negotiations and returning to Japan. If this were to happen, Korea would regret it. Tabohashi, I, 510-511, note 13.

54. *SJW, ILSN* 175:68a-70a, 72b-73a, *KJSL* 13:9a-b, 1876.1.20; Tabohashi, I, 469.

55. See note 54.

56. *ILSN* 175:73a, 78a-b, 1876.1.20.

57. *ILSN* 175:78b.

58. *SJW, ILSN* 176:20a-b, 1876.1.23.

59. Chang was exiled on February 20. *ILSN* 176:32b, 1876.1.26.

60. For the text of Ch'oe's memorial, see *ILSN* 176:21b-24a, 1876.1.23; Tabohashi, 514, note 15, 511-512.

61. *CSS*.6.4., 1876.1.27; Tabohashi, I, 512. On February 21 Ch'oe was impeached by the censorate and exiled to an island off Chŏlla province.

62. For memorials on February 21 and 22, see *SJW, ILSN* 176:31b-32a, 1876.1.25.

63. *ILSN* 176:36b-37a, 1876.1.27. Protests continued to February 29 when a final order was issued for Ch'oe's exile. For censorate memorials see *ILSN* 176:43b-44b, 1876.1.28; *ILSN* 176:48b-49a, 1876.1.29; *ILSN* 177:n.p., 1876.2.1, 2.2, 2.3, 2.4.

64. *ILSN* 176:36b, 1876.1.27.

65. *ILSN* 176:36b.

66. *ILSN* 176:38b.

67. *ILSN* 176:42a, 1876.1.28.

68. *ILSN* 176:42b.

69. Ibid.

70. ILSN 176:43a.

71. CSS.6.4.401-402, 1876.2.3.

72. ILSN 177:14b-15b, 1876.2.5.

Bibliography

Primary Sources

Ch'oe Ik-hyŏn, *Myŏn'am sŏnsaeng munjip* (The collected works of Ch'oe Ik-hyŏn), 24 *kwŏn*, 1908.

Chŏng Kyo, *Taehan kyenyŏnsa* (A history of the late Yi dynasty), no. 5 of the Han'guk saryo ch'ongsŏ series. Seoul: Kuksa p'yŏnch'an wiwŏnhoe ed., 1957.

Chŏng Yag-yong, *Mongmin simsŏ*. Seoul, 1961 ed.

———— *Yŏyudang chŏnsŏ* (The complete works of Chŏng Yag-yong), 152 *kwŏn*, comp. Kim Sŏng-jin, Kyŏngsŏng: Sin Chosŏnsa, 1934.

Chōsenshi (History of Korea), 37 vols. Keijō: Chōsen Sōtokufu, 1935.

Chosŏn wangjo sillok (The veritable record of the Yi dynasty), 48 vols. Seoul: Kuksa p'yŏnch'an wiwŏnhoe ed., 1955-58. Index, 1963.

Chŭngbo munhŏnbigo (Encyclopedia, enlarged and supplemented), preface dated 1907.

Dai Nihon gaikō monjo (Japanese diplomatic documents), comp. Gaimushō chōsabu. Tokyo: Nihon kokusai kyōkai.

"Hop'ae samok" (Regulations for the household tally system), ms. dated 1625.7.28 lunar.

Hwang Hyŏn, *Maech'ŏn yarok* (The memoirs of Hwang Hyŏn). Seoul: Kuksa p'yŏnch'an wiwŏnhoe ed., 1955.

Ilsŏngnok (Record for daily reflection), 2,375 *kwŏn*, 1760-1910.

Imsullok (Record of the 1862 uprisings). Seoul: Kuksa p'yŏnch'an wiwŏnhoe ed., 1958 ed.

Kim Kyu-rak, "Unha kyŏnmunnok" (Observations while on duty at the Taewongun's palace), ca. 1871, ms., Asami collection, University of California at Berkeley.

Kim Yun-sik, *Unyangjip* (Collected works of Kim Yun-sik), 16 *kwŏn*, preface dated 1913.

Kojong sillok (The veritable record of King Kojong), part of *Yijo sillok* (The Veritable record of the Yi dynasty), 10 vols. Peking: Chosŏn kwahagwŏn and Chung-kuo k'o-hsüeh yüan, 1959.

Kyŏngguk taejŏn (Great code of the Yi dynasty, promulgated 1471). Keijō: Chōsen sōtokufu, 1934.

"Kyŏngju Yi-ssi sebo" (Genealogy of the Kyŏngju Yi clan), ms. Harvard Yenching Library, Harvard University.

Bibliography

"Kyunyŏk samok" (Regulations of the equal service law), 1752. ms., Kyujanggak collection, Seoul National University Library.

Man'gi yoram (Government handbook), 2 vols., comp. ca. 1808. Keijō: Chōsen sōtokufu chūsūin ed., 1937.

"Nikkan kōshō jiken roku" (A record of the Japanese-Korean negotiations), in Nikkan gaikō shiryō shūsei (Documents pertaining to Japanese-Korean relations), VII. Tokyo: Gannandō shoten, 1963.

Pak Che-ga, Chŏngyujip. Seoul: Kuksa p'yŏnch'an wiwŏnhoe ed., 1961.

Pak Ir-wŏn, Takchiji (Record of the Ministry of Taxation), dated 1796, Seoul National University Classics edition. Seoul, 1967.

Pak Kyu-su, Hwanjaejip (The collected works of Pak Kyu-su), preface by Kim Yunsik, dated 1911.

Pibyŏnsa tŭngnok (The record of the Border Defense Command), 28 vols. Seoul: Kuksa p'yŏnch'an wiwŏnhoe ed., 1959-61.

Soktaejŏn (Great code of the Yi dynasty, continued, promulgated 1744). Keijō: Chōsen sōtokufu, 1935.

Sŭngjŏngwŏn ilgi (Records of the Royal Secretariat), 1,674 kwŏn. Cited as SJW. Kyujanggak collection, Seoul National University Library.

_____ (Records of the Royal Secretariat), Kojong's Reign, 15 vols. Seoul: Kuksa pyŏnch'an wiwŏnhoe ed., 1967-68. Cited as SJW, Kojong.

Taejŏn hoet'ong (Great code of the Yi dynasty). Comp. 1865. Keijō: Chōsen sōtokufu 1939.

Taejŏn t'ongp'yŏn (Great code of the Yi dynasty). Comp. 1785. Pŏpchech'o ed. Seoul, 1963.

Tongmun hwigo (Diplomatic documents of the Yi dynasty), Kyujanggak collection, Seoul National University Library.

Ŭigŭmbu, choein Ch'oe Ik-hyŏn kug'an (State tribunal, the trial of the criminal Ch'oe Ik-hyŏn), n.d., Kyujanggak collection, Seoul National University Library.

Ŭigŭmbu, choein, Pak U-hyŏn kug'an (State tribunal: the case of the criminal Pak U-hyŏn), n.d., Kyujanggak collection, Seoul National University Library.

Ŭigŭmbu, choein Son Yŏng-no kug'an (State tribunal, the trial record of the criminal Son Yŏng-no), n.d., Kyujanggak collection, Seoul National University Library.

Waesa ilgi (Diary of the negotiations with the Japanese). From ŭrhae (1875).12.26 lunar to kyŏngjin (1880).12.29 lunar, in 14 ch'aek, Kyujanggak collection, Seoul National University Library.

Yi Hang-no, Hwasŏjip (Collected works of Yi Hang-no). 22 kwŏn, 1899.

Yi Na-yŏng, Chosŏn minjok haebang t'ujaengsa (History of the struggle for liberation of the Korean people). Pyongyang, 1958; Japanese translation, Tokyo, 1960.

Yi Ik, Sŏngho sasŏl, 2 vols. Seoul: Kyŏnghŭi ch'ulp'ansa ed., 1967.

Yi Kŭng-ik, Yŏllyŏsil kisul (Record of Yi Kŭng-ik). 6 vols., supp. 3 vols. Keijō: Chōsen kosho kankokai ed., 1912-13.

Yi Kyu-gyŏng, Oju yŏnmun changjŏn san'go (Collected writings of Yi Kyu-gyŏng). 2 vols. Seoul, 1959.

Yi Tŏng-mu, Ch'ŏngjanggwan chŏnsŏ, 3 vols. Seoul: Seoul National University, Kojŏn ch'ŏngsŏ series, no. 1, 1966.

Yi Yu-wŏn, Imhap'il (Writings in retirement). Seoul: Sŏnggyun'gwan ed., 1961.

"Yŏngho hallok." 25 kwŏn. ms. Kyujanggak collection, Seoul National University Library.

Bibliography

Yu Hyŏng-wŏn, *P'an'gye surok*. Seoul: Tongguk munhwasa ed., 1958.

_____ *P'an'gye surok*. Korean trans. Kim Sang-gi. Seoul: Nong'ŏp ŭnhaeng chosabu, 1959.

Yu Su-wŏn, *Usŏ* (ca. 1729-37). Seoul: Seoul National University Press ed., 1971.

Works in Western Languages

Bodde, Derk, "Henry A. Wallace and the Ever-Normal Granary," *Far Eastern Quarterly*, 5 (1946), 411-426.

Chang, Chung-li, *The Income of the Chinese Gentry*. Seattle, Wash.: University of Washington Press, 1962.

Choe, Ching Young, "Kim Yuk (1580-1658) and the Taedongbŏp Reform," *Journal of Asian Studies*, 23:1 (November 1963), 21-36.

_____*The Rule of the Taewŏn'gun, 1864-1874: Restoration in Yi Korea*. Cambridge, Mass.: East Asian Research Center, Harvard University, 1972.

Ch'oe, Yŏng-ho, "The Civil Examinations and the Social Structure in Early Yi Dynasty Korea: 1392-1600." Ph.D. diss., University of Chicago, 1971.

_____"Commoners and Yangban in the Civil Service Examination in Early Chosŏn Dynasty Korea, 1392-1600," paper delivered at the 23rd annual meeting of the Association for Asian Studies, Washington, D.C., March 28-31, 1971.

_____"Commoners in Early Yi Dynasty Civil Examinations: An Aspect of Korean Social Structure, 1392-1600," *Journal of Asian Studies*, 33:4 (August 1974), 611-631.

Ch'ü Tung-tsu, *Local Government in China under the Ch'ing*. Cambridge, Mass.: Harvard University Press, 1962.

Chun, Hae-jong, "Sino-Korean Tributary Relations in the Ch'ing Period," in John K. Fairbank, ed., *The Chinese World Order*. Cambridge, Mass.: Harvard University Press, 1968, 90-111.

Conroy, Hilary, *The Japanese Seizure of Korea, 1868-1910*. Philadelphia, Pa.: University of Pennsylvania Press, 1960.

Crowley, James B., ed., *Modern East Asia: An Interpretation*. New York: Harcourt, Brace and World, Inc., 1970.

Cumings, Bruce G., "Is Korea a Mass Society?" *Occasional Papers on Korea*, no. 1 (April 1974; reprint of June 1972 ed.), 65-81.

Dallet, Charles, *Histoire de l'eglise de Corée*. 2 vols. Paris: Victor Palme, 1874.

Deuchler, Martina, "The Opening of Korea, 1875-84." Ph.D. diss. Harvard University, Cambridge, Mass., 1967.

Eisenstadt, S. N., *The Political Systems of Empires*. New York: The Free Press of Glencoe, 1963.

_____"Post-Traditional Societies and the Continuity and Reconstruction of Tradition," *Daedalus* (Winter 1973), 1-27.

Elvin, Mark, *The Pattern of the Chinese Past*. Stanford, Calif.: Stanford University Press, 1973.

Etzioni, Amitai, *A Comparative Analysis of Complex Organizations*. New York: The Free Press of Glencoe, 1961.

Fairbank, John K., ed., *The Chinese World Order*. Cambridge, Mass.: Harvard University Press, 1968.

_____ and S. Y. Teng, "On the Ch'ing Tributary System," in *Ch'ing Administration: Three Studies*, Harvard-Yenching Institute Studies 19. Cambridge, Mass.: Harvard University Press, 1961, 107-246.

Food and Money in Ancient China, trans. and annotated by Nancy Lee Swann. Princeton, N.J.: Princeton University Press, 1950.

Grajdanzev, Andrew J., *Modern Korea*. New York: The John Day Co., 1944.

Geertz, Clifford, *Agricultural Involution*. Berkeley, Calif.: University of California Press, 1970.

Han, Woo-keun, *The History of Korea*. Honolulu, Hawaii: East-West Center Press, 1971.

Harootunian, H. D., *Toward Restoration: The Growth of Political Consciousness in Tokugawa Japan*. Berkeley, Calif.: University of California Press, 1970.

Heaton, Herbert, *Economic History of Europe*. Hew York: Harper and Row, 1948 rev. ed.

Henderson, Gregory, *Korea: The Politics of the Vortex*. Cambridge, Mass.: Harvard University Press, 1968.

Henthorn, William A., *A History of Korea*. New York: The Free Press, 1971.

Ho, Ping-ti, and Tang Tsou, eds., *China in Crisis*. 2 vols. Chicago: University of Chicago Press, 1968.

Hsiao, Kung-chuan, *Imperial China: Rural Control in the Nineteenth Century*. Seattle, Wash.: University of Washington Press, 1960.

Hucker, Charles O., "The Tung Lin Movement of the Late Ming Period," in John K. Fairbank, ed., *Chinese Thought and Institutions*. Chicago: University of Chicago Press, 1957, 132-163.

The I Ching or Book of Changes. trans. Richard Wilhelm, rendered into English by Cary F. Baynes. New York: The American Book-Stratford Press, 1950.

Ike, Nobutaka, "Triumph of the Peace Party in Japan in 1873," *Far Eastern Quarterly*, 2 (May 1943), 286-295.

Johnson, David, "Remarks on the Medieval Chinese Oligarchy," paper presented at the Columbia University Seminar on Traditional China, ca. 1972.

Kahn, Harold L., *Monarchy in the Emperor's Eyes: Image and Reality in the Ch'ien-lung Reign*. Cambridge, Mass.: Harvard University Press, 1971.

King, Frank H. H., *Money and Monetary Policy in China: 1845-95*. Cambridge, Mass.: Harvard University Press, 1965.

Kuhn, Philip A., *Rebellion and Its Enemies in Late Imperial China: Militarization and Social Structure, 1796-1864*. Cambridge, Mass.: Harvard University Press, 1970.

Li, Dun J., ed., *The Essence of Chinese Civilization*. Princeton, N.J.: D. Van Nostrand, 1967.

McCune, George M., "The Exchange of Envoys between Korea and Japan during the Tokugawa Period," *Far Eastern Quarterly*, 5:3 (May 1946), 308-325.

Mayo, Marlene J., "The Korean Crisis of 1873 and Early Meiji Foreign Policy," *Journal of Asian Studies*, 31:4 (August 1972), 793-819.

Meskill, John, "Academies and Politics in the Ming Dynasty," in Charles O. Hucker, ed., *Chinese Government in Ming Times: Seven Studies*. New York: Columbia University Press, 1969), 149-174.

Nelson, M. Frederick, *Korea and the Old Orders in Eastern Asia*. Baton Rouge, La.: Louisiana State University Press, 1945.

Palais, James B., "Korea on the Eve of the Kanghwa Treaty, 1873-76," Ph.D. diss., Harvard University, Cambridge, Mass., 1968.

_____ "Stability in Yi Dynasty Korea: Equilibrium Systems and Marginal Adjust-

367

Bibliography

ment," paper presented at the Conference on Tradition and Change in Korea, Seoul, Korea, Sept. 1, 1969; published in Korean in Han'guk yŏn'gusil, ed., *Han'guk ŭi chŏnt'ong kwa pyŏnch'ŏn* (Tradition and change in Korea). Seoul: Koryŏ Taehakkyo, 1973, 283-300.

Parsons, James B., "The Ming Dynasty Bureaucracy: Aspects of Background Forces," in Charles O. Hucker, ed., *Chinese Government in Ming Times: Seven Studies.* New York: Columbia University Press, 1969, 175-231.

Perkins, Dwight, *Agricultural Development in China, 1368-1968.* Chicago: Aldine Publishing Co., 1969.

Sakai, Tadao, "Confucianism and Popular Educational Works," in Wm. Theodore de Bary, ed., *Self and Society in Ming Thought.* New York: Columbia University Press, 1970), 331-366.

Schurmann, Franz, *Ideology and Organization in Communist China.* Berkeley, Calif.: University of California Press, 1966, 2nd ed.

Schwartz, Benjamin, *In Search of Wealth and Power.* Cambridge, Mass.: Harvard University Press, 1964.

_____"Some Polarities in Confucian Thought," in Arthur Wright, ed., *Confucianism in Action.* Palo Alto, Calif.: Stanford University Press, 1959, 50-62.

Shin, Susan, "The Social Structure of Kŭmhwa County in the Late Seventeenth Century," *Occasional Papers on Korea,* no. 1 (April 1974; reprint of June 1972 ed.), 9-35.

Smith, Warren, "The Rise of the Sowon: Literary Academies in Sixteenth-Century Korea." Ph.D. diss., University of California at Berkeley, 1972.

Sohn, Pow-key, "Social History of the Early Yi Dynasty, 1392-1592: With Emphasis on the Functional Aspects of Governmental Structure." Ph.D. diss., University of California at Berkeley, 1963.

Song June-ho, "The Government Examination Rosters of the Yi Dynasty," in Spencer Palmer, ed., *Studies in Asian Genealogy.* Provo, Utah: Brigham Young University Press, 1972, 153-176.

Wagner, Edward W., ed., "The Harvard Edition of the Mansŏng taedongbo," Cambridge, Mass., 1967.

Wagner, Edward W., "The Korean Chokpo as a Historical Source," in Spencer Palmer, ed., *Studies in Asian Genealogy.* Provo, Utah: Brigham Young University Press, 1972, 141-152.

_____"The Ladder of Success in Yi Dynasty Korea," *Occasional Papers on Korea,* no. 1 (April 1974; reprint of June 1972 ed.), 1-8.

_____"The Literati Purges." Ph.D. diss., Harvard University, Cambridge, Mass., 1959.

_____"Social Stratification in Seventeenth-Century Korea: Some Observations from a 1663 Seoul Census Register," *Occasional Papers on Korea,* no. 1 (April 1974; reprint of June 1972 ed.), 36-54.

Weber, Max, *Economy and Society.* New York: Bedminster Press, 1968.

Wright, Mary, *The Last Stand of Chinese Conservatism.* Palo Alto: Stanford University Press, 1957.

Yang, Key P., and Gregory Henderson, "An Outline History of Korean Confucianism," in *Journal of Asian Studies,* pt. 1, 18:1 (November 1958), 81-101; pt. 2, 18:2 (February 1959), 259-276.

Bibliography

Works in Non-Western Languages

Ajia rekishi jiten (Dictionary of Asian history). 10 vols. Tokyo, 1959-62.

Arii Tomonori, "Richō hojūgun kō" (A study of the supplementary soldiers (*p'o-ch'unggun*) of the Yi dynasty), *Chosen gakuhō*, 31 (April 1965), 58-101.

_____ "Richō shoki no shiteki tochi shoyū kankei" (Private land tenure relations in the early Yi dynasty), in *Chōsen shakai no rekishiteki hatten* (The historical development of Korean Society), *Chōsenshi kenkyukai rombunshū*, 3 (October 1967), 63-92.

_____ "Richō shoki no yōeki" (Labor service in the early Yi dynasty), pt. 1, *Chōsen gakuhō*, 30 (January 1964), 62-106; pt. 2, ibid., 31 (April 1964), 58-101.

_____ "Tochi shoyū kankei: kōdenron hihan" (Land tenure relations: Critique of the national ownership thesis), in Hatada Takashi, ed., *Chōsenshi nyūmon* (An introduction to Korean history). Tokyo, 1970, 125-154.

Asō Takekame, *Chōsen tensei-kō* (A study of the Korean land system). Keijō, 1940.

_____ *Shakanmai seido* (The grain loan system). Keijō, 1933.

Ch'a Mun-sop, "Chosŏnjo hugi ŭi yŏngjang e taehayŏ" (Regiment commanders in the late Yi dynasty), *Sach'ong*, 12-13 (September 1968), 495-518.

_____ "Imnan ihu ŭi yangyŏk kwa kyunyŏkpŏp ŭi sŏngnip" (The commoner-service system after Hideyoshi's invasions), pt. 1, in *Sahak yŏn'gu*, 10 (April 1961), 115-131; pt. 2, in ibid., 2 (July 1961), 83-146.

_____ "Sŏnch'o ŭi Ch'ung'ŭi, Ch'ungch'an, Chunsunwi e taehayŏ" (The loyal guard units of the early Yi dynasty), *Sahak yŏn'gu*, 19 (April 1967), 1-48.

_____ "Sŏnch'o ŭi kapsa e taehayŏ" (The armored soldiers of the early Yi dynasty), pt. 1, *Sach'ong*, 4 (November 1959), 115-136; pt. 2, ibid., 5 (November 1960), 38-55.

_____ "Sŏnjojo ŭi Hullyŏn-dogam" (The military training agency of Sŏnjo's reign), *Sahakchi*, 4 (November 1970), 11-30.

Chang Kuk-chong, "Sipch'il segi kŭmsok hwap'e (tonghwa) ŭi yut'ong e taehayŏ" (The circulation of metallic currency in the seventeenth century), *Yŏksa kwahak*, 6 (1961), 44-55.

_____ "Sipp'al segi ŭi tonghwa chujo wa chŏnhwang munje" (The minting of copper cash and the problem of shortage in money supply in the eighteenth century), *Yŏksa kwahak*, 1 (1963), 40-54.

Ch'ŏn Kwan-u, "Chosŏn ch'ogi Owi ŭi hyŏngsŏng" (The formation of the five guards in the early Yi dynasty), *Yŏksa hakpo*, 17-18 (June 1962), 515-546.

_____ "Chosŏn ch'ogi Owi ŭi pyŏngjong" (Types of soldiers in the five guards in the early Yi dynasty), *Sahak yŏn'gu*, 18 (September 1965), 59-95.

_____ "Han'guk t'oji chedosa" (History of the Korean land system), II, in *Han'guk munhwasa taegye* (Grand outline of the cultural history of Korea), Seoul, 1965. II, 1381-1430.

_____ "P'an'gye, Yu Hyŏng-wŏn yŏn'gu, sang" (A study of P'an'gye, Yu Hyŏng-wŏn, pt. 1, *Yŏksa hakpo*, 3 (January 1953), 87-139.

_____ "Yŏmal sŏnch'o ŭi hallyang" (The *Hallyang* in the late Koryŏ and early Yi periods), in *Yi Pyŏng-do Paksa hwagap kinyŏm nonch'ong* (Memorial volume on the sixtieth birthday of Dr. Yi Pyŏng-do). Seoul, 1956, 333-356.

Chŏng Ku-bok, "P'an'gye Yu Hyŏng-wŏn ŭi sahoe kaehyŏk sasang" (Yu Hyŏng-won's ideas on social reform), *Yŏksa hakpo*, 45 (March 1970), 1-53.

Chōsen jimmei jisho (Korean biographical dictionary). Keijō, 1937.

Chōsen kyōikushi (History of education in Korea), trans. Song Chi-hak from the North Korean original. Tokyo, 1960.

Bibliography

Chosŏn minju juŭi inmin konghwaguk kwahagwŏn yŏksa yŏn'guso (Korean Democratic People's Republic Institute of Science, History Research Institute), *Chosŏn t'ongsa* (A comprehensive history of Korea). 2 vols. P'yŏngyang, 1962.

———*Chōsen kindai kakumei undōshi* (History of the modern revolutionary movement in Korea), Japanese trans. ZaiNihon Chōsenjin kagakusha kyōkai shakai kagaku bumon rekishi bukai. Tokyo, 1964.

Chosŏn t'ongsa (A comprehensive history of Korea). 2 vols. Pyongyang, 1962.

Fukaya Toshigane, "Chōsen ni okeru kinseiteki tochi shoyū no seiritsu katei" (The process of the establishment of early-modern landownership in the Yi dynasty), pt. 1, *Shigaku zasshi*, 55:2 (1944), 1-37; pt. 2, ibid., 55:3 (1944), 77-98.

———"Sensho no tochi sedo, ippan, jō: iwayuru kadenhō o chūshin to shite" (An outline of the land system of the early Yi dynasty, pt. 1: the so-called *kwajŏn* system), *Shigaku zasshi*, 50:5 (1939), 47-82; pt. 2, ibid., 50:6 (1939), 32-78.

Han'guk kunjesa: kŭnse Chosŏn chŏn'gip'yŏn (History of the Korean military system: the early Yi dynasty). Seoul, 1968.

Han'guksa: yŏnp'yo (History of Korea: chronology). Seoul, 1959.

Hanhandaesajŏn (Grand dictionary of Sino-Korean), Yang Chu-dong, Min T'ae-sik, Yi Ka-wŏn eds., Seoul, 1963.

Han Woo-keun, "Chŏngjo pyŏng'o sohoe tŭngnok ŭi punsŏkchok yŏn'gu" (An analysis of the record of recommendations presented to King Chŏngjo in 1786), *Seoul taehakkyo nonmunjip*, 11 (November 1965), 3-51.

———"Sŏngho, Yi Ik ŭi sahoe wa sasang" (A study of the thought of Sŏngho Yi Ik), in *Yijo hugi ui sahoe wa sasang* (Society and thought in the late Yi dynasty). Seoul, 1961, 133-325.

———"Taewŏn'gun ŭi sŏwŏn kwangjangch'aek ŭi iltan (A part of the Taewongun's policy of expanding the tax base), in *Kim Chae-wŏn Paksa hoegap kinyŏm nonch'ong* (Memorial volume in honor of the sixtieth birthday of Kim Chaewŏn). Seoul, 1969, 295-310.

———*Tonghangnan kiin e kwanhan yŏn'gu* (Studies on the origin of the Tonghak rebellion). Seoul, 1971.

———*Yijo hugi ŭi sahoe wa sasang* (Society and thought in the late Yi dynasty). Seoul, 1961.

Hayashi Taisuke, *Chōsen tsūshi* (A comprehensive history of Korea). Keijō, 1912.

Hiraki Makoto, "Jūshichi-hachi seiki ni okeru nūryosai shosei no kisoku ni tsuite" (On the status of offspring of male slaves and commoner wives in the seventeenth and eighteenth centuries), *Chōsen gakuhō*, 61 (October 1971), 45-75.

———"Sipch'il segi e issŏsŏ ŭi nobi chongnyang" (The attainment of commoner status by slaves in the seventeenth century), *Han'guksa yŏn'gu*, 3 (March 1969), 89-121.

Hŏ Chong-ho, "Uri naraesŏ ŭi hwap'e chidae ŭi palsaeng e taehayŏ" (The development of the cash land rent in Korea), *Yŏksa kwahak*, 3 (1964), 12-25.

Hong I-sŏp, *Chŏng Yag-yong ŭi chŏngch'i kyŏngje sasang yŏn'gu* (A study of the political and economic thought of Chŏng Yag-yong). Seoul, 1959.

Kang Chin-ch'ŏl, "Han'guk t'oji chedosa, sang" (A history of the Korean land system), I, in *Han'guk munhwasa taegye*. Seoul, 1965. II, 1229-1379.

Kang Chu-jin, *Yijo tangjaengsa yŏn'gu* (A study of factionalism in the Yi dynasty). Seoul: Seoul Taehakkyo ch'ulp'anbu, 1971.

Kikuchi Kenjō, *Kankoku kindai gaikōshi: Taiinkunden* (Modern diplomatic history of Korea: the biography of the Taewongun). Tokyo, 1910.

——— *Kindai Chōsen shi* (History of Modern Korea). 2 vols. Keijō, 1937.

Kim Chin-bong, "Imsul millan ŭi sahoe hyŏngjejŏk paegyŏng" (The socioeconomic background to the 1862 peasant rebellion), *Sahak yŏn'gu*, 19 April 1967), 89-127.

Kim Haeng-ja, "Minbi chipkwŏn'gi Hanjŏn taeoe kwan'gye ŭi kukche chŏngch'ijŏk koch'al" (A study of the diplomacy of the Korean court during the regime of Queen Min). Master's thesis, Ihwa taehakkyo, 1966.

Kim Kwang-jin, *Chŏng Tasan ŭi kyŏngje sasang* (The economic thought of Chŏng Tasan). Pyongyang, 1962.

Kim Sŏk-hyŏng, *Chōsen hōken jidai nōmin no kaikyū kōsei* (The class structure of the peasantry in the Korean feudal period). Japanese trans., Suematsu Yasukazu and Yi Tal-hŏn. Tokyo, 1960.

Kim Sun-dong, ed., *Han'guk kosa taejŏn* (Dictionary of Korean antiquities). Seoul, 1965.

Kim Un-t'ae, *Chosŏn wangjo haengjŏngsa: kŭnsep'yŏn* (Administrative history of the Yi dynasty: recent period). Seoul, 1970.

Kim Yong-sŏp, "Chosŏn hugi e issŏsŏ ŭi sinbunje ŭi tongyo wa nongji chŏmyu: Sangju yang'an yŏn'gu ŭi ildan" (The disruption of the social status system and land tenure in the late Yi dynasty: a portion of the study of the Sangju land registers), *Sahak yŏn'gu* 15 (April 1963), 1-46.

_____ "Chosŏn hugi ŭi nong'ŏp munje: Chŏngjo mallyŏn ŭi ŭngji chinnongsŏ ŭi punsŏk" (Problems in agriculture in the late Yi dynasty: an analysis of recommendations for the promotion of agriculture at royal request at the end of Chŏngjo's reign), *Han'guksa yŏn'gu*, 2 (December 1968), 53-103.

_____ *Chosŏn hugi nong'ŏpsa yŏn'gu: nongch'ong kyŏngje sahoe pyŏndong* (Studies in the agrarian history of the late Yi dynasty: the peasant economy and the changing social structure). Seould: Ilchogak, 1970.

_____ *Chosŏn hugi nongŏpsa yŏn'gu: nong'ŏp pyŏndong, nonghak sajo* (Studies in the agrarian history of the late Yi dynasty: changes in agriculture, trends of thought in writings on agriculture). Seoul: Ilchogak, 1971.

_____ "Kwangmu yŏn'gan ŭi yangjŏn saŏbe kwanhan ilyŏn'gu" (A study of the cadastral survey in the Kwangmu period), *Asea yŏn'gu*, 11:3 (September 1968), 81-202, English summary, 203-210.

_____ "Nongch'on kyŏngje" (The peasant economy), part of the Conference on Social Change in the Late Yi Dynasty, *Sahak yŏn'gu*, 16 (December 1963), 96-105.

_____ "Sagung changt'o ŭi chŏnho kyŏngje" (Tenancy on palace estates), *Asea yŏn'gu*, 19 (September 1965), 113-146.

_____ "Sagung changt'o ŭi kwalli: Tojangje rŭl chungsim ŭro" (The management of palace estates: the *tojang* system), *Sahak yŏn'gu*, 18 (September 1965), 573-626.

_____ "Sok, Yang'an ŭi yŏn'gu, sang: Chosŏn hugi ŭi chŏnho kyŏngje" (Continued: studies on land registers, pt. 1, Tenancy in the late Yi dynasty), *Sahak yŏngu*, 16 (December 1963), 1-64.

_____ "Yang'an ŭi yŏn'gu: Chosŏn hugi ŭi nonka kyŏngje" (A study of the land registers: the economy of peasant households in the late Yi dynasty), pt. 1, *Sahak yŏn'gu* (May 1960), 1-95: pt. 2, *Sahak yŏn'gu*, 8 (November 1960), 59-119.

KuHanmal choyak hwich'an (Treaties of the late Yi dynasty). Seoul, 1965.

Kuksa-daesajŏn (Great dictionary of Korean history). 2 vols. Yi Hong-jik, ed. Seoul, 1962.

Kwŏn Sang-no, *Han'guk chimyŏng konghyŏk-ko* (A study of the history of Korean place names). Seoul, 1961.

Kwŏn Sŏk-pong, "Yi Hong-jang ŭi tae Chosŏn yŏlguk imnyak kwŏndoch'ae e taehayŏ" (Li Hung-chang's policy of urging Korea to sign treaties with the powers), *Yŏksa hakpo*, 21 (August 1963), 101-130.

Bibliography

Mansŏng taedongbo (Grand genealogy of the 10,000 names). Seoul, n.d.

Min Pyŏng-ha, "Chosŏn sŏwŏn ŭi kyŏngje kujo" (The economic structure of Yi dynasty private academies), *Taedong munhwa yŏn'gu*, 5 (August 1968), 75-96.

Miyahara Toichi, "Richo no gun'eki seido, ho, no seiritsu" (The establishment of the support system as part of military service in the Yi dynasty), *Chōsen gakuhō*, 28 (July 1963), 112-131.

Nakamura Eikō, *Nissen kankeishi no kenkyū* (A study of the history of Japanese-Korean relations). 3 vols. Tokyo, 1965-69.

Oda Shōgo, "Richō no hōtō o ryakujo shite Tenshukyō ni oyobu" (A brief discussion of factionalism in the Yi dynasty as it pertained to Catholicism), *Seikyū gakuso*, 1 (1931), 1-26.

_____"Rishi Chōsen jidai ni okeru Wakan no hensen" (Changes in the Waegwan during the Yi dynasty), in *Chōsen Shina bunka no kenkyū* (Studies in the culture of Korea and China). Tokyo, 1929, 93-140.

Pak Chong-gŭn, "Tasan, Tei Jyaku-yō no tochi kaikaku shisō no kosatsu: kōsaku (noryoku ni ojita) tochi bumpai o chushin to shite" (A study of Tasan, Chŏng Yag-yong's ideas on land reform: in particular the distribution of land in accordance with labor), *Chōsen gakuhō*, 28 (July 1965), 75-112.

Pak Kwang-sŏng, "Chosŏn ch'ogi ŭi ŭich'ang chedo e taehayŏ" (The righteous granaries of the early Yi dynasty), *Sach'ong*, 7 (November 1962), 48-79.

Pak Pyŏng-ho, "Han'guk kŭnse ŭi toji soyukwŏn e kwan han yŏn'gu" (A study of landownership rights in recent Korean history), *Seoul taehakkyo pŏphak* (Seoul University law journal), 8:1 (1966), 63-93; 8:2 (1966), 78-104; 9:1 (1967), 157-185.

_____ *Han'guk pŏpchesa t'uksu yŏn'gu: Yijo sidae ŭi pudongsan maemae kŭp tanbobŏp* (Special studies on the history of the Korean legal system: sale and guarantee of immovable property). Seoul, 1960.

Pak Si-hyŏng, *Chosŏn t'oji chedosa* (History of the Korean land system), II. Pyongyang, 1961.

Richo jidai no zaisei (The financial administration of the Yi dynasty), n.p. Chōsen sōtokufu, 1936.

Shikata Hiroshi, "Richo jinkō ni kansuru ichi kenkyū" (One study on population in the Yi dynasty), *Chōsen shakai hōseishi kenkyū* (Studies in the social and legal history of Korea). Tokyo, 1937.

_____"Richō jinkō ni kansuru mibun kaikyūbetsuteki kansatsu" (Investigation of Yi dynasty population in terms of status and class), *Chōsen keizai no kenkyū* (Studies in the Korean economy), 3 (Tokyo, 1938), 363-482.

Sin Kuk-chu, "Kankoku no kaikoku, Unyō-go jiken o megutte" (The opening of Korea, the Unyō incident), in *Nihon gaikōshi kenkyū: Bakumatsu-Ishin jidai* (Studies in the history of Japanese foreign policy, the period of late Tokugawa and Meiji restoration). Tokyo, 1960, 124-142.

_____ *Kŭndae Chosŏn oegyosa* (Diplomatic history of modern Korea). Seoul, 1965. Japanese trans., *Kindai Chōsen gaikōshi*. Tokyo, 1966.

Sin Yong-ha, "Yijo malgi ŭi tojikwŏn kwa ilcheha ŭi yongsojak ŭi kwan'gye: sojangnon tojikwŏn ŭi soyukwŏn ŭro ŭi sŏngjang kwan mollak e taehayŏ" (The relationship between the right of *toji* in the late Yi dynasty and the long-term tenancy of the Japanese colonial period), *Kyŏngje nonjip*, 6:1 (March 1967), 29-75.

Song Ch'an-sik, "Yijo sidae ŭi hwanja" (Grain loans in the Yi dynasty), *Yŏksa hakpo*, 27 (April 1965), 23-64.

Song June-ho, *Yijo saengwŏn chinsa si ŭi yŏn'gu* (A study of the saengwŏn and chinsa examinations of the Yi dynasty). Seoul, 1970.

Bibliography

Song Nak-hun, "Han'guk tangjaengsa" (History of Factionalism in Korea), in *Han'guk munhwasa taegye* (Grand outline of Korean cultural history). Seoul, 1965. II, 282-288.

Sudō Yoshiyuki, "Chōsen kōki no dendō bunki ni kansuru kenkyū" (A study of land deeds in the later Yi dynasty), pt. 1, *Rekishigaku kenkyū*, 7:7 (July 1937), 2-48; pt. 2, ibid., 7:8 (August 1937), 39-65; pt. 3, ibid., 7:9 (September 1937), 23-68.

Tabohashi Kiyoshi, *Kindai Nissen kankei no kenkyū* (A study of Japanese-Korean relations in recent times). 2 vols. Keijō, 1940.

Taga Akigorō, *Chūgoku kyōikushi* (History of education in China). Tokyo, 1955.

Terada Gō, *Sōdai kyōikushi gaisetsu* (Survey of the history of education in the Sang dynasty). Tokyo, 1965.

Urakawa Wasaburo, *Chōsen junkyōshi* (A history of Korean martyrs). Tokyo, 1944.

Wada Ichiro, *Chōsen no tochi seido oyobi jisei seido chōsa hōkokusho* (Report on the Korean land and land tax systems). Keijō, 1920.

Watanabe Manabu, *Kinsei Chōsen kyōikushi kenkyū* (Studies in the history of education in Korea in recent times). Tokyo, 1969.

Wŏn Yu-han, "Sipp'al segi e issŏsŏ ŭi hwap'ye chŏngchaek saŏp chungsim" (Currency policy in the eighteenth century: the minting of copper cash), *Sahak yŏn'gu*, 19 (April 1967), 49-88.

_____ "Tang'ojŏn-go" (A Study of the 5-cash) *Yŏksa hakpo*, 35-36 (December 1967), 313-339.

_____ "Yijo hugi ch'ŏngjŏn ŭi şuip yut'ong e taehayŏ" (The import and circulation of Chinese currency in the late Yi dynasty), *Sahak yŏngu*, 21 (September 1969), 145-155.

_____ "Yijo Sukchongjo ŭi chujŏn tonggi" (The motives for the minting of cash in Sukchong's reign), *Tongguk sahak*, 9-10 (1966), 37-52.

Yi Hyŏn-jong, *Chosŏn chŏn'gi tae-Il kyosŏpsa yŏn'gu* (A study of the history of diplomatic relations with Japan in the early Yi dynasty). Seoul, 1964.

Yi Ki-baek, *Kuksa sillon* (A new interpretation of Korean history). Seoul, 1961.

Yi Nŭng-hwa, *Chosŏn kidokkyo kŭp oegyosa* (A history of Christianity and foreign relations in Korea). Keijō, 1928.

Yi Pyŏng-do, *Han'guksa taegwan* (Grand outline of Korean history). Seoul, 1964.

Yi Sang-baek, "Chŏnja sumo-go" (A study of the inheritance of mother's status by ch'ŏnmin), *Chindan hakpo*, 25-27 (December 1964), 155-183.

_____ *Han'guksa kŭnse chŏn'gip'yŏn* (History of Korea: recent times, early period). Seoul, 1962.

_____ *Han'guksa kŭnse hugip'yŏn* (History of Korea: recent times, late period). Seoul, 1965.

Yi Sŏng-mu, "Sŏnch'o ŭi Sŏnggyun'gwan yŏn'gu" (A study of the National Academy in the early Yi dynasty), *Yŏksa hakpo*, 35-36 (December 1967), 219-268.

Yi Sŏn-gŭn, *Han'guksa ch'oegŭnsep'yŏn* (History of Korea: most recent period). Seoul, 1961.

Yi Ul-ho, *Tasan kyŏnghak sasang ŭi yŏn'gu* (A study of Tasan's ideas on the classics). Seoul, 1966.

Yu Hong-nyŏl, "Chōsen ni okeru shoin no seiritsu" (The establishment of private academies in Korea), pt. 1, *Seikyū gakusō*, 29 (August 1937), 24-91; pt. 2, ibid., 30 (October 1939), 63-116.

_____ *Kojong ch'iha Sŏhak sunan ŭi yŏn'gu* (A study of Catholic persecution during King Kojong's reign). Seoul, 1962.

Bibliography

_____ *Han'guk chŏnjugyohoesa* (A history of the Catholic church in Korea). Seoul: Kat'orik ch'ulp'ansa, 1958.

Yu Sŭng-u, "Chosŏn hugi kunsu kwanggong'ŏp ŭi palchŏn" (The development of mining and industry for munitions in the late Yi dynasty), *Sahakchi*, 3 (July 1969), 1-35.

Index

384

Index

210-212; fails to influence Taewongun, 263; on grain loan corruption,
in 1862, 144; on Japan policy, 260,
264; on liquidation of grain loan ·
funds, 222-223; on monetary policy,
203; on prices and the market, 212-
214; protests leniency for Pak U-
hyŏn, 240
Pak U-hyŏn, 238-240
Palace estates (kungbang), 74, 101,
147, 277; amount of, 77; land of, 78-
82; restrictions over taxes of, 97;
fishing and salt revenues of, 104
Palace Treasury, 76
Pangmok, 253 n.1. See also Examina-
tions
Paper money. See Currency
Parkes, Sir Harry, 261
Patriarch's faction (noron), 15, 47-51,
57, 123, 305; and Mandongmyo,
119-120, 122. See also Factionalism
Peasants, poverty of, 58, 63-67
Personal service taxes (sinyŏk), 98-99
Pinch'ŏng (separate conference), 260
Pinch'ŏng yŏnmyŏng-gye, 34
Pin'gye, 194-195
Poin. See Support personnel
Policy conferences, 56
Ponggŏn, 94
Pongnim-daegun (later King Hyojong),
330 n.74
Pŏnnam Pak clan, 356 n.48
Population, 12, 64, 228, 312 n.20, 321
n.35
P'oryang, 310 n.9
P'oryangmi. See Artillery provision
rice tax
Posol (tax-exempt support personnel),
119
Post-station land (yŏkchŏn), 74, 78, 84
Poverty, of peasants, 63-67
Pragmatism, 273, 283; of Taewongun,
274, 279
Pragmatic-statist orientation, of policy,
133, 142-144
Prebends, 64, 75, 78, 311 n.17
Price fixing, 278
Price stabilization, 134, 143, 163, 212-
214
Prince Wanhwa (Wanhwagun), 45
Prince Yŏn'in (Yŏn'in'gun), 47. See also
Yŏngjo, king
Princely estates, 18
Princely men (kunja), 35
Princesses' Consorts, Office of the
(ibinbu), 36
Private academies. See Academies,
private
Private schools (sŏdang), 112. See also
Schools
Profit, prejudice against, 165
Property, private, 64, 292 n.34,
310-311 n.16. See also Land
Protected officials (ŭm, ŭmsa), 36, 356
n.48
Pug'in, 15. See also Factionalism,
Northerners
Punbu (private directive), 107, 297 n.36
P'ungyang Cho clan, 25, 37, 281, 297
n.39, 305 n.19
Punjŏng, 101
Purchase, of office or rank, 8
Pyŏkp'a, 48, 304 n.15, 305 n.19. See
also Factionalism
Pyŏlbihwan (special reserve loan fund),
222
Pyŏlch'i (special reserve fund), 207
Pyŏltan (list of regulations), 299 n.71
Pyŏng'in pyŏlbigok (1866 Special
Reserve Grain), 153

Queen Min (Yŏhŭng Min clan, of King
Kojong), 4, 45, 176, 274, 279, 345
n.51, 354 n.27, 359 n.21; offspring
of, 45, 216; possible relations of,
with Ch'oe Ik-hyŏn, 196; relations
of, with Kojong, 242-244; rivalry of,
with Taewongun, 237
Queen Min (of King Sukchong), 49,
122.

Rank land system (kwajŏn), 64, 75, 311
n.17
Rebellion, 63, 66, 272; of 1862, 100-
104, 144; and grain loans, 132; in
Ulsan, 262
Recommendation, 53-54; system, for
examinations, 128
Recording fee (hoerok), 137
Red Turbans, 180
Reform, 272-279; ineffectiveness of,
220; reasons for failure of, 3-4, 22;
weariness with, 227-228
Reform Bureau, of 1862 (ijŏngch'ong),
103-106, 144
Regencies, 25-29, 294 n.12
Regular lectures (kwŏn'gang), 32-33
Relief, 35, 132-135, 277
Relief Agency (chinhyŏlch'ong), 134,
331 n.2
Remonstrance, 11, 34, 180, 191, 197-
200, 230, 240, 250, 267-268, 283;
Kojong's toleration of, 184, 237; lack
of, 184; repression of, 245

Restoration (*chunghŭng*), 39, 42, 300 n.84
Revenues, totals of, in eighteenth century, 166. *See also* Finances, Taxation
Righteous Granaries (*ŭich'ang*), 134-136, 144, 156
Rites, 126, 189
Royal Clan, Office of the (tollyŏngbu), 36-37, 56
Royal genealogy (*Sŏnwŏn kyebo*), 37
Royal Genealogy, Office of the (chongch'inbu), 36-38, 40
Royal lectures. *See* Lectures, Royal
Royal Library (kyujanggak), 50
Royal Secretariat. *See* Secretariat, Royal
Royal Treasury (naesusa), 79
Ryukyu Islands, Japanese takeover of, 253

Sa, 98. *See also* Aristocracy; Yangban
Saaek, 115. *See also* Charters
Sabu, 91, 322 n.37. *See also* Aristocracy; Yangban
Sabuga, 101. *See also* Aristocracy; Yangban
Sach'ang. *See* Village Granaries
Sado seja. *See* Changhŏn, Crown Prince
Saengwŏn, 112. *See also* Examinations
Saengwŏn-chinsa pangmok, 299 n.75
Sagara, mission of 1872, 293 n.42
Saganwon (Office of the Censor-General), 344 n.24
Sahak. *See* Four Schools
Sahŏnbu. *See* Inspector-General, Office of the
Sajok, 108, 321 n.36. *See also* Aristocracy; Yangban
Sale, of office, 55
Salt taxes, 105, 147
Sama, 112. *See also* Examinations
Samgunbu. *See* Three Armies Command
Samsuryang. *See* Military Training Agency surtax
Sanggye, Prince, 305 n.19
Sangnap, 210. *See also* Tribute, royal
Sangp'yŏng t'ongbo. *See* Ever-normal circulating treasure
Sangp'yŏngch'ang. *See* Ever-normal granaries
Sangp'yŏngch'ŏng. *See* Ever-Normal Agency
Sansŏng hwan'gok (mountain fortress grain loans), 137

Sap'ae (royal grant), 78
Sasaek. *See* Four colors
Sasu, 155
Sayŏ (royal grant), 78
Sayŏgwŏn (Office of Interpreters), 216
Schall, Adam, 330 n.74
Scholars. *See* Confucian scholars; Literati
Schools: provincial (hyanggyo), 112, 327 n.10; government neglect of, 111-113. *See also* National Academy; Private Schools
Seclusion policy, 270
Secret censor. *See* Censor, secret
Secretariat, Royal (Sŭngjŏngwŏn), 29, 231, 296 n.23, 344 n.24; accused of obstruction by king, 249; accuses Chang Ho-gŭn of slander, 265; indicts official for improper remonstrance, 268
Seigniorage, 167-168, 174, 278
Seikan (conquer Korea) debates, 22, 293 n.43
Sejo, king, 296 n.23, 351 n.41
Seriousness (kyŏng), 240
Shamans, 6
Shang dynasty, 189
Shenandoah, The, 30
Shen-tsung, emperor (Ming dynasty), 229-230, 329 n.58
She-ts'ang (village granaries), 226. *See also* Chu Hsi; Granaries; Village Granaries
Shih-chi, on currency and inflation, 214
Shih Huang-ti (of Ch'in dynasty), 182
Shishi (men of will), 42
Shrines, 113, 125, 280, 282; proliferation of, 117. *See also* Confucius; Mandongmyo; Munmyo
Shu-yüan, 327 n.18
Silgyŏl (taxable land), 61
Silho, 91
Silhwan, 146
Silk letter, of Hwang Sa-yong, 178
Silla dynasty, 11, 38, 144
Silver, 167, 210. *See also* Currency
Silver jar money (ŭnbyŏng), 161
Sim clan, 306 n.38
Sim Ŭi-myŏn, 294 n.16
Sin Ch'ŏl-gu, 232
Sin Ch'ŏl-gyun, 354 n.27
Sin Hŏn, 195, 263, 306 n.34, 360 n.53
Sin Kwan-ho. *See* Sin Hŏn
Sin Suk-chu, 296 n.23
Sin Ŭng-jo, 207, 223
Sin Wan, 322 n.39

Harvard East Asian Monographs

151. James Polachek, *The Inner Opium War*

152. Gail Lee Bernstein, *Japanese Marxist: A Portrait of Kawakami Hajime, 1879–1946*

153. Lloyd E. Eastman, *The Abortive Revolution: China under Nationalist Rule, 1927–1937*

154. Irmela Hijiya-Kirschnereit, *Rituals of Self-Revelation: The History and Theory of Shishōsetsu*

155. Richard J. Smith, John K. Fairbank, and Katherine F. Bruner, *Robert Hart and China's Early Modernization: His Journals, 1863–1866*